SARATOGA

A Military History of the Decisive Campaign
of the American Revolution

John F. Luzader

SB
Savas Beatie
New York and California

Cataloging-in-Publication Data is available from the Library of Congress.

ISBN 978-1-932714-44-9

05 04 03 02 01   5 4 3 2 1

First edition, first printing

SB

Published by
Savas Beatie LLC
521 Fifth Avenue, Suite 3400
New York, NY 10175
Phone: 610-853-9131

Editorial Offices:

Savas Beatie LLC
P.O. Box 4527
El Dorado Hills, CA 95762
Phone: 916-941-6896
(E-mail) editorial@savasbeatie.com

Savas Beatie titles are available at special discounts for bulk purchases in the United States by corporations, institutions, and other organizations. For more details, please contact Special Sales, P.O. Box 4527, El Dorado Hills, CA 95762, or you may e-mail us at sales@savasbeatie.com, or visit our website at www.savasbeatie.com for additional information.

To my wife Jean, my sons, John and David, my daughter Alice.

And to the National Park Service, which supported
my family while I indulged my hobbies.

Contents

Contents *(continued)*

Maps

Photos and Illustrations

Photos and illustrations have been placed throughout the book for the convenience of the readers.

Note: A glossary for the explanation of military terms is provided as Appendix J

Foreword

According to many historians, history is replete with "turning points." Each is a catalyst upon which a social movement, a government, a technology, or a war made a decisive turn and forever changed the destiny of the overall historic event.

Properly speaking, the "turning point" of the American Revolution—the most singular decisive moment of the Revolution as a whole—must be Congress' resolution for independence voted on July 2, 1776. That event marked the point of no return, and the ratification of the Declaration of Independence that followed manifested the position of what was then a majority of Americans: the United States was a free nation of independent states no longer subject to the rules and laws of Britain. A declaration by a rogue citizenry assembled in Philadelphia was one thing. Validating Congress' bold action in the eyes of the enemy and other nations of the world, which could only happen through military means, was an entirely different matter.

The military events of 1775 generally favored the Patriots' cause, largely because the British were caught off-guard during the war's early months. Their operational plan for subduing the American rebellion, however, nearly ended the war the following year. That it did not was due largely to General George Washington's masterful end-of-year attacks on Trenton and Princeton, New Jersey, and Thomas Paine's timely and uplifting *Crisis*. The stunning reverses in the field saved the American cause from its pending ruin born of continual British victories and its own disillusionment. Such was the precarious state of the revolution in early 1777, and why that year promised to be a decisive one.

Operating under the belief that the end of the rebellion in America was in sight, British military strategy for 1777 was even more ambitious than it had been in 1776. While the British Army of the North American Colonies (lying on the Atlantic coast) commanded by General Sir William Howe orchestrated an invasion to take the American capital of Philadelphia, General Sir Guy Carleton's British Army of the Province of Québec (and its dependent territories and the frontiers) would engage in the more audacious design of moving a pair of armies from Canada in order to combine their strengths at Albany, New York. As is so often the case in history, politics intervened. Command of the invasion passed from Carleton to an excessively overconfident, dashing, and eager-to-prove-himself lieutenant general named John Burgoyne.

The 1777 British invasion from Canada is often referred to as the "Burgoyne Campaign" because he personally planned, proposed, lobbied for, organized, and commanded the operation. Though the "Burgoyne Campaign" promised much, success eluded British arms. A lack of coordination, overconfidence, and a dangerously-low opinion of the Army of the United States—together with American determination, brilliant defensive strategy, and the stellar leadership of soldiers like Benedict Arnold, John Stark, Daniel Morgan, and Thaddeus Kosciuszko, to name just a few—carried the day. No single American was responsible for the tremendous victory, but the lion's share of the credit rests with Northern Department commander Horatio Gates. His decision to fight on the west side of the Hudson River, and then aggressively pursue and surround Burgoyne's retreating army resulted in the catastrophic British surrender. And it was the surrender at Saratoga, not its several battles and satellite operations, which marked the true "turning point" of the American Revolutionary War.

There are many reasons why the Saratoga surrender proved to be such a decisive pivot point in the war's fortunes. The most important was that it convinced France to openly recognize the independence of the United States and join it in a commercial and military alliance against Great Britain. The recognition of American independence by France, one of the age's great world powers, gave necessary legitimacy to the self-proclaimed United States. That recognition provided French soldiers, money, credit, and matériel to the Patriot cause, all of which combined to bring about the decisive battlefield victory at Yorktown in October 1781, where the majority of the Franco-American allied force was comprised of French soldiers and sailors.

Saratoga's impact did not end with the involvement of France, for truly great moments in history create shock waves that are not restricted to place or time. French, and later Spanish and Dutch, involvement in the American War for Independence elevated the conflict from a colonial rebellion to the international stage. To the dismay of Great Britain, the warring colonial powers clashed in Florida, the West Indies, India, Africa, Gibraltar, the islands in the English Channel, and the Mediterranean Sea. French involvement in the war proved expensive, however, and ended up ruining the French economy. Deteriorating economic circumstances on the continent were a major cause of the French Revolution and the eventual ascension of Napoléon Bonaparte, the Napoleonic Wars, and a continued upheaval of European government and society well into the 20th century. The success of the American Revolution channeled energies into other national movements of independence throughout the world in countries in Central and South America, Africa, and Asia. The people whose lives were affected by the success of the American forces at Saratoga number in the hundreds of millions.

Due in great measure to President Franklin Delano Roosevelt, Saratoga National Historical Park was authorized in 1938 in order to preserve and protect the grounds of the battlefield, as well as interpret for the public its monumental significance. It's ironic that the fields of fighting, which had such an impact on the shaping of world events, are so well preserved. Nearly 100% of the battle sites are located inside the boundary of the park, as are perhaps 90% of the encampment and fortification sites. That, in combination with a stunningly beautiful viewshed, is a monument to 20th and 21st century historic preservation.

Over the years, a number of books have focused on the military and political events that brought Burgoyne's and Gates' armies together in upstate New York in September and October of 1777. Unlike previous authors, however, John Luzader writes with a thorough understanding of the subject, made possible from decades of writing and research. As a former park historian of Saratoga National Historical Park, he is able to bring to bear his years of methodical and experienced study and deep access to the park's unparalleled collection of source material related to the Northern Campaign, which he helped to build. Mr. Luzsader has walked the grounds of the battlefield countless times, is intimately familiar with the landscape he writes about, and understands the critical role it played in both the strategic and tactical situations faced by the armies. In addition, Mr. Luzader personally collected copies of valuable unpublished manuscript sources from Germany and Great Britain, which are necessary for a proper understanding of the chain of events that led to Saratoga. His excellent history of the military and political aspects of this campaign, and keen discussion of its principal players, is the result of his analytical approach and extensive use of primary sources. No one who has ever written a book about the Northern Campaign of 1777 knows more about this subject.

It is my great honor to introduce *Saratoga: A Military History of the Decisive Campaign of the American Revolution*, by former park historian John Luzader.

Eric H. Schnitzer
Park Ranger / Historian
Saratoga National Historical Park
July 2008

Introduction

The Long Road to Saratoga

America's northern strategy in the early period of the War for Independence was dominated by the matter of Canada. The Continental Congress was obsessed with making it the fourteenth member of the revolutionary coalition, but the American invasion to achieve that end failed at Quebec at the close of 1775, exacting in return a heavy cost in men, treasure, and political credibility. In spite of that campaign's tragic record, Congress remained committed to driving the British out of North America before reinforcements could strengthen General Sir Guy Carleton, the British commander in Canada, and General Sir William Howe, the British commander in the middle colonies.

Congress received the shocking news of the death of the American commander, General Richard Montgomery, on January 17, 1776. Throughout the early months of that year, Congress struggled to redeem American fortunes in the North. Its immediate reaction was to order recently-raised Pennsylvania regiments to march north within ten days and to direct New Hampshire, New York, and Connecticut to raise additional regiments to reinforce units already in Canada. The plan did not proceed as smoothly as Congress hoped it might.[1]

Various American generals' attempts to salvage the situation failed in the face of Guy Carleton's superior professional leadership, the impact of disease, a lack of medicine and supplies, and appalling morale. The defining combat took place at Trois Rivieres on June 8, when Colonel (later Brigadier) Simon Fraser defeated troops from New Jersey and Pennsylvania. By the first days of July 1776, the pox-ridden, impoverished, defeated wreck of the army that ten months earlier had departed from Crown Point on Lake Champlain in upstate New York on the crusade to add a fourteenth American state staggered back to where the campaign had begun.

The American defeat in Canada had complex and important results. An immediate one that contemporaries did not recognize was that it saved the Americans from having to try to hold what they would have won—an undertaking far exceeding their resources and capabilities. A more apparent result, as mentioned, was the great loss of men, materiel, money, and political capital.[2] The American invasion also roused the British to turn to more forceful plans to put down a stubborn rebellion that had proved itself to be aggressive in its attempts to spread its virus, while at the same time delaying William Howe's intended campaign against New York City.

During the winter of 1775-76, even as the American invasion dwindled down through its last fitful stages into a disappointing withdrawal, Guy Carleton was already preparing to exploit American discomfiture and dissension by launching a counter-invasion from Canada that, if successful, would carry the British into the rebellion's interior.

In May of 1776, the American commander-in-chief, General George Washington, received disturbing intelligence that Britain had concluded treaties with German princes. The agreements provided some 17,000 German soldiers for employment in America, most or all of whom would be available to sail that April. He also learned that fifteen British regiments were probably already at sea. The combination meant approximately 30,000 enemy soldiers would be available to employ against the rebellious colonists by the end of June 1776.[3]

The previous failure in Canada and limited resources at New York City precluded an American initiative in response. The most the American political and military leadership could do was to try to make a stand in Canada, preferably at the mouth of the Richelieu River, and do all in their power to keep Carleton out of New York. By enlisting additional members into the Continental army, calling upon the colonies to mobilize 30,000 militiamen to defend the interior, and encouraging friendly Indians to threaten Detroit and Niagara, they might distract the British from New York.[4]

While these deliberations were under way, the Canadian situation continued to deteriorate. A new commander, General Horatio Gates, reached Albany on June 25 to take over the northern army.[5] Daunting problems awaited him. After the army had suffered its decisive defeat at Trois Rivieres in Canada on June 8, the American commander on the scene, General Benedict Arnold, had wisely retreated to St. Johns, Canada, with 3,000 invalids. By the time Gates arrived at Albany, the force he was to command had retreated from Isle aux Noix to Crown Point in New York state. That put the command back into the Northern Department of the American military structure, commanded by General Philip Schuyler of New York.

Fortunately for the various American generals and the cause they served, Sir Guy Carleton faced a critical problem: his chance to advance successfully depended upon his regaining control of Lake Champlain. He had anticipated that necessity, and months earlier requested the boats, naval stores, and artificers needed to assemble a flotilla. But Sir William Howe's more urgent need for landing craft to use in taking New York City, scarce building materials, and too few skilled workers kept the British government from providing all that Carleton required. The most it could manage were some small gunboats armed with one small-caliber gun each, and flat-bottomed bateaux for transporting men and supplies. Carleton had to undertake construction of a fleet with whatever men and materials he could find.[6]

The Americans were doubly fortunate in that the British went about building their flotilla without a sense of urgency, while leaving their enemy virtually unmolested. In contrast, while the Americans lacked important martial qualities, dilatoriness was not among their salient faults. They worked diligently strengthening and extending the works at Fort Ticonderoga, the main American fortress in the north, and adding to the size of their own three-boat flotilla. As part of their defensive plan, Schuyler and Gates decided to abandon the old ruined works at Crown Point. Gates put Arnold in charge of shifting the men from Crown Point to Ticonderoga, leaving a small garrison under Lieutenant Colonel Thomas Hartley of the 6th Pennsylvania Battalion.

At Ticonderoga, Gates did what he could not only to improve the physical defenses but to change the quality of the force he commanded, which was plagued by sickness, fatigue, and desertion. Morale depended upon his and Schuyler's receiving and transporting the materiel required to improve shelter, clothing, rations, and arms, and upon getting a handle on the ravages of smallpox. Gates attacked these problems decisively and effectively. The men's health and morale, as well as discipline in the units, steadily improved through the summer and fall.[7]

Arnold, meanwhile, proceeded to prepare the American flotilla to contest control of Lake Champlain. An inventory of the Northern Department's vessels revealed to Gates that those captured by Schuyler's men during 1775 included a sloop and three schooners, which he reported to Congress were unarmed and "solely employed in Floating Waggons [sic];" they went to Crown Point to be armed. Schuyler also had ordered construction of gondolas [gunboats] and row galleys in a makeshift boatyard at Skenesborough. Ignorant alike of boat building and naval tactics, and knowing that Arnold had experience in the West Indian trade, Gates directed him to take charge of the race to build and command the new vessels. The choice proved fortuitous, as results would eventually establish.[8]

Schuyler and Gates gave unstinting support to Arnold's undertaking, and the former's aide-de-camp, Captain Richard Varick, from his post in Albany, labored beyond duty's requirements to forward everything needed.[9] By dint of unselfish cooperation and Arnold's amazing energy, a sloop, three schooners, and five gondolas soon rode at anchor at Crown Point. The gondolas, the backbone of Arnold's motley fleet, resembled large whaleboats. Each averaged fifty-seven feet long with a seventeen-foot beam, mounted two 9-pounders amidships, and a 12-pounder in the bow. With only one mast and a square sail, they were clumsy and hard to maneuver. Oars provided critically needed mobility.[10]

Arnold joined his little lake flotilla on August 14, with orders to sail down (northward) Lake Champlain as far as the Ile de Tetes, where he would try to determine the enemy's strength and, if it exceeded his own, would withdraw without making an "unnecessary display of power" or taking any "wanton" risk.[11] Arnold wrote to Gates on September 18 that he intended to move to Valcour Island, where there was a good harbor, offering to return to Ile de Tetes if his commander disapproved of the move.[12] Gates replied on October 12 that Arnold's change of station pleased him. By that time, the flotilla included sixteen vessels: one sloop, three schooners, eight gondolas, and four row galleys, mounting a total of 102 guns and manned by 856 men.[13]

Carleton and his army were still strangely inactive while the Americans built their fleet and improved Ticonderoga's defenses. Aside from assembling twelve gunboats and 560 bateaux on Lake Champlain and 120 more bateaux at other Canadian sites, the British did nothing to develop the kind of inland navy needed to satisfy the projected invasion's needs.

But by the end of August, Sir Guy rejoined his army from Quebec, where he had been busy reestablishing civil government, and gave his attention to deploying a fleet on Champlain. His fleet consisted initially of four vessels: two schooners (one of twelve, and the other of fourteen, guns) which had been disassembled and portaged around the Richelieu rapids; a large sixteen-gun radeu; and a six-gun gondola captured from the Americans. The armament totaled seventy-two pieces.[14] Seven hundred officers and men manned the boats and guns. Ever cautious, Carleton delayed advancing until a square-rigged, three-masted vessel, *Inflexible*, mounting eighteen guns, could be dismantled and brought from the St. Lawrence River. The operation consumed only twenty-eight days—a remarkably brief but fateful period.

By October 4, when Carleton departed Isle aux Nois, the campaigning season was already drawing to a close. His plan to reach Albany, New York, from whence he would cooperate with William Howe, was hopelessly behind schedule. The most Carleton could realistically hope to achieve was to take Fort Ticonderoga, from which he could launch a new offensive the next year. Even that was a long shot that would depend upon the Americans' either losing their nerve or putting up a feeble resistance.

Advancing slowly southward up the lake, on October 11 he sighted Arnold's boats strategically anchored between the lake's western shore and Valcour Island. The outmatched Americans fought heroically against a skillful enemy able to deliver twice their firepower, but an advantageous position and heroism were not sufficient. Under cover of fog and darkness Arnold maneuvered past the British, who renewed the fight on the twelfth; Arnold lost his flagship, *Royal Savage*. On the thirteenth, he beached his wrecked vessels at Buttonhole Bay on the Vermont shore. With 200 men, he eluded an Indian ambush and joined the small garrison at Crown Point, where he found *Enterprise*, *Trumbull*, *Liberty*, and *Revenge*—all that remained of his heroic fleet that had delayed Carleton's inland thrust for weeks.[15] Colonel Hartley and Arnold abandoned and burned the old fort at Crown Point and marched to Ticonderoga, where they joined its garrison in improving the works and constructing an outpost on nearby Mount Independence.[16]

Fort Ticonderoga and its dependencies were objectives tempting to Carleton. Possessing them would provide a forward base when, as was fully expected, the British renewed their campaign for control of the Champlain-Hudson route into the American interior. This was the situation Carleton faced: at the end of September 1776, Gates commanded 6,221 "Present Fit for Duty & On Duty" at Ticonderoga.[17] By October 14, reinforcements (including 1,085 New England militia), brought the total to 8,594[18]; Carleton's army outnumbered the defenders by more than 4,000. But Carleton suspected that only a siege would capture the fort, a suspicion confirmed by probes launched on October 27 and 29. Even if the siege were successful, maintaining a garrison through the winter was a commitment the general would not undertake.

On November 3, the British evacuated Crown Point and withdrew to St. Johns. Arnold, Gates, Schuyler, and the soldiers they commanded had delayed the first British invasion of the northern frontier sufficiently to end it. The fate of the second British campaign in 1777—and indeed the independence of the United States of America—would turn on the pivotal Saratoga Campaign.

Acknowledgments

Many people have helped me over the years, and I apologize in advance if I have overlooked anyone.

I conducted most of the research for this book while my work in Washington made possible daily access to the Library of Congress, the National Archives, and frequent use of materials in the sources found in libraries located in Philadelphia, New York, Harvard, Ann Arbor, and other locations. While on assignment in the United Kingdom and Germany, I had access to the manuscripts in the British Public Record Office, British Museum, Oxford's Bodleian Library, the excellent municipal libraries in Leeds, Manchester, and Exeter, and the library in Alnwick Castle. In Germany, the state and city libraries in Ansbach, Cassel, Frankfurt, Wolfenbuttel, and Marburg contained valuable manuscripts cited in this book. The passage of the years has made my acknowledgment more than tardy. The staffs of these institutions were thoroughly professional, and without their cooperation I could not have prepared this study.

I owe a debt of gratitude to Francis Wilshin, Charles Shedd, and especially Charles Snell, my predecessors at Saratoga National Historical Park whose research efforts in the 1930s and 1950s laid the groundwork upon which I built. I owe them more than they would have claimed. Stewart Harrington, Saratoga NHP's maintenance foreman, and seasonal ranger-historians Sam Manico and Peter Heavey, and schoolteachers who helped me understand the service's educational responsibilities, made my four-year introduction to this book's subject productive and enjoyable.

Finally, I owe more than I know to my publisher, Savas Beatie, its director, Theodore P. Savas, and his helpful staff. Editor Rob Ayer utilized his outstanding skills to turn my manuscript into what you now hold; Sarah Keeney and Veronica Kane read various versions and helped proofread for mistakes. Ted arranged for park ranger-historian H. Eric Schnitzer to write his gracious Foreword and provide substantial input; for Jim McKnight, formerly of the Associated Press, to take the battlefield photos that grace this book, and he helped prepare the original maps inside this study with assistance from another Savas Beatie author, J. David Dameron. Thank you.

Dramatis Personae

John Adams (1735-1826) was born in Braintree (now Quincy) Massachusetts, graduated from Harvard in 1755, and was admitted to the Boston bar three years later. He was highly intelligent, vain, argumentative, and incorruptibly honest. During the period covered in this study, Adams was the leader of the New England delegates and of the New England-Virginia bloc critical of General Philip Schuyler and advocates of his replacement by General Gates. Later a member— with Benjamin Franklin and John Jay—of the commission to negotiate the peace treaty with Great Britain, his postwar career included the vice-presidency and presidency. David McCullough has ably chronicled this remarkable life in *John Adams*.

Born in Norwich, Connecticut, **Benedict Arnold** (1741-1801) was the great-grandson of a Rhode Island governor and the beneficiary of a common school education. Apprenticed to an apothecary at fourteen, he ran away at fifteen, enlisted in 1758 in a New York company, and deserted. Arnold enlisted again in 1760, deserted, returned home, and completed his apprenticeship. After moving to New Haven he opened a shop to sell drugs and books. His success earned him enough to buy his own ships and engage in the West Indian and Canadian trade, which he augmented by smuggling. Elected captain of a militia company, he reached Cambridge, Massachusetts, ten days after the Concord-Lexington fight in 1775. Arnold received a Massachusetts colonel's commission and participated in Ethan Allen's dramatic capture of Fort Ticonderoga. With a flair for the dramatic, Arnold engaged in a series of spectacular adventures including the remarkable Valcour Island naval engagement on Lake Champlain (October 11-13, 1776), which aborted Sir Guy Carleton's 1776 invasion from Canada. Driven by ambition, avarice,

and vainglory, Arnold eventually betrayed the Revolution, his new country, and his comrades, and became a British general. He returned under the Union Jack to burn New London, Connecticut.

John Burgoyne (1722-1792) was a scion of an old Lancashire family, educated at Westminster School. He began his military career in the dragoons,

but made his professional reputation as a commander of light cavalry. After serving with some distinction in Portugal, he entered Parliament during 1761. As a moderate Tory, he proved an effective politician. Burgoyne was made colonel of the 16th Light Dragoons in 1763, and while retaining that rank became a major general nine years later. He also launched a literary career in 1774 with the performance of "Maid of the Oaks." His sinecures included the post of governor of Fort William in Scotland. Burgoyne's first American service was in Boston under General Thomas Gage, and later served in Sir Guy Carleton's failed 1776 invasion of New York. After his 1777 campaign came to grief at Saratoga, Burgoyne spent much time and effort defending himself before a parliamentary inquiry, and published his defense entitled *State of the Expedition*. He was a brave, competent, humane soldier whose misfortune was to command an expedition doomed by badly coordinated planning by Whitehall and a reorganized and well-led American Northern Department.

Sir Guy Carleton (1724-1808), a member of an Anglo-Irish family, was a capable and dedicated professional soldier, governor of Canada, veteran of lengthy service in North America, and the leader of the first invasion from Canada (1776). His solid service in Canada did much to defeat American efforts to add a fourteenth province to the rebellion. One of the obstacles to his military advancement was the enmity of Lord George Germain.

George Clinton (1739-1812) was New York's first elected governor. An attorney with brief military experience before the war, he also served as a member of the Continental Congress, and later received a brigadier general's commission in March of 1777. Although he was elected governor on April 20, 1777, Clinton also commanded the unsuccessful American defenses against Sir Henry Clinton's Expedition into the Hudson Highlands. One of Alexander Hamilton's rivals, Clinton served as vice-president under both Thomas Jefferson and James Madison. He died in office in 1812.

Sir Henry Clinton (1738?-1795) was the only son of Admiral George Clinton, one time governor of Newfoundland (1732-1741) and New York (1741-1751), and the cousin of the Earl of Newcastle. He grew up in New York and seemed to have a genuine interest in the colonies. His military career began as captain-lieutenant in the New York Militia. Returning to England with his father, he began a lifetime career in the Coldstream Guards in November 1751. Clinton served with distinction at Bunker Hill and became a "local" lieutenant general and second in command to General Sir William Howe in September 1775, succeeding to the senior British command in America in March 1778. He served in that capacity until after Yorktown. Clinton is the subject of an outstanding biography by William B. Wilcox entitled *Portrait of a General: Sir Henry Clinton in the War of Independence* (New York, 1964).

A Scottish-born professional soldier, *Simon Fraser* (1729-1777) was a veteran of the War of Austrian Succession and Seven Years' War, and lieutenant colonel of the 24th Regiment of Foot. He commanded a brigade comprised of his regiment and the grenadiers and light infantry of Sir Guy Carleton's army in 1776. He commanded General Burgoyne's Advanced Corps during the Saratoga Campaign and was fatally wounded during the fighting on October 7, 1777. Nineteenth century writers, upon no contemporary evidence, attributed his death to rifleman Timothy Murphy, a man who, on the basis of his widow's pension application, was not even present at Saratoga.

Peter Gansevoort (1749-1812) was a member of a long-established and prominent Albany family, though little is known about his life before he served with General Montgomery's troops in the invasion of Canada as a major in the 2nd New York Regiment. Gansevoort became colonel of the 3rd New York Regiment on November 21, 1776, and in that capacity commanded the defense of Fort Stanwix.

Horatio Gates (1728-1806) was the English-born successor of General Philip Schuyler to command of the Continental Army's Northern Department. He spent most of his adult life in the British Army, serving in North America. He was present at Braddock's Defeat (1755), was a brigade major at Forts Pitt and Stanwix, and became the first adjutant general of the Continental Army. In that capacity, Gates performed yeoman service in helping General George Washington organize the American forces. After the successful conclusion of the Saratoga Campaign, he served during 1778 in Boston as commander of the Eastern Department. Unfortunately, Gates suffered a humiliating defeat in South Carolina at Camden in 1780. That, along with an ill-conceived move by some to have him succeed Washington made him, along with Charles Lee, one of the most maligned general officers of the Revolution. More competent than nineteenth century writers acknowledge, Gates' substantial talents were dimmed by ethical ambivalence. He was, however, well-suited for the role he filled at Saratoga. Contrary to some writers, he and Burgoyne never served in the same regiment. (Burgoyne entered the army in 1742 and served, except for brief duty during 1758 with the 2nd Regiment of Foot, all of his service with mounted troops in Europe before arriving at Boston in 1775. Gates entered the army in 1749 and served in infantry regiments in North America.) The architect of the Saratoga victory died in 1810. He was buried in the Trinity Church graveyard on Wall Street in an unmarked grave.

Lord George Germain (1716-1785) George Sackville (known as Lord George Sackville from 1720 until 1770, and Lord Germain until he became Viscount Sackville in 1782) was born in 1716. The son of the First Duke of Dorset, he entered the army and served on the Continent during the 1740s and 50s, while taking part in parliamentary affairs, becoming Secretary of State for Colonies, technically Secretary of State for the Southern Department, a post he held until February 1782. In that position, Lord Germain was responsible for the conduct of the war. His papers in the University of Michigan's William L. Clements Library are among the most important sources for any study of the American Revolution. He was more competent than his political opponents and many American writers have portrayed him. He had the misfortune to be one of Sir John Fortesque's favorite targets, but Sir John usually found civilian leaders lesser men than their military contemporaries.

A German-American leader and military commander of the Tryon County, New York, patriots, **Nicholas Herkimer** (1728-1777) led his men in relief of Fort Stanwix. He was mortally wounded when the British ambushed his column at Oriskany on August 6, 1777.

A competent combat general, Scotsman *James Inglis Hamilton* (? - 1803) led the 21st Regiment of Foot (Scots Fusiliers) during the American rebellion. At Freeman's Farm (September 19, 1777) Hamilton commanded General Burgoyne's Center Column. He served as a major general in the 1790s campaigns in the West Indies at the head of the 15th Regiment of Foot. His only son, whom he adopted while a prisoner following Saratoga, was a colonel with General Wellington's army, and was killed at the Battle of Waterloo.

Richard Howe (1726-1799) was the brother of General Sir William Howe and Commander in Chief of the Royal Navy's American Station from 1776-1778.

The British commander-in-chief in North America from 1775 to 1778, **William Howe** (1729-1814) first gained attention as a commander of a light infantry battalion that led General Wolfe's force onto the Heights of Abraham on September 13, 1759. A Whig member of Commons from Nottingham, Howe disapproved of Parliament's coercive colonial policies. His role in developing Britain's plans for 1777 is examined in detail in this study. Contemporaries and students have condemned his indolence while commanding in the colonies. Troyer Anderson, in his provocative masterpiece *The Command of the Howe Brothers During the American Revolution* (New York, 1936) wrote: "It is my belief that the failure of the Howes is a mystery only because the conventional division between military and political history had diverted attention away from the points that serve best to explain the conduct of British operations in America," and did not "adjust their methods to the support that the government was willing to provide." Sir William and his brother, Admiral Richard Howe, were grandsons of one of George I's mistresses, making them illegitimate uncles of George III.

Brilliant, eccentric, and unstable, ***Charles Lee*** (1731-1782) served in the British Army in America during the Seven Years' War and then in the Polish Army, attaining the rank of major general. Wounded while fighting the Turks, Lee migrated to America in 1773. Identifying with the Continental cause, he bought land in Berkeley County, Virginia. A half-pay [retired] British lieutenant colonel with impressive military experience and above-average intelligence, he impressed the Revolution's leaders, who appointed him major general on June 17, 1775, subordinate only to George Washington. Real accomplishments and controversy, however, accompanied his checkered career. The Continental Congress named him General Schuyler's successor to the northern command in January 1776, but countermanded the order by assigning him to lead the Southern Department. Contemptuous of political generals (i.e., most Americans), Lee ran afoul of Washington's explosive temper at the Battle of Monmouth on June 28, 1778, and was court-martialed. Lee is the subject of two outstanding examples of historical scholarship: John R. Alden's *Charles Lee, Traitor or Patriot* (Baton Rouge, 1951) and John W. Shy's essay in George Allen Billias, editor, *George Washington's Generals* (New York, 1964). Both do much to revise the traditional image of this strange but capable and much maligned character.

Henry Brockholst Livingston (1757-1823), a member of the powerful Livingston clan, graduated from Princeton in 1774, entered the Continental Army the following year, and served on the staffs of both Generals Philip

Schuyler and Benedict Arnold. As his surviving letters plainly indicate, Livingston played an active and insidious role in promoting the unfortunate rupture between Arnold and Horatio Gates that followed the fighting at Freeman's Farm on September 19, 1777. After the war, Livingston became a successful attorney and an anti-Federalist politician. In 1807, President Thomas Jefferson appointed Livingston to the U. S. Supreme Court.

After vigorous service with the Massachusetts militia, **Benjamin Lincoln** (1733-1810) became a Continental major general on February 17, 1777. Dispatched northward to assist General Philip Schuyler with directing militia in the Northern Department, Lincoln was responsible for much of Horatio Gates' successful use of militia on the eastern side of the Hudson River, as well as with the intelligence utilization of the difficult, but important John Stark. It was Lincoln's misfortune to have to surrender the important post of Charleston, South Carolina, on May 12, 1780. However, that disgrace was tempered in 1781 when he formally accepted the British surrender at Yorktown. Like so many officers who served during the American Revolution, Lincoln still awaits a good biography.

Born in either Bucks County, Pennsylvania or Hunterdon County, New Jersey, **Daniel Morgan** (1736-1802) left home at seventeen and settled in the Shenandoah Valley. After serving in the Seven Years' War and Dunmore War, he received a captain's commission and the command of two Virginia rifle companies, which he marched 600 miles to Boston without losing a man. He participated in the disastrous Quebec assault of December 31, 1775, and took over for the wounded Benedict Arnold, with fateful result. Paroled and later exchanged, Morgan received a colonel's commission as commander of the 11th Virginia Regiment. He raised a body of sharpshooters drawn from various Virginia, Maryland, and Pennsylvania units. These men formed the famous corps he marched to the Northern Department, where he and his men distinguished themselves. After a checkered service that included resignation, he was promoted to brigadier general and commanded the American army at the important Battle of Cowpens on January 17, 1781. His unusual choice of tactics that day changed the course of the war in the South. Don Higginbotham's *Daniel Morgan: Revolutionary Rifleman* (Chapel Hill, 1961) is an admirable study of a remarkable man.

Enoch Poor (1736-1780 was a native of Massachusetts, a shipbuilder, and a merchant. He became colonel of the 2nd New Hampshire Regiment, and brigadier general in February 1777. Poor served well in several campaigns, including the Saratoga operations, where his cool handling of his troops during the fighting on October 7, 1777, repelled a veteran British bayonet assault. When Poor died in 1780 (probably from typhus), George Washington lamented his passing by writing, "He was an officer of distinguished merit, one who as a citizen and soldier had every claim to the esteem and regard of his country."

Freiherr (Baron) Friedrich Adolph von Riedesel (1738-1800) attended the University of Marburg's law school and served in England and on the Continent during the Seven Years' War. After the Duke of Braunschweig

(Brunswick) contracted with Britain to provide 3,936 infantrymen and 336 dismounted dragoons for service in America, von Riedesel served with General Burgoyne in his offensive from Canada into New York. His contemporary writings reveal a distinct unease about his service in America under British command. A thorough professional, he left a valuable body of papers that were widely used in preparation for this study.

A fellow of St. Peter's College, Cambridge, and native of Ireland, **Barry St. Leger** (1737-1789) joined the British Army in April 1756 and served in America during the Seven Years' War, participating in the siege of Louisbourg and the capture of Montreal. As lieutenant colonel of the 95th Foot, with the "local" rank of brigadier, St. Leger commanded the expedition down the Mohawk River that ended with the failed siege of Fort Stanwix.

Richard Varick (1753-1831) served as military secretary to both General Schuyler and Benedict Arnold and as deputy Mustermaster General of the Northern Department from April 1777 to June 1780. Along with his friend, Robert Livingston, Varick actively promoted the damaging Arnold-Gates quarrel that broke out during the Saratoga operations.

James Wilkinson (1757-1825) was a native of Benedict, Maryland, and a medical student who enlisted in Thompson's Battalion in September 1775. He served capably in Canada and became deputy adjutant general of the Northern Department. Though a thoroughgoing scoundrel involved in avaricious and treasonable acts, Wilkinson prepared a solid two-volume memoir that stands up reasonably well when checked against other, more respectable, sources.

British Plans for 1777:
Fight the War "From the Side of Canada"

Proposals Galore

On November 30, 1776, while General George Washington's demoralized men retreated across New Jersey, General William Howe, recently knighted for his Long Island victory, wrote two letters to Lord George Germain, the Secretary of State for America. The first reported on the recent Westchester campaign and Fort Lee's capture. The second advised Germain that he intended to quarter a large body of troops in "East Jersey," and that he expected the Americans to try to cover their capital city, Philadelphia, by establishing a line on either the Raritan or Delaware River.

More important for future events, Howe also proposed a plan for the next year's campaign. Sir William noted that he had received word that Sir Guy Carleton had abandoned his southward drive down the Champlain-Hudson line. Howe fully expected, however, that Carleton would renew his campaign in the spring, but that he would not reach his objective of Albany until September 1777. Sir Guy's 1776 performance made that a reasonable assumption.

"In that persuasion," Howe proposed a plan that he believed might "finish the War in one year by an extensive and vigorous Exertion of His Majesty's arms." He intended to continue the current strategy against New England, "the cradle of rebellion." Howe proposed two simultaneous offensives: one from Rhode Island to take Boston, and a second from New York City up the Hudson to rendezvous with the renewed advance from Canada. That was not, however, the sum of Howe's strategy for 1777. Howe wanted a third force to operate in New Jersey to check Washington by exploiting American concern for

Philadelphia's security, which he "proposed to attack in the Autumn, as well as Virginia, provided the Success of the other operations will admit of an adequate force to be sent against that province." Subduing South Carolina and Georgia could wait for the winter of 1777-78.

Howe's plan to end the war in one campaign lasting a little more than one year was an ambitious one. But he was not the only British general proposing plans designed to bring the expensive American war to an end. The various plans of different generals made different assumptions, aimed at different strategic goals, required different resources—and even envisioned different commanders. Howe himself would supplant his own plan at least twice, as successive British and American successes altered the equation.[1] Out of these various intentions and realities would come the campaign of 1777, one that would result in, and then be so affected by, the battle of Saratoga.

Howe Initiates the Debate

Howe's initial proposal of November 30 required 35,000 men and ten additional ships of the line to assure success against the 50,000 men the Continental Congress had resolved to raise.[2] To provide Howe with 35,000 men would require a reinforcement of 15,000 rank and file, which he hoped might be "had from Russia, or from Hanover, and other German states, particularly some Hanoverian Chasseurs, who I am well informed are exceedingly good troops."

Sir William's second letter, especially its latter part, reflected an important strategic assumption. He believed that only the hope of French aid kept the rebellion alive, and that if the threat of foreign support were neutralized and the force he proposed was "sent out, it would strike such Terror through the Country, that no Resistance would be made to the Progress of His Majestys Arms in the Provinces of New England, New York, the Jerseys & Pennsylvania, after the junction of the Northern and Southern Armies." Howe's objective continued to be recovery of territory rather than the destruction of the rebel army. Like Henry Clinton and unlike Germain and Lord Cornwallis, Howe believed that victory required expansion of the area of effective imperial control. He thus aspired to take only so much territory as he expected to be able to occupy. The royal army's continued presence in that territory would enable the loyal majority to declare itself, enroll in provincial corps, and assume an expanding role in restoring imperial authority.[3] Sir William intended to achieve victory by moving with impressive strength through centers of rebellion, relying upon overawing the disaffected, animating the loyal, and demonstrating to the wavering the futility of resistance, rather than upon hard and costly fighting against an elusive and resilient adversary.

The Cabinet Begins its Considerations

Sir William's letters reached Germain's office on December 30, 1776, and the Cabinet began discussing them on January 10, 1777. Like most Britons, the ministers anticipated an early victory in America. Many civilian observers were less sanguine than were army and naval officers. The general's first letter, by reporting the autumn's successes, confirmed the official optimism and so set the tone for responding to the second letter. Because Howe's strategy for 1777 did not dispel the prevailing euphoria and conformed to the objectives of the 1776 campaign, it was acceptable.

But Howe's projection of manpower requirements made the colonial secretary and his colleagues uneasy. Germain did not trust his fellow countrymen's determination to continue to support the war if it became too costly in men and money. In fact, he had been resisting committing more troops to North America since mid-autumn, when he told Prime Minister Lord North that he would not want more men, and that it was "sufficiently difficult to keep up and recruit what we had, that he hop'd Expences would rather diminish."[4]

Ministerial unease found faithful reflection in Lord Germain's January 14 letter to the general. "When I first read your Requisition of a Reinforcement of 15,000 Rank & File," began Germain,

> I must own to you that I was really alarmed, because I could not see the least chance of being able to supply you with the Hanoverians, or even with Russians in time. As soon, however, as I found from your Returns that your Army is reinforced with 4,000 more Germans (which I trust will be procured for you) 800 additional Hessian Chasseurs, & about 1,800 Recruits from the British, & about 1,200 for the Hessian troops under your Command, will consist of very near 35,000 Rank & File. I was satisfied that you would have an Army equal to your Wishes, especially when I considered that the Enemy must be greatly weakened and depressed by late Successes, and that there was room to hope that you would not find it difficult to embody what number of Provincials you might think proper for Particular Parts of the Service.[5]

But since the ministry in its unease most wanted to be reassured, the correspondence was marked by wishful thinking, ambiguity, and flawed interpretation. Because the most recent returns reported that Howe had some 27,000 "effective men," Germain and his colleagues persuaded themselves that a 15,000-man reinforcement would raise Sir William's strength to some 42,000, substantially more than the 35,000 figure the general said he needed. Interpreting the returns uncritically and accepting the 35,000 figure as representing Howe's assessment of his immediate requirements led the ministers into successive misapprehensions. Failing to analyze the returns provided them with what seemed to be a good prima facie basis for claiming that 7,000 men would bring Howe's force to "very nearly 37,000 Rank & File." But while Howe's return used the term "effective men," it was not a realistic representation of his strength because it included men who were on detached service, sick, and prisoners of war. Howe really reckoned from an estimated 20,000 men present and fit for duty, not 27,000.[6]

Timely assembly and then transport of the reinforcements as well as their numbers were also critical. Sir William's goal of taking only as much territory as he could effectively occupy presupposed manning garrisons, so the need for a 15,000-man reinforcement was a long-term one that included provisions for occupation troops. In brief, Howe's strategy for defeating the revolutionaries required a continuing expansion of military re-conquest until it encompassed all of the colonies. That meant that the closer the British came to success, the more men would be required to both occupy areas already won and simultaneously carry on the campaign against those remaining in rebellion.[7] Thus, his proposal that Russian or additional German soldiers be engaged made sense: if the reinforcements were to support long-term as well as immediate operations, there was sufficient time to complete the necessary negotiations and transport the auxiliaries to North America.

Whitehall deferred comment on Howe's operational plans until after the Cabinet learned more about the existing situation in the war theater at the end of 1776. Germain advised the general that judgment was suspended until "His Majesty . . . shall have an Opportunity of taking into consultation the whole State of this Momentous Affair."[8]

Howe's Second Thoughts

As events tend to do in time of war, the situation changed. On December 20, ten days before his November 30 correspondence reached London, Sir William sent Lord Germain a radically new plan for the 1777 campaign—one that reflected a dramatically different situation in the Middle States. Events in New Jersey had moved with stunning speed. Instead of being on the Raritan as the end of the year neared, his army had chased Washington across the state to the Delaware-Pennsylvania line. The American seat of government in Philadelphia was temptingly vulnerable, and the rebellion seemed to be tottering toward dissolution. Jerseymen and Pennsylvanians were daily foreswearing their disloyal ways and seeking pardons to restore them to their former allegiance. Those who persisted in the perverse course of resistance were rapidly losing the capacity to give force to their seditious designs.

While British opinion was unanimous in viewing New England as the seed bed of rebellion, informed men on both sides of the Atlantic knew that Pennsylvania was critically important to America's future. It was politically mature, with a diverse, comparatively well-informed, prosperous citizenry that included a larger proportion of men of liberal sentiments than any other region. Its capital, Philadelphia, was the major American port, a lively cultural and economic center, the third largest city in the empire, and—since the First Continental Congress' convening there during the autumn of 1774—the Revolution's political seat.

But Pennsylvania's people, like their fellows in the other Middle Colonies, were less militantly hostile to imperial policies than New Englanders and Virginians. Not only was their more diversified economy less vulnerable to Parliament's measures, many Pennsylvanians sensed that they profited from the imperial connection. Half a century later, William Livingston recalled what a wrenching experience it was for the people of the Middle Colonies to break their ties with Britain. "They had themselves suffered little, if at all, under imperial rule," he wrote. "Under it they had prospered and multiplied."[9] These colonists living in the very middle of the pluralistic middle of British North America already enjoyed to an important degree the kind of society that other Americans aspired to, and it had become a reality without needing a revolution. An effective majority for resistance to parliamentary "Intolerable Acts" developed only with difficulty and over articulate and reasoned opposition.[10]

Because Sir William believed that Washington's reverses in the other middle states of New York and New Jersey strengthened opposition to rebellion, it was logical to conclude that threatening Philadelphia would force Washington to stand and fight. Victory, therefore, was within his grasp. "[T]he opinions of the people being much changed in Pennsylvania," Howe summarized, "and their minds in general, from the progress of the army, disposed to peace, in which Sentiment they would be confirmed by our getting possession of Philadelphia, I am from this consideration fully persuaded the Principal Army should act offensively on that side where the enemy's strength will certainly be collected."[11]

Changing the order of priorities required postponing the New England offensive until after reinforcements arrived from Europe, so "that there might be a Corps to act defensively on the lower part of Hudson's River to cover Jersey and facilitate in some degree the approach of the Canada Army."[12] In this proposal Sir William lowered his manpower requirements from 35,000 to 19,000 men. Of these, 2,000 would remain in Rhode Island, while 4,000 would defend Manhattan. He would employ 10,000 against Philadelphia, and 3,000 to defend New Jersey and operate on the lower Hudson to "facilitate the northern army's advance."[13] Three thousand men could really do little to support action on the northern frontier, but Howe did not expect that such support would be needed before September, by which time the flow of events and the arrival of requested reinforcements would enhance British capabilities.

Howe's December 20 letter departed from the assumptions that had informed British strategy since 1775. Instead of concentrating the combined power of the Canadian and "Principal" armies against New England, he proposed to leave the former force to make its way southward largely alone toward an ill-defined objective, while he overran the Middle States, captured the rebel capital, and ended organized resistance to imperial authority.[14]

Washington Provokes Howe's Third Plan

Before Lord Germain and his colleagues had received *either* of Howe's proposed plans, the military situation in New Jersey took yet another dramatic turn that blasted the general's fragile optimism and reordered his strategic priorities. With audacity inspired by desperation, General Washington attacked and captured most of Howe's German troops at Trenton on the morning of December 26, defeated Lord Cornwallis' rearguard under Lieutenant Colonel Charles Mawhood at Princeton on January 3, and executed a skillful withdrawal into the hills around Morristown. Washington's army, crowded to the precipice of dissolution shortly before, not only survived but regained West Jersey.[15]

When Lord Germain wrote his January 14, 1777, letter, he was still ignorant of the events that made Trenton and Princeton immortal in the annals of military history. He could look back on 1776 with justifiable satisfaction. His administration had raised, equipped, and transported large armies to North America. Canada remained British, Manhattan and Long Island were reclaimed, and—so far as the secretary knew—New Jersey and Rhode Island were secure. The rebellion seemed almost crushed. In fact, at the time Germain made his assessment, Britain was closer to winning the war than she would ever be again.

While the colonial secretary did have reason to congratulate himself, the failure to end the American war during 1776 exposed Britain to perils that only a victory in 1777 could dispel. The concentration of so much of her military capability in America was a bold, calculated gamble taken in the face of French hostility. Against that danger weighed the advantages of ending the colonial rebellion before European neighbors could intervene to Britain's disadvantage. That the rebellion was almost crushed was not good enough; its actual defeat had to be accomplished, and soon, because French conduct during 1776 made it clear that European peace depended upon an early British victory. Throughout the summer France inched toward war, watching and hoping for an opportunity to recoup interests and prestige lost during the Seven Years' War. Everything she sought depended upon events in America. Would Britain and her rebellious children reconcile? Could the Americans continue to fight and make independence a reality? When British success on Manhattan seemed to answer the second question in the negative, the French drew back from internationalizing the conflict. But England still needed an early and unequivocal victory to make the withdrawal of her perennial nemesis permanent.

Washington's New Jersey victories, then, were indeed a turning point and perhaps the most important one in the war. Coming after an unbroken series of defeats, they revived the languishing revolution and discouraged loyalists who had recently anticipated an early vindication of their decision to stand by the Crown. The battlefield successes gave force to Thomas Paine's pamphlet *The Crisis*, published on December 23. The value of Continental currency rebounded. Military morale, which had verged on collapse, recovered immediately, and recruiting parties, which had failed to obtain enlistments only days before, enrolled whole companies in Pennsylvania, Delaware, and Virginia. Interested European observers, especially the French, began to believe that the American rebellion, which after British successes on Long Island and

Manhattan had seemed a hopeless cause, might again be worth encouraging and exploiting.[16]

The effect of Washington's phoenix-like recovery on General Howe was immediate and profound. It doomed the peace efforts in which he and his brother, Admiral Lord Richard Howe, had invested their energies and prestige. And their pacification-directed strategies stood exposed in all their inadequacy. The general who had just days earlier on December 20 confidently predicated his plans for the next campaign on nurturing American desires for peace, eleven days later predicted that achieving victory would require another major campaign.[17] By mid-January deepening pessimism persuaded him that he did not "now see a prospect for terminating the war but by a general action and I am aware of the difficulties in our way to obtain it, as the Enemy moves with so much more celerity than we can. . . ."

Because that "general action" must engage Washington's revitalized army, Howe required reinforcements. Twenty thousand more men would not be too many, but he could make do with 15,000. The larger figure would make possible an advance against Pennsylvania by land and water. The main force would move through New Jersey, while the balance would ascend the Delaware River. Such numbers would enable Sir William, at the same time, to post a large enough force in Rhode Island to raid New England.[18]

Burgoyne Weighs In

A third party to British planning for 1777 appeared when Lieutenant General John Burgoyne returned to London during the night of December 9. Like other officers who were members of Parliament, Burgoyne returned to attend the winter sessions, and in his case to also attend to family matters that had been affected by his father-in-law's death in February and his wife's in June of 1776.[19] Sir Guy Carleton had given Burgoyne a memorandum to deliver to Lord Germain. The document contained general proposals and manpower and materiel requisitions for the renewed northern offensive, and he recommended Burgoyne to Germain as a source of firsthand information.

Carleton's memorandum requested a 4,000-man reinforcement, a part of which would be employed to increase regimental strengths by 100 men each. "With a reinforcement to the above amount, and well composed, a large Corps may be spared to pass Lake Ontario, and to operate upon the Mohawk River. Another Corps might possibly be employed to penetrate to Connecticut River." Carleton's main force would ascend Lake Champlain southward, take

Ticonderoga, effect a junction with the Mohawk diversionary column, and establish a base for attacking Massachusetts and Connecticut.[20] Although he did not identify Albany as his destination, including for a rendezvous with a force of British soldiers moving northward from New York City, Sir Guy assumed that such a junction would occur if he were to cooperate with Howe. Carleton, however, intended to carry out the northern invasion without assistance from the lower Hudson.

Carleton's memorandum, however, was little more than a first draft, a few brief sentences on a single sheet of paper, and he had asked Burgoyne to enlarge upon that outline. This the latter did during his homeward voyage. The result was entitled "Memorandum & Observations relative to the Service in Canada, submitted to Lord George Germain," a sixteen-page detailed synoptic report organized under the headings of "General Carleton Requisitions" and "Observations." Because preparing the report helped Burgoyne organize his thoughts in a manner that influenced the drafting of his own plan for 1777, a detailed review is useful.

Burgoyne's first observation responded to Carleton's requisition for a battalion of seamen, numbering at least 300 men, to man the transports and frigates needed to support the southward advance. Anticipating some possible arguments against the idea of attaching 300 seamen, Burgoyne endorsed his commander's requisition in concept, but argued instead for the assignment of watermen recruited from the rivers of England, supervised by naval officers, to man the "Battalion Boats" that carried stores and supplies, as "particularly in those of the foreign Troops, who cannot learn to row well, [they] would be of great use in point of regularity and Expedition." Burgoyne considered and rejected alternatives. He noted that the practice of detailing rowers from the regiments should not apply in a situation in which men had to be detailed as boat and supply guards, and that relying upon Canadians for the service was not a realistic solution because "their great practice upon the water being in canoes which paddle; they are very awkward with an Oar, they are besides under no discipline, continually desert, or pretend sickness." If instead the commander had the proposed corps of watermen available, he would be able to dispense with a greater part of his naval complement once the army passed the lakes and reached the Hudson's upper reaches.[21]

Carleton's second requisition was entitled "Augmentation of Artillery Consisting of two Companies & the whole number [of] Companies in the Service . . . completed to an hundred Men each." Burgoyne's endorsement noted that "The Artillery, after the light [infantry] troops, is the [most] important Arm in the American war. The Assistance obliged to begin from the Line to that Service [during] the last Campaign was a great weakening to the Regiments at the same time that it is a very inadequate Substitute for trained Artillery men."[22]

Next, Sir Guy reported he would need, early in the spring, provisions for six months "at the full Ration for one third more than the Effectives of Soldiers & Seamen." In a lengthy observation, Burgoyne supported the one-third augmentation as necessary to provide supplies for the Canadians, Indians, artificers, and provincials, and to make up for inevitable losses due (substantial losses were inevitable in a wilderness campaign) to accidents, lost items, and waste.[23] The expedition could not succeed without the services of Canadians, Indians, and loyalist provincials, and they had to be assured of adequate rations and stores. Men making decisions at Whitehall without the benefit of colonial experience needed educating about conducting a campaign "from the side of Canada," and Burgoyne was a willing didact. He was "persuaded that the demand of Genl. Carleton in the Article will be found to be put as low as can be made consistent with the probable Emergencies of the Service."

Burgoyne then wrote his longest and most relevant comments concerning Carleton's need to requisition 4,000 men to reinforce his current army. The army in Canada, observed Burgoyne, numbered only 10,174 men, "in which number is comprised a good deal of useless stuff, viz. men recruited in Germany for the British Regiments, and sent over last year. Not one tenth of which will be fit for the ranks, from Infirmities, malingering Habits, Dejection, or Profligacy of Disposition. Many of the Irish Recruits and Drafts," continued Burgoyne, "are equally bad. In the Germans are also many unserviceable Men."

In addition, the Royal Highland Emigrants included a number recruited from among American prisoners of war during the summer of 1776. Their conduct before being captured had not impressed Burgoyne, and he expected many of them to desert at the first opportunity.[24] The men of another loyalist unit, the Royal Regiment of New York, were "not yet anything like Soldiers, having wanted Commissioned Officers & Serjeants to train them."

Burgoyne summed up his assessment of British military strength in Canada as follows:

> Upon the whole therefore, when a moderate Deduction of Sick is added to the useless, the whole of the Canada Army as it now stands, allowing for the Recruits arrived in the Autumn, and I believe not all comprised in the returns, will not exceed eight thousand men of such troops as I believe

your Lordship would wish to risk the fate of an offensive Campaign upon, or the Reputation of any General you may think proper to recommend to his majesty.

He recommended leaving 3,000 men in Canada, although "Genl. Carleton may possibly think a thousand more necessary." Citing Benedict Arnold's march to Quebec, the American attack on Three Rivers [Trois Rivieres], and "the project . . . conceived by Washington for penetrating into Boston with a corps of five thousand men, and thereby changing Ground with Genl. Howe, at the time he meant to attack the Works at Dorchester," Burgoyne noted that the Americans were "capable and inclined" to undertake rash offensives. Even if such a riposte did not occur, there was a need to guard against "small incursions to secure your convoys of Supply, which must all pass first up the St. Lawrence to Sorell, and afterwards by that River and Lake Champlain."

Like others who served in Canada, Burgoyne suspected that some of its people were inclined towards subversion and that many were reluctant to honor the "Duty of Corvies, which will be indispensably necessary for the Supply of the Army, even among the well affected." An adequate force was necessary to support the British government and give effect to its writ, and he proposed the disposition of the regular troops left in Canada reflected in the table below:

Quebec Garrison	500
Posts on the Chandiere and disaffected Parishes [to] Point Levis	300
Montreal Garrison and posts between that town and Oswegatchie	300
Trois Rivieres	100
Chain from Sorrell to Chamblee	100
St. John's	200
Isle Aux Nois, LaPrairie, Vergere, towns on the south shore of St. Lawrence and communication posts to St. John's	200
Escorts for Convoys over Lake Champlain	400
Allowances for Sickness, Desertions & other Casualties	600

Such piecemeal use of troops for garrisoning purposes was in keeping with Howe's long-term strategic approach of expanding the territory held, but it would vitiate the army's strength as a striking force, and weaken its ability to defend itself against the enemy's striking force.

Because the British could not afford to have these additional security requirements back in Canada satisfied by regulars alone, it would be necessary to have Canadians available to provide support services. Arrayed behind the regulars, approximately 500 men would carry out patrols and man posts to intercept enemy communications, prevent desertions, procure intelligence, and generally keep the country quiet. Another 2,000 would work on fortifications, and a similar number, with carts and horses, would transport artillery, provisions, other stores, and baggage to the water and across the portages. (Burgoyne perceptively noted that this need for horses and carts would coincide with the Canadians' corn-planting season.) A final 1,500 to 2,000 men, Burgoyne hoped, would be attached to the army pursuing the Americans.

From this bounty of manpower the general believed Canada could afford to contribute only 2,000 men, and more than it would provide if "any Diminution is made in the number of Regulars left among them." And even this number was bound to be affected by any plans, overt or otherwise, by France to recover Canada. In that case, "All the Reasons for having a respectable force there, will derive double Weight, for safe as the Country may be against a second Seduction by the Rebels it is obvious to the slightest Observation that many parts of it are liable to be seduced by the French."

On his own initiative, Burgoye added a concluding requisition that proposed construction of twenty-four gunboats capable of carrying light twenty-four-pounders, heavy twelve-pounders, and eight-inch howitzers. He supported that suggestion with a letter from Major General William Phillips to Carleton, and argued that prefabricated boats would be superior to any that could be built of green lumber during the campaign.

Burgoyne concluded his "Observations" by arguing that in order to carry out "a vigorous opening of the Campaign," nearly all the requested commodities (personnel and supplies) needed to be assembled altogether and to arrive in Canada "early in the year," and then should leave Montreal by June, after which the St. Lawrence became problematical for transportation purposes.[25]

Burgoyne, Carleton, and Germain

Burgoyne returned to England under some apprehension about his reception. How men perceived his relations with Carleton was critical. Would that general's detractors associate the subordinate with the commander's flawed 1776 campaign? Just what, exactly, was Sir Guy's standing at Westminster?

It certainly was not obvious that Carleton was out of favor. A man who had so recently as the past July received the red ribbon of a Knight of the Order of the Bath, along with a special warrant permitting him to assume the title and wear its insignia before being formally invested, would not be naked to his enemies. His father-in-law, Howard, Earl of Effingham, boasted an old and noble lineage with kinship to the Duke of Norfolk and descent from a cousin of Elizabeth I who had commanded the fleet that defeated the Spanish Armada. Those sorts of ties still counted. More important, Sir Guy had a supporter in the King, who valued him enough to award him the Order of the Bath over Lord Germain's objections.[26]

Against those favorable odds stood Germain's and Carleton's mutual hostility, of which Burgoyne was keenly aware. He would need to take careful account in his dealings with the secretary of state. Gossip and newspaper stories represented Burgoyne as being in Sir Guy's bad graces, which could have helped lessen the effect of Burgoyne's famously haughty manner.

"Gentleman Johnny" sought to smooth the path to his reception with a letter written to Germain from Portsmouth explaining that he was coming to Whitehall at Carleton's behest to expound on the plans for the next year's campaign, assuring his Lordship of his zeal for the King's service.[27] Burgoyne presented himself to Germain's cabinet at noon on December 10, bringing with him Carleton's proposals and his own "Observations."

He may also have delivered Sir Guy's most recent dispatch, dated October 22.[28] In it, Carleton reported that cold weather precluded reactivating the post at Crown Point and that he had withdrawn his army into Canada. He expected the Americans to construct another lake flotilla during the winter.

Carleton's letter closed by commending his emissary Burgoyne:

> I cannot omit on this Occasion mentioning to your Lordship the great satisfaction I have received from the Services of General Burgoyne, not only for the Zeal and readiness with which he concurred with me in promoting his majesty's Service, but from the attention and assiduity which he showed in his countenancing & preventing all faction and party in this Army. Dispositions to which your Lordship must be sensible, when unfortunately they are encouraged by Persons eminent by their Stations, are capable of defeating the most zealous Endeavours, and of rendering abortive the best concerted plans of Operation . . . .[29]

By seemingly making him a party to his own personal feud with the secretary, Carleton compromised Burgoyne. Sir Guy represented him as having known about Germain's subversion of the 1776 campaign by introducing malcontents into the Canadian army and having acted to thwart its designs. For his part, Burgoyne always professed loyalty to Sir Guy, though he likely believed that Carleton's effort to insert him into the dispute justified tempering that loyalty.

Whether Burgoyne actually went beyond criticism to intrigue has been the subject of much historical debate. Some contemporaries and many students contend that he came to realize that Carleton's abandonment of Crown Point and withdrawal to Canada, once known, had so damaged Carleton's reputation at court that Burgoyne decided to conspire to supplant him as commander. That allegation only surfaced after the defeat at Saratoga, however, and Burgoyne would vigorously defend himself against this accusation during the subsequent Parliamentary debate in November 1777.[30]

As 1776 gave way to 1777, however, Burgoyne's star was in the ascendent. He could not have been in London long before learning Germain intended him, and not Carleton, to lead the new year's advance south from Canada. The secretary was determined that Sir Guy would not command the next campaign. Burgoyne did not have to intrigue to displace Carleton, and he knew it.

Lord Germain sent Carleton's dispatch and the memorandum to the King and asked to meet with him to report on his interview with Burgoyne.[31] Burgoyne attended the royal levee at St. James Palace during the morning of December 11 and met with the King that afternoon. Two days later, George III wrote to Lord North informing him that he would not dismiss Carleton because that would be unjust in the face of his valuable services. He observed, however, that "Perhaps Carleton may be too cold or not so active as might be wished, which may make it advisable to have the part of the Canadian army which must attempt to join Gen. Howe led by a more enterprising commander . . . Burgoyne may command the Corps to be sent from Albany . . . ."[32] Lord Germain's desires notwithstanding, the King at this point seems not to have yet made a firm decision to invest Burgoyne with the invasion's command.

Enter Clinton

Another general was on his way home from America. The disgruntled Henry Clinton returned to England at the end of February with two objectives in mind.

The first was to obtain redress for the affront he believed Lord Germain had offered him in a statement published in the *Gazette* soon after receiving Clinton's and Admiral Sir Peter Parker's reports of the Carolina expedition. That statement implied that Clinton had landed on Long Island in Charleston harbor, found the channel separating it from Sullivan's Island too deep to ford, and passively waited for the navy to reduce the Americans' "palmetto fort."[33] Clinton believed that he had a potent double-barreled weapon of self-defense: he could threaten to both resign his commission, and to publish the complete text of his Sullivan's Island dispatch. A comparison of the latter with the slanted extract Germain had released would expose how the secretary had twisted facts and maligned the general and his troops.

The second objective was to obtain an assignment that would release him from serving under Sir William Howe. Clinton's personality made him an unsatisfactory subordinate. As Professor Wilcox observed: "He was vociferous in suggestions and criticism, and hurt when they were brushed aside; he was quick to take the initiative, as at Bunker Hill and White Plains, and resented being called to heel."[34] By the end of 1776 Clinton knew that he disliked Howe, with whose strategy and tactics he had disagreed during operations around New York. As noted, Howe strategically focused upon capturing territory—in that instance Manhattan and its environs—with a minimum risk in men, a strategy that precluded an early decision at arms. Clinton, by contrast, favored aggressive tactics that included concentration and attack, the primary objective being the destruction of the enemy's army—which was what he had proposed at Manhattan. Exploiting British naval superiority in a joint amphibious operation that would envelop Washington's army went hand-in-hand with his land-based operation. The only time that Howe's headquarters accepted his suggestions, and then only reluctantly, was during the battle of Long Island, when he led the main assault around the Americans' left wing, an enveloping thrust that carried him behind the enemy center and produced perhaps the most brilliant tactical success Britain obtained during the war. Clinton wanted no more duty under the commander who had given him the most onerous assignments, spurned his advice, never thanked him for service well-performed, and squandered the fruits of that service.

He had a third, personal, reason for returning home. The general was a devoted father, and he missed his motherless children who were in the care of his sisters-in-law, Elizabeth and Martha Carter. His homesickness for Weybridge and its household was palpable in his private correspondence.

Clinton sent Captain Duncan Drummond ahead to test the political climate at Whitehall. The captain's reception was encouraging. Germain and the King seemed sympathetic, and George III was "thoroughly well satisfied with every part of his conduct: I have as high an opinion of him as any officer in my service."[35] Gratifying as the King's flattery may have been, Henry Clinton wanted solid proof of the government's good graces.

Clinton pursued his goals with uncharacteristic circumspection. His careful offensive was the product of his realization, soon after he arrived in London, that Carleton and Howe, rather than he, were out of favor in some quarters. Standing just below them, if their futures were at risk he might profit from their discomfiture. Under such circumstances, discretion might serve his desired ends more effectively than pique.

The *Experiment*, Captain James Wallace commanding, reached London with news of the German debacle at Trenton on February 12. Eleven days later Howe's official report on Trenton, together with news of Lord Cornwallis' defeat at Princeton and the British withdrawal from West Jersey, reached Whitehall.[36] The ministry blamed Howe for the state of affairs that resulted following Washington's brilliant recovery at Trenton and Princeton, but it was careful to keep that censure from becoming common knowledge and grist for opposition mills. Clinton had it in his power to embarrass the government by raising questions about his commander's management of the recent campaign. This he refrained from doing. Instead, he was prudent in public statements and in a letter to *The Public Advertiser* that minimized the importance of Washington's successes and represented prospects for victory as being better than they appeared to be.[37]

Discretion aside, Clinton found himself in a strong position to command the next invasion from Canada. He was Burgoyne's senior, he wanted the post, and he enjoyed the King's favor. Indeed, on February 24, four days before he arrived, George III advised Lord North that he intended to propose Clinton for the northern command and Burgoyne for his replacement as Howe's second.[38] Thus, the position seemed Clinton's for the asking. But as much as he coveted it, he did not ask for it—probably because he expected Howe to give it to him when the army from Canada came under his authority.

And so it came to pass that the government selected John Burgoyne instead of Henry Clinton. The ministry offered Clinton another post, that of military commander in Canada, which in effect demoted Carleton to civil governor. It was an attractive offer to a man who hungered for independent command, but he rejected it out of regard for Sir Guy.[39]

An unhappy Henry Clinton was left with two very unappealing alternatives: resignation or returning to the uncongenial post under Sir William Howe. He still wanted to correct the public record of the Sullivan's Island fiasco—a revision ardently dreaded by the ministry. The King would not consent to his retirement. The Order of the Bath sweetened a deal that returned the newly-invested knight to Sir William's "family" with a dormant commission to succeed Howe should he resign or become incapacitated. For the moment, Sir Henry's ardor to publicize the interesting dispatches relating to the failed Carolina campaign cooled.[40]

Burgoyne's Proposal

On February 28, the day Clinton arrived in London, John Burgoyne submitted to Lord Germain his lengthy memorandum "Thoughts for Conducting the War from the Side of Canada."[41] The document contained no novelties. Instead, it proposed a continuation of the strategy that had informed British planning since 1775, and repeated much that Burgoyne had "observed" when he presented Carleton's October 22, 1776, dispatch to Germain on December 10. It did embody, however, proposals for the forthcoming campaign that were, in essence, discussions of alternatives.

The initial objective would be to secure navigation of Lake Champlain. Reoccupied Crown Point would provide a temporary base of operations. After retaking Ticonderoga in early summer, the old fort and its satellites would "become a more proper place for arms than Crown-Point." With the lake and the "Gibralter of the North" secure, he explained, "The next measure must depend upon those taken by the enemy, and upon the general plan as concerted at home." If that "general plan" required Howe's entire army to operate on the Hudson, and "if the only object of the Canada army is to effect a junction with that force," Burgoyne proposed advancing to Albany by way of Lake George. Although he expected the Americans "to be in force upon the lake," he hoped to use "savages and light forces" to force them "to quit it without waiting for naval operations." Failing that, he might resort to the South Bay-Skenesborough route, which would entail "a great deal of land-carriage for the artillery, provision, &c which can only be supplied from Canada." If the Americans continued in strength around the lake, it would be necessary to leave "a chain of posts, as the army proceeds, for securities of your communication, which may too much weaken so small an army." If land operations failed to overpower the enemy, making necessary an attack by water, the army had to be prepared by having available "carriages, implements, and artificers, for conveying armed vessels from Ticonderoga to the lake."

The general reiterated that a part of his "Thoughts" was the product of the "supposition that it be the *sole* purpose of the Canada army to effect a junction with General Howe, or after co-operating so far as to get possession of Albany and open communication to New York, to remain upon the Hudson's-River, and thereby enable that general to act with his whole force to the southward" [emphasis added] in conformity with Sir William's November 30 plan, which Germain received on December 30.

A potential alternative, continued Burgoyne, would be to operate directly against New England by forming a junction on the Connecticut River with the "corps in Rhode Island. Should the junction between the Canada and Rhode Island armies be effected upon the Connecticut," he explained, "it would not be too sanguine an expectation that all New England provinces will be reduced by their operation." Burgoyne also suggested that an important secondary offensive along the ancient Lake Ontario-Mohawk River route would provide "a diversion to facilitate every proposed operation."

If the army from Canada was judged inadequate "for proceeding upon the above ideas with a fair prospect of success, the alternative remains of embarking the army at Quebec, in order to effect a junction with General Howe by sea, or to be employed separately to co-operate with the main designs, by such means as should be within their strength upon other parts of the continent." Burgoyne noted that a sea-borne expedition would be less threatening to the Americans, nor "so effectual to close the war, as an invasion from Canada by Ticonderoga. This last measure ought not to be thought of, but upon positive conviction of necessity."

That final option was really a counsel of desperation, justified only if the strategic situation became drastically worse in the spring. It would require leaving too large a force in Canada, reducing the reinforcement force's tactical and strategic value. A large fleet, already committed elsewhere, would have to be diverted. The troops could not reach New York City until September, and all of the advantages inhering in a two-pronged attack would be lost.

Nowhere in Burgoyne's discussion of these alternatives does he infer that establishing a chain of forts along the Champlain-Hudson line and isolating New England were campaign objectives in and of themselves. British successes on both the upper and lower Hudson might happily result in New England's strategic isolation, but the campaign's purpose, in the final analysis, was primarily to make a strong additional force in the American interior available to Sir William Howe for use in executing whatever plan was adopted across the Atlantic at Whitehall.

Because his "Thoughts" discussed alternatives Burgoyne believed could accomplish the required overall goal, he did not precisely identify any intermediate objectives. Once Ticonderoga was again British, the "general plan of the campaign concerted at home" would determine the course the campaign would follow and identify the incidental objectives. He assumed that the ministry would develop and promulgate a definitive plan that would prescribe how he and Sir William would coordinate their respective operations. The closest that he came to anticipating an ultimate objective was when he based his first alternative upon the assumption that his campaign's "sole" purpose would be to form a junction with Howe, or "after cooperating so far as to get possession of Albany open communication to New York, to remain upon Hudson's River, and thereby enable that general to act with his whole force to the southward." That "whole force" would, of course, include the troops from Canada. And so Burgoyne expected to act in concert with Howe, but he did not define the form that cooperation would take. For that, "Gentleman Johnny" looked to the King and his ministers for direction.

Optimism born of high self-esteem attended all of John Burgoyne's public career, but when he planned to move an army from Canada into New York's interior, optimism did not blind him to the difficulties nature and the enemy could throw in his way. He assumed the Americans would strongly reinforce Ticonderoga (whose works could hold about 12,000 men), station a large flotilla on Lake George, and block the crude roads from Ticonderoga via Skenesborough to Albany by felling trees, destroying bridges, and erecting fortifications, "Thereby obliging the King's army to carry a weight of artillery with it." Because he expected to meet determined resistance, Burgoyne suggested that the "operating army" required at least 8,000 regulars, plus a strong train of artillery, a corps of watermen, 2,000 Canadians, and at least 1,000 Indians.

The King Responds

Prerogative made the King the captain-general of all the realm's armed forces. No constitutionally-responsible minister administered the military establishment. The King might appoint a commander-in-chief, but the Hanoverian kings had a strong military tradition and prided themselves on personally exercising their military prerogative. Like his grandfather, George III preferred to dispense with the services of an intermediary, so from 1770 until 1776, when Lord Jeffrey Amherst received the post, the army had no commander-in-chief.[42]

King George cherished his prerogative, but he did not presume a monopoly on military expertise. Wisely, he had either Lord Jeffrey Amherst or Adjutant General Edward Harvey review Burgoyne's "Thoughts."[43] The solicited critique of his proposals guided George III when he responded to the projected plan, in his own hand, in "Remarks on the Conduct of the War from Canada." Indifference to detail was not one of the King's attributes, and the following excerpts from his holographic "Remarks" illustrate the seriousness with which he addressed his royal duties. "The outlines of the plan seem to be on a proper foundation," he began.

> The rank and file of the army in Canada (including the 11th of the British, McClean's corps, the Brunswicks and Hanover) amount to 10,527; with the eleven additional companies and 400 Hanover Chasseurs, the total will be 11,443.

> As sickness and other contingencies must be expected, I should think not above 7,000 effectives can be spared over Lake Champlain, for it would be highly imprudent to run any risk in Canada.

> The fixing of the stations of those left in the province may not be quite right, although the plan proposed may be recommended. Indians must be employed, and this measure must be avowedly directed . . . .

> As Sir William Howe does not think of acting from Rhode Island into Massachusetts, the force from Canada must join him at Albany.

> The Diversion on the Mohawk ought, at least, be strengthened by the addition of 400 Hanover Chasseurs.

> The provisions ought to be calculated for a third more than the effective of the soldiery, and the general ordered to avoid delivering these when the army can be subsisted from the country.

> Burgoyne certainly undervalues the German recruits.

The idea of carrying the army by sea to Sir William Howe would certainly require the leaving of a much larger part of it in Canada, as in that case the rebel army would divide that province from the immense one under Sir W. Howe. I greatly dislike that idea.[44]

In his memorandum the King effectively selected from the alternatives Burgoyne proposed when he wrote "the force from Canada must join him [Howe] at Albany," underlining his words. Thus, when he drafted his memorandum, the King expected a junction of forces at Albany. There was, however, a possibility that his servants might interpret those words in critically different ways—as the unfolding of events would prove. Nonetheless, King George III's reply bestowed royal approval upon Burgoyne's plan.

On March 1, John Burgoyne received command of the army that would invade New York from the side of Canada.[45]

The Government Formulates its General Plan

The colonial secretary had begun drafting the government's plan long before the King wrote his memo. Germain's first draft had been written in response to Howe's optimistic second plan, contained in Sir William's letter of December 20, and then Burgoyne's royally-approved "Thoughts for Conducting the War from the Side of Canada." Before Germain completed that draft, he received Howe's considerably more pessimistic January 17 and 20 correspondence. Burgoyne's plan assumed cooperation with Sir William—to the end (in the King's problematical words) that "the force from Canada must join him at Albany."

However, Howe's three letters, optimistic and pessimistic alike, made it obvious where ultimate responsibility for determining strategy and assigning missions resided. In his December 20 dispatch, he "desired that any other Plan might be mentioned to him that might be thought more advisable." Burgoyne similarly had committed himself to act in conformity with "the general plan of the campaign concerted at home."[46]

Germain and his ministerial colleagues, responsible for determining what that general plan would be, could take justifiable satisfaction in how they had met the rebellion's challenges—at least until the final days of 1776. True, Washington's eleventh-hour recovery had blasted hopes of immediate victory, but some optimistic observers professed to believe that the recovery was merely the final spasm of a dying revolt. Germain himself was still captivated by his own optimism, still intent on avoiding asking Parliament to provide more troops for America, and still eager to believe that Sir William, his personal nominee, would win the war if he could be persuaded to act more ruthlessly.

Still, Germain was unable to resolve the various proposed plans' inherent inconsistencies in assumptions, strategic goals, and required resources. In that state of mind, he wrote to Howe the following ambiguous directive:

> In my despatch of 14 January . . . you were informed that His Majesty thought proper to defer sending you his Sentiments on your Plan for the next Campaign, until He was enabled to take the whole into His Royal Consideration.

> I am now commanded to acquaint you that the King entirely approves your proposed Deviation from the Plan which you formerly suggested being of the Opinion that the Reasons which have induced you to recommend this Change in your Operations are solid and decisive.

The King also recommended . . .

> [a] 'warm Diversion' against Massachusetts and New Hampshire coasts that would not only impede Levies for the Continental Army, but tend much to the Security of Our Trade, and indeed, it scarcely admits a doubt but that these Benefits must inevitably result from such an Arrangement; For as, on one hand, it is scarcely to be expected that those Provinces will part with Men when their Presence must be wanted for the internal Defence of their own respective Districts; so on the other, a salutary Check will unavoidably be put to the Successes of the Privateers, when we have destroyed or taken Possession of the Ports.[47]

General Howe's sights were on Philadelphia and the Middle Colonies as central to victory and pacification, but George III still saw New England as the rebellion's nursery, and correctly appreciated the importance of Yankee military and marine contributions to that rebellion. As the King's servant, Lord Germain could not be faulted for transmitting the King's proposal that the Howe brothers take operations against New England into "serious Consideration, so far as your intended Plan will admit." But the colonial secretary's responsibilities went beyond the duty to make the royal pleasure known to the Crown's servants. Germain was the minister most directly involved in the process of concerting a "general plan." He played a major role in shaping the King's perceptions, and was the principal architect of the strategies necessary to make the royal pleasure a reality.

How realistic was Germain's directive to Howe? Did the secretary believe that General Howe could, with the force available to him, take and secure Philadelphia, immobilize Washington, raid New England, *and* form a junction with Burgoyne at Albany? Unless the rebellion was truly in its death throes, only the most ill-informed and optimistic official could have been that naive. In fact, the secretary was poorly informed—but he could not help being so. He was dependent upon Burgoyne, Carleton, Howe, and others for intelligence that was flawed and out of date when he received it, and he was captive to the logic of his relations with them.

Whatever his flawed perception, Germain nonetheless brought to his responsibilities a singular determination, a devotion to duty, and a high opinion of his own capacities. Within a few days, however, he would be guilty of an act of negligence that would color later assessments of those supposed qualities.

The Generals Are(n't) Instructed

Sir Guy Carleton was the first to receive direction. On March 26—the same day Burgoyne again attended the King's noon levee and received his oral instructions—the secretary informed Carleton that as soon as he had driven "the rebel forces from the frontiers of Canada, it was his Majesty's pleasure that you should return to Quebec, and take with you such parts of your army as in your judgement and discretion appeared sufficient for the defence of that province; that you should detach Lieutenant General Burgoyne, or such other officer as you think most proper, with the remainder of the troops, and direct the officer so detached to proceed with all possible expedition to join General Howe, and put himself under his command." With those words, Lord Germain advised his enemy that he would not lead his army in the renewed campaign.

The secretary continued, delivering a gratuitous, if veiled, criticism of Sir Guy's aborted 1776 campaign by implying that another commander would redeem that lost opportunity:

> With a view of quelling the rebellion as soon as possible, it is become
> highly necessary that the most speedy junction of the two armies should
> be effected; and therefore, as the security and good government of
> Canada absolutely requires your presence there, it is the King's

determination to leave about 3000 men under your command, for the defence and duties of that province, and to employ the remainder of your army upon two expeditions, one under the command of Lieutenant General Burgoyne, who is to force his way to Albany, and the other under the command of Lieutenant Colonel St. Leger, who is to make a diversion on the Mohawk River.

His Lordship continued with the slyly insulting admonition, "I am to acquaint you, that as soon as you shall have fully regulated everything relative to these expeditions (and the King relies upon your zeal, that you will be as expeditious as the nature of the business will admit) it is his Majesty's pleasure that you shall detain for the Canada service" a total of 3,770 soldiers, which the secretary specifically detailed, and put under the command of Burgoyne a total of 7,173 soldiers, which he also specified, "together with as many Canadians and Indians as may be thought necessary for this service."

After furnishing Burgoyne "in the fullest and completest manner with artillery, stores, provisions, and every other article necessary for his expedition, and secured to him every assistance which it is within your power to afford and procure," Carleton was to give him "orders to pass Lake Champlain, and from thence, by the most exertion of [the] force under his command, to proceed with all expedition to Albany, and put himself under the command of Sir William Howe." Germain concluded with this final, crucial, paragraph:

> I shall write to Sir William Howe from hence by the first packet; but you will never the less endeavour to give him the earliest intelligence of this measure, and also direct Lieutenant General Burgoyne and Lieutenant Colonel St. Leger, to neglect no opportunity of doing the same, that they may receive instructions from Sir William Howe, it is his Majesty's pleasure that they will act as exigencies may require, and in such manner as they shall judge most proper for making an impression on the rebels, and bringing them to obedience; but that in so doing they must never lose view of their intended junction with Sir William Howe as their principal objectives.[48]

Unfortunately for the cause of British arms, the secretary failed to fulfill his obligation to "write to Sir William Howe . . . by the first packet." When Germain stopped by his office on his way to depart for a weekend in Kent, he discovered that neither his undersecretary nor his deputy secretary had finished preparing the clean copy of the order to Howe. With his horses standing in the street, Germain refused to wait for the job to be completed. His deputy proposed to simply inform Howe by sending him a copy of Burgoyne's instructions. The order intended for Howe was soon finished, but Germain by this time was on his way to Kent. Lacking a signature, the order was filed and never sent.[49] And so it came to pass that neither Lord Germain nor his aides sent explicit orders to General Howe directing him to move troops northward to Albany to rendezvous with Burgoyne and St. Leger.

Germain's Concept

In the absence of such instructions, Howe was left to interpret his role instead of doing so in keeping with what was supposedly required of him by the "general plan concerted at home," which reflected the ideas and requirements contained in Burgoyne's "Thoughts for Conducting the War from the Side of Canada."

Germain's later letter of May 18, 1777, notifying Howe that the King and his ministers seemingly approved of whatever the general thought wise, contained this phrase regarding a campaign against Philadelphia: "trusting, however, that whatever you meditate, it will be executed in time for you to cooperate with the army ordered to proceed from Canada."[50] The secretary seemed to anticipate that Sir William could make a flying excursion to Philadelphia, occupy it without serious effort, spend a few days organizing a loyal government, and return to New York to take whatever action was needed to cooperate with the forces moving south under Burgoyne. So strong was Germain's conviction that Howe could and would return to New York City in time to personally cooperate with Burgoyne, or that he would leave a force adequate for that purpose in the city, that he neither issued definitive orders to Howe nor advised Burgoyne of everything else the former intended doing.

Confident of Sir William's judgment, the secretary contented himself with stating his trust that the general would not permit the Philadelphia campaign to jeopardize the northern expedition's success. Such trust, of course, is a poor substitute for clarity. Germain's benign hope, in the form of his May 18 letter, reached Howe on August 16—too late to influence events. By then, Howe was on his way to Philadelphia, and Burgoyne was advancing down the Champlain-Hudson line.

Behind Lord Germain's optimistic leaving Sir William free to act as his discretion dictated was the secretary's concept of the plan he was responsible for concerting and articulating. That plan, as he claimed to conceive it, did not require the three forces to operate in concert to meet at Albany (although he did expect an unarticulated degree of "co-operation"). Rather, he expected Burgoyne and St. Leger independently to reach Albany, where they would become parts of Howe's command, hold the territory gained, and be available for Howe to employ in future operations. That interpretation seemed consistent with Burgoyne's statement in his "Thoughts" when he wrote, "the sole purpose of the Canada army [is] to effect a junction with General Howe; or after co-operating so far as to get possession of Albany and open communication to New York, to remain upon Hudson's-River, and thereby enable that general to act with his whole force to the southward."[51] Germain apparently did not envision Howe needing to contribute directly to the junction at Albany. Burgoyne and St. Leger would operate independently until they became available to Sir William at their Albany rendezvous.

"[W]ith regard to the Canada campaign," Lord Germain later informed the House of Commons on November 18, 1777,

> the honourable gentleman was under a mistake when he imagined that General Burgoyne had orders to fight his way to New York and then join Sir William Howe; his entire orders were to clear the country of rebels as far as Albany, which town was prescribed to him as the boundary of his expedition, unless circumstances might make it necessary to co-operate with General Howe, in which case he was to assist him to the utmost of his power.[52]

The final sentence implied that Germain expected Howe—and not Burgoyne nor St. Leger—to need assistance securing the Hudson valley.

Given this conception of the intended 1777 campaign, it was unnecessary for Germain to send direct personal orders to Sir William. With a copy of Burgoyne's instructions and the secretary's approval of the Philadelphia expedition, Howe had been told all that he needed to know.

Howe's Intentions

The absence of such orders would not excuse Howe for failing to act on the Hudson, if a reasonable assessment of the strategic situation dictated doing so.

That makes it necessary to attempt to determine how he conceived his role, whether that concept was valid, and whether his actions were consistent with his concept.

Sir William certainly was aware that a junction at Albany was contemplated, and that he was the avowed beneficiary of Burgoyne's and St. Leger's missions. For his part, his letter of November 30 had predicated his first plan for 1777 upon the success of renewed aggressive action down the Hudson. Germain had also dropped hints. In his letter of April 19, the secretary advised the general that the Hessian chasseurs, mentioned in his letter of March 3 as intended for Howe's army, were to be part of St. Leger's force, which was to become part of Howe's command when it reached Albany. He also told the general that the men holding local commissions as brigadiers would cease to hold that rank when they joined him.

But Sir William was not a subtle man, and hints did not make a very profound impression on him. As early as April 5, when he learned that reinforcements from England would fall short of the number requested and that his southern campaign had already been so delayed that he could not take Philadelphia in time to enable him to cooperate with any expedition from Canada, he wrote to Sir Guy Carleton. Howe's missive advised Carleton that he must not expect a cooperating column to come up the Hudson during the early phases of the next campaign. Any army coming down from Canada must, therefore, make its way on its own.[53]

That Sir William acknowledged some obligation to cooperate in the campaign's execution is apparent in the following paragraph:

> The further progress of this Corps, depending so much upon the enemy's movements cannot be foreseen at this Distance of Time; still I flatter myself and have Reason to expect, the Friends of Government in that part of the country [the Hudson Valley] will be so numerous, and so ready to give every aid and assistance in their power, that it will prove no difficult task to reduce the more rebellious part of this Province; In the meantime I shall endeavour to have a Corps upon the lower part of the Hudson's River sufficient to open the communication for shipping thro' the Highlands, at present obstructed by several forts erected by the Rebels for that purpose, which Corps may afterwards act in favor of the Northern Army.[54]

Like Burgoyne and Germain, Sir William invested more confidence in loyalist capabilities than he should have. But more to the point, while giving priority to Pennsylvania, he promised to commit a "Corps" to acting in Burgoyne's behalf by exerting pressure on the Americans from the lower Hudson.

Howe was prudently concerned about Washington's potential for affecting events in the north. He knew that if the American commander-in-chief turned his attention in that direction and moved against Burgoyne, that general would be in grave danger. "Washington is waiting our motions here, and has detached Sullivan with about 2,500 men to Albany," Howe advised Burgoyne on July 17. "My intention is for Pennsylvania, where I expect to meet Washington, but if he goes to the northward contrary to my expectations, and you can keep him at bay, be assured I shall soon be after him to relieve you."[55] Howe had, by the summer of 1777, absorbed the hard-learned lesson not to underestimate Washington's capacity for exploiting strategic opportunity.

Sir William explained his concern in greater detail in a letter he wrote Germain on July 16. He expected the American commander to try to cover Philadelphia by following him to Pennsylvania, in which case he thought that Burgoyne would experience few difficulties (except the logistical problems inherent in the type of expedition being undertaken) in reaching Albany. "[O]n the other hand," continued Howe,

> if General Washington should march with a determination to force General Burogyne, the strength of General Burgoyne's army is such as to leave me no room to dread the event; but if General Washington's intrusion should be only to retard the approach of General Burgoyne to Albany, he may soon find himself exposed to an attack from this quarter and from General Burgoyne at the same time; from both which, I flatter myself, he will find it difficult to escape.

Howe went on in an effort to justify approaching Philadelphia by ascending the Delaware River:

> Under the circumstances I propose going up the Delaware, In order to be nearer his place than I should be by taking The course of the Chesapeake which I once intended, or preferred to that of the Delaware provided the enemy had discovered a disposition to defend Pennsylvania.[56]

Clinton Returns, and the Sparring Continues

Newly-knighted Sir Henry Clinton returned to New York on July 5, the day Howe embarked upon his Pennsylvania campaign. Clinton recorded a conversation he had with Howe on July 13, ten days after he rejoined his commander.[57] "I told him I thought Washington had before this detached a great force to meet Burgoyne," recalled Sir Henry. "He [Howe] said he hoped he would go with his whole Army, for that he could never come back, and could not live there . . . Said I did not know whether he could come back, but was sure Burgoyne could not come forward, upon which depended the whole campaign. He said he hoped to see Burgoyne no further than Albany, and he wrote him word he could not cooperate with him early."[58]

Howe convinced himself that Burgoyne and St. Leger were strong enough to reach Albany unaided unless Washington went to Philip Schuyler's aid, in which case the two British armies would unite to crush him. That happy possibility persuaded Howe that approaching Philadelphia via the Delaware would place him in the best position to exploit whatever strategic opportunities his enemy's movements offered.

Clinton, however, long opposed to such an expedition,

> took the liberty . . . to say that it was highly probable that [while] the fleet was gone to sea that Mr. Washington would move everything that he could collect against General Burgoyne or me, and crush one or the other; as neither would be capable of withstanding such superior force unless time intelligence should fortunately bring the fleet to our relief. My arguments were at first little attended to, tho' from a conviction of the solid grounds upon which they were founded repeated perhaps oftener than was agreeable. By degrees, however, I thought I was listened to; [but] the momentary suspense which seemed to have been occasioned by what I said, soon yielded to predilection Sir William had for his own plan, which he told me could not with propriety be laid aside on account of its having been approved at home.[59]

Clinton concluded that Howe was aware of the dangers inherent in the Philadelphia campaign, but believed that, because it had the royal approval, he had little choice but to go ahead.

Nonetheless, Clinton continued to press upon his superior the alternative to Howe's plan, emphasizing its positive potential. "I told him with regard to his present plan was a good one but that I thought the time of the year bad, and that the better move would be to act upon the Hudson in force, if possible the junction and then the four provinces were crushed."[60]

In other venues, such as a letter to General Edward Harvey, Clinton instead emphasized possible negative consequences: "The only thing therefore in my opinion left for us now in the middle of July, is to cooperate in force with the northern army, not by a junction with it (for that I can never advise) but that sort of communication which will give us possession of Hudson's River; as it is, I almost doubt whether the northern army will penetrate as far as Albany."[61] Thus, in either coloration Clinton dissented from Sir William's optimistic appraisal of Burgoyne's chance for success, contending that the lower Hudson would have to be secured if the troops from Canada were to even reach Albany successfully.

His protests continued without any result other than Howe's admitting that he did not expect Burgoyne to advance south of Albany. Sir Henry recorded the following overall assessment of the strategy:

> When the design of employing an army under General Burgoyne on the Upper Hudson was mentioned to me; I took the liberty of suggesting the Hazard of miscarriage unless it was supported from below; and the consequent propriety of directing an early cooperation of Sir William Howe's whole force on the lower District of the River. For the attacking [of] Philadelphia (which I understand to be the object of that General Officers first operations in the ensuing campaign) could be undertaken only upon the principal [sic] of drawing on a general action with the Rebels; I humbly presumed that End (if anything could effect it) was more likely to be obtained by a vigorous exertion of the two British Armies on the Hudson; the passes of which must consequently fall under their power.[62]

Instead of a mere junction at Albany, Clinton favored cooperating in a conquest of the Hudson. The British could then turn their combined attention to taking Philadelphia.

Howe admitted that he had formerly believed that to be the best plan, but reports of large numbers of loyalists in Pennsylvania had persuaded him that the southern move would be better. Clinton agreed that there might be "friends of the Government" there, but similar expectations in New Jersey had ended in disappointment. He also pointed out that Howe would have to maintain a defensive force in New York and Rhode Island while prosecuting the Pennsylvania offensive. But Howe only replied by falling back upon the royal approval—though *without* invoking its admonition to undertake action there *only if* doing so did not jeopardize the northern campaign's success.

Clinton also recorded the curious fact that, even after Howe's expedition got under way, he (Clinton) could not bring himself to believe Philadelphia was Howe's real objective. He suspected the move was a feint intended to conceal a quick return and an advance up the Hudson to cooperate with Burgoyne. In his account of the American war entitled *The American Rebellion*, Clinton claimed that he was "persuaded he intended to deceive us all, though he was pleased to say he was going to sea with the present northerly wind, I should expect to see him return with the first southerly blast and run up the North River."[63]

In spite of Clinton's arguments and Howe's own apparent occasional misgivings, Sir William did launch the campaign that gained him the capture of Philadelphia—a pyrrhic success because, as many scholars have noted, the city figuratively took him captive while the American Congress simply moved the government first to Lancaster and then to York.

In a letter of October 22 to Lord Germain, after Burgoyne had surrendered his army at Saratoga and Howe learned that his defeated colleague had declared that he expected to meet a cooperating force at Albany, Howe wrote:

> In my last letter to Sir Guy Carleton, a copy of which was transmitted to your lordship in my despatch of April 2nd 1777, no. 47, and which His Majesty was pleased to approve, I positively mentioned that no direct assistance could be given to the northern army. This letter I am assured was received by Sir Carleton and carried by him to Montreal before General Burgoyne's departure from thence.[64]

Sir William never deviated from that self-exculpation.[65]

The Planning Ends

Our study of British plans for "the War from the Side of Canada" has examined Carleton's proposals and requisitions, Burgoyne's 'Observations' and his 'Thoughts,' and Germain's and Howe's perceptions of what implementation of those 'Thoughts' entailed.[66] Planning for the American campaign of 1777 began with numerous proposals by multiple generals, which were then responded to and modified by other government officers.

Given the dilatory communications and transportation technology of the day, some difficulty with efficient exchange of proposals, the effective production of a consensus, and the authoritative delivery of the resulting plan would have been predictable anyway. Add to that the personal likes and dislikes, the past rivalries, and the continuing career competition amongst the various officials involved, military and civilian alike, and the likelihood of differing interpretations of any less-than-clear directions were magnified.

Under those directions each particular general and minister had either obligations he was himself to fulfill, or obligations that he delegated to others to fulfill, or both. Whether any particular one of the variant interpretations of those obligations that developed were the result of honest confusion, willful disobedience, or shameful negligence is impossible to absolutely establish at this late date. What is certain is that these questions became the subject of bitter argument and the casting of many aspersions.

What can be said with certainty is that the residue of ambiguity and confusion that adhered to the plans and their execution contributed to the military situation in which General John Burgoyne and his soldiers found themselves when the 1777 campaign began to unfold: that of an army making its way, unsupported, deep into hostile territory, with the season advancing, and supplied with insufficient men and materiel to meet the challenges with which its enemies and the circumstances would confront it.

2

Invasion from Canada

Burgoyne Takes Charge of his Forces: The Good News

General John Burgoyne attended the royal levee at noon, Wednesday, March 26, where he had an audience with King George III. During the meeting, he received oral instructions from the King about his upcoming assignment in Canada. That same day, Lord Germain wrote a letter to Sir Guy Carleton containing the only written orders concerning his campaign Burgoyne ever received, and which Carleton would later turn over to him on June 10 when he formally invested him with the command of the Canadian Army.[1] On March 27, Burgoyne left London for Plymouth, where he dispatched a brief message to Sir William Howe advising him of the instructions he had received during his audience with the King, boarded the frigate *Apollo*, and after a moderately rapid crossing, arrived at Quebec on May 6. Six days later he traveled to Montreal to assume command of his army.

As of July 1, Burgoyne's army consisted of some 4,400 British troops and almost 4,700 German soldiers. The British contingent included 400 artillerymen, but was mostly made up of seven regiments of foot, each numbering between 500 and 600 men. The German contingent's equivalents were 100 artillerymen and five regiments of 500 to 700 infantry each, plus one regiment each of dragoons, grenadiers, and chasseurs, or jägers. In total, 8,671 infantrymen and 516 artillerymen, or 9,187 regulars, reduced by the retention in Canada of 343 British and 447 Germans to 8,177, were committed to the campaign to invade the northern colonies. By July 1, fifteen additional regulars and 886 auxiliaries joined him, giving Burgoyne a grand total of 9,078 white troops.[2]

An unusually large artillery train accompanied the army. The "Gibraltar of the North," Fort Ticonderoga, was the expedition's first major objective. Burgoyne had no intention of repeating General James Abercrombie's disastrous attack of 1758 when, because they lacked adequate artillery support, his men were slaughtered assailing the rock fortress. In 1776, Lord Germain dispatched a "huge battering train" to Canada for use in retaking Quebec from the Americans, but when the rebels did not occupy the city the cannon proved unnecessary. Sir Guy Carleton and General William Phillips had their choice of guns from that train, from which they selected 138 pieces: thirty-seven heavy guns, i.e., 12- and 24-pounders; forty-nine mediums, i.e., 3- and 6-pounders; and fifty-two howitzers and mortars. Phillips was officially tasked to serve as Carleton's chief of artillery, but Burgoyne, ignoring army regulations, made him second-in-command. The direction of the British artillery devolved upon Major Griffith Williams. Captain Georg Pausch commanded the German guns.[3]

Burgoyne organized the regulars into three divisions. As General James Lunt observed, "This was merely an instrument for organizing control, and there was nothing standard about the size or composition of a division."[4] Brigadier Simon Fraser commanded the first division, or Advanced Corps; Major General Phillips of the Royal Artillery, the army's new second-in-command, had the Right Division consisting of two brigades; and the Left Division was entirely German, also consisting of a pair of brigades, under the command of Major General Friedrich von Riedesel, Freiherr zu Eisenbach.[5] Lieutenant Colonel Heinrich von Breymann led the army's reserve, with Major Griffith Williams, as noted, commanding the Royal Artillery.[6]

In addition to the regulars listed above, two Canadian companies commanded by Captains Rene Amable de Bouchville and David Monin, together with the Indians brigaded with the Advanced Corps John Peters' and Edward Jessup's Provincial Battalions were assigned "out of the Line."[7] These units, Burgoyne wrote Lord Germain on July 11, were "in embryo," but he expected them to increase in maturity when the army reached the part of the invasion route where loyalists were numerous. Some recruits for the 33rd Regiment, under Lieutenant George Anson Nutt, who were later brigaded with the provincials, were temporarily detailed for duty with Lieutenant John Schank's Royal Navy contingent.[8]

The invaders included British regiments rich in battle honors and tradition. Like their British counterparts, the German regiments included officers and men who had seen combat and earned honors during the Seven Years' War. The field and company grade officers were as competent as any who served in North America, including a remarkable number who survived to become generals in the British Army.[9]

The army's enlisted men hailed from Great Britain's social orders whose members did not possess resources to purchase commissions. Some accepted the King's coin unwillingly, swept up by recruiting parties or driven into service by economic desperation. Many had known grinding poverty with no promise of a better future, illiterate and unfit for productive lives in a pre-industrial economy. Through severe and often brutal discipline, noncommissioned and company-grade officers managed to turn most of them into brave and effective soldiers. They were the men who marched into battle in close-order formation and received enemy fire from large-caliber muskets and rifles at a time when a puncture wound to the head or torso usually proved fatal, one to a limb often meant amputation, and every wound was more likely than not to become septic. Poorly paid and subject to wretched living conditions in the field, most of them endured their plight with courage and loyalty. Man-for-man, they gave as good an account of themselves as any eighteenth-century soldier. Once the battle was joined, even the most competent or lucky commander could exercise little control, leaving success or failure at the tactical level to the company officers and enlisted men.

The campaign began under favorable circumstances. "I have reason to be exceedingly satisfied," was how Burgoyne began a letter from Montreal to Adjutant General and acting Commander-in-Chief Edward Harvey on May 19, 1777,

> with all that has been done, and with most things that are doing: exertions have been made during the winter, which were remarkably favourable, in all the departments, and preparations are very forward; those that have been committed to the diligence of General Phillips have been executed with a diligence, precision, and foresight, that entitle him to the fullest praise. The troops are in a state of health almost unprecedented, and their spirits and general improvement are equally objects of great pleasure and promise. To this agreeable representation I have the happiness to add, that Sir Guy Carleton has received me, and the orders I brought, in a manner that, in my opinion, does infinite honour to his public and private character.[10]

Burgoyne was, perhaps, praising Sir Guy for his disinterested support somewhat more effusively than facts warranted.

Burgoyne's Forces: The Bad News

In that same May 19 letter to Harvey, Burgoyne predicted that his first major step would be to take Ticonderoga by siege ("for a siege I apprehend it must be"), though he ended with a nagging worry: "I had the surprise and mortification to find a paper handed about at Montreal, publishing the whole design of the campaign, almost as accurately as if it had been copied from the Secretary of State [Germain's] letter."[11] He feared, reasonably enough, that if knowledge of his plans was public property in Canada, they must be well-known among the Americans. Still, Burgoyne overestimated his enemy's perspicacity. If they had agents operating in Montreal, as they almost certainly did, they proved singularly deaf and blind, or their employers were too occupied with preconceptions to credit the widely circulated intelligence. General George Washington believed the British were not strong enough to undertake the conquest of the Champlain-Hudson route to Albany, and so would undertake to join Sir William Howe by sea. General Philp Schuyler believed Burgoyne would reverse Lord Amherst's 1760 route. Horatio Gates, as will be discussed in a later chapter, managed to divine Burgoyne's objective, but how much he owed his analysis to operatives in Montreal is not apparent.

A small cloud on the strategic horizon appeared in Sir William Howe's letter of April 5 to General Carleton, which the latter showed to Burgoyne. Sir William warned his colleague that because his army would be operating in Pennsylvania, he could provide the commander of the army from Canada with neither instructions nor more help than "a corps upon the lower Part of Hudson's River sufficient to open the communications for shipping through the Highlands . . . which corps may afterwards act in Favour of the Northern Army."[12] Perhaps because he believed that Lord Germain had sent definitive orders to Howe to clear the valley south of Albany and actively effect a physical junction with Burgoyne, or because he was confident that he could reach that town without a major commitment from New York City, the letter from Sir William did not unduly worry Burgoyne. His response was "a second letter to Sir William Howe, wherein I reported that I was entrusted with the command of an army destined to march from Canada, and that my orders were to force a junction with his excellency."[13]

A matter that gave Burgoyne more immediate concern was the disappointing response by Canadians to British recruiting. He had expected to exploit their presumed skill in wilderness fighting, but not even Carleton could persuade many of the habitants that Britain's cause was their own. They had developed their prowess in forest warfare in a setting of emotional loyalty to France and hostility to Protestants. That military tradition collapsed in the climate created by British rule. Fewer than 150 Canadians joined Burgoyne's banner. The general voiced his disappointment in a letter to Lord Germain dated May 14. "I cannot speak with much confidence of the military assistance I am to look for from the Canadians," he cautioned the secretary. "The only corps yet instituted, or that I am informed can at present be instituted, are three independent companies of 100 men each, officered by Seigneurs of the country, who are well chosen; but they are not able to engage many volunteers." The men were largely drafted from the militia, Burgoyne continued, "according to a late regulation of the legislative council. Those I have yet seen afford no promise of use of arms—awkward, ignorant, disinclined to service, and spiritless." There were a host of reasons explaining "this change in the natives since the time of the French government," he continued. "It may be partly owing to the disuse of arms, but I believe principally to the unpopularity of the Seigneurs and the poison which the emissaries of the rebels have thrown into their minds. . . ."[14]

Much more serious than the Canadians' reluctance to join the imperial fight was the shortage of wheeled vehicles and horses, a problem immediately apparent. On May 20, Burgoyne informed Carleton that he required up to 800 horses. When Sir Guy objected that the number was excessive, Burgoyne replied that, although he did not need that many before taking Ticonderoga, he would require them after that because he would become dependent upon land carriage after leaving Lake Champlain.[15] Although he promised to collect the horses, Carleton failed to do so. The problem was unresolved when, on June 4, General Phillips wrote to his commander about his concern for what would happen when the army—and especially its artillery—had to leave behind transportation on the lakes and strike out overland. Phillips had been led to believe that more carriages and horses would be available once the army reached Albany—but what would be available for him to rely upon in between?[16]

Burgoyne responded the same day by asking Phillips "to give in your opinion the mode of procuring horses and carriages from the country, combining the considerations of dispatch, sufficiency, economy towards government; and I wish to know the opinion as soon as possible."[17] As soon as possible was the next day, when Phillips reviewed for his commander the two possible modes of procurement: purchase and contract hire.

The former was problematical, Phillips noted, because it involved trusting too many procurers and inspectors who could be counted on to place monetary gain over the suitability of the animals for the King's service. Experience had taught him that purchasing animals nearly always failed to procure the requisite horses at a reasonable price, and that under the conditions prevailing in Canada it would cost between 20,000 and 30,000 pounds.

The second possible mode of procurement, advised Phillips, was "[t]he contracting for a certain number of horses at a fixed price for the hire by day, [which] reduces the whole to a very simple, and therefore generally a certain plan." Its success, he continued, depended upon "making as cheap, as fair, and just, [a] bargain, on the part of government, as can be: And, being so made, that the military and civil officers do their duty, by attending to the receiving of horses only as they are fitting for service. . . ." Phillips believed that contractors would recognize that fulfilling the contracts would be in their interest, and that the "care of the government will be, that it be done honestly and completely."[18]

By his answer, Phillips proved himself a dedicated, honest servant to the flag under which he served. While awaiting Phillips' opinion, Burgoyne asked Commissary General Nathaniel Day to calculate the number of horses and vehicles required to transport thirty days' provisions for 10,000 men, "together with 1000 gallons of rum."[19]

Acting upon the information provided by Phillips and Day, Burgoyne submitted a requisition on June 7 for "an expeditious supply of horses for the artillery, and 500 carts, with two horses each, for the other purposes." He concluded his request with this fateful paragraph:

> Your Excellency will observe, that, in order to save the public expense as much as possible, I have reduced this requisition much below what would be adequate for the service, and I mean to trust to the resources of the expedition for the rest: 500 carts will barely carry fourteen days provisions at a time, and Major-General Phillips means to demand as few horses as possible, subject to whatever future augmentations future services may require: the present number wanted will be about 400; there will then remain unprovided for (for expeditious movement) the transport of bateaux from Lake George to Hudson's River, and the carriage of the

tents of the army, and many other contingencies that I need not trouble your Excellency to point out to you.[20]

Difficult as it would have been to accomplish, Burgoyne's failure to assemble adequate vehicles and horses had deleterious logistical and tactical consequences. He began his campaign with too few of either to manage an efficient transport of equipment and arms, and without mounts for his German dragoons, limiting them to functioning as infantry and depriving his army of a cavalry capability. The logistical implications became immediately apparent when, as the army moved to St. John's, "more than half of the Carriages were broken & we did not get to St. Johns 'till night."[21] The logistical problem worsened with every advancing mile. The attempt to secure mounts for the dragoons led, that August, to the campaign's first disaster.

Burgoyne addressed a final dismaying issue in a letter to Adjutant General Edward Harvey, from his camp on the Bouquet River after he had already set out. Its opening paragraph, after briefly describing the difficulties attendant to getting his expedition underway, paid tribute to the men who overcame "the obstructions we have met with." The second paragraph is important for three reasons: 1) It explicitly states what he believed to be his objective; (2) It revealed a serious weakness in the government's failure to provide for a rational staff organization; and (3) It exhibited concern for the careers of the lieutenant colonels (Fraser, Hamilton, Powell) who, as "local" brigadiers, led his British soldiers. "I have been exceedingly distressed in regard to the brigadiers of this army," explained Burgoyne. "Sir Guy Carleton," he continued,

> the day I took leave of him, put into my hands an extract of a letter from the Secretary of War [Lord Barrington], approving the appointment, but observing, that whenever any of them should lead their brigades out of the province of Canada, in order to join the troops under General Howe, there would be a necessity for their command ceasing as brigadiers, &c.

> Were this to be put into execution, according to the letter of the order and the geographical limits of Canada, and supposing Major General Phillips at the same time to be employed solely in the artillery, I should find myself at the head of an army to undertake a siege, and afterwards pursue objects of importance, and possibly of time, without a single intermediate British officer between the lieutenant-general, commanding pro tempore in chief, and a lieutenant-colonel. It would be preposterous and impertinent in me

to say one word more to you, as an officer, upon the impossibility of methodising or conducting such an army with such a total deficiency of staff. . . .

Burgoyne decided to solve the problem by keeping the acting brigadiers in that rank throughout his campaign as members of "the Canada army till such time as I am in communication with General Howe, so as to make part of his force."[22] He solicited Harvey's support for what he intended to do. There was, of course, no time to await an assurance from the adjutant general of his approbation. The three officers functioned throughout the campaign as brigade commanders. Only two of them would survive the ordeals ahead, after which they would revert to their permanent rank when they rejoined their respective regiments.

The Battle for Hearts and Minds

General Phillips arrived at St. John's on the 10th of June, with Burgoyne and Riedesel joining the main columns the next day. Burgoyne received his written orders from Carleton on June 10, and was now fully vested in his command. Carleton made his appearance on the twelfth.

On June 14, the Royal Standard was raised on the vessel *Radeau* and saluted by the guns inside Fort St. John's and those within the flotilla. The standard had special symbolism. The square flag with the national arms covering the entire field without any supporting accessories normally signified the presence of a member of the royal family. In this case, according to the *Continental Journal* and *Weekly Advertiser* of Boston's September 19, 1776 issue, "When all the troops that gone out arrive in America, it is said that the Royal Standard is to be hoisted in three different parts of the country, when it is thought, many thousand people, friends of government, finding them selves likely to be supported (who were afraid before to take [sides]) will flock to it."[23]

When all was as ready as it would ever be, Burgoyne set out with his command to carry the war into the interior of the Northern Colonies. But even as he advanced against them militarily, Burgoyne decided that the time had arrived for him to address the benighted colonials and recall them to lawful allegiance with an awesome proclamation. The announcement to the people of New York and New England from his camp at Bouquet Ferry on June 20 opened turgidly, listing all of Burgoyne's official titles, including commander of "an Army and Fleet on an expedition from Canada." That army and fleet were

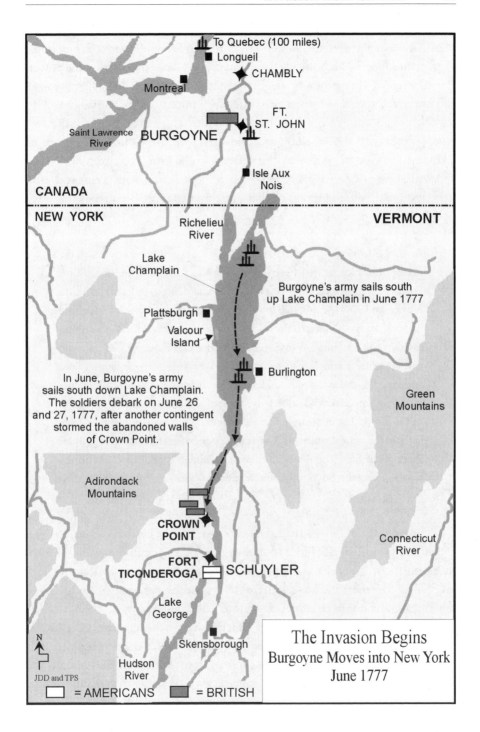

To Quebec (100 miles)

Longueil

CHAMBLY

Montreal

Saint Lawrence River

BURGOYNE

FT. ST. JOHN

Isle Aux Nois

CANADA

NEW YORK

Richelieu River

VERMONT

Lake Champlain

Burgoyne's army sails south up Lake Champlain in June 1777

Plattsburgh

Valcour Island

In June, Burgoyne's army sails south down Lake Champlain. The soldiers debark on June 26 and 27, 1777, after another contingent stormed the abandoned walls of Crown Point.

Burlington

Green Mountains

Adirondack Mountains

CROWN POINT

Connecticut River

FORT TICONDEROGA

SCHUYLER

Lake George

N

Skensborough

Hudson River

JDD and TPS

The Invasion Begins
Burgoyne Moves into New York
June 1777

☐ = AMERICANS   ▨ = BRITISH

"designed to act in concert, and upon a common Principle, with the numerous Armies and Fleets which already display in every quarter of America, the power, the justice, and when properly sought the mercy of the King." The King's cause, he continued, appealed "to the most effecting interests of the human heart." In an effort to appeal "To the Eyes and Ears of the temperate part of the Public," Burgoyne blasted the rebellion as "unnatural . . . the completest system of Tyranny that God in his displeasure suffer'd for [a] time to be exercised over a forward and stubborn Generation." After more in the same vein, and after vowing to extirpate the forces of that unnatural tyranny, Burgoyne concluded with a threat to devastate "the willful outcasts":

> In consciousness of Christianity, my Royal Master's clemency, and the honour of Soldiership, I have dwelt upon this invitation, and wished for more persuasive terms to give it impression; and not to be led to disregard it by considering the distance from the immediate situation of my Camp. I have but to give stretch to the Indian Forces under my direction, and they amount to thousands, to overtake the harden'd enemies of Great Britain and America (I consider them the same) wherever they may lurk. If not withstanding these endeavours, the sincere inclinations to effect them, the phrenzy of hostility should remain, I trust I shall be acquitted in the Eyes of God and Men in denouncing and executing the vengeance of the state against the willful outcasts. The messengers of justice and wrath await them in the field, and devastation, famine, and every concomitant horror that a reluctant but indispensable prosecution of military duty must exercise.[24]

The next day Burgoyne surpassed even that bombastic declaration when he called his 400 Indian allies to a council at the falls of the Bouquet, about forty miles north of Ticonderoga. There, he delivered a true oratorical effusion, ascribing to the Indians satisfactory conduct, sagacity, faithfulness, incorruptibility, honor, restraint, affection, valor, and a burning desire to fight for justice, law, and the king. After an indictment of the rebels and a call to arms, the general delivered a fatuous exhortation to conduct the war against their common enemies according to the canons of civilized combat. "Should the enemy, on their part, dare to countenance acts of barbarity towards those who may fall into their hands," he concluded, it shall be yours also to retaliate; but, till severity be thus compelled, bear immovable in your hearts this solid maxim (it cannot be too deeply impressed), that the great essential reward, worthy service of your alliance, the sincerity of your zeal to the King, your father and never-failing protector, will be examined and judged upon the test only of your steady and uniform adherence to the orders and counsels of those, to whom his Majesty has entrusted the direction and honour of his arms.[25]

How faithfully the translator relayed that stilted piece of bombast, and how much of it the warriors understood, is questionable. It was traditional to attribute to the natives a particular responsiveness to oratory, so it is possible they enjoyed the general's performance without knowing or caring precisely what he said. Whatever their understanding, after consulting amongst themselves, an "old Chief of the Iroquois" rose and delivered a reply on behalf of all, in which he ascribed to his fellows attentiveness, approbation, affection, sincerity, bellicosity, obedience, and good wishes for the success of Burgoyne, the King, and everything they sought to do.[26] At least, that is the message Burgoyne attributed to the "old Chief." More credible is the report that after the council adjourned, the Indians, well-supplied with liquor, held a war dance. And well they should have: they were "having the white man on," while enjoying his speeches and libations.

Contemporaries and their descendants have found ridiculing Burgoyne's verbosity and purple prose easy. The rebellious Americans, naturally, found nothing in the words to admire, and Francis Hopkinson authored a parody, a fine piece of Americana that, widely circulated in both America and Britain in an age not yet numbed by sound bites, produced considerable mirth at the general's expense.[27] Burgoyne's address to the Indians was even more roundly ridiculed than his proclamation to the New Englanders and New Yorkers. Simply put, the proclamations represented its author at his worst. Burgoyne was an articulate and intelligent man, but these were silly, and not worthy of him.

There were other aspects that did not go down easily. Employing "savages" did not sit well with many British consciences, including Burgoyne's. William Pitt and Edmund Burke bitterly condemned the practice, and the opposition in Parliament fixed upon the issue to level violent criticism against the ministry. Burke rose in the House of Commons to attack the policy and the general's address. He imagined a riot at Tower Hill, with the keeper of the animals housed there admonishing his charges before he loosed them upon the rioters: "My gentle lions, my humane bears, my sentimental wolves, my gentle-hearted hyenas, go forth: But I exhort you as ye are Christians and members of a civilised society, to take care not to hurt man, woman, or child." Horace Walpole wrote that fat Prime Minister Lord North found Burke's satire so funny that he "almost suffocated with laughter."[28]

The Americans were, of course, outraged by the prospect of their foe's enlisting Indians in the war. The fear of native warfare was never far from their consciousness, and few things struck more terror into the whites than a threat of this nature. Many of the older families had memories of relatives or neighbors who had been victims of frontier fighting.

It remains easy to condemn using Indians to try to suppress the rebellion. But it is fair to note that failing to employ them, and every other legitimate resource available, would have meant the British government had fallen short of its obligation to exploit all potential resources to bring the war to a successful close. The Americans implicitly acknowledged that themselves by seeking to bring Indians into the war as allies against the Crown, with very limited success. Experience had taught the natives that Americans posed a greater threat to their interests than the imperial government, and they took counsel of that experience. British policy, as expressed in the Treaty of Easton and the 1763 Proclamation Line, as executed by John Stuart in the South and Sir William Johnson in the North, had been more humane than the conduct of the Americans, most of whom believed that the red man deserved expulsion or extermination.

High-flown and ridiculous, Burgoyne's address to the Indians represented an effort, however foredoomed, to regulate his allies' conduct and humanize an inhumane practice. He was less culpable than he was futile, and his proclamation was no more bombastic and pompous than the public utterances of some of his contemporaries on both sides of the Atlantic. If Burgoyne had succeeded, his oratory would have been more favorably remembered—perhaps as a model of how to craft such words in such terrible times. Because he failed, however, it sounded then, and still sounds today, hollow and ridiculous.

In a final effort to overawe the locals, Burgoyne's fleet sailed southward up Lake Champlain in an incongruously brilliant display for a wilderness stage. The Indians—apparently recovered from the general's post-oration hospitality— the Loyalists, and the Canadians formed the vanguard in their canoes. The grenadiers of Fraser's Corps followed in gunboats, lending substance to the advance parties. The main column followed in bateaux, the British regiments on the right, the German on the left. Field grade and general officers stood erect in their pinnaces, and their commander, in full dress, was conspicuously visible aboard the *Maria*. Behind that brave spectacle glided the vessels carrying women and children, cooks, artificers, drivers, stores, live cattle, sutlers, and all the impedimenta that accompanied an eighteenth-century army on the offensive in hostile country. Over the water, martial music provided a quasi-operatic air to the scene.[29] Despite the fanfare, the soldiers came ashore during June 26 and 27 to an anti-climactic debarkation, landing after Lord Balcarres' light infantry battalion had rushed Crown Point's abandoned and derelict walls.

On June 30, while still in his new camp at the old colonial fort, Burgoyne issued this oft-quoted order, perhaps as a final effort to overawe, or at least to encourage, his own forces:

> The Army embarks tomorrow to approach the Enemy. We are to contend for the King and the Constitution of Great Britain, to vindicate the Law and to relieve the Oppressed. A Cause in which His Majesty's Troops and those of the Princes His Allies, will feel equal Excitement.

> The Services required of this particular Expedition are critical and conspicuous. During our progress occasions may occur, in which neither difficulty nor labour nor life are to be regarded. THIS ARMY MUST NOT RETREAT.[30]

But two days before that, on June 28, Burgoyne had issued orders intended to be operative for the campaign's duration. They prescribed signals to be used if it should become necessary to initiate a sudden embarkation, with baggage, etc., to be stowed in the boats, and also for a sudden departure by land, with baggage abandoned rather than loaded.[31] Perhaps this merely reflected a preparation for the unexpected, surely suitable for any commander. Perhaps, however, it also reflected a particular awareness by Burgoyne of the tendency of his American opponents to carry off the military surprise.

In any case, the "War from the Side of Canada" opened as Ticonderoga's promontory and the fort that crowned it loomed athwart the invasion route.

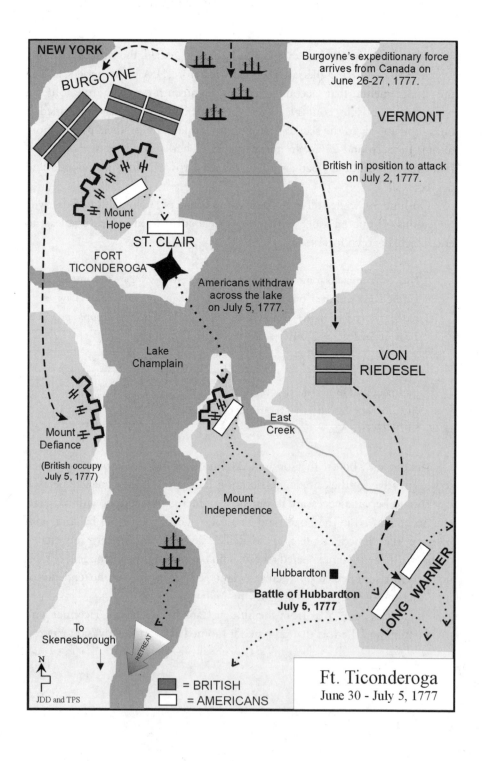

NEW YORK

BURGOYNE

Burgoyne's expeditionary force arrives from Canada on June 26-27, 1777.

VERMONT

British in position to attack on July 2, 1777.

Mount Hope

ST. CLAIR

FORT TICONDEROGA

Americans withdraw across the lake on July 5, 1777.

Lake Champlain

VON RIEDESEL

East Creek

Mount Defiance

(British occupy July 5, 1777)

Mount Independence

Hubbardton

Battle of Hubbardton July 5, 1777

LONG

WARNER

To Skenesborough

N

RETREAT

JDD and TPS

= BRITISH
= AMERICANS

Ft. Ticonderoga
June 30 - July 5, 1777

Fort Ticonderoga
and the Battle of Hubbardton

Ticonderoga: Its Importance, Strengths, and Vulnerabilities

Ticonderoga, hyperbolically dubbed the "Gibraltar of the North," is a conspicuous, blunt promontory three-quarters of a mile long jutting out of Lake Champlain's western shore. At the base of its southwest shoulder a narrow mile-long gorge carries Lake George's waters into Champlain. At its highest point, the promontory is slightly more than seventy feet above the lake's water.

From across Lake Champlain, Mount Independence, about fifty feet high, protrudes into the lake toward Ticonderoga's southwest shoulder. The quarter-mile wide passage between the headlands is the gateway between upper and lower Champlain. Once through it, the way is open by water into the lake's narrow southern end, and from there up Wood Creek to within a few miles of the Hudson River. An alternative route to the river ran westward through the gorge into Lake George and southward down that lake to a point equally near the Hudson. Two miles northwest of Ticonderoga was Mount Hope, commanding the road that ran up the gorge to Lake George. A mile northwest of the promontory Sugar Loaf, renamed Mount Defiance, rises 750 feet above the water. Except where Ticonderoga had been cleared for fortification and fields of fire, the countryside in 1777 was thickly wooded, with only an occasional farmstead settled since the last colonial war.

The French built a star-shaped fort, with bastions, on Ticonderoga in 1755. When General Jeffrey Amherst attacked Fort Carillon four years later, its garrison retreated, blowing up large portions of the works. The British repaired the fort and renamed it Fort Ticonderoga, but they allowed it to fall into disrepair after the Peace of Paris ended the Seven Years' War in 1763. The disappearance of the Anglo-French frontier reduced the post's importance, and it was manned by a very small garrison. The opening of the American Revolution restored its significance, and its capture was an early American objective. Ethan Allen and his "Green Mountain Boys," accompanied by Benedict Arnold, seized the stronghold on May 10, 1775.

The Americans invested considerable effort and treasure enlarging and strengthening the defenses, repairing the original fort, extending the "French lines" that formed an arc across the promontory, and erecting a blockhouse to cover the lines' flanks and rear. Other blockhouses, redoubts, and breastworks defended the northern and southern slopes. A barbette battery protected Mount Hope, dominating the outlet from Lake George, the sawmills powered by the outlet, and the road that lay between the lakes. A stream and swamps protected the rear of Mount Independence. Batteries, an eight-pointed star fort, and stone breastworks comprised Ticonderoga's defensive works. A boom of heavy logs, bound together by massive chains, closed the water passage at the lake's southern end. Behind the boom lay a bridge of boats. Water batteries on both shores covered the boom and bridge. Americans disagreed about many matters concerning their northern frontier, but they were virtually unanimous in assigning an exaggerated importance to Ticonderoga; their investments testified to that opinion.

Mount Defiance's ominous bulk loomed over Fort Ticonderoga and its satellites, and Polish-born engineer Thaddeus Kosciuszko—and perhaps John Trumbull—favored fortifying it. The latter, with Generals Arnold and Anthony Wayne, climbed the height in the summer of 1776. Some believed artillery on those heights would be able to threaten the fort itself; others disagreed.

Well-placed field pieces certainly could, however, seriously threaten to cut off retreat by water. No boats could safely lie at anchor off the American works. Equally important, occupation of the mountain would afford excellent observation of all troop activity within the works. Their possession by the enemy could adversely affect the defenders' morale in a period during which conventional wisdom placed an exaggerated value on the advantage possession of higher ground afforded.

In any case, the Americans, like the British and the French before them, did not incorporate the mountain into the defenses. That decision, given the scarcity of manpower, was inevitable. There were not enough men available in 1776 to erect and man additional works, and there were too few men present during the summer of 1777 to defend the works that were included in the system, much less Mount Defiance. Regardless of whether it was Horatio Gates or Philip Schuyler who made the decision not to fortify the mountain's summit, its occupation during General Burgoyne's operations and the resultant American evacuation provided fertile ground for later partisan recrimination that all parties exploited enthusiastically.[1]

Divining Burgoyne's Intentions

The Americans were woefully ill-prepared to thwart Burgoyne at Ticonderoga. The British commander had worried while in Montreal that his orders and plans were common knowledge. American intelligence collection in the old French town was so inept, however, that if indeed street gossip had made details of the campaign's plan public property, the agents failed miserably to profit from it. As a result, American generals and politicians still shared an uncertainty about what John Burgoyne and his army would do after leaving Montreal. General George Washington believed the British were too weak to advance down the Champlain-Hudson route to Albany. He and a majority in Congress expected Burgoyne to move southward by sea to join Sir William Howe. Schuyler believed Burgoyne would reverse Lord Jeffrey Amherst's 1760 route by ascending the St. Lawrence River, crossing Lake Ontario, and descending the Mohawk to Albany.

One American, General Gates, predicted that the British would "make the entire Conquest of the State of New York the first and main Object of this ensuing Campaign." He supported this analysis with a number of reasons: French and British military history, both longer-term and more recent; the military geography of America; the stance of the Indians and the Tories; and the availability of provisions. On the basis of his analysis, Gates noted that the Americans were too weak on the Hudson and Mohawk rivers, and he feared that Washington's main army would be drawn into New Jersey. Gates also worried, with good reason, about the security of the Hudson Highlands, and that, if his concerns were well-grounded, Howe would have access to the sea. The general wanted the Congress to know his views, and he asked President John Hancock to bring them to the delegates' attention.[2]

Gates' analysis was not perfect, but it reflected a sound knowledge of strategic facts logically examined, and was more nearly prescient than those of his fellow generals.[3]

The American Defense of Ticonderoga?

By mid-June, when Schuyler had his first concrete intelligence of Burgoyne's intentions from a captured British agent, the enemy was a few miles north of Crown Point at Bouquet River.[4] Fort Ticonderoga's new commander and the department commander now knew that Gates' analysis was correct: the British intended to retake Ticonderoga.

The fort's newest commander, Arthur St. Clair, reached his post on June 12. For the Scottish-born aristocrat and veteran of the Seven Years' War, it was not a happy occasion. On the thirteenth he wrote to General Schuyler that if the enemy attacked, "we are very ill prepared." St. Clair was being realistic. The fortifications were weaker than they had been during the previous autumn because the soldiers had burned the abatis for firewood. Stores were low, the pontoon bridge to Mount Independence was unfinished, and the garrison numbered only 2,089 infantrymen present and fit for duty, bolstered by 238 gunners.[5]

The American generals had options—every one of which would challenge their sagacity and moral courage. Because St. Clair had too few troops to man the works on both sides of Lake Champlain, James Wilkinson and General Schuyler discussed evacuating the sick, the garrison cannon, and all but 1,500 effectives to Fort George. Those men, with the light artillery, would defend the fort against a feint, but retreat if the enemy mounted a determined attack. According to Wilkinson, the general favored that idea, but contended that he could not abandon the fort without prior congressional approval.[6]

Abandoning the "Gibraltar of the North" without a fight was politically unthinkable. Yet, equally unthinkable for military reasons would be to make the garrison a forlorn hope, sacrificed to an exaggerated sense of the post's importance. The garrison had to be preserved at all costs to form a nucleus of future resistance. Between Ticonderoga and Albany there were only about 700 Continentals manning various old posts that were, during the summer of 1777, functioning as stockaded depots. If the fort's defenders failed to repel an attack, as was very likely, they must retire immediately while the retreat corridor remained open.[7]

When General Schuyler assembled St. Clair and Brigadier Generals Enoch Poor, John Paterson, and Alexis de Fermoy in a council on June 20, they faced desperate pressures and unpromising options. The department commander "requested the Council to take into consideration the state of this post, with respect to the number of troops necessary for its defence, the disposition of the troops, and mode of defence, the state of the fortifications, and the quantity of provisions that may be depended upon."

The result of those deliberations, constituting the Council's "most serious consideration," was ten points, delivered "clearly and unanimously of opinion." In those points the generals resolved that, although they did not have enough men to defend the entire works, they would hold Ticonderoga and Mount Independence as long as possible. But if, as was probable, they would have to evacuate one of those positions, they would concentrate on holding Mount Independence. Meanwhile, most stores would be moved to Mount Independence, and Jeduthan Baldwin's artificers would improve that post. Efforts would be made to strengthen the obstructions between lower and upper Lake Champlain, although they knew that doing so would require six weeks. If their men could not hold Mount Independence, everyone would retreat southward, employing the bateaux being collected and held in readiness. The Council concluded with the resolution to ask General Washington for reinforcements, knowing all too well that the commander-in-chief in Pennsylvania could not send them in time to repel the enemy.[8]

The Council, however, left some important questions unasked and, therefore, unresolved. How would troops driven from Ticonderoga reach Mount Independence, in the presence of an enemy possessing the former and able to interdict the floating bridge and the boom over which the men must withdraw? How could they preserve and load the bateaux, with the enemy in possession of both forts and capable of bringing the water gap between lower and upper Lake Champlain under effective fire? The generals had prepared a justification for doing what was inevitable—knowing that the inevitable would be unpalatable to General Washington and the members of the Continental Congress.

Having provided for a doomed defensive strategy, and anticipating the storm of opprobrium that would follow news that the "Gibraltar of the North" was no longer American, General Schuyler departed on June 22 to do what he could to improve logistics and plead for reinforcements. St. Clair remained at Ticonderoga to conduct the best defense he could.

Burgoyne Begins

While the commander of the American Northern Department and his subordinates wrestled with their problems, Burgoyne and his army at Crown Point prepared for what the British commanding general expected to be a major test. He attached great strategic and symbolic importance to retaking Ticonderoga. The fort blocked his route to Albany, and its hold on British perceptions rivaled that of the Americans'. The British had fought the French for possession of it during the final war for North American empire. Its earlier loss to the "Green Mountain Boys" was a bitter blow to British pride, and a bone in the throat of any commander who aspired to redeem imperial fortunes on the northern frontier. Restoring it to the empire would make heroes of Gentleman Johnny and his soldiers.

Burgoyne expected retaking the fort to be a heroic undertaking, the centerpiece of which would entail employing heavy artillery supporting siege operations. When he drafted his "Thoughts for Conducting the War from the Side of Canada," he assumed that "the enemy would be in great force at Ticonderoga." That assumption led to the decision to include heavy twelve- and twenty-pounders in the original artillery train.[9] He intended to conserve precious manpower by bombarding the Americans into submission from gunboats and land batteries. Burgoyne anticipated that the Americans valued the fort as highly as he did and would therefore fight to retain their prize. He also had a healthy respect for their ability to defend a fortified position.

On June 26—the day Burgoyne, Major General William Phillips, and Major General Friedrich von Riedesel, with their army's main column, reached Crown Point—Brigadier Simon Fraser's advanced corps embarked toward Ticonderoga and landed at the mouth of Putnam's Creek on Lake Champlain's western side. Captain Alexander Fraser, with his Indians and Canadians, followed Otter Creek and joined the advanced corps. Gunboats followed to cover the advance parties.[10]

Because the Americans occupied both sides of the lake, Burgoyne divided his main force, posting British regiments on the west side and Germans on the east. The men were ordered to carry 100 rounds per man; if there was insufficient ammunition for that distribution, the supply would be divided equally among the units. The tents, knapsacks, blankets, provisions, and extra ammunition would be stored in the bateaux. All other baggage was to remain behind until ordered brought forward with the officers' tents and baggage. The British battalions would use seventeen boats, the Germans twenty-two. The previously-mentioned general order of the twenty-eighth directed what should be done with the baggage if it became necessary for the line regiments to move out suddenly, whether by water or land.[11]

On June 30, Burgoyne issued his most important preparatory orders: after naming the brigadiers and brigade majors for the day, and exhorting his men with the words earlier recorded ("THIS ARMY MUST NOT RETREAT"), he directed that an hour after dawn the next day, "Each Wing to form a Column of Batteaux . . . . The Right Wing keeping to the West Shore, the Left Wing the East . . . The Dragoons of Riedesel [to] form the Advanced Guard. . . ."[12]

The first day of July dawned clear and calm. The boats and bateaux almost covered the mile-wide passage between Crown Point and Ticonderoga. The regimental bands "contributed to make the Scene and passage extremely pleasant." The British disembarked about four miles above Ticonderoga and camped in line. The Germans, except for Lieutenant Colonel Heinrich Breymann's Jägers, which formed Fraser's reserve, and the dragoons, who guarded Burgoyne's gear, landed on the lake's eastern shore.[13] The soldiers spent the rest of the day clearing fields of fire in front of their camps and cutting roads of communication between the several brigade positions. Fraser's Corps remained at its post at Three Mile Point, a mile in advance of the British camps.

Early the next day General Phillips, with Fraser's Corps and General Hamilton's Brigade, advanced against Mount Hope, whose garrison prudently fired their works and fled to the old French lines, leaving the enemy in control of the portage to Lake George. Fraser's effort to cut off their retreat from Mount Hope failed. Phillips' men went into position less than 100 yards from the Americans, took cover, and opened fire. St. Clair believed that the British actions signaled the prelude to the hoped-for frontal assault and ordered his men to remain under cover and to hold their fire until the command to commence firing was given.

A British soldier, emboldened by the apparent American passivity, crawled toward to the American lines. James Wilkinson, whose lust for fame rivaled Benedict Arnold's, ordered a sergeant to shoot the bold Britisher. The sergeant dutifully obeyed. Assuming that his shot was the signal to open fire, the entire American line leapt to its feet and poured successive volleys in the direction of the enemy. The artillery zestfully joined in. When American officers finally restored fire discipline, the enemy had withdrawn a distance of 300 yards, leaving the sergeant's target lying on the ground. The Americans fired at least 3,000 musket balls and eight cannons at a 500-man force, killing one man and wounding two more—all at a range of but 100 yards. A burial party ventured out to dispose of the object of Wilkinson's attention, still lying uninjured and dead drunk on the field.

Other players in the day's drama also overindulged during July 2. Some Indians got drunk and ventured too close to the American lines. Lieutenant William Houghton of the 53rd Regiment received a wound trying "to bring them off;" one Indian was killed and another injured.[14] While that noisy business was in progress, von Riedesel's Germans moved to a stream behind Mount Independence, reaching there too late in the day to attack its fortifications.

Burgoyne's men spent a very busy third of July. Lieutenant Colonel Powell's Brigade replaced Hamilton's on Fraser's left at Mount Hope, and Hamilton's men returned to the main camp and prepared to advance the next morning.[15] Light artillery attached to Fraser and Powell rejoined their parent brigades. Burgoyne shifted von Gall's Brigade of von Riedesel's command to Fraser's former position at Three Mile Point on the Ticonderoga side of the lake, giving von Riedesel, in exchange, Alexander Fraser's Canadians, Indians, and Provincials; presumably, the exchange gave the baron a light infantry capability. The hospital remained at the point.[16]

Burgoyne cherished the common British article of faith that the rebels' ranks contained many men who were secretly loyal to their old allegiance. Eager to facilitate their joining him in their liberation, he included this injunction in the orders for July 3:

> It is known that there are many men in the rebel Army who are well effected to the Cause of the King. Some have been compelled into the Service, others engaged only with a view of joining the King's Troops. The Savages are therefore cautioned against firing upon any single men or small parties that may be endeavouring to come over, and the Army in general will consider these men in a very different light from common Deserters, and treat them with all possible encouragement; and should it unfortunately happen that any Soldier of this Army should fall into the hands of the Enemy, it will be his Duty to let this order be known to the Enemy's Army.[17]

The effectiveness of this order is not reflected in the records of either army. But men did desert from the Northern Department, especially militiamen; British sources refer to accepting additions to Jessup's and Peters' Loyalist units. Much of the local population was indeed Tory in sympathies, and the general's policy probably did encourage men enrolled in the New York militia to join him.

During July 3, the armies engaged in a fitful artillery duel whose only significant result was the further depletion of the American magazine.

During the fourth, Burgoyne moved his headquarters from his flagship *Royal George* to high ground behind Fraser's Corps, where German dragoons provided security.[18] More important, either Burgoyne or his artillery chief, Phillips, directed Lieutenant William Twiss to reconnoiter Mount Defiance, which a detail of light infantry occupied during the night. Twiss reported that the mountain had "the entire command of the works and buildings both of Ticonderoga and Mount Independence, at a distance of about 1,400 yards from the latter, that the ground might be leveled so as to receive cannon, and that the road to convey them, though difficult, might be made practicable in as little as twenty-four hours."[19]

The engineer's estimates of the distances were too low. From the crest of Mount Defiance to the masonry fort is about 1,760 yards and to Mount Independence approximately 2,100 yards, an error of 360 and 600 yards, respectively. Because the maximum effective range of even the heaviest pieces did not exceed about 1,200 yards, cannon emplaced upon the summit could not seriously threaten the fortifications.[20] Burgoyne knew, however, that even if Twiss' estimates were correct, the artillery threat would not be to the fort, but to the stronghold's communications, making it strategically untenable. "The hill also commanded, in reverse," he explained, "the bridge and communication, saw the exact situation of the vessels, nor could the enemy, during the day, make any material movement or preparation, without being discovered, and having their numbers counted."[21]

British artificers made a road up the mountain during July 4. Some 400 men detailed from the regiments constructed a battery for "light twenty-four pounders, and medium twelves" during the next day, working with such dispatch that the weapons could have been in place by July 6.[22]

The American (Non-)Defense

General St. Clair experienced a transitory period of optimism when 900 militiamen arrived. That they taxed his meager supplies tempered that brief glimmer of hope. Still, he continued to expect an assault on some part of his fortifications, in which case the reinforcements might be decisive. He could detect, however, no activity that revealed the point from which a massed attack might come.

During the morning of July 5, St. Clair noticed movement on Mount Defiance that dashed any optimism he still harbored. Standing with the omnipresent James Wilkinson, he watched the enemy's artillery initiative threaten his avenue of retreat and the survival of his garrison. In response, he quoted the eloquent lines from Joseph Addison's tragedy "Cato" that celebrated the Roman Republicans' last stand for popular liberty: "Tis not in mortals to command success. But we'll do more Sempronius, we'll deserve it."

The Scotsman needed all the stoicism he could summon. Saving his troops demanded immediate action. Calling a council of his commanders, he solicited opinions; they unanimously agreed to retreat as soon as darkness fell.[23]

The schooners *Revenge* and *Liberty*, the sloop *Enterprise*, and the galleys *Gates* and *Trumbull*, survivors of Arnold's 1776 lake fleet, lay at anchor in line behind the boom and bridge. Behind them were more than 200 bateaux and other craft that would transport invalids and stores up the lake to Skenesborough. The effectives were to rendezvous on the lake's eastern side and march by a road that ran behind Mount Independence southward to Hubbardton, thence to Castleton and west to Skenesborough. Ticonderoga's defenders maintained a continuous cannonade to cover the noise of preparations for withdrawal and to divert the enemy's attention.

But while it may have drowned the sounds of preparation, the firing also alerted the British that something was afoot with their American cousins. By the next morning, Fraser learned from deserters that the retreat was under way. General Roche de Fermoy's imprudent firing of the works on Mount Independence also announced to Burgoyne that his prey was preparing to escape.

Fraser's headquarters were on the west side of the lake, a mile and a half from the bridge to Independence. After learning from the deserters that the retreat had begun, he hurried to the bridge, which he found partially razed, with cannon aimed along its length. Four gunners "manned" the pieces, with orders to fire upon the enemy when they tried to cross the bridge, and then to retreat. But the artillerymen had raised their morale by attacking some spirits, and by the time Fraser's men approached they were too drunk to do anything but sleep. Compounding the farce, an Indian accidentally fired one of the cannon, which was elevated so high that the only damage was to the advanced party's nerves.

And so Ticonderoga's commandant and garrison fled. Burgoyne's army, with unexpected ease, had retaken the "Gibraltar of the North."

Recriminations

Ticonderoga's abandonment shocked military and political leaders unprepared for such a bloodless defeat. Ignorance of conditions in the North and of British intentions combined with political factionalism to nourish confusion and recrimination. No one was immune to the infection.

Even George Washington, for all his moral courage, was dismayed. The most recent intelligence from Schuyler's department had reached him at Middlebrook, New Jersey, on June 26. The report merely confirmed news that Burgoyne was indeed advancing. The commander-in-chief even believed that the British threat to Ticonderoga might be a feint to cover other, more dangerous objectives. Washington now realized that it was Horatio Gates who had been correct about Burgoyne's intentions, and that the British commander had already overcome his first major obstacle to descending the Hudson and uniting with Sir William Howe's command. In Washington's case, the fort's loss, while it shocked him, did not lead to paralysis. He moved his Grand Army closer to the Hudson Highlands, alerted the posts on the lower Hudson to be vigilant in expecting Howe to move upriver to cooperate with the army from Canada, and called upon the eastern states to send militia to reinforce Schuyler.[24]

Others reacted less moderately. Delegates to the Continental Congress and many soldiers believed that Ticonderoga's fall could have been due only to incompetence, cowardice, or treachery, and they indulged in that ancient blood sport of scapegoating. St. Clair and Schuyler were the obvious candidates for sacrifice.

St. Clair received censure from men who argued that "honor" required him to defend his post until surrounded and forced to capitulate. In the event, St. Clair's was in fact a brave decision, and one that conformed to the resolutions of General Schuyler's council of June 20: that the garrison should defend Ticonderoga and its dependencies as long as possible before retreating, consistent with preserving the garrison and stores.

Although the decision was consistent with his own council's resolution, Schuyler himself was quick to condemn St. Clair's decision to evacuate Ticonderoga. His anger stemmed from the fact that St. Clair issued his evacuation decision without explicit orders or the department commander's approval. St. Clair, of course, had no immediate access to Schuyler's headquarters. An effort to communicate with Schuyler to solicit his approval for a withdrawal to save his men would have required, under the best of circumstances, four or five days. Such a luxury of time St. Clair did not possess. Once the guns on Mount Defiance interdicted the retreat route (another day at most) Ticonderoga and Mount Independence would have been isolated, their garrisons taken prisoner.[25]

Members of Washington's staff also excoriated St. Clair for abandoning a citadel in which so much hope and so many resources had been invested. Alexander Hamilton, whose opinions of his own military talents were not modest, wrote to John Jay on July 13. "The stroke at Ticonderoga is heavy, unexpected and unaccountable," seethed the future Secretary of the Treasury. "If the place was untenable why was it not discovered to be so before the Continent has been put to such amazing expence [sic] in furnishing it with means of defence. If it was not untenable, what, in the name of common sense could have induced the evacuation? I wish to suspend my judgment on the matter; but certainly present appearances speak to either the most abandoned cowardice or treachery."[26] Hamilton was not criticizing Schuyler, his future father-in-law; St. Clair was his target. Benedict Arnold, never loath to fault colleagues in disfavor, also denounced St. Clair, declaring that "some person must be sacrificed to an injured country." Even some members of St. Clair's command joined the chorus and hinted at cowardice or treachery.

The Continental Congress, where the people's tribunes carried the burdens of government, was the theater in which ultimate judgment played out. Here, Schuyler's congressional foes were unsparing in their condemnation, some stooping to speculate about that general's loyalty. He, in turn, blamed that home of egalitarian malcontent, New England, averring that if its states had complied with requests for reinforcements, Ticonderoga would still be in American hands. (Schuyler conveniently ignored the fact that most of the men New England raised for the Northern Department had, at Washington's direction, been diverted to the lower Hudson and New Jersey.) Of the reinforcements Schuyler did receive, his disparagement was vehement. But he assured General Washington on July 18 that he would soldier on, in spite of the "malice of my enemies."[27] Having regained command of the Northern Department, the general refused to share the responsibility for its failures.

Throughout July, while Burgoyne's army advanced and Schuyler, in spite of his querulous correspondence, did as much as an American general could do under prevailing conditions, Congress wrestled with problems inherent in maintaining civil control without the benefit of adequate machinery of government. One of its earliest and more constructive acts was to respond affirmatively to Washington's July 10 recommendation that it direct Benedict Arnold to collect militia from New England and New York to reinforce Schuyler. On the same day, however, Arnold—furious at well-founded congressional suspicions of financial malfeasance and having been passed over for promotion during the previous February—submitted his resignation from the Continental Army.[28]

The delegates heard Washington's letter read during the eleventh of July session and, officially ignorant of Arnold's letter of resignation, ordered him to report to Washington's headquarters, where on July 12 he heard Washington reiterate his wishes that Arnold join Schuyler.[29] Arnold asked Congress to suspend his resignation, and he joined Schuyler's forces in the North.

Castigated on every hand and abandoned by men who should have defended him, St. Clair asked Washington to convene a court-martial, and that Arnold, who had vehemently censured him, be excluded from sitting on the court.[30] Cleared in 1778, St. Clair continued to serve in subordinate assignments throughout the war.[31] Schuyler, the other target of vituperation, also sought vindication. A court-martial, with General Benjamin Lincoln presiding, convened at Fredericksburg, New York, on October 1, 1778. Found not guilty of "Neglect of Duty," Schuyler resigned from the Army and served in Congress.[32] Neither man merited the opprobrium he suffered for the loss of Ticonderoga.

The Americans Withdraw . . .

One Scot, St. Clair, left Ticonderoga to face censure; to another, Simon Fraser, fell the honor of sending an express messenger to his commander shortly after dawn on July 6, reporting that the citadel was again British. His brigade, supported by German grenadiers and light infantry, immediately took up the pursuit of the American effectives as they retreated toward Hubbardton in the Hampshire Grants. General Burgoyne, "knowing how safely I could trust that officer's conduct," concentrated on marshaling his forces to exploit the initiative gained by his first victory.[33]

Leaving the British 62nd Regiment at Mount Independence and the German Regiment Prinz Friedrich [Regiment Erb Prinz] at Ticonderoga under the command of Brigadier James Hamilton, Burgoyne took the rest of his army and its flotilla up the southern end of the lake to Skenesborough.[34]

Dazed, weary, grumbling Americans sweated and cursed through the oppressive heat along the rutted military trace that served as a road to Hubbardton, where it joined an older, less-primitive road leading to Castleton. Maintaining march discipline, always difficult during a retreat, was made especially so by green, three-month militia regiments, two of which had arrived at Ticonderoga only two days before the evacuation. The inexperienced and frightened men, who wanted more than anything else to get as far away as quickly as their legs would carry them, repeatedly broke ranks. By constantly riding along the column St. Clair and his staff succeeded in imposing a degree of order. In that state, two Continental and four militia regiments proceeded, with Colonel Ebenezer Francis' 11th Massachusetts forming the rearguard.[35]

When about three miles from Hubbardton, St. Clair received an exaggerated report that a combined loyalist-Indian party occupied the settlement. He pressed on and found that the raiders, about fifty in number, had left in the direction of Castleton with several captives. The women and children had fled, leaving the village deserted. The raiders' presence posed a problem that he could not resolve until he knew more than he did when he reached Hubbardton. He realized that the raiders had not come from Ticonderoga; perhaps they came from farther north. If so, were they part of an advanced corps, with regular troops behind them? That would create a situation that the Americans were not prepared to deal with, one possibly more dangerous than a pursuit from Ticonderoga. For more than an hour St. Clair waited for Colonel Francis to bring up the rearguard. But stragglers slowed Francis' march, and he halted near where St. Clair had learned about the raid on Hubbardton.[36]

The general might have delayed longer, waiting for Francis to join the column, but he could not restrain the militiamen. He moved toward small-but-important Castleton, where roads leading to Connecticut and the Hudson met. Prudently concerned to keep his force from fragmenting, he left Colonel Nathan Hale's 2nd New Hampshire Regiment and Colonel Seth Warner's battalion of "Green Mountain Boys," about one-third of his force, under the latter's command, with orders to await and take command of the rearguard when it arrived, and then to rejoin the main column.[37]

Francis arrived with his rearguard and more than 100 stragglers in mid-afternoon. Excluding the stragglers, Warner now commanded about 953 officers and men, of whom only about 520 were in good condition. Of those, only his own battalion was fit to march immediately: the New Hampshiremen were too tired, after a day's march that had covered twenty-four miles, to move on; the rearguard was less fatigued, but it too needed rest; and the stragglers included sick, feeble, and demoralized men who had reached the limit of endurance. The colonel could not hope to start toward Castleton until after the men had rested and eaten, which would require the rest of the day.[38]

There was another important reason for staying where he was until morning: his assignment was to protect the rear of the main column, delay pursuit and, if necessary, engage the enemy long enough to give the main column time either to escape or to assume an effective defensive posture. Athwart the military road along which pursuit from Ticonderoga would come and six miles from Castleton, the site he occupied was suitable for both defense and bivouac. Of the options available that evening, remaining at Hubbardton was the best.[39]

Having decided to spend the night, Warner arrayed his composite force, deploying the 2nd New Hampshire and the stragglers along Sucker Brook and astride the road from Mount Independence. The 11th Massachusetts moved up Zion Hill slightly northward to a position on a ridge dominating the road from Crown Point. He posted his own battalion on the slope behind the New Hampshiremen to function as a tactical reserve. The Americans were in position to react to a hostile advance along either of the two possible routes.

The key to the position was John Sellick's farm at the intersection of the road from Mount Independence and the one to Castleton. Sellick's was a typical frontier farm, with a field fence of logs and felled trees, stumps, and brush. Warner's and Hale's men spent the late afternoon and what energy they could marshal improving the field's northern and western boundaries. Concerned about Indian and loyalist raiders, Warner posted pickets around his position's perimeter. Because he did not expect the enemy's pursuit column to march so rapidly as to pose an immediate threat, he did not post any patrols on the road from Mount Independence—a fateful decision, as events would prove. The exhausted Americans, certain that they had done what they could to secure their bivouac, bedded down for a chilly, uncomfortable night.

About two miles south of the rearguard, Colonel Benjamin Bellows and two militia regiments encamped along the road. Other troops were scattered between them and Castleton, which the main body occupied. St. Clair's column was in what was apparently a reasonably secure state. The fifty raiders had vacated the settlement as his force approached. The three-unit rearguard occupied a tenable position. Bellows' militia and the troops along the road should provide communications between the rearguard and the main force.

. . . But Not Far Enough

Seth Warner's men were unaware, as they slept that night, that Fraser's Advanced Corps was only three miles away. Three miles behind them, von Riedesel's infantry, Jägers, and grenadiers camped. Their combined strength was approximately 1,950 men: 850 British and 1,100 Germans. With an energy that gave the lie to fond American illusions about European lack of initiative, the combined German and British column started toward Hubbardton at three o'clock in the morning. As Fraser approached the sleeping camp, Indian and provincial scouts reconnoitered along the road and through the woods to test the American perimeter security. The 24th, Fraser's own regiment with Major Robert Grant commanding, followed by Lord Balcarres' light infantry and Major John Dyke Acland's grenadiers, advanced along the road. Brigadier Fraser accompanied the light infantry, the best position from which to control his column.[40]

The brigadier surveyed the broad valley below from a knob west of the road. A mile and a half away, rugged, stony Zion Hill dominated the scene. As he watched, musket fire signaled contact between the 24th Regiment's vanguard and American pickets. The regiment's lead company deployed from column into line and into the underbrush on the fringe of Sellick's field. Major Grant opened the attack, and the entire column engaged.

The light infantry company obliqued to the left of the battalion companies toward what would later be called Monument Hill. From that point, the regiment would sweep the valley below. But the field's key to success was Zion Hill, possession of which would seal the American escape route. Fraser sent the necessary orders to Lord Balcarres and Major Acland, sent couriers to General von Riedesel, and hurried to join the light infantry as it moved to the left of Grant's battalion companies.[41]

The men of Nathan Hale's 2nd New Hampshire had gathered in small groups around their fires preparing and eating their breakfast when the 24th Regiment attacked, turning the bivouac into a churning mass of panicked confusion. A few men rallied and returned fire from behind felled trees, but the majority fled into the forest; their commander became a prisoner. Major Grant's six companies mopped up the futile resistance and pursued those in flight through the woods for about 300 yards, when a volley from Warner's Green Mountain Battalion stopped them in their tracks and killed Major Grant. Meeting stout resistance, and with their commanding officer down, the men of the 24th took cover and returned a desultory fire.[42]

Colonel Warner had intended to march for Castleton after first light, and his men may have been forming when the New Hampshiremen came under attack. The intensity of the fire told him that it was too late to move out. Saving St. Clair's main column required immediate, determined resistance by the rearguard. And so Warner rushed his men into the woods and across the military road to stop the British before they cleared Sucker Run. Their almost

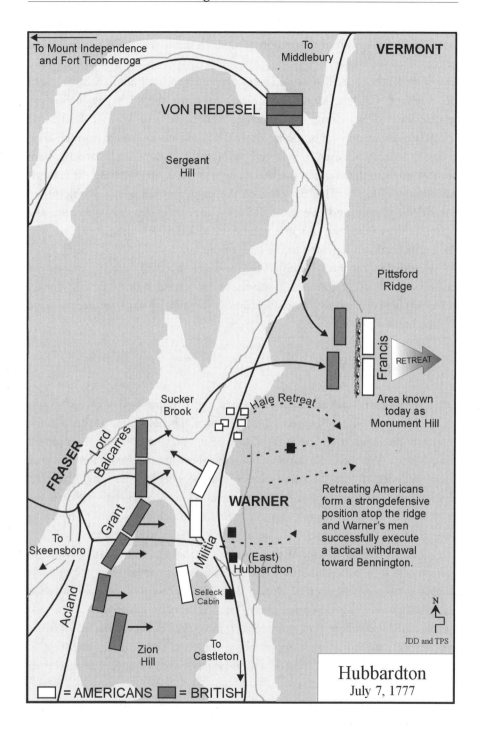

To Mount Independence
and Fort Ticonderoga

To
Middlebury

VERMONT

VON RIEDESEL

Sergeant
Hill

Pittsford
Ridge

Francis

RETREAT

Sucker
Brook

Hale Retreat

Area known
today as
Monument Hill

FRASER

Lord
Balcarres

Grant

WARNER

Militia

(East)
Hubbardton

Retreating Americans
form a strongdefensive
position atop the ridge
and Warner's men
successfully execute
a tactical withdrawal
toward Bennington.

To
Skeensboro

Acland

Selleck
Cabin

Zion
Hill

To
Castleton

N

JDD and TPS

☐ = AMERICANS ▥ = BRITISH

Hubbardton
July 7, 1777

point-blank volley into the battalion company's ranks was the Americans' first act of effective resistance.[43]

With Warner at Sellick's cabin was Colonel Ebenezer Francis, who had sent his adjutant, Captain Moses Greenleaf, to form the 11th Massachusetts, preparatory to marching to Castleton. When he and Warner heard the increasing crescendo of battle he dashed to join his regiment, formed it in column, ordered the men to load and prime their muskets, and marched them southward until they sighted the British light infantry approaching the crest of Monument Hill. The 11th deployed to the right, formed a line, double-timed toward the enemy, and opened a withering fire. Balcarres' lead elements, the light infantry of the 29th and 34th regiments, reeled back with heavy losses, and the entire battalion retreated to the base of the hill.[44]

Francis, momentarily gratified by the local success of having driven the enemy off the hill, regrouped along the crest behind a stone fence. Warner reformed his battalion to Francis' left across the military road, setting the stage for the battle's second phase.

Surprises on Both Sides

Lord Balcarres and his officers rallied his light infantry and advanced slowly up the hill from which Francis had driven them. The 24th moved through the woods immediately to the earl's right. Out of sight of the troops on Monument Hill, Major John Acland's battalion of grenadiers approached Zion Hill in a move intended to turn the American left and interdict an American retreat via the road to Castleton. Two of Acland's battalion's companies deployed to make contact with the 24th Regiment and prevent an attack on its flank. The move brought them into the open field between Zion Hill and the military road.

The erupting fire alerted Warner to the fact that the grenadiers intended to turn his flank by occupying the hill.[45] The American commander immediately deployed part of his Green Mountain Battalion to Zion Hill, which until then had not figured in his defensive plans. The Vermonters resorted to a ruse that outraged the grenadiers: they clubbed their muskets, i.e., shouldered them in the reverse with the butts up, a universally recognized signal of the intention to surrender, and when they stepped within range of their enemy, presented their pieces and opened fire.

Warner's ploy, deviously clever though it was, failed to halt the grenadiers, who slung their muskets and clawed their way up Zion's rocky slope, grabbing bushes and trees as they pulled themselves to the summit. During the fight for

Zion Hill a musket ball struck the grenadier commander in the thigh. A small guard remained with him while the rest of his men rushed down the reverse slope toward Warner's left flank and the road to Castleton.

It was at this time in the battle that the American commander executed a maneuver worthy of a professional officer schooled in 18th-century tactics.[46] Warner, his left flank dangerously hanging in the air, refused it by curving it into the rear and anchoring it in the corner of a log fence on the east side of the Castleton road south of John Sellick's house. He now occupied a very strong position that the grenadiers could reach only by traversing open fields, exposed to fire from behind cover. The skill with which Warner controlled his men—retreating in the presence of an attacking enemy, halting when he gained favorable ground, refusing his flank, and then resuming the fight—was a remarkable achievement.

Remarkable also were the events unfolding on the American right, where Colonel Francis faced the 24th Regiment and Balcarres' light infantry. Fraser was confident that, once his troops gained Monument Hill's crest, disciplined British skill with the bayonet would prevail. The dense woods made maintaining a properly-dressed line impossible, but the officers kept their men advancing under effective control, firing and reloading as they drew near the American line.

Francis now courageously resorted to an unexpected tactic: he led his men from behind their cover in a counterattack that confronted their enemies in the woods halfway down the hill, where they fired at close range at individual targets. Francis made himself conspicuous as he encouraged his men, and a ball shattered his right arm. The counterattack caught the British completely by surprise, and in spite of their officers' desperate efforts, the light infantrymen recoiled and staggered down the slope, carrying the 24th on their right with them. Lord Balcarres received a superficial shoulder wound while trying to rally his men.[47]

Simon Fraser's well-conceived twin offensive had failed. Warner and Francis had executed difficult and dangerous maneuvers that would have challenged better-trained and more-experienced soldiers. They and their men displayed a disciplined courage that was rarely, if ever, surpassed during the War for Independence. In what only could have come as a grave shock to Fraser, he found himself in battle not with a retreating, inexperienced enemy, but with a foe that seemed stronger near the end of the fight than before the engagement began—an opponent encouraged by unexpected success against brave, professionally-led Regulars. The brigadier's last hope lay with Freiherr von

Riedesel's Germans. The aide Fraser sent back found von Riedesel with his advance party on the same knob from which Fraser had first reconnoitered the field.

When the German general surveyed the scene of action, the American lines inscribed a half-moon in which Warner's Vermonters occupied an arc from a point across the Castleton road from Sellick's cabin, thence in front of the house to the end of a stone wall; Francis' 11th Massachusetts manned the rest of the line, a position to which he had skillfully withdrawn after repelling the second light infantry attack. Studying the scene through his Fernglass, von Riedesel watched the distant puffs of smoke and small human figures that told the experienced combat veteran that the Americans were adopting Fraser's turning movement in reverse by driving back his left.[48]

His reaction to what he saw was as swift as his assessment of the tactical situation. He ordered Captain Carl von Geyso's Jäger company to double-time to support Balcarres' light infantry. Captain Maximillian Christoph Ludwig von Schottelius led his grenadier company farther left into the battle line, where he could turn southward along Monument Hill's crest and fall upon the American right and rear. For added psychological effect, the Jägers' band of hautboys and Waldhorns played their riflemen into battle. The general sent a courier back to Oberstlieutenant [Colonel] Heinrich von Breymann with orders to bring up the more than 900 men of the German main column.[49]

Fraser, apparently unaware that the Germans were going into action, made another desperate bid for victory. He knew that the grenadiers from Zion Hill had gained the road to Castleton and were moving northward against the American left flank. He therefore ordered the 24th Regiment and the light infantry to fix bayonets and charge up Monument Hill for the third time. This time, he ordered that neither enemy fire nor difficult terrain were to prevent them from engaging the Americans, using their bayonets against a foe against whom that weapon was almost always effective.[50]

But before the tired, much-mauled soldiers could mount their charge, an alien sound reached American and British ears. To the accompaniment of their band, lusty voices sang old German hymns—probably "Ein feste Burg ist unser Gott" and possibly "Herr Gott, dich loben wir, regier." The Brunswickers of von Riedesel had arrived. When they stepped within effective range of Francis' line, the Germans fired volleys by platoons, advancing slowly in close order as they overlapped the American right. The 11th Massachusetts fell back in disorder onto the plateau to the right side of the road to Castleton, where their colonel rallied them behind a log fence.[51]

Across the plateau and out of range of the Massachusetts muskets, the combined British and German regiments and the Jägers and light infantrymen dressed ranks, preparatory for a charge. Hoping a preemptive strike would abort that charge, Francis led his men back across the plateau in a desperate gamble that cost him his life. At the same time German grenadiers advanced along the Castleton Road toward the American right. Overwhelmed, the brave men of the 11th Massachusetts finally broke and fled into the woods.[52] Seth Warner, fighting on the American left and facing British grenadiers advancing from the south, watched as his right wing vanished into thin air. Realizing the battle was over, he ordered the Vermonters to fall back. The men evaporated into the wilderness, with directions to reform at Rutland.

By 8:45 in the morning the Battle of Hubbardton was over. The vicious, closely-fought, and bloody fight, which had lasted slightly more than two hours, served as a testament to the bravery of both Americans and Europeans. It also bore witness to the especially effective leadership of Seth Warner and Ebenezer Francis.

Skenesborough, Forts Anne and Edward, and Beyond

Initial Skirmishes

While General St. Clair led his beaten column southward, his bateaux fleet sailed unhurriedly toward Skenesborough. Its commander, Colonel Long, felt no urge to hurry. He placed great trust in the massive boom of logs strung along its massive chain of inch-and-a-half iron bars, backed by a bridge supported by twenty-four timber piers. Between the piers were log floats fastened together by double chains secured by iron bolts. Long was certain it would take the British a long, long time to break through. His confidence was sorely misplaced.

British gunboats smashed the chain with a few well-placed shots, and the piers were cut. Within a few hours Burgoyne's fleet was running before a northerly wind. The Americans landed at 1:00 p.m. on July 6. By 4:00 the British were less than three miles away. Burgoyne landed his first three regiments to arrive—the 9th, 20th, and 21st—on South Bay's east side, with orders to cross Wood Creek and occupy the road to Fort Anne, the only route southward. Moving those units through the woods to their assigned positions required longer than expected, and they were not ready when the general launched his attack up the mouth of Wood Creek.

Knowing that Skenesborough's stockaded fort was too weak to withstand an attack, Colonel Long sent the invalids and women up Wood Creek, accompanied by a party to row the boats transporting them. Once the boats were away, he set his men to burning the fort and fleet. They succeeded in destroying the stockade, its building, and *Enterprise*, *Gates*, and *Liberty*, but the enemy would arrive in time to capture the schooner *Revenge* and galley *Trumbull*.

The Americans destroyed everything combustible that had been salvaged at Ticonderoga, and what would not burn was abandoned. Their desperate task completed, the colonel and about 150 men fled toward Fort Anne.

Burgoyne's attack on Skenesborough opened before his three regiments were into position to cut off Long's retreat, but he ordered Lieutenant Colonel John Hill to pursue the Americans with his 9th Regiment. Hill set out during the morning of July 7, his progress painfully slow.[1] The road to Fort Anne was execrable, even by contemporary standards—meaning it was all but impassable. The Americans rendered it even worse by destroying the crude bridges that spanned the numerous streams. The result was that the 9th Regiment managed only ten miles during the seventh and stopped within a mile of the fort. An American appeared early the next morning claiming to be a deserter. When questioned, he explained to Colonel Hill that there were 1,000 men manning Fort Anne. Because he had only 190 men with him, Hill sent a message to Burgoyne asking for reinforcements. The "deserter" promptly slipped away and informed Colonel Long of Hill's weakness.

Unbeknownst to the British, a 400-man body of New York militia sent by General Schuyler under the command of Colonel Henry Van Rensselaer had arrived from Fort Edward. Emboldened by his agent's report, Long turned on his enemy and attacked Hill about 10:30 on the morning of July 8.[2] The scene of the action was a defile about three-quarters of a mile northeast of the fort, where the British were caught on a narrow ledge with Wood Creek on their left and a steep hill on their right. As at Hubbardton, the woods were thick and the terrain so precipitous that Hill's men of the 9th Regiment could neither form a cohesive line nor obtain a clear field of fire. Some Americans crossed the stream and slipped into the enemy's rear. To avoid being surrounded, Hill sent his men up the steep slope that hemmed them against the creek. Once on the summit they held the Americans at bay for two hours. Just as they were running out of ammunition, they heard what was described as a "war whoop." The Americans heard it too, and broke off the attack against the embattled 9th Regiment.[3]

There had indeed been a "war whoop," but no warriors—just a lone Englishman, Captain John Money, trying to lead a party of Indians to his regiment's support. The tribesmen were so unenthusiastic about getting involved in a pitched fight that they lagged behind, leaving Captain Money to strike ahead without them. When he reached the scene of battle, he—with remarkable presence of mind—sounded what he hoped would resemble an Indian war cry. The Americans, by now also low on ammunition, had no stomach for taking on a fresh war party. Thinking prudence the better part of heroism, they beat a hasty retreat to Fort Edward, setting fire to Fort Anne as they withdrew. As unlikely as it was, Money's ploy succeeded.[4]

General William Phillips soon arrived with the 47th and 53rd regiments and escorted the remnants of the battered 9th back to Skenesborough. Phillips left the wounded at the scene of the battle under the care of Sergeant Roger Lamb, who sometimes functioned as assistant surgeon, and a soldier's wife. In that lonely spot they ministered to their charges until three of the twenty-four wounded had died and the rest were deemed fit to travel.

At Castleton, meanwhile, General St. Clair could only try to save his column from destruction by retreating. Burgoyne was at Skenesborough, forcing the American commander to "change his line of march, and by a circuitous route through Pawlet, Manchester, and Bennington, he struck the Hudson at Battenkill and joined Schuyler at Fort Edward on the 12th July."[5]

Except for the units left at Ticonderoga and Mount Independence, by July 10 the British army was reassembled at Skenesborough and Castleton. That day's general order recited the successes of Hubbardton and Fort Anne and announced that "Divine Service will be performed on Sunday next [July 13] at the head of the Line, and at the head of the Advanced Corps, and at sun set on the same day a feu de joye will be fired with Cannon and small arms at Ticonderoga, Crown Point, the Camp at Skenesborough, and at the Post of Breeman's [sic] Corps."[6]

General Burgoyne and his soldiers had reasons aplenty to congratulate themselves and to have recourse to the God of Battles, thanking Him for past mercies and beseeching future guidance and protection. The 18th century was not conspicuous for religiosity, and soldiers were notoriously impious. But men respected forms, and faith or superstition moved those who faced danger to invoke supernatural help.

Burgoyne Ponders His Options

The British commander stood in special need of guidance, for he stood now on the horns of a difficult—and what would prove to be controversial—decision. If his campaign had later been successful, few would have faulted him for the decision he was about to make. But because it failed, and failed so catastrophically, contemporary and future analysts freighted that decision with much of the burden for that failure.

In his "Thoughts on Conducting the War from the Side of Canada," Burgoyne identified Lake George as providing the "most expeditious and most commodious route to Albany."[7] That route would take the army to Fort George, the northern terminus of a sixteen-mile road to Fort Edward and the portage to the Hudson River. He believed it to be the shortest route from Ticonderoga to the river, and the least vulnerable to delaying action, ambush, and flank attack. He noted further that an alternative was "the route by South-Bay and Skenesborough . . . but considerable difficulties may be expected, as the narrow parts of the river [Wood Creek] may be easily choked up and rendered impassable; and at best, there will be necessity for a great deal of land-carriage for the artillery, provisions, &c: which can only be supplied from Canada."[8] As was the case with all of his "Thoughts," the general was projecting proposals, and he did not commit himself to following specific courses of action in the face of changing tactical situations.

For instance, the general had not foreseen that the Americans would retreat from Ticonderoga by way of Skenesborough. He had, in fact, hoped to capture the garrison when he took the fort. To the extent that he may have thought about an American evacuation and retreat while he formed his proposals, he probably expected them to withdraw down Lake George. From his perspective in 1776, that seemed the most logical course for a garrison driven from Ticonderoga to take.

St. Clair did not act as Burgoyne had hoped. The American commander had not waited for his enemy to besiege or assault his post, and refused to reward Burgoyne by allowing him to make the men of the garrison prisoners of war. Nor did St. Clair retreat down the lake nor along the road that ran parallel to the lake's western shore, for the British seizure of Mount Hope interdicted that route by dominating the gorge and its waterway between the lakes. The American general took the only feasible route left to him, the waterway up South Bay and the land route to Skenesborough.

Burgoyne correctly considered defeating the retreating Americans more important than capturing posts. He needed to employ a tactic for pressing the pursuit and, if possible, to bring his quarry to battle—an elusive objective in the northern frontier's forests and scattered clearings. He thus had to decide whether to adhere to his original proposal, which might enable him to get between St. Clair and Schuyler, or to follow another course in light of new problems and opportunities.

One option available to Burgoyne was to employ his advanced corps, supported by light artillery, as a flying column to attack Fort Edward, which during July's third week would have fallen quickly. His main force could have descended Lake George and seized the fort of the same name with its forty cannon and store of ammunition, cutting off St. Clair's retreat. General Gates, a better strategist than some of his contemporaries, British and American, believed that if Burgoyne had chosen that option he would have reached Albany by the end of July. But separating his advanced corps from his main column would have been a gamble, and Burgoyne, while an "old gamester," would not take the risk inherent in that option.

Two other options remained open for the British commander. First, he could break off the pursuit of the retreating American army, return to Ticonderoga, drag his bateaux, gunboats, artillery, and stores up the gorge from Lake Champlain to Lake George, move his entire force down the lake to Fort George, and portage overland to Fort Edward and the Hudson. That was the course favored by most of his critics. Alternatively, he might continue moving his troops along the land route from Skenesborough, but send the gunboats, bateaux, and heavy artillery by Lake George. Burgoyne chose the second alternative.[9]

Some of the expedition's officers believed that the general's deviation from the route he originally proposed entailed excessive effort and delayed reaching Fort Edward and the Hudson.[10] Parliamentary critics, especially among the government's supporters, argued that it contributed materially to the defeat at Saratoga. Contemporary and later writers vied with one another in finding language adequate to express their condemnation and eagerness to discredit his motives and execution.

Of these critics, the author of the best Loyalist history of the war in New York, Judge Thomas Jones, claimed that if Burgoyne had returned to Ticonderoga and embarked his army upon Lake George, he might have passed the lake in twenty-four hours. He attributed the general's contrary decision to Phillip Skene's corrupting influence, writing that if Burgoyne had

> fairly and openly told the truth, he would have declared that the route he pursued was by the advice of Colonel Philip Skene, the proprietor of Skenesborough, and whose estate there, by clearing out Wood Creek, and making a firm substantial road from thence to Fort Edward, with strong bridges over all creeks, and causeways through the swamps and morasses, had Great Britain succeeded in the contest, would have been rendered more valuable by several thousand pounds.[11]

Hoffman Nickerson embellished the judge's indictment of Colonel Skene's character with an apocryphal story to the effect that Skene had kept his mother's desiccated corpse in his basement for years instead of burying it so that he could continue to collect her annuity, supposedly proving that he was the sort who would not be above advising a general with an eye to his own profit. So much for how some detractors interpreted the general's motives for making the choice he did.[12]

But what does an examination of Burgoyne's own rationale for his decision reveal? Most students of the campaign have noted what Nickerson labeled "weak" reasoning by Burgoyne: that taking the Lake George route would have entailed a retrograde move back to Ticonderoga. That was part, but not the sum, of Burgoyne's explanation. "Questions have been made by those who began at this period to arraign my military conduct," Burgoyne wrote later in his own defense,

> whether it would not have been more expedient for the purpose of rapidity, to have fallen back to Ticonderoga, in order to take the convenient route by Lake George, than to have persevered in the laborious and difficult course by land to Fort Edward? I considered not only the general impressions which a retrograde motion is apt to make upon the minds both of enemies and friends, but also that the natural conduct of the enemy in that case would be to remain at Fort George, as their retreat could not then be cut off, in order to oblige me to open trenches, and consequently to delay me, in the meantime they would have destroyed the road from Fort George to Fort Edward . . . .[13]

The great number of boats also, which must necessarily have been employed for the transport of troops over Lake George, were by this course spared for the transport of the provisions, artillery, and ammunition.[14]

This single passage from the "Narrative" section of his *State of the Expedition* encompasses or suggests several factors—strategic, tactical, and logistical—affecting Burgoyne's choice of options, which will be addressed in more detail below.

The Loyalist Angle

First, let us examine Burgoyne's statement concerning "the general impressions which a retrograde motion is apt to make upon the minds of both enemies and friends." An important strategic consideration favored continuing to operate in the country east of Lake George. Abandoning the land route to

Fort Edward would remove even an implied threat to New England, one of the alternatives included in Burgoyne's "Thoughts." To make that threat credible, he posted von Riedesel at Castleton to "assist my purpose of giving jealousy to Connecticut and keeping in check the whole country called the Hampshire Grants."[15] Both Baroness von Riedesel and Lieutenant Colonel Kingston, Burgoyne's adjutant general and military secretary, later confirmed this motivation, with Kingston adding that the hope was that the "alarm towards Connecticut" would "give encouragement to the loyal inhabitants, if any such there were."[16]

The subject of encouraging loyalism merits more attention from historians than it has received, with the lack of study due at least in part to the fact that it did not figure explicitly in the papers documenting plans for the campaign's eastern phase. But the goal was problematical. Supporting loyal Americans and recalling the disaffected were objectives that at once inspired and complicated military and political objectives; vanquishing the rebellious, however, simply required their military defeat and restoring political and social order. In any case, Britain both overestimated loyalist strength and failed to exploit effectively what real and potential sources of popular support did exist.

Although explicit discussion of loyalism received limited attention in the Burgoyne-Germain correspondence, all parties assumed that both Burgoyne and St. Leger would be operating in regions containing many people who would, given the opportunity, declare for the King. Their assumptions were not founded entirely upon illusion. Exact figures are unobtainable, but many who lived along the Champlain-Hudson line and in the Mohawk Valley were either secret or open loyalists or persons at least lukewarm to rebellion. Many inhabitants of the Hampshire Grants, like other border people, were susceptible to the influence of a military presence in determining their political commitment. Whatever the actual or potential number of loyalists, Philip Skene probably exaggerated it to Burgoyne, and the general's native optimism provided fertile ground in which hope became certitude.[17]

With his army providing the military presence he expected would be decisive in restoring political loyalties, Burgoyne's general order for July 12 appointed Colonel Skene "to act as Commissary to administer the Oath of Allegiance, and to grant Certificates of Protection to such Inhabitants as sue properly for the same, and to regulate all other matters relative to the Supplies and assistance that shall be required from the Country or voluntarily brought in." The general's expectations had already received apparent confirmation by the arrival of

Some hundreds of men, a third part of them with arms . . . professing themselves loyalists, and wishing to serve, some to the end of the war, some for the campaign. Though I am without instructions on the subject, I have not hesitated to receive them, and, as fast as companies can be formed, I shall post the officers till a decision can be made upon the measure by my superiors.[18]

Burgoyne intended to employ them to "keep the country in awe," and bring in cattle. Their most important contribution would be psychological, in the "impression which will be caused upon public opinion, should provincials be seen acting vigorously in the cause of the King . . . ."[19] The new arrivals were embodied into the provincial units then "in embryo but very promising," commanded by Lieutenant Colonels John Peters and Ebenezer Jessup of the skeleton Queen's Loyal Rangers and King's Loyal Americans.

But for all of his and Skene's optimism, the local recruits would not measure up to the commander's hopes in either numbers or effectiveness.

Consideration of the Routes

The water route led along Lake George and thus through Fort George, at its southern end. Lack of intelligence affected Burgoyne's assessment of Fort George's potential role. His knowledge of its physical condition was limited. He did know, of course, that the lake protected its front, a steep hill defended its rear, and marshes made its sides difficult to attack. If the Americans at the fort made a determined resistance, they would delay him until after he could post cannon on the hill. That would buy them time to destroy the sixteen-mile portage road to the Hudson, and he would not reach Fort Edward within a month. On the other hand, if he followed the land route, he could threaten Fort George from the rear, obliging its defenders to retreat or risk capture. Burgoyne certainly overestimated the fort's strength, but, in light of what he knew, his concerns were logical.

Other factors made the choice of the land route less patently foolish than has been claimed. Lake George lies 221 feet above the level of Lake Champlain. Access between lakes was via a gorge up which boats, artillery, and supplies had to be dragged more than three miles, a task that, when eventually undertaken, required eleven days of arduous labor. Lieutenant Hadden's terse account is worth a read in this regard:

From ye 14th to the 25th we were employed in bringing forward the guns, Stores, and provisions; and in transporting Guns & Batteaux's from ye Saw Mills Creek to Lake George. The road is tolerably level, and where it wanted repairs the Rebel Prisoners were employed[,] being furnished with Tools and working under Guard. We had about Two hundred of them confined in a barn, and when they were not wanted either for the above purpose or Removing Guns and Stores, amused themselves in beating Hemp.[20]

Subjecting the expedition's line and flank companies to that fatiguing ordeal would have adversely affected their combat readiness. The land route was demanding enough; using the Lake George route would have been that much worse.

Comparative distances presented problems that Burgoyne and his staff had to weigh in deciding how to move toward the Hudson and their enemy. If the entire army or the main column, less the advanced corps, followed the Lake George route, it first would have to return from Skenesborough to Ticonderoga, a distance of thirty-six miles by water. The length of the "Carrying Place from Saw Mill Creek to Lake George," up the gorge was, as noted, slightly more than three miles. Lake George, according to Governor Thomas Pownall's reckoning, was thirty-six miles long.[21] The length of the portage between Lake George and the Hudson was sixteen miles. Therefore, if troops and stores were transported by the water route, starting from Skenesborough, then going by way of Lake George, the shortest possible distance was ninety-one miles.

Was there another alternative—perhaps following the Lake George route, but not descending the lake by boat? In the previously-quoted passage from his defense of his decision to advance by land on the Skenesborough side, Burgoyne argued, "The great number of boats also, which must necessarily have been employed for the transport of the troops over Lake George, were by this course spared for the transport of provisions, artillery, and ammunition."[22] That statement seems to imply that no road paralleling the lake existed. However, Major Samuel Holland's 1776 map, "The provinces of New York, New Jersey, with a part of Pennsylvania and the province of Quebec (drawn by Major Holland, surveyor-general of the northern district in America), shows a road west of and running parallel to the lake."[23] Was Burgoyne ignorant of the map's existence? That was possible, but unlikely, for the map was known in Canada. Any general who presumed to plan a campaign on the northern frontier would certainly avail himself of all relevant cartographic information.

That is assuming, of course, that the map, published in 1776, was actually available to Burgoyne when he drafted his "Thoughts" during the early weeks of 1777. But he had, in any case, participated in Sir Guy Carleton's 1776 campaign, and thus may have known about the road even before the publication of Holland's map.

Assuming Burgoyne knew a road lay west of the lake, it is possible that he rejected it as a feasible route for moving troops because it was about fifty miles long, and because of its condition. If, as was probable, it resembled contemporary frontier tracks, his decision to reject it would not have been an unreasonable decision.

A summary of the various routes' comparative features is in order. The distance from Skenesborough to Fort Edward via the lake entailed seventy-five miles of water transport, a three-mile "carrying Place," and a sixteen-mile portage between Forts George and Edward. In contrast, if the main column marched southward from Ticonderoga, it would have to traverse at least sixty-six miles of rough, muddy, wilderness road to reach the Hudson. In favor of the latter option was the fact that there had been no Americans between Ticonderoga and Fort George to render that part of the road hazardous.

The length of the next section of the route Burgoyne's army would have to traverse, from Skenesborough to Wood Creek, was twenty-three miles, including a four- or five-mile portage. In May 1777, Colonel Udney Hay reported to General Gates that the road was reasonably easy, the worst part being a three-mile stretch between Forts Anne and Edward that required constructing a causeway, a task that would take thirty men three weeks.

As discussed in the next section, General Schuyler would soon commit a large body of men to obstructing that very road, changing it from "tolerably easy" to almost impassable until cleared and repaired; but comparing the routes as they existed during the second week of July makes approaching the Hudson by land less the result of whim or corrupt influence than a considered professional decision.

It is also important to note that, once Burgoyne made his decision and set things in motion, the army reached Fort Edward on July 29, while General Phillips and the supply fleet arrived at Fort George about noon on the twenty-eighth. Moving the bateaux, gunboats, artillery, and stores over the portage from Lake George to the Hudson consumed even more time. Thus, transporting the army down the lake route would have saved no time at all. If the men as well as the impedimenta had moved by boat, the army would have

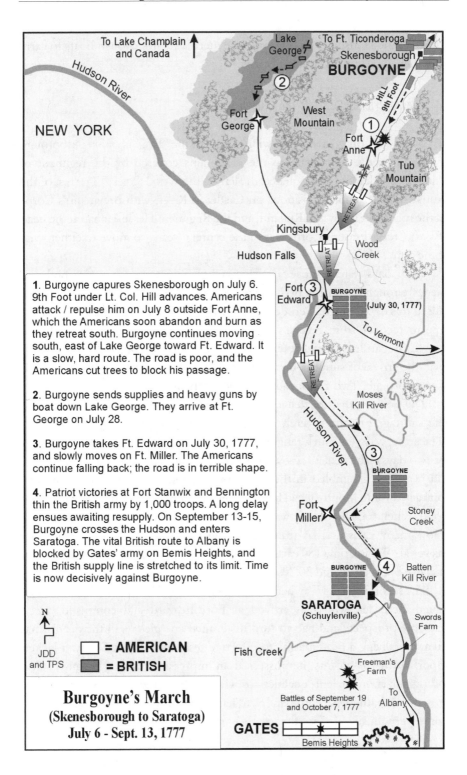

To Lake Champlain and Canada

Lake George

To Ft. Ticonderoga

Skenesborough

BURGOYNE

Hudson River

Hill 9th Foot

NEW YORK

Fort George

West Mountain

Fort Anne

Tub Mountain

RETREAT

Kingsbury

Hudson Falls

Wood Creek

RETREAT

1. Burgoyne capures Skenesborough on July 6. 9th Foot under Lt. Col. Hill advances. Americans attack / repulse him on July 8 outside Fort Anne, which the Americans soon abandon and burn as they retreat south. Burgoyne continues moving south, east of Lake George toward Ft. Edward. It is a slow, hard route. The road is poor, and the Americans cut trees to block his passage.

2. Burgoyne sends supplies and heavy guns by boat down Lake George. They arrive at Ft. George on July 28.

3. Burgoyne takes Ft. Edward on July 30, 1777, and slowly moves on Ft. Miller. The Americans continue falling back; the road is in terrible shape.

4. Patriot victories at Fort Stanwix and Bennington thin the British army by 1,000 troops. A long delay ensues awaiting resupply. On September 13-15, Burgoyne crosses the Hudson and enters Saratoga. The vital British route to Albany is blocked by Gates' army on Bemis Heights, and the British supply line is stretched to its limit. Time is now decisively against Burgoyne.

Fort Edward

BURGOYNE
(July 30, 1777)

To Vermont

RETREAT

Moses Kill River

Hudson River

BURGOYNE

Fort Miller

Stoney Creek

BURGOYNE

Batten Kill River

SARATOGA
(Schuylerville)

Swords Farm

N

JDD and TPS

☐ = **AMERICAN**

■ = **BRITISH**

Fish Creek

Freeman's Farm

Burgoyne's March
(Skenesborough to Saratoga)
July 6 - Sept. 13, 1777

Battles of September 19 and October 7, 1777

To Albany

GATES

Bemis Heights

arrived at the Hudson even later, because there were not enough boats to carry both men and supplies simultaneously.[24]

The Americans Degrade the Chosen Route

By July 10, Burgoyne's right wing occupied the "heights of Skenesborough in two lines; the right flank to the mountains covered by the regiment of Reidesel [sic] dragoons en potence: the left on the Wood Creek." The rest of the Brunswickers occupied positions on Castleton River, with Breymann's Corps on the roads to Putney and Rutland, and the Regiment Hesse-Hanau at the head of East Creek. Fraser's Corps was in the center, "ready to move to either wing of the army."[25]

Two days later, those outlying units rejoined the main body at Skenesborough,[26] and for two weeks the British army remained there. What caused this delay, one that eroded that army's initiative and gave the Americans time to recover from reverses and gain strength in numbers, materiel, and morale? Regardless of the route chosen and its condition, Burgoyne had to await the arrival of supplies from Canada before he could move his army from Skenesborough. Two factors added to his problem.

The first was that the delivery of stores was delayed by deficient transport. The shortage of carts severely affected the arrival of every type of materiel. "The army, was very much fatigued (many parts of it having wanted provisions for two days," the general wrote on July 11, "almost the whole [of] their tents and baggage), assembled in their present position."[27] Most of the 500 carts contracted for in Montreal had broken down because they were built with green wood. When Captain Money was asked during the parliamentary investigation, "How many carts and ox-teams could be mustered at any one time?" he answered, "I think only 180 carts . . . the number of ox-teams I really forget, but I believe between 20 and 30."[28]

The second factor was what General Schuyler had his men doing while they waited. Schuyler, who had arrived at Fort Edward and command, faced fearsome prospects and had to turn his limited energies to all the details that attended rallying a beaten army to effective resistance. While Schuyler lacked important martial talents, he possessed an impressive fund of business sense and organizational talent, qualities for which, at that moment, were in greater need than a battle-wise commander. What Schuyler did was put his ax men to work, very busily. In so doing, they made a significant contribution to

Burgoyne's eventual failure by rendering the road to Fort Edward so nearly impassable as to require its practical rebuilding.

"The British," wrote Sergeant Lamb in a brief but graphic description of this American handiwork,

> were obliged to suspend all operations for some time and wait and wait at Skenesborough for the arrival of provisions and tents; but they employed the interval clearing a passage of the troops, to proceed against the enemy. This was attended with incredible toil. The Americans, under the direction of General Schuyler, were constantly employed in cutting down trees on both sides of every road, which was in the line of march. The face of the country was likewise so broken with creeks and Marshes, that there was no less than forty bridges as to construct, one of which was over a morass two miles in extent.[29]

Lieutenant Hadden's journal entry for July 12 contributes commentary about what Burgoyne's army could not do as a result of the American activity:

> After the Action at or near Fort Anne, the 9th Regiment were withdrawn and joining the Army at Skenesborough, no other Detachment was sent out, and the Enemy tho' not victorious were the real gainers in this affair, the advantage they made of it was to Fell Trees across Wood Creek and the Road leading by the side of it to Fort Anne. The clearing of which cost the Army much labour and time, and gave the enemy spirits & leisure to wait those reinforcements which enabled them to retire deliberately, always keeping near enough to prevent our sending out small Detachments: a large Corps advanced to Fort Anne (in place of the 9th Reg't) wou'd have increased the Enemies Fears and prevented these delays.[30]

Schuyler's delaying tactic and the labors of his men succeeded decisively. British and German work details slaved daily until July 21 restoring the road, rebuilding bridges, constructing a causeway, and clearing Wood Creek. This backbreaking, enervating labor sapped vigor and did nothing to enhance morale.

While his ax men bought valuable time with their valiant efforts, much more remained for Schuyler to do. The morale of dispirited men had to be restored. Reinforcements had to be marshaled. Scarce supplies had to be collected and allocated. Schuyler had to solicit additional provincial human and material resources from governments hard-pressed to meet existing demands. He had to enlist time to serve those vital ends.

American folklore, sometimes given credence by serious students who should know better, has depicted a pleasure-loving Gentleman Johnny Burgoyne living a sybaritic life in Philip Skene's wilderness mansion while allowing a crippled but virtuous foe to recover. He did so while exposing his weary, exploited men to the fatigues of reopening an invasion route that an abler, more humane commander would have avoided.[31] The general was indeed fond of high living and very responsive to feminine graces, and he may well have lightened the hours with drink and dalliance. Generals, including some who have enjoyed distinguished careers in more recent wars, have often done so. Contemporaries, however—including that sometimes-censuring gossip Baronin von Riedesel—who were in a position to know about how Burgoyne spent what free time he had are silent on the subject. What can be documented is that the time he spent at Skenesborough was not passed in idleness.

Sunday, July 13, was so sodden that Burgoyne ordered the soldiers to not strike their tents. But the weather did not cause him to cancel the feu de joye and prayers. Because the day was "set apart for rejoicing, all working Parties are to be remitted, except such as may be necessary for the cleanliness of the Camp."[32] The inclement weather forced the troops to form in the front instead of in the line of battle, i.e., by battalions drawn up in line facing the designated front. The artillery fired first, then the advanced corps, followed by the brigades firing in turn. The ceremony concluded with the chaplains reading appointed collects from the Book of Common Prayer. The locals who witnessed it would never forget it.

While British fatigue parties worked at reopening Wood Creek and the road to Fort Edward, other soldiers performed camp duties and assembled supplies preparatory to resuming the march, tasks that rain and mud rendered more than normally arduous.[33]

Burgoyne's Artillery Millstone

The artillery train was a significant part of Burgoyne's plan and the conduct of the campaign, but it also progressively increased the burden the army bore in the ever-more-difficult advance.

Like Sir Guy Carleton, Burgoyne expected stiff American resistance at Ticonderoga and Forts George and Edward. Since the winter of 1775-76,

Burgoyne had been impressed by American skill in entrenching, a fact emphasized in his "Reflections on the War in America." He anticipated that he would need an overwhelming preponderance of firepower to overawe the Americans and destroy the cover behind which they could mount strong resistance. Thus, the original train provided by Carleton consisted of 138 guns, including heavy, medium, and light cannon, together with howitzers and mortars of different sizes. When Ticonderoga fell with surprising ease, the general reduced the original train by dispersing eighty of his guns—some to his ships, some to remain at Ticonderoga, and some back to Canada. The field train that accompanied the army after those reductions amounted to 43 guns ranging from twenty-four-pounders to three-pounders, with howitzers and mortars. These were divided between the British and German forces, and on the British side between some guns for Fraser's Advanced Corps, with the remainder apportioned into three brigades of Royal Artillery.[34]

Critics have condemned the train of forty-three pieces as being excessive, and as having conspired with the choice of the Skenesborough-Fort Edward route to fatally flaw the campaign's execution. Burgoyne's eventual defeat has tempted analysts to seek out and magnify individual contributing factors, but persuasive analytical assessment has been more elusive than some have admitted.

Every gun, its ammunition, and their transport obviously added to Burgoyne's problems, and those burdens became more onerous with each additional mile. Yet no one would have argued that he could achieve his objective without artillery at all. In fact, because the campaign was an offensive one, success required that his artillery capability exceed his opponent's. Carleton, Burgoyne, and Phillips—the last an experienced artillerist—also believed that American tactics and the war theater's character imposed peculiar requirements. This conviction informed Burgoyne's justification of the size and composition of his field train. In his later defense he began by citing truisms supported by experienced observation. Artillery, he wrote, "was extremely formidable to raw troops," and "in a country of posts it was essentially necessary against the best troops; that it was yet more applicable to the enemy we were to combat," he continued,

> because of the mode of defence they invariably adopted, and at which they were beyond all other nations expert, that of entrenchment covered by a strong abbatis, against which cannon, of the nature of the heaviest above described, and howitzers, might often be effectual, when to dislodge them

by any other means might be attended with continued and important losses. . . . [B]ut further reasons for not diminishing the proportion of guns to six-pounders in this train, were first, their use against block-houses (a species of fortification peculiar to America); secondly, a probability that gun-boats might be requisite for the security of the water transport; on some part of Hudson's River; but principally the intention of fortifying a camp at Albany, in case I should reach that place, should meet with a sufficiency of provision there (as I was led to expect) and should find it expedient to pass the winter there, without communication with new York.[35]

Admittedly, there was an element of obvious post-facto rationalizing in that lengthy and labored defense.

There was more, however. The general was painfully aware that the Americans could field more men than he. But he also knew that, man for man, the British soldier was a better campaigner. That fact made trained men especially valuable. They were scarce in Britain—hence the reason for hiring men of German extraction. England could not easily replace soldiers lost in America. Artillery was especially effective against green, part-time soldiers, entrenchments, and fortifications. Cannon would help neutralize the American numerical advantage. Burgoyne's reasoning was similar to American reliance upon technological weaponry in overcoming comparable disadvantages during the Korean, Vietnamese, and Iraqi campaigns, and more cogent than some have conceded.

Provision for moving the heavier guns, gunboats, bateaux, and stores down Lake George proceeded while headquarters remained at Skenesborough House. The transfer from Lake Champlain to Lake George continued from July 14 until July 25. On Saturday, July 26, the descent of Lake George got underway, and about noon two days later, the supply flotilla arrived at Fort George.[36]

Burgoyne Receives More "Help" and Reaches the Hudson

At Skenesborough, meanwhile, Burgoyne's army received an augmentation that quickly became a liability. The western Indians raised by Charles de Langlade and Saint Luc de la Corne put in their appearance on July 20. The general had hoped for 500 "brave and tractable" warriors. Shadowy events in Canada frustrated that hope. Funds provided to Langlade to engage Indians disappeared. The Frenchman claimed that someone had stolen most of the money, which was true enough, but Captain Arent De Peypster, commandant at Mickilimackinic, suspected that it was Langlade—whose reputation for chicanery was well-earned—who had embezzled the missing cash. With what Langlade had left he recruited about 150 outcasts intent on murder and looting, with as little risk to themselves as possible. Burgoyne greeted them with the same fatuous oration he had delivered at the camp at Bouquet Ferry on June 21. Events subsequent to that exercise in moral suasion demonstrated two unpleasant facts: (1) The Indians' contributions to military success were almost nil, and (2) Burgoyne, even with Alexander Fraser's help, could not control them.

On the day the army departed Skenesborough, a raiding party provided grisly confirmation of the general's concerns. After a foray into Camden Valley in the vicinity of modern Salem in Washington County, New York, the warriors paused at the farm of loyalist John Allen, where they killed and scalped the entire family and ransacked the house. It was a gruesome prelude of trouble to come.[37]

By July 22, fatigue details completed reopening the road to Fort Edward. Fraser's Corps advanced to Fort Anne during the twenty-third. Burgoyne prepared to follow with the main column; invalids and prisoners were sent back to Ticonderoga. One hundred fifty convalescents and "men least able to march," together with fifty men each from among the Germans, British, and Provincials, remained at Skenesborough "for some days" under command of Major Paulus Aemilius Irving of the 47th Regiment. Rations for the rest of the month were issued. Still without their mounts, von Riedesel's dragoons formed the advanced guard, and a company of the rear regiment constituted the rearguard. The Provincials marched behind the British regiments, and the carts carrying the baggage followed immediately ahead of the rearguard. Provost Lieutenant Hetherington and his provost guard followed a "quarter of a mile in the Rear of the whole . . . to take up all stragglers." The British, Canadians,[38] Loyalists, and Indians moved the fourteen miles to Fort Anne and Fraser's Corps at Jones' Farm in the "Pitch Pine Plains" during July 25. Two days later, Burgoyne ordered the 21st Regiment to reinforce Fraser, leaving a subaltern and twenty men to function as the commanding officer's escort. While the main column marched southward, headquarters remained at Fort Anne until July 24, when it moved to the camp at the Pitch Pine Plains.[39]

Fraser's Corps reached the crossroads about two miles from Fort Edward, where it was joined by the main column minus the 21st Regiment left at Jones'

Farm to cover communications with Skenesborough. Before leaving the Plains, Burgoyne issued orders in anticipation of arriving at Fort Edward. The Advanced Corps would camp on the heights beyond the fort while the Loyalists, Canadians, and Indians would be in front, in line with Fraser's left flank. Headquarters, guarded by the German dragoons, would be near the fort in the "Red House." The British right wing took up a position on "rising ground on this side of the Plain." The left [German] wing remained at Fort Anne to aid in transporting provisions and stores until ordered to rejoin the British.[40]

The British, Provincials, and Indians occupied the vacant fort during July 30. Twenty-three days had elapsed since Burgoyne's men arrived at Skenesborough. Some American writers, failing to give Schuyler and his ax men their due, have contemptuously noted that the rate of Burgoyne's advance was only one mile a day. Negotiating those twenty-three miles under the conditions Schuyler imposed, however, was a creditable performance. "It was no small feat that Burgoyne should have reached Fort Edward on the 30th of July," observed Sir John Fortesque.

Arriving at the dilapidated and recently-abandoned colonial fort meant that Burgoyne's army had finally reached the Hudson River, which Carleton had failed to do in 1776. One stage, the passing of the lakes, was past. But the riparian approach to Albany lay ahead, and the British commander knew that still more daunting tests would attend the campaign's next phase. The impressive distances covered had lengthened and made more vulnerable his line of communications while compounding his logistical problems—all without yet seriously engaging his enemy. It was true that, except at Hubbardton, the enemy's performance had been unimpressive, but Burgoyne and his subordinates were professionals who realized that as long as the American Northern Department's military capability survived, British objectives remained unfulfilled.

Reaching Fort Edward and the Hudson was the campaign's turning point. Every advance after July's final week was to be illusory, exacting humiliating and unavailing sacrifices. The rest of this narrative is a history of the destruction of John Burgoyne's plan for "conducting the War from the Side of Canada."

The Infamous Murder of Jane McCrae

Even before the British army reached Fort Edward, an event occurred that has entered American folklore and proved to be a curious harbinger of the future. An Indian band arrived at Fraser's camp at the Pitch Pine Plains with captives and a scalp. One captive was a militiaman named Samuel Standish; another was Mrs. McNeil, a corpulent Scots widow whom Benson Lossing nearly three-quarters of a century later identified as Brigadier Fraser's cousin.[41] The scalp came from the head of Jane "Jenny" McCrae. Fortunately for history, Samuel Standish gave an eyewitness account—the only documented one—of what had happened to the two women.

Jane, a daughter of a Presbyterian domine, came north from New Jersey to live with a brother, Colonel John McCrae of the 13th Regiment of the Albany County Militia, whose home was about half way between Fort Edward and Schuyler's Saratoga estate. Like many Hudson Valley families, the McCraes were divided in their loyalties. Jane and perhaps two of her brothers were loyalists; her fiancé was a neighbor, David Jones, a lieutenant in Peters' Corps serving with Burgoyne. When Colonel McCrae's family sought refuge in Albany, Jane elected to await her lover at Mrs. MacCrae's house at Fort Edward. Sometime during July 27, the women left for Fraser's camp with a party of Indians.

Fifty-six years later, Samuel Standish filed a brief sworn account of Jane's murder when he submitted his claim for a Revolutionary War pension. He was a twenty-three-year-old militiaman living in West Stockbridge, Massachusetts, when he received his second summons for duty. On July 8, he marched with Captain Aaron Rowley's Company, Colonel John Brown's Regiment, to Fort Anne. He was on guard detail at Fort Edward on July 17 when Indians attacked the picket post, firing upon the guard. Standish was (according to this account) unwounded and ran down the hill toward the fort, but was captured before he could reach safety. He subsequently saw Jane McCrae and Mrs. McNeil, who Standish identified as Jane's aunt, with another group of Indians. The two parties quarreled, and one of the warriors shot and scalped the young woman. Standish said that he recognized the women because American soldiers had offered to escort Jane southward, but she had declined, saying that she was not afraid to stay.[42]

Samuel told a more detailed but unsworn story when Jared Sparks interviewed him in 1830. After recalling how he had been on picket duty about half a mile from Fort Edward and was attacked, wounded in the foot, and captured, he related that he and his captors

> arrived at the top of the hill at the place where he had stood centinell [sic], near a large pine tree & spring of water. Several Indians were gathered round the spring, and in a few minutes he saw Jenny McCrae and Mrs.

McNeil walking up the hill with a party of Indians. They came near the spring and stopped. In a short time violent language passed between the Indians and they got into a high quarrel, beating each other with their muskets. In the midst of the fray, one of the Chiefs in a rage shot Jenny McCrae in her breast, & she fell & expired immediately. Her hair was long & flowing, and the same chief took off the scalp, cutting so as to unbrace nearly the whole part of the head on which her hair grew. He then sprang up, tossed the scalp in the face of a young Indian standing by, brandished it in the air, and uttered a savage yell of exultation. When this was done the quarrel ceased, & the whole party moved off quickly, for the fort had already been alarmed. They went as soon as possible to Genl. Fraser's camp, which was then five miles distant on the road to Fort Anne.[43]

Although they are in substantial agreement, Standish's accounts differed in some details, which is not surprising given his age and the passage of more than fifty years since the events described. The statement given when he applied for his pension is the more credible—it was in his own words and sworn before a local magistrate; the account in the Sparks manuscript is in Sparks' words—and it is possible, even probable, that he embellished the old man's words for dramatic effect and to conform more closely to developing tradition. Standish's identifying Mrs. McNeil as Jane's aunt is interesting. There was more likelihood that they were kin than that the older woman was General Fraser's cousin, for which we have only Benson Lossing's second-hand identification, based, according to him, on the woman's granddaughter's statement. Lossing loved the dramatic too much to be skeptical about a good story.

Even before the old veteran swore to his spare, straightforward story, legend and romance were already at work creating myths that Hoffman Nickerson wove into a compelling narrative. He built upon Standish's account, consolidating several apocryphal strands to tell how a "beautiful girl of twenty-three, tall and noted for her long and lustrous hair, which would reach to the floor when she stood to let it down" received a letter from her Tory lover, went to Fort Edward to meet him, and died at the hands of Britain's savage allies.

After claiming that Standish was a descendant of Miles Standish of Plymouth Plantation fame and that he was the source of Nickerson's version, Nickerson told that after capturing the militiaman, the Indians "chanced upon the house of Mrs. McNeil, entered it, and dragged out the old woman and Jane McCrae." They hurried the women along a wagon track, tried to mount them on horseback, but could not lift the fat old woman. She and some of the Indians fell behind and out of sight of Jane and her captors. As the girl passed Standish, an Indian shot and scalped her.

The captain continued the story with a description of the scene at Fraser's camp:

> Meanwhile Mrs. McNeil, together with those of the Indians who had remained with her, also reached the camp. Although she had not been injured, the Indians had stripped her to her chemise, perhaps of every stitch she had on, and in this state they turned her over to her cousin, General Fraser. At this point a brief flash of humor lightens the tragedy for a moment, for the embarrassed general was not able to find in camp any women's clothes large enough for the fat old woman . . . , and out of his own wardrobe only his officer's greatcoat was ample enough to cover her nakedness. Meanwhile she was (somewhat excusably) scolding him with even more than her usual fluency for sending his rascally Indians after her.[44]

Nickerson interpreted the tragedy's significance, relating how Burgoyne failed to punish Jane's murderer, and the impact thereof upon the people of the region. No one, not even the affianced sweetheart of a Tory officer and sister of a Patriot colonel, was safe. An "enormous" reaction to the murder gradually manifested itself, as the men of the upper Hudson Valley rallied to the colors.

Nickerson's imaginary version synthesized generations of mythologizing that turned the young Tory maiden into an American heroine whose brutal murder brought outraged volunteers into Schuyler's desperate, demoralized army to inflict fitting punishment upon an unprincipled foe. Those vestals of the patriotic flame, the Daughters of the American Revolution, even named a local chapter for the martyr—the only loyalist so honored.

Writers with varying scholarly pretensions, including William L. Stone, F. J. Hudleston, C. H. Van Tyne, John Fiske, S. G. Fisher, George Otto Trevelyan, and Christopher Ward, repeated and burnished the tradition.[45] Predecessor mythmongers, not eyewitnesses and contemporary testimony, informed their successive narratives and interpretations.

Evidence, in fact, rebuts them. No news accounts that circulated among the area's scattered farms and small settlements publicized the McCrae murder. Local loyalists must had heard rumors of the killings of the Allen family and Jane, fellow loyalists, with dismay. Adherents of the rebellion, except those who knew the victims personally, were probably less horrified; given current passions, some may have believed that they received their just desserts for supporting an evil and oppressive cause. Because surviving contemporary documents are silent, we can deduce, not prove, those assumptions.

There are firmer grounds for doubting that Jane's death brought large numbers of volunteers to the American colors. Muster rolls do not record numerous enlistments. To the contrary, they report that desertions continued to be a serious problem. The militiamen who joined the Northern Department's troops did so not as individuals but as members of units called to duty by state and county executives. The men of the Hampshire Grants, whom folklore has seizing their flintlocks and rushing to battle when they learned of Jenny's cruel murder, were already with General John Stark and Colonel Seth Warner by July 24—three days before the killing. The number of militia regiments attached to Schuyler's main force did not increase in numbers between the end of July and August 19, when Gates succeeded Schuyler, and no militia from the upper Hudson and Hampshire Grants joined Gates prior to September 19, the date of the Battle of Saratoga's first major engagement.[46]

The genesis of Jane's apotheosis was a letter General Gates wrote to General Burgoyne on September 2. The British commander had protested treatment of German, British, and loyalist prisoners taken at Bennington, alleging that some had been killed after surrendering, and others dragged through nearby towns and abused by local civilians. Gates responded by accusing Burgoyne, "in whom the fine Gentleman is united with the Soldier and Scholar," of hiring savages to scalp white people and paying a bounty for each scalp. Among the innocent victims of that barbarity, continued Gates, was Jane McCrae, "a young lady lovely to the sight, of virtuous character and amicable disposition," who had been "scalped and mangled in a most shocking manner [by] a murderer employed by you."[47] When the contents of the letter became public, Gates—in a letter to Governor Jonathan Trumbull—bragged that he had exploited the incident for propaganda purposes.[48] The impact was less immediately dramatic than traditionally represented. Gates' letter was the first chapter of a romantic legend.

The atrocities perpetrated by Burgoyne's allies had a negligible impact upon American fortunes. They did, however, affect those of the British by demonstrating a fateful problem for a white commander who tried to use Indians as auxiliaries. Their effective employment to achieve military ends depended upon a degree of control that eluded most British leaders.

The news of the McCrae murder, which reached Burgoyne in the evening, shocked him deeply. A humane product of the Enlightenment, he subscribed to canons of civilized warfare that reprobated wanton murder. That the Indians' victims were adherents to the cause he served made the killings especially reprehensible and stupid, offending at once his personal honor code and compromising his moral authority. As he wrote to Brigadier Fraser, "I would rather put my commission in the fire than serve a day if I could suppose Government would blame me for not discountenancing by some strong acts such unheard [of] barbarities."[49]

During the morning of July 28, the army commander took himself to the Indian camp to assert his military and moral authority by demanding delivery of the murderers for execution. But in his relations with the Indians he dealt from a position of weakness. Lord Harrington was a captain of the 29th Regiment's grenadier company. During the parliamentary inquiry into the campaign, he described what followed:

> There were many gentlemen in the army (and I own I was of the number) who feared that he would put that threat into execution. Motives of policy, I believe alone, prevented him from it; and if he had not pardoned the man, which he did, I believe the total defection of the Indians would have ensued, And consequences, on their return to Canada, might have been dreadful, not to speak of the weight they would have thrown into the opposite scale, and gone over to the enemy, which I imagine would have been the case.[50]

The author of *Anburey's Travels* accurately summarized Burgoyne's dilemma. "The situation of the General, whose humanity was very much shocked at such an instance of barbarity," he explained, "was very distressing and critical, for however inclined he might be to punish the offender, still it was hazarding the revenge of the savages, whose friendship he had to court, rather than seek their enmity."[51]

The compromised commander surrendered to the apparent logic limned by the Earl of Harrington and whoever penned the *Travels* by pardoning the Indians. He had, about a month before reaching Fort Edward, required that "a British officer or proper conductor" accompany each Indian party. St. Luc de la Corne's followers ignored that policy as a restraint upon their conduct and made it a source of discontent, threatening their continued service. John Burgoyne learned what most commanders should have known already: that motives other than loyalty to a distant king informed Indian involvement in white men's wars. A Sir William Johnson or Daniel Claus could deal with native leaders of Joseph Brant's stature; but Burgoyne was not a Johnson, and St. Luc de la Corne was a duplicitous and vicious partisan, possessing none of Brant's statesmanship.

Pardoning Jane's murderer did not satisfy the Indians. As early as the morning after the "council" in their camp, they began to desert. The lure of easy pillage was fading, and they refused to acquiesce even to the British commander's ineffectual effort to control them.

The Beginning of the End

After reaching Fort Edward, Burgoyne's fortunes began to decline. American victories at Fort Stanwix (August 3) and Bennington (August 16) damaged Burgoyne more than he realized and broke the pattern of inevitable British success. Reaching Fort Edward stretched his supply line to its effective limit, a limit that an approaching autumn would render even more tenuous.

Fatefully, Burgoyne had failed to bring General Schuyler to battle. The Northern Department's main force continued to exist, growing stronger as reinforcements joined it. Schuyler, together with Benedict Arnold, Benjamin Lincoln, Horatio Gates, and the North's civilian governments had not only preserved it, but were making it into a vehicle for potential victory. On August 10, Schuyler began the slow withdrawal from Stillwater, to which his men had retreated, to Van Schaick's and Havers Islands at the confluence of the Hudson and Mohawk rivers. There, first under his command and then under General Gates, the Americans recovered strength, morale, and the strategic initiative.

At Fort Miller, Burgoyne again had to choose between two routes to his objective at Albany. One lay along the east side of the Hudson, and the other along the west side. Albany was on the west side, the river was wider and deeper there, and the road on that side offered closer access to the town. But the Northern Department's main army was also on the western side, in a position and strength not definitely known to the general.

Slightly strengthened by 300 men, Burgoyne chose the western road. His British regiments crossed to the village of Saratoga (modern-day Schuylerville) during the thirteenth, followed by the Germans. In three columns, they began their three-day march to near the mouth of the Krummach Kill, less than three miles north of the American fortified position on Bemis Heights—setting the stage for a decisive trial at arms.

The Bennington Raid

Genesis of the Raid

John Burgoyne took stock of his campaign's progress as he descended the upper Hudson. His men had stood up well thus far to the rigors of the difficult march. They were in good health, and their morale was also good in expectation of ultimate victory. True, some Germans suffered from their peculiarly virulent form of Heimveh, a type of homesickness that was often disabling and sometimes fatal. But most of them, led by officers who commanded their loyalty, conducted themselves creditably in the alien environment. True, the provincials were less numerous and effective than the general wished, but his native optimism promised improvement on that score—especially as the Empire's military presence came to be perceived as overwhelming and permanent.

The rebels' continued retreat was persuasive evidence that the effect of the Crown's presence was rapidly sinking in. Success had attended every engagement, and now American Philip Schuyler had crossed to the Hudson's western bank, leaving the water route from the Battenkill to Canada in British hands. Loyalists and wavering locals were renewing their allegiance in the presence of Colonel Philip Skene and British Chaplain Brudenell. Burgoyne was confident that he would be in Albany before the end of August, and that Brigadier Barry St. Leger would join him there—even if no troops from the lower Hudson did likewise.

Only a lone cloud marred the happy horizon, though it was one that, if not scattered by decisive action, could expand to threaten all prospects of success.

Transport and supply dependent upon the lengthening line of communications seemed a greater threat than Schuyler's retreating American soldiers who, except for Colonels Ebenezer Francis' and Seth Warner's men at Hubbardton, had manifested little martial spirit and competence. Burgoyne hoped that relief from reliance upon the Canadian depot was available if horses and cattle believed to be plentiful in the Hampshire Grants [Vermont] could be procured.

And the Grants might hold other attractions. Could their people be wooed from attachment to the rebel cause? While encamped at Castleton, Major General Friedrich von Riedesel, whose unemployed dragoons became more of a liability with every mile, proposed a horse-collecting raid eastward behind the Americans in the Arlington-Manchester area.[1] Burgoyne believed that detaching an adequate force so far north would take it too far from the march route to Albany, and so rejected the German's suggestion.[2] One month later, however, the worsening logistical situation persuaded him to reconsider the plan, and the generals drafted orders for a raid into the Grants.

The expedition would march from the Battenkill to Arlington, where loyalists under Captain Justin Sherwood would join it. From there, it would proceed by way of Manchester to Rockingham on the Connecticut River, "the most distant part of the expedition." From Rockingham the soldiers would descend the river to Brattleboro, "and from that place, by the quickest march . . . to return by the great road to Albany."[3] The raid had several goals: "to try the affections of the country, to disconcert the councils of the enemy, to mount Reidesel's [sic] dragoons, to complete Peters' corps, and to obtain large supplies of cattle, horses, and carriages."

The generals' instructions were less quixotic than they seem in retrospect. The hope Burgoyne harbored that the Grants' inhabitants nourished latent loyalist sentiments that would become overt with an imperial military presence was not unreasonable. He had found more sympathizers south of Ticonderoga than some later generations have wanted to remember. New Yorkers in general—and General Schuyler in particular—were cordially disliked by many settlers, some of whom expressed as much enthusiasm for fighting "Yorkers" as for killing redcoats. Colonel Skene and other local Tories exaggerated the loyalty of their neighbors to the east, but the presence of royal soldiers could be expected to test the country's sentiments. Enlarging the army's provincial contingent would result from arousing the people's affection for the old order.

Burgoyne continued to hope to "disconcert" American councils by making them believe that he posed a threat to New England. Some Americans did fear that Britain would strike at the rebellion's heart by bringing the war into the

Yankee interior. To delude his foe, the general instructed the raid's leader to "use all possible means to make the country believe that the troops under your command are an advanced corps of the army, and that it is intended to pass Connecticut on the road to Boston. You will insinuate that the main army from Albany is to be joined at Springfield [Massachusetts] by a corps from Rhode Island."[4]

While hoping for additional enlistments was reasonable, expecting the raid to garner some 1,000 horses and a significant number of livestock was not. Horses and livestock in these numbers were not available under the most favorable conditions, and conditions were very unfavorable. Farmers have always been notoriously unwilling to donate their animals to military purposes, even when they favor the army's cause. Frontier New Englanders were no exception. Unless the Grants' settlers' "affections" for the Crown were unusually sacrificial, they could be expected to make the conversion of their beasts into mounts, draught horses, and rations as difficult as possible.

Burgoyne also deluded himself into believing the expeditionary force could be self-sufficient by living off the country, and could accomplish its mission within about two weeks (by which time he expected to be in Albany). He did, however, include the proviso that "should the army not be able to reach Albany before your expedition be completed, I will find means to send you notice of it, and give your route another direction."[5]

From its inception, unreality marked the planning and execution of the Bennington raid. The officer best qualified by experience and the composition of his corps to conduct it was Brigadier Simon Fraser, yet he was not party to either phase. There is no evidence that he disapproved of the decision to undertake a diversion eastward, but Lieutenant Colonel Kingston's testimony during the parliamentary enquiry was explicit in stating that the brigadier did not approve its being conducted by Germans.[6] Although the adjutant general urged him to do so, Fraser declined to intrude into his superiors' deliberations. Burgoyne and von Riedesel foolishly ignored Fraser's expertise and the skills peculiar to his corps when they drafted instructions for the man who was to lead it.

Two fatal errors doomed the raid. The first was the composition of the column. The raiding party numbered 486 men from the following units: Brunswick [Braunschweig] dragoons, 150; Peters' Provincial Corps, 150; Captain Alexander Fraser's light infantry, fifty; Loyalists and Canadian Volunteers, fifty-six; German grenadiers, fifty; Hesse-Hanau gunners, thirty; and Indians, 100.[7] Fraser's light infantrymen and Sherwood's men from Peters' loyalists were English speakers, but only some of the latter were familiar with the region in which they were to operate. Two light field pieces accompanied the column.

The second error was selecting dragoon Lieutenant Colonel Friedrich Baum, a man as innocent as his troops of the mission's requirements, to command the column. Baum had seen action during the Seven Years' War in Europe, but he had little command experience. Philip Skene, "from whose supposed knowledge of the country and influence among its inhabitants much was expected," and the Loyalists bore the impossible task of relating the undertaking and its inexperienced command to the strategic realities they would face.

Why Burgoyne and von Riedesel dispatched a German dragoon officer and a predominantly German force into the American interior is difficult to understand. Military protocol helps provide a partial explanation. The German division made up the army's left or eastern wing, and operations in that sector would normally be entrusted to it. Gerald Howson, in his biography of Burgoyne, wrote that the Germans "were still resentful at remarks that had been passed about the Trenton affair and had tried to restore their national pride by claiming that only their action had saved Fraser from defeat at Hubbardton, a claim that had brought some sarcastic replies. Burgoyne probably felt . . . to send the Germans would do much to restore their morale."[8] The idea of the raid originated with von Riedesel, and it was his dragoons who required the mounts. Most important, Burgoyne could not spare his British and German flank companies, the indispensable core of his offensive capability. The dragoons, provincials, and Indians were less essential to success in a set battle and more expendable if the raid failed.

The Raid Begins—and Changes

Baum's dragoons, in their leather breeches, clumsy spurred jackboots, and large cocked hats, marched away from Fort Edward during an oppressively hot August 9. Their immediate destination was Fort Miller, eight miles down a rough and dusty road, where they were to join the men who were to accompany them from Fraser's advanced corps. According to von Riedesel's report to the Duke of Braunschweig, that contingent had moved southward to Stillwater. To make up for that deficiency, 100 Germans from Lieutenant Colonel Heinrich Breymann's Corps were drafted to join Baum. Some Canadians and Indians also joined, but fewer than originally intended.[9]

While the column halted at Fort Miller during the tenth, Burgoyne "changed the route originally intended for the detachment, and ordered Baum to march directly to Bennington, intelligence being received that the rebels had a considerable magazine there."[10] That change radically altered the expedition's objective. Seizing a garrisoned military depot replaced the intent to project a military presence that would produce men, horses, and cattle while confusing the Americans about British objectives. It was hoped that the original mission might be accomplished without encountering serious armed resistance; capturing the depot was more likely to involve force, if only against despised militia.

When Burgoyne wrote his account of the raid to Lord George Germain on August 20, the general reported that the Americans had done his foraging for him by assembling at Bennington cattle collected in the Hampshire Grants, as well as a "large deposit of corn and wheel[ed] carriages" guarded by militia whose numbers varied daily. He believed that "possession of the cattle and carriages would certainly have enabled the army to leave their distant magazines, and to have acted with energy and dispatch; success would also have answered many secondary purposes."[11] Burgoyne anticipated that taking the Bennington depot would meet logistical needs more quickly and with a greater degree of certainty than a fortnight's excursion through thinly-settled frontier settlements.[12]

Baum's assembled column left Fort Miller during August 11 and marched about four miles to the mouth of the Battenkill, where fifty Jägers from Major Ferdinand A. von Barner's Regiment joined it.[13] It advanced another fifteen miles over the crest of the watershed separating the Battenkill and the Hoosick to Cambridge during the twelfth, where its advance guard defeated a party of militia, captured eight prisoners, 1,000 bushels of wheat, and 150 bullocks, which Baum sent back to the main army.

The ease of this victory led to Baum's undoing. According to von Riedesel, Baum "was informed that there were from 15 to 1,800 of the enemy at Bennington, and that they had a very considerable magazine there, besides 2,000 bullocks and 300 horses. Encouraged by the success of his first attack," explained von Riedesel, "Lieutenant-Colonel Baum proposed to march the next day towards Bennington, and dislodge the enemy from that post."[14]

The decision to attack a reported 1,000-man post with a force about one-third that strong was suicidal. His success against forty or fifty militia at Cambridge could not justify the optimism the baron attributed to Baum. His ignorance surpassed his hubris, for important developments had effected dramatic changes in the local military situation.

Enter Stark and the Frontiersmen

The altered scene in the Hampshire Grants had its focus in that personification of Yankee cussedness wed to Scotch-Irish combativeness named John Stark. A product of the New England frontier, Stark was medium-sized, muscular, brave, and pithily articulate in a manner that invited quotation that was often apocryphal. He was also contentious, suspicious, opinionated, so fiercely individualistic that he refused to serve any cause on terms other than his own, and contemptuous of authority to the point of insubordination.

Few American commanders, including General Washington, had more raw firsthand combat experience than John Stark. His association with matters military began in 1755, when he participated in Sir William Johnson's operations against Baron Ludwig von Dieskau, followed by service as an officer in the legendary Robert Rogers' Rangers. After participating in Lord Jeffrey Amherst's capture of Crown Point and Ticonderoga in 1759, Stark returned to the Hampshire Grants and enthusiastically opposed New York efforts to annex what became Vermont. New England's resistance to British colonial policies appealed powerfully to the congenial rebel, and on April 23, 1775, he became commander of the 1st New Hampshire Line and led his regiment at Bunker Hill. From January 1 until November 8, 1776, Stark served as colonel of the 5th Continental Infantry and commanded that regiment in Canada during the summer of 1776. The 5th became the 1st Continental New Hampshire in November, with Stark commanding and participating in the dramatic miracle of Trenton and Princeton. Passed over for promotion to brigadier general, he resigned in disgust on March 23, 1777, and returned to the Grants.[15] He took home with him valuable combat experience that enhanced a native gift for leadership.

Stark also carried away other, less useful, baggage. As proud and obsessed with "honour" as Benedict Arnold, Stark despised the Continental Congress. Local loyalty weighed more heavily than identification with a nebulous concept like a nation, a trait shared by more than a few of his contemporaries. But Stark threatened to mortgage important talents and a powerful personality to destructive provincialism. He was gratuitously contemptuous of colleagues, only some of whom merited his low esteem, and he detested General Schuyler on personal, political, and professional grounds. Still, Stark possessed an attribute that made an important and immediate contribution to American victory and opened the way for him to reclaim a place in the fight for independence: more than anyone, including Ethan Allen, he personified the virtues and flaws of the frontiersmen who peopled the troubled country between the Connecticut and the Hudson.

And that country was undergoing a wrenching transition. While British soldiers invaded the Hudson Valley, political leaders in the Grants were forging an organization that on June 8, 1777, declared itself a new, independent commonwealth named, first, New Connecticut, and then Vermont, with a revolutionary constitution: the first in North America to prohibit slavery. Under the able administration of Governor Thomas Chittenden, his colleagues, and successors, the infant state maintained a uniquely independent existence until its admission to the Federal Union after New York relinquished claims to land west of the Connecticut River in 1790.[16]

Providing an effective defense against hostile military force was obviously beyond the resources of the embryonic state. Only its parent, New Hampshire, was prepared to meet that need, and its General Court did so on John Stark's demanding terms. On July 18, 1777, it commissioned him a brigadier general of militia, expressly making him accountable only to the General Court or to New Hampshire's Committee of Safety. During the next day it enhanced his independence by explicitly authorizing him to cooperate with the troops of other states or the Continental Army, or to act "separately as it shall appear expedient to you for the protection of the people or the annoyance of the enemy." That authority was a lodestar that Stark followed willingly—even willfully. The General Court commissioned a second brigadier, William Whipple, a signer of the Declaration of Independence.[17]

The extreme localism that informed New Hampshire's response to the British threat testified to the weakness of national claims to people's loyalties. It was also a prescription for military disaster that only a remarkable combination of factors avoided.

The first factor was the remarkable speed with which Stark's militia brigade mobilized. Partly this was because the terms upon which he and the General Court agreed stimulated volunteering. Field and company grade officers literally rounded up men of their townships. Taverns, shops, and churches became recruiting centers. The General Court commissioned Stark on Friday, July 18. By nightfall the following day 221 men had enlisted for two months of active duty, filling three of the authorized twenty-five companies. By Tuesday, July 24,

1,492 officers and men, almost ten percent of the qualified voters, had enrolled—an eloquent manifestation of local loyalties and the energy of the region's leaders.[18] By July 30, Stark's Brigade was ready to march, or at least tramp, its way to Charleston, New Hampshire, on the east bank of the Connecticut River.

As one historian observed, the men who joined Stark's colors were not a "mere mob."[19] They included many veterans of the Seven Years' War, and most were as good marksmen as the limitations of the accuracy of the smooth-bore musket would allow. Their lives on the rural frontier conditioned them for field duty. If they were short on discipline, they had physical courage in abundance. The men who answered New Hampshire's call to arms and Colonel Warner's veterans of Hubbardton provided the critical contribution to victory. Many were dangerously undisciplined, but their personal courage and resourcefulness carried the day in an action for which formal tactics were ill-suited.

A second factor, sometimes overlooked, was Major General Benjamin Lincoln, whom General Schuyler placed in charge of the New England militia. The Northern Department's commander intended that Lincoln bring those paragons of individualism to join his main army on the Hudson. That was a potentially explosive problem involving dealing with a stubborn, reckless man who would not scruple at insubordination and who enjoyed the enthusiastic support of the people he led. But Lincoln would have the wisdom and moral courage to treat Stark as an ally even when it became obvious that his fellow Yankee would subordinate himself to neither Lincoln nor Schuyler.

The third factor was Stark's skill in conducting the kind of battle that made the best use of the type of men who comprised his brigade, against the kind of force Baum and then Breymann led against them. With all his faults and professional limitations, Stark was a superb leader: bold, willing to take responsibility for his actions, and keenly attuned to and sharing the prejudices and strengths of the men he commanded.

A fourth and critical factor that helped decide the outcome of the Bennington Raid then underway was the qualitative and quantitative deficiencies of the forces Burgoyne committed to the raid. They represented too large a commitment for the probable benefits to be obtained, and yet at the same time were not equal to a successful foray into a little-understood region from which livestock and stores were to be seized and removed. The raid's commanders, Friedrich Baum and Heinrich Breymann, undertook operations in an environment and against an enemy under tactical conditions for which they had no preparation. They were dependent upon appallingly inaccurate intelligence, and led troops inexperienced in, and poorly equipped for, irregular warfare in a hilly wooded country traversed by execrable roads.

From Charleston, Stark sent his brigade to Manchester, where Colonel Warner's regiment, joined by Massachusetts and New Hampshire militia, were assembled under the command of General Lincoln. General Schuyler had intended that Lincoln remain in the Hampshire Grants to respond to any move the British might make against New England and to interdict foraging raids. But by the first week of August he finally realized that Albany, and not New England, was Burgoyne's objective. Lincoln was directed to leave Warner in Vermont and march the Massachusetts and New Hampshire militia to reinforce the main army on the Hudson. Complying with these orders, Lincoln directed Stark's Brigade to accompany him westward.[20]

Stark arrived on the scene and promptly refused to place himself and his men under any command other than his own. Stark and his soldiers owed obedience to no authority but New Hampshire's General Court, and he was determined not to rejoin the Continental Congress until that body made him a Continental general.[21] Lincoln tried to persuade him that he was arrogating to himself a responsibility that could have dangerous consequences. Stark hotly responded that he was accustomed to taking responsibility for his conduct. When Lincoln reported the brazen insubordination to the Congress, that body resolved to notify the General Court that its granting Stark command autonomy was destructive to military authority, and request that it direct its general to "comport himself to the same rules which other general officers of the militia are subject to, whenever they are called out at the expense of the United States."[22]

Lincoln knew that even a successful appeal to the Congress could not be timely enough to break the immediate impasse that Stark had created. Rather than standing upon his obviously valid prerogative as the senior general officer bearing a national commission, he decided to treat Stark as an ally and endorsed his intention to move against the vulnerable British communications line by trying to persuade Schuyler to approve the move. Given Stark's intransigence and the support he enjoyed from his men, that unstable accommodation was the best solution available. Happily for the Americans, it did not produce the disaster that under most conditions should have followed.

Lincoln immediately left for Stillwater to confer with the beleaguered departmental commander, whose days in that troubled post were rapidly drawing to a close. Warner and his regiment of Continentals, along with about 200 recently-enrolled rangers, remained at Manchester.

Stark Encounters the Enemy

On the day of his confrontation with Lincoln, Stark marched his men to Bennington, halfway between Manchester and Schuyler's headquarters. At Bennington was the depot for supplies on their way from the upper Connecticut River to Schuyler on the Hudson. Stark—supposedly—was to remain there, awaiting Lincoln's return with the results of his conference with his commander.

Like most actions taken by Stark, the move to Bennington had the potential for disaster—from which events delivered him. Remaining at Manchester offered a better base from which to threaten Burgoyne's communications, as Stark had proposed. In contrast, Bennington was too far southwest, and to have tried to encircle the British from there would have exposed Stark to attack by Burgoyne's left wing. On the other hand, being at Bennington enhanced the depot's security and halved the distance between Stillwater and Manchester, making contact with Lincoln easier.

John Stark was no patient man, and when word from Lincoln failed to arrive by August 13, he prepared to leave Bennington, apparently for Cambridge. His reason for deciding to move is obscure. He may have experienced an uncharacteristic pang of remorse and intended to join Schuyler. More probably, he decided to harass Burgoyne's rear without waiting for Schuyler's approval. Most probable, his restlessness led him to move without really knowing what he intended. Before he could get his inexperienced men on the march, however, Stark received intelligence that persuaded him to change his mind and earned him an enviable place in history: an enemy column was approaching Bennington.

Colonel William Gregg, whom Stark had dispatched with 200 men to deal with Indian raids, posted himself at a mill on the Owl Kill called variously Van Schaik's, St. Coick's, and Sancoick's. At 8:00 on the morning of August 14, the head of Lieutenant Colonel Baum's column appeared. Gregg's men fired a volley and retreated across the stream. Writing on a barrel head an hour later, a pleased Colonel Baum reported that the Americans "broke down the bridge, which retarded us above an hour; they left in the mill about 78 barrels of very fine flour, 1,000 bushels of wheat, 20 barrels of salt, and about 1,000 worth of pearl and pot ash." Thinking defensively, Baum ordered "thirty provincials and an officer to guard the provision and pass of the bridge."[23]

The Indians were, as usual, proving a serious threat to the British-German expedition's success, looting indiscriminately and destroying what they could not carry away. On a more encouraging note, a number of local people who professed loyalty "flocked in hourly, but wanted to be armed."

Five prisoners taken at the mill, perhaps supported by the professed loyalists, told Colonel Philip Skene's interrogators that between 1,000 and 1,800 militia guarded Bennington's stores, but that they intended to withdraw whenever their enemy appeared. Emboldened by that piece of misinformation, Baum continued his approach march until coming within sight of Stark's advancing column at St. Luke's Bridge over Little White Creek, about four miles west of Bennington.

When he learned that Baum had seized the mill, Stark sent a courier to Manchester with orders directing Colonel Warner to join him, and moved west to engage the largely German enemy. The two columns faced one another while Baum digested some new, disturbing information. As von Riedesel later reported to the Duke of Braunschweig, the Americans expected "a large reinforcement . . . and intended to attack as soon as the reinforcement joined them." When he received this information, Baum "very properly deferred his intention of pushing on to Bennington, and halted at his post, sending off an express to inform General Burgoyne of his situation, and desiring that Some troops may be ordered to sustain him."[24]

Stark reacted to his foe's presence by withdrawing more than two miles, while Baum occupied a steep hill 300 feet above the Walloomsac River. In those positions, the two forces settled down for the night. Rain made the fifteenth miserable for the men facing one another among the hills north of the river. Movement became especially difficult. Drenched soldiers carried out their officers' commands as best they could, preparing and eating sodden rations while endeavoring to keep their powder dry.

For Baum's men, the situation was made marginally less trying by the arrival of ninety local loyalists under the command of Francis Pfister (or Phister), a half-pay lieutenant formerly of the "Royal American" Regiment of Foot. This addition increased Baum's total strength to about 700, including Indians.[25] But Stark's strength also increased, to more than 2,000 with the arrival of 400 Vermont militia, a company from Berkshire County, Massachusetts, and a band of Stockbridge Indians.[26]

Baum was aware of Stark's numerical advantage, but he was also confident that his men possessed superior combat capability. Instead of retreating, he deployed his troops in a hastily-conceived, widely-dispersed defensive perimeter. Engineer Lieutenant Andrew Durnford, who survived the coming battle, drafted a map entitled "Position of the Detachment under Lieut. Col.

Baum at Walmscock near Bennington," the best source of information concerning Baum's deployment. The dragoons and half of Alexander Fraser's light infantrymen (rangers) occupied the steep hill above the river where the column had spent the night of the fourteenth. Taking advantage of the wooded site, they raised a redoubt and mounted within it a three-pound gun. The rest of the rangers positioned themselves across the Saratoga-Bennington Road about fifty feet from St. Luke's Bridge and 140 feet north of the rangers. German grenadiers threw up a small work in which the Hesse-Hanau gunners mounted a second three-pound piece. Other grenadiers, Jägers, and Provincials took positions left of the road from Saratoga. Canadians occupied four houses near the bridge, while Loyalists occupied a redoubted post across the Hoosick River about 840 feet southwest of the bridge. Another body of Jägers was in position on the slope of the hill overlooking the river. Durnford did not identify where the Indians were positioned. The lieutenant's plan includes errors that distort the physical setting, but no contemporary document refutes his data's fundamental accuracy.

Colonel Baum's situation was more dangerous than he and his superiors on the Hudson understood. He faced more than 2,000 men with fewer than 800 of his own. His force was too widely dispersed in an effort to defend positions whose extent exceeded his resources. In addition to the strong American force in the immediate vicinity, Seth Warner's troops were on their way from Manchester; any reinforcements for Baum would have to march a long and very muddy twenty-five miles.

As unpromising as his tactical situation was, the German colonel had no other real option available to him. He had to stand and fight. Retreating through the mud, at the mercy of a much larger, aggressive enemy capable of and more than willing to turn retreat into a death march, would be suicidal. Besides, thought of surrender to Stark's ill-disciplined mob probably never occurred to Baum: he was a professional soldier, whose best hope was to hold off the militia until reinforcements arrived, or somehow beat them in the field. After all, most of his men were Regulars, and his enemy was a motley pick-up gang of untried farmers and woodsmen.

Baum's men took up their positions almost under American eyes. Stark watched while the dragoons and rangers fortified the top of the hill, and took in the evidence of activity at the bridge and the Loyalists' redoubt. Individual scouts probably reported details that were not within range of the general's telescope and the personal observations of his staff. The clouds were parting, and the result was a tactical situation more clearly understood.

The American Gamble

The American response was astonishingly ambitious, yet fatefully successful. Colonel Warner arrived ahead of his regiment, and he and Stark decided to employ the most difficult tactic available to them: a double envelopment. Daunting enough with seasoned veterans, they dared to attempt it with men who, except for Warner's Green Mountain Boys, were as inexperienced as any who ever fought a major engagement. They intended to encircle Baum's position by simultaneously attacking his front, both flanks, and his rear. Improbably, their execution of that maneuver turned out to be flawless.

The rain that had drenched everyone for more than thirty hours ceased during the morning August 16, and the envelopment got underway about noon. Colonel Samuel Herrick led a 300-man composite force of Vermont rangers and local militia against the enemy's right flank. Colonel Moses Nichols took 200 New Hampshire militiamen on a long circuit to get around Baum's left. Two hundred additional New Hampshire men under Colonels David Hobart and Thomas Stickney moved against the Loyalists in their redoubt southwest of the bridge, while another 100 distracted Baum by demonstrating against the dragoons' redoubt. The plan was that when the sound of firing from Herrick's and Nichols' flanking parties reached him, Stark would launch the decisive frontal attack with his remaining 1,300 men.

Baum may have watched the flanking columns disappear into the woods, but if he did, he failed to understand their import.[27] In any event, the two columns remained undetected as they approached their objectives through heavy woods until they were almost in Baum's rear. What Baum did see were small, unorganized groups of men in their shirtsleeves carrying clubbed muskets, the universally recognized signal of peaceful intent, or wearing white cloths, which indicated they were Tories. In the naive faith that their foe subscribed to such rules of conduct, and believing that the majority of the local people were loyalists, the Europeans welcomed the newcomers as allies. Amazingly, Baum's pickets withdrew to allow the enemy to enter their lines unmolested.

Both Herrick and Nichols were in position by 3:00 p.m. The latter opened fire first, followed by Herrick. Once this firing was obvious to everyone, Hobart and Stickney attacked the Loyalists' redoubt, and Stark's main body rolled forward with its frontal assault.

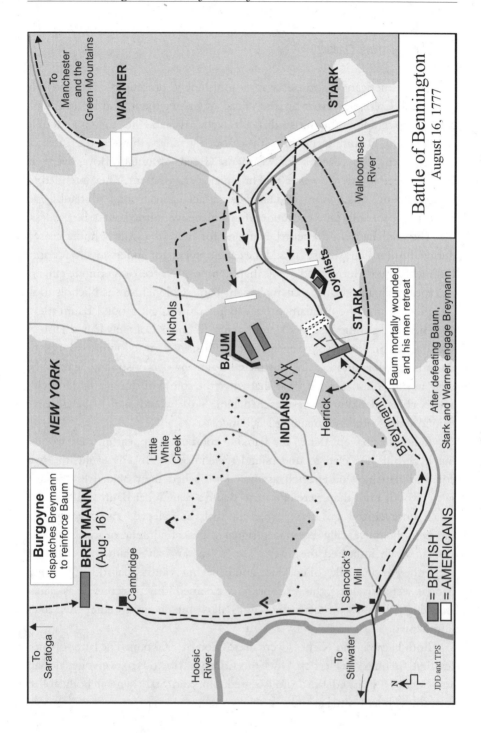

Battle of Bennington
August 16, 1777

To Manchester and the Green Mountains

WARNER

STARK

STARK

Wallooomsac River

NEW YORK

Nichols

BAUM

Loyalists

STARK

Baum mortally wounded and his men retreat

INDIANS

Herrick

Breymann

After defeating Baum, Stark and Warner engage Breymann

Little White Creek

Burgoyne
dispatches Breymann to reinforce Baum

BREYMANN
(Aug. 16)

Cambridge

To Saratoga

Hoosic River

Sancoick's Mill

To Stillwater

N

= BRITISH

= AMERICANS

JDD and TPS

The provincials abandoned their redoubt after firing one volley. The American attackers reached the fortification while its defenders were falling back and reloading. The Canadians in the houses at the bridge and the Indians fled without offering any resistance at all. As the chaos spread, the casual parties who had infiltrated Baum's ranks morphed into a fifth column that joined their countrymen and repaid their hosts' gullibility in murderous coin.

Some fugitives from the rear positions joined the dragoons and light infantry in their hilltop fortification, where doomed men sold their lives and freedom dearly. Militia from the flanking units attacked across the open ground behind the redoubt while the American main party under Stark's immediate command scrambled up the steeply wooded slope in Baum's front. They charged in no particular formation and fired individually at close range from the cover of rocks and trees—tactics the defenders were uniquely unprepared to resist.

For two hours, Baum's 200 Regulars, reinforced by the unknown number of fugitives from the rear, repulsed attackers who outnumbered them almost ten to one. When their powder wagon exploded in a spectacular eruption of flame and smoke, the will to continue the lopsided fight went up with it. Practically out of ammunition and exhausted, Fraser's rangers scattered. Baum and his dragoons made a desperate effort to break out. Drawing their heavy sabers, they began cutting their way through the knots of attackers. Having no bayonets, the militia crowded about the frantic Germans, too close to effectively use their muskets. Shocked by the sudden counterattack, the American militia fell back before the slashing sabers, but then gathered themselves and closed in again. When Colonel Baum fell with what would prove to be a fatal stomach wound, the survivors surrendered.[28]

Burgoyne Sends a Relief Column

General Burgoyne received Baum's request for support at his headquarters in the Duer house at Fort Miller during the night of August 14-15. Major General von Riedesel reported to his sovereign that the colonel's "[r]eport was written in such high spirits, that the General was induced to believe that he requested reinforcements more to enable him to attack the enemy than from any fear of his Corps being in danger of being attacked."[29]

Although a sense of urgency was missing, to Burgoyne's credit he responded to Baum promptly. James Hadden recorded in his journal that the general first considered sending Fraser's Advanced Corps, but decided that it was too large to be "risqued."[30] At 8:00 on the morning of the fifteenth, Sir Francis Clarke, aide-de-camp to the commander, ordered Lieutenant Colonel Heinrich Breymann to march with his Brunswick grenadier battalion and Major Ferdinand von Barner's Jäger battalion, together with a pair of guns, to reinforce Baum. Breymann's approximately 700 men set out one hour later. Because wagons were scarce, each soldier carried forty rounds in his pouch, and two boxes of ammunition were loaded onto the artillery carts.

The relief column got underway quickly enough, but it could not sustain its initial momentum. "[T]he troops being forced to wade the Battenkill," Breymann reported to von Riedesel, "were detained a considerable time—the number of hills, excessively bad roads, and continued rain, slowed our march so much, that we scarcely made half an English mile an hour." Each gun and ammunition wagon had to be "dragged up the hills one after another." One wagon overturned, explained Breymann, "and was put into condition to proceed with the greatest difficulty.[31]

When Breymann's guide lost his way, and a search for the correct route proved unsuccessful, Major von Barner located a more reliable man who led the column in the proper direction. Progress was so slow that nightfall found the muddy, tired men still seven miles west of Cambridge, where they slept on their arms without shelter. Before halting for the night, Breymann sent a note to Baum to alert him that help was on the way. The courier, Lieutenant Johann Caspar Hannemann, reached Lieutenant Colonel Baum about 11:00 that night. Baum acknowledged receipt of the message, and Breymann resumed his march at 6:00 on the morning of August 16.

The horses dragging the two cannon were so weak from hunger that the second day's advance threatened to be as slow as the first. Major von Barner's advance guard commandeered replacements, and the march resumed until the column covered about nine miles, or two miles beyond Cambridge. There it halted while officers closed up the ranks because men were straggling as they slogged through mud churned by horses, cannon carriages, ammunition carts, and marching men.

About 2:00 in the afternoon, a pair of Philip Skene's Loyalists brought in a request that Breymann post an officer and twenty men to secure Sancoick's mill against an expected attack. Breymann sent even more substantial assistance in the form of a sixty-man detachment of grenadiers and Jägers under Captain Gottlieb von Gliessenberg to occupy the mill. The main body of the column followed and, although an ammunition cart broke down, caught up with the advance guard at 4:30. Although Baum's men were at that moment fighting for their lives, Breymann claimed he did not hear any gunfire.

At the mill, meanwhile, Colonel Skene told the German commander that Baum was only two miles distant, and together they moved off to join him. Before they had gone far, fugitives from the fighting blocked their route. The panicked men offered confused and conflicting accounts of the battle. Neither Breymann nor Skene seem to have understood that Baum's command had been destroyed. As the former reported to von Riedesel, "I at that time did not know of his engagement being over; If Colonel Skene knew, I cannot believe that he had reasons for concealing it from me. If I had known, I certainly would not have engaged the enemy."[32]

Knowing Baum was in trouble, but acting under the belief he was still fighting, Skene and Breymann hurried forward with their men to support him. About 1,000 yards from the bridge, they encountered a "large number of armed men, some in jackets, others in shirts who were trying to possess a height that was on my left." Clinging to his illusions, Skene assured Breymann they were royalists, and rode toward the men to ask them to declare themselves. He "received no answer other than a discharge of fire."[33]

Like Baum, Breymann and Skene were the wrong men for the mission. They were also brave and dedicated soldiers who would persevere. Barner's Jägers charged up the slope against the party that had fired at Skene, while Breymann led the grenadiers and Captain Carl von Geyso's rifle company along the road. Unfortunately for British arms, the Breymann's "army of relief" was in poor condition for a fight. Its men had dragged themselves along an exhausting march for more than a day and half to meet, not comrades on the offensive, but aggressive enemies. Both forces had suffered from the heat and humidity that made every discomfort and danger harder to bear, but Stark's Americans were in much better condition, with soaring morale and a victory under their belts. Although they had just fought a brisk two-hour engagement and were scattered to chase retreating enemy and loot their abandoned camps, they were less heavily accoutered and had enjoyed at least a brief rest.

Firing down from higher wooded positions, the Americans inflicted disproportionate casualties upon the exposed Regulars, who struggled to deploy along the road while other Americans staged frontal attacks against them. Repeated attempts to overwhelm the Germans failed when Stark's men met the Regulars' steady and disciplined determination to stand their ground and close with their enemy.

Shortly before sunset, Seth Warner's 330 rangers and Green Mountain Men under Lieutenant Colonel Samuel Safford joined the battle. They had arrived about one mile short of Bennington about midnight after marching from Manchester through the same downpour that soaked every man who fought on the Walloomsac. Their approach was about as slow as Breymann's. They ate breakfast and dried their muskets, stopped at the depot, and drew ammunition. It was shortly past noon when they took the road west toward St. Luke's Bridge. About two miles along the road, the men heard fitful fire from the day's first action. Instead of quick-stepping to the firing line, they stopped at Stark's camp, where they drew a ration of rum and dropped their packs. They halted again after crossing the bridge to drink from the river, a stop that the oppressive heat made all but imperative.

Warner's men reached St. Luke's Bridge just as Baum's dragoons rushed down the hill from their redoubt into defeat, ending the Baum-Stark fight. The reinforcements halted here for the third time before continuing along the road almost another one-half mile. By that time Stark had assembled some of his scattered militia and, with Warner's assistance, engaged Breymann near the site of the modern hamlet of Walloomsac. Warner's soldiers deployed to the left into swampy land bordering the river. They soon realized their mistake and, after firing a few volleys, began an orderly move to higher wooded ground north of the road. The position was less than one mile southwest of the abandoned dragoons' redoubt.

Breymann took the initiative by committing his Jägers to an effort to turn the American right flank, and initially the German reinforcements gained ground. But half of Warner's corps countered, as they had at Hubbardton, by adopting their enemy's maneuver in reverse and turning the German left flank. The other half extended its own left in an effort to threaten the Jägers' right flank. With the front stabilized, Stark's men, who had been about to break again, rallied. The fight was equal, briefly, until the German light infantry had nearly exhausted their forty rounds and the gunners had not a shot remaining.

Breymann's desperate men were ignorant of Baum's fate, but it must have been obvious that the men whose attack they had been sent to support were not engaging the enemy. Their cannon were useless, their ammunition gone, and they were outgunned by a howling mass of Americans intent upon their destruction. Their options were limited: retreat or surrender. The latter choice offered little hope for survival. After trying to drag away the guns by hand and losing more men in the attempt, Breymann issued the order to withdraw shortly after sunset.

Their retreat began in good order, with the soldiers maintaining their formations and effectively using their dwindling supply of shot to keep their pursuers at bay. But the overwhelming weight of well-armed numbers drove them so mercilessly that the retreat threatened to degenerate into a rout. The drummers beat the parley, but the militia did not recognize the signal or ignored it. Some men, demoralized by the saturation of short-range fire, took to the woods, where their cumbersome gear made escape all but impossible. It seemed that Breymann's fate, like Baum's before him, was sealed.

That he and his men did not share that fate was due to their personal courage. Breymann suffered a superficial leg wound, but kept his Regulars (by now all but incapable of retaliating against their tormentors) from disintegration. When darkness fell, his men survived to continue their flight to rejoin the main army, twenty-five long and weary miles away on the Hudson River.

Stark prudently called a halt to his pursuit. Controlling his men was difficult enough in daylight, but it would be impossible in the darkness. In his August 22 report to General Gates, Stark reported, "We pursued them till dark but had the daylight lasted one hour longer, we should have taken the Body."[34]

Significantly, the Americans did nothing the next day or thereafter to convert their tactical success into a strategic coup. Lincoln led a force of 500 to 600 men from Schuyler's army to join Stark in the projected attack against Burgoyne's left-rear, a move that promised results that would have been more damaging than those accruing from Baum's destruction. The moment was an auspicious one, but Stark's militiamen were not capable of sustained action. Their general was ill, and he and his brigade "seem to have been more paralyzed by their easy victory than regular troops would have been by a check."[35] Those men who did not immediately return home contented themselves with enjoying their booty at the scene of triumph—an unheroic anticlimax to a remarkable feat of arms, one about to be compounded by their refusal to remain in service hours before the men of the Northern Department finally confronted Burgoyne himself on September 19.

Assessing the Outcome

Sources disagree in assessing the cost of the Bennington raid. What is not in dispute is that Burgoyne lost nearly 1,000 men compared to fewer than 200 for the Americans. The loss was compounded by the capture of field artillery, muskets, and other arms and supplies.[36]

The Northern Department and the Continental cause benefited in other ways from the Bennington raid's failure. The depot's stores saved by that failure remained available to Horatio Gates' army while it challenged the British advance. After the victory on the Walloomsac, mere mundane problems of administration and transport of those supplies replaced security concerns. The victory also signaled the disappearance of an organized enemy threat in the country between the Connecticut and Hudson valleys. Baum's destruction and Breymann's subsequent defeat cleaved away almost one-seventh of the strength of Burgoyne's army. Significantly, most of those lost were Regulars. The defeat of those European professionals by a force whose largest component was a newly-raised and untrained militia was a boon to American morale at a critical time in the revolution's history. The fact the victors significantly outnumbered the vanquished did not diminish the impact of the American success.

The region's sizable loyalist element and their potential allies among the uncommitted responded to the raid's failure in a manner that was predictable but difficult to quantify. Whatever they had hoped for from the foray into their country, nothing associated with the battle—except the personal courage displayed by men such as Philip Skene—redounded to their credit. The loyalists generally did not distinguish themselves in valor or sagacity, and optimistic predictions that the presence of royal troops would produce effective provincial support proved hollow. The raid's defeat discouraged overt, potential, and crypto-loyalists from committing themselves to a palpably weakened cause. Fond illusions of latent Toryism was among Bennington's casualties.

Arguably, Bennington was the American Revolution's luckiest victory, one produced by a fortuitous conspiracy of circumstances. As one student of the battle put it, the combat "can only be compared to the turning up of the double zero three or four times in roulette," to wit:[37]

- Burgoyne's detaching the wrong kind of force, led by men who compounded the general's error by bad tactical decisions, contributed to American luck;

- Stark's being at Bennington without the enemy's knowing it and in time to intercept Baum was the product of chance. He might have remained at Manchester or marched westward to harass Burgoyne's left wing, which is what he originally intended to do;

• The foul weather favored the Americans by delaying Breymann's march, then cooperated by clearing just in time for Stark to destroy Baum;

• Stark's and Warner's resort to a double envelopment, difficult enough with seasoned veterans, invited disaster when attempted by the kind of men available during the engagement's opening phase; it should have failed;

• Even the dilatoriness of Warner's corps operated to American advantage by delaying its arrival in time to provide a rallying force for Stark's men as they were breaking, and to apply the coup de grace to Breymann's attacking column.

It is fair to say that success at Bennington was the progeny of audacity wed to fickle fortune.

John Stark and his victorious militia received the lion's share of the credit for the victory, and on October 4 the Continental Congress rewarded Stark with the coveted prize of a brigadier general's commission.[38] The militia merited much of the praise they received, but alone they would have failed to repel Breymann: Stark's militia were breaking before the Germans when Seth Warner's tardy corps arrived to save the day.

However one analyzes the battle, John Stark and Seth Warner had combined to inflict a body blow against Regular troops with a victory that set the stage for Saratoga.

To Control the Mohawk:
The Battle of Oriskany and Siege of Fort Stanwix

Secondary, But Important

Indians, traders, and settlers all followed an ancient route that ran from the Atlantic to Lake Ontario. Nature made the site of modern Rome, New York, key to that route's use and control. The Mohawk rises northeast of that city and flows east until it unites with the Hudson River to reach the Atlantic. On Rome's northern flank is Wood Creek which, with the Fish Kill, the Oswego River, and Lake Oneida, provides a waterway in the other direction to Lake Ontario. Men following that riparian highway had only to traverse the nearly level portage between the Mohawk and Wood Creek to travel by water from the sea to Lake Ontario and Canada's interior. That short portage was the Great or Oneida Carrying Place, and its possession was essential to controlling access to the northwest frontier.

Indians and colonists knew from experience that the Mohawk was a gateway to a vast region. Maps and reports taught the same lesson to officials in London and Versailles.[1] There was another, more salient, reason why it was important: the country between the upper Hudson and Lake Erie was home to the Six Nations of the Iroquois Confederacy. They numbered no more than 10,000 to 12,000 and could field fewer than 2,000 warriors by the second half of the eighteenth century. Their Confederacy, however, was the strongest native force in North America and one with a hostility, hallowed by bloodshed and tradition, to France and her respective Indian allies. But for this Confederacy, the French and their Huron and Algonquian clients would have flanked British North America on the north and west. The Six Nations were also entrepreneurs of a fur trade that made the northwest frontier an important economic resource.[2]

At the close of the colonial period, much of northern and western New York continued to be frontier. Much of it was Iroquois country, but the Six Nations were weakened and their people, especially the Mohawks, Oneidas, and Onondagas, had closer and more dependent contacts with whites. The latter were a mix of English, German, and Highland Scot, with a minority of Dutch families. The valley's preeminent personality was Sir William Johnson, who from 1756 until his death in 1774 served as superintendent of Indian affairs for the tribes north of the Ohio River.

The half of New York bordering on Canada and the Iroquois lands, including the Mohawk Valley from two miles west of Schenectady, was separated from Albany County in 1772 to form Tryon County. Its people entered the Revolutionary era with families and communities divided. Some joined rebellious fellow-colonists, while others remained faithful to old ties or hoped to remain neutral. Others found the choice wrenching as they chose between competing claims to their allegiance. The English and Dutch, most of whom were native-born, probably included more dedicated "Patriots" than the other ethnic groups. Highlanders could be found in both camps. Those who were British army veterans, with little affection for the Hudson Valley gentry who provided most of the province's leadership, tended to remain loyal to the Empire. The Germans, without strong emotional ties to England, found choices less agonizing and many favored rebellion. Others remembered shabby treatment from the aristocratic families whose scions provided the rebellion's leadership, and preferred a royal government to a native oligarchy. Some tried, as they or their elders had during the last imperial war, to remain neutral in a quarrel they believed was not theirs.

The Revolution along the Mohawk was, as elsewhere in frontier communities, more a civil war than a social revolution. Sir William Johnson's extended family provided loyalist leadership. The heir to his title and some of his political influence was his son, Sir John, whose Palatinate mother gave the Johnsons a useful tie with local Germans, to whom Sir William had been a sympathetic patron. Guy Johnson was Sir William's nephew, son-in-law, and successor to the Indian superintendency. Daniel Claus was another son-in-law, and John Butler was a loyal lieutenant to the senior Johnson. Closely associated with those men was Joseph Brant [Thayendaga], Sir William's secretary and brother of Molly Brant, Sir William's Indian mistress and mother of six of his children.

Sir John tried to organize the valley's loyalists and Indians into a coherent provincial force, but the revolutionary party frustrated his efforts and placed him and some of his supporters on parole. Apprehensive of his influence, New York's revolutionary government decided to arrest Sir John. When he learned Colonel Elias Dayton with a party of men was about to seize him, Johnson fled to Canada, where he raised the King's Royal Regiment of New York.[3]

Sir John's flight did not dispel American worries about the Mohawk Valley. The region's economic potential, its political and military significance, and the importance of the Six Nations made its security absolutely essential. Few men knew more about New York's affairs than General Schuyler, and he had a long-standing personal interest in the region that included 8,000 acres of Cosby's Patent that he acquired in 1772. On June 8, 1776, that canny gentleman, as commissioner of Indian affairs and commander of the Northern Department, wrote a letter to the President of the Continental Congress recommending stationing soldiers at the Oneida Carrying Place and, significantly, that the Indians be informed that the Americans intended to maintain a military presence in the Mohawk country.[4]

Without waiting for congressional action, Schuyler wrote to General Washington on June 11 that he was "preparing everything I can with the utmost secrecy for taking post at Fort Stanwix, which I propose to do immediately after the conference with the Indians."[5] Congress acted on June 14 by passing a resolution directing Schuyler to hold his conference with the Indians and to build a fortification at Fort Stanwix. The resolution also directed Washington to support these efforts. The commander-in-chief complied accordingly.[6]

Schuyler and the commissioners did not succeed in persuading the Indians to enter into early negotiations, but the general did not allow that to delay preparations for occupying the Carrying Place. He ordered Colonel Elias Dayton of the 3rd New Jersey Regiment of the Continental Line to occupy Fort Stanwix with 500 men of his regiment, Colonel Cornelius Wynkoop's 4th New York Continental Regiment, and seventy-five Tryon County militiamen. Dayton's composite force reached the fort on July 23. Schuyler, meanwhile, had moved to German Flats to meet with Indians who, he reported to Washington, raised no objections to American occupation of the Mohawk portage.[7]

A "New" Fort and its Garrisons

Colonel Dayton found Stanwix's fort dismantled and ruined.[8] Instructions directed him to secure the Carrying Place, provide a base for patrols, and either rebuild the fort or erect a new one. General Schuyler left selecting the alternative to the colonel, noting, "As I never was at Fort Stanwix, I cannot positively recommend any particular place for erecting a Fortification, but from the best Information I have been able to procure, I am led to believe that Spot on which the Fort stood the most Eligible, of this you must be the Judge."[9]

To save time and have a structure ready to occupy before winter, Dayton elected to rebuild. His engineer was Nathaniel Hubbell, one of those quiet heroes of the Revolution about whom we know too little. Within less than a fortnight Dayton wrote to the general, praising his men's industry and predicting that the "Fort will be Tenable by 15 August."[10] Schuyler, in turn, wrote to Washington on August 1, "Fort Stanwix is repairing and is already so far advanced as to be defensible against light artillery."[11]

Dayton reported to the department commander on the same day that "The Fort here which at present is very defensible against almost any Number of Small Arms we had this day the pleasure to name Fort Schuyler."[12] By the beginning of September, General Schuyler, who had spent most of the latter part of the summer at German Flats talking to Indian delegations, believed the new fort could withstand any force the enemy was likely to use against it that year. Hubbell and the men under his supervision had accomplished their task in spite of disturbing rumors of enemy activity, continued demands on time and manpower to provide patrols, and the departure of the 4th New York's detail, which was ordered eastward on August 2.[13]

Like most of the Continental Army's men, Colonel Dayton's New Jersey troops' enlistments expired at the end of 1776. To replace them, Schuyler ordered Colonel Samuel Elmore's Connecticut State Regiment to move from German Flats to Fort Schuyler [Stanwix]. That unit occupied its new post on October 17, but because there were barracks for only 200 men, part of the regiment returned to German Flats to winter at nearby Burnet's Field.[14]

The Mohawk frontier was quiet during the winter of 1776-77, but there was little reason for complacency. Sir Guy Carleton's 1776 invasion had been an earnest of British intent to carry the war into the interior. Although he had withdrawn into Canada during November, evidence was persuasive that the campaign was merely deferred, to be resumed the next season. The politics of command of the Northern Department, sectional and personal rivalries and loyalties, and chronic shortages sapped energies and tested commitment to the Revolution. Washington's desperation-born aggressive action at Trenton and Princeton had preserved the army and boosted morale, but to many it seemed the odds still greatly favored the Empire—and that the next major campaign might well end the rebellion.

Fort Stanwix stood unfinished and, although defensible against small arms and light artillery, remained vulnerable to a determined attack supported by heavier field pieces.[15] Nathaniel Hubbell had made excellent progress repairing the fort during the summer of 1776 and had begun collecting materials during the autumn in anticipation of resuming construction the next spring. One of the Continental Congress' last acts of 1776 was a resolution on Saturday, December 28, directing that the winter be spent strengthening Fort Schuyler and building other fortifications on the Mohawk, and that all departments of the army were to contribute what was needed to support those efforts.[16]

Sometime early in 1777 a new and rather mysterious Frenchman replaced Hubbell. Bernard Moussac de la Marquisie was a volunteer assigned to the Northern Department whom Schuyler ordered to the Carrying Place to "repair this fort in the same form it was last war."[17] Declaring that the fort was too ruined to repair, Marquisie persuaded Schuyler to authorize construction of a new post—an incredibly foolish decision that, if carried out, would have destroyed American defensive capabilities in western New York. To begin with, the previous year's labors would have been wasted. Building a new fort would exceed available resources and could not be completed before the summer's end, whereas every informed person expected aggressive enemy action during the coming campaign season. As it was, a critical shortage of men for fatigue details plagued Colonel Gansevoort's 3rd New York, which replaced Elmore's command during April and May. Marquisie's decision was especially indefensible in light of Schuyler's conviction that Burgoyne's invasion would reverse Amherst's march, descending the Mohawk.

The Frenchman soon gave Gansevoort and his second-in-command, Marinus Willett, ample reason to wish themselves rid of his services. His plan to raze the existing fort in the face of time and manpower constraints was dangerously imprudent. His construction of buildings within the fort's field of fire and design of the covert way pickets impeached his professional qualifications. He also intruded himself into Indian affairs and bragged to General Gates that representatives of the Six Nations had insisted upon treating with him, and that it was his good offices that had secured their neutrality. (The historical record indicates no such thing.) In his hubris, Marquisie urged the general to order a Captain Florimont to Stanwix, where "the sight of another French officer will confirm to the savages what I have already told them—and also you may be assured he is an honest man."[18]

Notwithstanding the Frenchman's overweening confidence, Colonel Gansevoort reported on June 15 that "nothing of any importance is yet done towards strengthening the fortification . . ."[19] Marinus Willett wrote thirty years later that Marquisie's incompetence prompted Colonel Gansevoort to order Willett to arrest the engineer sometime in July, after it became known that the enemy was approaching.[20] Whatever the circumstances, on July 10 Schuyler ordered Gansevoort to "send Capt. Marquisie down & let Major Hubbel [sic] superintend the works."[21]

Contemporary sources do not record the work done under Hubbell's supervision between July 10 and August 3, the day British Lieutenant Colonel Barry St. Leger began his siege. The evidence is clear, however, that no new fort as proposed by the French captain replaced the older work. Twenty-three days were insufficient for razing the existing structures and building the fort that the British commander described as

> a respectable Fortress strongly garrisoned with 700 men and demanding a train of Artillery we were not masters of for its speedy subjection. Its form is a kind of Trapezium or four sided figure with four Bastions freized and picketted, without them is a good ditch with pickets nipping out a considerable way at the salient angles of the Bastions . . .[22]

That description still fit the pre-revolutionary fort precisely.

British Considerations

The primary purposes of the campaign that John Burgoyne proposed for 1777, as contained in his "Thoughts for Conducting the War from the Side of Canada" are detailed in an earlier chapter dealing with that subject. It is necessary, however, to revisit the general's treatise and relate it to the proposals for the Mohawk expedition.

"To avoid breaking in upon other matters," Burgoyne explained, "I omitted in these papers to state the idea of an expedition at the outset of the campaign, by the Lake Ontario and Oswego, to the Mohawk-River; which as a diversion to facilitate every proposed operation, would be highly desirable, provided the army should be reinforced to afford it." He went on to propose:

> that Sir John Johnson's corps, a hundred British from the second brigade, and [a] hundred more from the 8th regiment, with four pieces of the

lightest artillery, and a body of savages; Sir John Johnson to be with a detachment in person, and an able field-officer to command it. I should wish Lieutenant-Colonel St. Leger for that employment.

I particularize the second brigade, because the first is proposed to be diminished by the 31st Regiment, remaining in Canada, and the rest of the regiment, drafted for the expedition, being made also part of the Canada force, the two brigades will be exactly squared.[23]

Burgoyne's "thought" about the Mohawk expedition ambivalently proposed a diversion while questioning its efficacy. It is important, however, to remember that his "Thoughts" discussed alternatives. He did not argue persuasively for the western expedition's military utility. True, it would create a diversion, but would it be effective enough to justify the commitment of the scarce regular troops the operations required? In the event, his decision to provide for a diversion on the Mohawk was undertaken more to serve political ends than to secure military objectives.

Informed men at Whitehall understood that the Mohawk was the gateway to an extensive interior whose importance would eventually rival that of the Champlain-Hudson country. Pontiac's Conspiracy of 1763 was fresh in their memories, and prudence dictated that the western tribes become accustomed to giving precedence to imperial interests. More pressing was the need to nurture the loyalty of the Six Nations: two of them were refusing active support to their traditional allies, and one, the Oneidas, was actively assisting the rebels. Victorious British soldiers in the valley would guarantee the fidelity of the faithful and recall the wavering and alienated to a proper relationship.

This included as well the local loyalists, who figured significantly in the Government's decisions—not only the active ones such as the Johnsons and their associates, but also crypto-loyalists and passive sympathizers. The former had suffered self-exile for their principles, raised a force of "provincials," and persuaded authorities at home that the majority of the valley's people would rise for King and empire whenever a British army gave substance to royal governance.

St. Leger Assembles His Expedition

The marriage of military and political purposes induced the ministry to commit itself to the Ontario-Mohawk expedition, and Lieutenant Colonel St.

Leger of the 34th Regiment, scion of an old Anglo-Irish family, received the "local" rank of brigadier.[24]

His expeditionary force was to include 100 men from each of the two regiments stationed in Canada, the 8th and 34th; Sir John Johnson's Regiment (the Royal Greens); Walter Butler's ranger company; 342 Hanau Jägers, of whom only about eighty men actually joined the expedition; and forty artillerymen to serve two 6-pounders, two 3-pounders, and four 4.4-inch Coehorn mortars. Auxiliaries would include "a sufficient number of Canadians and Indians." The returns found during Colonel Willett's raid on St. Leger's camp on August 6 reveal that the British force of 1,400 included 800 white troops (200 British regulars, 300 Royal Greens, seventy rangers, eighty Germans, and 150 provincials) and 600 Indians.[25]

The white troops left from Lachine, across the river from Montreal. On June 23, St. Leger received intelligence that "there were 60 men in a picketed place" at the Carrying Place. That inaccurate report persuaded him to hurry through the wilderness and storm what he believed to be a weak frontier post incapable of defense against his artillery. Skeptical of the intelligence, Colonel Daniel Claus dispatched a reconnaissance force that returned to report a very different situation. In a letter to William Knox, Claus recorded St. Leger's fateful selection of which intelligence to believe and thus act upon:

> Between 60 & 70 Leagues from Montreal my reconnoitering party returned and met me with 5 prisoners (one a Lieut) and 4 scalps having defeated a working party of 16 rebels, as they were cutting Sodd [sic], towards repairing and finishing the old Fort which is a regular Square, and garrisoned by upwards of 600 Men, the Repairs far advanced, and the Rebels expecting us, and were well acquainted with our Strength and Rout[e]. I immediately forwarded the Prisoners to the Brigr [Brigadier] who was about 15 Leagues in our Rear. On his Arrival within a few Leagues of Buck Island he sent for me, and talking over the Intelligence the Rebel Prisrs. gave, he owned that if they intended to defend themselves in that Fort, our Artillery were not sufficient to take it, however he said he was determined to get the Truth of these Fellows. I told him that [?] examined them separately they agreed in their story; and here the Brigr. still had an opportunity & time of sending for a better train of artillery, and wait for the junction Chasseurs [Jägers] which must have secured us success as every one will allow, however he was still full of his alert, making little of the Pris[one]rs Intelligence.[26]

Although St. Leger refused to await the arrival of more Jägers or to send back for additional guns, he agreed to go to Oswego, which he had intended bypassing, to join the Indians assembled there.

This was evidence of trouble in that quarter. Daniel Claus had been the expedition's superintendent of Indians since July 8. The junction with the warriors occurred at Oswego on July 23. When Claus arrived he met with Joseph Brant, who informed him that 300 of his Indians would arrive that day, but that they were almost destitute of supplies, especially ammunition, because Colonel John Butler had supplied them so minimally that spring, and they had been on service for two months. The next day Claus received an order to join up with St. Leger at Salmon Creek. When Brant learned of Claus' intention to depart, he went to Claus' tent and remonstrated with him. Brant, recalled Claus, "told me that as no person was on the Spot to take care of the Number of Indians with him, he apprehended in case I should leave them they would become disgusted & disperse, which might prevent the rest of the 6 Nations to assemble, and be hurtful to the Expedition." Brant begged Claus to explain the situation to St. Leger. As Claus explained it, the Indians were not only short on supplies, but lacking nearly every attribute the campaign and the British required. "St. Leger mentioned in-deed my going was chiefly intended to quiet the Indns. with him who were very drunk & riotous, and Captn. Tice who was the Messenger informed me, that the Brigr. ordered the Indians a Quart of Rum apiece which made them all beastly drunk and in which Case it is not in the power of Man to quiet them."

Claus continued:

> Accordingly I mentioned to the Brigr. by Letter the Consequences that might affect his Majestys Indn Interest In case I was to leave so large a Number of Indns that [were] Come already, & still expected. Upon which Representation and finding the Indians disapproved of the Plan and w[ere] unwilling to proceed, the Brigr. came away from Salm[on] Creek, and arrived the next day at Oswego with the Compy of 8th & 34 Regt. and abt 250 Indians.

> Havng equpd [sic] Josephs party with what necessities and Ammunition I had, I appointed the rest of the 6 Nations to Assemble at the 3 Rivers a convenient place of Rendezvous & in the way to Fort Stanwix, and desired Col. Butler to follow me with the Indians he brought with him from Niagara and equip all at the 3 Rivers.[27]

This episode serves to further demonstrate that securing and retaining effective Indian support was both critical and difficult. Some of the Indians were reluctant to take an active part in serving imperial interests. They had retentive memories that included broken promises and exploitation. Sir William Johnson, the white man who had held title to their loyalty and affection, was dead, and none of his heirs inherited enough influence to assume his mantle. John Butler and Daniel Claus knew the Indians and enjoyed their trust, but mutual antagonism limited their usefulness. Joseph Brant, who could identify with both races, tried to obtain fair treatment for his people, while committing them to British interest. Sir John, who did not inherit his father's political skills, had the bad luck to operate in a climate very different from the one in which Sir William had functioned so effectively. St. Leger was unfit by training, experience, and temperament for leading these warriors. The Indian was always an uncertain factor in white men's campaigns—as Burgoyne and St. Leger were about to find out.

The Continentals Garrison, and the Militia Marches in Relief

While Continental troops garrisoned Fort Stanwix, defense of the Mohawk Valley settlers fell to the Tryon County militia under the command of Brigadier General Nicholas Herkimer [Herkheimer], leader of the pro-revolutionary German settlers. Herkimer had the task of preparing a divided people to defend themselves, and he struggled with hostile forces both external and internal. That many Germans, whose forebears had suffered exploitation at the hands of Hudson Valley grandees, were among the county's militia made the general's task more difficult. Criticisms of almost every decision he made aggravated his problems.

A case in point was his handling of a meeting in July at Unadilla with Joseph Brant. Details are obscure and susceptible to conflicting interpretations. Knowing too well the horror that would attend Indian participation during the fighting that was certain to come, Herkimer may have urged Brant to keep his people neutral. The Mohawk leader instead declared for the King and, without interference from the militia, who outnumbered the warriors 380 to 130, withdrew to Canajoharie Castle.

Herkimer's cool-headedness did not win him the plaudits of a grateful public, and his leadership was weakened with tragic consequences when he tried to succor Fort Stanwix early the next month. Yet with a perversity that taxed Philip Schuyler's much-taxed patience and understanding, the people of

Tryon County neither replaced nor fully trusted their county chairman and militia commander.

A few days before the Unadilla conference, while Burgoyne was at Crown Point, General Schuyler received explicit information about enemy plans. In a letter dated June 29, Schuyler wrote to the Tryon County commander that Sir John Johnson was on his way to Oswego and planned to attack Fort Stanwix. He ordered Herkimer to prepare his militia to support the fort's garrison "at a moment's notice."[28] Schuyler followed that order with a message to Colonel Gansevoort, informing him that "A report prevails that Sir John Johnson intends to attack your post. You will therefore put yourself in the best posture of defence . . . I have written General Herkimer to support you with the militia, in case you should be attacked. Give him therefore the most early intelligence if any enemy should approach you."[29]

Gansevoort was already aware of the danger. Oneidas had reported to him that they had encountered hostiles who intended to attack the fort.[30] The colonel and his garrison drove themselves almost to exhaustion to render their post as defensible as possible and to block Wood Creek. A severe shortage of men and the colonel's fear of a surprise attack during the work made the task as stressful as it was arduous. Schuyler acted to provide Gansevoort with additional manpower, ordering Herkimer to set 200 men to clearing the road between Forts Dayton and Stanwix so that reinforcements could reach the latter more quickly, and to detail an equal number to reinforce the garrison.[31]

There was irony in ordering the militia to provide 400 men at a time when Tryon County's committee of safety was pleading with the general to dispatch Continental troops to defend the Mohawk frontier. Schuyler had available in the Hudson Valley 5,193 Continentals and an artillery detachment to oppose Burgoyne's thus-far-successful army of 6,341 regulars and an uncertain number of Indians, Canadians, and provincials. "I am sorry, very sorry that you should be calling upon me for assistance of Continental troops when I have already spared you all I could [the 3rd New York]," the harried department commander responded on July 10 from his temporary headquarters at Fort Edward. "For God's sake do not forget that you are an overmatch for any force the enemy can bring against you, if you will act with spirit."[32]

The spirit that actually animated Tryon County's patriots at the time is revealed in a long letter from the harassed Nicholas Herkimer. In compliance with Schuyler's instructions, he had ordered 100 men to reinforce the fort's garrison. But the county chairman, Lieutenant Colonel William Seeber, and some committee members countermanded the order. Herkimer succeeded in getting that problem resolved, but because the militiamen feared for their families' safety they were reluctant to obey orders to muster. They expressed special fear of the Indians, openly declaring "that if the enemy shall come, they will not leave home, but stay with their families, and render themselves over to the enemy." Herkimer claimed that "whole numbers of men in each district are so far discouraged, that they think it worthless to fight, and will not obey orders for battle, if the county is not in time succored with at least 1,500 Continental troops." The loss of Ticonderoga "made the greatest number of our affected inhabitants downhearted, and maketh the disaffected bold. . . ."[33]

Schuyler responded to Herkimer's realistic pessimism by ordering Colonel James Wessons' 9th Massachusetts Continental Regiment into Tryon County to put some steel into the backbones of the "downhearted" and awe the "disaffected."[34] Reinforcements for the fort's garrison arrived from the 3rd New York Continental Regiment and the New York militia.[35] To enhance security and improve local morale, Schuyler placed all troops in the county under the command of a senior colonel of the 1st New York named Goose van Schaick, who was recovering from a wound received at Ticonderoga on July 6.[36]

Fort Stanwix's garrison was acutely conscious of the dangers it faced. While militia fatigue details protected by Continentals worked at obstructing Wood Creek, scouts reported the enemy column's approach. More immediately ominous were the hostile Indians found prowling the woods trying to ambush members of the garrison and local civilians. On Sunday July 27, three girls went raspberry picking about 500 yards from the fort. Indians fired on them, killing and scalping two and wounding the third. To prevent ambushes and consolidate his force, Gansevoort withdrew the fatigue parties.[37] On July 28, he sent downstream "those women who belonged to the Garrison which had children with whom went the Man that was Scalped the Girl that was Wounded Yesterday & Sick in the Hospital."[38]

At great risk to themselves, Oneidas and friendly Mohawks brought the colonel intelligence of St. Leger's progress and the activities of native war parties. The quality of that intelligence was difficult to assess.

Captain Thomas De Witt, who had remained at Fort Dayton, arrived during the thirteenth with about fifty men of Gansevoort's regiment, and Major Ezra Badlam brought in 150 of Colonel Wesson's 9th Massachusetts. The fort's commissary, a man named Hanson, brought word that seven bateaux loaded with ammunition and provisions were coming upstream. Within twenty-four hours Oneidas came into the fort with information that 100 "Strange Indians" were at the ruins of the old "Royal Block House" and approaching the fort.

Fearing that the hostiles intended to intercept the boats, Gansevoort detailed 100 men to reinforce the bateaux-guard.[39]

There was much that the fort's commander did not know, but he was certain of one thing: within a few hours the enemy would arrive. Colonel Willett's Orderly Book recorded the garrison's deployment, with pickets on night watch, alarm signals to spur the manning of the bastions, and assignments for each of the garrison's detachments.[40]

St. Leger Approaches; Surrender or Siege?

The Americans' blocking of Wood Creek had been so effective that St. Leger's column was advancing too slowly for his purposes. His fear was that additional men and supplies would reach the fort before he could invest it. In order to obtain intelligence and intercept any relief parties, he ordered an advance guard under Lieutenant Bird toward the fort. Most of the Indians would not cooperate with the lieutenant and refused to move. Bird conducted a personal reconnaissance, and his report to his commander closed with his quixotically volunteering to "invest" the fort.

St. Leger's reply represents an interesting reflection of the range of possibilities, both favorable and unfavorable, he envisioned. "[Y]our resolution of investing Fort Stanwix is perfectly right," he began, "and to enable you to do it with greater effect, I have detached Joseph [Brant] and his corps of Indians to reinforce you." St. Leger continued:

> You will observe that I will have nothing but an investiture made; and in case the enemy observing the discretion and judgment with which it is made, should offer to capitulate, you are to tell them that you are sure I am well disposed to listen to them: this is not to take any glory or honour out of a young soldier's hands, but by the presence of the troops to prevent the barbarity and carnage which will ever obtain where Indians make so superior a part of a detachment . . .[41]

Ridiculing the brigadier's optimism in imagining that the Americans might surrender to so limited a show of force is tempting. But St. Leger shared some of his contemporaries' common views: disdain for colonial arms and a justified fear of what Indians would, in the absence of a large number of regular troops, do to a surrendered garrison. While he certainly hoped that a mere show of force would persuade the defenders that they could honorably surrender, he probably did not expect that to happen; St. Leger's orders simply provided for that possibility.

The bateaux that Colonel Gansevoort expected approached the fort shortly after St. Leger's advance party arrived at Fort Newport's ruins. The contents of the four bateaux were successfully unloaded and conveyed into the stronghold. Nearly simultaneously, the main fort's sentinels detected the proximity of St. Leger's advance troops, and the garrison manned its posts. Just then, the bateauxmen who had stayed behind with their boats ran up to the fort, having been fired upon and chased back from the river by the enemy, with a loss of two wounded, one missing and one captured. That evening, thirty men sortied to set fire to two barns near the fort. They took the precaution of taking with them a field piece, with which they first fired grapeshot into the barns, "to of[f] the Enemys Indians that might have been Skulking about them."[42]

St. Leger's advance party had failed to intercept the supply boats, but the fort's "investiture" was now underway. He was unable to commit all of his men to the siege, however, because 110 of them worked for nine days clearing obstacles from Wood Creek, and another party was busy cutting a temporary road from Fish Creek over which to move artillery and supplies.[43]

There is a tradition that on August 3, the siege's opening day, St. Leger paraded his troops to overawe the garrison. Contemporary American and British reports are silent on the subject, although Ensign William Colbreath noted in his journal entry for August 3, "about three o'clock this afternoon the Enemy shewed [sic] themselves to the Garrison on all Sides Carry'd off some Hay from a Field near the Garrison."[44] His description falls far short of any theatrical show of force. Even if one did occur, it might have had the opposite of the desired effect: such a "review must have shown them [the American garrison] that in white men alone the numbers of St. Leger's force were at most equal, if anything inferior to their own," as Nickerson noted.[45] In any case, at 3:00 p.m. that afternoon, St. Leger sent Captain Tice under a flag to demand the fort's surrender, and to promise protection to the garrison—if the demand was met. Colbreath recorded that Gansevoort rejected both demand and promise "with disdain."[46]

Knowing that the enemy would attack whenever he could emplace his artillery and bring up the men working on the temporary road and clearing the passage on Wood Creek, the garrison continued to strengthen the defenses. Harassing fire from the Indians forced the fatigue parties to confine work to the night time. During the night of the fourth, details ventured out to bring in twenty-seven stacks of hay for the cattle impounded in the fort's ditch, and to

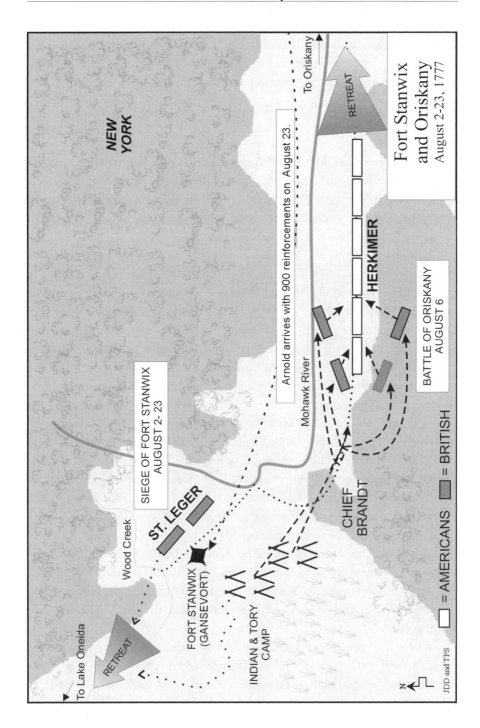

Fort Stanwix
and Oriskany
August 2-23, 1777

NEW
YORK

To Oriskany

RETREAT

Arnold arrives with 900 reinforcements on August 23.

Mohawk River

HERKIMER

BATTLE OF ORISKANY
AUGUST 6

SIEGE OF FORT STANWIX
AUGUST 2-23

ST. LEGER

Wood Creek

CHIEF
BRANDT

FORT STANWIX
(GANSEVORT)

INDIAN & TORY
CAMP

RETREAT

To Lake Oneida

N

□ = AMERICANS   ▨ = BRITISH

JDD and TPS

burn a house and barn obstructing the field of fire. The Indians' fire wounded six and killed two men during the fourth and sixth. Late on the afternoon of the fifth, the British burned the barracks that Marquisie had built outside.[47]

The Battle of Oriskany

During the same afternoon of August 3, St. Leger received word from Sir William Johnson's Indian mistress, Molly Brant, that a relief column was approaching the fort and would be within ten or twelve miles of his camp by that night. The British commander now faced the serious tactical problem of sustaining a siege while repelling a relief column.

The relief column was General Herkimer's response to learning of the British advance on the fort. On June 30, he ordered the Tryon County militia to muster at Fort Dayton. By August 4, between 800 and 900 men had assembled and begun marching to raise the siege. During the night of August 5, Herkimer dispatched scouts forward to inform Gansevoort of his advance and to ask him to cooperate if the enemy attacked the militia. He also asked him to fire three shots to affirm his willingness to make a sortie when Herkimer's column approached, then to engage the men besieging the fort to prevent their concentrating on the militia.

Herkimer reached a critical point in his approach march during the morning of August 6. No shots had been heard from the fort. Should he continue to advance or await the requested signal? He convened a council to discuss the question. Herkimer wanted to wait for the signal, but the overwhelming majority of his officers favored an immediate advance. The general maintained his position with traditional Teutonic stubbornness, and the discussion became heated. Some of the officers accused him of Tory sympathies, making much of one of his brothers being an officer in Sir John Johnson's regiment. Berated and maligned, the elderly farmer-soldier yielded and gave the order to march. With his Oneida scouts in the lead, Herkimer took the head of a double column of some 600 men, followed by a 200-man rearguard.

When he received Molly Brant's message, St. Leger dispatched approximately 400 Indians and the light infantry company of Johnson's regiment, under Sir John, Colonel Butler, and Joseph Brant, to ambush Herkimer's column.

With fatally poor march security, the Tryon County men tramped to a place about six miles from the fort where the road crossed a broad ravine about fifty feet deep with very steep banks. There, the Anglo-Indian party had laid an ambush, with the light infantrymen on the west and the Indians along the ravine's margin in a rough half-circle, leaving the eastern side open to Herkimer's men. When the middle of the column was deep in the ravine, the light infantrymen intended to check its head while the Indians closed their circle around the rearguard.

The column's main body had made its way into the ravine and up the western side when the Indians east of the ravine opened fire and rushed the road-bound militia, springing their trap too early to surround the rearguard, which promptly fled. The light infantry and the Indians on the west rushed forward. While rallying his men, General Herkimer was wounded in one of his legs, and his horse was killed. According to some accounts, he sat on his saddle, stripped from his dead horse, where he smoked his pipe and directed the defense of his embattled command.

With skill and steadfastness, the ambushers completed their circle while the Americans took cover behind trees, formed in small circles, and fought with a valor born of desperation, and often hand-to-hand. After perhaps three-quarters of an hour a cloudburst opened, soaking the muskets' priming; the fighting paused. During that lull, Herkimer's men took cover by twos, so that when one had fired and was reloading, the other would be ready to shoot any enemy who moved against them. The Tryon County men gave a good account of themselves that day. The Indians, who experienced heavy casualties, became more cautious as the minutes ticked past.

At this point in the action, a second British detachment under Major Watts arrived on the scene. Johnson ordered his men to turn their coats inside out to conceal their uniforms so they could advance under the guise of a sortie from the fort. When Herkimer's militia discovered the ruse they attacked, triggering a fierce hand-to-hand fight that ended when the Indians retreated, followed by their white allies. Too badly mauled to pursue, the militia collected their wounded, including their general, and marched back to Fort Dayton. Herikimer's severely injured leg was eventually amputated, and he succumbed to his wounds on August 16.

A Sortie Becomes a Raid

That same morning of August 6 was a time of uncertainty at Fort Stanwix. The garrison observed that the Indians, who had been maintaining a sniping fire, were leaving the immediate area for the lower landing on the Mohawk. The officers and men feared that something was afoot in the valley, and that the loyalty of its inhabitants would weaken if the fort were reported taken. "This Morning the Indians were seen going off from around the Garrison towards the Landing as they withdrew we had not much firing," a concerned Colbreath recorded in his journal. "Being uneasy least [sic] the Tories should Report that the Enemy had taken the Fort [.] Lieut. Diefendorf was Ordered to get Ready to set of[f] for Albany the Evening to Inf[orm] Genl Schuyler of our Situation."[48]

Before the lieutenant could leave, the men Herkimer had sent with his message announcing his approach arrived at Stanwix. As Colbreath recorded, now "the Communication which has been Entirely Blocked up" was opened; now the garrison learned of the imminent arrival of 1,000 militiamen to relieve them; now they learned of the three-gun signal which Herkimer awaited. The latter was immediately fired off, "followed by three cheers by the whole Garrison." Further responding to Herkimer's requests, Colonel Gansevoort dispatched 200 to 250 men with a field piece under Lieutenant Colonel Willett to rendezvous with the militia.[49]

Willett set out down the old military road that ran between Albany and Oswego. When his column was about half a mile from the fort it came upon Sir John Johnson's unoccupied camp and instantly changed its mission. Forgotten was the sortie's purpose to support the embattled Herkimer. The troops instead raided the abandoned camp, a nearby Indian one, and perhaps Lieutenant Bird's at "Lower Landing Place," about one-half mile distant. "Nothing could be more fortunate than this enterprise," Willet reported with less than self-effacing satisfaction. He continued:

> We totally destroyed routed two of the enemy's encampments, destroyed all their provision that was with them, brought off upwards of fifty brass kettles, and more than a hundred blankets (two articles which were much needed by us) with a number of muskets, toma-hawks, spears, ammunition, cloathing, deer skins, a variety of Indian affairs, and five colours, which on our return to the fort, were displayed on our flagstaff, under the Continental flag.[50]

Willett's men skirmished with some fleeing Indians before turning about to return to the fort. A detachment of British regulars tried to intercept them, but "The ambush was not quite formed when we discovered them, and gave them a well directed fire.—Here especially, Major Badlam, with his field piece, did considerable execution," reported Willett. "[H]ere, also, the enemy were annoyed by the fire of several cannon from the fort, as they marched round to form the ambuscade. The enemy's fire was very wild, and though we were very much exposed, did no execution at all."[51]

The loot taken from the camps, as Willett later revealed, included "several bundles of papers and a parcel of letters belonging to our garrison, which they had taken from our [Herkimer's] militia, but not yet opened . . . . There were likewise papers belonging to Sir John Johnson, and several others of the enemy's officers, with letters to and from Gen. St. Leger, their commander; their papers have been of some service to us." Willett's men also captured prisoners who were carried into the fort and interrogated. They reported the disturbing news of the fight at Oriskany, the size of St. Leger's force, and the number and types of his artillery.[52]

The raid on the Indian camp did have some unintended though important results. The loss of clothes, blankets, and provisions, coupled with the loss of several of their chiefs at Oriskany, dampened the native warriors' enthusiasm for what threatened to be a long and unrewarding siege—a species of operation for which they rarely had an affinity. In fact, the British situation was not nearly good enough to give much promise of success, unless St. Leger could persuade the fort's garrison that defending its post was doomed to failure.

St. Leger put the best possible face on recent events when he reported the series of events to Burgoyne. Herkimer's militia "fell into it [ambuscade]. The completest victory was obtained," the brigadier continued, stretching the truth for his superior. "Above 400 lay dead on the field, amongst whom were almost all the principal Movers of Rebellion in that Country." The fighting, he boasted, crushed enemy morale—"The Militia will never rally" and nothing stood in the way that will "retard my progress in joining you [except] the reinforcement of what they call their regular troops by way of Halfmoon up the Mohawk River. A diversion therefore from your army by that quarter will greatly expedite my junction with either of the grand armies."[53]

At this time, however, Burgoyne was many miles north of Halfmoon and in no position to send St. Leger's Mohawk expedition any form of assistance.

Again: Surrender or Siege?

Fort Stanwix's garrison enjoyed a respite from enemy fire during most of August 7, although "at 11 o Clock [sic] this Evening," wrote the journalist Colbreath, "the Enemy came near the Fort called to our Centinels, telling them to come out again with Fixed Bayonets and they should give us Satisfaction for

Yesterdays work, after which they fired 4 small Cannon at the Fort we laughed at them heartily and they returned to Rest."[54] The fort's defenders now knew that the enemy had finally brought up their artillery, and during the eighth, the besiegers fired more shots, which the garrison "in order to Return the compliment, they [the enemy] were Salutted [sic] with a few Balls from our Cannon."[55]

About 5:00 p.m. on August 8, St. Leger's adjutant, Major Ancrum, accompanied by Colonel Butler and a surgeon, approached the fort under a flag. In essence, the parley consisted of the British urging the Americans to surrender, and the Americans refusing to do so. During the first day of the cease-fire that followed the parley, St. Leger again sent a flag to the fort with a written statement of the oral demands made the previous day. These exchanges included the British issuing dire warnings of what their Indian allies would do to the American soldiers and their families if the garrison was defeated. As far as the defending Americans were concerned, any blood shed in that manner would be on British hands. When St. Leger played on the Americans' responsibility for avoiding a bloodbath, the Americans retorted that the responsibility lay with the British, who as officers, gentlemen, and the supposed representatives of civilization, had a duty to not allow the slaughter of their innocents.[56] Neither side yielded its position.

The post-parley armistice was to have lasted three days, but the British began a bombardment that night at 10:30, a "well directed fire" that continued all night. Gansevoort had the fort's papers and money stored in the southwest bastion's bomb-proof. An exchange of artillery continued at intervals during the next week, with very little effect on the garrison and none on the fort's fabric.[57]

And then, recorded Ensign Colbreath, "The Enemy threw some Shells Horrisontally [sic] at out Works."[58] The explanation behind Colbreath's journal entry is found in St. Leger's report to Burgoyne. "It was found that our cannon has not the least effect upon the sod-work of the fort," observed the brigadier, "and that our royals [mortars] had the power of teasing, as a six-inch plank was a sufficient security for their powder-magazine, as we learnt from deserters." Lieutenant Glenie, one of St. Leger's artillerymen appointed to act as an assistant engineer, devised a rather ingenious method for reducing Fort Stanwix. Glenie, explained St. Leger, "proposed a conversion of the royals (if I may use the expression) into howitzers. The ingenuity and feasibility of this nuance striking me very forcibly, the business was set about immediately, and soon executed." When field trials revealed that "nothing prevented their operating with the desired effect but the distance, their chambers being too small to hold a sufficiency of powder," a decision was made to "approach the fort by a sap to such a distance that the ramparts might be brought within their portice, at the same time all materials were preparing to run a mine under the most formidable bastion." St. Leger, it seemed, had found a way to solve the vexing problem of Fort Stanwix.[59]

A map drawn by Colonel Francois de Fleury, a French engineer fighting for the Americans, depicts a portion of St. Leger's deployment of positions for the siege. The absence of a scale limits its usefulness in determining distances, but an estimate (based on the size of the square formed by the fort's bastions, 335 to the side, except for the eastern face) of the distance between the original battery positions and the fort was approximately 350 yards. The sap or approach trench was directed toward the northwest bastion.[60]

While the besiegers worked at the sap, the garrison and its enemies maintained an exchange of fire. The fort suffered little or no damage, although a few casualties occurred among the defenders. On August 21, a woman in the fort who was "big with Child" was wounded in the thigh by artillery fire. The next day she gave birth to a daughter in the southwest bastion's bombproof. According to Colbreath, mother and child "do well with the Blessing of God."[61] The enemy also diverted the stream that supplied the fort with its main source of water, forcing the garrison to dig wells inside the fort. Sorties went out for a variety of purposes, and both sides lost men through desertion.

The Threat to the Mohawk Valley: Schuyler Responds with Arnold

The British did not ignore the region Fort Stanwix defended while the stronghold itself was under siege. After the battle of Oriskany, Sir John Johnson proposed to take 200 men and "a sufficient body of Indians" down the valley to bring the people back to the royal cause. St. Leger, however, "said he could not spare the men, and disapproved of it."[62] A few days later Walter Butler took two regulars and three Indians to German Flats in an effort to enlist the inhabitants' assistance in persuading the fort's garrison to surrender. Butler carried with him a proclamation signed by Sir John, Daniel Claus, and John Butler that combined a clumsy combination of cajolery and threats. "Surrounded as you are by victorious armies, one half (if not the greater part) of the inhabitants friends of the government," concluded the proclamation, "without any resource, surely you cannot hesitate a moment to accept the terms proposed to you, by friends and well-wishers to the country."[63] Fort Dayton's garrison captured the little party, aborting the venture into psychological warfare.

While Gansevoort and St. Leger contended for control of the Mohawk country, events were underway elsewhere that would prove decisive in frustrating British designs. General Schuyler was retreating southward along the Hudson before Burgoyne's hitherto victorious advance, struggling to retard that advance and prepare his main army for a stand that would repel the British invasion. Shortages, personality clashes, political rivalries, and a succession of disheartening reverses conspired to bring his task to the brink of failure. Still, the general did not neglect his responsibilities in the western sector of his command. During July, Schuyler devoted hours trying to obtain additional Continental troops for Tryon County, and sought the state's help in finding militia units to send up the Mohawk, as evidenced by his previously-noted letters to the county's committees and General Herkimer in which he tried to encourage and advise them.

On August 6, Schuyler's assistance took a more concrete form when he ordered Brigadier General Ebenezer Learned's Brigade of Massachusetts Continentals to march from Van Schaick's Islands to Fort Stanwix's relief. He also wrote to Tryon County's committee requesting its militia's cooperation.[64]

The main body of Schuyler's army lay at the village of Stillwater, and from that place Major General Benedict Arnold departed on August 13 to command operations on the Mohawk.[65] The department commander ordered Arnold to "repair thither [to Tryon County] with all convenient speed and take upon you the command of all the continental troops & such of the Militia as you can prevail upon to join your troops. Fort Schuyler is being besieged you will hasten to its relief and hope that the Continental troops now in the county of Tryon, if joined by some of the militia will be adequate to the business."[66] Arnold set out immediately for Albany, where he met Colonel Willett, and together they hurried to Fort Dayton, which they reached on August 20.

The next day, Arnold convened a council consisting of Brigadier General Learned; Colonels Willett, John Bailey (2nd Massachusetts), Cornelius Van Dyke (1st New York), Henry Beeckman Livingston (4th New York), and James Wesson (9th Massachusetts); and Lieutenant Colonel John Brook (8th Massachusetts). The members discussed the possibility of enlisting Indians, and the information brought to Fort Dayton by Oneidas reporting that St. Leger's force included "upwards of 1,000 Indians . . . and other forces are near 700, besides some Tories. . . ." Arnold noted that the members of their own column "are 933, and 13 artillerymen, exclusive of a few militia, the whole not exceeding 100 on whom little dependence can be placed."

What options were open to Arnold's small command? To answer that question, he put the matter before the council, asking its members "whether it is prudent to march with the present force and endeavour to raise the siege of Fort Schuyler, or to remain at this place, until reinforcements can be solicited from below, and more of the militia turned out to join us, and until the Oneidas had determined if they would join us, of which they give encouragement." The council's conclusion was as follows:

> Resolved, That in the Opinion of this Council, our force is not equal to that of the enemy, and it would be imprudent and putting too much to the hazard to attempt the march to the relief of Fort Schuyler, until the army is reinforced: the council are of the opinion that an express ought immediately to be sent to General Gates, requesting he will immediately send such reinforcements to us as will enable us to march to the relief of the fort, with a probability of succeeding and that in the meantime the army remain at the German Flatts, at least until an answer can be had from General Gates, and that all possible method be taken to persuade the militia and Indians to join us.[67]

As this episode makes clear, Benedict Arnold—who had a well-earned reputation for audacity equaled by few, if any, of his contemporaries—approached the relief of Fort Stanwix with uncharacteristic caution. While it was true that St. Leger's force outnumbered Arnold's column, the total American strength, including the fort's garrison, was more than equal to that of the enemy. At most, St. Leger's white troops numbered 700 to 800 men, of whom 300 were Canadian militia, not the most reliable of units. The Indians, who may have numbered 800 at that time, were of limited usefulness in a pitched battle, and even their total had been reduced by losses suffered at Oriskany. Between Arnold and Gansevoort the Americans had a maximum of 1,746 men, of whom all but about 100 were Continentals.[68] St. Leger could not have both maintained the siege and repelled Arnold's relief column. If he abandoned the siege, the Stanwix garrison would be free to cooperate with Arnold to attack him. Perhaps the responsibility of an independent field command sobered the flamboyant general who, when he did not hold ultimate responsibility for the conduct of a campaign, so often made his superiors appear pedestrian.

If Arnold was not prepared to march on, he was at least prepared to sound aggressive. A proclamation he issued over his name denounced the enemy's barbarity, claiming that "Humanity to those deluded wretches, who are hastening blindfold to destruction, induces me to offer them, and all others concerned whether savages, Germans, Americans or Britons PARDON, provided they do, within ten days from the date hereof, come in lay down their arms, sue for protection, and swear allegiance to the United States of America." To the obdurate, he addressed these words: "But if blind to their own interest and safety, they obstinately persist in their wicked courses, determined to draw to themselves the first vengeance of Heaven, and of this exasperated country, they must expect no mercy from either."[69]

Willett once again returned eastward to deliver the council's resolution to General Gates and to request a reinforcement of 1,000 light infantrymen. Arnold was playing games. He knew Gates did not have 1,000 light infantry to send to him. In fact, Gates' only light troops were Dan Morgan's riflemen, who numbered fewer than 500 effectives, and Gates had not yet brigaded them with drafted infantry into a composite corps of riflemen and light infantry. Arnold was positioning himself, in case his mission failed, to plead inadequate support from headquarters—a ploy not unique in military history.

Without waiting for reinforcements, Arnold resorted to his own application of psychological warfare that has few parallels in American history and folklore. The local patriots had uncovered a particularly inept Loyalist plot in the vicinity of German Flats. Among the prisoners taken was one of the least impressive members of the numerous Schuyler clan, a mentally deficient eccentric named Hon Yost Schuyler. Hon Yost had lived among the Indians, who apparently believed that his affliction gave him a peculiar relationship with the supernatural. The local whites held him in neither awe nor affection, and they condemned him to death for his part in the plot. His brother Nicholas and their mother came to Arnold's camp to plead for the unfortunate man's life.

Retaining Nicholas as a hostage for his brother's performance, Arnold promised to spare Hon Yost if he would enter the enemy's camp and play upon the Indians' emotions by exaggerating the size of Arnold's force. Delighted with the opportunity, the half-wit enthusiastically entered into the spirit of the charade with a cunning that belied his intellectual limitations. To give credibility to his story that he had escaped from captivity, he had bullets shot through his clothes. A conspiratorially-inclined Oneida agreed to follow Hon Yost, at a credible interval, to confirm his story.

Because they had heard disturbing news that a large relief force was on its way, the Indians were susceptible to the young man's deception. When they asked him how many men were in that force, he looked up and pointed to the leaves on the trees—the implication obviously clear. The dramatic episode left a profound impression upon those who watched it. Taken before St. Leger, he enlarged upon his story and predicted that Arnold with 2,000 men would be upon the besieging force's rear within twenty-four hours.

At that propitious moment the cooperative Oneida appeared with some Indians he had met in the woods. Arnold, explained the helpful Indian, had no quarrel with St. Leger's Indian allies, and intended to attack only the British and the Tories. One enthusiast added that a talking bird had warned him that great numbers of hostile warriors were on their way to destroy the fort's assailants. The Indians, already disheartened by the bloody Oriskany fight and becoming impatient with the paucity of loot, prisoners, and scalps, found irresistible the reason for going home.[70]

St. Leger, Sir John, and the Indian superintendents, Butler and Claus, tried to persuade their allies not to overreact to the wild tales of Arnold's advance. The commander convened a council at which he learned that 200 warriors had already deserted. The chiefs announced that if he did not retreat, they would abandon him.[71]

We cannot know how much Hon Yost's story influenced the Indians. We do know that the campaign had been unprofitable and that they had no stomach for a prolonged siege and another pitched battle. For them, Hon Yost's fortuitous appearance offered an excellent excuse for doing what they wanted to do: abandon the expedition. Daniel Claus put the best possible face on the debacle. "The Indians," he explained,

> finding that our besieging the Fort was of no Effect, our troops but few, a reinforcement as was reported of 1500 or 2000 Men with Field pieces, by the way, began to be dis[pi]rited & file off by Degrees: The Chiefs advised the Brigr to retreat to Oswego and get better Artillery from Niagara & more men to return and renew the Siege, to which The Brigr agreed and accordingly retreated wch. was on The 22 of Augt.[72]

The withdrawal was so precipitous that the troops left most of their equipment behind, to the garrison's satisfaction.[73]

At German Flats, meanwhile, General Arnold learned of the enemy's attempt to dig approach trenches at Fort Stanwix. Fearful that an attack might carry the fort, Arnold finally decided to hurry to its relief. An express message met him when he was about two miles on his way, advising him of St. Leger's withdrawal. Arnold pushed 900 men forward in an effort to catch up to and engage the enemy's rear, but they reached the fort at 5:00 p.m., too late to press the pursuit. The next morning, he dispatched 500 men to continue the chase, but bad weather forced him to abandon the effort. A small party that pressed on reached Oneida Lake in time to see the last of the British regulars crossing it in boats.[74]

The Northern Command: Personalities and Politics

The Two Contenders

The history of the Continental Army's northern command revolves around two men of radically different origins, political principles, military experience, and command styles. Without a full understanding of who these men were and how one came to lead the Northern Department during the summer of 1777, it is impossible to completely grasp and appreciate the rich complexity that was the Saratoga Campaign in general, and American involvement in those operations in particular.

The first of these men, Philip John Schuyler, descended from New York's patroon stock, an aristocrat by birth, wealth, and demeanor. Patrician that he was, he was far from being an effete product of privilege. Schuyler willingly followed a routine of economic and political activity that taxed his less-than-robust constitution. His public service began during the Seven Years' War as a captain, commissary, and major, when he displayed the same talent for logistics that marked his Revolutionary career. Like most of the Hudson River grandees, he was a reluctant revolutionary. Politically, he stood somewhat to the right of such main-line conservatives as George Washington, John Adams, and Roger Sherman. But unlike Adams and Sherman, Schuyler committed little of his philosophy to paper, and the record does not document his personal political philosophy. When the Continental Congress turned to creating generals, its members recognized the political necessity of naming a New Yorker by appointing him a major general, ranked only by Washington, Artemas Ward, and Charles Lee. Schuyler's leadership of the American invasion of Canada of 1775-1776, however, produced a growing chorus of criticism that was a prelude to the fourteen months of political in-fighting over the northern command.

Schuyler's assets were his political and social connections, an administrative capability that made him a master of detail, and devotion to his state's and nation's interests as he perceived them. His weaknesses included an arrogance toward those he considered his social inferiors (which compromised his effectiveness when dealing with undeferential men and less patrician politicians), a lack of aggressiveness that invited censure, and a penchant for blaming others when things went wrong.[1]

The second man under consideration, Horatio Gates—the godson of that sometimes-venomous diarist, correspondent, man of letters, and gossip Horace Walpole—was born in England, probably at Hornby Castle, Yorkshire, or Malden, Essex, in 1728 or 1729. According to Walpole, Gates' mother Dorothy was a housekeeper for the Second Duke of Leeds, and Robert, his father, may have been a butler or a journeyman tailor before becoming collector of customs at Greenwich. Their son somehow managed to acquire an above-average education and in 1749 entered the British Army at the rank of lieutenant. His plebian birth made his entry into an officer class dominated by gentry and aristocrats unusual.

After a few months service with his regiment at Halifax, Gates became a captain-lieutenant in Colonel Hugh Warburton's Regiment, and in September 1754 a captain in the Fourth Independent Company Foot, stationed in New York City. He participated in General Edward Braddock's 1755 campaign and was wounded at Turtle Creek. After recovering, Gates served in the Mohawk Valley as brigade major under Generals John Stanwix and Robert Monckton and accompanied the latter to Martinique. In April 1762, he received a major's commission in the 45th Regiment, posted in Nova Scotia. Two years later he transferred in that rank to the 60th [Royal American] Regiment, which he exchanged for a half-pay majority in the 74th Regiment.

Despairing of further preferment, Gates resigned from the army. In 1772, he emigrated to America where, early the next year, he settled on a plantation near Shepherdstown, [West] Virginia. While stationed in New York during the mid-1750s Gates had become associated with members of the Whig Club, and for the rest of his life espoused the liberal sentiments that eventually found expression in Jeffersonian republicanism. Those views made him a critic of British imperial policies, and he was an early advocate of independence.[2] The former British major resumed his military career when the Congress named him adjutant general of its new army with the rank of brigadier general on June 17, 1775.[3] In that capacity he performed yeoman service helping organize and train the fledgling Continental Army.

Excepting Benedict Arnold and Charles Lee, Gates proved to be the war's most complex American general. Physically brave, intelligent, a competent administrator, blunt, profane, and quarrelsome, he was capable of mortgaging his substantial talents to overarching ambition and ethical inconstancy. Contemporaries as diverse as Benjamin Franklin, John and Samuel Adams, Jefferson, James Madison, and Henry Cruger respected him, and contemporary evidence portrays him as popular with the soldiery. Yet, for more than a century, American writers were almost unanimous in calling him incompetent, cowardly, scheming, dishonest, a worse leader than David Wooster and Artemas Ward—and Arnold's moral inferior.[4]

Certainly Horatio Gates was cast in an unheroic mold. Even soldiers who liked him called him "Granny Gates." He lacked Washington's commanding presence and Schuyler's icy dignity, and he had none of Arnold's and Anthony Wayne's charismatic flair. Gates' political views were anathema to some who feared the threat of social revolution. Still, anti-Gates bias has been more visceral and longer-lived than other antipathies because he was allegedly party to and beneficiary of what conspiracy-mongers termed the Conway Cabal. According to their demonology, a corps of malcontents, including army officers and congressmen, combined to replace Washington with the intriguer— Horatio Gates. Worthington C. Ford, editor of the *Writings of George Washington*, attributed a new dimension to the spurious victor of Saratoga's perfidy when he wrote in 1911 that

> Washington had stripped his army of an essential part of his strength to place Gates beyond risk of defeat, and facing the British at Brandywine he had lost a battle because, as he thought, Gates had not promptly returned those loaned troops. No doubt exists of the intention of Gates in retaining them, in spite of the urgent sending of [Alexander] Hamilton by Washington to hasten their return. To enjoy the full sweets of victory, to magnify his own success and importance, and to make sharper the contrast between his victory and Washington's want of it, Gates was willing to risk the destruction of the "main" army under Washington.[5]

To construct that damning indictment, Dr. Ford misrepresented relevant facts. The "loaned" troops were Daniel Morgan's riflemen, who joined Gates in

August. The battle of Brandywine occurred on September 11, just eight days before the first engagement at Saratoga. Washington did not ask for their return (if they were no longer needed), until September 24, thirteen days after Brandywine. Gates obviously needed them for the final fight with Burgoyne on October 7. The British general surrendered on October 17, and Morgan left to rejoin Washington the next day. Hamilton visited the Northern Department between October 31 and November 5, but not to request the return of Morgan's riflemen, who had departed thirteen days earlier. What he did request were reinforcements from three Continental brigades still with Gates: those of Paterson, Glover, and Nixon. On November 7, two days after Hamilton left, Paterson's and Glover's men marched south, leaving Nixon's the only Continental brigade in the entire department.[6]

Ford's grossly inaccurate account of events was an extreme expression of the virulence even a reputable scholar could resort to in discrediting the man he believed betrayed the national hero. Criticism of Washington, whatever its nature and motivation, was treasonous. To aspire to replace him, as Gates' traducers claimed he had done, could not be the ambition of a man capable of defeating Burgoyne. Ergo, he was not the real architect of victory; others, notably Schuyler and Arnold, deserved the credit. The disastrous battle of Camden in August 1780 confirmed their judgment of the man they agreed had intrigued against the noble Washington and the selfless Schuyler. Underhandedly securing the command of the Northern Department was thus, for Gates, but a prelude to becoming commander-in-chief.

What was at Stake?

The story of how Horatio Gates became commander of the Northern Department in 1777 has implications not limited to the political ramifications of Congress' other appointments. Every general officer's appointment was political—it could not be otherwise. No military establishment existed from which the Congress could select candidates qualified only by merit and seniority. It had created (or adopted) an army, and it had to create an officer corps using the only mechanism at its disposal—politics. Therefore, place of residence, social status, prominent friends and supporters, political views, and military experience influenced Congressional nominations and the order of appointment. When Congress gave the northern command to Schuyler or Gates, most of those considerations were in play, along with others peculiar to the time and prevailing circumstances. "I take notice of this appointment of

Gates because it had great influence on my future fortunes," penned honest John Adams in his *Autobiography* about how Gates came to find himself in command. "It soon occasioned a competition between him and Schuyler, in which I always contended for Gates, and as the rivalry occasioned great animosities among the friends of the two generals, the consequences of which are not yet spent." Adams continued:

> Indeed they have affected the essential interests of the United States and will influence their ultimate destiny. They effected an enmity between Gates and Mr. [John] Jay who always supported Schuyler, and a dislike in Gates of Hamilton who married Schuyler's daughter . . . . I never had in my life any personal prejudice against Schuyler . . . But the New England officers, soldiers, and inhabitants knew Gates in the camp at Cambridge. Schuyler was not known to many, and the few who had heard of him, were prejudiced against him from the former French War. The New Englanders would not enlist to serve under him, and the militia would not turn out. I was, therefore, under a necessity of supporting Gates.[7]

Adams, like other delegates, responded to regional issues that had political implications—whether in support of Gates or Schuyler.

Alexander Hamilton avenged his father-in-law on Adams in his *Letters from Alexander Hamilton Concerning the Public Conduct and Character of John Adams, Esq.*, by attempting to sabotage his election campaign in 1796. He also intrigued against him from within the cabinet during his presidency, a vendetta that contributed to the eventual defeat of the Federalist party.[8]

Professor Jonathan G. Rossie, who devoted the major part of his *The Politics of Command in the American Revolution* to a detailed study of the Gates-Schuyler rivalry, argued that the rivalry was, in part, a product of the important debate about the meaning of the American Revolution. Gates' supporters were principally, but not exclusively, found among men who believed that liberty required that the states be the seat of ultimate power, whereas Schuyler's support came almost exclusively from nationalists who wanted to hedge the Revolution with limits that would lead to creating a strong central government, safely dominated by a political and social elite. The contest anticipated the divisions that produced the new nation's political parties.[9] Professor Rossie's interpretation deserves respectful consideration because, while other forces operated, the struggle for the northern command did provide the Revolution's left and right wings an arena before coherent parties existed as vehicles for political competition.

Previous Leadership Controversies: The Canadian Command

Selecting a replacement for General Richard Montgomery as field commander in the North after he was killed during the 1775-1776 American invasion of Canada posed especially difficult problems. Montgomery's death and Arnold's serious wound caused the command to devolve upon Brigadier General David Wooster who, in addition to detesting and being detested by Schuyler, was sixty-five years old, incompetent, and in poor health. Because the general commanding in Canada was subordinate to the commander of the Northern Department, mutual hostility between the two was bound to affect adversely the army's effectiveness.[10]

Wooster soon made the inevitable a reality when he issued orders regulating the troops in Canada. Schuyler complained to Congress that his subordinate was being insubordinate, and demanded that orders affecting the force in Canada be cleared through him. Wooster argued that the man in the field with the troops, not the department commander in Albany, was the proper person to issue such orders.[11] As long as Schuyler remained in command of the department and continued to exercise that command from Albany or his country estate at Saratoga, anyone named to the Canadian post would almost certainly fail.

There were men in Congress and the Continental Army who believed that Schuyler would make solving the command problem easier by resigning. Henry Knox told Gates "from Schuyler's conversation that he wished to be excused acting as general."[12] Rumors to that effect reached members of Congress, and some were delighted to hear them, relay them, and hope that they were true. New Englanders, with whom his unpopularity approached unanimity, were not alone in wishing to see the New Yorker replaced. Others were severely critical of his management of the Canadian campaign, recognizing that he was not the best choice to lead that kind of quixotic venture to a successful conclusion.

Indeed, Schuyler was not the best choice to lead any martial venture. "In depth and breadth of mind, in stability of intention, in firm decisiveness to plan and to execute, in the ability to meet a confused situation, discern its essentials, and expend his energies upon them," wrote even a sympathetic student, "Schuyler was somewhat deficient." The New Yorker, continued the writer, lacked the executive power required to make a man an "effective and successful general officer." Nor had his "slight" military experience as a captain during the French and Indian War "been sufficient to induce a habit of command." Finally, he noted, Schuyler "had not the physical vigor nor ruggedness needed to cope with the hardships and deprivations of a wilderness campaign."[13]

General Schuyler might have overcome his military limitations and personal haughtiness if he had been able to gain his men's confidence and respect by sharing their hardships and dangers, and if he had displayed the kind of dynamic leadership that men such as Benedict Arnold, Richard Montgomery, and Daniel Morgan were capable of achieving. But ill health plagued him, especially during moments of stress and crisis. For example, after spending two weeks of September 1775 with his troops, Schuyler thereafter remained at Ticonderoga, his Saratoga estate, or his Albany mansion while the department's soldiers suffered privation, death, and defeat. His absence from the battle zone contributed to the indiscipline, low morale, and inadequate combat performance that characterized too much of the campaign. Many in Congress knew that, and hoped the general would accommodate them by resigning—which he would not do.

Since the commander of the Northern Department would neither exercise personal command in Canada nor quit his post, to whom could the Congress give an assignment that promised more travail than glory? Charles Lee seemed to be the only major general with the qualifications required for such demanding duty. Lee, however, was Schuyler's senior in rank, with a commission dated June 17, 1775, while Schuyler's was dated two days later. In spite of the inherent potential for trouble, in that his seniority precluded his being Schuyler's subordinate, the delegates unanimously elected Lee commander in Canada.[14] He would vacate his post at New York City; and Schuyler would replace him there, implying that Lee would control operations both on the New York frontier and in Canada.

While Congress' arrangement was already fraught with potential for trouble, President of the Continental Congress John Hancock's letter of February 1776 advising Schuyler of Lee's appointment guaranteed that the potential would become a certainty. Intent upon placating the New York general, he told him that appointing Lee did not reflect a lack of confidence in his generalship. In fact, he gilded the lily by writing that the delegates would have preferred seeing Schuyler lead the restoration of American fortunes in the North. Because, however, they were "apprehensive should you be sent on so fatiguing a service as that of Canada must be, especially at this inclement season, your country would be deprived of the advantage of your services . . . it was thought best to send General Lee to Canada, reserving for you the command of the forces and conduct of military operations in the colony of New York."[15]

Schuyler thus retained effective command of the Northern Department, while Lee was expected to lead the troops in Canada. The delegates in Congress expected them to cooperate as equals, each to "as Far as in your power give mutual aid in supporting the cause of freedom and liberty."[16] Expecting two vain, hypochondriacal, rank-conscious men to work for "the cause of freedom and liberty" rather than for themselves was supremely naive. Lee was eccentric, capable, and irascible. As a career officer, he entertained a low opinion of generals of less experience who owed their commissions to their political positions. Schuyler was determined to retain command, and intelligent enough not to fall for Hancock's flattery. He knew all too well that many in Congress blamed him for the Canadian debacle. On the same day that the president of Congress penned his letter, Schuyler wrote one of his own disputing Wooster's assertion that the commander in Canada was in any degree independent of the man commanding the Northern Department. The field command had never been a separate one, and General Montgomery had always conducted himself as a subordinate.[17] His letter had the virtue of disabusing the most optimistic delegate about the wisdom of naming a general to the field command who was senior to the departmental commander. Creating an independent Canadian Department seemed the logical solution.

There was at the same time, however, a need to establish a department in the South, where the British threat was rapidly worsening. Loyalist sentiment there was strong. In South Carolina, Tories tried to seize control of the government in a virtual civil war. And a strange conversation between Lee and British General Henry Clinton that took place in early February, when they had a chance meeting in New York, assumed a newly-ominous importance. Clinton told Lee that he was leading a major offensive against Charleston, South Carolina. Lee was skeptical, observing to Washington that for him "to communicate his full plan to the enemy is too droll to be credited."[18] As Professor Rossie later noted, in so doing, Clinton "revealed both a whimsical nature and an utter contempt for American military power."[19] But it became alarmingly apparent that Clinton had been candid with the former British lieutenant colonel who had turned his coat and become a rebel general.

The thoroughly-alarmed Congress did what its severely-limited mandate allowed it to do: it authorized fourteen Continental battalions for service in the South and undertook an extensive reorganization of the army, dividing the country into four departments. The Eastern Department included New

England; Washington would be both commander of that department and commander-in-chief. Schuyler would command a Middle Department, comprised of New York, Pennsylvania, Maryland, Delaware, and New Jersey. Lee would command the department in Canada. To counter Clinton's threat, Congress made Virginia, the Carolinas, and Georgia a Southern Department.[20] But who would be its commander?

The only major generals without department commands were Artemas Ward and Israel Putnam. Even if they had been military geniuses—which they were not—they were unacceptable to the Southerners, who wanted Virginian Charles Lee. On February 27, the day Congress created the Southern Department, Edward Rutledge of South Carolina nominated Lee. But the Canadian command's importance and the conviction that Lee was the only general in whom all interested parties would have confidence made Congress reluctant to send him south. Lee thus continued, until the first week in March, to try to improve the Americans' grip on New York City, at once outraging the state's Provincial Congress and earning the equivalent of a censure from the Continental Congress for administering loyalty oaths and arrogating civil authority to himself.

Finally, on March 1, Congress decided to invest Lee with command of the Southern Department and, without Washington's advice or approval, appointed John Thomas to the Canadian command with the rank of major general.[21] Neither Washington nor Lee approved of that arrangement. In spite of his earlier reluctance to take on the Canadian command, Lee, noting that he alone among the candidates spoke French, expressed the logical opinion that "it would have been more prudent to have sent me to Canada." The commander-in-chief shared that view. "As a Virginian I must rejoice at the change," he wrote Lee on March 14, "but as an American, I think you would have done more essential service to the common cause in Canada. For besides the advantage of speaking and thinking in French, an officer who is acquainted with their manners and customs and who has traveled in their country must certainly take the strongest hold on their affections and confidence."[22] Washington also knew that, as a New England veteran of King George's War and the French and Indian War, Thomas was not the man to win the habitant's support.

As Rossie observed, appointing Thomas to the Canadian command without Washington's advice and concurrence set an unfortunate precedent that made the commander in the North directly responsible to the Continental Congress rather than to the commander-in-chief, a degree of independence justified on neither military nor political grounds.[23] Congress compounded its folly by failing to produce a definitive statement of Schuyler's position in the chain of command, and as long as that remained unresolved, the potential for trouble remained undiminished. Charles Lee was his senior, and Schuyler would have accepted his appointment without demur. But Thomas, in addition to being a New Englander (a species unloved by Schuyler) was the army's most junior major general. The fact that he possessed combat leadership experience that the New Yorker lacked did not compensate for his other attributes.

If Schuyler had complied with Congress' order to replace Lee in New York City as soon as his chronically troublesome health permitted, the problem of his role might have been mooted. But he refused to go to the city, offering the argument that leaving Albany would cause supplying the troops in Canada to suffer. Congress accepted the logic of his contention and countermanded its directive. From his headquarters at his home in Albany, Schuyler would command the Middle Department, while managing logistics for the army in Canada. Presumably, Thomas would enjoy the same degree of independence that the delegates had vested in Lee. That presumption, however, fell short of certainty because they disagreed among themselves about whether, in the changed circumstances, Canada was really a separate department, and whether Thomas or Schuyler held the chief command in the North.[24]

The Aftermath of Defeat in Canada

Schuyler's, Thomas', and Benedict Arnold's best efforts, coupled with the diplomacy of a congressional commission made up of Benjamin Franklin, Samuel Chase, and the brothers Carroll, Charles and John, could not prevail in Canada. Thomas died of smallpox on June 2, just one month after taking command. Brigadier Generals William Thompson and John Sullivan failed in their attempts to salvage the situation against Sir Guy Carleton. By July, the defeated wreck of the American army that only ten months earlier had departed Crown Point staggered back to where the campaign had begun.

During the search for scapegoats upon whom to cast the sins of omission and commission that marked that campaign, bitter personal and regional animosities surfaced in disgraceful mutual recrimination. General Schuyler unreservedly blamed every failure and mistake on New Englanders, and some of his indictments were plausible enough to convince delegates from middle and southern states of their justice. New England tardiness in sending reinforcements and the conduct of some New Hampshire soldiers at Quebec were especially damaging.[25] When Congress' emissaries returned to Philadelphia, their reports reinforced anti-New England sentiment. They were particularly unsparing in their condemnation of David Wooster, declaring him "totally unfit," and that his presence with the troops was "prejudicial to our affairs; we would humbly advise his recall."[26]

Samuel Chase, an uncritical partisan of General Schuyler and to whom New England egalitarianism was anathema, also insistently held that region and its soldiers responsible for every American failure.[27] John Adams, whose normal discourse was argumentation, found Chase's accusations especially galling. Leading the defense of his native region, he denounced the Marylander for fomenting discord between Northern and Southern soldiers during his stay with the army.[28] The impenitent Chase continued unabated his castigation of Yankees and unqualified support of Schuyler's every act. Not to be outdone in vituperation, some irresponsible New Englanders resorted to slandering Schuyler, even going so far as to suggest he was disloyal.

The period immediately following the Canadian debacle was not the Continental Congress' finest hour. Disappointment and helplessness conspired to make even normally responsible men debase the coinage of political discourse. When delegates from New Jersey, New York, and Pennsylvania united to cast the odium of defeat on New England they ignored their own states' slowness in responding to the call for reinforcements, and the fact that when their soldiers belatedly arrived at the front, their effectiveness in resisting the British advance did not surpass that of the New Englanders'. In fact, all of the troops defeated by the British under Simon Fraser, in the defining fight at Trois Rivieres on June 8, were from New Jersey and Pennsylvania.[29]

Yet, even more than David Wooster's inept leadership and the tardiness of reinforcements, time played a significant role in defeating the Americans in Canada: Congress wasted weeks before authorizing the invasion, Schuyler wasted as much time organizing it, and the British bought additional time for themselves by their excellent defense at Fort St. Johns in the autumn of 1775.[30]

A Commander—for Canada?

As the British made preparations to launch their 1776 counter-invasion from Canada, Congress wrestled with choosing a new commander for the 1,000 pox-ravaged, dispirited, near-mutinous men who comprised the northern army—most of them embittered New Englanders. To expect General Schuyler to rebuild that army into an effective fighting machine required an optimism few objective observers could muster. The Congress desperately needed to select a major general with organizational experience who was untainted by defeat, did not share the animus against Yankees, and who did share their brand of republicanism. One man, Horatio Gates, had those qualifications.

Gates was the army's senior brigadier general, commissioned on June 17, 1775, two days after Washington was named commander-in-chief. As adjutant general, a position for which Washington may have nominated him (the Virginian had served with him during Braddock's campaign and was well aware of his service as a brigade major), Gates had played a significant part in organizing and training the Continental Army.[31] As ranking brigadier general, Gates—and not Thomas—would normally have been promoted in March, but his importance as adjutant general probably persuaded Congress to defer his advancement. Artemas Ward's resignation on April 23 created a vacancy for Gates to fill on May 16.[32]

On May 18, before either Gates or Washington knew of the former's promotion, the latter received from George Merchant, an escaped prisoner of war, papers that included copies of treaties concluded between Britain and German princes providing for the employment in North America of some 17,000 German soldiers.[33] Merchant also brought a letter to Benjamin Franklin covering one dated February 13, 1776, purporting to be addressed to Cadwallader Colden, Royal Lieutenant Governor of New York. That piece of correspondence reported that fifteen British regiments were probably at sea bound for America. These organizations, combined with German mercenary reinforcements who could sail in April, totaled approximately 30,000 enemy soldiers the King would be able to employ against the rebellious colonists by the end of June 1776.[34]

In addition to that alarming report, the letter included venomous criticism of Franklin and John Jay and a suggestive reference to replacing Washington with "A general of the first abilities and experience [who] would go over if he could have any assurance from Congress of keeping his rank; but being very high, he would not admit to have anyone but an American his superior, and that only in consideration of the confidence due to an American in a question so peculiarly American." A second letter dated February 14 announced that "A general of first rank and abilities would go over, if the Congress would authorize anyone to promise him a proper reception. This I had from Mr. Lee, agent for Massachusetts, but it must be a secret with you, as I was not to mention it."[35]

The "Mr. Lee" in question was Arthur Lee, the unstable and trouble-making brother of Washington's long-time friend and supporter, Richard

Henry Lee. The implication was clear. In Arthur's opinion (and one certainly shared by others), Washington was not a man of "first abilities," and the command should go to a European soldier possessing those abilities, probably the Comte Francois de Broglie.[36]

Washington forwarded the original to Franklin, the addressee, with a copy to Richard Henry Lee. More important, he sent his adjutant general—Horatio Gates—to Philadelphia with the copies of the Anglo-German treaties. They were so important that Washington knew Congress would need to act without delay. Because he was reluctant to leave New York while the probability existed that the British fleet might appear, he sent Gates to represent him in developing a strategy for dealing with the new situation. Washington made it clear to President Hancock that his adjutant general enjoyed his confidence and had important latitude in representing his commander. "[Gates'] military experience and intimate acquaintance with our affairs," explained Washington, "will enable him to give Congress the fullest satisfaction about measures necessary to be adopted at this alarming crisis, and with his zeal and attachment to the cause of America, have a claim to your notice and favors."[37] During the evening of the day Washington penned that endorsement, he received an urgent invitation from Hancock to come to Philadelphia for rest and consultation with Congress. At the same time, headquarters received notification that Gates had been promoted to major general and that Quartermaster General Thomas Mifflin had been made a brigadier general.[38]

John Hancock's letter notifying Gates of his advancement contained the flattering news that Congress had promoted him because of "the very great service you have performed for America by introducing order and discipline into the Army of the United Colonies, as well as your zeal and ardor for the American cause."[39] Those words certainly gratified the new major general, who was no more immune to flattery than his commander and several of his colleagues. They also accurately summarized his services and confirmed his confidence in Congress' perspicacity.

Washington shared the good opinion of Gates' services, but he did not welcome Hancock's request that the newly-promoted generals be assigned to Massachusetts. The threat of a British offensive there was too remote to justify posting them in a strategic backwater. Gates, who departed New York on May 19 before the arrival of the notice of his promotion, learned of it after arriving in Philadelphia on the twenty-first. Because by that time Washington had accepted Hancock's invitation to consult with Congress in person, Hancock deferred consideration of the documents from Merchant until the commander-in-chief was present.[40] Washington reached the capital on May 23, where consultations involving Washington, Gates, Mifflin, and a congressional committee continued for a week.[41]

While the deliberations were under way and the Canadian situation continued to deteriorate, Congress wrestled with what to do about the Canadian command. John Sullivan believed that his service in the North had earned him the right to the post. Washington obliquely but effectively scotched that chance in a letter by observing that Sullivan obviously wanted it, but "Whether he merits it or not, is a matter to be considered." Sullivan, continued Washington, "was active, spirited, and zealously attached to our cause. . . . But he has his wants, and he has his foibles. The latter are manifest in a little tincture of vanity, and an over desire of being popular, which now and then leads him into some embarrassments."[42] After paying tribute to Sullivan's personal attributes, the commander-in-chief observed "as the security of Canada is of the last importance to the well being of these Colonies, I should like to know the sentiments of Congress, respecting the nomination of any officer to that command." He obviously did not believe that Sullivan was the man for the job.

Congress' delegates had all but made their decision by June 13, when Schuyler's faithful supporter, Samuel Chase, wrote to Gates that a general "is to be sent [to Canada] with the powers of a dictator. Many have their eyes upon you, and I doubt not, that you will be appointed to this great and important [post]."[43] After more discussion, they made it official on June 17, resolving "that General Washington be directed to send Major General Gates into Canada to take command of the forces in that province." The decision granted Gates authority that John Adams ironically described this way: "We have ordered you to the post of Honour, and made you Dictator in Canada for six months, or at least until the first of October . . . . We don't trust you generals, with too much power, for too long Time."[44] The comment was more than a puckish aside. It was a reminder of the traditional Anglo-colonial distrust of generals and military establishments.

General Washington carried out Congress' directive on June 24, when he informed Gates, who was now back in New York City, that he was to command in Canada. He did not presume to give his old adjutant general detailed orders, noting that "The distance of the scene and frequent changes which have happened in the state of our affairs in Canada do not allow me to be more particular in my instructions. The command is important, the service difficult but honorable; and I most devoutly pray that Providence may crown your arms with abundant success."[45]

The new major general left New York City to take over his new duties on June 25. Daunting problems awaited him. The decisive defeat at Trois Rivieres had taken place earlier that month, followed by Arnold's retreat to St. Johns with 3,000 invalids. "Where, or in what Condition I will find the Army, I have no conception," Gates wrote John Adams. "The Prospect is too much clouded to distinguish Clearly."[46]

Overshadowing everything was the ambiguity of his mandate from Congress. Buoyed by words like those written by Adams and Chase and his own wishful thinking, Gates flattered himself that it conferred plenary powers in the northern theater. Congress had, however, significantly circumscribed his authority when it did not define his command relationship with General Schuyler, who remained commander of the Northern Department, which was the base for all operations. The delegates clearly meant for Gates to exercise substantially independent command of the field force in Canada, which Montgomery, Wooster, Thomas, and Sullivan had exercised in practice. If, as was all too probable, that force withdrew into New York and reentered the Northern Department, what would be its commander's relationship with the department commander? Failure to provide for that eventuality compromised Gates' position and provided fertile ground for official and personal conflict that could only make resisting British aggression from Canada more difficult.

Congress compounded its error by leaving the embittered John Sullivan with the northern field army. In his June 7 letter to Washington hinting that he wanted the Canadian command, Sullivan declared himself unwilling to serve under anyone other than Washington or Charles Lee. That declaration persuaded the commander-in-chief that leaving Sullivan in place was unwise. Unfortunately, not enough delegates shared that concern.[47]

Sullivan's resentment was neither the sole nor the most serious problem plaguing command of the northern troops. By the time Gates arrived at Albany and was a guest in Schuyler's mansion, the force he was to command had retreated from Isle aux Noix to Crown Point—back into his host's Northern Department. So long as the army remained south of the Canadian border, Gates, the junior major general present, would remain Schuyler's subordinate.

Instead of possessing the powers described by Adams and Chase, Gates faced a reality he was unwilling to accept: that his commission was dormant except in Canada, where there were no longer any American troops and where none would be in the foreseeable future. Insisting, however, that Congress intended him to command the northern force wherever it was, his appointment of Morgan Lewis and Joseph Trumbull to deputy quartermaster general and deputy commissary, respectively, brought matters to a head in a confrontation with Schuyler.[48] Although willing to confirm whomever Gates appointed, Schuyler clarified the command relationship by asserting "that he conceived the army to be altogether under his command when on this side of Canada subject however to the control of General Washington; that in his absence General Gates commanded the army in the same manner as General Sullivan did now and only as the eldest officer."[49] In brief, Gates was succeeding Sullivan. Because everyone, including Schuyler, knew that his chronic poor health would preclude his commanding in the field, Gates would, indeed, enjoy a considerable degree of independence—but at the sufferance of Schuyler, who would continue to possess plenary authority in the North. The seeds of discord in the later Saratoga operation were now firmly planted and already beginning to bear poisonous fruit.

Both men realized that Washington and Congress needed to remove all ambiguity. "As both General Gates and myself mean to be candid, and wish the matter settled without any of the chicane which would disgrace us as officers and men," wrote Schuyler to Washington in an effort to clarify the situation,

> we have agreed to speak plain, and to show each other what we have written to you upon the occasion, and he has accordingly read the whole of what I have said . . . . If Congress intended that General Gates should command the Northern Department, wherever it may be, as he assures me they did, it ought to have been signified to me, and I should have immediately resigned the command to him; but until such intention is properly conveyed to me, I never can, I must entreat your Excellency to lay this letter before Congress . . . to avert the dangers and evils that may arise from a disputed command.

The commander-in-chief promptly forwarded the letter to Congress, warning of the "evils which must inevitably follow a disputed command." He also observed that the troops on the northern frontiers would now be limited to defensive operations and that one of the two major generals—obviously Gates—could be more usefully employed with the Grand Army.[50]

Congress' delegates quickly reconfirmed its decision to vest Schuyler with overall command, resolving on July 8:

> That Major General Gates be informed, that it was the intention of Congress to give him command of the troops whilst in Canada, but had no

design to vest him with a superior command to General Schuyler, whilst the troops should be on this side of Canada; that the president write to General Schuyler and Major General Gates, stating this matter, and recommending to them to carry on the military operations with harmony, and in such a manner as shall best promote the public business.[51]

While the resolution affirmed that, with the army back within the bounds of the Northern Department, Gates did not possess a "superior command" to Schuyler, it did not indicate that Gates was the subordinate, implying that the two generals would share command. President Hancock's letter to the principals clearly indicates that that was the delegates' naive intent.

Not every delegate believed that the Solomonic decision would stand up under the strains inherent in two ambitious, strong-willed men sharing the burdens of command in a theater that provided a stage for intense sectional and ideological rivalries. Samuel Adams, whose bluntness and realism were probably unsurpassed among his colleagues, prophetically predicted the arrangement's failure when he wrote, "Admitting that both generals have the accomplishments of Marlborough and Eugene, I cannot conceive that such a disposition [of the northern command] can be attended with any happy effects, unless harmony subsists between them. Alas!" Adams continued, "I fear this is not the case—already disputes have arisen, which they have referred to Congress! And although they appear to treat each other with a politeness becoming their rank . . . altercations between commanders who have pretensions so nearly equal, I mean in point of command, forbode a repetition of misfortunes."[52]

"Command carried with it the concomitant of responsibility," Professor Rossie aptly noted in his interpretation of Congress' effort to order command relations. "Both Schuyler and Gates would be acutely aware that a mistake by one would ruin the reputation of the other. The joint command, therefore, demanded a complete selflessness on the part of the two generals—a quality neither Gates nor Schuyler ever had in abundance."[53]

Ridiculing the Continental Congress for its management of military affairs has been all too easy. The manifest absurdity of its arrangements for command on the critical Canadian frontier cast its deficiencies in high relief. Justice and accuracy, however, require recognizing the complexity of the problems it faced and the limited resources it could bring to their solution. Congress—the creature of an emergency, endowed with ambiguous authority by suspicious member colonies, and lacking decisive coercive power—had nevertheless formed a union of confederated colonies, created a military establishment, opened diplomatic relations, and borrowed money. During May, June, and the first days of July, while trying to cope with the Gates-Schuyler problem, the delegates also consulted, debated, and approved the final draft of the Declaration of Independence. No other revolutionary body has wrought so well.

Gates' reaction to clarification of his status was mixed. On the one hand, he wrote to John Adams from his command post at Fort Ticonderoga, "I am no Dictator here . . . I have been Deceived and Disappointed in being removed from a place where I might have done the Publick Service"—an obvious sarcastic rebuttal to Adams' allusion to the dictatorial authority of the commander in Canada.[54] In a more politic vein, he told Hancock that he had written to Schuyler "to assure him of my entre [sic] satisfaction and acquiescence in the Resolve of Congress. And my unalienable resolution to obey his Commands."[55] Once again secure in his position as northern commander, Schuyler could be and was generous toward his unwilling second, and professed himself pleased by the "perfect harmony" prevailing between them.[56] Both men did, indeed, seem determined to subordinate personal ambitions to the public service to which they repeatedly vowed devotion, and cooperated in preparing to resist Carleton's southward advance.

Carleton's Offensive and the American Response

While Guy Carleton constructed his fleet for his southward invasion and the American forces at Ticonderoga worked on its defenses, Schuyler and Gates made their decision to abandon the old ruined works at Crown Point. Arnold, Sullivan, and Frederick William von Woedtke concurred. But twenty-one officers, led by Colonels John Stark, William Maxwell, and Enoch Poor, drafted a protest petition. They argued that the army must dispute every foot of ground. Abandoning the old fort would provide the enemy with a strong position from which to attack Ticonderoga and make it impossible for the American boats to operate north of Crown Point. They also feared the British would use the works at Crown Point to support Indian incursions against the New England frontier.[57]

General Schuyler summarily dismissed their protest, declaring that abandoning Crown Point was "Indispensably necessary for a variety of reasons," and that their arguments did not "bear sufficient weight" to justify reversing the decision.[58] His tone so angered the colonels that at least one of them leaked the news of the controversy to a friend serving with Washington, who brought it to his commander's attention. Washington consulted some of his subordinates, one of whom, Nathanael Greene, reflected his New Englander's bias when he wrote to Governor Nicholas Cooke of Rhode Island that Schuyler has reached "one of the most mad resolutions I ever heard of, that is to quit Crown Point . . . we lose all the advantage upon the lake [Champlain]; we have so much suprimity [sic] that the enemy could not enjure [sic] us this summer. We lay all the back parts of New England open."[59] Greene was Washington's ablest lieutenant, and his views carried weight with his chief and his fellow officers.

Washington shared the opinions of Greene and other members of his staff and addressed a letter to Schuyler, whom he held responsible for what he believed was an ill-conceived decision.[60] The letter's tone, however, was too reserved to convey the full measure of his disapproval. On July 19, he wrote a more candid reflection of his opinion to Gates, with whom he was (at that time) on more intimate terms. Washington professed himself skeptical of Schuyler's claim that his troops were not capable of defending Crown Point. He further opined that the field officers' dissent seemed to cast doubt upon the professed motives behind the decision. Washington went on to rehearse the colonels' arguments, declaring that

> [n]othing but a belief that you have actually removed the army from the Point to Ticonderoga, and actually demolished the former; and the fear of creating dissension, and encouraging a spirit of remonstrating against the conduct of superiors by inferiors, have prevented me, by the advice of the general officers here, from directing the post at Crown Point to be held until Congress should decide upon the propriety of its evacuation. . . . I must . . . express my sorrow at the resolution of your council, and wish, that it had never happened, as everybody who speaks of it also does; and that the measure could yet be changed with propriety.[61]

Gates' reply to Washington's suggested strictures came in the form of a letter as blunt as any the commander-in-chief ever received from a subordinate. Simply put, the major general defended Schuyler without reservation. "Your Excellency Speaks of those Works to be Destroyed at Crown Point," began Gates. "Time, & Bad Construction of those Works," he continued, had Completely Effected that business long before General Schuyler came with me to Crown Point. The Ramparts are Tumbled down, the casemates are Fallen in. The Barracks Burnt, and the whole so perfect a Ruin, that it would take Five times the Number of Our Army for several Summers, to put Those Works in Defensible [sic] Repair. Your Excellency also mentions the Troops expected to reinforce this Army; it would be to the last Degree improper, to Order Those Troops to Crown Point, or even hither [Ticonderoga] untill [sic] Obliged by The most pressing Emergency, as that would only be heaping One Hospital upon another . . . . Everything about this Army is infected—The Cloaths, The Blankets, The Air & The Ground they walk upon.[62]

Gates not only presumed to correct Washington's misapprehensions concerning Crown Point's condition and the general situation on the northern frontier, he voiced resentment that general officers of Washington's staff, of whom only Israel Putnam had personal experience in the North, had subjected his and Schuyler's decision to uninformed review.

The commander-in-chief's response reflected the not-too-surprising fact that he found the letter's tone offensive. He did, however, retreat from his unqualified condemnation of the decision to withdraw from Crown Point, and assured Gates that "there was council called" to review the matter and that he had merely discussed it with his general officers. Washington concluded that he would "not take up more time upon the subject, or make it a matter of further discussion."[63]

Schuyler responded to the growing criticism with a letter to Washington, written on August 6, that his censure by the generals' council in New York City was such an insult that he would resign unless Washington and/or Congress, in turn, censured the council's members. Washington repeated what he had told Gates and advised Schuyler to drop the subject. If, however, he should persist, his letter threatening to resign would be forwarded to Congress.[64] The New Yorker did not persist, but neither did he not forget the matter, which he believed proved there were men in the army and Congress intent on ruining him. His suspicions were exaggerated, but not altogether unfounded, for there were some who seized every opportunity to discredit his conduct. When, on July 17, Washington informed Congress of his disapproval of abandoning Crown Point, John Hancock quickly announced that the commander-in-chief had the authority to deploy all Continental troops, including those assigned to the Northern Department, a clear signal that Washington was empowered to reverse Schuyler's command decisions.[65]

Schuyler's relations with Congress suffered additional damage during a series of conflicts with Congress, the later recounting of which will be an important part of the details of this story.

Carleton's Offensive and the American Response: Gates and Arnold

While Schuyler conducted bootless duels with Congress and Carleton's men prepared to penetrate the American interior, Gates at Ticonderoga did what he could to change the quality of a force that had ceased to be "an army but a mob . . . ruined by sickness, fatigue and desertion, and void of any ideas of discipline and subordination."[66] Morale depended upon his and Schuyler's receiving and transporting the materiel required to improve shelter, clothing, rations, and arms.

Smallpox's ravages still jeopardized the health of men whose exposure to the disease had been so limited as to make them especially vulnerable. Inoculation was effective in reducing its severity, but field conditions rendered its administration difficult. Gates attacked the problem by ordering that all pox-stricken men be confined in a hospital at Fort Edward, that inoculating incoming recruits cease, and that the newcomers go into quarantine at Skenesborough.[67] His efforts paid dividends: by mid-August the army was free of the disease.[68] As the summer progressed, the men at Ticonderoga improved in health and morale. Strict, consistently-applied discipline reinforced unit effectiveness. By the end of October, Gates reported to Schuyler that the troops "here are in good spirits and think only of victory."[69]

The most important lieutenant serving the commander at Ticonderoga was Benedict Arnold. Although Arnold was sometimes a difficult subordinate himself, relations between Gates and the Connecticut general were at this time amicable and productive. Arnold's relations with lower-ranking officers created additional headaches for his military superiors and Congress, but his dealings with Captain Jacobus Wynkoop, whom Schuyler had placed in command of the lake flotilla, were judicious and demonstrated a firm grasp of the type of tactics peculiar to inland naval operations. Gates directed Arnold to supercede the inadequate temporary commodore. When on the night of August 15 Arnold arrived at Crown Point to assume command, Wynkoop refused to recognize his authority. While still trying to cope with that insubordination, Arnold heard, during the afternoon of the nineteenth, that an enemy force was approaching and, without informing Wynkoop, sent two schooners to investigate. Claiming that he suspected the boats' crews of deserting to the enemy, Wynkoop halted them by firing a signal gun. A furious Arnold threatened him with arrest, and Wynkoop, arguing that only Congress could place another officer over him, nevertheless ordered the schooners to continue their investigation.[70]

When informed of the incident, Gates ordered Arnold to arrest Wynkoop and send him to Ticonderoga. Arnold complied, but softened the blow with a letter recommending leniency. "I believe the Commodore was really of opinion that neither of us had the authority to command him," explained Arnold. "He now seems convinced to the contrary and sorry for his disobedience to orders. If it can be done with propriety, I wish he may be permitted to return home without being cashiered."[71] Gates concurred and allowed the stubborn Dutchman to ride to Albany with his pride largely intact. Arnold had behaved responsibly and generously, effectively ridding the Northern Department of an unfortunate appointment whose continued involvement in matters concerning the inland flotilla would have been disastrous. The matter of the Hazen court-martial was more serious and less admirably managed.

Moses Hazen was almost as complex a character as Arnold, frequently the object of suspicion, yet often an important and useful American officer. He had fought honorably at Crown Point, Louisbourg, Quebec, and Sillery during the Seven Years' War, winning a commendation from General James Wolfe and retiring at half-pay from the 44th Regiment of Foot. A wealthy landowner in Canada by 1775, Hazen's conduct during the Revolution's first year was sufficiently ambivalent to earn the suspicions of both armies. The British imprisoned him for a time, and both they and General Montgomery confiscated his property. He redeemed himself with the Americans during the invasion of Canada, and on January 22, 1776, was commissioned colonel of the Second Canadian Regiment.

Unfortunately, Hazen and Arnold embroiled themselves in a confusing and compromising dispute over confiscated goods, and Arnold charged him with insubordination. Gates authorized a court-martial with Colonel Enoch Poor, at that time commanding the 8th Continental Infantry, presiding. Between them, Arnold and members of the court turned the proceedings into a farce that saw him denouncing the court and challenging its members to duels and the court's refusing to hear his prime witness. After trying to extract an admission of fault from Arnold, Poor turned the minutes over to Gates with the request that Arnold be arrested and the Congress advised of the general's contempt for military law. Arnold, for his part, wanted the delegates to investigate the court's conduct.

Gates reviewed the transcript, dissolved the court, and declined to arrest Arnold, observing in his report to Congress that "the wrath of General Arnold's temper might lead him a little farther than is marked by the precise line of decorum to be observed before and towards a court martial." Understanding the circumstances, continued Gates, "I am convinced if there was a fault on one side there was too much acrimony on the other. Here again I am obliged to act dictatorially and dissolve the court martial. . . . The United States must not be deprived of that officer's services at this critical moment." Gates added that, while he was required to forward the matter to Congress, he believed that the delegates "will view whatever is whispered against General Arnold as the foul stream of that poisonous fountain detraction."[72]

By rescuing Benedict Arnold from almost certain disgrace, Horatio Gates did in fact make sure that "the United States [was] not . . . deprived of that officer's services at [a very] critical moment." It was at this juncture that Arnold went off, prepared his fleet, and fought the battle of Lake Champlain, foiling Sir Guy's 1776 invasion of the Northern colonies.

Schuyler Besieged

While Arnold's ad hoc sailors and Gates' Ticonderoga garrison of Continentals and militiamen thwarted Carleton's designs, military politics continued with barely perceptible abatement. In the midst of an unseemly fight over the Northern Department's commissariat, Walter Livingston, Commissary of Stores and Provisions and a Schuyler protégé, submitted his resignation, which Congress accepted on September 14. On that day Schuyler submitted his own resignation as "a major general in the army of the American States," but promised to remain at his post until a successor was appointed, which he assumed "need not exceed a fortnight."[73]

One can sympathize with the New York general's frustrations and growing suspicions that critics were conspiring against him. But resigning at a juncture when Washington faced victorious Sir William Howe at New York, and the delegates were struggling with more problems than their slender resources were intended to bear, was irresponsible. He knew if Congress accepted his resignation, Horatio Gates would become departmental commander—and he did not intend to advance that rival's cause. Evidence deduced from subsequent events suggest that Schuyler expected Congress to reject his untimely resignation, unequivocally endorse his performance, and "prevail" upon him to continue to command the northern army.[74] If he did, in fact, expect the delegates to respond in that fashion, the sarcastically self-righteous correspondence that soon issued from his pen testified to either self-destructive hubris or a remarkable political ineptitude on the part of a man who was not a political naif.

Schuyler took particular umbrage to a September 14 congressional resolution—passed nine days before receipt of his resignation—consigning fifteen tons of powder, 20,000 flints, and 200 reams of cartridge paper to Gates' Ticonderoga garrison.[75] Because the resolution consigned those supplies "to General Gates for the use of the army in the Northern Department," Schuyler interpreted the measure as by-passing his authority. Not even a letter from hard-pressed General Washington, trying to reassure him that the resolution was a response to a requisition from Gates, and that the words "for use of the Northern army" inferred no denigration of his authority, could mollify him.[76] The department commander's emotion-charged misinterpretation marked the end of the fruitful spirit of cooperation between him and his lieutenant that had prevailed since early July.

Professor Rossie's examination of the political ramifications of the tortured relations with Congress is useful. "Increasingly convinced of Gates' ambition, Schuyler may well have regretted his letter of resignation," writes Rossie. "Needless to say," he continued,

> there was no such regret evinced by the New England congressmen. Elated by Schuyler's resignation, Elbridge Gerry predicted that "harmony will ensue" in the Northern Department. There was another reason to rejoice. "We have obtained Colonel Moylan's resignation and General Mifflin is come again into the office of quartermaster general," he jubilantly informed Gates on September 27. Thus the Lee-Adams junto—the powerful congressional faction led by the Lees of Virginia and the Adamses of Massachusetts of which Gerry was a member—could be well satisfied. Bound together by the common conviction that reconciliation [with Britain] was now hopeless, the junto sought to advance those who shared that belief. . . . Livingston had been disposed of, Schuyler was on his way out, and Gates would almost certainly succeed to the command of the Northern Department.[77]

The anti-Schuyler faction's rejoicing proved premature. Its members underestimated the political skills of another strong bloc—one not yet fully committed to independence, but very committed to General Schuyler and, like him, "reluctant revolutionaries."

The New York Convention immediately took the offensive with a "spirited remonstrance" warning that "fatal and total destruction" would follow if Schuyler ceased to command in the North. Connecticut delegate William Williams suspected that Schuyler had personally initiated the remonstrance.[78] Congress appointed Edward Rutledge and William Hooper of North Carolina and Thomas McKeen of Delaware to take the remonstrance under consideration and report back. All three were known Schuyler partisans, and Phillip Livingston assured the convention's president that their report would "without question, be satisfactory."[79]

Williams correctly predicted that Schuyler's advocates would be so numerous and aggressive that those who would have been willing to accept his resignation "will give way to such a torrent in his favor for the sake of peace." President Hancock rather abjectly apologized to the general for tardiness in responding to letters, pleading the press of business, and promised to mend his ways. More important, Congress on October 2 resolved:

> That the president be desired to write to General Schuyler, and inform him that the Congress cannot consent, during the present situation of our affairs, to accept his resignation, but request, that he continue the command which he now holds; that he be assured, that aspertions [sic], which his enemies have thrown against his character, have had no influence upon the minds of the members of this house, who are fully satisfied of his attachment to the cause of freedom, and are willing to bear testimony of the many services which he has rendered to his country; and that, in order effectually to put calumny to silence, they will, at an early date, appoint a committee of their body, to enquire fully into his conduct, which, they trust, will establish his reputation in the opinion of all good men.[80]

The resolution was not a model of consistent logic. After declining to accept the general's resignation, condemning critics of his performance for casting aspersions upon his character, and fulsomely praising him, it promised expeditiously to appoint commissioners to "enquire fully into his conduct," trusting their inquiry would confirm the delegates' opinion. There was sound logic behind the internal contradictions, even if first glance suggests otherwise. The resignation's timing virtually insured its rejection. On August 27, the British had driven Washington from Long Island to Manhattan, which he had to abandon, leaving New York City to the enemy. It seemed for a while that the American army's central force might disintegrate. Schuyler and both his supporters and his critics knew this, and the delegates' resolution reflected fundamental reality. Schuyler had adroitly maneuvered the Congress into endorsing his stewardship.

Nor was the general finished with Congress. Before passing its resolution of October 2, it had, on September 25, enacted another one that appointed commissioners to "consult with the commanding officer of the northern department, and such other officers as may be thought proper." Because Congress had not yet acted upon his resignation, Schuyler was still commanding the Northern Department, and thus was the one, pending that action, with whom Congress' agents would consult.

But the general interpreted the matter very differently. In a letter dated September 27, and before formal rejection of the resignation, President Hancock informed Schuyler that the commissioners were on their way to discuss with him matters pertaining to his command. Schuyler, on October 6, instructed Hancock that he had erred in notifying him because "I find by the resolution of 25th ult. that the commissioners are to confer with General Gates," wrote Hancock. "My name is not so much as mentioned in any of the resolutions of that except in the second, and by that it would seem as if I acted under General Gates. Indeed from the resolution of that day it seemed unnecessary to have sent me any of the other papers, as it strongly implied that I do not any longer command in this department."[81] He also wrote to Washington on the same day that, without advising him that his resignation had been received and that he no longer commanded the Northern Department, Congress was sending George Clymer of Pennsylvania and Richard Stockman of New Jersey on their way to Ticonderoga to consult Gates "with respect to the army under his command."[82]

The general's letters to Hancock and Washington were not consistent with the facts. The resolution of September 25 contained no reference to Gates, but did refer to Schuyler twice. Schuyler either misrepresented the resolution's language or, on the basis of erroneous information, was responding without having seen it. His letter to Washington with the quotation concerning Clymer and Stockton was made up out of the whole cloth. Congress did not name the delegates until September 26, and their instructions did not direct them to confer with Gates.[83]

General Washington chose to ignore Schuyler's letter. So, once again from his Saratoga country house, Schuyler picked up his quill and wrote to Hancock a letter dated October 16. "The calumny of my enemies has risen to its height, their malice is incapable of heightening the injury," blasted Schuyler, who continued:

> I wish for the sake of nature they had not succeeded so well, I wish they had not been countenanced by the transactions of those whose duty it was to have supported me. In the alarming situation of our affairs, I shall continue to act some time longer, but Congress must prepare to put the care of this department into other hands: I shall be able to render my country better services in another line, less exposed to the repetition of the injuries I have sustained.[84]

The general's complaints were unwarranted. Congress had done more than confirm him in his command. It had expressed itself fully satisfied with his dedication to the common cause and acceded to his own request for an enquiry "effectually to put calumny to silence." Schuyler responded by yet again offering to resign, accusing the delegates of conspiring with his critics.

One week later he fired another salvo in his attack on Congress. This time, Schuyler alleged that its August 17 resolution exonerating General David Wooster of misconduct was

> couched in such terms as to leave even to the candid and judicious no alternative but that of supposing that Canada was not properly supplied either by Congress or me. Judge on whom the public censure would fall and let every gentleman in Congress fancy himself in my situation. . . . Is it consistent with the dignity which should be inseparable with the most respectable body on earth, partially and precipitantly to enter into a resolution which leaves so much room for the public to consider me a faithless servant? Deeply sensible of the injury I have sustained from the hand which ought to have supported me, I shall endeavor to be patient [and] do my duty in this critical juncture with zeal, alacrity and firmness.[85]

Even loyal supporters found that letter distressing. When the delegates acquitted Wooster, they did nothing to impugn Schuyler's integrity and devotion. If, as Robert R. Livingston warned him, they should have to choose between him and Congress, "your very friends must take part against you, or contribute to lessen the influence of a body on whose power their very salvation depends. Should any unfortunate accident happen, it would be charged and perhaps justly, to your precipitate conduct (for such it would be called) & God knows whether you could escape the blind resentments of the people."[86]

Schuyler's faithful friend Edward Rutledge undertook to repair the general's relations with Congress with a proposal that Schuyler come to Philadelphia to confer with the delegates, who, after hearing his plans for defeating Carleton's "making an Impression from Canada; and having obtained full powers for that purpose, let him return to his command to carry those measures into execution." Since Schuyler already possessed all the powers that Congress could grant, Rutledge probably hoped that the general's presence would be enough to confound his critics. He also noted that a visit from Schuyler would also have a much-desired political result, by helping suppress democratic "popular spirit."[87]

Gates on the March

Sir William Howe's successes against Washington on Manhattan and in New Jersey aborted Schuyler's projected visit. After failing to raise an adequate response from Pennsylvania and New Jersey militias, Congress on November 23 resolved "That General Washington be directed forthwith to order, under his immediate command, such of the forces, now in the Northern Department, as have been raised by the states of Pennsylvania and New Jersey."[88] Because Carleton had by that time withdrawn into Canada, veteran soldiers could safely march south to reinforce Washington's disintegrating Grand Army.

After a summer of defeat, retreat, and despair, the troops under the commander-in-chief's immediate command were reduced to a total of 3,765 "Present Fit for Duty & on Duty."[89] Ignorant of Howe's decision to suspend operations and bivouac his army on the Delaware River side, Washington feared an attack on Philadelphia. His existing force was too small to defend the city. Since many of the men's enlistments expired December 1, and most of the rest would be free to leave at the year's end, survival required early and effective reinforcement.

On November 26, Washington ordered Gates to march the New Jersey and Pennsylvania Continental regiments to Philadelphia.[90] Gates had anticipated Washington's need when, on November 15, he wrote to Schuyler that he believed Howe's objective was the American capital, and that a "large body of Troops could not be too soon assembled upon the west side of the Delaware." Gates, therefore, would order eight Continental regiments to march to Albany for winter quarters, "or be at Hand to Succour the Southern Army, as occasion might require."[91]

After receiving Schuyler's order to place Colonel Anthony Wayne of the 4th Pennsylvania Battalion in command at Ticonderoga, Gates started southward with eight regiments on December 2.[92] Six days later, when they were in Orange County, the New York Council of Safety urged Gates to join forces with Generals Charles Lee and George Clinton, who together had a combined Continental and militia force of about 9,000 men.[93]

Washington had detached Lee for service east of the Hudson, but when conditions worsened in New Jersey he urged him to rejoin the main army. Contemptuous of Washington's capacity for command, Lee responded with perilous tardiness. The Council of Safety's members wanted to retain Lee's, Clinton's, and Gates' forces to defend the Hudson Valley. Ignoring Washington's and the nation's greater need, Lee contributed an unpalatable morsel to the disgusting stew when, on December 13, early on the same day that a British patrol captured him, he wrote Gates a letter condemning Washington's allowing Fort Washington to fall, with the gratuitous observation that he had "unhing'd the goodly fabrick we had been building—there never was so damn'd a stroke—entre nous, a certain great man is damnably deficient."[94]

Gates immediately rejected the Council's proposal to join with Lee and Clinton, and persuaded its members that what they suggested was patently foolish.[95] Since it was clear the general was determined to join Washington, the Council's spokesman informed him that Clinton would accept orders respecting his New York militia.[96] Although Gates would have been very pleased to add the militiamen to his force, they were unwilling to leave their state, and Gates lacked the authority to coerce them.

After a march marked by rain and snow, Gates led his column across the Delaware during December 16 and arrived at Washington's camp on the twenty-second. Once reunited with the commander-in-chief, Gates volunteered advice that, fortunately, Washington rejected: withdraw across the Delaware and abandon Philadelphia. Gates believed the retreat from New York City and across New Jersey had so demoralized the soldiers that they could not be rallied north of Maryland.[97] But Washington, reinforced by the 600 effectives Gates brought in and approximately 2,000 Pennsylvania militia, had a total of

7,659 men. And it was with those soldiers that Washington wrought the miracle of Trenton-Princeton.[98]

Gates, however, did not participate in that miracle. With Washington's assent, he rode to Baltimore, whence Congress had adjourned because of Philadelphia's vulnerability. The general claimed that his health had so declined as to limit his capacity for active combat command. Critics, however, have unfairly attributed Gates' trip to a combination of cowardice and ambition. But at least three contemporaries who were in a position to know—Thomas Nelson, Elbridge Gerry, and John Hancock—referred to his poor health in correspondence.[99]

Professor David Nelson, who carefully studied the details of the general's career, argued that if ambition was Gates' lodestar, he would not have absented himself from Washington's staff. "In fact, if politics had been uppermost in his mind, he would have realized that to serve under Washington in a military skirmish . . . could only bolster his reputation with Congress, not to mention with Washington himself," explained Nelson, "who would certainly have appreciated Gates' remaining with him in an hour of need. Better to have arrived on the doorstep of Congress as a victorious, or even defeated, general who had stood high in Washington's favor than to sit idly by while others fought.[100]

Gates reached Baltimore on December 28, and he certainly contacted delegates who had supported him and still favored a change in the northern command, as is reflected in Samuel Adams' note to kinsman John: "Congress is very attentive to the northern army and care is taken effectually to supply it with everything necessary this winter for the next campaign."[101] The New England-Virginia bloc continued intent on replacing Philip Schuyler.

The Vexatious Problem of Rank: Appointments, Seniority, Promotions, and Assignments

The Congress that convened in Baltimore at the end of 1776 included a number of new, inexperienced delegates, some of whom lacked their predecessors' political acuity. Pressing problems tested them. The national military establishment needed enlarging and staffing, and the chronically inefficient logistical system had to be reformed if the army were to survive. Personal ambition, provincial jealousies, and philosophical principle made Congress' task more difficult than a catalogue of issues would reveal.

Take, for instance, the need to create a larger army. How large must it be? How should its ranks be filled? Hard experience convinced many officers that they could not win the war without a large regular army that could quickly respond to enemy initiative or exploit promising opportunities. On September 16, while Washington was directing the successful delaying skirmish at Harlem Heights, Congress authorized enlisting eighty-eight regiments through state quotas "to serve during the present war." Units already enrolled and recruited for the war's duration would be counted toward the total authorized strength. Every enlisted man would receive a bounty of twenty dollars and entitlement to allotments of 100 acres. Officers received congressional commissions, but "the appointment of all officers and filling up vacancies (except general officers) [would] be left to the governments of the several states."[102]

Conceding the power to appoint company and field grade officers to the states did not resolve a fundamental issue. Did ultimate authority over the Continental Army reside in the states or with Congress? If the latter was, in reality, "merely a forum for the individual states, then the appointment of officers and their promotions should rest with the states. If, on the other hand, Congress was more than the sum of its parts, then it should exercise the final authority in all matters touching upon the Continental Army—including the promotion of its officers." Some delegates realized that dividing the appointment authority posed more problems than it solved. Fearing that the states would appoint unqualified men, Congress requested of General Washington that he send it a list of officers he wished to have retained in the army. Congress expected to "send the list with a Member of Congress to their respective states who have been ordered to stress the necessity of appointing men of education . . . ."[103]

Matters came to a head during February 1777, when Washington notified Congress that it needed to appoint three major generals and ten brigadiers. The delegates responded with a debate that Thomas Burke of North Carolina described as "perplexed, inconclusive, and irksome."[104] There was general dissatisfaction with the performance of several commanders, and members disagreed about how to select and promote generals. John Adams, who was disinclined to view them with awe, wrote to his wife Abigail that "Schuyler, Putnam, [Joseph] Spencer, and [William] Heath, are thought by very few to be capable of the great commands they hold. . . . I wish they would all resign."[105] Although Adams himself had faults that some contemporaries delighted to contemplate, he also enjoyed important assets, among them intelligence and honesty—and other testimony supports his statement. Schuyler, for example, had more critics than committed champions, and "Old Put" was often an object of condescension that approached ridicule. In 1779, Major General Alexander McDougall described Spencer as a fool and Heath as an "honest, obstinate man." Consistent with his distrust of generals, Adams suggested, "For my part I will vote upon the general principles of a republic for a new election of general officers annually, and every man shall have my consent to be left out, who does not give sufficient proof of qualifications."

Other delegates were not ready to go along with Adams' application of the ancient practices of the Roman Republic. Some believed that the Congress should establish rules for promotion, and proposed several. Delegates from Virginia, Maryland, and North Carolina proposed that the states recommend appointments based upon the number of men they provided: "three battalions, one brigadier, nine [battalions] one major general;" the members rejected that apportionment. Some delegates favored the simple solution of promoting according to seniority.[106] Others, however, found that criterion unacceptable. Thomas Burke had an idealistically orderly streak that found expression in a profound distress at Congress' failure to agree upon a standard for promotions, and that led him to favor basing promotion upon the number of regiments [battalions] raised by the states.[107]

Everyone agreed that, regardless of the standard adopted, Congress had to reserve the right to reward outstanding merit. Finally, on February 19, the delegates passed a resolution intended to be a compromise including all the diverse proposals: "That in voting for general officers, a due regard shall be had to the line of succession, the merit of the person proposed, and the quota of the troops raised, and to be raised, by each state."[108] That catch-all effort to comprehend every shade of opinion so nearly approached the meaningless that it, when applied, worked manifest injustice to Benedict Arnold, John Stark, Jedediah Huntington, and Jeremiah Wadsworth. "The overall effect of the promotions was to breed dissatisfaction among many of the officers who felt they were unjustly passed over, and to pose a dilemma for Congress," summarized one scholar. Many high-ranking officers were unfit for command, but if Congress ignored their seniority and promoted more capable junior officers, "it was subjected to insults and threats." Contrarily, if Congress tried to promote men solely on seniority, its efforts were lampooned "by those states whose tardy support of the war had deprived them of general officers, while the present quotas of troops they were contributing entitled them to positions of high rank. But if Congress chose to take this into consideration, and thereby passed over able senior officers from states which had their 'quota' of generals, then they did these men an injustice and risked their resignations."[109]

Application to Schuyler and Gates

The politics of appointments and mutual resentments produced the poisoned environment into which the Gates-Schuyler contest for the northern command was revived by another exercise in politics. On September 12, 1776, Gates named John Trumbull, artist son of Connecticut Governor Jonathan Trumbull, deputy adjutant general of the Northern Department. The young man did not receive his commission until February 22, 1777—more than five months after Gates named him. Noting that he had been serving as acting deputy in that position since June 28, 1776, Trumbull asked Congress to date his commission from that date.[110] It was an unexceptional request, but personalities and politics kept compliance with it from being routine. Four factors were at play: 1) The president of the Continental Congress, John Hancock, did not like the Trumbulls; (2) Gates made the appointment, a fact that could not fail to embarrass Trumbull with Schuyler's supporters; (3) The delegates were in a testy mood about appointments and criticism; and (4) Trumbull couched his request in terms that fed that mood. He believed he was the object of deliberate animosity, not the victim of an oversight caused by the press of business, and so he intended to "lay aside my cockade and sword."[111] Gates, together with Trumbull's friend and supporter James Lowell, tried to persuade him not to resign. The major general asked Hancock to recommend that the commission be "reinstated from the time of his embarking with me at New York, to join the Northern Department."[112] The delegates, though, were by now quite impatient with complaining letters from officers, including an especially hectoring one that arrived from the pen of General Schuyler.[113] A less-provocative request from young Trumbull would have mollified them, but his response was so belligerent that they resolved to ask Gates to select a replacement; Trumbull resigned.[114]

While young Trumbull was busy irritating members of Congress, Gates was lingering on their doorstep, playing the game that engaged 18th-century generals: politics. New Englanders were especially hospitable. When they learned Sir Henry Clinton had captured Newport, Rhode Island, Samuel Adams and other Yankees suggested that Gates or Nathanael Greene (another favorite of theirs) be detailed to retake the town. Washington aborted that scheme when he replied that Benedict Arnold and Joseph Spencer had received the assignment.[115]

On February 5, Washington made Gates commandant at Philadelphia.[116] Fifteen days later Congress resolved that future enlistments be for three years or the war's duration, and that Gates resume the post of adjutant general.[117] Washington endorsed the proposal. "I look upon your resumption of the Office," he wrote Gates, "as the only means of giving form and regularity to our new army."[118] Gates was now firmly impaled on the horns of a dilemma, torn between his ambition for an independent command and not offending Washington and friendly delegates. He hesitated to place himself again under the commander-in-chief's personal command., and knew that his supporters were working to have him replace Schuyler in the Northern Department, whose commander would preside over the campaign to repel the next British invasion. Most of the soldiers for that campaign would come from New England, and few northerners believed Schuyler was the leader who would successfully turn back the invaders.

Working to Schuyler's disadvantage was his chronically unpleasant relations with Congress, which worsened as the general, convinced that the delegates harbored men committed to his downfall, penned a succession of letters reflecting his frustrations and suspicions. Certainly many facts justified his suspicions, and military conditions in the North would have frustrated a commander more resourceful than Schuyler. But the tone of his correspondence discomfited his supporters and was grist for his critics' mill.

In its December 9, 1776, issue, Hugh Gaines' *Gazette and Weekly Mercury* published what purported to be an intercepted letter from Commissary Joseph Trumbull to Delegate William Williams of Connecticut. Williams, a veteran of the Seven Years' War, signer of the Declaration of Independence, a dedicated patriot who on several occasions volunteered his money and credit to the Revolutionary cause, was an implacable Schuyler critic. The letter attributed to Trumbull contained an "odious suspicion" of Schuyler's character.[119]

Believing in the letter's authenticity was easy enough for Schuyler: he had opposed Joseph Trumbull's appointment, and he knew of Williams' open opposition to himself. On February 4, 1777, Schuyler wrote a letter upbraiding Congress for not immediately defending him against his calumniators.[120] The letter did nothing but fuel the increasingly adversarial climate and convince Congress to resolve

That it is altogether improper and inconsistent with the dignity of this Congress, to interfere in the disputes subsisting among officers of the army; which ought to be settled, unless they can be otherwise accommodated, in a court martial, agreeable to the rules of the army; and that the expressions in General Schuyler's letter of the 4th of February, "that he confidently expected Congress would have done him justice, which it was in their power to give, and which he humbly conceives that they ought to have done," were, to say the least, ill-advised and highly indecent.[121]

President Hancock informed the general of the resolution and advised him to moderate his style. Schuyler ignored that wise counsel and decided to plead his case before Congress as a member of the New York delegation, departing Albany on March 24. In the meantime the Adams duo introduced, and the delegates passed, a resolution installing General Gates as the independent commander at Fort Ticonderoga. Hancock executed the resolution on March 25, directing Gates to "immediately repair to Ticonderoga, and take command of the army there."[122] By underlining those six words, Congress made clear its intent: Schuyler retained nominal command of the department, but Gates would be the operational commander—a point accented by Gates' being permitted to select Major General Arthur St. Clair as his second-in-command.

The politics of command was producing ill-conceived decisions that could only exacerbate a disgraceful commingling of ambition, factionalism, and provincialism that corrupted all parties.

Gates Takes Charge

When Horatio Gates reached Albany on April 17, Schuyler had already left to attend Congress, leaving Gates the senior officer present. Establishing his headquarters in Albany, he promptly began to function as de facto department commander, technically exceeding the authority granted him by Congress. But the Northern Department had to be prepared to meet the challenge of the renewed offensive every informed person expected would come during the upcoming summer. The northern winter had severely limited what could be done, and April was rapidly drawing to a close. A commander attending Congress could not make the daily decisions now required.

This does not mean Schuyler had been derelict in his duties. Plagued as he was by poor health, he had done what he could to administer his extensive department and perform his duties as Indian Commissioner. Acutely conscious of American vulnerability in the Mohawk Valley, he had assigned French engineer Captain B. de la Marquisie to rebuild the ruined Fort Schuyler [Stanwix] (although that assignment did not end satisfactorily, as previously discussed). Before he left he replaced Colonel Samuel Elmore's Connecticut troops with Colonel Peter Gansevoort's 3rd New York Regiment of the Continental Line.[123] Preparations at Forts Stanwix and Dayton had a special urgency because Schuyler and Washington expected the next invasion would descend the Mohawk Valley, reversing Jeffrey Amherst's 1760 route. Schuyler felt more secure about the Champlain-Hudson country, with its massive Fort Ticonderoga standing athwart that route.

But Gates rightly believed that preparations to repel the coming British campaign could not be deferred until the uncertain date of Schuyler's return. Conditions at Ticonderoga were especially worrisome. Much of the barracks' fabric was ruined, and the barracks were too far from the defensive works. An undiplomatic plea to Washington for tents succeeded only in irritating the commander-in-chief. Supplies desperately needed at the fort were lying undelivered in the Albany depot.[124]

Expecting the British to field more than 11,000 men, Gates sent a requisition for 13,600 men to Congress. But the New England militia was tardy in arriving, and Gates, darling of the region's legislators, asked Joseph Trumbull, "What infatuation has Seized my Yankees [?] They take the Field as tardily as if they were going to be hanged."[125]

Loyalism was strong in New York, and Gates committed soldiers to dealing out summary judgment. He evinced more satisfaction with their effectiveness than the facts justified when he told Hancock that Toryism was "diminished this way; About Twenty have been killed . . . many are in the several Goals [jails] of this and Neighboring Counties, and the rest offer to Surrender."[126]

Gates must have realized there were officers in the Northern Department whose loyalty to General Schuyler was undiminished, and he could not have been surprised to learn that Lieutenant Colonel Richard Varick, the Deputy Commissary General of Muster and erstwhile aide to Schuyler, was corresponding with the general. Schuyler asked Varick to learn all that he could about the ramifications of Gates' appointment to Ticonderoga. After conversations with Dr. Jonathan Potts and Colonel Morgan Lewis, both Gates confidantes, Varick reported, "I have the greatest pause of suspicion, that there is more on the carpet, than either he [Potts] or Col. Lewis choose to have mentioned to any person who they are not certain of being equall[y] prejudiced in General Gates favor as themselves." Gates made a point of letting the young colonel know that the correspondence had been intercepted. A justifiably dismayed Varick wrote Schuyler on April 18, "It is rumored that he [Gates] is to command in the department & that he has the appointment of all the staff for this army."[127] Divided loyalties, however natural, did not augur well for affairs in the North.

An important product of Gates' brief stay in Albany was his analysis of what he expected the enemy to undertake during 1777. General Howe's primary objective would be the conquest of New York state by effecting a junction of troops from New York City with an invading expedition from Canada. Interestingly, Gates anticipated that Sir William, either deluded by non-military factors or acting upon uninformed orders from London, might be so distracted as to undertake to capture Philadelphia. Whatever happened, Gates expected that the British army in Canada would advance south along the Champlain-Hudson line, with Fort Ticonderoga its first objective.[128] The unfolding of events during 1777 confirmed his analysis. Horatio Gates was no military genius, but he did possess a core of professionalism that served the Americans well during this critical period.

Push Comes to Shove

While Gates worked to prepare the Northern Department for the inevitable invasion, important events moved Congress into another chapter in the politics of command. And it finally gave Schuyler the formal inquiry he craved. Since no one had charged him with any offence, nor had he been the object of any action that dishonored him, some delegates opposed the inquiry, arguing that it was in itself an implied censure. The New York members, however, effectively countered with the question, "If the general had done his duty faithfully, why was his authority pared away to nothing and the command of the army, in effect, transferred from him to General Gates, a junior officer?"[129] Congress responded on April 17 by appointing a thirteen-member committee to investigate the total record of Schuyler's service.[130]

Everyone expected the committee to vindicate the general. But Gates' continued service as field commander with extraordinary authority was incompatible with Schuyler's powers as department commander. The latter rightly recognized the delegates' inconsistency in retaining him in command in his department while bestowing upon Gates a separate command that made him the effective commanding general in the North. Schuyler would not agree to serving at Albany unless he received absolute command "over every part of the Northern department"; he would return to Albany only as a civilian.[131] Three days after making that declaration, he informed Washington that he intended to resign.[132]

A summary of the rather complex military-political situation is in order: Gates commanded at Ticonderoga with authority that made him the Northern Department's field commander and, in Schuyler's absence, de facto department commander as senior officer present; Schuyler, the department's commander, was attending Congress as a New York delegate, intent upon salvaging his military reputation and authority; Congress instituted an investigation, at the general's insistence, into his conduct that everyone expected would endorse his stewardship in the North; Schuyler threatened to resign if Gates occupied a command at Ticonderoga that was, in reality, independent of the department commander; and finally, Schuyler's opponents intended for Gates to emerge as northern commander.

Those men who desired Gates' elevation to northern commander were too optimistic. They underestimated the pro-Schuyler faction's political resourcefulness and their grasp of logic. In the first place, that faction undertook more than just obtaining an endorsement of the general's past performance—they sought to restore him to unqualified command. To that end, they exploited the accurate perception that New York harbored many who would welcome British success. Only General Schuyler's military and political leadership stanched the flow of disaffected folk into overt Toryism. To remove him just as a King's army was poised to enter the state would ensure its loss.

The shift in sentiment occurring as the delegates deliberated both disappointed and angered Gates. He saw no reason why the man commanding on the northern frontier should not have his headquarters at Ticonderoga, just as the British had done during the Seven Years' War. The fort was the primary obstacle on the invasion route and would be the enemy's first objective. Further, it acted as the nerve center for any defensive action to interdict that route, and was where the general directing the American forces should be—and Gates was determined to be that general. Gates resolved not to serve on the front if Schuyler were to exercise superior command at Albany. If that was Congress' will, he would request dismissal from its service.[133]

With the able leadership of New York delegates, General Schuyler's supporters rallied to vindicate the general and have him exonerated of all accusations of improprieties in managing funds sent during 1775 for operations in Canada. The general submitted a remonstrance to Congress that justified "himself in every particular."[134] The delegates responded by resolving that his "memorial was satisfactory, and that the Congress entertained the same favorable opinion of the general as they entertained before passing the resolution"—which constituted "a complete and honorable vindication of the general's character and conduct." The New Yorkers believed that neither they nor Schuyler had to worry about the thirteen-member committee's inquisition.[135]

That optimism received official confirmation when, on May 15, the Board of War recommended to Congress

> That Major General Schuyler be directed to proceed to the Northern department, and take upon himself the command there. . . . That a letter be written by the President to Major General Gates, informing him, that Major General Schuyler is ordered to take upon him the command of the Northern department; and that Congress remains desirous that Major General Gates should make his own choice, either to continue in the command of the Northern department, under General Schuyler; or to take upon him the Office of Adjutant General in the Grand Army immediately under the Commander in chief, with the rank he now holds.[136]

The Board's recommendation offered Gates the Hobson's choice between serving as Schuyler's subordinate or accepting the post of adjutant general—which in February had been deemed a demotion, and under the conditions obtaining in May would be even more demeaning.

Gates' supporters attacked the Board's report, but—by a vote of five states to four, with two divided and two not present—the delegates accepted it on May 22. The New England states—excepting Rhode Island, which had no delegates present—and Richard Henry Lee opposed acceptance. The majority of the Virginia delegates, Maryland, New York, North and South Carolina, and Pennsylvania voted to return Schuyler to the Northern Department. Georgia and New Jersey divided. The unexpected Virginia majority for Schuyler was decisive.[137]

Jonathan Trumbull and James Lowell immediately reported Congress' action to Gates, who was outraged, as his opponents had expected and hoped he would be.[138] He had, after all, on the eleventh of the month declared that he would seek an "Honourable Dismission" if his cause did not prevail. However, if they were intent on calling his bluff, he frustrated them by obtaining

Schuyler's permission to appear before Congress. His opponents were not deeply disturbed by the prospect of his demanding a hearing, believing themselves "indifferent about his resentment."[139]

At Roger Sherman's request, Gates on June 18 gained admittance before the delegates "to communicate Intelligence of importance."[140] Prefacing his presentation with a few general remarks, he quickly turned to his reason for appearing before men who "a few days since without having given any cause of offence, without accusation, without trial, without hearing, without notice" had reduced him by supercession, and proceeded to denounce the New York delegates, especially James Duane, as authors of his humiliation. During the donnybrook that ensued, the New Yorkers demanded his expulsion, while New Englanders clamored for him to be heard. The former prevailed, and Gates withdrew.[141]

The fiasco was a thoroughly unedifying performance during which the general and those who had urged him to appear made a serious tactical blunder that played into the hands of the New Yorkers. Just a few months earlier in February, not a single delegate from that state had attended the Continental Congress; its influence was at low ebb. But by mid-April, William Duer, John Jay, Philip Livingston, and James Duane led a six-man delegation, and by the end of June those able men had conducted a bold campaign that salvaged General Schuyler's career and seized the initiative in ordering affairs on the northern frontier.

Candid and perceptive men spelled out to Gates the nuances of the politics of command. The Congress had really not intended for him to command the Northern Department. Hubris and political machinations had misled him. Though he now realized that he and his partisans had made a fool of him, he neither resigned nor continued to protest. A cool-headed reassessment revealed his situation to be less bleak than it had seemed. Schuyler was running against Brigadier General George Clinton for governor of New York. If, as seemed probable, the former won election, Gates would succeed him in the Northern Department. State domestic politics promised to give him what the politics of command had withheld.

With John Burgoyne preparing to invade, the time for the commander of the department charged with repelling that invasion to seek the governorship of the state that would be the invasion's theater was unpropitious; but Schuyler, expecting to win, did not campaign aggressively. To Schuyler's and Gates' shared surprise, George Clinton won the election. Schuyler was less popular with farmers and tradesmen than with the state's political and social elite, and

Clinton was a formidable popular leader. Thus, Schuyler continued as department commander.

The War Intervenes in the Politics

It was during this point that Burgoyne re-took Ticonderoga without an assault. On July 8, three days after the Americans evacuated the great northern citadel, Congress disposed of Gates by ordering him "to repair to headquarters and follow the directions of General Washington."[142] While he awaited the commander-in-chief's orders, he made a brief visit to his home at Traveller's Rest. After returning to duty he again rejected the post of adjutant general, and Washington placed him in temporary command of General Benjamin Lincoln's division. On July 24, Lincoln had gone northward to take charge of organizing the Northern Department's New England militia.[143]

In a series of further reverses, Schuyler's main force retreated southward, to the accompaniment of a rising chorus of criticism of the general's conduct of the defensive campaign. Even men who had steadfastly supported him were having second thoughts. His future son-in-law, Alexander Hamilton, admitted in a letter to Robert R. Livingston that "I am forced to suppose him inadequate to the important command with which he has been intrusted. There seems to be no firmness in all his actions . . . ."[144] By early August, the Americans had retreated to Stillwater on the Hudson's west side, where they began preparing field fortifications. But after eleven days Schuyler again ordered his men to retreat, and by August 18 his main camp was only nine miles from Albany.

Meanwhile, Congress and Washington received news of Fort Ticonderoga's loss with shocked disbelief. The commander-in-chief took what tardy measures he could to relieve the pressure on Schuyler by marching from Middlebrook, New Jersey, to Morristown, posting General John Sullivan at Pompton, and sending General Samuel Holden Parsons to relieve John Nixon's brigade at Peekskill, so that it could rush northward to reinforce Schuyler.

As noted in the previous chapter, Arthur St. Clair, Ticonderoga's commander, became the scapegoat upon whom everyone, including Schuyler, placed the blame for not repulsing the enemy. But Schuyler, as he had in 1776, also held New England responsible, arguing that if that region had reinforced him the fort would not have fallen. He conveniently ignored the fact that in March, Washington had diverted most of the New England units intended for Ticonderoga to New Jersey and Peekskill, a deployment of which Schuyler was properly informed. Schuyler characterized the replacements he did receive as being one-third blacks and boys, then assured Washington that he would smile "with contempt on the malice of my enemies, and attempt to deserve your esteem, which will console me for the abuse which thousands may unjustly throw out against me."[145] New Englanders eagerly entered the lists against their old adversary, accurately gauging the shift taking place when Congress communicated directly with Benedict Arnold without going through Schuyler. The politicians directed the former to assemble militia to "check the progress of Gen. Burgoyne, as very disagreeable consequences may be apprehended, if the most vigerous [sic] measures are not taken to oppose him."[146]

Others, including some New Yorkers who had special cause for concern—their state was, after all, the one most immediately affected by Burgoyne's invasion—wanted Schuyler and St. Clair called to account. On July 26, New Jersey delegate Jonathan Sargeant introduced and Daniel Roberdeau of Pennsylvania seconded a motion to recall both men and direct Gates to replace Schuyler.[147] During the debate that followed, New England delegates, anticipating victory, argued that both St. Clair and Schuyler had forfeited their soldiers' confidence. Exaggerating the role of the militia, they claimed that, while their region's militiamen would not serve under the Northern Department's senior generals, they would gladly do so under Gates. More damaging to Schuyler was that New Yorkers had come to share the growing disaffection—a fact of which the general was painfully aware.[148] Congressional opponents engaged in some hyperbole in limning Gates' comparative military virtues.[149]

Opponents of Sargeant's motion were quite willing to recall St. Clair and investigate his evacuation of Ticonderoga, but recalling Schuyler was another matter. Conditions in the North, not the general, were to blame they argued—neglecting to remember that they and the department commander bore at least some of the responsibility for those conditions. In light of those conditions, they claimed, no one could have repelled the enemy. And, as usual, they charged that Yankee machinations were behind all criticism of the general. Yet, every report from the North made their contentions less plausible. Finally, the New York delegation advised the state's Council of Safety that they doubted the wisdom of continuing to oppose Schuyler's recall and believed doing so would serve neither the general's nor the state's best interests.[150]

On July 29, Congress resolved to inquire into the evacuation of Ticonderoga and Mount Independence and "into the conduct of the general officers at the time of the evaquation." A committee of five members, three of them New Englanders, would recommend the mode for conducting the investigation.[151] James Lowell succinctly assessed the reason for and the risk inhering in the resolution when he wrote to New Hampshire delegate William Whipple that he was certain Gates would receive the northern command, and that "I hope the militia of New England will do justice to our labors by turning out and behaving well. The unpopularity of the Northern commander has been declared a bar to our hopes—therefore the change."[152]

So Congress' delegates had, with varying degrees of willingness, decided to recall their discredited northern generals, leaving Gates as Schuyler's logical replacement. However, the politicians wanted Washington to accept the responsibility of naming "such general officer as he shall think proper" to command the Northern Department.[153] Washington would have none of it. He thanked President Hancock for the "high mark of confidence" that Congress reposed on him, but wished "to be excused. . . ."[154]

No longer able to defer their decision, the delegates on August 4, by a vote of eleven states to one, conferred the northern command upon Horatio Gates.[155]

Summation

Intrigue marked the process by which the Continental Congress chose the commander of the Northern Department, and students have looked upon that intrigue with appropriate distaste. But intrigue characteristically marks struggles for power, and the American Revolution was, in the final analysis, a struggle for power—where it would reside and who would exercise it. Determining who would command the Revolution's forces aptly illustrated that fact.

The loser in the contest for command, Philip Schuyler, deserved well from the country he served. His negotiations with the Abenaki and Iroquois Confederacy were skillful, if not uniformly successful. He administered a wide-flung and difficult command. No available general could have more effectively slowed the British advance between Forts Anne and Edward. Schuyler was also the principal architect of American success in the Mohawk Valley. Unfortunately for the New Yorker, he was not an accomplished strategist or tactician, enjoyed generally poor health, had never personally commanded men in battle, and was not an inspiring leader whose personality and resourcefulness could restore American fortunes in the North.

Horatio Gates, who won the contest, had spent his adult years in military service. In 1777 he received the responsibility for restoring those fortunes. The rest of this study is an account of how he executed that charge.

8

The New Commander Rebuilds

Gates Assembles his Army

The Northern Department's new commander joined its main body of troops in its encampment at the junction of the Hudson and Mohawk rivers on August 19.[1] The men present, about 4,000 fit for duty, were organized into four brigades commanded by Brigadier Generals John Paterson, John Glover, John Nixon, and Ebenezer Learned. Learned's Brigade was on detached service with Major General Benedict Arnold's expedition to relieve Fort Stanwix. Units not assigned to brigades included approximately 300 artillerymen and eighty engineers or artificers.[2] Other departmental troops were in the Mohawk Valley under the overall command of Colonel Goose Van Schaick of the 1st New York Regiment and east of the Hudson and in the Hampshire Grants with Major General Benjamin Lincoln.

Horatio Gates outlined the disposition of the men under his immediate command in an August 22 letter to General Washington:

> . . . I found the main body of the Army encamped upon Van Schaicks Islands, which are made by the Sprouts of the Mohawk River Joining with Hudsons River; Nine Miles North of Albany—A Brigade under Genl. [Enoch] Poor [is] encamped at Londons [Loudon's] Ferry on the so[uth] Bank of the Mohock [sic] River, five miles from hence; a Brigade under Genl. Lincoln, had joined Genl. Stark at Bennington; & a Brigade under Genl. Arnold Marched the 15th to Join the Militia of Tyron [Tryon] County, to raise the Siege of Fort Stanwix. . . .[3]

All of the men at Van Schaick's Islands and Loudon's Ferry were Continentals and overwhelmingly New Englanders: eleven of the fourteen regiments were from Massachusetts, three from New Hampshire.[4] A New York unit, the former 1st Canadian, together with three Massachusetts regiments were operating with Benedict Arnold. The force's preponderance of New Englanders had been an embarrassment to General Schuyler, contributing to his alienation from the men he commanded and compromising his effectiveness. An aggressive and victorious commander could have overcome the inherent sectional imbalance; Schuyler was neither.

George Clinton, New York's first elected governor, acted on August 1 to increase his state's contingent when he complied with a congressional requisition and set in train the mobilization of militia to contribute to the Northern Department's manpower requirements. He dispatched from his capital at Kingston two important letters. One was to Colonel Morris Graham of the Dutchess and Ulster County Militia explaining that "[t]he operations of the Enemy against this State to the Northward as well as the exposed situation of the Southern Counties, renders it expedient to call into actual service a very considerable Proportion of the Militia." Ulster County regiments commanded by Colonels Snyder and Pawling were to supply 160 men each, while four Dutchess County regiments were to supply 350 men each.[5] Clinton's order concluded with this injunction: "As the Safety of the State may depend upon the instant Execution hereof it is expected that the Men to be raised in Consequence of these Orders will be in the City of Albany within ten Days of the Delivery hereof."[6]

Governor Clinton's second letter was to Brigadier General Abraham Ten Broeck, commanding the Albany County Militia, the state's largest military unit. "The late Operations of the Enemy in your Quarter," explained the governor, "renders it necessary to use every Exertion to collect a Force to prevent their pursuing the advantage they have already gained by penetrating farther in this State." He informed the general that he had ordered reinforcements for the garrisons in the Hudson Highlands to enable General Washington "to draw from thence a Part of the Continental Troops to reinforce the Northern Army." He also told Ten Broeck about the orders to the Dutchess and Ulster County militias and directed the militia commander to detach from his brigade 1,000 men in two regiments to reinforce the Northern Department.[7]

The governor's executive acts bore impressively early fruit. Within three weeks, on the day after Gates assumed command, the general was able to issue an order establishing two new regiments of 500 men each from the Albany county force.[8] Colonel Graham's composite regiment from Dutchess and Ulster Counties arrived at Van Schaick's Islands on the last day of August. Thus, all three units ordered north by Governor Clinton on the first day of August had joined Gates by month's end. Two regiments of New York Continentals, the 2nd and 4th, Colonels Philip Van Cortlandt and Henry Beekman Livingston, respectively commanding, arrived on the twenty-second.[9] New York's contributions to the Northern Department's main force now totaled three Continental and three militia regiments.

The 2nd and 4th were in camp only one day when they found themselves on the march to reinforce Arnold's column moving to the relief of the besieged Fort Schuyler. At a council of war convened by him at German Flats on August 20, the expedition's senior officers had resolved to request reinforcements, and Colonel Marinus Willett left for Gates' headquarters to ask for 1,000 light infantry. The department commander did not have them, but he responded by sending the newly-arrived New York infantry regiments. Because British Brigadier Barry St. Leger raised his siege on the same day the units left camp, they returned to camp on the twenty-ninth.[10]

The most important addition to Gates' command joined him on August 30, when Colonel Daniel Morgan arrived with his 451 riflemen.[11] Morgan's Rifle Regiment had its origin in General Washington's creation, during the summer of 1777, of an elite light infantry battalion of 500 picked Continental sharpshooters from western Maryland, Virginia, and Pennsylvania. Most of the Virginians were drafted from Morgan's 11th Virginia Regiment; the others hailed from several Virginia, Maryland, and Pennsylvania regiments. On August 16, the commander-in-chief ordered Morgan to march his new command to Peekskill, New York, where General Israel Putnam would provide boats to transport it to Albany, where Morgan would report to Gates. Washington testified to the confidence he had in the new elite unit when he wrote, "The approach of the Enemy in that Quarter, has made further reinforcement necessary, and I know of no Corps so likely to check their Progress in proportion to its Numbers as that under your command. I have great dependence on you—officers & men, and I am persuaded, you will do honour to yourselves & essential services to your country."[12] Daniel Morgan and his men would justify that confidence.

Gates, however, expected Morgan to join him on the twenty-third with "1,000 Picked men."[13] He was disappointed on both counts: contrary winds delayed departure from Peekskill, and the corps' strength was only slightly more than half the number Gates, for some reason, expected to receive. Finally assured of Morgan's imminent arrival, he wrote to him on August 29 that he had "much satisfaction in being acquainted by General Washington of your march for this Department." Gates had the quartermasters supply Morgan with carriages, tents and other equipment, and usher his men to a camp laid out for them at Loudon's Ferry. He "[d]raughted one Sub[altern], One Serjeant, and One Corporal, Fifteen pickt Men from Each Regiment to Serve with your Corps & under your Command."[14]

While the riflemen settled into their camp, Benedict Arnold returned from the Mohawk Valley with Learned's Brigade. The march to and from Fort Stanwix had been exhausting, leaving ninety-four men "sick-present" and 135 "sick-absent" when it mustered on September 7. Gates ordered the men to rest at the main camp for one day before moving on to Loudon's Ferry at daylight on September 10.[15]

The Challenges of Supply: Ammunition, Clothing, Shoes, Blankets, Bayonets, Wagons . . .

In spite of the department's enhanced numerical strength, its commander still faced formidable tasks to prepare it to defeat enemy designs. He might have rendered them less daunting if he had not summarily rejected General Schuyler's conciliatory overtures. The New Yorker's loyal partisans would probably have been less zealous in their efforts to promote discord among the staff if their patron had received more deferential treatment from his successor. For his part, Schuyler worked diligently to increase the flow of supplies, and he continued to carry out his diplomatic responsibilities in dealing with New York tribes.

Administration consumed endless hours of Gates' time, although in this he was very much in his professional element. Since his days as a brigade major during the previous war, he had acquired additional experience and developed a grasp of detail that helped him be an effective adjutant general during the American army's first year. That background served him well during his early weeks in the Northern Department. He was doubly fortunate that his predecessor was also a skillful administrator. The command that he assumed in mid-August had many problems, but neglected administration was not one of them. However, if the northern army was to become more aggressive, its management had to respond to that posture's demands. Even with good luck, the requirements taxed his competence and patience.

Logistics to support a reversal of American fortunes strained the army's resources. On the day he took command, Gates received a report from Major Ebenezer Stevens, commander of his artillery battalion, directing the general's attention to a "Return of Ordnance Stores wanted in the Northern Department." Twelve ammunition wagons with harness and horse, fifty sets of harness for field pieces, twelve tons of bar lead for musket balls, a ton of 3-pound shot, papers and flannel cartridges, twenty sets of "Mens Harness" to help gunners manhandle their cannon, an ammunition wagon for every regiment, 100 yards of sail cloth for covering ammunition, and twenty tons of grape shot were only some of the supplies required.[16]

Commissary of Artillery Ezekiel Cheever's response to the major's requisition was willing, if discouraging. He could not fill the orders, especially the one for twelve tons of bar lead, for he had no more than five tons in stock. He promised to forward "one half or more, as it may come to hand." The other articles would be on their way "as soon as Q Master Pynchon can furnish teams . . . as fast as in my power."[17] Lieutenant Colonel David Mason, Deputy Commissary-General of Military Stores at Springfield, promised that he would ship the ordnance supplies as soon as teams and guards became available, coupling that positive news with a complaint that Colonel Cheever had assumed unwarranted authority "in relation to the Department of Supplies."[18]

On the day the allegedly officious Cheever penned his discouraging report, Colonel Hugh Hughes, whose post as assistant to Quartermaster General Thomas Mifflin provided him with opportunities to observe the Continental Army's supply operations, responded to Gates' request for additional logistical support. Hughes' letter was an informative yet depressing discussion of the sorry state of affairs obtaining in the Commissary Department:

> . . . In fact the whole Place of Commissaries, Ins and Outs, if I may be allowed to use a vulgar Phrase, look like Cats in a strange Garret at one another, and not one of them knows what he is about[.] Such are the unhappy effects of Shifting Hands in the Midst of a Campaign Sir, and of which, I am well informed, your worthy Predecessor, avows himself the Contriver! I don't verily believe any Age had produced a Mathematician capable of Calculating the Eccentricity of this All-governing Planet.[19]

Procuring adequate clothing and shoes, a chronic problem for all 18th-century armies, was especially critical for the new nation. Commissary of Clothing Major George Measam, Deputy Commissary-General of Purchases

Jacob Cuyler, and other military and civilian agents invested countless hours of continuous effort to provide minimal supplies to the army engaged in an autumn campaign on the northern frontier.

Two days after he took over his new command General Gates received from Major Measam a report that included the welcome news that 1,000 coats and 380 shirts would reach the northern army from Philadelphia. The coats Measam described ranged from red coats faced with red, to blue faced with red, to drab with red, to brown with white; some were faced with green or blue; still others were "Brown turned Green." Few Northern Department soldiers actually wore the "Buff and blue" favored by tradition and patriotic artists.

Less welcome was word that the shipment would include no shoes, the shortage of which never completely ended.[20] Some relief, however, came from Major General William Heath, commander of the Eastern Department, who sent what shoes he could from Massachusetts stores.[21] By the second day of September Measam managed to have 850 pairs available, but of "Good shoes fit for Campaign there is but 606 pairs—Besides which, there are upwards of 300 pairs very Thinn [sic] Pumps, french made, not fit for Campaign purposes."[22]

Major Stevens' letter of September 3 provides a glimpse of the hardships common soldiers suffered when he explicitly described his artillerymen's needs. The gunner asked the general to

> issue an order to the Commissary of Cloathing [sic] to procure sixty blanketts [sic] for my men as they are much in want, having not more at present than six to a Company likewise a proportional number of shoes and Stockings and other Cloathing understanding that some Cloathing and blanketts have arrived [at Albany] and my men being in Suffering Condition is the reason of my application to your honor.[23]

Three days before Gates' men began their march northward, Measam provided encouraging news that he had a "fine parcel of Uniform Coats . . , there is Blue faced red sufficient for two middling full regiments and Brown faced red for one regiment." There were additional articles of clothing at Albany, Boston, and "to the southward." But he needed a full accounting from the regimental quartermasters to match needs with supplies. He did not have enough hats, but he had a "great plenty of Mill's Caps both red and blue which I hope will be a very good substitute."

George Measam's letter provides a rare insight into a neglected subject: the callous indifference some revolutionary officers demonstrated toward their men's welfare. He was keenly aware of the soldiers' physical needs and the difficulties attending meeting even the most basic ones. Blankets were in critically short supply. As of the third of September he had on hand only 187 of them. Dr. Jonathan Potts, deputy director-general of hospitals, was pressing him for as many blankets as he could get. Although shipments made more available, by the tenth Gates told General Schuyler, who wanted some to use in negotiations with Indians, that none were left in the stores. "Some gentlemen are very pressing to obtain the fine Large Blankets," reported Measam, who was disgusted by the entire state of affairs. "I think it not generous of them—taking two Blanket[s] for one person upon your Unlimited order. I have delivered to Col. Kosiceusko [sic] one very fine Large Blanket with which he is not satisfied, he says I will get your positive order for another." The artilleryman took matters into his own hand. "As I am informed there are great numbers in camp without a blanket I thought it not a fair Distribution to give two large Blankets to one man without your particular order upon some particular occasion, and I flatter myself what I have done will meet your approbation."

Gates supported Measam and also approved the distribution of fifty much-needed blankets to the hospital, though fewer than Dr. Potts requested, making the surgeon "angerey [sic]."[24]

General Schuyler conscientiously responded to his successor's letter of September 10 by assuring him, on the eleventh, that he would arrange for moving surplus blankets from Fort Stanwix to the Hudson.[25]

Richard Varick provided General Gates and future students with a brief assessment of three of the army's five brigades (excluding the riflemen and artillerymen) when he reported the results of musters. Nixon's Brigade was "pretty well clothed and well armed except for the want of a few Bayonets, that their arms were clean & in such order as does Honor to the officers commanding them." Inspecting Paterson's Brigade revealed that the soldiers kept their muskets clean but many lacked bayonets and that "most of the Non Commissioned Officers & privates stand greatly in need of Clothing." Learned's field-wise veterans were "well armed, their Arms in good order, but deficient in bayonets, their Clothing is tolerably good."[26] The shortage of bayonets, of course, aggravated a weakness that too often plagued Americans in combat against British regulars.

Requisitioning wagoneers compounded the transport problems. From Albany, less than one day's drive from Gates' headquarters, the army's quartermaster Morgan Lewis wrote, "One of the persons sent out after waggons [sic] has returned Without any Kind of Success. He has brought me a List of Such Persons as have been applied to and refuse to go, who amount to almost forty; most of them alledging [sic] the Want of Drivers in excuse; owing to the late [recent] Draughts of the Militia." Lewis closed with the good news that he had, while writing his letter, learned that one of his assistants, whom he had sent seventy miles downriver, had succeeded in engaging ninety-seven wagons and drivers—a major coup, and one that served Gates well during the shift northward.[27]

The Challenges of Supply: Food

Food was of course vital, and maintaining a consistent, reliable schedule of rations challenged quartermasters and purchasing agents. In 1775, the Continental Congress prescribed a soldier's ration as follows:

> Resolved, That a ration consist of the following kind and quantity of provisions: 1 lb. Beef, or 3/4 lb. Pork or 1 lb. salt fish per day; 3 pints of peas or beans per week, or vegetables equivalent, at one dollar per bushel for peas or beans; 1 pint of rice, or one pint of Indian corn, per man per week; 1 quart of spruce beer or cider per man per day or nine gallons of molasses, per company of 100 men per week; 3 lbs candles to 100 men per week, for guards: 24 lbs soft, 8 lbs hard soap, per 100 men per week.[28]

Officers were authorized extra rations ranging from one for lieutenants to five for a general. Women and children accompanying the army also received a daily ration, and efforts to limit their numbers failed: their presence was an important morale factor for which the army paid a high price in provisions, shelter, and discipline.

Despite whatever Congress might resolve about a soldier's rations, commissioners frequently were unable to procure the prescribed foods. Substitutions were so common as to be the rule. Fresh vegetables were usually impossible to find in sufficient quantities to be significant (spoilage being the main culprit). Beer, cider, and rum were chronically scarce. Wartime inflation, profiteering, and corruption conspired to make providing for the soldiers' needs a thankless and exhausting task.[29]

Poor and inadequate supplies were chronic, but General Schuyler and his agents had forestalled a subsistence crisis during 1777. Their efforts made possible the optimistic report that Deputy Commissioner General for Issues John Bleecker prepared for Jacob Cuyler concerning provisions in store at Albany on the last day of August. On hand were thirty-eight tierce [casks] and twenty-two barrels of bread, sixty barrels of flour, forty cattle, 400 sheep, and sixteen hogsheads and eighty barrels of rum. Future supply seemed assured because

> . . . A large quantity of Flour is minutely Expected in from Esopus and Kinder Hook. The Commissary at New Haven has been wrote to. . . send a thousand barrels of Pork or Beef to the landing at Fish Kill, as soon as the Express return, Genl. shall be made acquainted what I have to depend on from that quarter for Salted meat.—a number of purchasers of Live Stock are Employed in Several parts of New England, so as on Computation, to furnish the army weekly with 100 head of Cattle, but as his Honr. Genl. Gates has by Verbal message of [to] yourself Signified that provisions ought to be made for 15,000 men, the purchases of live Stock shall be increased, and Every measure to the Utmost of my Endeavours shall be pursued to accomplish the Victualling of that Body of Men.[30]

General Gates' administrative experience persuaded him prudently to base his victualing requirements upon the abovementioned projection of 15,000 men. His command never included that large a complement, but given the number of extra rations required for officers and camp followers and the accidents that attended field supply, his projection was realistic. Setting so high a requisite produced increased effort to purchase larger numbers of stock. Even so, the supply of meat failed to keep up with demand. General Washington intervened and released half the salt meat on hand at the magazine in Ulster County for shipment northward, but that store had only 433 barrels of beef and pork on September 7.[31] General Heath again provided critical support when he ordered on September 12 that 300 barrels of pork and 700 barrels of beef be moved to the magazine at Bennington.[32] On the same day, General Lincoln wrote from Pawlet that he expected a shipment of flour.[33]

Gates' army consumed at least eighty head of cattle daily, and prices climbed to twenty pounds per head as beasts became harder to find. Schuyler was forced to request additional money because, "A Supply of money must always be in the hands of my Purchasers for without it nothing can be Done[.] flour and many other articles must be procured for the Army."[34] By September 14, the supply of flour on hand at the Albany magazine was down to thirty barrels, which could not be forwarded for lack of casks. However, two sloops laden with flour, salt beef, and pork were due that evening, which quartermaster Morgan Lewis promised to send immediately to the camp.[35]

Brigadier General Joseph Palmer of the Massachusetts Militia visited the Northern Department during the first week of September and departed with a clear understanding of the urgency of expediting a steady flow of supplies from the Eastern Department. Six days after returning to Boston, he informed Gates that he had stopped at Westfield, where he found "Several hundred Blankets and large Quantities of rum, Rice, Port-wine and Oatmeal, but . . . no positive orders for forwarding them; these were Continental Stores, so we cou'd only advise to their being forwarded as soon as possible." When he reached Springfield, Palmer learned that sixteen wagon loads would immediately set out for the Hudson Valley.[36] The situation at Westfield illustrates that chronic communications problems delayed distribution of supplies, even when stores were available. Gates' correspondence reveals that by September's third week, his men were receiving a reasonably consistent flow of foodstuffs, and other sources do not contradict that conclusion.

Logistics remained a serious concern, but they were not serious enough to dominate command decisions. Gates did have the decisive advantage of operating on interior lines with access to sources of resupply. Logistics, on the other hand, often drove his foe's decisions. Burgoyne operated far from his supply base and was dependent upon a vulnerable line of communication that precluded timely delivery of the sinews of war.

The Ultimate Challenge of Supply: Information

Flawed intelligence has been a bane to commanders throughout recorded history. Before Prussia bureaucratized its command structure during the 19th century, no army had a staff recruited and trained specifically to collect and evaluate intelligence. Both Burgoyne and Gates were professionals who appreciated the importance of informed knowledge about the enemy, his strength, deployment, and intentions—but neither had access to a system capable of providing requisite data.

The situation on the northern frontier was especially difficult. Because they commanded a department extending westward from the Connecticut Valley and the western border of Massachusetts to the upper reaches of the Mohawk Valley, and northward to the Canadian frontier, Schuyler and Gates devoted significant energy and time to soliciting and studying reports from a widely-scattered field. Because both armies lacked an adequate cavalry component, the commander's traditional eyes and ears, scouts—often drawn from light infantry—provided most of the raw information about immediate conditions. They reported on the terrain and enemy deployment, and brought in captives and local people for interrogation. The generals also relied upon their staffs, subordinates, civil authorities, and private persons for collecting routine and specialized intelligence. Both commanders even conducted personal reconnaissance. In the final analysis, they were their own G-2. Ultimately, both officers performed their command functions hampered by limited, imprecise, and conflicting information about their own forces and the enemy.

Limited reconnaissance and intelligence abilities notwithstanding, Gates managed to correctly divine Burgoyne's strategy. From his headquarters at Van Schaick's, Gates learned more about Burgoyne, residing at William Duer's Fort Miller house, than the British general knew about American capabilities and movements.

News from the Mohawk

Gates, as had Schuyler before him, keenly understood the need to invest heavily in thwarting British designs on the Mohawk. As earlier discussed, on his first day as department commander Gates solicited information from Benedict Arnold, who was at Fort Dayton in German Flats. The dashing son of the Havens had caught up with Ebenezer Learned, whom Schuyler had dispatched to reinforce Gansevoort at Fort Stanwix. Arnold received his new commander's letter during the evening of August 20 and replied the next day. He told Gates he intended to leave that morning with 1,000 Continentals and a "handful" of militia to raise Brigadier St. Leger's siege of Stanwix. With his customary flair, Arnold assured Gates that "you will hear of my being victorious or no more, & as soon as the Safety of this part of the Country will permit I will fly to your assistance." Arnold also reported that General Nicholas Herkimer had died from his wounds suffered a fortnight earlier at Oriskany, and that he was "credibly informed that gen. St. Leger has sent to Gen. Burgoyne for reinforcement," suspecting, however, that the latter had none to spare. Still, added Arnold, the matter might be "worth inquiring into."[37] Gates, of course, knew that a paucity of manpower was not the only thing that precluded Burgoyne's sending men to the Oneida Carrying Place; the distance was too great to permit providing timely reinforcement.

Arnold also sent Gates the minutes of the council he had called on the twentieth that resolved to request reinforcements from the main army. Arnold really wanted his commander to send Morgan's riflemen, the only "light troops" in the department until September 11, when Gates created a battalion of light infantry under the command of Major Henry Dearborn. The commanding general was not about to send Morgan's Corps on what was really a secondary mission, but he did immediately detach the 2nd New York Regiment and Livingston's New York regiment to support Arnold. (The British withdrawal before they reached Arnold's column aborted their assignment.)[38] Arnold delayed his departure from Fort Dayton for Fort Schuyler long enough to write another letter—this one to General Schuyler telling him that he believed St. Leger's enemy force outnumbered his own two to one (which he probably knew was untrue), and that the Oneidas and Tuscaroras would arrive at German Flats on the twenty-second. Arnold also congratulated Schuyler, as he had Gates, on Stark's and Warner's stunning victory at Bennington.[39]

Bad roads and security concerns that attended a march through the woods had the same delaying effect upon Arnold's advance that they had on the movements of less flamboyantly aggressive leaders. He progressed only ten miles during two days after leaving Fort Dayton. Fortunately, the moment he had negotiated that distance, an express brought the following message, which he forwarded to Gates:

1777 Aug. 22
Fort Schuyler
Gansevoort to the Honble. General Arnold or Officer Commanding the Army on their March to Fort Schuyler.

This morning at 11 o'clock I began a Heavy Cananade [sic] upon our Enemies Works which was immediately returned by a number of Shells and Cannon—About 3 o'clock usual Deserters came in who informed me that Genl. St Leger with his army was retreating with the utmost Precipitation—soon after which I sent out a party of About Sixty men to enter their Camps, who soon returned and confirmed their accounts. . . . About 7 o'clock this Evening Hanjost Schuyler arriv'd here and informed me that General Arnold with Two Thousand Men, were on their march for this Post in Con-sequence of which, I send you this information.[40]

Arnold professed to be at a loss "to Judge of their real intentions, whether they have returned home, or retired with a view of engaging us on the road, I am inclined to the former from the Acct. of the Deserters & from their leaving their tents and Considerable Baggage. . . ."[41] Leaving his own artillery and tents, Arnold and 900 of Learned's men began a forced march, hoping to catch up with St. Leger's rear and capture his guns and heavy baggage. As noted in a previous chapter, Arnold reached Fort Stanwix during the evening of August 24, "too late after so fatiguing a March to pursue the Enemy that Evening." A 500-man detachment followed the British until heavy rain forced the return of all but a "small party," which reached Oneida Lake in time to watch the last of the invading enemy crossing in boats.

Arnold left Gansevoort's and Van Schaick's 700 men at Fort Schuyler with two month's provisions. In spite of General Schuyler's best efforts to woo the Indians of the Mohawk Valley, only the Oneidas and Tuscaroras proved friendly. Still, Arnold believed that the American garrison had little reason for concern, so decisively had St. Leger and the Johnson faction been frustrated.

Focusing on Burgoyne

Soon after Gates arrived at Van Schaick's Islands, he received from the vigilant George Measam especially valuable intelligence that helped him assess less reliable reports. The source was an obligingly garrulous Hanoverian soldier who deserted from the British 53rd Regiment at Fort Edward. According to the prisoner, Burgoyne's army numbered 6,000 men when it landed at Quebec. His command included:

- Ten British regiments of about 300 men each;
- Six German regiments of about 500 men each;
- Ten grenadier companies of about 30 men each;
- Ten light infantry companies of about 30 men each;

Of this number, the following remained behind in Canada:

- Three British regiments;
- One captain, two lieutenants, and fifty men from each British and German battalion;

About 800 men garrisoned Ticonderoga:

- A British regiment;
- A German detachment;

The resulting main army, at Fort Edward (as of when the man deserted), was comprised of the following:

- Six British regiments (the 9th, 20th, 53rd, 24th, 21st, and 47th), each with 300 men, totaling 1,800;
- Five German regiments, totaling 2,200 men;
- Indians and loyalists between 400 and 500, of whom 200 to 300 were Tories (whom the "General looked upon in a manner of spies");

The Lake Champlain fleet was comprised of:

- The "Floating Battery," armed with twenty-four 12-pounder guns;
- The *Royal George*, armed with twenty 12-pounders;
- The *Carleton*, armed with twenty 12-pounders;
- Two other vessels armed with eleven or twelve 6-pounders each;
- Gunboats (approximately twenty-four);
- "One gun Batteaus[:] a vast number sufficient for the Army and Provisions."[42]

Although flawed in its report of regimental strengths, the man's account provided a generally accurate description of Burgoyne's army.

While Arnold's assessment of the relative security of the northwestern frontier was realistic, the northeastern sector was still in grave danger. The British held Ticonderoga and dominated Lakes Champlain and George. True, Gates could be certain that Burgoyne would not receive reinforcements from Canada, and that his line of communication was vulnerable. But so long as the enemy maintained a substantial presence in northeastern New York and the Hampshire Grants, Gates needed reliable intelligence about conditions north and east of the main area of operations. He was fortunate that in Benjamin Lincoln he had a dedicated surrogate whose self-effacing patience and tact faithfully served his commander and the cause they shared.

An early message from Brigadier General John Fellows of the Massachusetts militia was an example of the misinformation the department's commander had to guard against. Writing on August 22 from Sheffield in northern Massachusetts, Fellows reported that a prisoner had told his captors on the day Lieutenant Colonel Friedrich Baum's troops marched to Bennington (or the previous day), that "Genl. Burgoyne detached Brig. Gen. Frasier [sic] together with the Light Infantry, Grenadiers and Savages to the Westward—if this intelligence is true his object is beyond doubt Fort Schuyler [Stanwix]." Fellows probably was skeptical, since he added in his message to Gates that he thought it his duty to transmit the prisoner's story.[43] The report worried Gates not at all. He knew no corps-sized force could ascend the Mohawk from Fort Miller without colliding with elements of his own army.

Collecting supplies and intelligence could be only a prelude to making decisions that would determine whether the Northern Department's new commander and his men could frustrate John Burgoyne's designs. By the first week of September Gates commanded a stronger, better-equipped army with higher morale than General Schuyler ever had at his disposal. His enemy was correspondingly weaker—having suffered two serious defeats at Bennington and Fort Stanwix—and pursuing Schuyler's retreating force had dangerously stretched his line of communications. The strategic tide had turned away from Gentleman Johnny Burgoyne in the Americans' favor. Exploiting that sea change, however, required sagacity, a clear-sighted strategy, and good luck.

Horatio Gates was in command of an army comprised of brave and motivated soldiers. Only time would tell whether he was the man who could lead them to victory.

Prelude to Bemis Heights and "the Airy Scheme"

Assembling the Fractious Forces

The time for developing new initiatives for frustrating John Burgoyne's designs was at hand. General Gates knew the British could not long remain at Fort Miller and must soon retreat to Ticonderoga or continue the advance on Albany. There was nowhere between those places they could winter, and spending the cold season at the former would not be an attractive option.

Albany, for strategic and logistical reasons, offered a much better alternative. The lower Hudson provided communications with the premier British base at New York City, and occupying Albany would make supply resources much more readily accessible and in greater quantity than would be the case at the more isolated northern fortress. Finally, bringing his army to Albany and making it available to Sir William Howe for the next campaign was the expedition's primary purpose. Retreating to Ticonderoga, therefore, would be tantamount to admitting defeat without having engaged the Americans in major combat. Sir Guy Carleton had done exactly that in 1776; Burgoyne was not about to reprise that role in 1777.[1]

By August 22, Gates was convinced Burgoyne would push on. That conclusion required the Americans to move northward toward the enemy and take up a position suitable for either defensive or offensive operations. Van Schaick's Islands and the junction of the Hudson and Mohawk rivers were not suitable for either purpose. Where should the army move?

The army that would march, however, was growing stronger by the day. Excluding Dan Morgan's riflemen, the artillerymen, and artificers, the

Continentals numbered 6,043 present and fit for duty. Including those additional personnel, the total number of effectives was some 7,000. Militia continued to arrive and be integrated into brigades. The 2nd and 17th Albany County regiments, commanded by Colonels Abraham Wempel and William Bradford Whiting, respectively, and Colonel Morris Graham's Dutchess and Ulster County Regiment were tucked into John Glover's Brigade.[2] Colonels Thaddeus Cook and Jonathan Latimore's Connecticut regiments joined Enoch Poor's Brigade.[3]

Some 700 to 800 of John Stark's men from New Hampshire arrived on the Hudson on September 11.[4] The arrival of these veterans seemed, for the moment, to reward the patient efforts of Gates and Benjamin Lincoln to persuade their fractious commander to commit the heroes of Bennington to the common cause. The story, however, is not that simple.

On his return to Manchester from conferring with Gates about strategy, Lincoln stopped at St. Croix on the Walloomsac to discuss with General John Stark the role required of him, which was to "take command of the one thousand troops, and move toward the [Hudson] river." Stark "appeared perfectly satisfied" with the plan. A review of his returns, however, revealed that he had only slightly more than 750 men present and fit for duty. Colonel William Williams was to reinforce Stark with about 200 men from the Hampshire Grants, and Lincoln ordered a Colonel Robertson "to join with his few men." Taught by experience how volatile Stark could be, Lincoln followed their conversation with a letter dated September 6 reiterating Stark's mission and Gates' explicit wish to have him occupy high ground east of the river opposite Stillwater.[5]

Stark's immediate response did not promise wholehearted cooperation. "I received yours informing me of Genl. Gates movement," he began. "I should be glad to move to the height opposite him on the east side, but the task is too hard for me in my present circumstances. I have but about 800 men, and not one man knows the ground (not so much as one foot)." Not content with that weak demurrer, Stark advanced a transparently specious argument: "The whole of Mr. Burgoynes army is on this side of the river—General Gates may as well tell me, go attack Genl. Burgoyne['s] army with my Brigade, as to desire me to march between him and the enemy."[6]

Stark followed this piece of nonsense with another written to Lincoln on the seventh in which he pretended that Lincoln had indicated that Gates would depart Van Schaick's Island during September 6. Stark, however, knew that he had not done so by noon of that day. Because the seventh was rainy, Gates would not reach Stillwater during the eighth. Colonel Williams had only 60 men (not 200) fit for duty, "which together with my brigade will not exceed 700 men, and many of that number are now sick with the Meazels—besides all this I have not one carriage with me to transport my provisions from this place."

Stark went on to add, with gratuitous effrontery, the following note in an effort to shift the onus of his situation onto Lincoln's shoulders:

> N. B. There is more difficulty prevails—my mens time is almost out and [I] do find it out of my power to detain them longer than while the time is expired, and they are further pleased to say (notwithstanding my endeavours to persuade them to the contrary) that they are looked upon as a very disrespectable body which (they say) may be evidenced by your letter to the State of Massachusetts Bay, in which the continental Troops were placed in the front of the battle [Bennington]—and had the applause of victory—your men immediately after and mine the last of all—these circumstances sir are so implanted in their minds that in no case they should exert themselves as heretofore, once more they think that they should be treated in like manner.[7]

Stark not only misrepresented the tenor of Lincoln's report, but whatever his men learned about the report's contents came from their commander, and thus any ideas "implanted in their minds" were derived from him.

In spite of that provocation, Lincoln offered a tempered reply. "In my letter to the Council of Massachusetts Bay, I meant to speak of the troops engaged in the late action in the most respectful terms," he wrote. "If the arrangement [list of units] is wrong it was not so designed." Indeed, nothing in the letter impugned the conduct of any soldiers who had served at Bennington.

Lincoln devoted the rest of his letter of September 8 urging Stark to fulfill his assigned role and assuring him that any support needed for the slightly more than one-day march from the Walloomsac to the Hudson would be available. He regretted that Stark's men used the date of their service expiration "as a reason why they should not act the little time they are to continue in camp."[8]

That Gates also controlled his temper is evident in a pair of letters he sent from Stillwater on September 10. "I am astonished," he penned Lincoln,

> at my Friend Stark hesitating to perform what he had previously, and with entire approbation, consented to execute; the post I wished him to Occupy, is not more than half [a] cannon Shot from [the] Right of this

Army, & by Twelve at Noon, I shall have a good Bridge of communication finished across the River. Inclosed is my letter to him upon the Subject[;] after reading it I think he will not delay one moment the march to that Ground.[9]

Gates' second, slightly more pointed letter, was directed to the man who had so "astonished" him. "I am exceeding Surprised and Disappointed," Gates informed Stark,

at not finding you at the place, where I understood from General Lincoln you had agreed to take post, to Cooperate with me—so far from your being between me & the Enemy's whole Army; the post is not half [a] cannon shot from my Right; & in a line with it; and this forenoon, a good bridge of Communication will be finish'd across the River—I entreat you will not Tarnish the Glory you have gain'd, but march immediately to the post assigned you.[10]

Stark had, in the meantime, realized that his insubordination might very well tarnish his laurels, and on the ninth informed Gates that his brigade would move to the heights opposite Stillwater. Stark was too ill to accompany it, but indicated he would rejoin his men as soon as he recovered. Pending that recovery, "I am Dear Sir in the Greatest Agony of Grief and Pain. . . ."[11]

In this manner, after almost one month of inactivity on the Walloomsac, and led by Colonel Samuel Ashley, the militiamen reached their assigned position during September 11.[12] Their commander, still pleading bad health, did not appear until the morning of the eighteenth—the day his men's terms expired. About noon on that day, in an act of irresponsible localismo, with battle imminent, and despite Gates' offer of a ten-dollar bounty for each man who remained, Stark led his men back to the Hampshire Grants.[13]

The American Position

When Gates decided to take up the place where he intended to stop Burgoyne, he commanded a force that had increased in size to at least 9,000 men, approximately 1,800 more than the British general commanded. The Europeans' professionalism and experience significantly reduced that numerical advantage, but a well-fortified position could more than restore the balance in favor of the Americans.

The search for such a position began on September 8, when the Americans set out on their northward march. During the morning of the next day they were at Stillwater, across the Hudson from the high ground Gates expected Stark to occupy. But the valley west of the river was too broad to afford a strong position, and Gates moved his men three miles farther to Bemis Heights. There, he discovered that the high ground, if properly fortified and manned, met his tactical requirements. A westward curve of the river and a marsh bordering it crowded the road to Albany onto a narrow shelf of solid ground dominated by bluffs more than 100 feet high on the eastern face of the heights. American occupation of the high ground would inevitably force Burgoyne onto the horns of an unappealing set of choices. If he continued his advance southward, tactical disadvantages awaited. Forcing his way along the road would dangerously expose his men to the American guns, while turning into the hills to drive his enemy from their position would trigger a major engagement against a fortified enemy. If Burgoyne decided against an attack and attempted to retreat north—thereby aborting the campaign—the larger American army would pursue his outnumbered and outmaneuvered Europeans. Any option Burgoyne chose forced him to act on Gates' terms. The selection and occupation of Bemis Heights was a strategic coup for the Americans, and a turning point in the campaign.[14]

At the base of Bemis Heights was a tavern operated by Jotham Bemus. Abutting Bemus' land was a farm belonging to John Neilson. The property contained an older log home, a newer frame house, and a barn with a steeple. Just south of Neilson's farm was another small farm belonging to Captain Ephraim Woodworth, which included his farmhouse. The fortified American camp encompassed all three properties. A sketch drawn by Colonel Richard Varick on the back of a letter to General Philip Schuyler on September 12, the day the Americans occupied their new camp, identified Bemus' Tavern, the Woodworth [Red] House (which Gates selected as his headquarters), three other Woodworth buildings (which became the hospital), Neilson's home, and the brigade camps.[15]

With the camp selected, Gates marched his men into position. John Nixon's Massachusetts brigade manned the right wing overlooking the Albany Road. Next, on line with Nixon and facing north were the brigades of John Paterson and John Glover. The left end of their line rested just below the crest of the hill. Gates' left wing, the two brigades of Benedict Arnold's Division under Enoch Poor and Ebenezer Learned, faced west. Morgan's Corps camped north of the apex and angle formed by the two wings and athwart the road running from Woodworth's farm north to Quaker Springs. The road and another that climbed the hill from the tavern to Woodworth's and thence northwest to Saratoga Lake provided crucial interior lines of communication for the American army.

Although it was a naturally strong position, Gates ordered his front fortified. Soldiers under the watchful supervision of Thaddeus Koscuiszko and Baldwin began immediately to improve upon nature by raising extensive field fortifications, an endeavor that engaged them through September 18 and again from September 20 to October 6.

During the first week of military occupation, the farms on Bemis Heights were fortified with a perimeter protected by a series of breastworks, entrenchments, redoubts, and outposts. By week's end they still did not constitute one continuous line of works, but they dominated the most vulnerable terrain features and interdicted those that might shield an approaching enemy.

The defenses would eventually evolve into a solid line extending from the second ridge west of the Albany Road in an arc to its terminus about 750 feet south of the Woodworth House. Extensive redoubts were built along the ridge immediately above and parallel to the Albany Road, in the low-lying land between the river and road, behind the tavern, at the bridge of boats, and on high ground 2,400 feet southwest of Woodworth's. Work begun on a redoubt 2,400 feet west of the apex of the main line of resistance was still unfinished on October 7. A line of picket outposts provided perimeter security, and trees felled with the branches pointing away from the fortifications formed an abatis.

Having interdicted the route to Albany with works above and athwart the road, the commanding general and his engineers turned to preventing the British from flanking those works and dislodging the Americans. They secured the area from the river to the ridge west of the crest, incorporating topography into an integrated defensive system. The streams and ravines dictated the locations of the main line of resistance and its complementary outworks. The fortifications were erected to enfilade those features, precluding their use by the enemy. They also needed to command the defiles and the opposite slopes in order to provide the defenders with targets-in-depth should the enemy attempt to cross. Reducing dead areas the British might otherwise exploit required that the defensive components be mutually supportive.[16]

The manner in which the fortification plan responded to strategic requirements and opportunities offered by the terrain testified to the professionalism found within Gates' army. The measures the defenders took would anticipate and frustrate every tactic Burgoyne would employ against them. As events would bear out, the field fortifications on Bemis Heights met the requirements of the local tactical situation to a degree seldom, if ever, surpassed during the war.

Americans had proved especially adept at raising field fortifications, and had been doing so since the beginning of the war. But that Gates' soldiers were able to accomplish as much as they did while simultaneously carrying out patrols, manning outposts, performing camp fatigue, and fighting a day-long battle—all within a period of twenty-four days—was an impressive testimony to their leadership, discipline, and stamina.

The Camp on Bemis Heights

Contemporary sources do not reveal the details of the camp's internal organization. Informed conjecture, however, provides us with a generally accurate reconstruction. By 1777, the Continental Army was less amateurish than is generally believed. Many of its officers and men had served during the previous imperial war, during which they became, to some degree, familiar with British practices and precedents. A remarkable number, including men too young to have served previously, read current British publications and English translations of French and German studies of military science and tactics. Experience gained during the war was instructive, and Continental regiments and some militia units contained veterans with two years of service behind them. Finally, Gates and his chief engineer were professional soldiers who had spent their adult lives in European armies. Conditions in America dictated modifications in practice, as local conditions always did, but they created practical exceptions rather than new standards. In a conjectural reconstruction of Gates' camp one can assume that it generally conformed to prevailing British practices with the modifications imposed by terrain, the wishes of the commander, the size of the regiments, and the availability of tents. Remembering to use the terms "regiment" and "battalion" synonymously, we can develop a representative regimental field encampment.

The standard battalion/regimental encampment had a depth of 320 yards arranged in the following manner:

• At the head was the Quarter Guard, a small detachment commanded by a subaltern [lieutenant] posted 84 yards in front of the battalion's line;

• ,Fifty-four yards behind the Quarter Guard lay the Parade, a thirty-yard-deep area where the troops assembled for formations, guard mount, and other purposes;

• Immediately behind the Parade was a line upon which the colors, surplus drums, and the "bell tents," in which the muskets were stacked when the men did not "lie upon their arms," were aligned;

• The tents of the several companies lay four yards behind the line of "bell tents," aligned to a depth of thirty to forty-five yards, depending upon the number of enlisted men. Wagons, usually one to a battalion in Europe, more in America, transported the tents, with the men carrying the poles. Common tents for the men measured six and half feet square and five feet high and could accommodate six men, although they were sometimes pitched together in a manner that would shelter as many as eighteen. The camp's streets ran between the company tents;

• To the companies' right stood the battalion's organic artillery, wagon, and gunners' tents;

• Twenty or thirty-two yards behind the companies was a line of subalterns' tents; and twelve to twenty-four yards to their rear were the captains' tents, separated by a street from those of the field officers;

• Behind those was the battalion commander's tent. Then came the tents of the staff officers (normally not present in American regiments);

• Behind those was a line where the officers' horses were tethered;

• Next was the officers' mess tent, and twenty yards behind it were the battalion's kitchen, behind which were the tents of the butchers and sutlers;

• Finally, fifteen yards in the rear were the tents of the rear guard.

A cavalry encampment closely resembled the infantry's except that the horses were tethered in the street between the rows of tents. At Bemis Heights there were neither "bell tents" nor artillery because most, if not all, of the guns were in place along the fortified line. The camp, therefore, had no need for an artillery park. The bodies of men who died in camp were, if conditions permitted, buried in front of the encampment facing the enemy. This was not true for prisoners of war, however. If they died in a hospital or in camp, they were interred as conveniently as possible in the rear.[17]

Because of the nature of the ground and the number of regiments present, the camp on Bemis Heights was certainly more compact than the conventional one described above.

Gates' Strategy and Burgoyne's Options

The American fortifications defined their commander's strategy as he had matured it by September's second week. The defensive-minded Gates wanted to avoid a pitched battle in an open field. As in 1776, he intended to "Defend the main Chance; to attack only by detail; and when a precious advantage offers." His men would continue to improve their position while they settled in to await their enemy's advance. Gates happily released the initiative to Burgoyne: he could throw his troops into a frontal attack against the strong works, try an advance through the densely-wooded area across broken ground against the American left flank, or retreat. As Gates wrote President Hancock two days before occupying Bemis Heights: "[A] few days, perhaps hours, will Determine whether General Burgoyne will Risque a Battle, or Retire to Tyconderoga for I cannot think he will stay long inactive in his present position."[18]

Gates' strategy was more prudent than heroic. His career in the British Army and knowledge of military history had given him a healthy respect for European fire discipline and skill with the bayonet. He knew firsthand how brave the British veteran could be. He respected his Continentals' capacity for courage and resilience, and his opinion of militia was better than that of most professional soldiers. But he was also keenly aware of the limitations posed by militia, and knew they would perform best fighting under cover of fortifications. Defending a fortified position was also less costly than fighting in the open, and Gates was never profligate with soldiers' lives. As we shall see, he modified his strategy during both of the major engagements at Saratoga. But until the second one had ended, his posture was essentially defensive: holding Bemis Heights, and forcing his enemy to choose his poison. This, then, was the centerpiece of his plan for defeating Burgoyne.

The American Order of Battle

The American army on Bemis Heights included twenty-six regiments of foot (twenty-one Continental and five militia) totaling 7,146 men. Gates merged Colonel Morgan's Rifle Regiment with a battalion of light infantrymen drafted from the several Continental regiments commanded by Major Henry Dearborn into a 694-man elite corps under Morgan. Because bayonets could not be fitted onto rifles, and reloading rifles was relatively slow, riflemen were vulnerable to attack between volleys. Brigading musket-armed light infantry with riflemen to protect the latter made taking advantage of the rifle's accuracy more militarily effective. The only cavalry present with the army was Major Elijah Hyde's troop of Connecticut Light Horse, about 200 men. The army's artillery consisted of Stevens' Independent Battalion, 248 men serving twenty-two guns of unknown caliber. Seventy-one men of Baldwin's Detachment of Engineers and Artificers provided important core construction capability. Excluding wagoners, staff, Stark's New Hampshire militia (who marched home the day before the first engagement), and an unrecorded number of Indians, Gates' effective combat strength was 8,359. (See also Appendices C and D.)

Gates organized his infantry into five brigades and an independent light corps. He personally commanded the right division, three brigades of Massachusetts men under Glover, Paterson, and Nixon numbering 3,787 men. General Arnold commanded the left division, comprised of Learned's and Poor's brigades numbering 3,359 men. (Morgan's officially independent corps was tactically part of that left wing.) The small cavalry contingent probably served as a headquarters guard. Contemporary cartographic sources do not reflect the locations of the twenty-two artillery pieces, but given Baldwin's and Stevens' skill and the commanding general's experience, they most certainly would have distributed the pieces to cover the Albany Road and the field of fire along the main line of resistance.[19]

Gates' army was well-organized and led by generally competent officers. It was numerically superior to Burgoyne's command and it was posted in a position that was, given Burgoyne's resources, almost impregnable. If American morale remained good and unity prevailed, the only way to defeat them was to entice or drive them off Bemis Heights. Surviving sources reflect a confidence among the Americans that even the departure of Stark's Brigade did not shake.

Intrigue over Generals

There was, however, a germ of dissension that soon festered into a potential threat to the unity of command. The overwhelming majority of New Englanders welcomed Gates' succession to command of the Northern Department. This was important for many reasons, not the least of which was that New England provided most of the department's soldiers. But some New Yorkers preferred serving under their native son, General Schuyler—even though the "Proud Patriot" was not personally popular with the soldiery. If the officers of the New York regiments felt strongly about his displacement, they did not commit their sentiments to sources that have survived. Even men such as James Livingston (commander of the New York regiment that had formerly been the 1st Canadian), Henry Beekman Livingston (Schuyler's former aide-de-camp and now colonel of the 4th New York), and Philip Van Cortlandt (commander of the 2nd New York), all members of patrician families and related to the general, subordinated personal feelings to serve loyally the man who superceded their kinsman.

There were, however, two important exceptions: Major Henry Brockholst Livingston, Schuyler's former aide-de-camp who now served General Arnold as an unassigned volunteer in the same capacity, and Lieutenant Colonel Richard Varick, Schuyler's former military secretary who in 1777 served as deputy commissary-general of musters. Both men were fiercely devoted to Schuyler and loathed his successor. They penned almost daily letters to their patron indicting Gates' character and competence.

For example, Colonel Varick's letter of September 12 reporting the move to Bemis Heights criticized the camp's position and layout. "Should we unfortunately be defeated will it not be in Burgoyne's power to take our Baggage [?] I think it past a Doubt," he wrote. "However, we must not think of It. It is a just maxim that Inferiors should silently obey the Orders of Superiors." Varick honored that maxim by condemning the reconnaissance details as "too few but those too small to know the movements of the Enemy . . . they may come Near or run far from us for Aught . . . [Gates?] Knows."[20]

Varick wrote two letters to Schuyler on September 16, one at 8:00 a.m. and another three hours later. "I wish to God we had a Commander who could see a little Distance before him without Spectacles [a snide dig at Gates' wearing eyeglasses to correct his nearsightedness] and we would probably make as Brilliant a stroke as at Bennington," Varick lamented in the first letter of the day.

"Wishes are Vain; with [a] cheerful March we shall proceed & rely on American Good Fortune." A sketch accompanied the second, longer, letter. Varick expected an attack within the next three days, a reasonable "guess" since as a member of the commander's staff he was privy to Gates' assessment of enemy intentions. If that attack came during the day, Varick would assure the British commander "a crip[p]led Army at least provided Matters are Managed agreeable to my Ideas of the propriety of our Mode of Defence." Modesty was not Colonel Varick's salient attribute.[21]

Varick was also unhappy with Kosciuszko's fortifications, which did not meet the twenty-four-year-old colonel's high standards. "I don't approve of the more Advanced Works, next the River on the Ridge," he complained to Schuyler, "for the Moment they drive our Troops out, it serves as Work for them against the small Redoubt, as it is at least level, if not higher than It." Varick's eagerness to discredit Gates was leading him to resort to absurdity: the fortified ridge was the crest of a 100-foot bluff so steep that ascending under peaceful conditions taxes a climber's agility and lung power. That was the only part of the American position the British had an accurate view of, and its strength was so obvious that Burgoyne was persuaded he had to get his foe off Bemis Heights.

Varick also claimed that high ground in front of Paterson's and Nixon's brigades dominated their camp. At first blush, there seems to be merit in his observation concerning ground north of Paterson's position: parts were indeed higher. But the British would have found it too broken and densely wooded for battalion formation attacking a main line of resistance, and American outposts occupied the strategic high point. Varick compounded his absurdity when he claimed that high ground covered Nixon's camp as well. The strong "Advanced Work" he deplored earlier formed Nixon's front and covered the main line, behind which the brigade's camp lay; no higher ground threatened it. He also disapproved of the outposts "on all the Hills worth Contending for in our Front," because he abhorred "Detaching the Army in so many parts."

On the day before Burgoyne launched his first attempt to knock Gates off Bemis Heights, Colonel Varick sent General Schuyler more examples of his commander's conduct, one at 8:00 p.m., another three hours later. In the latter he castigated the plans worked out by Gates and Lincoln, of which his staff position gave him some knowledge, telling Schuyler that he "lamented that Lincoln is [off] on some airy Scheme when it is possible that the Enemy may drive us & ruin all he can possibly Effect if he is in North of the Enemy & A

Stroke was meditated against Tyconderoga & Fort George, Where he is now we know not with certainty."[22]

The second Gates detractor, Henry Brockholst Livingston, was the son of New Jersey's first elected governor and scion of a famous New York clan. He would lead a public life in the orbits of powerful men and end it as an associate justice of the United States Supreme Court. Livingston began his military career in 1775 as a young captain and aide-de-camp to General Arthur St. Clair. In 1779 he would take a leave of absence to serve his brother-in-law, John Jay, as private secretary during the latter's diplomatic mission to Spain. The New Yorker sorely tried Jay's patience by being sulky, captious, and bad-mannered. More damaging was his penchant for "making indiscreet remarks to Europeans hypercritical of Americans and their government."[23] Captured by the British on his way home in 1782 and jailed in New York City, he was eventually paroled by Sir Guy Carleton. In the summer of 1777, the 19-year-old was a volunteer aide-de-camp to Benedict Arnold, a position in which his tendency to discover, identify, and deplore trivial matters bore mischievous fruit.

The young schemer apparently received a letter from Schuyler criticizing Gates' strategy, because in his own September 13 letter he wrote that he was "perfectly in opinion with you." The Hudson River, he continued,

> will render it almost impossible for our two Armies [Gates' and Lincoln's] to act in junction against the Enemy and the great distance between us will put it out the power of one to support the other in Case of an Attack - - - Gen. Lincoln remains at Paulet [sic], and by his own account, has short of 2,000 Militia, nor can I learn that he has orders to make any further movements toward the rear of the Enemy.[24]

Livingston continued, decrying . . .

> [the army's being] greatly at a loss for Intelligence - - No large Parties have been sent out to harass them - - and the small scouts seldom bring in any information of consequence - - I should think Detachments of 200 or a thousand might be [of] great Service in Skirmishing with the Enemy - - It would make fighting familiar to our Troops and dishearten the Foe.[25]

The future Supreme Court jurist contradicted himself by reporting to Schuyler that three detachments, one numbering 200 men, had reconnoitered the enemy and brought in prisoners.[26] His next three letters reported the activities of *nine more scouting sorties*.[27] Despite these obvious contradictions, he continued in the same vein, accusing Gates of insufficient aggressiveness. "It is really astonishing that we have lain so long near together without the least Skirmishing - - - I should [think] our numbers were such to justify sending out Parties of 200 or 2000 without much danger to the Army," he argued. "These might harass the Enemy by attacking their detached parties, and could always retreat or be supported in case of necessity."[28] Moving beyond mere words and behind-the-scenes treachery, Livingston further distanced himself from order and harmony on Arnold's staff by waging a duel with Major Leonard Chester, an "extra aide" to the general, in which neither principal was injured.[29]

In persons less closely associated with the American command echelon, Varick's hubris and Livingston's captiousness—as documented in what the former termed "sub rosa" correspondence with General Schuyler—might be dismissed as silly products of immaturity and immodesty. But because these men were close to Arnold, the question whether their criticisms reflected that general's views can be neither ignored nor answered conclusively. If they did reflect Arnold's opinions or, more important, contribute to them, their letters to embittered Philip Schuyler were important and provide useful insights into the dangerous quarrel that would erupt between Arnold and Gates following the combat of Freeman's Farm (the details of which Varick and Livingston would report to Schuyler with obvious relish). An omen of that rupture appeared in a postscript to Varick's September 12 letter: "I forgot to tell you that a little Spurt happened on Wednesday Eveng between Gates and Arnold Inter Nos."

The unhappy truth is that these young officers perceived themselves as Schuyler's agents, and their personal loyalty to him compromised their professional commitment to the common cause.

The Two Armies Probe Each Other

While Livingston, Varick, and Schuyler exchanged embittered opinions of Gates' preparations for defeating Burgoyne, the officers and men on Bemis Heights exerted themselves in further strengthening their fortifications and trying to assess their enemy's strength and discern his intentions.

During the first night in their new camp, his deputy adjutant general, Colonel James Wilkinson, led a light cavalry detachment within sight of Burgoyne's encampment at Saratoga. There, he found a 70-man picket at General Schuyler's manor house, listened while enemy drums beat assembly, and captured three uncooperative men of the British 20th Regiment.[30] During the next day, 200 of Morgan's riflemen under Lieutenant Colonel Richard Butler reconnoitered the country around Saratoga Lake and Jones' Mill, where a party of Lieutenant Colonel Ebenezer Jessup's Provincials were posted with orders to attack the Loyalists "if he finds it practicable." According to Henry Livingston, that "Enterprize failed for want of knowledge or through Cowardice of the Guide - - - Butler was misled, & returned without Effecting any thing - - -." On September 14, Arnold and 200 riflemen scouted the area between Bemis Heights and Van Vechten's Mill to determine whether it provided a more "eligible" place to encamp. A 100-man British picket guard saw them and deployed, but Arnold decided not to attack them because they could be too easily supported by the enemy's main body.[31] The reconnaissance found no alternate height of sufficient size, so the Americans continued fortifying Bemis Heights.

The next day, September 15, Arnold repeated the maneuver. Varick reported to Schuyler that "Genl. Arnold is this day gone out with a Large Party. I don't know his Intentions, probably to try the East Side of the River, as he seemed very desirous to have a prospect of the Enemy's Camp from the High Hill on that Side—if he proceeds on this Side he may fall in with some of the Enemy."[32] No other source records the nature or results of that reconnaissance.

Lieutenant Colonel Andrew Colburn of Alexander Scammell's 3rd New Hampshire Continental Regiment directed what turned out to be the most productive reconnaissance. Colburn crossed the river on the fourteenth and from a height later called Mount Willard, observed British movements on the far side. He reported that the enemy had crossed to the Hudson's west side and was camped near the Continental Barracks north of Schuyler's country house, with an advanced post located about one mile south of the main body, i.e., a short distance south of the house.[33] Colburn returned to Bemis Heights during the evening of the fifteenth and reported that Burgoyne's men had struck camp at 2:00 in the afternoon and advanced about a mile and half. Scouts on the western side of the river captured a member of the British 29th Regiment's grenadier company, who confirmed the accuracy of Colburn's observations.

Prelude to Battle

Horatio Gates now knew beyond any doubt that John Burgoyne intended to advance against his position. At 3:00 in the morning of September 16, the

American army commander ordered his men to stand at arms.[34] This was a prudent—if somewhat premature—precaution because substantial probing, reconnaissance, and skirmishing preceded the main combat.

While Burgoyne's command was camped above Van Vechten's Mill, he dispatched scouting parties downstream by boat that approached within three miles of the American lines. Expecting the enemy to repeat that ploy, Arnold ordered Colonel Philip Van Cortlandt of the 4th New York Regiment to take a party by bateaux to within two miles of Van Vechten's, conceal their boats, wait for the scouting craft to pass, and get into their rear and cut them off. Van Cortlandt returned to camp at 11:00 the next morning. When his quarry did not venture down river, he aborted his mission in favor of a reconnaissance of the British position and reported, inaccurately, that they were camped on both sides of the river.[35]

The aggressive American scouting confirmed that Gates' expectation was correct: Burgoyne was going to try to force him off Bemis Heights. The American general ordered his men to strike their tents and load their baggage onto the unit wagons—normal preparations for battle—by daybreak on September 18.

According to Gates himself, he would attack his enemy "only by detail, and when a precious advantage offers." He now decided that his opponent was offering him just such a precious advantage, and so ordered Arnold to attack the enemy during their approach march while they were at a tactical disadvantage.

With his entire division and Morgan's Corps, Benedict Arnold moved out of the American camp's left wing and marched to a point slightly more than two and one-half miles north of Bemis Heights, where about 10:00 a.m. he and his men came upon a small party of enemy soldiers and women digging potatoes in a field northwest of Taylor's house, south of the British encampment. Instead of driving ahead to capture them, Arnold's Americans opened fire, killing or wounding several of the foragers.[36] Varick told Schuyler that, because the "Woods was thick & very brushy the Genl. did not think proper an Engagement there Least [sic] our Own Men should kill Each Other & he ordered his Troops to return . . . ." By 4:00 that same afternoon, Arnold's Division was back in the American camp.

The eighteenth of September was not a happy day for General John Burgoyne, for he remained ignorant of his enemy's strength and his fortifications. Gates' pickets had plagued his march all the way from Saratoga. Now, Burgoyne had lost soldiers while foraging, killed by an obviously alert and active foe. From his headquarters in the Swords house, Burgoyne issued a combination general order that both dealt with the foraging issue and made dispositions for the approaching battle. Deploring the loss of effective soldiers for mere potatoes, the British commander decreed that commanding officers were authorized to hang any man caught trespassing beyond the army's advanced sentries. Two days' rations were to be issued, baggage would remain in the wagons, and as soon as the bridges were repaired, the men would resume their advance toward Bemis Heights. The British leader also directed that one subaltern officer orderly from each of the three corps was to be sent, on horseback, to attend the commander. Anticipating immediate action, Burgoyne concluded: "In the case of an Action, the Lieut. General will be found near the center of the British Line, or will leave word there where he may be followed."[37]

Gates was already certain that combat was imminent, and Burgoyne reinforced the belief lingering within British ranks: a battle for Bemis Heights was now inevitable.

Benjamin Lincoln and the 'Airy Scheme'

In his letter to General Schuyler, Richard Varick scoffed at Benjamin Lincoln's move—"Lincoln is [off] on some airy Scheme." Varick could not have been more wrong. Before we continue with the main narrative and bring the armies within shooting distance of one another, it is important to discuss and understand Benjamin Lincoln's contributions to the Colonial victory. Underrating Lincoln and his service in the Northern Department has become such an easy and common exercise that some students have emphasized his "great bulk and loose jowls" at the expense of his important contributions to American success. Horatio Gates was fortunate to have in Lincoln a dedicated surrogate whose self-effacing patience and tact faithfully served his commander and the cause they shared.

At the end of August, General Lincoln was at Bennington, still trying to act as an honest broker between the Continental Army and John Stark while working to enhance the effectiveness of the militia east of the Hudson, a region rich in loyalists and peevishly sensitive frontiersmen. Lincoln reported to Gates on August 26 his plans for utilizing militiamen as they arrived, expecting five companies to come in before the end of the day. He added intelligence brought to him by three of his men who had returned to camp after escaping captivity. These men reported that the enemy had a large number of ox teams and supplies at Fort George; that there was some artillery at Fort Anne; that the

British 62nd Regiment, some Germans, and the artillery train were located at Fort Edward; and that Burgoyne's main force was at Fort Miller, planning to locate its winter quarters in Albany.[38]

The letter Lincoln wrote to his commander on September 4 provides a brief but helpful glimpse of his plans for operations in his sector. Lincoln dispatched a "person" to Burgoyne's headquarters in William Duer's house at Fort Miller who contrived somehow to collect the following intelligence: the British "flying camp," Fraser's Corps of 1,700 men, was three miles below Fort Miller; the Germans were encamped about halfway between Fraser and headquarters; about 300 men, commanded by a major, remained at Fort Miller; and there were some 150 men at Fort George and 500 at Ticonderoga. Lincoln was tantalizingly silent about the identity of that "person" and how he succeeded in collecting his useful information. Another informant claimed that an "English regiment and 15 or 16 light pieces were at Fort Anne," and that Burgoyne intended moving his heavy artillery across the river to Stillwater.[39] The number of field pieces was inaccurate, but the other information was generally reliable.

Collecting intelligence, however, was not General Lincoln's most important function. He was to do what he could with the available resources to coordinate operations against Fort Ticonderoga and other enemy posts along the long and tenuous British line of communications, and to cope with a difficult John Stark, whom victory along the Walloomsac had not made less fractious. As time would prove, Lincoln realized more success in the former than in the latter.

Despite having no more than 2,000 men available at Pawlet, Vermont, Lincoln anticipated his commander's needs when, on September 13, he detached 500 Massachusetts militiamen on each of three missions under Colonels John Brown, Central Berkshire County Regiment; Samuel Johnson, Essex County Regiment; and Benjamin Ruggles Woodbridge, 1st Hampshire County Regiment. Lincoln described their assignments when he reported to Gates in a letter written at Pawlet on September 14. The department commander forwarded to Gates a letter received from Massachusetts Brigadier General Joseph Palmer describing "the weak state of Ticonderoga." In addition to that tempting bit of information, Lincoln had learned from informants that the enemy held a considerable number of prisoners at "Lake George landing" under a "very small guard," and that there was, at the same location, a large magazine of stores. Taking advantage of that intelligence "would perfectly coincide with the original design of my being sent there; vizt. If possible, to divide and distress the enemy. . . ."[40]

Lincoln anticipated Gates' approval. While he remained at his Pawlet headquarters with his remaining 500 men, his three subordinates promptly put the plan into operation. Because the British had evacuated Skenesborough, Woodbridge's assignment was accomplished there without incident. Woodbridge's next objective was to secure Brown's avenue of retreat, should that become necessary. Brown, Arnold's old nemesis, had the more ambitious mission of the triumvirate of colonels: (1) to attack the enemy outpost at the "landing at Lake George," located at the lake's northern terminus, release the prisoners held there, and destroy its magazine; and (2) "attempt Ticonderoga," where Brigadier Henry Powell with some 900 men of the British 53rd and the Prinz Friedrich [Erbprinz] Regiments and some Canadians manned Burgoyne's line of communications' strongest post. Colonel Johnson had orders to support Brown by engaging the Germans on Mount Independence.[41]

Powell was too secure in the old French masonry fort to be overawed by Brown, who lacked the siege artillery necessary to carry the bastion. His response to the American's demand for surrender was a terse one: "The garrison entrusted to my care I shall defend to the last." Brown and Johnson bombarded Mount Independence without any noticeable result except the expenditure of precious gunpowder. After four fruitless days, Johnson and some of Brown's men retired.

With his remaining 420 men, Brown embarked upon Lake George to attack Diamond Island, about twenty-five miles south of Ticonderoga and three miles north of Fort George, where Captain Thomas Aubrey, with two companies of the British 47th Regiment, guarded a supply depot. By the time Brown's flotilla, which had been delayed by unfavorable winds, attacked about 9:00 a.m. on September 24, a British prisoner captured and paroled at Ticonderoga reached the island and warned Aubrey. After engaging in an artillery duel, the Americans burned their boats and retired to Pawlet via Skenesboro.[42]

Varick was wrong again. The attempts to seize Ticonderoga and Diamond Island were unsuccessful, but Lincoln's "airy Scheme" accomplished its missions: the release of the American prisoners at Lake George Landing; the discouragement of Burgoyne's troops (who learned of these events immediately after having failed to dislodge their foe from Bemis Heights); the securing of intelligence that those troops had no more than four weeks' supplies; and the raising of American morale on Bemis Heights. Lincoln's "airy Scheme" also demonstrated the vulnerability of Burgoyne's line of communications.

10

Freeman's Farm

On Tory Ground

John freeman and his wife Effelina moved onto "Great Lot 16" of the Saratoga Patent, about one and one-half miles north of Bemis Heights sometime during 1766. On January 2, 1768, they leased 170 acres for "three lives" from the patentee, General Philip Schuyler, at a rent of six pence per acre, with the first payment due January 1, 1773.[1] By the autumn of 1777, John was a moderately successful farmer living in a solid, probably frame, house. Three other buildings—a log barn and two farm structures—stood near his home. After selling most of his livestock to the British army, he still owned thirteen sheep, an unspecified number of "Young Cattle," and some hogs, probably a sow and her litter.[2] Lieutenant William Cumberland Wilkinson's map of the battlefield shows two of Freeman's buildings, fenced cultivated fields and meadow, and a fenced and partially cleared pasturage.[3]

Sometime prior to 1770, the Freemans acquired new neighbors when James McBride leased ninety-seven acres from General Schuyler. Wilkinson's map shows five McBride buildings, three fenced cultivated fields, and three fields in pasture.[4]

Like neighbors Jotham Bemis and Ezekial Ensign, John Freeman, his son Thomas, and James McBride were loyalists. The older Freeman's fidelity was especially active. According to Thomas' testimony supporting his claim for compensation, his father served as a guide during the British advance from Canada. After the army reached the Stillwater area he sold most of his animals to the commissary, and father and son enlisted in "Jessup's Corps," the unofficial designation for the King's Loyal Americans.[5] They were among the loyalist Provincials whom Burgoyne permitted to leave the British camp before the army's surrender. Thomas served until 1783; John died at South River prior to 1788.[6]

Also like Jotham Bemis, the Freemans and McBrides were not stereotypical Tories. The deep-rooted conflicting interests that obtained between patentee landlords and their tenants complicated New York's role in the Revolution. The great majority of the population were tenant farmers holding their farms by indentures. Mutual resentments occasionally flared into open hostility, as they did in 1740, 1757, and more recently in 1766, when 200 armed tenants on Livingston Manor—which, like most of the Saratoga Patent, lay in Albany County—rose against their landlord. The Saratoga Patent was spared the worst features of those troubles, partly because leases were longer and less blatantly exploitative. But even when the causes for friction were less grievous, conflicts of interest were present. If the landlord happened to be a loyalist, his tenants tended to adopt the revolutionary cause; if he was a prominent Whig, as in the case of the Schuylers and Livingstons of Albany County, tenants were often pro-British.

Burgoyne's expedition converted many of the tenantry from crypto-loyalists into overt supporters of the Empire, and a substantial number enlisted in Peters' and Jessup's Corps. Others, such as Jotham Bemis and his wife, were sufficiently active to attract the attention of the Commissioners for Detecting and Defeating Conspiracies.[7]

Burgoyne's Dilemma

The nineteenth of September of 1777 dawned unseasonably warm. Fog hung over the Hudson, blanketing both the American fortifications on Bemis Heights and Burgoyne's bivouac north of Kromma Creek (or the Great Ravine). The British commander had arrived at the proverbial moment of truth—the soldier's most dreaded predicament: forced to act on his enemy's terms.

It was unthinkable for Burgoyne to remain where he was, suspended between Canada and his objective of Albany. His camp was indefensible, vulnerable alike to attack from the hills that would pin his soldiers against the river and to being cut off to the north, ending all hope of extracting himself from his intolerable situation. Retreat was even less feasible. There was no way he could move his men and stores 100 miles to Ticonderoga without turning the withdrawal into a death march, harassed and eventually destroyed by Gates' 9,000-man army, General Benjamin Lincoln's force of 2,000 militia, and Colonel Seth Warner's Green Mountain veterans. In the unlikely event that Burgoyne could reach Ticonderoga, the post's supplies could not sustain the survivors against the rigors of a northern winter without resupply from Montreal, a difficult and dangerous undertaking.

Burgoyne's only viable option was to fight Horatio Gates. That reality reduced him to choosing one of two very unattractive alternatives. He could keep his army in column on the road to Albany and try to force his way past batteries posted athwart the road and on Bemis Heights' bluff. While he might be able to overrun the former, the fortified batteries on the bluff were secure against attack from the river valley. Any column marching broadside to that line could not survive an attempt to march through the narrow passage between Bemis Heights and the Hudson. The choice was nearly no choice at all.

The second option was to somehow lure or drive the Americans out of their fortified camp and open the way to Albany. Courage, determination, and professionalism might yet beat the obvious odds, save Burgoyne's army, and redeem British fortunes in the north. Perhaps snatching victory in this quarter, added to Sir William Howe's occupation of Philadelphia, would deal the rebellion the body blow that would end it. Burgoyne, "the old gamester," chose the latter of two unattractive options: he would advance against Gates' fortifications and engage him in battle.

A Primer on Warfare of the Era

Before describing the first major engagement, a brief digression examining Revolutionary-era infantry combat is useful for understanding the form the battle assumed.

One of the most enduring and treasured American traditions attributed to American success in its war for independence was a stark difference in tactics. The British and their German auxiliaries, captives of an antique, outmoded military heritage born on Europe's open battlefields, marched into battle in close formation against American sharpshooters fighting as individuals from the cover of trees, boulders, and walls. The events at Concord in 1775, and King's Mountain in 1780, lent apparent support to that perception, but even in those atypical firefights American marksmanship has been overrated. The overwhelming majority of battles did not take place under frontier conditions. "It was certainly not the backwoods rifle, a weapon virtually unknown in New England in 1775," explained one writer, "and which was not for another three-quarters of a century to develop into a practicable arm for general use, that won the war."[8]

The infantry's basic weapon was the flintlock smoothbore musket that fired a lead ball approximately ¾-inch in diameter (.75 caliber), to which a fourteen-inch bayonet could be attached (diminishing its accuracy). Loading required twelve motions, in the course of which the soldier tore off one end of a paper cartridge with his teeth, sprinkled a few grains of powder into the priming pan, and finally rammed cartridge and ball down the muzzle with the ramrod. The average soldier could fire two (and sometimes three) rounds a minute. Some experts might get off as many as five shots. Because the bayonet made it more difficult to use the ramrod, effectively only one round could be fired once bayonets were fixed. Some men in their haste did not bother to use the rod at all, pounding the musket butt on the ground to lodge the cartridge and ball. This method diminished the shot's effectiveness. Too rapid a rate of fire compromised the musket's effectiveness, which depended upon volley fire delivered by unit.

The battle line consisted of two ranks usually formed in open order (rather than shoulder-to-shoulder) with minimum depth between ranks. A rank of "file closers" sometimes followed about six paces behind to replace casualties. In the attack, the soldiers advanced while maintaining their alignment, knowing they were relatively safe until they stepped within about 100 yards of the enemy. Because deferring fire until about fifty yards distant from their opponents was desirable, strictly enforced fire discipline was essential. In fact, prevailing professional opinion held that it was better to receive, not deliver, the first fire, to sustain the inevitable losses, and then fire when close enough to the foe to ensure that every shot found a mark.

Firing was normally by volley as opposed to "at will" or individual firing. Loading and firing were done by command, with little or no aiming at a specific target. Except at close range, marksmanship was generally quite poor. The musket's smoothbore, rudimentary sight, and fixed bayonet militated against accuracy. Target practice received less attention than drill, and supply problems made powder and ball, always expensive, too dear to permit frequent target practice anyway. The volley was directed, on command, simply ahead, or perhaps to the left or right oblique. The objective was to lay down a curtain of fire ahead of one's troops at the desired rate of one shot every fifteen or twenty seconds, assuring at least two volleys before closing with the enemy. The men then resorted to clubbing with their muskets or stabbing with the bayonet, with which the British were famously effective.

It is important to remember that the ranks were normally in close, not extended, order. They thus formed a compact mass, presenting a solid target while firing at another compact body of men at pointblank range. Smoke produced by black powder quickly enveloped the line, making effective personal control of the unit difficult. While accuracy was superfluous, controlled speed was imperative. Speed allowed defenders to pour as many bullets into the attacking force as possible; speed allowed the attackers to close with the enemy before they had been too severely decimated to retain strength sufficient to carry their objective. But speed had to be subject to control. Many officers agreed with General James Wolfe when he wrote that firing very rapidly was unnecessary and that "a cool well-leveled fire with the pieces carefully loaded is more destructive and formidable than the quickest fire in confusion."[9] Because the men usually carried no more than thirty rounds, uncontrolled fire was not only less effective, but quickly exhausted the ammunition supply. Burgoyne's General Order for September 21, which praised the conduct of officers and men during the fighting on the nineteenth, tempered his praise with a revealing paragraph in which he again reinforced the preference for the bayonet over the ball, and the particular importance of firing only on an officer's order.[10] These were the words of an experienced officer—wise advice that reflected knowledge of the foot soldiers' basic weapon.

Burgoyne's General Order also reflected an easily forgotten truism of military history: there are limits to the degree to which tactical doctrines and the commanders who apply them can control the actions of even the best-disciplined soldier during the confusion, fear, and excitement of combat. In that environment, fire discipline tended to deteriorate into "rolling fire," a euphemism for firing "at will," with every man reloading and pulling the trigger as rapidly as he could, with the company officers losing control in the resulting din. The rigid drill upon which volley fire depended worked against regaining control. The soldiers were so absorbed in the mechanics of reloading and firing and in dulling the natural desire to run away that the only way officers could break the routine was to get in front of the men and strike up their muskets' muzzles—a dangerous and difficult undertaking. British light infantrymen and fusiliers also carried regular muskets; artillerymen were usually armed with carbines, a shorter and lighter version of the musket.[11]

And then there was the rifle. In spite of this weapon's limited military utility, some German light infantry units, called Jägers (German for hunters), carried a short rifle. Interestingly, the Continental Congress' first military decision, even before naming George Washington commander-in-chief, was a resolution "that six companies of expert riflemen be immediately raised in Pennsylvania, two in Maryland, and two in Virginia."[12] Pennsylvania's response was so enthusiastic that Congress raised that state's quota to nine companies, organized as Colonel William Thompson's Pennsylvania Rifle Battalion, later the 1st Continental Infantry. Disciplinary problems compromised their usefulness during the siege of Boston, and riflemen fell from favor as reliable soldiers.[13]

The regiment was the British Army's basic organization, but that was an administrative, rather than a tactical, term. The titular or administrative commander was the colonel who contracted with the Crown to raise and equip a regiment. Except for units designated "Royal," the regiments were their colonels' property, and they intended to profit financially and socially from that species of property by selling commissions, receiving a bounty for each recruit, negotiating lucrative contracts for uniforms, and retaining for each colonel the captaincy of one company. A captain-lieutenant exercised personal command of the "colonel's company." The Crown paid the colonel an annual sum he was expected to use in paying the soldiers, buying clothing, and enlisting replacements. Because there was no pay scale for general officers, the salary of each depended on his being titular colonel of a regiment—that might or might not be part of his command as a general. For example, Burgoyne's regiment was the 16th ("Queen's") Light Dragoons, from whose ownership as the colonel and the captaincy of one company he derived his income; but his regiment did not accompany him on his expedition.

The tactical unit was the battalion, but the terms "regiment" and "battalion" were practically synonymous during this era because regiments usually consisted of one battalion. The active tactical commander, the man who commanded in garrison or in the field, was the lieutenant colonel, who also had the captaincy of the "lieutenant colonel's company," personally commanded by his company's lieutenant. The standard regiment/battalion had ten companies, eight of which were "battalion companies." The other two were "flank companies," one of grenadiers and one of light infantry. Flank companies were often brigaded together to form grenadier and light infantry corps or battalions.

Americans modeled their regiments on the British, though that modeling was not precise. They never formed grenadier companies, for example, and colonels were the regiments' tactical commanders until after January 1778, when Congress created the rank of "Lieutenant Colonel, Commandant" to facilitate grade-for-grade exchange of captured regimental commanders. The Americans did organize light infantry companies and, like the Europeans, they sometimes merged them to form elite corps for special missions. Morgan's Rifle Regiment was technically light infantry. The number of companies and the strength of American regiments varied from state to state and from time to time.

A cherished tradition, one fostered by admiring biographers and some generals, represented general officers as personally leading their armies into battle in the heroic mode of Alexander the Great and Henry V.[14] Although general officers did continue to personally command on the battle line when a crisis required them to show themselves, as the Duke of Marlborough did at Blenheim in 1704, they normally exercised command from positions from which they could receive intelligence and issue orders through aides and couriers.

The advent of firearms and field artillery wrought a tactical revolution that changed the way officers, especially generals, functioned. The diminished dependence upon the shock effect of massed formations caused a gradual reduction in the number of ranks, from eight or ten at the beginning of the seventeenth century to two or three by the end of the eighteenth. That thinning and attendant extension of the front rendered impossible the personal control of large units.

Under the pressure of a crisis that required his physical presence, a general might inspire his troops or retrieve a deteriorating situation by taking over direct command. He always did so, however, at the expense of being able to provide overall direction. In addition to placing his person at risk, he limited himself to experiencing the battle from the common soldier's perspective, became inaccessible to subordinates, and ceased to be able to influence events occurring outside his severely limited field of view. Killing was the soldier's business; the officer's was to lead and exercise immediate command; the general's obligation was to direct. It should go without saying that such precise compartmentalizing did not always obtain in combat, but violating it was so risky as to limit doing so to moments when extreme conditions demanded extreme measures.[15]

Application to the Engagement at Freeman's Farm

Most early accounts by participants in the fighting of September 19 agree that the American generals followed prevailing command practice. "It is worthy to remark, that not a single general officer was on the field of battle the 19th Sept until the evening when General Learned was ordered out," explained James Wilkinson. "General Gates and Arnold were in front of the center of the camp, listening to the peal of small arms . . . ." Two enlisted men, John Neilson and Ezra Buel, told Jared Sparks that "there were no general officers in the action. At one time Buel said he saw Genl. Poor, with two or three other officers, quite in the rear of the American Army, and taking no part in the action. The fighting was chiefly under the eyes of [Colonels] Morgan, Scamil and Cilley."[16]

General Gates, in his fortified camp on Bemis Heights, enjoyed advantages not available to his opponent. He occupied a defined, relatively compact position, one that dominated all probable combat arenas. He could, from the crest of the heights, direct the response to Burgoyne's initiative without subjecting himself to the limitations that direct physical involvement on the battlefield imposed. In contrast, the dominating vantage point nearest to where Burgoyne camped is Fraser Hill, two and one-half miles west of Swords House and almost three and one-half miles by road. For much of that distance, the road lay between the steep banks of the Kromma Kill. Thus, there was no point from which the British commander could oversee and direct the battle.

Burgoyne labored under other disadvantages. His reconnaissance parties were unable to obtain accurate intelligence about the configuration and strength of Gates' left wing. His transport tied him to the river and the road that paralleled it, and their security required posting the 47th Regiment's six available battalion companies to guard bateaux and supplies. Because his real objective was reopening the route southward, he had to divide his army by leaving a force on the road strong enough to exploit any weakening of Gates' interdictive posture.

The British commander tried to mitigate his problems by adopting the solution employed by Ferdinand of Braunschweig during the Battle of Krefeld in 1758.[17] He followed his critical wing, the one moving against Horatio Gates' left flank, relinquishing effective control over his own reserve and the left wing posted along the river, hoping that sufficient coordination between his two wings would be maintained. The competence of General Freiherr von Riedesel,

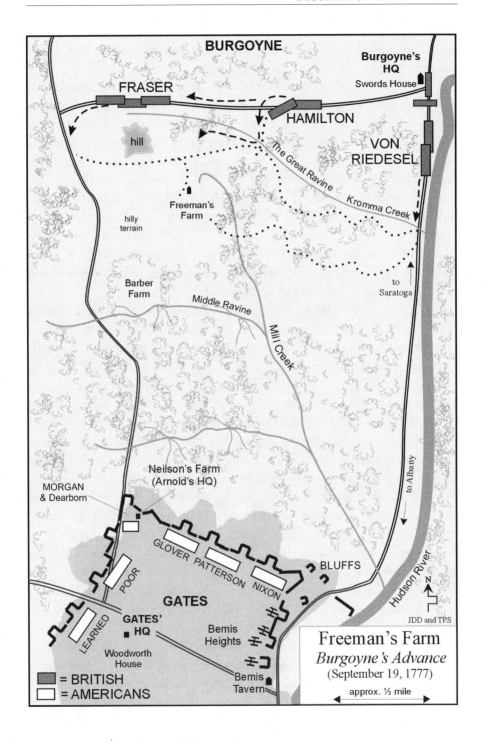

BURGOYNE

Burgoyne's
HQ
Swords House

FRASER

HAMILTON

VON
RIEDESEL

hill

The Great Ravine

Kromma Creek

Freeman's
Farm

hilly
terrain

Barber
Farm

Middle Ravine

Mill Creek

to
Saratoga

Neilson's Farm
(Arnold's HQ)

MORGAN
& Dearborn

to Albany

GLOVER PATTERSON NIXON

POOR

BLUFFS

Hudson River

GATES

LEARNED

GATES'
HQ

Bemis
Heights

N

JDD and TPS

Woodworth
House

Bemis
Tavern

= BRITISH
= AMERICANS

Freeman's Farm
Burgoyne's Advance
(September 19, 1777)

approx. ½ mile

who commanded the left wing, reduced, but did not eliminate, the risk Burgoyne took.

The 3,011-man left wing was the tactical key to Burgoyne's advance, the base upon which Fraser's Corps right wing and Hamilton's central column deployed. Because its role was initially passive, the von Riedesel column's importance is easy to underestimate. Its core was the four German regiments: von Riedesel, von Rhetz, and Specht under General Specht, and the Hesse-Hanau Erbprinz, commanded by General von Gall; 100 Jägers, and eighty dismounted dragoons. Captain Pausch's sixty artillerymen and their four 6-pounders and Lieutenant Dufais' two 6-pounders completed the German column. In addition to the six companies of the 47th Regiment guarding the stores, the force proceeding down the river valley included the bulk of the British artillery train: two 24-pounders, four 12-pounders, four 6-pounders, two 8-inch howitzers, and three 5 ½-inch howitzers.[18]

Marching about 9:00 a.m. along a road running westward from Swords house for three miles from the river to a junction with the road from Bemis Heights to Quaker Springs, Fraser's Corps formed the right column. It contained ten companies each of grenadiers and light infantry, Fraser's rangers, four companies each of German grenadiers and light infantry, an under-strength Jäger company, the British 24th Regiment's eight battalion companies, two Canadian companies, and Provincials [Loyalists]. Captain Walker's 140 men serving six 6-pounders and two 5 ½-inch howitzers accompanied them. Fraser's strength totaled 2,547 men. His mission was to engage Gates' left wing and, if possible, turn it.

The smallest column, the center of Burgoyne's army, numbered 1,598 men under Brigadier James Hamilton. It consisted of the battalion companies of the British 9th, 20th, 21st, and 62nd regiments supported by Captain Jones' four 6-pounders. Burgoyne and his headquarters accompanied Hamilton's Division, which followed Fraser's route until it reached a junction with the first southbound road, then followed it across the Kromma Kill's ravine southward across a plateau until reaching a rough track running westward from the river. Burgoyne and Hamilton turned right onto that trail, which led them up a steep draw to a wooded tableland between the Great Ravine and the stream later called the North Fork. The column halted about one-half mile west of the draw, and faced left (southward) in line. A picket occupied an abandoned house on a knoll south of the road. There it waited for the two flank columns [Fraser's and von Riedesel's] to get into parallel positions.[19]

Gates' Choices

Horatio Gates had scouts out on both sides of the river. The patrols on the east side were especially useful, observing the enemy from the vantage point of the height later called Mount Willard. From these reports Gates acquired three important pieces of intelligence: (1) Burgoyne had resorted to the risky tactic of dividing his army into three elements, widely separated by ravines, woods, and small clearings; (2) the British general intended to engage the American left; and (3) working parties were repairing bridges on the river road, and a large infantry force, supported by artillery, was advancing toward the Bemis Tavern. Gates knew where his enemy was, how he was deployed, and from this information correctly divined his purpose. He now had to devise a tactic to frustrate that design.

His first decision was to intensify the concentration of forces facing the enemy. To that end, he immediately dispatched an order to General Benjamin Lincoln at Pawlet to march the troops not already committed to "distressing the enemy" in the Lake George-Ticonderoga sector to join the main force on the Hudson, where he should post 500 or 600 men on the hills across from Bemis Tavern. The rest of Lincoln's men were to occupy the former camp at Stillwater Village.[20] Gates knew Lincoln could not arrive before September 22, and so did not intend to employ him in defending Bemis Heights against Burgoyne's immediate threat. What he did intend was to have him in position to be available for two eventualities: if the Americans on Bemis Heights failed to repel the British decisively and Burgoyne persevered in moving along the shelf of land between the river and the right flank of the American fortifications, the troops on the hills above the east bank and in the Stillwater camp would reinforce the road's interdiction. If, on the other hand, the enemy were repulsed and forced to retreat, being on the Hudson would position Lincoln to cooperate in pressing the American advantage.

More immediately pressing was the problem of how to counter the enemy's three-column advance. Should the Americans remain in their fortifications waiting for the enemy to attack? There was much to recommend that course of action. The natural advantages enjoyed by men defending themselves behind cover were multiplied in this instance by a numerical superiority. The Americans' performance when employing linear tactics in the open against disciplined, determined professionals whose better fire discipline and skill with the bayonet was proverbial had not been impressive; whereas, their record while fighting from cover was more than respectable. Defense was also more economical in manpower. Standing on the defensive in their works might postpone the decision at arms—a postponement that could only benefit the defenders. The Americans operated on interior lines, with access to reinforcements and resupply, while their enemy could be neither reinforced nor resupplied. In addition, troops deployed by Lincoln along his lines of communication jeopardized Burgoyne's contact with Ticonderoga and Canada. Orthodox military doctrine, reinforced by history, argued for remaining in the fortified camp and forcing the British commander to resort to the attack, a costly option with prospects for success that diminished hourly. These factors explain why remaining on the defensive had been Gates' original intention.

There was, however, another, more aggressive alternative, and one that Benedict Arnold strongly favored.[21] That option called for attacking the British before they came within range of the American camp. Engaging them in the woods and the small, stump-studded farm clearings north of Bemis Heights could reduce the effectiveness of superior European skill in linear, close-order tactics and prevent their bringing artillery into play against American fortifications. Morgan's riflemen would be especially effective in the woods, exploiting the broken ground cover to break up cohesive enemy formations. If the Americans failed to completely repel their enemy, they could withdraw and re-form behind their works, where they stood a strong chance of frustrating and defeating Burgoyne.[22]

But invoking that proactive tactic involved risks that made Gates hesitate to employ it, in spite of the cogency of arguments in its favor. A fundamental reason for caution was the difference in the quality of soldiers. Although the Americans outnumbered their enemy in terms of raw numbers, they were inferior in training, discipline, and experience. Most of Gates' men were Continentals, but not all were battle-hardened veterans. The militia could not be depended upon to stand firm against well-led veterans, especially if asked to fight outside the works. The broken terrain that made well-ordered European formations difficult to maintain made their maintenance by less-experienced Americans even more so. Using riflemen armed with their slow-loading pieces in the open invited disaster. Finally, Gates was a product of European doctrine and practice. He was more economical of manpower than was Arnold, whose faith in American ability to field larger numbers of men made him more aggressive and less prudent.

Contrary to what his detractors alleged, Gates was determined to fight Burgoyne, but he meant to do it on his own terms. He intended to force his

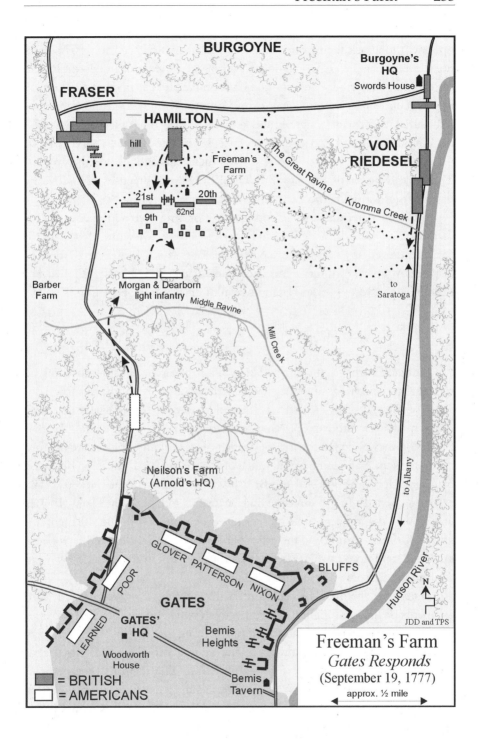

Freeman's Farm
Gates Responds
(September 19, 1777)
approx. ½ mile

opponent to attack the fortified camp, which he was certain the British could not capture. That failure would doom Burgoyne's expedition and defeat British plans to have a northern army on the Hudson for Sir William Howe to employ in prosecuting a future campaign. If the Americans did not permit themselves to be lured from their stronghold and kept their nerve, they must win. Gates did not intend to be lured, and he did not expect his men to lose their nerve. And so the Americans prepared for battle, striking their tents and loading the wagons. These acts were not preludes to withdrawal, but normal practices when an army readied itself for trying the fortunes of war.[23]

Although determined to defend his position from behind the cover of his fortifications, Gates did not commit himself to a passive defense. He was all for harassing the enemy's offensive deployment. To that end, he directed Arnold to dispatch Morgan to observe and harry the advancing columns, an intelligent exploitation of resources and an indication of his intent to give battle.[24]

The First Phase: Morgan Probes

Morgan's corps of riflemen and light infantry marched in column along the road to Quaker Springs until they reached the woods north of the field of fire in front of Arnold's Division. There they deployed in open-order lines, with Morgan in his customary place slightly to the rear of the center. In that formation they obliqued toward the British center column until, shortly before noon, some riflemen came within range of John Freeman's house-lot, occupied by Major Gordon Forbes of the British 9th Regiment and his pickets.[25] The riflemen opened a fire so effective that, according to Lieutenant Digby, Forbes was wounded and every other officer killed or wounded.[26] The riflemen, not known for their caution and their discipline, rushed into the cleared field—and ran headlong into a formidable fire that caught them in the open, converting their weapons from an asset into a liability.

Hamilton deployed his column, with the 9th, 21st, 62nd, and 20th regiments on line from right to left respectively, while Fraser detached two light infantry companies toward the sound of the firing.

A crisis of command and discipline among Morgan's men arose that threatened to confirm Gates' fears about committing them in open combat. Gates and members of his staff were inspecting a newly-positioned battery when they heard firing from the direction of Freeman's farm. Colonel James Wilkinson rode toward the sound to find out what was happening.[27] After entering the woods he found Major Dearborn, who was "forming about thirty or forty file" to intercept the light infantry companies Fraser had dispatched. He also met Major Morris, who reported the details of the initial engagement with Forbes' pickets and accompanied Wilkinson to Freeman's house, which "was almost encircled with dead." After leaving the house, he found Lieutenant Colonel Butler with three men, "all treed," who told him that they had "caught a Scotch prize [meaning, no prize at all],"

> that having forced the picket, they had closed with the British line, and been instantly routed, and from the suddenness of the shock and the nature of the ground, were broken and scattered in all directions. . . . We changed our position and the Colonel inquired what were Morgan's orders, and informed me that he had seen a heavy column moving towards our left. I then turned about to regain the camp and report to the General [Gates], when my ears were saluted by an uncommon noise, which I approached, and perceived Colonel Morgan attended by two men only, who with a turkey call was collecting his dispersed troops. The moment I came up to him, he burst into tears, and exclaimed, "I am ruined, by G – d! Major Morris ran on so rapidly with the front, that they were beaten before I could get up with the rear, and my men scattered God knows where. I remarked to the Colonel that he had a long day before him where I had seen his field officers, which appeared to cheer him, and we parted."[28]

Morgan's riflemen rallied in the woods bordering the farm, while Dearborn's light infantry covered their left, facing lead elements of Fraser's Corps.

While Morgan's riflemen in this instance exhibited the indiscipline that often marred American combat effectiveness, some of Brigadier Hamilton's men also conducted themselves with less than the cool-headed self-control battle-wise British veterans were expected to display. They reacted to the unaccustomed experience of being shot at by almost invisible, highly accurate marksmen by shooting back individually without orders. With the contagion that can attend lapses in discipline, the confusion spread among the British units closest to the Freeman farm, killing several of Forbes' own pickets as they withdrew into the line. Deputy Adjutant Robert Kingston ordered Lieutenant James Hadden to fire a signal gun, which quickly restored fire discipline.[29]

No match for restored volley firepower, Morgan's command retreated to rising ground about 275 yards south of Freeman's house. Wilkinson returned to camp and reported to General Gates, who ordered Arnold to commit reinforcements.[30] Colonel Joseph Cilley's 1st New Hampshire engaged "a Body of the Enimy [sic] with a great Deal of Spirit."[31] Dearborn's light infantry moved to the right, in line with the reinforcement, but the British forced Cilley back until Lieutenant Colonel Winborn Adams and Colonel Alexander Scammell brought their regiments, the 2nd and 3rd New Hampshire, forward into line on Morgan's left.[32]

By 2:00 p.m., Burgoyne's three columns had responded to their signal and begun to advance simultaneously. Gates had little choice but to alter his tactics. He could have adhered to his original design by covering Morgan's withdrawal into the camp, and then defended that position with the advantages accruing to holding fortifications against numerically weaker assailants. By his decision to support Morgan with the New Hampshire regiments, he adopted Arnold's more aggressive tactical option. But he continued to be determined not to be lured into diluting the strength of the interdicting right wing blocking the route to Albany. He did, however, anticipate rather than await an attack on his left. He thus converted Morgan's harassing action into the prelude to a pitched battle—one that would be fought according to conventional, linear, field practices. The fighting that followed exposed the dangers attendant to that conversion.

Morgan's Corps and the three New Hampshire regiments, more than 1,700 men, deployed into a crescent-shaped front around the southern and southwestern fringes of Freeman's fields. The riflemen's right lay between a field and a ravine. To their left, the 3rd, 2nd, and 1st New Hampshire regiments linked up with Dearborn's light infantry, which continued to skirmish with the point of Fraser's column. Opposing the Americans were five regiments numbering about 1,600 men. The British line included, left to right, the 20th, 62nd, and 21st regiments from Hamilton's Division. The 9th formed to the rear in reserve, with two companies occupying buildings between the Freeman and McBride houses. General Fraser detailed the battalion companies of his own 24th Regiment under Major William Agnew toward Hamilton's right, deploying *en potence* (that is, drawn back at an angle) to his column. The British light infantry and German Jägers occupied high ground 260 yards northwest of the British 9th Regiment.[33]

The American efforts to turn Hamilton's right flank met with transitory success, pushing his line northward across the weed-covered fields. They briefly captured one 6-pounder cannon, but because they lacked linstocks and

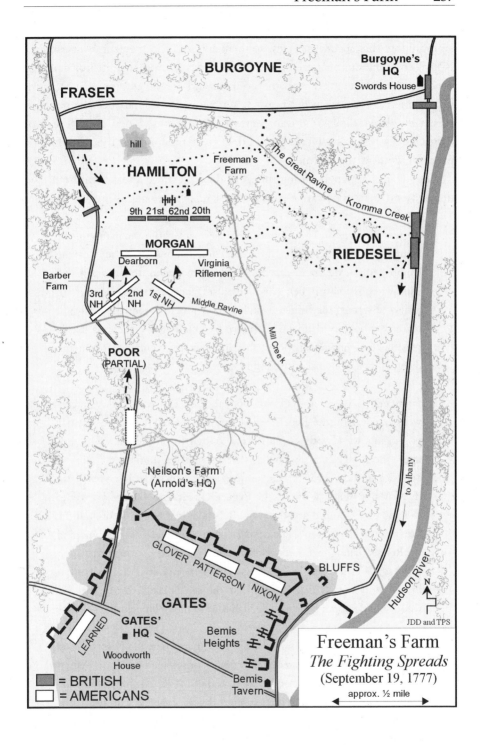

BURGOYNE

Burgoyne's
HQ
Swords House

FRASER

hill

HAMILTON

Freeman's
Farm

The Great Ravine

Kromma Creek

9th 21st 62nd 20th

VON
RIEDESEL

MORGAN

Dearborn

Virginia
Riflemen

Barber
Farm

3rd
NH

2nd
NH

1st NH

Middle Ravine

Mill Creek

POOR
(PARTIAL)

Neilson's Farm
(Arnold's HQ)

to Albany

GLOVER PATTERSON NIXON

BLUFFS

Hudson River

N

GATES

JDD and TPS

GATES'
HQ

Bemis
Heights

Bemis
Tavern

Woodworth
House

Freeman's Farm
The Fighting Spreads
(September 19, 1777)
approx. ½ mile

LEARNED

= BRITISH
= AMERICANS

ammunition, the piece was useless to them and was soon retaken by its original British crew. Hamilton's men quickly recovered from their initial disciplinary breakdown and behaved with the courage and steadiness for which British infantrymen were deservedly praised. With a series of bayonet charges they repeatedly drove their American enemy back into the woods. But there their own charges lost cohesiveness and effect over time, giving the Americans a precious window to reform.

For what happened during this period of the early afternoon, useful and detailed first-person narratives from three British combatants are available.

> *Sergeant Roger Lamb:* The Americans being unable from the nature of the country, of perceiving the different combinations of march (as the country is thickly covered with woods, movements may be effected without a possibility of being discovered) advanced a strong column, with a view of turning the British right, here they met the grenadiers and light infantry, who gave them a tremendous fire. Finding it was impossible to penetrate the line at this point, they immediately counter-marched and directed their principal effort to the centre.[34]

> *Joshua Pell (volunteer):* About two o'clock the 9th, 21st and 62nd regiments were engaged by the Rebels near Freeman's Farm, they were strongly posted in a wood with a deep Ravine to their front, the fire was so hot upon the 20th, 21st, and 62nd, that they broke, but by the spirited behavior of their Officers were immediately rallied, and drove them from there. Major Agnew with the 24th Regt. advanced into the woods in order to flank them; on the first onset the Rebels retired in confusion, but the fire from the [Hamilton's] line having abated considerably at this time, and the Rebels finding their Left Flank in danger, poured a strong force upon this Regt. Which caused them to retire about one hundred yards behind an inclosure in a grass field [McBride's]; the rebels fought bravely in the woods but darst not advance one inch toward the open field.[35]

> *Royal Artillery Lieutenant James Hadden:* The Enemy being in possession of the wood almost immediately attacked the Corps which took post behind two log huts on Freeman's Farm. Capt. [Thomas] Jones' Brigade [company] was hasten'd to their support, I was advanced with two Guns to the left of the 62nd Regt. And ye two left companies being formed en potence I took post in the Angle. Lieut [George] Reid remain'd with Capt

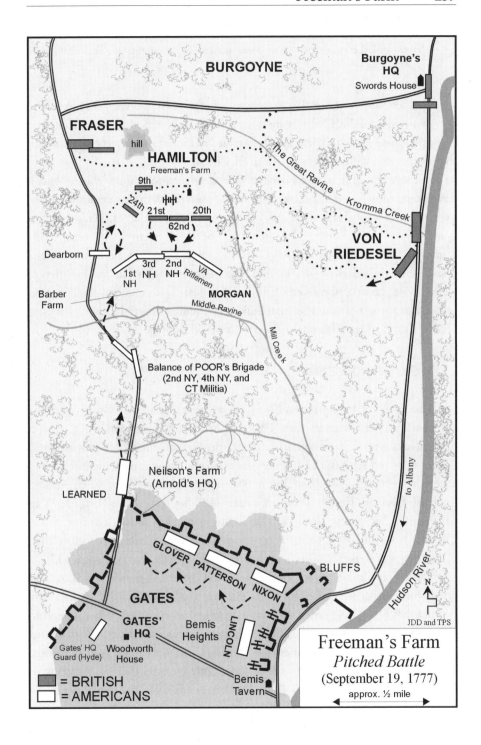

FREEMAN'S FARM
Pitched Battle
(September 19, 1777)
approx. ½ mile

= BRITISH
= AMERICANS

JDD and TPS

Jones and the other two [guns] was posted between the 9th and 21st Rgts.[36]

Hadden added to Pell's narrative of the 24th's involvement: "Five companies of the 24th Regt. were advanced into the wood in their front, and being repulsed a second attempt was made by the whole Regiment, in which they succeeded with the loss of about fifty men."

Because the 21st wheeled back to face westward to counter the American enveloping movement, the 62nd found itself converted into a salient in the line, exposed to fire on both flanks and suffering heavy casualties. Hadden's two guns, posted in the angle, lost nineteen of their twenty-two men. While requesting infantry support from General Hamilton, who was present on the line, a shot passed through Hadden's hat. The brigadier had no infantry to spare, so the lieutenant moved off to plead his case with General Phillips, who joined Burgoyne near the Freeman buildings. Phillips ordered Captain Jones to accompany Hadden with one of Lieutenant Reid's crews.[37]

A General Action Ensues

The fight in the center had become much more than a British probing action and an American ambush. The two armies had engaged in heavy, though indecisive, combat interrupted by lulls during which their units reformed to deliver renewed attacks and counterattacks. For all its intensity, there remained a certain tentativeness about the action until mid-afternoon, when Arnold directed General Enoch Poor to order out the rest of his brigade: Van Cortlandt's 2nd New York, H. B. Livingston's 4th New York, and the Connecticut Militia.[38] Americans on the firing line now numbered more than 2,200 men, substantially more than the number of British troops engaged.[39]

The effect on the fighting of the increased American numbers was to wear down the British 62nd Regiment to the point where it fell into confusion. Almost half its officers and men had been killed or wounded. When forced to abandon the hill on which it had been fighting, Lieutenant Hadden's two guns moved off with it. The Americans pressed the retreating British troops, following at a distance of a mere 100 yards. Only General Phillips' throwing of the 20th Regiment into the woods on the British left saved the remainder of the 62nd from probable destruction.[40]

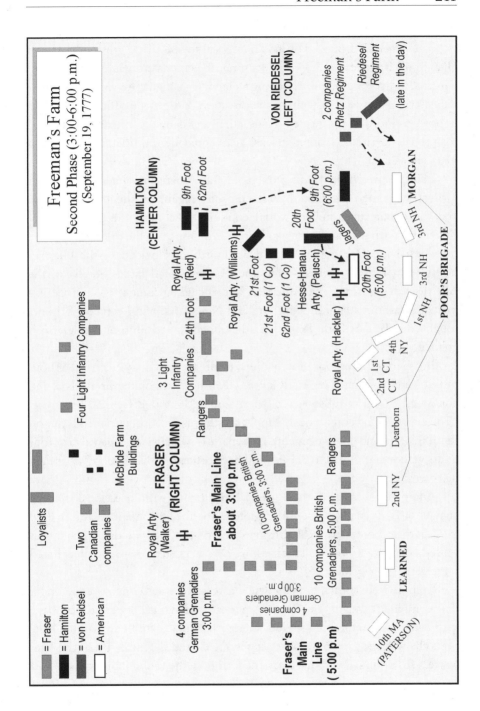

Freeman's Farm
Second Phase (3:00-6:00 p.m.)
(September 19, 1777)

The Americans, buoyed by their numerical superiority, aggressively pressed Hamilton's Brigade and Fraser's Corps, but the latter's entry into the fight had frustrated the early attempts to turn Hamilton's right. Relying upon their increased manpower but without the direction of a general officer who could impose a more sophisticated tactic, the regimental commanders limited themselves to simple frontal attacks, augmented by the riflemen's harassing marksmanship.

Later, between 4:00 and 5:00 p.m., the American right, consisting of Morgan's riflemen, the three New Hampshire regiments, the 4th New York, and the Connecticut militia, would continue to contest the possession of Freeman's farm with a reorganized British left. Opposing the riflemen were the men best suited for coping with their unorthodox practices—the German Jägers from Fraser's Corps—while the 21st and 62nd faced the rest of the American right wing. The American left, including Latimore's and Cook's militia, Dearborn's light infantry, the 2nd New York, and Learned's Brigade, fought the British 24th Regiment, the rangers, and British and German grenadiers.[41]

But by mid-afternoon, the battle was already reaching its crisis. "About three o'clock the action began by a very vigorous attack on the British line, and continued with great obstinacy till after sunset," reported General Burgoyne. "The enemy being continuously supplied with fresh troops, the stress lay upon the 20th, 21st, and 62nd regiments, most parts of which were engaged near four hours without intermission; the 9th had been ordered early in the day to form in reserve."

Burgoyne supported these central regiments with occasional spirited charges by his grenadiers, the 24th regiment, and the light infantry. He also used the Jägers and other parts of Breyman's corps but, not wanting to endanger Fraser's control of the heights on which he was posted, these too constituted mere partial engagements.[42]

Cumulatively speaking, Burgoyne's forces were suffering severely under the combined weight of three American strengths: superior numbers; surprising (to some) courage; and telling marksmanship. "Few actions have been characterized by more obstinacy in attack and defence," Burgoyne later wrote. He continued with his assessment of how the action unfolded:

> The British bayonet was repeatedly tried ineffectually. Eleven hundred British foiled in these trials, bore incessant fire from fresh troops in superior numbers, for above four hours; and after a loss of above a third

of their numbers (and in one of the regiments above two thirds). . . . Of a detachment of a captain and forty-eight men, the captain and thirty-six were killed or wounded. . . .The tribute of praise due to such troops will not be wanting in this generous nation; and it will as certainly be accompanied with a just portion of shame to those who have dared to deprecate or sully valour so conspicuous—who have their ears open only to the prejudice of American cowardice, and having been always loud upon that courtly topic, stifle the glory of their countrymen to maintain a base consistency.[43]

Other British veterans agreed in describing the heaviness of the fighting. Lord Balcarres testified that the "enemy behaves with great obstinacy and courage." Deputy Quarter Master Money was impressed by the gunfire's intensity, as were Lord Harrington, Major Forbes, and Lieutenant Colonel Kingston, confirming American accounts.[44]

Burgoyne attributed the disproportionately large number of officer casualties to the "great number of marksmen, armed with rifle-barrel pieces: these, during an engagement, hovered upon the flanks in small detachments, and were very expert in securing themselves, and in shifting their ground. In this action," continued Burgoyne, "many placed themselves in high trees in the rear of their own line, and there was seldom a minute's interval of smoke, in any part of our line without officers being taken off by [a] single shot."[45]

"Here the conflict was dreadfull [sic] for four hours a constant blaze of fire was kept up, and both armies seemed to be determined on death or victory," wrote Sergeant Roger Lamb of the 9th Regiment, providing a corroborating narrative from the enlisted man's perspective. "Men, and particularly officers, dropped every moment on each side. Several of the Americans placed themselves in high trees, and as often as [they] could distinguish a British officer's uniform, took him off by deliberately aiming at his person. Reinforcements successively arrived and strengthened the American line."[46]

Burgoyne and the British found great difficulty in countering this latter American advantage. The Indians and Canadians, whom Burgoyne had hoped "would be of great use against this mode of fighting," disappointed him. Of the former, "those that remained after the great desertion . . . not a man of them was to be brought within sound of a rifle shot." And after the best Canadian officer fell, his men soon lost their morale. In fact, not the Indians nor the Canadians but the German Jägers were "the best men to oppose as marksmen . . . . though their number was so small, as not to be one to twenty to the enemy."[47]

By late afternoon the battle was turning in the Americans' favor. They had savaged Hamilton's Brigade so thoroughly that it was in danger of ceasing to be an effective unit. Fraser's Corps retained its defensive capability and continued to be dangerous, but it could not have survived a collapse by Hamilton and the growing American numerical superiority. Only the injection of a new body of troops could save the day for the hard-pressed, exhausted Europeans as they faced ever stronger and more aggressive Americans on the firing line. Salvation arrived in the form of Burgoyne's left column.[48]

The Germans Rescue the British

While Fraser and Hamilton made their approach march and engaged Morgan's Corps and Learned's and Poor's regiments, General von Riedesel's work parties built and repaired bridges preparatory to launching the basic strategic strike: an advance against the American right wing. It is important to emphasize that Burgoyne's purpose was to reopen the road past Bemis' Tavern, the road interdicted by the fortifications athwart and above that route. Reopening the road required that the Americans be enticed or driven from their interdicting fortifications. The German column's mission was to exploit any success that Fraser and Hamilton had in dislodging the Americans from Bemis Heights. Remember also that von Riedesel's force was larger than either of the other two European commands, totaling slightly more than 3,000 men (excluding 300 sailors, engineers, and Canadian wagoneers).[49] The artillery train consisted of fourteen cannon, including two light 24-pounders, four medium 12-pounders, four light 6-pounders, two 8-inch howitzers, four 5 ½-inch mortars, and "several Coehorn Mortars" mounted on bateaux.[50] Thus, von Riedesel's was the best-armed column, the one best equipped to deal with the kind of strong, fortified position against which Burgoyne anticipated employing his unusually powerful artillery train.

As soon as the artificers had completed the bridge over a small stream 510 yards south of the Taylor house, von Riedesel signaled his regimental commanders to start down the road, with his own regiment in the lead, followed by the Rhetz, Specht, Erbprinz, and 47th regiments. Their advance got under way while work continued on a bridge over the Kromma Kill, which drains the Great Ravine.

About 2:00 p.m., Captain Thomas Blomefield of the Royal Artillery, who had accompanied General Phillips, reported to von Riedesel that the

Braunschweiger [Brunswick] Jägers were heavily engaged and that a general battle was developing on the Freeman farm. The German general ordered the captain to return to the line with "weniger grosse Kannon aus dem Artilleriensatz [a few heavy cannon from the artillery train]."[51] Soon after Blomefield left with an unrecorded number of 12-pounders, von Riedesel sent his English aide, Captain Samuel Willoe, to obtain more information from General Burgoyne. Ignorant of American deployment and intentions, von Riedesel made preparations against a surprise attack. He was especially concerned about the area between the two bridges.

Drawn up along a 500-yard line were the supply wagons and most of the artillery. Von Riedesel placed his own regiment in line about 400 yards west of the road. Two companies of Regiment von Rhetz formed on the right, and two of Captain Georg Pausch's 6-pounders covered an open field to the line's left and front. The remaining three companies of the von Rhetz regiment faced southward between Pausch's battery and the road; dragoons and Jägers formed a picket line to the left of the battery. Lieutenant F. Carl Reinking sent out patrols, which were to withdraw if they made solid contact with the enemy. Already, American patrols were active enough to be annoying—they shot one dragoon's horse out from under him.[52]

Captain Willoe soon returned with orders from Burgoyne directing von Riedesel to provide for the security of the artillery and baggage and then bring as many regiments as was feasible and attack the right flank of the American firing line. The baron immediately started his regiment, two von Rhetz companies, and Pausch's two-gun battery on the road to Freeman's farm, leaving General Specht with his regiment, the British 47th, the six remaining companies of the von Rhetz regiment, the Jäger company, dragoons, and the bulk of the artillery train in position along the Albany road.[53]

Intending to bring his men into battle fresh, von Riedesel halted them for two brief rests. By 5:00 p.m., they had completed their mile-long approach march and deployed to fall upon the exposed American right flank. The surprise blow struck Morgan's riflemen and the New Hampshire regiments, turning and bending them back behind the main line of resistance. As Hamilton's men on the British right rallied, the 10th Massachusetts from Paterson's Brigade arrived and formed on the American left, too late to stiffen the resistance of the embattled American line. Hit hard but holding their order remarkably well, the Americans conducted a fighting withdrawal across the Freeman, Coulter, and Barber farms to the Middle Fork, where they found safety from pursuit by their exhausted enemy. After catching their breath there, the men retreated within their prepared lines.[54]

Although no one knew it yet, the battle of Freeman's Farm was over. The fighting ended a little more than one hour after von Riedesel arrived on the field in dramatic fashion to fall against the exposed American flank. The British possessed the field, one of the telltale signs of the tactical winner of any engagement. However, the route to Albany remained closed, for Paterson's and Nixon's brigades were still in place on Bemis Heights overlooking that key road. Burgoyne might claim a tactical victory, but Horatio Gates and his men had won the more important strategic success.

Between Battles: Fortifying and Squabbling

The Fighting Does Not Continue

After sundown and the American withdrawal to Bemis Heights, General Burgoyne's men who had fought the battle of Freeman' s Farm lay down on the field in ranks and under arms. They had no time to bring up rations, tents, or baggage, and so shivered through the chill autumn night, listening to the cries of wounded men to whom they could not minister in the darkness. The cold at least spared them the stench that rises where men die violently—one which no veteran of combat can ever forget. The belief that they had won the day when their stubborn enemy quit the field may have made their discomfort less acute, but those most heavily engaged were too tired to savor any sense of victory.[1] The men of the left column under General Freiherr von Riedesel lay on their arms along the Albany Road, but they had access to food and blankets and so were less fatigued than their comrades on the battlefield.

Dawn brought relief from the night's cold, and wagons and carts arrived with rations and baggage for the men on the main line of resistance. Those carts and wagons carried wounded to the hospital located near the Albany Road, where the army had camped on the eve of battle. Burial parties collected the dead and interred them east of Freeman's house.[2]

The equally weary Americans of Arnold's Division spent a somewhat more comfortable night in their tents and, after hours without food, could prepare and eat their rations. Surviving sources are silent about how well they rested. Some likely slept the sleep of exhaustion. Others, even veteran campaigners, may have been too stimulated to relax, fearful that their successful interception of the advance on their camp was only a temporary purchase of time, and that they would have to fight again on the morrow. The men manning the American right wing, who had not participated in the fight, were alert to repel an enemy advance down the Albany Road. Before dawn, American scouts were out between their lines and Freeman's farm, observing and harassing their enemy.[3]

The men of both armies expected General Burgoyne to resume his offensive during the twentieth. The 53rd's Lieutenant William Digby wrote in his journal what may have been camp scuttlebutt, that Generals Phillips and Fraser urged an immediate renewed attack upon the American position, but that their commander postponed the action because of "our hospitals being so full and the magazines not properly secured to risque [sic] that movement."[4] According to American Adjutant General James Wilkinson, British General William Phillips later provided him a more plausible explanation:

> After the affair of . . . 19th September terminated . . . Burgoyne determined to attack you the next morning on your left, with his whole force; our wounded, and sick, and women had been disposed of at the river; the army was formed early on the morning of the 20th, and we waited only for the dispersion of the fog, when General Fraser observed to . . . Burgoyne, that the grenadiers and light infantry who were to lead the attack, appeared fatigued by the duty of the preceding day, and that if he would suspend the operation until the next morning, he was persuaded they would carry the attack with more vivacity. Burgoyne yielded to the proposition of Fraser; the orders were countermanded, and the corps returned to camp; and as if intended for your safety and our destruction, in the course of the night, a spy reached Burgoyne with a letter from General Sir Henry Clinton, advising him of his intended expedition against the highlands, which determined Burgoyne to postpone the meditated attack of your army, and wait events; the golden opportunity was lost—you grew stronger every day, and on the 7th of October overwhelmed us.[5]

Burgoyne did receive such a communication from Sir Henry Clinton, and the hope it engendered would have fateful consequences.

The Americans Continue to Fortify

During the seventeen days that elapsed between the main battles around the Freeman farm, more than 6,000 Connecticut, Massachusetts, New

Hampshire, and New York militiamen arrived, bringing Gates' force to slightly more than 15,000 rank and file. The Americans extended and strengthened their fortifications until they formed a continuous line from the river to Neilson's farm and thence southwestward for three-quarters of a mile.[6]

Among the first measures taken by the Americans to improve their defenses was constructing an abatis of felled trees in front of their line. Richard Varick wrote to General Schuyler on Monday, September 22, that "The woods round us are cut & cutting down to form an Abbattis [sic] against a charge of bayonets or sudden Surprise."[7]

In a letter to Major General William Heath, Brigadier General John Glover reported: "We are making every necessary preparation to receive them [the British], by felling Trees, & Abiteeing [sic] the passes between the North [Hudson] River, & Saratoga Lake about 6 miles distance."[8]

Colonel James Wilkinson provided the most complete description of the state of the fortifications on October 4:

> Gates' right occupied the brow of the hill near the river, with which it was connected by a deep intrenchment [sic]; his camp, in the form of a segment of a great circle, the convex towards the enemy, extended rather obliquely to his rear, about three-fourths of a mile to a knoll occupied by his left; his front was covered from the right to the left of the centre, by a sharp ravine running parallel with his line and closely wooded: from thence to the knoll at his extreme left, the ground was partially cleared, some of the trees being felled and others girdled, beyond which in front of his left flank, and extending to the enemy's right. . . . The extremities of this camp were defended by stoney batteries, and the interval was strengthened by breastwork without intrenchments, constructed of the bodies of felled trees, logs and rails with an additional battery at an opening left of the centre. The right was almost impracticable; the left difficult of approach.[9]

The British also Fortify

General Gates' defensive strategy, based upon denying Burgoyne access to Albany, made extending and strengthening his interdicting field fortifications eminently logical. Burgoyne's raising strong static works did not. His aggressive strategy required relentless pressure imposed by a mobile force that would not give its enemy an opportunity to marshal its resources. His purpose was to bring his army to Albany, where it would cooperate with Sir William Howe's 1778 campaign.

He may have hoped to accomplish that mission without active assistance from the lower Hudson. September 19 was the climax of an evolving epiphany. The battle at Hubbardton was small, but viciously fought; the Bennington raid was nothing short of an outright disaster. So by mid-September, the general was desperate for Sir Clinton to assist him by moving upriver toward Albany. The enemy he fought on Freeman's farm was very different from the one that had retreated from Fort Ticonderoga. These Americans had advanced northward from the Hudson-Mohawk junction, closed the route to Albany, and fought his veterans to a standstill with courage and skill. The news that Sir Henry was active below Albany added a welcome factor to the strategic equation. Burgoyne did not abandon his objective when he did not renew the offensive on September 20, but he did decide to buy time to allow Clinton's moves to distract the former major sitting on Bemis Heights with his newly-effective force of Continentals and militiamen. That required preparing field works that would serve as a base of operations from which he could, with renewed vigor, resume the initiative and unite with the forces from New York City in Albany.

Possessing the battlefield placed Burgoyne in a strong tactical position. A series of ravines, which began southwest of Freeman's farm and ran eastward to within half a mile of the river before turning south, covered his front. The ravine drained by Kromma Creek—which extended all the way from McBride's farm (north and west of Freeman's farm) to within 200 yards of the river—protected his rear. His engineers improved the position by erecting a series of small outworks along the northern crests of the southern ravines until those ravines turned southward. From that point the interval between the ravine systems forms a plateau that was occupied, in part, by the farm of Jeremiah Taylor. The British and Germans prepared a strong line of entrenchments along the axis of that plateau to the hill west of the river, where a series of redoubts ran north and south along bluffs north and south of the Kromma Creek that covered the Albany Road, artillery park, hospital, and bateaux. The three fortifications north of the Kromma Creek came to be called the Great Redoubt. Outposts north of the kill's ravine, later called the Great Ravine, protected the rear from American attempts to attack from that quarter.

The British fortified camp was thus a counterpart in its tactical role to the American position on Bemis Heights; and, like it, its most critical problem lay in providing for a defense against a turning attack from the west, where the British camp lacked a strong natural position at its western end comparable to the crest of Bemis Heights on the Neilson and Woodworth farms. To correct that

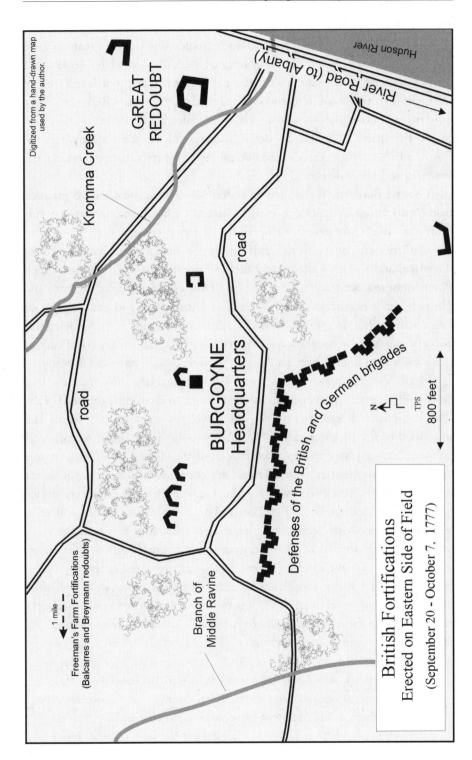

Digitized from a hand-drawn map used by the author.

Hudson River

River Road (to Albany)

GREAT REDOUBT

Kromma Creek

road

BURGOYNE Headquarters

Defenses of the British and German brigades

road

Freeman's Farm Fortifications
(Balcarres and Breymann redoubts)

1 mile

Branch of Middle Ravine

N

TPS

800 feet

British Fortifications
Erected on Eastern Side of Field
(September 20 - October 7, 1777)

deficiency, Burgoyne's men erected two redoubts: one on the Freeman farm that contemporaries called the Light Infantry Redoubt—and later generations the Balcarres Redoubt—and a second, smaller German post north and west of the Light Infantry Redoubt that would be called the Breymann Redoubt. There were two additional outposts, one west of the Balcarres Redoubt, another west of the Breymann Redoubt. To defend the rest of the interval between the fortifications, Canadians stockaded two cabins on the road that ran between the Freeman and McBride farms.

General Burgoyne had issued an order that defined the standard for such field fortifications in general as early as June 20, while his army was at Sandy Bluff on Lake Champlain: "Officers of all ranks commanding Forts, and Detachments, are constantly to Fortify in the best manner the circumstances of the place, and the implements at hand will permit. Felling Trees with their Points outward, barricading Churches and Houses, Breastworks of Earth and Timber, are generally to be effected in a short time, and the Science of Engineering is not necessary to find and apply such resources."[10] Applying this concept to particular cases always involved some adaptation. The fortifications Burgoyne's men built at Freeman's farm are discussed in more detail below.

The Light Infantry or Balcarres Redoubt had the dual purposes of defending the interval between the ravine systems, and covering the head of the southern ravine where it originates in a web of small "runs" south and southwest of the Freeman farm. "The Army immediately began to fortify its position," wrote Hauptmann Georg Pausch of the Hesse-Hanau Artillery in a letter to Hessian Adjutant General Baurmeister dated November 26. "[O]n the fields where the first battle was fought, General Fraser's corps encamped behind a great redoubt, built of timbers and earth. Its length must have been at least one hundred fifty chains [a conservative estimate]. The walls in some places were six feet high. Eight cannon—four light six, two light three-pounders, and two five and a half howitzers—were mounted in embrasures."[11] Pausch recorded in the September 20 entry of his valuable *Tagebuch* that the dead were buried on the battlefield, "instead of on the hill because breastworks were thrown up there [*anstatt auf der hohe, veil die Brustwerke war dort gebauen*]." He described the redoubt's construction:

> [An] entrenchment of newly felled trees laid on top of one another. . . The cannon and howitzers battery is placed on the hill, and the openings between the trees are filled with earth. And on the outside, too, earth is thrown over them [*Die Batterie fur Cannonen und Haunitzen ist auf die Hohe*

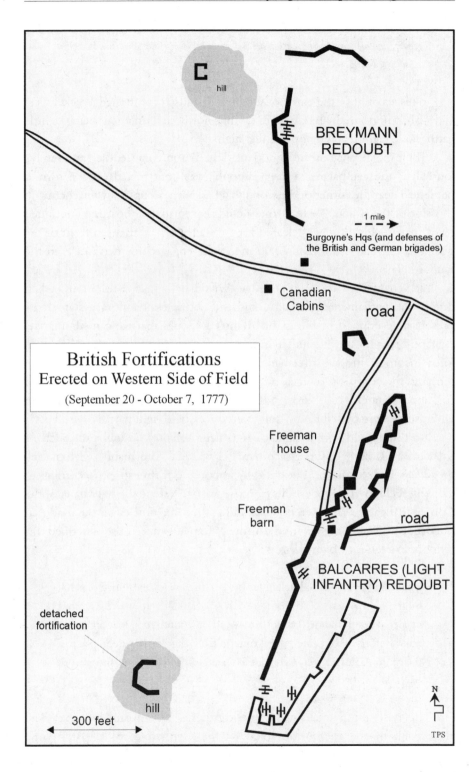

C
hill

BREYMANN
REDOUBT

1 mile

Burgoyne's Hqs (and defenses of
the British and German brigades)

Canadian
Cabins

road

British Fortifications
Erected on Western Side of Field
(September 20 - October 7, 1777)

Freeman
house

Freeman
barn

road

BALCARRES (LIGHT
INFANTRY) REDOUBT

detached
fortification

hill

300 feet

N

TPS

gesetzt, und die Eroffunger zwischen die Baume mit Boden gefullt, Draussen ist Boden sie uber gewerfen].

In his account of the battle of October 7, Pausch mentioned a picket west and slightly north of the Balcarres Redoubt's northern terminus as being "a little earth-work, eight feet long by five feet high."[12]

"[F]or the defence of the right flank," the Baron von Riedesel wrote in his journal of the campaign, "a large redoubt was constructed on the former battlefield near the corner of the wood that had been occupied by the enemy on this side of the ravine."[13] He further noted that fortifying the camp continued daily, that a field of fire was cleared for a distance of 100 paces in front of the position, and that more than 1,000 men were engaged for two weeks in the fatigue details.

Lieutenant William Cumberledge Wilkinson's maps, testimony taken during the parliamentary inquiry, and the above contemporary statements present a description of the Light Infantry Redoubt that we can summarize. Built on a roughly north-south axis, facing west, the fortification was 453 yards long, incorporating the Freeman house and barn. At the front's southern terminus the rampart turned eastward for about 180 yards, then northeastward for approximately 150 yards. Sally ports gave access into the fort, and embrasures were built into the wall to accommodate eight pieces of artillery.

Northwest and within sight of the Light Infantry Redoubt the men of Lieutenant Colonel [Oberstlieutnant] Friedrich Breymann's Brunswick grenadiers built a smaller, but critically important, fortification. According to General Freiherr von Riedesel, its purpose was "to defend the right flank of the Corps of Brigadier Fraser en potence and at the same time cover the road that ran over the hill into the rear of the army."[14] Captain Pausch also described this redoubt in a letter to Baurmeister:

> The Reserve Corps Riedesel under Lt. Col. Breymann encamped on a hill on the right, where a fortification of trees was built en potence. Its front occupied seven hundred fifty feet and stood about seven feet high with musket ports. Two three-pound cannon from our corps were in place in the center. The camp lay behind it at an angle, protected by a breastwork of trees.[15]

That description agrees with American James Wilkinson's account: "The right flank of the enemy, occupied by the German corps of Breymann, consisted of a breastwork of rails piled horizontally between perpendicular pickets, driven into the earth, formed en potence to the rest of his line, and extended about 250 yards across an open field, and was covered on the right by a battery of two guns. The interval from the right . . . was committed to the defense of the provincialists, who occupied a couple of log cabins."[16]

The descriptions provided by Pausch and Wilkinson agree, in general, with one given to Jared Sparks in 1831 by General Morgan Lewis, who had served as Gates' quartermaster during the Saratoga operations. Lewis described the German redoubt as being seven or eight feet high and built of small trees supported by strong posts, "with an opening about nine or ten inches wide, suitable for small arms . . . . It was a very excellent cover against infantry, being of sufficient thickness to prevent musket balls from passing through."[17]

Information about the several outworks erected west of the Light Infantry and Breymann Redoubts is diffuse and fragmentary. Wilkinson's map depicts a fairly strong post on the western slope, on a low ridge in front of the Light Infantry Redoubt that 19th century writers called the "Bloody Knoll," and a small work slightly north of the redoubt's northern terminus.

Wilkinson's map of the action of September 19 shows two buildings beside the road that ran south of the Kromma Creek's south branch between the homes of Freeman and McBride, one on either side of the road. His map of the encampment indicates that they were incorporated into two outworks, which von Riedesel wrote were occupied by the Canadian companies of Novin and Boicherville. Several accounts of the October 7 attack on Breymann's post refer to them as the "Canadian Cabins."

Another outwork of the Breymann Redoubt stood near the crest of the bank northwest of that fort's right end. It was a nearly square structure with an opening in the rear covered by a traverse.

The accompanying sketch, scaled at 1 inch : 800 feet, illustrates the Anglo-German fortifications east of Fraser's encampment behind the Light Infantry Redoubt. Because the works on the British right flank were involved in the battle of October 7 and their sites are easily identified and accessible for visitors to Saratoga National Historical Park, they have received more attention than the left wing of Burgoyne's fortifications, which were nonetheless important to his defense system.

Because he had some knowledge, albeit imprecise, of the details of Gates' fortified camp, Burgoyne did not operate in an intelligence vacuum. He sent scouting parties out, trying to learn what they could about their enemy, including his strength, deployment, and intentions. Possibly most productive was information collected from the numerous loyalists living along the Hudson. The nature of intelligence collection makes its documentation elusive, so only ambiguous hints survive among contemporary sources. But the British commander and his staff did know that the men on Bemis Heights outnumbered them, and the fight of September 19 had taught them not to underestimate their courage and resourcefulness. Fortifying their right flank on the Freeman and McBride farms defended them against the most likely threat: a turning movement emanating from the American left. But a movement against their artillery park, supply wagons, bateaux, and hospital, although less probable, could not be safely discounted.

General Burgoyne identified the reasons for fortifying his left in a letter to Lord George Germain. His troops, after "fortifying their right, and extending their left to the Brow of the heights, so as to cover the meadows through which the great river runs, and where their bateaux and hospital were placed[, t]he 47th regiment, the regiment Hesse Hanau, and corps of Provincials, incamped [sic] in the meadows for further security . . . . On our side it became expedient to erect strong redoubts for the protection of magazines and hospital."[18]

Burgoyne Pins his Hopes on Clinton

While his soldiers built fortifications, scouted, and exchanged fire with American patrols, General Burgoyne waited for the promise contained in the coded note he had received before dawn on Sunday, September 21, which Sir Henry had written in New York City ten days earlier. The two generals had agreed upon a system of apparently innocuous letters, which Burgoyne decoded using an hourglass-shaped cutout laid over the letter. Burgoyne lost the original from Clinton, but reconstructed it from memory: "You know my good will and are not ignorant of my poverty. If you think two thousand men can assist you effectually, I will make a push at [Fort] Montgomery in about ten days, but ever jealous of my flanks. If they [the Americans] move in force on either of them, I must return to save this important post. I expect reinforcement every day. Let me know what you wish."[19]

A commander whose situation was less desperate than Burgoyne's would have derived little hope from that ambivalent message. First, Sir Henry wanted Burgoyne's sanction for moves he had long hoped to make but dared not make unless they were specifically requested, because of the risk to New York City. Second, even if those reinforcements could arrive within a few days of departure, Clinton did not intend to depart for the Hudson Highlands for "about ten days," meaning that his force would not leave New York before the twenty-second. Third, if Clinton's flanks were threatened he would immediately return to defend the city. Burgoyne's forlorn assumption that 2,000 men advancing toward Albany could extricate him at that late date reflected his despair.

The Arnold-Gates Quarrel: Many Contributors

While Burgoyne's soldiers fortified their newly-won position and awaited confirmation of the hoped-for cooperation from Sir Henry Clinton, and while American Continentals and militia strengthened their lines and absorbed reinforcements, Generals Gates and Arnold engaged in a dangerous, unedifying quarrel.

Their relations previously had been amicable over a long period. Gates, while commanding at Fort Ticonderoga during the autumn of 1776, had provided critical support to Arnold's construction of the lake flotilla that fought Sir Guy Carleton's inland navy at Valcour Island from October 11 to 13, 1776. Earlier that same year, Gates salvaged his subordinate's career when the Hazen court-martial turned over its records to him and requested Arnold's arrest for contempt. Gates dissolved the court and refused to arrest the defiant general.[20]

For his part, Arnold had held himself aloof from Gates' and Schuyler's sometimes sordid competition for the Northern Department's command while carefully cultivating both men. His own difficult relations with some subordinates and fellow officers and his conflict with the Congress that had led to his tendering and then suspending his resignation gave Arnold reasons to court their good will: he needed all the influential help he could muster. For example, two letters dated August 21, one to Schuyler and another to Gates, congratulated both men on the American victory at Bennington, a victory to which Gates had contributed nothing and Schuyler little more, in almost identical words.[21]

His relations, while respectful with both men, had been more intimate with Gates than with Schuyler. In brief, the correspondence of Generals Gates and Arnold during 1776 and 1777 reflected friendship and mutual respect. Yet, within hours after dealing their enemy an important blow, the two men most responsible for the success or failure of American arms on the northern frontier were on the way to becoming irrevocably estranged.

Many students of the campaign have speculated about the estrangement's origins.[22] Suggestions include many alleged affronts Gates had committed on

Arnold: reassigning troops from his command; preventing Arnold from making the Freeman's Farm victory complete by withholding reinforcements and holding him back; displaying jealousy in general, but particularly by withholding credit for victory in reports to President Hancock and Congress; bumping Arnold from second to third in command in favor of Benjamin Lincoln; and general class and political differences.

Of those who have speculated on the estrangement, Professor Paul David Nelson was the most sympathetic to Gates. Thus, we must examine closely his contention that relations between the generals began to deteriorate shortly after Gates took over the Northern Department because he replaced Arnold with Lincoln as second-in-command. That interpretation rests upon four assumptions: (1) that Arnold had been the department's second-in-command under Schuyler; (2) that Lincoln joined the department after Gates became commander on August 19; (3) that Gates officially changed the chain of command after becoming commander; and (4) that Arnold had requested and Gates refused reinforcements during the fighting on Freeman's farm.[23]

Both Arnold and Lincoln joined Schuyler's command in July. Schuyler ordered the former to the front at Fort Edward and the latter to Manchester to assume general command of the New England militia operating east of the Hudson.[24] While the subject of who was second in the department's chain was not addressed in orders, seniority dictated that Lincoln was the second-ranking general officer, although Arnold's presence with the main body of troops made him temporarily second in Schuyler's absence (which was most of the time) or in the event of the commanding general's death or incapacitation. That de facto command structure prevailed so long as Lincoln was detached and Arnold was senior officer present. It would change whenever Lincoln rejoined the main body, when Arnold would revert to being the third in seniority. In so far as the department's command structure was concerned, relationships did not change when Gates succeeded Schuyler. Lincoln would be second-in-command with dormant right of succession whether Schuyler or Gates was department commander.

An important clue lies in a letter Richard Varick wrote to Schuyler at 2:00 p.m., September 12, the day the army occupied Bemis Heights. After describing the new position, Varick added this postscript: "N. B. I forgot to tell you that a little Spurt happened on Wednesday Eveng between Gates & Arnold. Inter Nos."[25] That morsel of gossip introduced a matter that was the seed of distrust that, nourished by personalities and events, matured into a dangerous clash. The "little spurt," as Varick flippantly reported it, probably grew out of an administrative confusion concerning the assignment of the 2nd and 17th Albany County Militia, Graham's Regiment of Dutchess and Ulster County Militia, and Cook's and Latimore's Regiments of Connecticut militia. On the ninth of September Gates directed Arnold to assign those units, and Arnold brigaded the New York militia with Enoch Poor's Brigade and the Connecticut troops with Ebenezer Learned's command.[26] The next day—not immediately before the fighting of the nineteenth—Deputy Adjutant General James Wilkinson published a general order that assigned the New York units to John Glover's Brigade.[27] When Arnold vehemently objected, Gates defended the officious young lieutenant colonel, mollifying Arnold by promising to issue an order reversing the assignments. Gates, in the press of events, did not keep that promise.

Although some students have written that disagreement about the conduct of the fighting on the nineteenth and Gates' alleged refusal to reinforce Arnold further damaged relations, a careful study of the battle does not support that interpretation. Gates acceded to Arnold's recommendation to engage the enemy on Freeman's farm and supported that decision with more than 4,000 men. There may have been undocumented disagreement over details, but Arnold, even during his bitterest dialogue with Gates, never accused his commander of dereliction nor failure to support the men committed to the fighting.

The immediate occasion for the rupture was Gates' report to President of the Continental Congress John Hancock, in which, after briefly describing the battle of the nineteenth, wrote: "The General good Behaviour of the Troops on this important Occasion cannot be surpas[sed] by the most Veteran Army, to discriminate in praise of the Officers, would be Injustice, as they all deserve the Honor & Applause of Congress; Lieut. Cochburn & Lt. Col. Adams with the rest of the unfortunate Brave who fell in their countrys cause deserve a lasting monument to their glory."[28]

Someone untruthfully told Arnold that Gates had referred to the troops engaged in the fight as a "Detachment of the Army." The informant was probably Varick, whose position as deputy commissary-general of musters gave him access to headquarters. His letters to General Schuyler during September and October document his knowledge of matters reported and discussed among the staff. In fact, in a letter of September 21, Varick bragged about stealing a copy of Colonel John Brown's letter of September 18 to General Lincoln that reported the former's action against Ticonderoga.[29] If Varick was the source, he also knew that what he reported to Arnold was false. Whoever reported the letter's contents obviously conveyed to Arnold the impression that the commanding general's report was worded in a manner that made it an intentional slur.

Almost simultaneously with dispatching the report of the battle of the nineteenth came a general order regularizing the status of Morgan's Corps. That unit, which was an independent organization composed of men detached from several Virginia and Pennsylvania regiments, had been sent by Washington to provide the Northern Department with a light infantry capability. Gates enlarged the Corps on September 11 by the organization of a battalion of light infantry under command of Major Henry Dearborn of the 3rd New Hampshire. The addition of those light infantrymen, who were drawn from several regiments and armed with smooth-bore muskets, significantly increased the Corps' firepower by providing it with a rapid-fire capability to match its marksmanship, derived from the accurate but slow-firing rifles. The Corps posted on the left wing of the American line, and although no orders assigned it to Arnold's Division, he had considered it a part of his command. The General Order of September 22 cited the unit's independent status and officially defined its commander's place in the chain of command with the following words: "Colonel Morgan's corps not being attached to any brigade or division of the army, he is to make returns and reports to headquarters only; from whence alone he is to receive orders."[30]

Gates acted completely within his prerogatives as the department commander to whom General Washington had detailed Morgan, but Arnold agreed with Livingston and Varick that the order was a studied insult.

The Rupture

Not one to suffer what he considered an insult silently, Arnold appeared at Gates' headquarters in the Woodworth House sometime during the evening of the twenty-second. Livingston described the meeting to General Schuyler:

> Matters were altercated in a very high Strain - - - Both were warm - - - the latter [Gates] rather passionate & very Assuming - - - Towards the End of the debate Mr. G - - - told Arnold - - - : He did not know of his being a Major General—he had sent his Resignation to Congress - - - He had never given him Command of any division of the Army.[31]

James Wilkinson similarly reported that Gates replied to Arnold's protest (which neither Wilkinson nor Livingston quoted) by discussing whether, in the light of Arnold's suspended resignation, the latter had any rank or command. That was followed by "high words and gross language; and Arnold demanded a pass to go to Philadelphia."[32] To Arnold's surprise, Gates did not plead with him to stay, but replied that "Genl. Lincoln would be here in a day or two, that he should then have no Occasion for him; and would give him a pass to go to Philadelphia, whenever he chose it."[33] Shocked and furious, Arnold returned to his quarters, where he wrote a letter that summarized his role in the recent action and recited his grievances. That letter is so important to the story that it merits quoting at length:

> . . . I have been informed that in the Returns transmitted to Congress of the killed and wounded in the action the troops were Mentioned as a Detachment of the Army, and in the Orders of this day I observed it is mentioned that Col. Morgan's Corps not being in any Brigade or Division of this Army are to make Returns and reports only to head Quarters, from whence they are alone to receive Orders - - - Altho it is notorious to the whole Army they have been in and done duty with my Division for some time past. - - - When I mentioned these matters to you this day, you were pleased to say in Contradiction to your repeated Orders you did not know I was a major Genl or have any Command in the Army - - - I have ever supposed a Major General's command of Four Thousand men, a proper Division and no Detachment when composed of two Brigades forming one wing of the Army and that the General and Troops if guilty of misconduct or cowardly behavior in the time of Action were justly Chargeable as a Division and that if on the other hand they behave with Spirit and Firmness in Action they were Instly entitled to the applause Due to a Brave Division not [a] Detachment of the Army would have thought extremely hard to have been Aminable [sic] for their Conduct.

"I mentioned these matters," Arnold continued,

> as I wish Justice done to their Division, as well as particular Regiments and Persons - - - For what reason I know not (as I am conscious of no Offense or neglect of Duty) but I have lately Observed little or no attention to Any Proposals I have thought it my Duty to make for the Publick Service, and when a measure, I have proposed has been agreed to, it has been

immediately contradicted, I have been received with the greatest coolness at Head Quarters, and often huffed in Such a manner as must mortify a Person with less Pride than I have in my station in the Army - - - You said you expected General Lincoln in a day or two when I should have no command of a Division, that you thought me of little Consequence to the Army, and that you would with all your heart give me a pass to have whenever I thought proper. As I find your observations very just that I am not, or that you wish me of little Consequence in the Army, as I have the Interest and Safety of my Country at heart, I wish to be where I can be of the most Service to Her - - -I therefore as soon as General Lincoln has arrived here request your Pass to Philade, with my two aides de Camp and their Servants, where I proposed to Join General Washington, and may possibly have it in my Power to Serve my Country altho I am thought of no Consequence in this Department.[34]

The letter is important for both what it included and what it omitted. It omitted any accusation that Gates had refused to reinforce the men Arnold committed to the fight on Freeman's farm. Nor did it claim that the commanding general had restrained Arnold from inflicting the coup de grace that would have defeated Burgoyne at the end of the nineteenth's battle. Arnold's three principal grievances were: (1) Gates' omitting specific reference to him and his division in his report to Congress; (2) The order defining Morgan's position in the chain of command; and (3) That his recommendations had not received the attention they were due, and that when they had been accepted they were "immediately contradicted." These were not issues that justified the violent rupture that ensued. But Arnold was persuaded to interpret them as personal affronts that could be addressed only by Gates' sending a new report to President Hancock, rescinding the order regularizing Morgan's status, and apologizing for not according Arnold the deference due him. Gates, not unnaturally, considered Arnold's manner and language insubordinate; to a man who had spent his career in the army, insubordination, from whatever source, was not tolerated. Both men had been under severe strains, and with their enemy still less than a mile and half away, those pressures continued to take their toll. Both were also under the influence of subordinates whose roles in the affair were, to put it charitably, irresponsible.

Gates read Arnold's letter late in the evening and replied the following morning. "I did not receive your letter until I was going to Bed last Night," explained the army's commanding general. "The permission you requested for yourself and Aids [sic] de camp to go to Philade is Inclosed."[35] Gates then addressed the following to President Hancock: "Major general Arnold having desired Permission for Himself and Aids de Camp to go to Philadelphia, I have granted his Request. His reasons for asking to leave the Army at this Time shall with my Answers be transmitted to Your Excellency."[36]

Arnold, who certainly believed that Gates really did not dare permit him to leave the Northern Department and carry his grievances to the Congress and General Washington, returned Gates' note with the following:

> When I wrote you yesterday I thought myself Intitled to an answer and that you would at least condescend to acquaint me with the reasons which induced you to treat me with the affront and indignity, in a publick manner, which I mentioned and which has been observed by many Gentlemen of the Army, I am conscious of none but if I have been guilty of any Crimes deserving such treatment I wish to have them pointed out that I may have an Opportunity of vindicating my conduct I know no reason for your Conduct unless I have been traduced by some designing Villain - - - -I requested Permission for myself and aids to go to Philadelphia, instead of which you have sent me a Letter to the Honble John Hancock Esqr which I have returned if you have any letters for that Gentleman which you think proper to send sealed, I will take charge of them. I once more request your Permission for myself and Aids to Pass to Philadelphia [37]

Arnold thus rejected the pass that Gates provided. He really did not want to present himself under prevailing conditions to a Congress with whom he was in bad odor and to which he already had tendered a letter of resignation. Nor could he have been eager to rejoin General Washington, whose low tolerance for insubordination was well known. Arnold may have expected Gates to ask him to remain in the department. Or he may have hoped that, when news that he intended leaving became known, officers and men would be so insistent that he stay that the commanding general would have no option but to beg him to stay and acknowledge his indispensability. His hubris was so great that he could not conceive of an American success without him. Whatever his reasons, Arnold remained on Bemis Heights without a formal command.

Underlings Stoke the Flames

While tensions in the camp on Bemis Heights were building to a dangerous pitch, Schuyler's protégés Livingston and Varick kept their patron informed with biased, detailed letters. Their devotion to Schuyler and hatred of Gates made them Arnold's partisans, and they described the developing controversy with unconcealed pleasure and no apparent consideration except that Gates be discredited. From the day that Gates replaced Schuyler, they kept up a running criticism of the new commander's motives and decisions, and while they piously called upon Heaven for victory, they made it manifest that Providence would have to grant that victory in spite of Gates' craven incompetence.

In a revealing note penned two days before the Freeman's farm fight, Richard Varick declared that "Should Fortune declare against Us, It may be Necessary that some Disposition be made by You for the Consequences of that important Event; I think it therefore my Duty to give You the Earliest Intelligence."[38] Varick was at least pretending that Schuyler would have to redeem American interests, justifying his detailed reporting of conditions and events in the American camp. In the letter of the nineteenth that described that day's fighting, Varick wrote concerning Gates, Arnold, and his own devotion to Schuyler: "I will sooner see him [Gates] downed and Quartered, than do anything for him out of my Line. But Arnold I will cheerfully serve.—It is not fit I should put it on paper lest the Letter may be seen by Others. I shall execute my Duty to You, as soon as I shall have the pleasure of being with You."[39]

Varick lost no time reporting the quarrel's opening to the general in a lengthy letter written during September 22, the day Arnold confronted Gates. Like Arnold's opening letter to Gates, it is central to any study of the Arnold-Gates conflict:

> . . . I am sorry for my Country['s] Sake to give You the following Intelligence, Which I beg You to keep Inter Nos.—Matters between Genl. Gates and Arnold got to such a Pitch, That I have the fullest Assurance, Arnold will quit the Department in a Day or two. . . . Gates has not treated him with Common Civility & politeness for these several Days past, I think I gave You a Hint of It in my first Letter.—Since which he has been unsufferably rude.—He seems to be piqued that Arnold's Division has the Honor of beating the Enemy on the 19th.—In Consequence of which he has this day declared in Genl. Orders, that Morgan's Corps & Light Infantry under Major Dearborn, belong to His Brigade or Division,

& are subject to No Orders but those from Head Qtrs. Altho a few days since he ordered Arnold to add them to one of the Brigades of his Division.—Matters came so high, that Arnold told him he would not suffer the Treatment & asked Gates' Pass to Philadelphia & Gates said he would give it with all his heart.—"He further told Arnold, he should not have a Division."—This I am certain of, Arnold has all the Credit of the Action of the 19th, for he was ordering out troops to It, while the other was in Dr. Potts tent backbiting his neighbors for which words had like to Ensue between him & me & this I further know, that he Asked where the Troops were going, when Scammell's Batt. Marched & upon being Answered, he declared no more should go, he would not suffer the Camp to be Exposed.

"[H]ad Gates complyed with Arnold's Repeated Desires," continued Varick,

he would have gained a Genl. & compleat Victory over the Enemy.—but it is evident to me, he never intended to fight Burgoyne, till Arnold, urged, begged & entreated him to do It—Nay, he meant by Moving the Army to cast an [illegible] on Your Reputation, in hopes that Burgoyne would be frightened by his Movement from the South & North. . . .I apprehend much that a certain person, whose Conduct much bespeaks the Character of a Sycophant, & who affects great Friendship for You, has no small share in attempting to injure Your Reputation when Set in Competition with Genl. Gates' & Is at Bottom of the Dispute between Arnold and Gates.—I apprehend if Arnold leaves us, we shant Move unless the Enemy run up the River.—He had the full Confidence of the Troops & they would fight gallantly under him.—If he quits I shall not stay longer unless I can probably see Saratoga [Schuyler's estate ten miles north of Bemis Heights at modern Schuyerville].[40]

This remarkable letter is a primary source of the traditional anti-Gates interpretation of both the fighting on Freeman's farm and the generals' quarrel.

"I am much distressed at Gen. Arnold's determination to retire from the Army at this important Crisis," Henry Livingston wrote to General Schuyler the following day, " . . . —His presence was never more necessary." Livingston continued:

He is the Life and Soul of the Troops – Believe me Sir, To him & him alone is due the honor of our late Victory.—Whatever Share his Superiors may claim they are entitled to None - - - -. He enjoys the Confidence & Affection of Officers & Soldiers.—They would, to a Man, follow him to Conquest or Death - - - - His absence will dishearten them to such a degree, as to render them of but little Service - - - The difference between him & Mr G - - - -has arisen to too great a height to admit a Compromise. I have, for some time past observed the great Coolness, & in many instances, even disrespect with which Gen. Arnold has been treated at Head Qr. - - - - His proposals have been rejected with marks of Indignity - - - His own orders have frequently been contravened—and himself set in a ridiculous light by those of the Commander in Chief - - - - [41]

After parroting Arnold's recitation of his grievances, Livingston continued his interpretation of events:

The Reason of the present disagreement between two old cronies, is simply this—Arnold is your friend - - - - - - - I shall attend the general down—Chagrining as it may be for me to leave the army, at a time when an Opportunity is offering for every young Fellow to distinguish himself, I can no longer submit to the Command of a man whom I abhor from my very Soul - - - - His Conduct is disgusting every One, but his Flatterers & Dependents, among who profess to be your Friends - - - A Cloud is gathering & may ere long burst on his Head - - - [42]

The young officers' letters and Arnold's catalogue of grievances are couched in language suggesting a common source expressed in interchangeable terms.

Two days after the quarrel erupted, Varick predicted that it would end in a duel between the generals and reported, with obvious relish, that Arnold had challenged General Benjamin Lincoln's authority to issue orders to units in the American left wing. According to his letter to Schuyler, Arnold observed Lincoln, who had arrived at Bemis Heights during the evening of the twenty-second,

giving some Directions in his Division, He applied to him to know whether Gates had given Orders about It, was answered in the Negative; he then told him he tho't Lincoln's Division. . . lay on the Right & that the

left belonged to him & Gates ought to be in the Center, he requests
Lincoln to Mention this to Gates & have it fixed Arnold is determined not
to suffer any one to Interfere in his Division & says It will be certain
Death, to any Officer, who does, in Action If it be not settled
before,—that Gates can't refuse him his Commd. & will not yield it Now
as the Enemy are expected - - -. . . & to thwart Gates' wish to have none
but such as will Crouch to him & his Humours, in Camp, he will Remain,
if I am not seriously Mistaken - - - [43]

If Varick's account can be trusted, Arnold pretended to believe that he
continued to command the left wing, and that Lincoln was to command the
right and Gates the center. Since that had never been the case, Arnold's
contention was patently spurious. Lincoln's arrival from east of the Hudson
River would, however, as earlier noted, pose a command problem—even if
Arnold and Gates had remained friendly. Lincoln was the former's senior, and
his presence relegated Arnold to being the third-ranking general officer present.
On the other hand, that would not necessarily have affected the distribution of
divisions among the three men. In fact, the distribution that Arnold pretended
to believe had been settled upon was a sensible one that may have been
discussed orally at the time Gates ordered Lincoln to join the main force on the
Hudson.

More serious was Arnold's denial that Gates had the authority to remove
him from his command and his threatening any officer who "interfered" with
his division with "certain death." Arnold knew that Gates had orally relieved
him and that a commanding general possessed such authority. His threat to kill
any officer who exercised any command in his old division "in Action If it were
not settled before" was puerile and indefensible. Regardless of whether he was
bluffing or in earnest, Arnold's conduct was irresponsible and mutinous.

There is, of course, a possibility that Varick's account was inaccurate or
exaggerated, and that his enthusiasm for Arnold's cause and his desire to exploit
the quarrel to discredit Gates led him to tell too lurid a story. Be that as it may, a
general order issued the next day formalized the command structure by vesting
Lincoln with command of the right wing and reserving the left to Gates'
personal command.[44]

The tone of the young men's letters of the twenty-second and twenty-third
approved Arnold's threat to leave the Northern Department. They seemed
almost to hope that his departure would result in an American defeat that would

discredit Gates and vindicate Schuyler. Their tone changed when they reported events that began to unfold on September 24.

Others Attempt Intervention

By the twenty-fourth of the month, "Arnold's Intention to quit this department is made public, and has caused great uneasiness among the Soldiers." Henry Livingston wrote to Schuyler that General Poor had proposed that he, Learned, and the colonels of Arnold's old division present an "Address" to Arnold thanking him for his leadership, especially "for his conduct in the late Action," and asking him to remain in camp. That Poor and Arnold were old adversaries heightened the proposal's dramatic implications. Poor's regimental commanders (Joseph Cilley, Wilborn Adams, Alexander Scammell, Philip Van Cortlandt, Henry Beekman Livingston, Thaddeus Cook, and Jonathan Latimore) signed the "Address." Learned's colonels (John Bailey, Michael Jackson, James Wesson, and James Livingston) agreed with the petition's "propriety, but declined to sign because they feared giving umbrage to General G [ates]. A paltry Reason for Officers of rank to allege for not doing their duty . . ." The refusal of the Learned's officers to sign, claimed Livingston, doomed the "Address."

Livingston next reported that only intervention by the general officers (Lincoln, Learned, Poor, Nixon, Paterson, and Glover) could "bring about a reconciliation." He claimed that General Lincoln, who was "anxious for Arnold's stay," had been proposed as the proper person to sponsor the negotiations—as, indeed, he was, as the senior officer present.[45]

Livingston's September 25 letter to Schuyler explained how the generals' efforts fared:

> I mentioned in Letter, Yesterday that I was in hopes the General Officers would take some measures to prevent Genl. Arnold's leaving the Army - - - - When the matter was hushed, some thro' jealousy, others for fear of offending Gates, declined having anything to do with the dispute - - -They all wish him to stay—but are too pusillanimous to declare their sentiments—There the matter rests - - - Some indeed were weak enough to propose that Arnold should make concession and thus bring about a compromise - - -His Spirit disdains any thing of the kind —- He seems more determined than ever, & I fear will too soon put his resolution into Execution - - - - [46]

The generals disappointed Livingston by trying to bring about a reconciliation through some negotiated compromise. At least some of the general officers believed that Schuyler's young champions were a source of trouble and undertook to relieve tensions by removing at least one of them from the camp. Varick reported to Schuyler that someone . . .

[Had] thrown out in an unmanly manner, that Arnold's Mind was poisoned by some of those about him, here I feel myself touched. Altho' the person alluded to in Mine (I think) the 10th . . . Who Affects great Friendship for You [James Wilkinson], was polite enough to tell Major Chester, Livingstons Antagonist, that the first step toward an accommodation, will be to get rid of Livingston. - - - This Arnold was informed of but disdains so ignoble an act. . . .

Livingston, for his part, "has too much Regard for his Country to remain, when by Sacrificing his own Pleasure he may possibly promote Its Wealth." He would leave for Albany the next day; Varick would follow, if there were no action by Saturday or Sunday, although it would give him "more pleasure, if I can see Saratoga First,—This pleasure I fancy I should have this Day enjoyed, if Genl. Gates had Either furnished Arnold with troops on the 19th or permitted us to go out on the 20th. . ."[47]

The sacrificial lamb, Livingston provided more details in his letter to Schuyler. He first reported that Arnold had consented to stay at Bemis Heights in response to a letter from all of the general officers, excepting Lincoln, "tho' no accommodation has taken place- - -" He continued with an account of the negotiations, as told him by Arnold:

I find myself under the necessity of returning to Albany, & merely to satisfy the Caprice & jealousy of a certain great person - - - - It has been several times insinuated by the Commander in chief to Genl. Arnold, that his mind had been poisoned & prejudiced by some of his family—And I have been pointed out as the person, who had this undue influence over him - - - Arnold has always made proper replies on these occasions, & despised the Reflection - - - But since the last Rupture, another Attempt has been made, in a low, indirect manner to have me turned from Genl. Arnold's Family - - - Major Chester, (who by the bye is an impertinent Pedant) attempted to bring about a reconciliation - - -For this purpose he consulted with the Dep: A Gen [Wilkinson]—And in the Course of their conversation, was told that some overtures were necessary on Arnold's Side - - - That Gates was jealous of me; & thought I had influenced Arnold's conduct - - - that of course it was necessary to get rid of me to open a way for an accommodation - - - When this was told to Arnold, he could scarcely contain himself & desired Chester to return for Answer—that his judgment had never been influenced by any man, & that he would not sacrifice a Friend to please the "Face of Clay" . . . .[48]

This interesting letter claimed that, even before the post-battle argument, Gates had accused Arnold of being unduly influenced by Livingston, that the latter had "despised the Reflection," and that after the "last Rupture" men working for a reconciliation made the young man's departure a condition. If Livingston's account was accurate, the general officers succeeded in persuading Arnold to remain in camp, hoping that he and Gates would reconcile. Arnold, while agreeing to remain, refused to make any concessions that would represent a retreat from the position he had taken during his confrontation with the commanding general. Then, according to Livingston, the generals addressed another letter to Arnold that formalized his agreement to stay without requiring any concession on his part. About the only firm conclusion to emerge is that the general officers concerned with effecting a reconciliation persuaded Arnold to stay, that Livingston was a troublemaker, and that all would profit from his leaving.

Why Varick was not also identified as a candidate for rustication is not clear, and he was exercised that he was not so honored. Perhaps the men involved in the negotiations knew more about the characters and actions of the two men than we do and believed that Livingston was more of a threat to harmony. As a mere volunteer aide to Arnold, he was also more readily expendable.

For his part, Richard Varick was determined to share his friend's distinction. After all, for one of his sense of importance, being reduced to being a comparative cipher was demeaning. He wrote Schuyler on the twenty-sixth:

. . . I told Arnold this morng. I should leave Camp soon on that Account.—As Livingston does not leave Camp, till to Morrow, I believe We shall go in Company, unless I hear that Something is in Agitation soon.—I am rather too great a check on the Director Genl. & some of his associates, too Staunch Friends to Gates to live with, without giving some of them a Rub, & It rather a Disagreeable Situation to check Others & be checked in Language Yourself. - - -I shall never fail to do the Duties, I owe Myself, be It who it may, that opposes me. - - - [49]

The details of what prevailed upon Arnold to decide not to make good his threat to leave the Northern Department, beyond the suspicion that he never really intended to leave, are elusive. We have only Livingston's and Varick's versions as they transmitted them to Schuyler. The petition Poor circulated has not survived. Of the colonels whose support in begging Arnold not to leave he solicited, four (Daniel Morgan, Joseph Cilley, Philip Van Cortlandt, and Rufus Putnam) left personal papers, but they contain no references to the petition. In fact, none mentions the quarrel. Papers of three of the generals (Lincoln, Glover, and Nixon) also exist. They, too, contain nothing that supports the story we have been following. Soldiers batten upon gossip and rumor, especially when it concerns headquarters and what officers are doing when they are not in view. One would expect the men on Bemis Heights—who certainly heard that something was afoot, and that the most dramatic member of the officer corps had threatened to leave them and been displaced—to have commented on that dramatic event in journals or memoirs. And yet, strangely, no contemporary diary, journal, nor later memoir (other than those already cited) mentions the controversy.[50] And none reflects a decline in morale.

The Unhappy Upshot of it All

So, Benedict Arnold remained in camp, ignored by Gates, without a command, and reduced to the cipher he had complained of being in his correspondence with the commanding general. But he took pains to demonstrate his contempt for authority by bestowing a fifty dollar reward, in direct violation to department policy, on a soldier who had killed an Indian during the retreat from Fort Edward. Gates reprimanded him. Arnold obviously hoped to develop another quarrel, but Gates dropped the matter by accepting Arnold's contention that he was, in Schuyler's absence, in temporary command when the Indian had been killed.[51]

On October 1, when militia were appearing daily to swell his ranks, and Gates was improving his position while he waited for an increasingly-desperate Burgoyne to make his next move, Arnold delivered his final round in the epistolary duel. Once again, this is worth quoting at length:

Notwithstanding the repeated ill treatment I have met with, and continued daily to receive, treated only as a cypher in the army, never consulted or acquainted with one occurrence in the army, which I know only by accident, while I have every reason to think your treatment proceeds from a spirit of jealousy, and that I have every thing to fear from the malice of my enemies, conscious of my own innocency and integrity, I am determined to sacrifice my feelings, present peace and quiet, to the public good, and continue in the army at this critical juncture, when my country needs every support. . . .I beg leave to say, that when Congress sent me into the department at the request of his excellency General Washington, they thought me of some consequence, and I believe expected the commander-in-chief, would consult with me, or at least would have taken my opinion on public matters. I think it my duty (which nothing shall deter me from doing) to acquaint you the army are clamorous for action. The militia who compose a great part of the army are already threatening to go home. One fortnight's inaction will, I make no doubt, lessen your army by sickness and defection at least four thousand men, in which time the enemy may be reinforced to make good their retreat. . . .I have reason to think, from intelligence since received, that had we improved the 20th of September it might have ruined the enemy, that is past, let me entreat you to improve the present time. . . .I hope you will not impute this hint to wish to command the army, or to outshine you, when I assure you it proceeds from my zeal for the cause of my country in which I expect to rise or fall.[52]

Gates did not respond. In fact, he never made further written reference to relations with his unhappy lieutenant.

The generals' quarrel did credit to neither man. Arnold was pathologically sensitive concerning his honor and toward any hint of disagreement or criticism. His violent temper got out of control, and he behaved toward Gates in a manner that he would not have tolerated had their roles been reversed. Gates acted within his prerogatives, but he was petty in dealing with a valuable, charismatic combat leader. Because he did not commit his version of the dispute to writing, we can only guess at why he did not do more to retain the friendship and services of a man with whom he had for more than two years maintained a mutually useful relationship.

Perhaps the generals would not have fallen into their disgraceful squabble if they had been free of the influences of others who sought to profit from it. We have noted the satisfaction with which Livingston and Varick reported their detailed versions of the quarrel. And we have their testimony that those seeking a reconciliation considered them provocateurs. They exploited whatever potential issues divided the two generals, feeding Arnold's vanity and sense of persecution, persuading him that he was the victim of Gates' malice. It was probably Varick who falsely told Arnold that Gates had called his division a "Detachment of the Army" in his report to Hancock, and that it was an intentional slur. If our knowledge of the quarrel is accurate, what Varick told Arnold was the immediate occasion for the generals' rupture. The young men hoped to discredit the man who had displaced Schuyler, to whom they displayed a loyalty that eclipsed the one they owed their country.

Omnipresent James Wilkinson was mischief's real work of art. Varick, in a September 22 letter to Schuyler, implied that Wilkinson was "attempting to injure" Arnold. The details of his role are more elusive, but he had an influence on Gates—who was no more immune to flattery than some of his greater contemporaries—that was less than benign.[53]

Finally, there was Philip Schuyler, who had reason to detest Gates and who could not bring himself to restrain his young protégés. He did nothing to dissuade them from being agents of discord, obviously encouraging their mutinous correspondence when he could have recalled them, with paternal firmness, to their duty. If we relied exclusively upon his papers deposited in the New York Public Library, we could assume that his role was passive—and he meticulously preserved his personal and official correspondence. But did he omit anything revealing that he was an active party to the quarrel? The Lloyd Smith Collection deposited in the Morristown National Historical Park's library contains a letter Schuyler penned to Varick at 6:00 on the morning of September 20. It suggests that an entrenchment be added between the Hudson and a swamp on the extreme right flank—an obvious response to the sketch of the fortifications on Bemis Heights that Varick had provided him.

But there was more. Schuyler wanted Varick to show the letter, not to Gates, Kosciuszko, or Stevens, but to Arnold, and warned Varick to destroy his letters, "lest an accident should [put] them into hands I do not wish they should fall into I mean the person you mention [Gates]."[54]

Unfortunately, General Schuyler was a party to a disgraceful and dangerous quarrel.

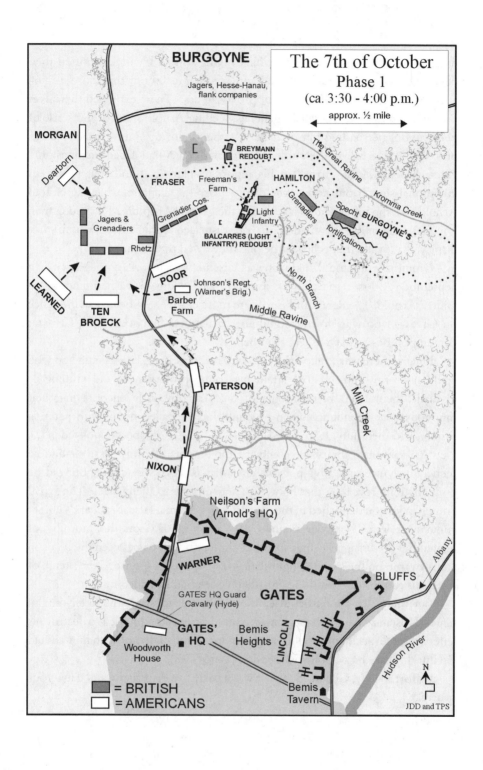

12

The Seventh of October

British Desperation

General Burgoyne's general order for October 3 opened with words calculated to sustain his men's morale even as he reduced their ration:

> There is reason to be assured, that other powerful Armies are actually in cooperation with these Troops; and although the present supply of provisions is ample, it is highly desirable to be prepared for any circumstances in the field that the King's service may require, without the delay of bringing Forward further stores for those purposes; the ration of Bread or Flour is, for the present fixed at one pound.[1]

Desperation caused Gentleman Johnny, normally unusually solicitous of his troops' well-being and morale, to dissemble. The other powerful cooperating army was still in New York City, and the Americans had severed his supply line from Canada. Only the labors of foraging parties supplemented the diminishing stores. And time favored his enemy: with every passing day the disparity between the armies' strength in both men and materiel increased. The autumn nights and seasonal rains announced winter's too-early approach. And in spite of his attempts to shift the responsibility for occupying Albany to Sir Henry Clinton, Burgoyne knew that he could not delay past mid-month the decision to act—either aggressively or in retrograde.[2]

On October 4, the commander summoned Generals Phillips and von Riedesel and Brigadier Fraser to his headquarters above Wilbur's Spring for a council of war. Burgoyne knew Gates' right flank along the Hudson River was impregnable and that ordering a frontal assault against the numerically superior, strongly entrenched Americans would be conspiring in the slaughter of his men. He therefore proposed a solution that earlier, greater captains had employed: an enveloping movement—this one around the American left flank. Except for an 800-man camp guard, he would commit his entire force to an attack on Gates' left and rear. A later report of this council by von Riedesel to the Duke of Braunschweig described the dilemma the Europeans faced and somehow had to resolve:

> On the 4th of October General Burgoyne called a council of war . . . and asked our advice on what should be done in this affair, proposing we could by a roundabout way turn the enemy on his left flank and attack the rear. As by such a movement, however, we have to remove ourselves from the water at least three whole days, we would risk losing all of the batteaux and provisions, and then have nothing at all to live on, because it was not expected that two battalions could defend the riverbank. On this occasion, I attempted to present the danger of our situation . . . and to urge a retreat to Ft. Edward as soon as possible, especially on account of the only slight possibility of the early arrival of General Clinton. However, we waited, nourished by hope.[3]

On that tentative note, the council adjourned and the generals inspected their camp's left wing, which covered the artillery park, supply train, and bateaux, and decided that it could not be defended by an 800-man camp guard. Another council convened on October 5, during which von Riedesel proposed a retreat to the Battenkill, which he believed would place the army in a better position to await more precise news of Clinton's movements. Fraser supported that suggestion, but Phillips withheld comment.[4] Burgoyne rejected the baron's proposal, and returned to his own for an envelopment of Bemis Heights. He defended his decision in his narrative of the campaign, writing:

> [O]n the second day after the action [of 19 September] I received intelligence from Sir Henry Clinton of his intention to attack the [Hudson] highlands about that time and I was hourly in expectation, I thought a justly founded one, of that measure operating to dislodge Mr. Gates entirely, or oblige him to detach a large portion of his force. Either of those circumstances, could have opened my way to Albany. In these

circumstances, could the preference upon these alternatives admit a moment's reflection? To wait so fair a prospect of effecting at last the great purpose of the campaign, or to put a victorious army, under all the disadvantages of a beaten one, by a difficult and dangerous retreat; relinquishing the long expected cooperation, and in the very hour of its promise, leaving Sir Henry Clinton's army, and probably Sir William Howe's exposed, with so much of the season of campaign to run, to the whole force of Mr. Gates, after he should have seen me on the other side of Hudson's River.[5]

This was not John Burgoyne at his best. Claiming that he premised his decision to move against Gates on October 7 upon concern for Clinton and Howe was special pleading, as was his invoking the tortured "long expected cooperation" argument, also advanced in an October 25 letter to Sir Henry. In that message he attributed his defeat to the absence of cooperation, adding that "I saw the desperate state of things and that nothing but a successful action could enable me to advance or retreat."[6] The theme that the alleged inflexibility of his order to advance to Albany robbed him of the power to make discretionary decisions was central to Burgoyne's shifting responsibility for his campaign's failure onto the government and fellow generals.

Special pleading aside, his situation was clearly desperate, and his resistance to the idea of retreat reflected that fact. He had to fear not only pursuit by Gates' larger army, but also the Americans he knew to be active along the route to Ticonderoga. Between them, those two forces could destroy a retreating army by either massed attack or decimation in detail. That reality and, probably, his sense of duty made trying to fight his way past Bemis Heights the lesser of two bad alternatives. General Burgoyne had no illusions that resorting to that alternative would be easy. Hubbardton, Bennington, Fort Stanwix, and finally the battle of September 19 had demonstrated American combat capability. His objective was, as it had been on September 19, to get Gates' army off Bemis Heights, the last good defensive position north of Albany available to the Americans.

British Intentions

For all his desperate boldness, a tentative imprecision characterized Burgoyne's description of the action he planned. That imprecision has led students of the campaign to interpret his tactic in different terms, such as a "reconnaissance in force," or a move to gain ground from which to attack the fortified troops on Bemis Heights. After briefly discussing possible motives, Hoffman Nickerson dismissed the subject by concluding that "The whole thing was vague."[7] The general contributed to the confusion when he wrote a letter dated October 20 to Lord George Germain. "[W]hen no intelligence having been received of the expected cooperation, and four or five days for our limited stay in camp only remained," the general explained, "it was judged advisable to make a movement to the enemy's left, not only to discover whether there were any possible means of forcing a passage should it be necessary to advance, or of dislodging him for the convenience of a retreat, but also to cover a forage of the army which was in greatest distress on account of the scarcity."[8]

Burgoyne's letter lends credence to the "reconnaissance in force" interpretation. But the general was not finished explaining his purpose. The other school of interpretation could find support in his narrative's statement: "[C]onfident I am, upon minute examination of the ground since, that had the other idea been pursued [i.e., had Gates received the attack in his fortifications], I should in a few hours have gained a position, that in spite of the enemy's numbers, would have put them in my power."[9]

Students have not been alone in their confusion. Von Riedesel wrote to his sovereign that "it was decided on the 7th of October to undertake a reconnaissance against the left wing of the enemy, and if it was found invulnerable to consider retreat." That described the move as being both a reconnaissance made in sufficient strength to take the offensive and as a probing action to determine whether to attack or retreat.[10]

More useful in determining the British commander's intent is examining the force he committed to the effort. The size and composition of the probing force reflected both the tentative nature of its mission and Burgoyne's tactical vulnerability. In officers and men, it included 1,700 of his best troops. The 1,500 regular soldiers and 100 Provincials comprised slightly more than twenty-two per cent of his 7,183-man army. Burgoyne's commitment of his best troops make it very probable that he contemplated something more serious than a reconnaissance of the American lines or a cover for foraging parties.

An even better clue to his intentions was his deployment of ten pieces of artillery. Cannon could be moved through the rough, wooded country only with great effort. One artillery officer observed that "Once a 12 pounder is removed from the Park of artillery it was gone." The deployed guns included six 6-pounders, two 12-pounders, and two 8-inch howitzers, the last being especially useful against entrenchments.[11] That commitment argues strongly that Burgoyne intended to attack Gates' left.

If that was his purpose, why were his orders so ambiguous? Perhaps experience had taught him that Gates was quick to divine an invading army's intentions—witness the former British major's correct analysis of the Burgoyne campaign's route and objective, in which Generals Washington and Schuyler had failed, and his foiling of Burgoyne's attempt to lure him out of his works on September 19. Another explanation for Burgoyne not identifying an objective on October 7 was the fear of failure that had been growing in his mind after the repulse of the nineteenth. He may have concealed his real objective because, realizing the mounting odds against success, he feared that failure to gain it would destroy the morale of soldiers already on reduced rations and deserting in growing numbers. Employing terms such as "reconnaissance" might reduce the impact of failure.

The position in which Burgoyne was most interested was a low north-south ridge 800 yards west of the angle formed by Gates' entrenchments on John Neilson's farm. Possessing it would enable William Phillips' experienced gunners to deliver enfilade fire into the Americans' camp. Equally important, it would provide the base for a flanking attack against its left and rear that, if successful, would force the Americans off Bemis Heights, realizing Burgoyne's goal of "forcing a passage and dislodging the enemy."

Gates and engineering officer Thaddeus Kosciusko were not blind to the ridge's importance and had begun entrenching along its military crest. Lieutenant William C. Wilkinson's map depicts an eastward-facing work labeled "Intrenchment which was only begun."[12] Contemporary sources do not reveal whether the British knew that its construction was underway. Wilkinson prepared his drawing after the surrender, when he could visit the site. Scouting parties may, however, have observed the work, and Burgoyne may have decided to act before the position became so strong as to foreclose any opportunity for a turning movement.

While the immediate objective was to seize the ridge, possessing it was to be preliminary to further action. Whereas the British generals later unanimously agreed that an attack on the American left and rear was to follow, von Riedesel subsequently cast the purpose in more tentative terms.[13] Because he was certainly party to the decisions taken and was recording impressions of events, not pleading an official interpretation, his accounts merit special, though not uncritical, attention.

After describing the conference of October 4, opining that the decision to entrust the camp's left wing to an 800-man guard was infeasible, and recording Burgoyne's rejection of the baron's proposed retreat to the Battenkill, the German general wrote that Burgoyne initially refused to entertain any suggestion of withdrawal. But after reconnoitering,

> [h]e said that on the 7th, he would undertake another great reconnoitering expedition against the enemy's left wing to ascertain assuredly his position and whether it would be advisable to attack him. Should the latter be the case, he intended to advance on the enemy on the 8th, with his entire army. If an attack was not advisable, he would, on the 11th, retreat back to the Battenkill.[14]

The baron was describing a probing expedition preliminary to deciding to attack or withdraw. Because a general assault would not be launched until the next day, the probing column was to be the aforementioned especially strong force of 1,500 men, eight field pieces, and two howitzers. If an attack seemed "advisable [ratsam]," they would occupy and hold the ridge until, on the eighth, the entire 7,183-man army joined them in a turning movement.

Lieutenant William Digby of the 53rd Regiment's grenadier company corroborated von Riedesel's account when he wrote in his journal that a "detachment of 1500 regular troops with two 12 pounders, two howitzers and six pounders were ordered to move on a secret expedition and to be paraded at 10 o'clock."[15] He later learned that Burgoyne's "intended design was to take post on a rising ground, on the left of their camp—the 7th—with the detachment, thinking they would not have acted on the offensive, . . . and on that night our main body was to move so as to be prepared to storm their lines by day break on the 8th . . . ."[16]

If Digby's version is reasonably accurate, General Burgoyne's tactic was more the product of desperation than mature judgment. If 800 men could not secure the British left, with its stores, bateaux, and artillery park, against an advance upriver from the American right, committing the "entire" army to an assault on Gates' left and rear on the eighth was risking everything on a gamble against overwhelming odds.

Burgoyne was betting that his probing force could gain and hold an advanced enfilading position against the Americans' strong, well-entrenched left where, according to Digby, he expected them "to not have acted on the offensive." After remaining in that exposed position overnight, he believed he could launch a general flank attack, all the while leaving the equally strong American right wing free to attack the vulnerable British camp and/or engage the attacking army's left. That was, indeed, taking council of desperation.

Still, probing the American left, enfilading it and, if feasible, developing a turning movement made sense, even in spite of unfavorable odds, whereas undertaking the attack von Riedesel described did not. This conclusion is based, of course, on the proposition that the probe would have produced a decision to attack. If it produced a decision to follow the baron's advice and withdraw, Burgoyne had delayed too long and worsened the odds against a successful disengagement in the presence of a larger, stronger foe.

The truth was that by waiting until the second week of October to act, the only chance Burgoyne had of avoiding a catastrophic defeat was for Horatio Gates to lose his nerve and make an egregious tactical blunder. This hope was a fatal substitute for strategy.

The British Attack

By October 6, General Burgoyne had determined to test his enemy, and he resorted to traditional methods to raise morale and prepare his men to risk their lives. To compensate for the recent reduction of rations he ordered that "On the next delivery of Provisions, two days fresh meat will be issued at the rate of one pound of beef per Ration, to each man." The soldiers would revert to salted meat for the next two days. To help prepare the men for renewed combat, he distributed amongst them twelve barrels of rum.[17]

The commander's solicitude confirmed the soldiers' suspicions that they were soon to test the enemy's mettle in another trial at arms and, fortified by four days' rations, they prepared for battle. The fighting of September 19 and daily harassment by American scouting patrols warned them that they faced a determined, battle-wise enemy who enjoyed a numerical superiority and both strategic and tactical advantages. But they were disciplined, experienced campaigners, and they trusted their officers and their own courage.

Accompanied by Phillips, Riedesel, and Fraser, Burgoyne led the probing force out of camp about noon. Generals Hamilton and Specht were left behind in charge of the troops posted on the high ground of the encampment's left flank, with General Gall responsible for the units positioned in the entrenchments extending from the Hudson River to Freeman's farm. Loyalist Lieutenant Joshua Pell, Jr., left a description of how Burgoyne deployed his probing force:

The detachments mov'd according to order by the right in three Columns; Light infantry and 24th Regiment with Bremens [sic] Corps form'd the column of the Right with two 6 pounders, taking their route thro the wood on the right of Freeman's farm. . . .The Grenadiers and the Regt. of Hesse Hanau [Pell included all German units under that heading], form'd the Center column with 2 12 pounders, and 2 eight inch Howitzers, marching thro the open field. The detachments of the Line, with the Canadian Volunteers and Provincials form'd the column of the left marching thro the wood, where the engagement of 19th September was fought.[18]

According to von Riedesel, a contingent of Indians and Loyalists deployed to the right to function as scouts and skirmishers.[19]

Divided into its three columns, the force marched southwestward to a low hill upon which the Barber family had a small, cleared farm. A fifty-man picket under Captain Joseph Blague of Cook's Connecticut Militia was already in position there. After driving the Americans out of the clearing, the European soldiers foraged in the fields while the generals pondered their next move.[20]

The Americans Defend—and Then Attack

Horatio Gates' force on Bemis Heights was more formidable than it had been when Burgoyne had tried to dislodge it in September, having grown from around 9,000 to 13,064 men. As he had on the nineteenth, Gates kept a strong division committed to interdicting the road to Albany. That right wing under General Benjamin Lincoln, twenty-three regiments totaling 6,368 men, included the brigades of Glover, Nixon, Paterson, and Warner. Benedict Arnold's former division, now under Gates' personal command, had twenty regiments totaling 5,399 men and included the brigades of Poor, Learned, and Ten Broeck, Morgan's Corps of riflemen and light infantry (552 men), and Wolcott's Brigade of Connecticut Militia Cavalry (which formed Gates' headquarters guard). Three hundred sixty-five artillerymen under Major Ebenezer Stevens served twenty-two cannon. Colonel Jeduthan Baldwin's seventy-two man detachment of engineers and artificers was attached to headquarters.[21]

The Americans thus enjoyed a more than two-to-one superiority and a tactical and strategic advantage that could only be wrested from them by a military miracle. Miracles, however, are unreliable sources of victory. As he had attempted on September 19, Burgoyne on this day had to entice or drive Gates off Bemis Heights. Brave British and German soldiers could burnish their regiments' reputations, but they could not produce the miracle that would open the way to Albany.

Alerted by the sound of British signal guns, General Gates ordered the lines manned about 1:00 p.m.[22] The enemy's appearance on the Barber farm confirmed his expectation that Burgoyne would repeat his attempt to turn the American left. Knowing that time was running out for the Europeans and that their commander must soon retreat or fight his way past the high ground blocking his way south, Gates was in daily anticipation of action. His reliance upon a reactive tactic that was economical of manpower and resources was about to be tested.

"[O]n the afternoon of the 7th October, the advanced guard of the centre beat to arms; the alarm was repeated throughout the line, and the troops repaired to their alarm posts," wrote James Wilkinson in what is the most detailed record of the events that attended Burgoyne's occupation of the Barber farm. No one has improved upon it. "I was at headquarters when this happened," he continued,

> and with the approbation of the General, I mounted my horse to inquire the cause, but on reaching the guard where the beat commenced, I could obtain no satisfaction but that some person had reported the enemy to be advancing against our left. I proceeded over open ground, and ascending a gentle proclivity in front of the guard, I perceived about half a mile from the line of our encampment, several columns of the enemy, 80 or 70 rods from me, entering a wheat field which had not been cut and was separated from me by a small rivulet; and without my glass I could distinctly remark their every movement. . . . After entering the field, they deployed, formed the line, and sat down in double ranks with their arms between their legs. Foragers then proceeded to cut the wheat or standing straw, and I soon after observed several officers, mounted on the top of the cabin. From which with their glasses they endeavoured to reconnoitre our left, which was concealed from their view by intervening woods.[23]

Wilkinson decided that the enemy did not intend to attack immediately and reported to Gates that "They were foraging and endeavouring to reconnoitre your left; and I think Sir, offer you battle . . . their front is open, and their flanks rest in the woods, under cover of which they may be attacked, their right is skirted by a lofty height. I would indulge them." The general responded: "Well, then, order on Morgan to begin the game."[24]

Morgan's Corps had by this time moved north from its position near John Neilson's house and formed in front of the entrenchments' center. Wilkinson delivered Gates' order and discussed with Morgan the enemy's deployment on the Barber farm, which he described as being "formed across a newly cultivated field, their grenadiers with several field pieces on the left, bordering on a wood and a small ravine . . . their light infantry on the right, covered by a worm fence at the foot of the hill before mentioned, thickly covered with wood, their centre composed of British and German battalions." Morgan knew the ground and proposed a circuitous approach that would post him on an elevation to the enemy's right, from which he intended to commence his attack "as soon as our fire should be opened against their left."

Gates approved Morgan's proposal and ordered General Enoch Poor to commit his brigade to an attack on the British front and left flank while General Ebenezer Learned moved his brigade against the British 24th Regiment and the German units on line between Burgoyne's right flank and the British grenadiers.[25]

Morgan immediately deployed his corps "to the left and ascend[ing] and advan[cing] in a direction to meet any part of the enemy that might be moving in that direction."[26] Delayed by the circuitous nature of their movement, Morgan's men could not attack Fraser's 24th regiment and light infantry until about 3:00 p.m., when the 1st, 2nd, and 3rd New Hampshire Continentals from Poor's Brigade came on line opposite the British grenadiers and guns of the Hesse-Hanau artillery.[27] The rest of Poor's regiments deployed facing the drafts from the British 9th, 21st, and 62nd Regiments, and Alexander Fraser's rangers and Provincials.

For about thirty minutes, fitful artillery and small arms fire echoed through the timber and open fields as American riflemen and advanced parties engaged components of the European probing force. By 3:30 p.m., as the firing became general, Learned's Brigade, reinforced by Ten Broeck's Albany County Militia, deployed between Morgan and Poor.[28] Within a few minutes exploding black powder blackened men's faces and shrouded the firing line in smoke, reducing visibility and impairing fire discipline. Uncontrolled "firing at will" increasingly replaced volley fire as contending lines wavered, broke, and reformed. Cohesion of even veteran units was difficult to impose. Combat's endemic confusion compromised the effectiveness of linear tactics.

With the armies so engaged, Morgan moved to turn the British right. The commander of that flank, Simon Fraser, had already been mortally wounded trying to rally his outnumbered troops.[29] Enoch Poor's 1,600-man brigade overwhelmed the grenadiers and assailed the thin red line of the British left wing, driving it into retreat toward the Light Infantry [Balcarres] Redoubt on Freeman's farm. The six regiments of Learned's Brigade, reinforced by one of Jonathan Warner's Massachusetts Militia regiments, attacked Germans who, even with their flanks exposed, stubbornly fought them off. A renewed charge finally forced von Riedesel's heavily mauled men to join the general withdrawal into the fortification on the Freeman farm.[30]

Burgoyne's "reconnaissance in force" had within a relatively short time suffered more than 400 casualties and lost all of its field pieces. At least 8,000 Americans—including Paterson's Brigade and the 5th, 6th, and 7th Massachusetts regiments from Nixon's Brigade—were present on the field, although not all of them participated in the fighting.

Arnold Returns to the Field

Sometime after Learned's Brigade launched its attack on the enemy's center, the most dramatic event of the day occurred when Benedict Arnold galloped from the camp on Bemis Heights onto the field and joined Learned's soldiers.[31]

Excluded from command by his threat to leave the Northern Department, Arnold had been riding about camp "betraying great agitation and wrath," remembered one eyewitness. His "ardent" and proud nature could not tolerate his former division dominating the battle without his personal participation. As soon as the Germans withdrew, Arnold, probably with some of Learned's men, joined elements of Poor's Brigade in forcing the enemy through the woods and across the fields of the Coulter and Freeman farms, overrunning a small outwork on "Bloody Knoll," and massing before the Light Infantry [Balcarres] Redoubt. That massive fortification, the strongest of the British line, measured some 500 yards long. The stronghold was "built of trees, some very large, with earth thrown between the trees and against the exterior to a height of from four to six feet," wrote Freiherr von Riedesel, "with four exterior sally-ports and eight interior entrances from the camp into the double-walled portion, which includes three-quarters of the work. There are embrasures for the cannon and a bacquet for the soldiers."[32]

Captain Georg Pausch confirmed the German general's observations: "The walls in some places were six feet high. Eight cannon—four light sixes, two light three-pounders, and two five and a half howitzers—were mounted at embrasures."[33]

The reinforced earthen redoubt now sheltered the more than 1,000 men who had retreated from Burgoyne's main line of resistance, plus seven battalion companies of the Regiment von Riedesel, bringing the number of its defenders to approximately 1,500 disciplined, determined soldiers.[34] From behind the redoubt's strong walls they could exact a heavy toll upon any assailant, especially infantry who had engaged in a firefight and pursued a retreating foe across rough woods and a meadow.

The Americans threatening the redoubt numbered about 3,300 men—1,400 of whom were fresh troops from Paterson's Brigade. Even without artillery—because they lacked linstocks, no one could fire the two pieces taken from the "Bloody Knoll" outpost—they could have neutralized the men in the fortification. Prudence dictated that Poor's soldiers, reinforced by Paterson, form a line behind the ridge parallel to the southern half of the redoubt, pin down the defenders with a heavy and steady fire, and await the development of a flanking movement around Burgoyne's right, which was defended by numerically weak German Jägers. But prudence was alien to Arnold's nature.

According to European combatants, he led Poor's and Paterson's men in a futile and costly attack against the stronghold. British and German sources agree on both the ferocity and futility of the assault. Burgoyne, in his letter of October 20 to Lord Germain, explained that his retreating soldiers "had scarcely entered the camp when it was stormed with great fury, the enemy rushing the lines under severe fire of grape-shot and small arms. The post of the light infantry under Lord Balcarres assisted by some of the line," he continued, "which threw themselves into the entrenchments, was defended with great spirit, and the enemy led by General Arnold was finally repulsed."[35]

In his *State of the Expedition*, the general paid tribute to American courage he faced at Saratoga:

> And if there can be any person, who, after considering the circumstance, and the positive proof of the subsequent obstinacy, in the attack on the post of Lord Balcarres, and various other actions of the day, continue to doubt, that the Americans possess the quality and faculty (call it whatever they please) they are of a prejudice that it would be absurd longer to contend with.[36]

"I must here again, in justice to the army," Burgoyne summarized, "recur to the vigour with which they were fought by the enemy. A more determined perseverance than they showed in the attack upon the lines, though they were repulsed by the corps under Lord Balcarres, I believe, is not in any officer's experience."[37] Blunt Lord Balcarres tersely testified before the parliamentary inquiry that his fortification was "attacked . . . with as much fury as the fire of small arms can admit" and his cannon were "of great use" in repelling the Americans. German participants also commented on the ferocity of the assault, although noting that in the end it failed, and that "we held it until the next morning."[38]

Contemporary American accounts are strangely silent about this phase of the battle, and many years passed before memoirs of veterans of the October 7 fighting appeared. The earliest to appear in print is this brief entry by Wilkinson:

> I then proceeded to the scene of renewed action, which embraced Burgoyne's right flank defence, and extending to his left, crossed a hollow covered with wood, about 40 rods to the entrenchments of the light infantry; the roar of cannon and small arms at this juncture was sublime, between the enemy behind their works, and our troops entirely exposed, or partially sheltered by trees, stumps, or hollows, at various distances not exceeding 120 yards.[39]

Wilkinson was describing not an aggressive assault led by Arnold, but a holding action. His version is very much at odds with those of the redoubt's defenders. His account of other, less dramatic actions is notably detailed, but about the assault on Balcarres' Redoubt, he was unusually reticent.

Samuel Woodruff, a loyal admirer of Arnold, wrote fifty years after the battle that although Arnold "had no command that day, he volunteered his services [and] was early on the ground and in the hottest part of the struggle at the redoubts."[40] Colonel Philip Van Cortlandt, commander of the 2nd New York Regiment of Poor's Brigade, was among the men who followed Arnold that day, and he left an "Autobiography" that was eventually published in *The Magazine of American History* in 1878. Van Cortlandt's description of the battle included this remarkable description:

> I being yet with Poor's brigade and advancing, the British retiring towards their battery, as the Hessians towards theirs. General Arnold, now on the field and in sight of the nine gun battery [the Balcarres Redoubt] sent his

aid [sic] to the right, ordering General Poor to bring his men into better order as we were pursuing. This order arrested our progress and prevented our taking the British battery in less than ten minutes; as we should have entered it almost as soon as the British, as Morgan did that of the Hessians, which Arnold discovered after sending the above order to General Poor, and as he had also sent another order by his aid, he now rode as fast as he could to counteract his own orders. . . .[41]

The colonel's account describes a confused and contradictory sequence of actions that may have been closer to the reality of combat than later, more structured accounts of clear-headed leaders commanding men and events.

Major Henry Dearborn, because he was with Learned and Morgan on the extreme American left, did not have firsthand knowledge of what transpired in front of the Balcarres strongpoint and did not refer to it in his *Journal*. However, his "Narrative of the Saratoga campaign," written in 1815, contains this brief but intriguing statement: "Our troops pursued and after dislodging those who occupied their outworks [on "Bloody Knoll"], General Poor with his brigade advanced to the main works of Fraser's camp, while Arnold with the light troops and several Regts of the line, assaulted the German entrenched camp."[42] Dearborn did not place Arnold at the head of Poor's and Paterson's brigades in attacking the Light Infantry [Balcarres] Redoubt, but with the units attacking the so-called Breymann Redoubt (an event discussed in detail below).

No American participants in the battle described the attack on Balcarres' fortification as being either dramatic or especially significant. Nor do they credit Arnold with leading the assault. In fact, Van Cortlandt claimed that by directing Poor to "bring his men into better order," Arnold actually *prevented* the Americans from taking the position, and then riding "as fast as he could to counteract his own orders." Interestingly, Richard Varick, Arnold's vehement advocate during the quarrel with Horatio Gates, did not place his hero in the fighting.

Most writers thereafter limned a very different scenario, one in which, under Arnold's inspired leadership, Americans threw themselves against Burgoyne's strongest fortification and, in spite of its strength, engaged its defenders in furious hand-to-hand fighting. Following (perhaps) Isaac N. Arnold's biography of his kinsman, they attributed to Arnold's commanding presence the most daring and decisive actions of the day, continuing the battle after the British withdrawal from the field, an interpretation Christopher Ward succinctly expressed when he wrote: "The fighting seemed to be over, and if

Gates had commanded in the field it would have been over; but Arnold was of different stuff. He was not content with driving the enemy from the field, he wanted a smashing victory."[43] Sir John Fortesque believed that Arnold's superior military instinct led him to seize "the opportunity for a general attack upon the British entrenchments."[44]

"Arnold and the Americans engaged, following the fugitives, arrived opposite Balcarres' post and promptly attacked," wrote Hoffman Nickerson, as always without bothering with sources. His account is the standard melodramatic version of events:

> Although without artillery they pressed forward through the heavy fire both of musketry and grapeshot from the British cannon. Darting to and fro and raging like a madman, Arnold was a host in himself. It was said of him [by whom?] that he struck an officer of Morgan's corps with his sword and wounded him in the head, remembering nothing of the incident afterwards and begging his pardon when told of it. Under his leadership the abatis in front of Balcarres' lines was stormed and a determined attack made upon the breastworks themselves. Nevertheless their strength, together with the fact that Balcarres' light infantry had been reenforced by the survivors of the reconnoitering detachment brought the assault to a stand . . . .[45]

Captain Nickerson's classic account synthesized the several traditional versions of the attack, including the improbable wounding of Morgan's officer (improbable because Morgan did not participate in the fight for the Light Infantry [Balcarres] Redoubt). No known contemporary source describes Arnold's "raging like a madman." Never one to sacrifice a dramatic opportunity for pedestrian prose, Nickerson apparently relied on British accounts of the ferocity of the action and filled the evidentiary vacuum with stirring invention.

Most writers who believed that Arnold inspired and led the attack approved of his decision and conduct, in spite of the attack's cost and futility. Enough heroism was manifest to render reality nugatory. Blind American courage in the face of certain failure has a seductive appeal, redeeming the sacrifice of brave men. But 3,300 brave Americans could not overcome the 1,500 brave Europeans who defended Balcarres' redoubt. They charged repeatedly, only to become entangled in the maze of fallen trees at the barricade's base. Whatever Arnold's role, most of the Americans who died on October 7 fell before the Light Infantry [Balcarres] Redoubt.

The Decisive Action: Breymann's Redoubt

A few hundred yards to the left and rear of the men contending for the Light Infantry (Balcarres) Redoubt, another American general, Ebenezer Learned, prepared for the battle's most decisive action. With him was his veteran brigade, now regrouped after its assault on von Riedesel's Germans, and Morgan's Corps, reinforced by the 5th, 6th, and 7th Massachusetts Regiments of Nixon's Brigade, a total of about 2,000 men.

The key to the American victory was not a direct attack on Burgoyne's strongest post, but a turning movement directed against his right wing, where 200 Jägers of the German reserves under Lieutenant Colonel Heinrich Christoph Breymann manned a weak log redoubt. General von Riedesel described the post's purpose: "The Reserve Corps of Lieutenant Colonel Breymann built their Emplacement beyond the Ravine to defend the right flank of the Corps of Brigadier Fraser en potence and at the same time cover the road that ran over the hill into the rear of the Army."[46]

Embedded in James Wilkinson's egocentric *Memoirs* is an accurate description of the tactical situation Ebenezer Learned exploited:

> I then proceeded to the scene of renewed action, which embraced Burgoyne's right flank defence. . . . The right flank defence of the enemy occupied by the German corps of Breymann, consisted of a breast-work of rails piled horizontally between perpendicular pickets, driven into the earth, formed en potence to the rest of his line, and extended abut 250 yards across an open field, and was covered on the right by a battery of two guns. The interval from the left to the British light infantry was committed to the defence of provincials, who occupied a couple of log cabins [of the McBride farm]. The Germans were encamped behind the rail breast-work, and the ground in front of it inclined in a very gentle slope for about 120 yards, when it sunk abruptly, our troops had formed a line under this declivity, and covered breast high were warmly engaged with the Germans. From this position, about sunset, I perceived Brigadier-general Learned advancing toward the enemy with his brigade, in open column. I think with Colonel M. Jackson's regiment in front.[47]

The most straightforward account of this critical post's capture that has come down to us is from one of the men involved, Colonel Rufus Putnam of the 5th Massachusetts Regiment.

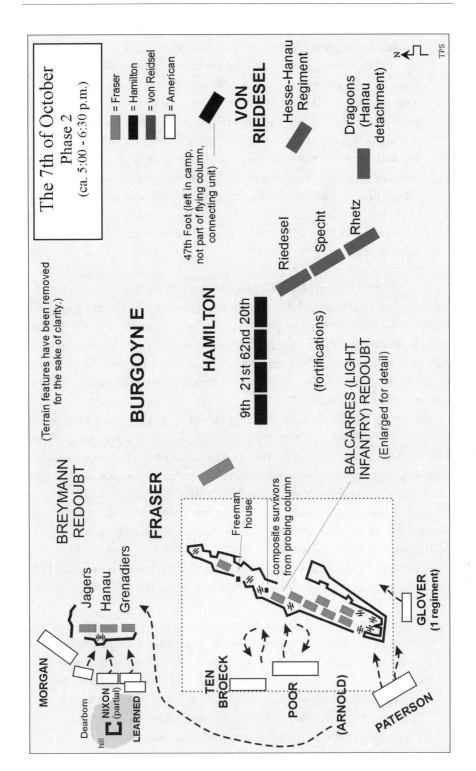

The 7th of October
Phase 2
(ca. 5:00 - 6:30 p.m.)

= Fraser
= Hamilton
= von Reidsel
= American

(Terrain features have been removed for the sake of clarity.)

47th Foot (left in camp, not part of flying column, connecting unit)

VON RIEDESEL

Hesse-Hanau Regiment

Dragoons (Hanau detachment)

Riedesel

Specht

Rhetz

BURGOYNE

HAMILTON

9th 21st 62nd 20th

(fortifications)

BALCARRES (LIGHT INFANTRY) REDOUBT
(Enlarged for detail)

BREYMANN REDOUBT

FRASER

Freeman house

composite survivors from probing column

Jagers
Hanau
Grenadiers

MORGAN

Dearborn

hill

NIXON (partial)

LEARNED

TEN BROECK

POOR

(ARNOLD)

GLOVER (1 regiment)

PATERSON

N

TPS

The facts are as follows, in the front of these works was a clear open field bounded by a wood at a distance of about 120 yards. In the skirt of this wood I was posted with the 5th and 6th regiments of Massachusetts[.] [T]he right and left of these works were partly covered by this wood and the rear by a thick wood. The moment orders were given to storm, I moved rapidly across the open field & entered the works in front, I believe the same moment that the troops of Learned's Brigade (of which Jackson's regiment was) entered on the left and rear. I immediately formed the two regiments under my command & moved out of these woods [works] (which was not enclosed in the rear) into the woods toward the enemies [sic] enclosed redoubt [Balcarres Redoubt] in the rear of their main encampment.[48]

Another officer from Nixon's Brigade, Captain Benjamin Warren of the 7th Massachusetts, recorded this terse description of his regiment's role in the fighting: "We marched to the right of Col. Morgan's riflemen to the lines within ten rods of a strange fort; fought them boldly for better than half an hour when they gave way; left the fort and fled. Our people marched in and took possession of their cannon and 600 tents, standing with baggage etc. The fire was very hot on both sides."[49]

According to Wilkinson, "[G]eneral Learned . . . incline[d] and attack[ed] to his right . . . with great gallantry, the provincials abandoned their position and fled; the German flank was by this means uncovered, they were assaulted vigorously, overturned in five minutes, and retreated in disorder, leaving their gallant commander, Lieutenant-colonel Breymann dead on the field."[50]

As the men of Learned's and Nixon's Brigades, with Morgan's Corps, stormed Breymann's post, Arnold, having left the troops engaged in front of the Balcarres Redoubt, joined the assault. As usual with any historical re-telling involving Arnold, there are numerous (at least partly) conflicting versions. Here is Wilkinson's description of Arnold's role in what is now a legendary event:

. . . [Arnold] finding himself on our right, dashed to the left through the fire of the two lines and escaped unhurt; he then turned to the right of the enemy, as I was informed by that excellent officer, Colonel Butler [of Morgan's Corps], and collecting 15 or 20 riflemen threw himself with his party into the rear of the enemy, just as they gave way, where his leg was broke, and his horse killed under him; but whether by our fire or that of the enemy, as they fled from us, has never been ascertained.[51]

One of the key figures in the attack against Breymann's Redoubt was Henry Dearborn, commander of the light infantry of Morgan's Corps. Dearborn left a pair of accounts of the fighting. The earliest brief account appeared in his *Journal*, and is consistent with evidence offered by the testimony of contemporaries.[52] His "Narrative," written in 1815—after he achieved national prominence and became the object of criticism for incompetence as secretary of war—differs substantially from his Journal, as well as with the accounts of other participants. It made no reference to Arnold's leading the attack on the Light Infantry [Balcarres] Redoubt, indicating that General Poor commanded there, and fixed the time of assault on Breymann's position as somewhat earlier than the one against Balcarres' position.[53]

A third Dearborn version of events appeared in H. A. S. Dearborn's *The Life of Major General Henry Dearborn*, prepared in 1822. The younger Dearborn exaggerated his father's command role. Like his father, he depicted General Poor leading the attacks on the Light Infantry [Balcarres] Redoubt. Arnold made his appearance on the field where "Morgan and Dearborn had united their corps in front of the German camp, together with Weston's regiment and some other detachments," wrote the younger Dearborn. His account is valuable and worth reproducing at length. "Arnold," he continued,

> came up to Morgan and Dearborn, who were conversing on the propriety of a forward movement, and clapping his hand on the shoulder of the latter, observed, with great energy and zeal, "within fifteen minutes we will carry those entrenchments." In reply to him, it was stated by Morgan and Dearborn, that the works appeared formidable against musketry; were well manned and that their troops were much fatigued and nearly exhausted. Arnold replied, with cheering confidence beaming on his countenance, "that the enemy were panic-stricken and would not fight: that he would take a small party and pass through the woods to the rear of the enemy's right, where there were no works; and when he opened fire on the right it was to be the signal for them to advance in front, and storm the works." The necessary arrangements were promptly made and, when it was discovered Arnold had gained the rear, the riflemen and infantry gave three cheers and pressed forward with spirit and impetuosity. . . .When General Arnold entered, on the right of the rear of the camp, he ordered the [German] troops, which had suddenly faced about to receive him, to lay down their arms—but a platoon, directly in his front, fired, by which his horse was killed, and he wounded, in the same leg that was shattered in

his attack on Quebec. The horse fell on the other leg, and Dearborn, having entered the front, at the same moment, ran up and extricating him, enquired if he was badly wounded; Arnold replied with great heat, "in the same leg that was wounded before; I never go into action without being shot; to be disabled at such a time - - - I wish to God the ball had gone through my heart . . . .[54]

Besides omitting General Learned's and Colonel Brooks' important roles, and emphasizing Dearborn's, this account ignores the fact that the terrain precluded Arnold's entering the redoubt from the enemy's right because the fortification's right overlooked an embankment so steep as to preclude anyone's ascending it on horseback. Every other account had Arnold entering the rear of the post from the enemy's left—the only direction from which a flanking movement could be made.

Before summarizing the evidence relating to the fall of Breymann's post, we should consult British and German sources for what they reported, and for their accurate assessment of the impact of the loss of that redoubt.

Freiherr von Riedesel penned two reliable reports of what to him was an especially tragic event. In his October 21 letter to the Duke of Brainschweig, he wrote that while the men in the Light Infantry [Balcarres] Redoubt were still under attack, a climactic assault carried the Breymann Redoubt. Here are his words, unmarred by the florid language that characterized the prose of many contemporaries when they corresponded with important people:

> At the same time [as the attack on the Light Infantry Redoubt], the latter attacked the entrenchment of Colonel Breymann, which was held for a long time, but the latter was shot dead, and the enemy came in the rear, in that manner the enemy captured the entrenchment, tents, and equipment. The larger part of the men, however, were saved. Colonel von Speth, who wanted to help Colonel Breymann, with forty men, was himself surrounded in the night by ten men and taken prisoner, and with that this unfortunate affair was ended.[55]

A more informative version of this affair appears in a draft manuscript of von Riedesel's "Reflections on the Campaign":

> Another body at the time attacked the embankments of Breymann's division in front and on his left flank. The Grenadiers composing this

corps fought bravely, but being only two hundred strong, and their commander—the chivalric Breymann—being shot dead, they were compelled to retreat. This latter misfortune resulted from the fact that the Canadian companies, belonging to the reconnaissance expedition, were absent from their place beside this corps, part of them being in the great [Balcarres] redoubt, and the others not having returned to their position. Had they been in their places, it would have been impossible to surround the left flank of Breymann.[56]

Burgoyne realistically assessed the loss of Breymann's stronghold when he wrote: "[U]nhappily the entrenchments of the German reserve, commanded by Lieutenant Colonel Breymann, who was killed, were carried and although ordered to be recovered, they were never so, and the enemy by that misfortune, gained an opening on our right rear. The night put an end to the action."[57]

Excepting the testimony in the Dearborn "Narrative" and Dearborn's excessively reverent biography, the evidence supports Learned's and Morgan's initiating the assault on the German post and Arnold's leaving the units attacking the Light Infantry [Balcarres] Redoubt and riding between the fire of the two armies through the gap made by the capture of cabins to Breymann's left and joining a party of riflemen entering the German rear from their left.

Aftermath: American Satisfaction

The fall of Breymann's Redoubt opened Burgoyne's line to attack from his right and rear. After Colonel von Speth's capture while trying to recover the fallen post, Burgoyne withdrew under the cover of darkness to the Hudson River valley, where the Europeans spent the next day under the protection of fortifications overlooking his artillery park, hospital, bridge of boats, and camp.

British Lieutenant Digby provided a succinct record of Burgoyne's move:

> During the night we were employed in moving our cannon Baggage &c nearer to the river. It was done with silence and fires were lighted to cause them [the Americans] not to suspect we had retired from our works where it was impossible for us to remain, as the German lines commanded them, and were then in possession of the enemy, who were bringing up cannon to bear on ours at day break. It may be supposed we had no thought of sleep, and some time before day we retreated nearer to the river. Our design of retreating to Ticonderoga then became public.[58]

Gates' men had fought a well-coordinated battle that, except for the ill-conceived assault on the Light Infantry [Balcarres] Redoubt, was characterized by mutual support among units and very professional brigade, regimental, and company deployment. The result was an economical victory, gained with relatively few casualties—150 killed and wounded—in contrast to the enemy's 700 killed, wounded, and captured. Gates' strategy of forcing Burgoyne to try to dislodge him from Bemis Heights and fighting on American terms succeeded.

"I have the satisfaction to acquaint your excellency with the great success of the Arms of the United States in this Department," wrote Gates in his October 12 report to President Hancock about the day's achievements. He continued:

> On the 7th last, the Enemy attacked our advanc'd Piquets upon the left which drew on an Action, about the same hour of the Day, and near the same Spot of Ground, where that of the 19th of Sept. was fought from 3 O'Clock in the afternoon, until almost Night, the Conflict was very warm and bloody, when the Enemy by a precipitate Retreat determined the Fate of the Day—leaving in our hands eight Pieces of Brass Cannon, the Tents and Baggage of their Flying Army, a large quantity of Fix'd Ammunition, Major Acland, who commanded the Corps of Grenadiers, Capt. Money, Q. M. General, and Sir Francis Clarke, principle aide to His Excellency General Burgoyne. The loss on our Side is not more than [blank] Killed and Wounded, amongst the latter is the Gallant Major General Arnold, whose Leg was fractured as by a Musket Ball, as he was Forcing the Enemy's Breast Work—Too much praise cannot be given to the Corps commanded by Col. Morgan, consisting of the Rifle Regiment and the Light Infantry under Major Dearborn; but it would be injustice to say that the whole Body engaged did not equally deserve the honour and Applause due to such exalted merit. . . .[59]

This report reveals Gates in a very different light than the one in which many writers depict him. His account was business-like in an era too often marked by stilted language. It honored a brave enemy and was generous in attributing victory to all who served. Finally, it contained a gracious tribute to the man who had been an implacable enemy and whose insubordination had held the potential to jeopardize the cause they both served.

It is worth noting that in no surviving document, including his private correspondence, did Horatio Gates ever disparage Benedict Arnold's service in the Northern Department.

Retreat, Pursuit, and the Siege of Saratoga

Retreat (and Recriminations) Begin

Early on during his advance southward from Canada, General Burgoyne proclaimed that "this army does not retreat." The fall of Breymann's Redoubt during the final hours of the fighting on October 7, 1777, reduced that proclamation to a hollow boast. The loss of the stronghold exposed the right wing of the British fortified camp to enfilade fire, making it untenable. With his men outnumbered and exhausted, his supplies fatally depleted, and his hopes of assistance from Sir Henry Clinton founded more on desperation than reality, the general ordered his battered army to withdraw to their fortified line's left wing. There, protected by what writers later called the Great Redoubt, his soldiers spent the eighth under a harassing sniping and artillery fire, preparing to retreat.[1] At dusk, the commander and his senior officers escorted the body of Brigadier Simon Fraser, who died that morning, to the redoubt, where Chaplain Edward Brudenel read the Church of England's Burial Office, and American gunners, unaware of the procession's nature, did their best to break up the burial party.[2]

Immediately following the burial service, with preparations for withdrawal complete, and the hospital, the wounded, sick, and attendants commended to General Gates' care, the army formed in column. Alexander Fraser's company of rangers, accompanied by the Loyalists and the few Indians who remained, formed the advanced party, followed by the Germans, the British 9th Regiment, the 47th Regiment, the artillery and wagons, and the rest of the British troops. Fraser's Advanced Corps, now commanded by Lord Balcarres, provided the rearguard. Alexander Fraser's rangers marched at 9:00 p.m., von Riedesel's Germans followed one hour later, and Balcarres' Corps moved at 11:00 p.m. The last men did not leave the encampment until shortly before 4:00 in the morning of October 9.[3]

"On the night of the 8th and the 9th we actually started," wrote von Riedesel in his October 21 letter to the Herzog von Braunschweig. "I was supposed to make the advanced guard with 4 battalions," he continued,

> the baggage following me, the army and rear guard. Thus as I came to Overgotta [Dovegat] House, I saw that the enemy had occupied the heights of Saratoga, which however, he left and placed himself across the Hudson behind the Battenkill. Here there was still time to get through, if we had continued our march leaving behind the heavy artillery, bateaux, and baggage; but we stopped at Overgotta House and remained there despite my pleas.[4]

The intention of this disingenuous summary was to advise the baron's sovereign of the campaign's failure in a manner that placed the onus for the loss of the men of his command squarely on the shoulders of General Burgoyne. The German's account was misleading because it implied that von Riedesel could, from Dovegat [modern Coveville], see that the Americans had occupied the village of Saratoga and that they had retreated across the Hudson behind the Battenkill. He could not have seen that from Coveville, and the Americans did not cross the river behind the Battenkill, but downriver of that stream. He probably learned that the enemy was on the hill above the village of Saratoga from Alexander Fraser's scouts, and the Americans under General John Fellows did not withdraw across the river until after von Riedesel and the retreating column left Dovegat. In her account, published in 1800, the Baronin von Riedesel repeated the substance of her husband's report.[5]

Burgoyne provided a description of prevailing conditions in an account that was more detailed, as well as free of recriminations. "A defeated army was to retreat from the enemy flushed with success in front, and occupying strong posts in the country behind," began the general's account, which continued thusly:

> We were equally liable upon that march to be attacked in front, in flank, or rear. The disposition of march had been concerted as much as circumstances would admit; and it was executed by the officers and troops

in general with a precision that experience in critical situations can only teach. The baggage, which could only move in one column, and in a narrow road, fell into the confusion which it is impossible to guard against in the dark, because a single accident of an overturned or broken wheel, or even the stupidity or drunkenness of a driver, may stop and often confuse the motion of the whole line. Care was taken that no such accident should break the order of the troops, and orders were sent to Major General Phillips, who commanded the rear guard, in case he was attacked, to pay attention only to the main object of covering the troops; or, if occasion were [offered], of taking a position to give them time to form. . . . At day-break the next morning [October 9] the army had reached very advantageous ground [Dovegat] and took a position in which to receive the enemy. A halt was necessary to refresh the troops, and to give time for the bateaux, loaded with provisions, which had not been able to keep pace with the troops, to come a-breast. A portion of the provisions was delivered also from the bateaux, not without apprehension that delivery might be the last: for there were parts of the river in which the boats might be attacked from the other side to great advantage, not withstanding the correspondent movement of the army. . . . The above purposes being effected, the army proceeded in very severe weather, and through exceeding bad roads.[6]

The general accurately described the situation he and his army faced. Contrary to the impression often given, General Gates had, even before engaging the enemy on October 7, taken measures to thwart his escape by ordering militia commanders to post themselves east of the Hudson River and in Burgoyne's rear. John Stark and his heroes of Bennington reappeared, captured Fort Edward's small British garrison, and advanced down the river toward Saratoga.[7] Two thousand New Hampshire militiamen under Brigadier General Jacob Bayley constructed an entrenched camp on high ground north of old Fort Edward. More immediately affecting the retreat, Gates ordered Brigadier General John Fellows, commanding about 1,300 Berkshire County, Massachusetts, militia to move northward up the east side of the river to the mouth of the Battenkill, cross the Hudson, and entrench on the heights of Saratoga.[8] Fellows' men were the troops von Riedesel claimed to have seen. They were too few in number to halt the retreat, but Gates could reinforce Fellows and follow Burgoyne so closely that the latter would be caught between pursuing and interdicting forces.

Sometime after the retreat march got under way, Lieutenant Colonel Nicholas Sutherland returned from reconnoitering Fellows' position at Saratoga and urged Burgoyne to permit him take his regiment, the 47th, and surprise the militiamen, whose perimeter security was temptingly lax. The general refused because he feared the loss of cohesive control. Like almost every decision taken by him, some writers have criticized Burgoyne for losing an opportunity to dislodge Fellows. There was a sound reason, however, for his decision. A successful retreat in the presence of the enemy required absolute control, and the detachment of an entire regiment without concert and support from the main column would jeopardize, and perhaps sabotage, that control. In addition, while Fellows' men were lax about security, as militia usually were, the 47th Regiment could muster no more than 250 men against Fellows' 1,300 fresh troops in a prepared position.[9]

As the above-quoted accounts reported, the army halted at Dovegat, about four miles north of where it began its retreat. At that point the road, for the first time, left the river flats and climbed to gently sloping higher ground where, to von Riedesel's avowed disgust, Burgoyne ordered a halt to distribute rations and secure communication with his bateaux. About this decision, too, critics have had much to say. The burden of their comments is that he should have pressed on, without concern for his baggage. This criticism does not explain, however, how the retreating army could have effected its retreat without taking along its supplies. The country north of Fort Edward was so sparsely settled and cultivated that it could not have supported a fraction of the army even under favorable conditions, which of course were nonexistent. Two armies had traversed the area within less than three months, and those incursions had occurred too late in the year for people to replant and restock.

An influential contribution to the litany of criticism emanated from Freifrau von Riedesel's industrious pen, reporting that Burgoyne so coveted an "Order"—promised him if he effected a junction with Sir William Howe—that he could not reconcile himself to retreating, and jeopardized his army by resorting to frivolous excuses for halting the withdrawal, including a pause to inventory his cannon. Instead of counting his guns, she argued, Burgoyne should have abandoned his artillery train, which would have enabled his men to march rapidly enough to have, within four miles, crossed the Hudson and been free of their pursuers.[10] Some students have subscribed to her interpretation, or have at least found it persuasive.[11] Yet, no evidence that the King and ministry had promised the general a peerage exists. More important was this question:

Would abandoning the artillery to the Americans have secured a successful escape?

That very question arose during the House of Commons' inquiry into General Burgoyne's conduct. Charles Stanhope, Viscount Petersham (after April 1, 1779, Earl of Harrington) was asked, "Would leaving the heavy artillery behind . . . have made a difference of four miles in the march?" His lordship answered. "I can't conceive that it would. The enemy were in force behind us; not having the numbers to contend with them, it would have been a very desperate circumstance to have abandoned our cannon in case of an attack." To the question whether the guns were of use during the retreat, he replied that they were not of "any use than that of their not being turned against us." When asked whether they could not have been rendered useless by spiking the vent and knocking off the trunnions, Stanhope responded, "I understand that spikes in the cannon are easily removed," and that breaking off the trunnions was "not an easy matter, I believe almost an impossibility, with any tools that are carried in an army." Later in the interrogation he testified that even without the artillery the soldiers were too tired to continue without a rest, saying "The army was certainly much fatigued, I believe they could have gone but little further. They were certainly not in a state for a long march."[12]

One of the most thoughtful journals kept by a veteran of the campaign was that of Lieutenant William Digby of the 53rd Regiment of Foot. After noting other criticisms of his commander, Digby penned the following:

> They also said that even [on] the 10th by spiking our cannon and destroying all baggage &c.—a paltry consideration in comparison, in our circumstances—we might have made our retreat good to Fort George, saving the troops and Musquetry: but then it was not certain that vessels were prepared to convey us over the lake [George]; in which case it would have been a worse post than Saratoga for the army. These were the opinions of unsatisfied and discontented men, who had never approved of anything that turned out contrary to their expectations. Had Burgoyne been fortunate, they would not have dared to declare them; as he was unsuccessful, they set him down guilty.[13]

The British commander wisely determined to keep his force concentrated and in possession of its artillery train and stores. As events soon demonstrated, he came very close to proving the wisdom of his decision when General Gates imprudently ordered an advance for October 11—a move aborted by the prudence of the American commander's subordinates.

That observation aside, contrary to the baroness, the Europeans would have had to march much more than four miles through torrential rain to be free of Gates' equally sodden army. The air-mile distance from Old Saratoga to Fort George, from whence boats might have transported them over Lake George to within a few miles of Ticonderoga, exceeds twenty-five miles. The shortest route, a primitive track west of the river, led to the ford at Fort Edward—the one taken by Colonel Sutherland—thence over the portage between the Hudson and Fort George. John Fellows with 1,300 men, Jacob Bayley with 1,300 men, and John Stark with 1,400 men were poised to contest that avenue of escape.[14]

An alternative to that route would entail crossing to the east side of the Hudson above Saratoga near the mouth of the Battenkill. Major Duncan Forbes of the 9th Regiment of Foot later testified concerning this route:

Q. Did the battery of the enemy on the other side of the river at Saratoga command the ford on that river?

A. It did. . . .

Q. Had the passage of the ford been affected, and then proceeded towards Fort Edward, on the east side of the river, must they most necessarily have passed Batten Kill?

A. Undoubtedly.

Q. Do you remember the ford at Batten Kill?

A. Yes.

Q. Would it have been possible for the army to have passed that ford without artillery to cover them, and the enemy posted on the other side?

A. Certainly not. I had an opportunity of seeing the twentieth regiment pass that ford [during September 13] without an enemy to oppose them, and they took a considerable time, owing to the depth of the water, the rapidity of the current, and the stones being remarkably slippery, so that several of them fell into the river.[15]

Fellows, Bayley, and Stark were even more prepared to interdict that route than the units west of the river. Burgoyne's parliamentary critics apparently saw no advantage in trying to exploit criticism of his decision to retain his supply and artillery, and the subject did not surface during the rest of the inquiry.

A sound strategic reason for preserving an artillery capability existed. If the opportunity presented itself to make a last-ditch stand and await action by Sir Henry on the lower Hudson, the guns might make the difference between survival and certain defeat. As has been noted above, such an opportunity briefly existed as the army went on the defensive on "the Heights of Saratoga." And Captain Hoffman Nickerson, who delighted in exposing the professional flaws of both Burgoyne and Gates, did not include the von Riedesel condemnation of the decision not to abandon the guns to the Americans, who would certainly have appreciated their foes' awarding them their supplies and ordnance.

The Europeans resumed their retreat through the cold drenching rain, crossing the Fishkill to the village of Saratoga [Schuylerville] during the evening of October 10. "[N]ot only does it rain incessantly, the roads are soaked and almost impassable," Schuler von Senden recorded in his diary. "We have burnt our tents and all encumbrances, because the troops can no longer carry them. We arrive at a river [the Fishkill] that flows into the Hudson. What the leadership only now realize, we built a bridge here during the advance march, but the enemy had destroyed it. There is nothing to do but wade the river, in spite of the water's depth and in spite of its being very cold to wade. It is rather dark."[16]

General Fellows had prudently, and in compliance with orders, withdrawn his militia to the east of the river and positioned them to interdict the ford at Saratoga and to cannonade the embattled enemy. Thus, von Senden continued, "The enemy artillery, nevertheless, fires at us during the crossing as they had sighted their guns at the ford during daylight. We suffer new losses. We assemble again before the small village, Saratoga, which we hopefully passed a short while ago in a southern direction."[17]

The exhausted soldiers tried to build fires to warm themselves and dry their clothing, but the American artillery targeted the flames from their positions across the river. In an effort to keep from freezing in the icy wind, the men trudged about constantly through the long night. "Towards morning the rain stops, but a heavy frost sets in," Senden wrote as he concluded the day's diary entry. "To make our desperation complete, the detachment which had been sent to build the bridge [over the Hudson] returns. General Burgoyne had recalled it. We are supposed to entrench here, but the ground is stony, the men are exhausted and half frozen to death."[18]

Baroness von Riedesel added titillation to the story of the soldiers' misery that delighted Americans who battened on British depravity for two centuries. After detailing how she and her children had to sleep on a bed of straw, she wrote of being visited by General William Phillips, whom she asked why they were halting instead of pressing northward. If her account is at all accurate, she must have known what everyone knew: that the men who had fought a battle and slogged ten miles along a road so muddy that a brass cannon sank out of sight were too near the end of their resources to continue. Even her redoubtable spouse had been so tired that he had, at one point, climbed into her carriage and slept with his head on her shoulder for three hours—and the baron rode a horse. The men marched, or rather slogged, on foot and were even more weary. Yet, the baroness professed not to understand why it was imperative that the column halt. By the time she finally published her story, General Phillips had been dead for nineteen years, so it was safe to quote him verbatim: "Poor lady, I admire you drenched to the skins you are, yet have the courage to go on in this weather. If only you were our commanding general. This halt is because he [Burgoyne] is very tired and wants to stay here this night and give supper."[19] The most generous alternative to considering the passage a complete invention is that the German noblewoman's English was so poor that she misunderstood Phillips.

But there is more to the tale. Instead of sharing his soldiers' exhaustion, Burgoyne was (alleged the baroness) "happily merry, spending half the night singing and drinking and amusing himself with the wife of a quartermaster who was his mistress and like he loved Champagne."[20] The callous commander was not only disporting himself with the wife of a member of his staff, he was doing so in the manor of patriot General Philip Schuyler, a house he soon wantonly burned. John Burgoyne was certainly a libertine. He was also a conscientious, humane commander who earned the sobriquet "Gentleman Johnny" because he treated his troops with unusual decency. To accept the baroness' unsupported testimony to the contrary, as many writers did, was more partisan than scholarly.

The truth was much more prosaic. Simply put, the commander, his officers, the enlisted men, and the women and children accompanying the column were too near collapse to go farther. Three days under arms—one day of battle and two of being subjected to harassment while expecting attack—and ten miles of moving themselves, their gear, their field guns, and wagons along a road that marching men, horses, cattle, and wheels had churned into a muddy trench had extracted a crippling emotional and physical toll.[21]

Because the bridge over the Fishkill was out when the main body of troops crossed, the cannon remained with Hamilton's Brigade south of the creek until the next day, when they too waded to its north bank and joined the main column on high ground overlooking the Schuyler estate and the river.[22]

Contrary to the baroness' allegation that Burgoyne was reluctant to continue the retreat, the general ordered Lieutenant Colonel Nicholas Sutherland to march his 47th Regiment, Hill's 9th Regiment, Alexander Fraser's Rangers, MacKay's Canadians, and the army's artificers about twelve miles up the Hudson's west bank to opposite Fort Edward. Because the 9th and 47th had been less heavily engaged in the fighting of the seventh, they were the freshest men available. Once opposite Fort Edward, Lieutenant William Twiss, since June 26 commander of the Corps of Engineers, would direct construction of a bridge to the eastern side of the river. Its obvious purpose was to provide for a retreat to Fort Ticonderoga. Given that Burgoyne had probably been informed by his scouts of Stark's and Bayley's presence east of the Hudson, he was aware that the odds facing him were indeed discouraging. Charles Stanhope (later Lord Harrington) testified that the general entertained even more desperate ideas, including trying to ford the river and making a forced march down the east side of the river to Albany.[23] Burgoyne was so determined to save his army from capture that he contemplated measures certain to fail.

About 4:00 in the afternoon of October 10, the American advance guard reached the Fishkill and found the enemy camped and entrenched on the "heights of Saratoga."[24]

Retreat and Pursuit Segue into Siege

While Burgoyne's men began their slow northward retreat, Gates' soldiers drew and cooked rations, replenished their ammunition rounds, and rested. Some writers have savaged the American commander for his tardy pursuit of a battered and outnumbered enemy. Indeed, he could have immediately committed the 2,856 men of Patterson's and Nixon's Brigades who had not engaged in the fighting of October 7. But the militia, who comprised those brigades, were not the men to undertake rapid, disciplined movements. The best troops, the Continentals, had been heavily engaged on the seventh and were as tired and hungry as the men they had fought. They needed to be re-provisioned and fully rested. The same rain that drenched their enemy and turned the Albany Road into a quagmire also fell upon the victors and so slowed their pursuit. Any veteran of ground combat understands "General Mud's" impact on operations.

Horatio Gates was in no great hurry to run his opponent to ground, for Burgoyne had no haven to which to flee. Bayley, Stark, and Fellows were east of the Hudson with 4,032 effectives.[25] "Granny" Gates knew that only a serious tactical blunder by him or his subordinates, or a British relief from the lower Hudson, would save Burgoyne. Patience and prudence had served him well, and he hoped to continue to enlist them in closing his campaign.

As soon as the Americans arrived at the Fishkill's south bank, Major Ebenezer Stevens deployed several cannon into battery and opened fire on the bateaux and working parties off-loading supplies.[26] The British defensive position north of the Fishkill was a strong one. Just north of the stream, a ridge stretches northward, breaking sharply on the east and flattening into a plateau toward the west. Behind a breastwork British Grenadiers, Loyalists, the British 9th, 24th, and 21st regiments, and Alexander Fraser's Rangers deployed, supported by field pieces. Most of the Germans deployed northeast of them and north of where Schuylerville now lies. The German Jägers and about 100 Canadians were athwart an east-west road. The other British regiments deployed north of the stream. The artillery park was on a low knoll southeast of the German regiments Riedesel, Rhetz, Specht, and Erbprinz [Hesse-Hanau]. The Hudson covered the eastern flank, and the Fishkill provided a moat on the south. Unlike the battlefield, cultivated fields and river meadows provided wide open fields of fire. The soldiers occupied entrenchments prepared by them during September 13 and 14 on their way south, took over ones begun by Fellows' men on September 9, and dug more of their own. Burning General Schuyler's country house, mills, and estate buildings expanded the field of fire south of the creek.[27]

Quotations from the journals of two officers, one British and the other German, provide glimpses of what the men of Burgoyne's army experienced in their new camp. First, Lieutenant William Digby of the 53rd Regiment of foot:

> [October] 11th. Their cannon and ours began to play on each other. They took many of our Batows [sic] on the river, as our cannon could not protect them. We were obliged to bring our oxen and horses into our

lines, where they had the wretched prospect of living but a few days as our grass was gone, and nothing after [that] but leaves of trees for them; still they continued fireing [sic] into us from Batteries they erected during the night, and placed their riflemen in the tops of trees; but still did not venture to storm our works. At night we strengthened our works and threw up more.[28]

"Today [October 11]," wrote Schuler von Senden of the Regiment von Specht, "the enemy appear in greater numbers on the other shore of the Hudson, so that there can be no further thought of our crossing."[29]

The Americans Abort an Attack

General Gates misinterpreted intelligence that a body of troops had moved northward (Sutherland's departure for Fort Edward). From that news, he assumed his enemy's main body was abandoning its position and resuming its northward retreat, presenting an opportunity to attack an outnumbered enemy deployed in column with every tactical factor in his favor. When he shared that assumption with his adjutant general, James Wilkinson, the young colonel warned that he would be exposing his army to a possible trap. The general insisted that Burgoyne had, in fact, retreated, leaving only a strong rearguard to cover his move.[30]

If Wilkinson was right—as he was—the American commander was about to do what he had so wisely refused to do while camped on Bemis Heights: engage the enemy on his terms. Anticipating an attack, Burgoyne had recalled Sutherland with the 9th and 47th regiments to reinforce his main body in its strong defensive position. "Had Burgoyne merely proposed to stand where he was . . . his position would have been strong enough to enable him to turn back his assailants with heavy loss," was how Hoffman Nickerson succinctly described the tactical situation. "Worn down as his army was, he still had his two chief assets, first, the ability of his disciplined regulars to defeat even a far more numerous body of the improvised troops of the rebels should the latter engage them on ground suitable to their close-order formations, and second, the fire of the twenty-seven guns remaining, exclusive of the mortars . . . ."[31]

Wilkinson recorded that he made an inspection of the outposts before going to bed. When he returned at 11:00 p.m., he found Gates still awake. The general showed him an order he had issued for a general attack at dawn on the

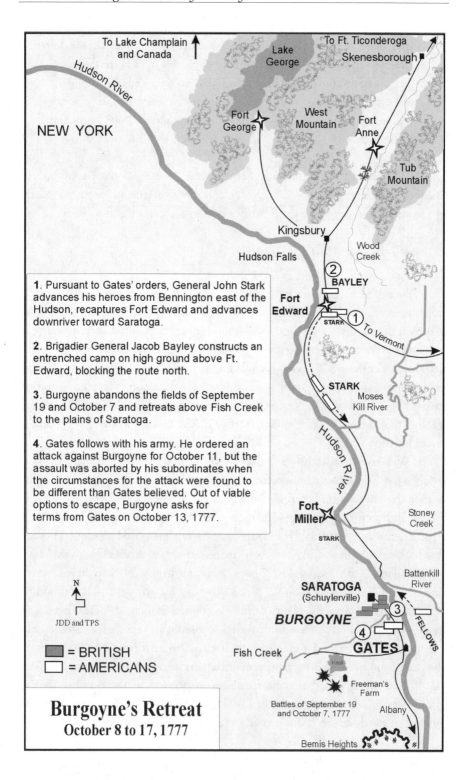

To Lake Champlain and Canada

To Ft. Ticonderoga

Hudson River

Lake George

Skenesborough

NEW YORK

Fort George

West Mountain

Fort Anne

Tub Mountain

Kingsbury

Wood Creek

Hudson Falls

② BAYLEY

1. Pursuant to Gates' orders, General John Stark advances his heroes from Bennington east of the Hudson, recaptures Fort Edward and advances downriver toward Saratoga.

Fort Edward

STARK ① To Vermont

2. Brigadier General Jacob Bayley constructs an entrenched camp on high ground above Ft. Edward, blocking the route north.

STARK
Moses Kill River

3. Burgoyne abandons the fields of September 19 and October 7 and retreats above Fish Creek to the plains of Saratoga.

Hudson River

4. Gates follows with his army. He ordered an attack against Burgoyne for October 11, but the assault was aborted by his subordinates when the circumstances for the attack were found to be different than Gates believed. Out of viable options to escape, Burgoyne asks for terms from Gates on October 13, 1777.

Fort Miller

Stoney Creek

STARK

Battenkill River

N
JDD and TPS

SARATOGA
(Schuylerville)

③ FELLOWS

█ = BRITISH
☐ = AMERICANS

BURGOYNE

④ **GATES**

Fish Creek

Knoll

Freeman's Farm

Burgoyne's Retreat
October 8 to 17, 1777

Battles of September 19 and October 7, 1777

Albany

Bemis Heights

eleventh. When the young officer remonstrated against that decision, Gates ordered him to make a predawn reconnaissance.

Gates planned to have Morgan's Corps deploy against the British right while the rest of the army advanced across the open river bottom south of the Fishkill. Before Wilkinson could report the results of his reconnaissance, Morgan moved out in a dense fog, crossed the creek about a mile southwest of its mouth, and cautiously probed the outposts of the units posted in the entrenchments on the heights of Saratoga. When pickets fired on his skirmishers Morgan halted, perhaps suspecting Burgoyne's army had not withdrawn as believed. If that hunch was correct, having the Fishkill at his back must have made Morgan uneasy. Being unfamiliar with the ground and surrounded by fog, however, he was uncertain of how to change position. At that moment, with characteristic fortuity, Wilkinson rode through the mist and saved Morgan, just as he had done on September 19. Because Wilkinson had become familiar with the terrain during the American retreat southward, he was able to advise the colonel to oblique leftward into a position that would make him less vulnerable to being pinned against the creek. After promising that he would secure support, Wilkinson hurried to Gates' headquarters and received orders to direct Learned's and Paterson's brigades to reinforce Morgan.[32]

Meanwhile, Nixon's and Glover's brigades, while preparing to cross the Fishkill not far from its mouth, captured a picket who reported that the main body of Burgoyne's army was still in position. Undeterred, the two brigade leaders continued their advance. Nixon, Glover's senior in rank, crossed first. Before Glover could follow, a British deserter informed the Americans that not only were the Europeans still in their entrenchments, but that Sutherland had returned with the two regiments detached toward Fort Edward. Nixon halted on the news and the fog lifted quickly, revealing the enemy in position and well prepared to defend themselves against any attack. Nixon's men immediately came under fire from artillery and small arms and fell back across the creek in disorder.[33]

Learned's Brigade forded the Fishkill about three-quarters of mile left of Nixon and almost directly in front of the British position's strongest point. Because a "standing order" issued the previous day mandated "[t]hat in case of an attack against any point, whether front, flank, or rear, the troops are to fall on the enemy at all quarters," Wilkinson feared that Learned, hearing the firing to his right, would go on the offensive. When he arrived with the intent of warning Learned, Wilkinson found the veteran Continentals resolutely advancing up the slope against the men of the British Grenadiers and Light Infantry, the British

9th, 21st, and 24th Regiments, Alexander Fraser's Rangers, and Loyalists, strongly entrenched and supported by cannon. Their commander was reluctant to disregard the standing order until after Wilkinson convinced him that Nixon and Glover had withdrawn. While his men drew back the British fired upon them, killing an officer and several enlisted men.[34]

The battle-wise prudence of Gates' adjutant-general, coupled with the leadership skills of the corps and brigade commanders, saved Gates from accepting the dangerous challenge that Burgoyne had offered. With no other viable option facing him, the American commander settled down to the siege that he hoped would break the back of the invasion "from the side of Canada."

The British Cast about for Options

When his opponent did not engage on his terms, Burgoyne's situation degenerated from desperate to hopeless. His logistical problem, always difficult, became insoluble when the Americans captured his bateaux and the supplies they carried. "[O]ur cattle began to die fast and the stench was very prejudicial in so small a space. . . . We now began to perceive their design by keeping at such a distance, which was to starve us out," was what Lieutenant Digby scribbled into his journal on October 12. After noting that he believed Burgoyne's "greatest wish" was to receive an attack, Digby complimented his enemy, labeling as "prudence" their decision to forego that opportunity, "well knowing what a great slaughter we must have made among them: they knew exactly the state of our provisions, which were [sufficient for] but 4 or 5 days more, and that upon short allowance."[35]

The baroness was the most prolific commentator on conditions in the beleaguered camp, and her description is graphic. But her animosity toward Burgoyne and her egotism detract from her testimony. The "greatest misery and utmost disorder prevailed in the army," wrote the noblewoman. The commissaries had forgotten to distribute rations; and although there were plenty of cattle, no one had slaughtered them. More than thirty starving officers came to her to be fed, and she exhausted her supplies and appealed to Stanhope (Earl of Harrington), "Come and see for yourself these officers, who have been wounded in the common cause, and are now in want of everything, because they do not receive that which is due them. It is, therefore, your duty to make a representation to the general." According to the baroness' creative imagination, she so shamed Burgoyne that he soon came to her and "pathetically" thanked her for reminding him of his duty and complained that he was poorly served and his orders not obeyed. He then asked the officers why they did not avail themselves of his kitchen, and they explained that doing so was not proper. In a less self-absorbed vein, she described shortages of food and water and the constant cannon and small arms fire.[36]

The elusive compiler of *Travels Through the Interior Parts of America* wrote that "incessant rain" fell from October 6 until the Convention [surrender]—an exaggeration, but the account is nonetheless quite evocative of conditions, and worth a careful reading:

> After our arrival at Saratoga, debarred of that very essential to the health and convenience of troops, water, although close to a fine rivulet, it being at the hazard of life, in the day time, to get any, from the number of riflemen the enemy had posted in trees, and at night the men were prevented, as they were sure to be taken prisoners, if they attempted it. All the water that the army was supplied with was from a muddy spring, and what they could get out of the holes the cattle made with their feet; by want of luxury, and render their provisions more palatable, when it rained hard, the men used to catch it in their caps, to mix with flour. Officers in general found the same as the soldiers, most of them young campaigners, and not so provident of their liquors, relying upon a fresh supply that was following the army. This was the only time in life I found money of little use; I was not the only one who, when drenching wet and shivering with cold, would have given a guinea for a glass of any spirit.[37]

In brief, the Royal Army's situation was desperate. Rations were almost exhausted, the Americans were subjecting the besieged to constant fire, the numerical imbalance was increasing daily in favor of the Americans, and hopes for relief from the south were hard to sustain. The hints of approaching winter were apparent in the frigid nights and frosty mornings. Every soldier and officer in the entrenchments at Saratoga feared that nothing could save them from defeat and surrender.

On October 12, General Burgoyne convened a council of war, with another the next day. Their minutes constitute some of the campaign's most important and revealing documents. They are excerpted at length as examples of how the bureaucratic processes of armies continue even when, or perhaps especially when, events teeter on the verge of disaster. Present on the 12th were the commander, Major General von Riedesel, Major General Phillips, and Brigadier James Hamilton.

The Lieutenant General states to the council the present situation of affairs. The enemy is in force, according to the best intelligence he can obtain, to the amount of upwards of 14,000 men, and a considerable quantity of artillery, are on this side of the Fish-Kill and threatens to attack. On the other side of the Hudson River, between this army and Fort Edward is another army of the enemy, the numbers unknown; but one corps which there has been opportunity of observing, is reported to be about 1500 men. They have likewise cannon on the other side of the Hudson's River, and have a bridge below Saratoga church, by which they can communicate. . . . The bateaux of the army have been destroyed, and no means appear of making a bridge over the Hudson's River, even if it were practicable from the position of the enemy.[38]

Having candidly described a situation of which all of them—even von Riedesel—were aware, the commander discussed the tactical options attending a retreat. "The only means of retreat, therefore, are by the ford at Fort Edward, or by taking [to] mountains in order to pass the river higher by rafts, or by any other ford which is reported to be practicable with difficulty, or by keeping to the mountains, to pass the head of Hudson's River, and continue to the westward of Lake George all the way to Ticonderoga," explained Burgoyne. "It is true, this last passage was never made but by Indians, or by very small bodies of men."

Important and immediate problems attended choosing from among those options:

In order to pass cannon or any wheel carriages from hence to Fort Edward, some bridges must be repaired under fire of the enemy from the opposite side of the river; and the principal bridge will be the work of fourteen or fifteen hours; there is no good position for the army to take to sustain the work, and if there were, the time stated as necessary, would give the enemy on the other side of the Hudson's River an opportunity to take post on the strong ground above Fort Edward, or dispute the ford while General Gates' army followed in the rear.[39]

Burgoyne next turned to the one forlorn hope that remained: Clinton's and Vaughan's campaign south of Albany:

The intelligence from the lower part of Hudson's River is founded upon the concurrent reports of prisoners and deserters [even with the British at Gates' mercy, some Americans deserted], who say it was the news in the enemy's camp, that Fort Montgomery was taken; and one man, a friend to government, who arrived yesterday, mentions some particulars of the manner in which it was taken. . . . The provisions of the army may hold out to the 20th; there is neither rum nor spruce beer.[40]

With these uncomfortable facts and bits of suspicions set forth, Burgoyne solicited his subordinates' "sentiments on the following propositions":

1. To wait in the present positions an attack from the enemy, or the chance of favourable events;

2. To attack the enemy;

3. To retreat, repairing the bridges as the army moves for artillery, in order to force the passage of the ford;

4. To retreat by night, leaving the artillery and the baggage; and should it be found impracticable to force the passage with musquetry, to attempt the upper ford, on the passage around Lake George;

5. In case the enemy by extending to their left, leave their rear open, to march rapidly for Albany.[41]

Von Riedesel and the British triumvirate of generals responded to those alternatives this way:

Upon the first proposition resolved, that the situation would grow worse by delay, that the provision now in store not more than sufficient for the retreat should impediments intervene, or a circuit of the country become necessary; and as the enemy did not attack when the ground was unfortified, it is not probable they will do it now, as they have a better game to play;

> The second inadvisable and desperate, there being no possibility of reconnoitering the enemy's position, and his great superiority of numbers known.
>
> The third impracticable;
>
> The fifth thought worthy of consideration by the Lieutenant-General, Major General Phillips, and Brigadier-General Hamilton; but the position of the enemy yet gives no opening for it.

While the three British generals were inclined to consider that option, the German vigorously opposed it and argued for adopting the fourth. After some debate, the council

> Resolved that the fourth proposition is the only resource, and that to effect it, the utmost secrecy and silence is to be observed; and troops are to put into motion from the right in the still part of the night, without any change in the disposition.[42]

The generals agreed to put their resolution into effect and move their troops out at 10:00 that night. Preparations were made, rations distributed and, according to von Riedesel, the Germans were ready to depart on schedule. The British were not yet prepared, and scouts reported that the American "position on the right was such, and they had so many parties out, that it would be impossible to move without our march being immediately discovered." Because secrecy was requisite for success, the orders were countermanded.[43]

That night, John Stark and his Bennington veterans crossed the river on rafts and closed the road that led up the west bank to Fort Edward. They had refused to remain at Bemis Heights and participate in the fight of September 19, but they were willing to close the gap that forced Burgoyne to capitulate—possibly influenced by the prospect of plunder. Stark's Knob, north of present day Schuylerville, memorializes their contribution to American victory.

The Last Recourse: Consideration of Surrender

With the last forlorn hope of escape lost, Burgoyne convened another council. Its minutes read as follows:

Minutes and Proceedings of a Council of War, consisting of the general Officers and Field Officers, and Captains commanding Corps, on the Heights of Saratoga, October 13.

The Lieutenant-General having explained the situation of affairs, as in the preceding council, with the additional intelligence, that the enemy was entrenched at the fords of Fort Edward, and likewise occupied the strong position on the Pine plains between Fort George and Fort Edward, expressed his readiness to undertake at their head any enterprise of difficulty or hazard that should appear to them within compass of their strength or spirit. He added, that he had reason to believe a capitulation had been in the contemplation of some, perhaps all, who knew the sequence to national and personal honour, he thought it a duty to his country, and to himself, to extend his council beyond the usual limits; that the assembly present might justly be esteemed a full representation of the army; and that he should think himself justifiable in taking any step in so serious a matter, without such a concurrence, of sentiments as should make a treaty the act of the army, as well as that of the general.

The first question therefore he desired from them to decide was, Whether the army of 3500 fighting men, as well provided with artillery, were justifiable, upon the principles of national dignity and military honour, in capitulating in any possible situation?

Resolved, nem. con. In the affirmative.

Question 2. Is the present situation of that nature?

Resolved, nem. con. That the present situation justified a capitulation upon honourable terms.

The Lieutenant-General then drew up the message, marked No. 2, and laid it before the council. It was unanimously approved, And upon that foundation the treaty opened.[44]

Including in the council the field officers and captains who, like Alexander Fraser, commanded independent units was certainly unusual, but Burgoyne was unwilling to accept the full responsibility for capitulating. He knew that losing not only a critical campaign but an army would meet violent political censure back home, and he wanted to make clear to the members of Lord North's ministry that his surrender met the approbation of his army's senior officers. Gentleman Johnny was a member of parliament and an experienced politician with no intention of allowing Lord Germain and the ministry to sacrifice him. He was preparing his defense even before he provided the occasion for censure.

Baron von Riedesel confused the deliberations of the two councils in his report to the Duke of Braunschweig. He was eager to convince his sovereign that the burden of responsibility for losing the troops entrusted to him by "His Serene Highness" rested squarely with the British commander. But the baron's letter contained important details, some of which may have been his personal interpretations or inventions to make the news more palatable to the duke. They also probably included information not included in the second council's minutes.

According to von Riedesel, Burgoyne presented four alternatives: (1) "to attack the enemy in a much more advantageous position than our present, but however, even if we could beat him, for want of provisions, we could not reach Fort George"; (2) "to remain as long as we could in our faulty position [which was, of course, a position taken in spite of the baron's advice], and when we ran out of food to surrender ourselves at discretion"; (3) "to capitulate on suitable terms, or (4) to permit each one to make his own way through the woods as well as he could to get to Fort George, which was possible for wild animals, but not for soldiers."

He reported that the staff officers, both British and German, unanimously agreed that if General Burgoyne "believed there was a possibility of attacking the enemy with success, they were willing to sacrifice life and limb." However, added the German officer,

> to effect a retreat of from 60 to 70 miles through pathless woods and to lose cruelly an entire army would be sheer sacrifice, as the army would have only enough for 4 days, so in case the enemy did not intend to attack, it would be better to think about an adjustment and honorable capitulation while it was still possible to consider the day when we had to surrender ourselves at discretion [i.e., on American terms] because of complete lack of provisions. After mature deliberation, and in order not to sacrifice completely the troops and subjects of your Serene Highness, I agreed to this opinion, and for the following reasons . . .[45]

The baron began his analysis by pointing out that even if the Europeans had attacked and beaten the Americans, their food supply was too small to support them until they reached Fort George, and that their horses were so weak that the baggage and artillery could not be transported. "If our army had been beaten, which was expected, on account of its weakness," he continued, "the terrain and its unfortunate position, and on account of the fallen spirits of the soldiers, all of the men would have been sacrificed. The king [of Britain] would lose an army of 3500 men and your Royal Highness your brave subjects." Because the Americans would not attack and "could pick the very day when we had eaten the last mouthful and take us prisoners at discretion," an American attack would have separated the British and German contingents and resulted in a rout. Trying to retreat across the Hudson with all of the fords interdicted by Americans was a "wild dream," and "to break our way separately through the woods, at the hazard of each, was also an impossible plan, and would sacrifice the whole corps, especially the Braunschweigers, who were not made to adapt themselves in pathless woods."

After noting the council's decision to send a flag to the American commander, the baron got to the heart of his message: "[B]efore we went our separate ways, I asked General Burgoyne in the presence of all the staff-officers to declare that he had never disclosed his plans to me, or asked my opinions, and that I had not the least part in all the events which had occurred, to which he not only agreed, but also declared that all events which had happened, even the situation in which he now found himself, were entirely his own and no other's responsibility."[46]

Von Riedesel was asking the British commander to be complicit in a lie when he asked him to agree that he had never informed the German of his plans nor asked his opinion. The baron attended every council of war and recorded their deliberations in his personal papers, making a point that he had contributed his opinions, including the instances when he dissented. That Burgoyne assumed full responsibility for the campaign's military fate was unremarkable. He did that, at least formally, during councils and before the parliamentary inquiry. (In every surviving document, Burgoyne's references to von Riedesel were favorable, while the baron and his lady, unknown to the Briton, often repaid Burgoyne in a different coin.)

Returning to the council of October 13, the letter Burgoyne drafted to Gates and submitted to his council reads as follows:

After having fought you twice, Lieutenant-General Burgoyne has waited some days in his present position, determined to try a third conflict against any force you could bring to attack him. . . . He is apprised of the superiority of your numbers, and the disposition of your troops to impede his supplies, and render his retreat a scene of carnage on both sides. In this situation he is impelled by humanity, and thinks himself justifiable by established principles and precedents of state, and of war, to spare the lives of brave men upon honourable terms. Should Major-General Gates be inclined to treat upon that idea, General Burgoyne would propose a cessation of arms during the time necessary to communicate the preliminary terms by which, in any extremity, he and his army mean to abide.[47]

Appended to the letter was the following message:

Lt. General Burgoyne is desirous of sending a field officer with a message to M. Genl. Gates upon a matter of high moment to both Armies. The Lt. Genl. requests to be informed at what hour Genl. Gates will receive him tomorrow morning.[48]

General Gates replied at 9:00 in the evening of October 13:

Major General Gates will receive a field officer from Lieut. Genl. Burgoyne, at the advanced post of the Army of the United States, at 10 o'clock tomorrow morning from whence he will be conducted to Head Quarters.[49]

14

The Convention of Saratoga

Negotiations Begin

When he received General Gates' agreement to receive a field grade officer authorized to negotiate on his behalf, General Burgoyne on October 14 sent Lieutenant Colonel Robert Kingston, his adjutant general and acting military secretary. (The colonel and his commander had an especially close relationship, beginning in 1759 when he became a lieutenant in Burgoyne's regiment, the 6th Light Dragoons.) Kingston, under a flag of truce, presented himself at an American advanced outpost at the southern end of the remains of the bridge over the Fishkill, where he was met by Gates' deputy adjutant general, James Wilkinson. The ever-officious Wilkinson tried to persuade Kingston to hand over his commander's message, but the Briton refused. "General Gates has agreed to receive the message," replied Kingston, "and I am not authorized to deliver it to any other person." Wilkinson blindfolded and escorted him about a mile down the Albany Road to Gates' headquarters, located southeast of the Dutch Church. There, the colonel and former British major greeted one another "familiarly." "General Gates, your servant," offered the former, to which the general responded, "Kingston, how do you do."[1]

After a few minutes of polite remarks, Kingston read a memorandum. It was a response to a somewhat petulant letter Gates had written on the twelfth, of which excerpts follow:

> I had the Honour to receive Your Excellency's Letter by Lady Ackland,
> the Respect due to her lady Ship's rank, the Tenderness due to her Person

and Sex, were alone Sufficient Recommendation to entitle her to my Protection; considering my Preceding Conduct, with Respect to those of your Army, whom the Fortune of War has placed in my Hands. I am surprised your Excellency, should think that I could consider the greatest attention to Lady Ackland in the Light of an Obligation. . . .The Cruelties which mark the Retreat of Your Army in burning the Gentlemen's and Farmer's Houses, as they pass along, is almost amongst civilized nations, without a Precedent, they should not endeavour to ruin those, they could not conquer, this conduct betrays more the vindictive Malice of a Monk than the Generosity of a Soldier. . . . At the Solicitation of Major Williams, I am prevailed upon to offer him and Major Meiborn in Exchange for Co. Ethan Allen—Your Excellency's Objection to my last Proposals for the Exchange of Col. Ethan Allen, I must consider as trifling, as I cannot but suppose that the Generals of the Royal Army act in equal Concert with those of the Generals of The Armies of the United States . . . .[2]

In his memorandum in reply, read by Kingston, Burgoyne defended the destruction of General Schuyler's manor and buildings as being militarily necessary because they shielded Americans advancing during the aborted attack of the tenth. He also pointed out that the old barracks had burned by accident, in spite of efforts to save them. Concerning the exchange of prisoners held by Gates for Ethan Allen, Burgoyne properly stated that he could not treat for the exchange of prisoners of war taken by Sir William Howe, especially as Allen's case had been the subject of negotiations between Howe and General Washington.[3]

After reading that thinly-veiled reminder to Gates to mind his manners, Kingston presented the letter that Burgoyne had prepared with the approval of the council of war of the thirteenth. Wilkinson is our witness for what followed:

So soon as he had finished, to my utter astonishment, General Gates put his hand in his pocket, pulled out a paper, and presented it to Kingston, observing, "There Sir, are the terms upon which General Burgoyne must surrender." The Major [sic] seemed thunderstruck, but read the paper, whilst the old chief surveyed him intently through his spectacles. Having finished the perusal of the propositions of General Gates, Major [sic] Kingston appeared exceedingly mortified, and said to the General, "I must beg leave to decline delivering this paper to Lieutenant-General Burgoyne, because although I cannot presume to speak for him, I think the propositions it contains cannot be submitted to." The General observed that he might be mistaken, and there could be no impropriety in his delivering them. Kingston requested that they might be sent by one of his own officers, which the general declined, and remarked "That as he had brought the message, he ought to take back the answer;" to which the Major [sic] reluctantly consented, took leave, and I again filleted him, and at his request conducted him to our advanced guard . . . .[4]

What was it about General Gates' preempting the opening of the negotiations by presenting a seven-article set of terms that so surprised Wilkinson and Kingston? And what made those terms so repugnant that Kingston insisted he not be required to transmit them? The answer to the first question is that traditional practice allowed the party initiating the negotiations to propose terms that the enemy could accept, reject, or modify. Answering the second question requires reviewing the terms Gates proposed:

• The first article rehearsed the conditions that had brought Burgoyne to seek terms. His army had suffered "repeated defeats." Desertions and casualties had reduced his numbers; shortages were crippling him; his enemy surrounded his encampment, and had cut off his retreat. Therefore his army could "only be allowed to surrender [as] prisoners of war."

• The second article proposed that the officers and soldiers could keep their personal property, accompanied by the gratuitous comment that "generals of the United States never permit individuals to be pillaged."

• The third article required that Burgoyne's troops be escorted to New England, "marching by easy marches, and sufficiently provided for . . . ."

• The fourth permitted the officers to wear their side arms, and in general to "be treated with the liberality customary in Europe, as long as they, by proper behaviour, continue to deserve it; but those who are apprehended having broken their parole, as some British officers have done, must expect to be close confined."

• The next article required the surrender of all "public stores, artillery, arms, ammunition, carriages, &c. &c."

• The sixth article—the core of his proposal—provided that once the articles were signed, Burgoyne's troops would form in their encampments, "where they will be ordered to ground their arms, and may thereupon be marched to the river side, to be passed over on their way towards Bennington."

• The final article extended the truce until sunset to give the British commander time to reply.

Gates had offered Burgoyne terms tantamount to a demand for unconditional surrender.[5]

The entire episode alarmed Wilkinson. As soon as he had escorted Kingston, he hurried back to his commander and asked whether "he had not given Burgoyne an advantage by not waiting to receive his overtures, before he presented his own terms?" Gates' perspicacity was not unlimited, and he could not see that he had done so. Skeptical about the wisdom of Gates' proposals, Wilkinson inquired "Whether he meant, in any extremity, to recede from the propositions he had made?" Gates admitted that he was bluffing, and that he "would relax a great deal to get possession of the enemy's arms."[6] He had essentially demanded unconditional surrender, but was prepared to accept less.

An old gamester, Burgoyne was no stranger to bluffs. He knew that, in spite of his bravado, Gates must be concerned about British moves between the Hudson Highlands and Albany. Burgoyne knew his position was hopeless and that he had to surrender, but he might yet exploit the victor's concerns to ameliorate the conditions. He was also a proud and brave man who commanded men who deserved the best he could gain for them, even if what he gained was more psychological than substantive. Conditions would have to become much worse before he would submit to an unconditional surrender.

After Kingston returned with Gates' draft proposals, Burgoyne convened his council and prepared his response:

• To the first proposal he replied that his army, however reduced, will never admit that their retreat is cut off, "while they have arms in their hands";

• He responded to the third article proposing his army's transfer under American escort to New England with one of his own providing that "free passage be granted to this army to Great Britain upon conditions of not serving again in North America during the present contest, and a proper port to be assigned for the entry of transports to receive the troops, whenever General Howe shall order";

• He replied to the article relating to officers' retaining their side arms that as, "There being no officer in this army under, or capable of being under the description of breaking paroles, this article needs no answer";

• He agreed to deliver all public stores, excepting arms. That exception was important to his rejecting . . .

• . . . the sixth article: "The article is inadmissable in any extremity. Sooner than this army will consent to ground their arms in their encampment will they rush on the enemy, determined to take no quarter." He would capitulate—with his men marching out of their positions under arms and entitled to the honors of war.[7]

Kingston returned to Gates' headquarters with Burgoyne's reply and the following: "If General Gates does not recede from the 6th article, the treaty ends at once. . . . The army will to a man proceed to any act of desperation, rather than submit to that article. . . . The cessation of arms ends this evening."[8]

The negotiations assumed a strange character because Horatio Gates was a victorious general uncertain whether he could impose his will upon the defeated foe. His legion of critics, contemporary and later, attributed that state to his inherently weak and craven character and to his not being the real architect of victory: that honor, his critics argue, belonged to others, notably Schuyler and Arnold. Gates, on the other hand, was merely the unworthy beneficiary of their heroic deeds. Does this verdict have any merit?

The fortunes of war gave the American commander overwhelming advantages. He had frustrated the enemy's strategic designs and inflicted a decisive tactical defeat. His army included thirteen infantry brigades and one light corps (Morgan's Corps of riflemen and light infantry). That corps and five of the brigades were Continentals; militia comprised the other eight. Also present were 498 members of Stevens' Independent Battalion of Artillery, 376 light cavalrymen, and seventy-one members of Baldwin's detachment of engineers and artificers. That army, exclusive of bateauxmen, totaled at least 20,365 effectives.[9] General Burgoyne's Orderly Book documents his strength as 6,350, excluding 1,100 sent to Canada, for a total of 5,250 officers and men.[10] The Americans enjoyed an almost four-to-one numerical advantage.

Gates' much larger force had the Europeans surrounded. Their supplies were down to four days' rations, and their ammunition stores had been severely depleted. Burgoyne's men were physically and emotionally drained. And their last realistic hope for relief had vanished when Burgoyne received Sir Henry Clinton's letter of the sixth of October.

The Clinton Factor

The British commander in the north had known since receiving Clinton's message of October 6 that although elements of Sir Henry's army would advance upriver toward Albany, Clinton would neither assume responsibility for the army at Saratoga nor undertake a breakthrough to rescue his embattled comrade.[11] But Gates did not know that Clinton's objectives were so limited. He knew with but imprecise detail of the fall of Forts Clinton and Montgomery. He had also received letters from General Israel Putnam, American commander in the Hudson Highlands, dated October 11 and 12, telling him that the enemy had penetrated to the town of Fishkill.[12] Gates was very much aware that after the forts' fall, British Major General John Vaughan was sailing upstream. However, neither Vaughan nor Burgoyne anticipated that he would be able to materially affect the latter's fortunes, unless Gates became sufficiently alarmed to divide the force surrounding Burgoyne at Saratoga or became distracted during negotiations.

Although he did not divide his force on the upper Hudson, Gates did become sufficiently distracted to wish to terminate those negotiations as early as possible. Although he frequently received information about British activity, he remained ignorant of the enemy's intentions. Hence the strained negotiations between the unimperious victor and the desperately opportunistic suitor.

Burgoyne followed his rejection of Gates' sixth article and the announcement that he considered the cease fire as ending that evening with proposed terms of his own and the stipulation that Kingston would return for an answer at 10:00 on the morning of the fifteenth for Gates' answer.

> • Burgoyne's first proposal: "The troops to march out of their camp with
> the honours of war, and the artillery of the entrenchments, which will be
> left as hereafter, may be regulated." Gates' response: "The troops to

march out of their camp, with the honours of war, and the artillery of the entrenchments to the verge of the river, where the old fort [Fort Hardy] stood, where their arms and artillery must be left."

• The second proposal provided for free passage of his army to a port from whence its men would be transported to Great Britain upon the condition of not serving again in North America during the war, "whenever General Howe shall so order." Gates agreed, but specified Boston as the port of embarkation.

• The third proposal provided for voiding the second one for persons exchanged.

• The fourth proposal provided for the officers' retention of their personal property and that their baggage not be searched, "the Lieutenant–General giving his honour that there are no public stores secreted therein. . . ." Gates agreed.

• The fifth proposed that the officers would not be separated from their men, and would be lodged according to rank. Gates agreed, so far as circumstances permitted.

• The sixth proposal covered the inclusion of the noncombatants in the treaty; Gates agreed.

• The seventh proposal provided that the Canadians be permitted to return to Canada and not be surrendered; the American raised no objection.

• The eighth proposed that three officers, not above the rank of captain, receive passports to carry dispatches to Sir William Howe, Sir Guy Carleton, and Great Britain by way of New York City, and that the dispatches not be opened; Gates agreed.

• The penultimate proposal stipulated that "the foregoing articles are to be considered only as preliminary for framing a treaty, in the course of which others may arise to be considered by both parties, for which purpose it is proposed that two officers of each army shall meet and report their deliberations to their respective Generals." Gates' response is revealing: "The capitulation to be finished by 2 o'clock this day, and the troops march from their encampment at five, and be in readiness to march towards Boston tomorrow morning."

Kingston received Gates' answers from Wilkinson at the stipulated hour and delivered them to his commander.[13]

The dispatch with which Gates agreed to so many of the proposals, especially his insistence that negotiations conclude by two o'clock and that the troops lay down their arms by five, confirmed Burgoyne in believing what he wanted to believe: that the British advance upriver toward Albany was, in fact, causing the American commander concerns that would operate in his favor.

Though events seemed to justify the Briton's innate optimism, the weight of his opponent's immediate worries became less onerous. Sometime during October 15 a letter, dated the eleventh, arrived from General Putnam with the welcome news that the British force operating in the Hudson Highlands was smaller than he had earlier reported, numbering no more than 3,000 or 4,000, too small to pose a serious strategic threat to Gates' rear.[14] In fact, even "Old Put's" revised estimate was too high, for Vaughan had no more than 2,000 effectives with him.

If he had been privy to Sir Henry Clinton's instructions, Gates would have had even less reason for being anxious. Vaughan was to probe his way northward toward Burgoyne, give whatever help he could, and join him if that proved necessary. But Clinton doomed any chance of success Vaughan could have had. He knew, or should have known from intelligence given him, that large vessels could not ascend the river beyond Livingston's Manor, about forty-five miles short of Albany. Beyond the Manor, only shallow-draft boats could move upstream. However, he embarked the soldiers on transports that drew too much water to approach Albany. By the fifteenth Vaughan reached Esopus, burned the village, and heard a rumor that Burgoyne had surrendered. During the seventeenth he reached Livingston Manor, where his pilots announced that they had reached the head of navigation and could go no farther. Vaughan spotted rebels observing his uncomfortable situation and learned from them that Gates had defeated Burgoyne on the seventh. A week later Clinton received orders from Sir William Howe to send him 2,000 men, and on the twenty-second he directed Vaughan to return to New York City.[15]

The details of those events were not clear to Burgoyne and Gates at Saratoga as their negotiations played out in an atmosphere of bluff. The former still read omens of hope in his suspicions of his opponent's liberality; and Gates, although feeling less pressure from downriver, remained determined to encompass the enemy's defeat as quickly as possible.

Burgoyne, having come to the quick conclusion that the reason Gates was so eager to conclude a treaty must be that Clinton's expedition was getting closer to Albany, sought to gain time to permit that expedition to come to his relief or, at least, to pressure Gates to grant even more favorable terms. The British general convened another council that decided to inform the rebel commander that, while the basis for an agreement was agreed to, some minor issues required additional exploration that would take more time than Gates had stipulated. Burgoyne would appoint two officers to meet with two from Gates "to propound, discuss, and settle those subordinate articles, in order that the treaty in due form may be executed as soon as possible."[16]

After receiving notice of the council's decision, Gates appointed Brigadier William Whipple, a signer of the Declaration of Independence and commander of a brigade of New Hampshire militia, and the omnipresent Wilkinson to meet the British commissioners, Lieutenant Colonel Nicholas Sutherland and Captain James H. Craig. Gates' aide-de-camp, Major Isaac Pierce, acted as the meeting's secretary. The commissioners met during the afternoon of the sixteenth near one of General Schuyler's sawmills. After lengthy discussion, they signed and exchanged articles of capitulation, and about 8:00 that evening parted to report to their respective commanders.[17]

When Wilkinson reached headquarters about 11:00, he found the following letter from Captain Craig:

Camp at Saratoga, 15 Oct.
1/2 past 10 o'clock

Sir,

Upon reporting the proceedings of this evening to Lieutenant-General Burgoyne I was happy to receive his approbation of and ready concurrence in every article that has been agreed upon between us; it however appears upon a retrospect of the treaty, that our zeal to complete it expeditiously has led us unto the admission of a term in the title very different from his meaning, and that of the principal officers of this army, who have been consulted on this important occasion. We have, Sir unguardedly called that a treaty of capitulation, which the army means only as a treaty of convention. With the single alteration of this word, Lieutenant-Colonel Sutherland and myself will meet you at the stipulated time tomorrow morning with the fair copy signed by General Burgoyne...

I hope, sir, you will excuse my troubling you so late, but I thought it better than by any delay to prevent the speedy conclusion of a treaty which seems to be the wish of both parties, and which may prevent the further effusion of blood between us, I beg your immediate answer...[18]

Gates did not believe the choice of terms was very important, except as a possible salve to the defeated enemy's pride. His adjutant responded: "Colonel Wilkinson's compliments to Captain Craig, Major General Gates will admit the alteration required."[19] Thus, the Articles of Capitulation became the Articles of Convention, and Gates believed that by substituting a word the wearisome negotiations were finally ended.

Final Delays

His hopes proved premature. General Burgoyne was playing for time, hoping that events on the lower Hudson would operate in his favor. The Freiherr von Riedesel recorded why Gates was too sanguine, and Burgoyne optimistic:

In the night from the 15th to the 16th a man came allegedly from Albany, who asserted that General Clinton was advancing to Albany, and was probably there by now. This perplexed us very much, particularly as this informer had not seen the corps of General Clinton, but had the information only third-hand from hearsay. General Burgoyne was filled with hope again, and wanted to break the already agreed preliminary terms, even if both the deputy officers had given their approval to the amendment. A council of war was called together again, and the first question was raised as to whether General Burgoyne could break the already approved convention with honor. This was answered by a majority with No. Then, whether the news which had been received could be accepted as true, and whether such would improve our situation or not, This was answered by No.[20]

In spite of his council's votes and against all odds, John Burgoyne continued to oppose surrender, nurturing the illusion that Sir Henry Clinton would save him. More revealing was the faith he had in the courage and skill of his soldiers. Burgoyne believed that operating on interior lines, able to counterattack at any point on their perimeter with support from his still-impressive artillery, would allow his men to gain time for reinforcements to arrive from the lower Hudson. He determined to stall for more time, and reached a compromise with the council's majority. To that end, he dispatched the following note to General Gates:

> [I]n the course of the Night [of October 15/16] Lieut. Genl. Burgoyne received intelligence that a considerable Force has been detached from the Army under the Command of Major General Gates during the course of the Negotiations depending between them, Lieut. General Burgoyne conceives this, if true, to be not only a violation of the Cessation of arms, but subversive to the principles upon which the Treaty Originated, Viz. a great Superiority of Numbers in General Gates' Army. Lieut. General Burgoyne therefore requires that two Officers on his part be permitted to see that the strength of the Forces now opposed to him is such as will convince him that no detachments have been made, and that the same principle of Superiority on which the Treaty First began still exists.[21]

Grasping for every conceivable delaying tactic, Burgoyne finally exhausted Gates' patience. The American commander dispatched Wilkinson with this terse reply: "No violation of the treaty has taken place. The requisition therefore contained in your message . . . is inadmissible. It now remains with your Excellency to ratify or Dissolve the treaty." Gates closed by adding that he expected "your immediate reply."[22]

Wilkinson recalled that after he had transmitted his commander's message Burgoyne tried to justify his conduct by declaring that not only his reputation but service to his King and the honor of British arms required the most cautious circumspection. He referred to the information derived from camp rumors, as well as authentic information supplied by a loyalist who had come through the lines the previous night. His informant had, no doubt, seen men moving southward. They were, however, New York militiamen who, their term having expired, refused to remain in camp. The British general went on to aver his men's spirit and the belief that there was not a man who did not "pant for action." The American called attention to the soldiers lining the hills on the east side of the river and those surrounding Burgoyne's troops on the south, west, and north. But the general continued to declare that he would not sign the convention and that the truce would end in one hour.

Wilkinson's narrative, detailed and lengthy, is important reading for a full understanding of these important events:

> [A]nd after a moment's pause, I added, "Be pleased, Sir, to favour me with your determination?" He [Burgoyne] answered, "I do not recede from my purpose; the truce must end." "At what time, Sir?" "In one hour." We set our watches, and on taking leave, I observed, "After what has passed, General Burgoyne, there can be no treaty; your fate must be decided by arms, and General Gates washes his hands of the blood which may be spilled." "Be it so," said he, and I walked off with the most uncomfortable sensations; for our troops were much scattered, having encompassed the British army in three parts out of four; the men had got the treaty in their heads, and had lost their passion for combat, and what was worse we had been advised of the loss of Fort Montgomery, and a rumour had just arrived that Esopus was burnt, and the enemy proceeding up the river; but I had not proceeded fifty rods, when Major [sic] Kingston ran after me and hailed; I halted and he informed me, that General Burgoyne was desirous to say a few words to me; I returned, when he addressed me by observing, that "General Gates had in the business depending between them, been very indulgent, and therefore he would hope for time to take the opinion of his general officers, in a case of such magnitude to the two armies; as it was far from his disposition to trifle in an affair of such importance.". . . . I asked what time he would require? He mentioned two hours; and we again set our watches, and I retired, promising to wait at our picket for his answer.[23]

One can wish for a less egocentric source than James Wilkinson, but he often preserved the most detailed, nuanced narrative available. The above quotation includes the clearest depiction of what Americans had riding on the outcome of these negotiations. He did not portray the men who defeated Burgoyne as heroic figures, eager to exact condign vengeance on a hated foe. Rather, they had expended their "passion for combat" and were worried about events south of Albany. Like men who have survived combat always have, they longed for at least a cessation of arms and palpable evidence that they were victors. They had "got the treaty into their heads."

Amidst the stench of dead animals, in cold, damp weather surrounded by loyal, but weary and hungry men, Burgoyne convened his final council. Its task was to consider whether the treaty, in light of prevailing conditions, was binding on the army, and if the commander's honor was engaged to sign it. He persuaded himself that he was not bound by events, and he would not execute the treaty upon the sole consideration of a point of honor. He continued to believe with almost pathetic faith that by great exertions and overcoming hardships the army might yet be relieved.

His generals did not share his optimism. Even if Sir Henry were where unreliable reports placed him, the distance from Saratoga was "such as to render any relief from him improbable during the time our provisions could be made to last." One general reported that his opinion was "if the convention is not signed, he apprehends there will be considerable desertion." Two others baldly stated that the British 47th Regiment could no longer be depended upon. Another believed that the morale of the soldiers in the 62nd Regiment was so poor that they were "not equal to their former exertions." Like the American soldiers, Burgoyne's men "have got the convention in their heads as desirable." Many of the ablest officers were absent, sick, or wounded. Some of the British officers thought their men would stand firm if attacked, but "the most sanguine do not think any part of the army in that elevation and alacrity of spirit necessary for undertaking desperate enterprises." Further, if the treaty were broken off, a renewal of fighting would be hopeless, and a defeat would be "fatal to the army," while a victory could not save them, "as they have neither provisions to advance nor retreat against an enemy, who, by experience, we know are capable of rallying at every advantageous post." Finally, the life and property of "every provincial and dependent of this army depends upon the execution of this treaty."[24]

The lengthy, lurching pace of the negotiations wore upon the American commander's nerves. A messenger was dispatched to learn from Wilkinson what had passed between him and General Burgoyne. The adjutant general sent him a report on the status of the situation, then waited near General Schuyler's burned manor, where he was joined by Gates' aide-de-camp, Major Isaac Pierce, to await the results of the enemy's council of war.

After three-quarters of an hour, Wilkinson watched as British Lieutenant Colonel Nicholas Sutherland crossed the creek and joined the two American officers. He brought discouraging word: "Well, our business will be knocked in the head after all." When asked why, he replied, "[T]he officers had got the devil in their heads, and could not agree." Wilkinson claimed that he answered, "I am sorry for it, as you will now lose not only your fusee [fusil, a light musket often carried by officers], but your whole baggage." The Briton expressed regret and helplessness.

Wilkinson again saved the day by suddenly remembering the letter Captain Craig had sent him the previous night, which resulted in designating the surrender document a "treaty of convention." Sutherland asked for it, but Wilkinson refused. "I shall hold it as a testimony of the good faith of a British commander," he replied. After Sutherland promised to return it within fifteen minutes, the American relented, turned over the document, and Sutherland raced back to headquarters. Gates, meanwhile, had sent orders to break off negotiations unless Burgoyne immediately ratified the convention. Wilkinson assured his commander that he was doing his best to bring the negotiations to a happy conclusion and would personally report to him in half an hour. Sutherland returned with Craig carrying the convention—ratified by General Burgoyne.[25]

Thus ended the bargaining by which John Burgoyne surrendered a British army to a former half-pay major.

The Resulting Convention

The convention by which General Burgoyne surrendered his army contained twelve articles, including:

> • The first and most important provided for the soldiers' marching out of their encampment "with the Honours of War" to the site of colonial Fort Hardy, where, at their officers' command, they would pile their arms and leave their artillery. They would thus receive the respect due men who had served faithfully as long as reasonable hope for success existed, according to the accepted practices of war;

> • The second, and eventually most controversial, article granted the army free passage to Great Britain, "on Condition of not serving again in North America during the present Contest," and designated Boston as the port of embarkation. This provision quickly became a major source of criticism of General Gates' negotiations, building upon the obvious fact that returning the army to Europe would free a comparable force for service against the Americans;

• The third article dealt with issues of exchange;

• The fourth and fifth articles dealt with moving the convention troops to Boston;

• The sixth article secured officers' personal property, "General Burgoyne giving his Honour that there are no public Stores secreted therein"— another source of controversy;

• The seventh article provided that officers would not be separated from their men, and that officers would be quartered according to rank and permitted to assemble their units for "necessary purposes of Regularity";

• The eighth article confirmed that everyone in Burgoyne's army, "whether composed of sailors, batteaumen, artificers, drivers, independent companies, and followers of the army, of whatever country," shall be considered British subjects for the purposes of these articles.

• The ninth article read: "All Canadians and Persons belonging to the Canadian Establishment, consisting of sailors, Batteau Men, Artificers, Drivers, Independent Companies, and many other Followers of the Army, who come under no particular Description, are to be conducted immediately by the shortest Route, to the first British Post on Lake George. . . ." This provision's purpose was to deliver loyalists from the vengeance of the victorious rebels;

• The tenth article granted three officers "not exceeding the Rank of Captain" passage to carry secured dispatches to Sir William Howe, Sir Guy Carleton, and to Great Britain;

• The eleventh article placed the officers on parole and permitted them to wear side arms;

• The twelfth article allowed the defeated army to send to Canada for its clothing and baggage.

The terms closed with these words: "These Articles are to be mutually signed and exchanged tomorrow Morning at 9 o'clock, and the Troops under

Lieut. General Burgoyne are to march out of their Intrenchments [sic] at three o'clock in the Afternoon. . . . To prevent any Doubts that might arise from Lieut. General Burgoyne's name not being mentioned in the above Treaty, Major General Gates hereby Declares that he is understood to be comprehended in as fully as if his name had been specifically mentioned."[26]

During the night, Captain Alexander Campbell of the 62nd Regiment, whom Burgoyne had sent to Sir Henry Clinton on September 28, returned to the British lines with a rather devastating reply to the former's request for orders:

> Not having any instructions from the Commander in Chief [Sir William Howe] relative to the northern army, and ignorant of even his intentions concerning its operations (except his wishes it may get to Albany) Sir Henry Clinton cannot presume to send orders to General Burgoyne. But he thinks it is impossible General Burgoyne could really suppose Sir Henry Clinton had any idea of penetrating to Albany.[27]

That depressing message confirmed yet again the hopelessness of Burgoyne's situation.

Surrender

Lieutenant Digby described the opening event that occurred in the British camp on the morning of October 17 under the heading, "A day famous in the annals of America":

> Gen. Burgoyne desired a meeting of all the officers early that morning, at which he entered into a detail of his manner of acting since he had the honour of commanding the army, but he was too full to speak; heaven only could tell his feelings at the time. He dwelled much on his orders to make the wished for junction with General Clinton, and as to how his proceedings had turned out, we must (he said) be as good judges as himself. He then read over the Articles of Convention, and informed us the terms were even easier than we could have expected from our situation, and concluded with assuring us, he never would have accepted any terms, had we provisions enough, or the least hopes of our extricating ourselves any other way. . . .[28]

The defeated army paraded about 10:00 a.m. and, with drums beating the "Grenadier's March," tramped to the site of Fort Hardy. At their officers' command they lay down their arms. Some embittered soldiers broke their pieces, and the Germans, in violation of the Convention, concealed their colors. With a rare respect for Burgoyne's men, Gates ordered that no Americans witness their humiliation. Doctor Thacher described these important historic events in his *Journal*:

> 18th—At the appointed hour yesterday morning the Americans marched into the lines of the British to the tune of Yankee Doodle, where they continued till the royal army had marched to the place appointed and deposited their arms according to the treaty. . . . It is a circumstance characteristic of the amiable and benevolent disposition of General Gates, that, unwilling to aggravate the painful feelings of the royal troops he would not permit the American soldiers to witness the degrading act of piling their arms. This instance of delicacy and politeness, at the moment of triumph, towards an enemy who had committed the most unprecedented outrages, is a mark of true magnanimity, and deserves the highest praise, though it deprives our army of the satisfaction to which they are justly entitled.[29]

Burgoyne—in full dress, accompanied by his general officers, and escorted by Wilkinson—rode to meet General Gates, who received them wearing a plain blue coat. Wilkinson, appropriately, introduced the two commanders. The commanders saluted in the then-current fashion by raising their hats. Burgoyne spoke first: "The fortunes of war, General Gates, have made me your prisoner." No stranger to military protocol, the former Royal Army major replied: "I shall always be ready to bear testimony that it has not been through any fault of your Excellency." Burgoyne introduced Major Generals Phillips and von Riedesel, who in turn presented their subordinate commanders. Gates introduced General Schuyler, who had arrived from Albany, the American brigade commanders present, and Colonel Morgan who, as commander of an independent corps, merited comparable recognition. According to some accounts, Gates invited the Europeans into his tent (or hovel); after a brief interval, the commanders appeared in front of the marquee, where Burgoyne silently presented his sword, which Gates promptly returned. The officers rejoined their parties and shared a dinner.[30]

While Gates and his unwilling guests dined upon a hastily-prepared meal and drank appropriate, if not candid, toasts, the disarmed and defeated soldiers, to the accompaniment of fife and drum, marched southward along the same muddy road they had followed twice before: once on the way to battle and defeat, and again in retreat to a siege and surrender. American Continentals and militiamen lined both berms, quiet and disciplined, impressing the observant among the defeated with their physical stature and martial mien—in spite of the absence of standardized uniforms. The conduct of the Americans was testimony enough to the quality of discipline and morale that General Gates and his officers had instilled in men not always noted for those soldierly qualities. By dusk the column reached the site of the camp they had occupied on October 8 and where their hospital continued to shelter the casualties of the fighting of September 19 and October 7.

Recriminations Begin on Both Sides

Generals Burgoyne and von Riedesel, with the latter's family and a number of officers, lodged in General Schuyler's Albany mansion. From such comfortable quarters the British commander, on October 20, wrote two letters to Lord George Germain, one an official dispatch and the other a personal note. The dispatch chronicled events following his crossing of the Hudson on September 13 and 14.[31] The private letter was the opening salvo of the defense he would develop more fully during the parliamentary inquiry of 1778. "I rest my confidence in the justice of the King and his councils," began Burgoyne, "to support the General they thought proper to appoint to as arduous an undertaking, and under as positive a direction, as perhaps a cabinet ever framed. It will, I am sure, be remembered my Lord, that a preference of exertions was the only latitude given to me, and that to force a junction with Sir William Howe, or at least a passage to Albany, was the principle, and the spirit of my orders."

The general was pleading his case that the inflexibility of the orders he received required him to force his way to Albany, where he would form a junction with Howe. Failing to obey that mandate would have earned him the censure of "every class and distinction of men in government, in the army and in the public." His apologia followed:

The expediency of advancing being admitted, the consequences have been honourable misfortune. The British have persevered in a strenuous and bloody progress. Had the force been all British, perhaps the perseverance had been longer. But as it was, will it be said, my Lord, that in the exhausted situation described, and in the jaws of famine, and invested by quadruple numbers, a treaty which saves the army to the state, for the next campaign, was not more than could have been expected? I call it saving the army, because if sent home, the state is thereby enabled to send forth the troops now destined for her internal defence; if exchanged, they become a force to Sir William Howe, as effectually, as if any other junction had been made.[32]

The general's defense on the one hand, and the ministry's attempt on the other hand to shift the onus of defeat onto the commanders in America led to the inquiry that prompted Burgoyne to write his *State of the Expedition*, so frequently cited in this and every study of his fateful campaign.

General Gates had little time to luxuriate in the sunshine of victory. Brigadier Henry Watson Powell, with the battalion companies of his 53rd Regiment, and the German Regiment Prinz Friedrich, Lieutenant Colonel Christian J. Praetorius commanding, continued to hold Fort Ticonderoga and its satellites with a total of about 900 rank and file. General Vaughan, whose troops burned Esopus on October 16, continued to threaten American interests on the lower Hudson. The only immediate response Gates could make was to start marching his Continentals and some of the militiamen southward toward Albany, while other militia returned home.[33]

Victory did not immunize Horatio Gates from controversy and censure. Not only did the Convention's terms expose him to criticism, but the manner in which General Washington received authentic information about Burgoyne's defeat reflected adversely upon Gates. As usual, he cooperated by providing grist for his critics' mill.

On October 18, Gates prepared a report of the conclusion of negotiations and Burgoyne's capitulation for John Hancock, president of the Continental Congress, and enclosed a copy of the Convention's articles, which was proper because he was directly under congressional orders, as Washington had noted on August 2 when he refused to appoint a commander for the Northern Department.[34] Gates entrusted that important and urgent correspondence to his adjutant, the ineffable James Wilkinson, who was recovering from a "convulsive colic." Wilkinson delayed his departure from Albany, and stopped en route to bask in the adulation of friends, including Ann Biddle, his inamorata. The distance between Albany and York, Pennsylvania, where Congress sat while General Howe occupied Philadelphia, was 285 miles. Wilkinson took eleven days to deliver his dispatches—an average speed of less then twenty-six miles per day—arriving on October 31.[35] The overjoyed delegates ordered a gold medal to the Victor of Saratoga and declared a day of thanksgiving.[36]

General Washington received formal word two days later, nearly two weeks after Burgoyne surrendered. However, he had not been completely ignorant of the events in the north. On October 30, he dispatched Lieutenant Colonel Alexander Hamilton to Albany to urge General Gates to send immediate reinforcements from his department. By the time Hamilton arrived Gates had already sent Morgan's Rifle Regiment to rejoin the commander-in-chief; Learned's and Poor's brigades and Colonel Seth Warner's Green Mountain Boys had marched southward to support Israel Putnam near New York City, leaving Gates with three Continental brigades, which he wanted to retain to use in regaining Ticonderoga and protecting the Albany frontier. At Hamilton's request, he immediately ordered Paterson to reinforce Washington, and soon after sent Glover's Brigade, retaining only Nixon's Brigade and almost no militia by November 7.[37]

General Gates' failure to directly report his success to the commander-in-chief was technically defensible, but reflected adversely upon him. Courtesy and respect for Washington's position dictated that the victorious commander of the Northern Department take the time to address at least a brief personal letter to his fellow soldier. Gates, who could be chivalrous to a defeated foe, should have been equally respectful of his senior commander.

The Congress that awarded him the gold medal also sent Gates orders to remain at Albany and to rid the Champlain-Hudson corridor of the enemy. The British did not wait for his challenge. On November 14, he learned that they had evacuated the posts at Ticonderoga, Mount Independence, and on Lakes Champlain and George.[38] (Securing the lower Hudson against Sir Henry Clinton in New York City would prove more difficult, and would engage Gates during the summer of 1778.)

The saga of Horatio Gates and John Burgoyne was finally ended. The loser returned home to face a parliamentary inquiry; the victor faced a future of criticism and accusations of intrigue, incompetence, and even cowardice.

Epilogue

Saratoga's Fruit: The Strategic Revolution

British Losses

The American victory at Saratoga radically changed the strategic dynamics of the American Revolution. Piers Mackesy, who wrote about Great Britain's defeat, noted "[t]hat in round figures the British loss at Saratoga was not large. But it would be difficult to replace, and more serious still was the proof of what the perceptive had long suspected: that the American country with its armed population might be beyond the power of Britain to reconquer with any force which she could raise and sustain in America. The grand design of 1775 lay in ruins."[1] This concluding chapter examines why Mackesy's assessment is so cogent.

The first and most obvious of Saratoga's fruits was the elimination of a British army, even one as modest as Burgoyne's. The rebellious Americans had one less army to worry about than they had during the summer and autumn of 1777, and the soldiers who surrendered on October 17 were well-trained, experienced veterans led by competent officers. Britain's limited manpower resources, which had obliged her to hire German regiments, made the loss of the slightly more than 7,000 men who had comprised Burgoyne's army on July 1 a more severe blow than simple numbers might otherwise indicate.

Also lost were thirty-seven guns left at Ticonderoga and Fort George, and another thirty-six field pieces that formed the artillery train committed at Freeman's farm and Saratoga.[2] Thus, the Americans gained seventy-three valuable pieces of ordnance during the autumn of 1777. In addition, the British losses included thousands of muskets, German Jäger rifles, flints, powder, and cannon balls captured and damaged during the course of the campaign. Bateaux, wagons, carts, and horses added to those losses. These figures do not include the materiel lost when Barry St. Leger failed to take Fort Stanwix. Although not every British article found its way into the American magazine, many—including all of the cannon—did. The result was the substantial enhancing of Patriot combat capability.

More important than Burgoyne's surrender was the defeat of the strategy that had informed Britain's campaigns of 1776 and 1777: using Canada as a base for invading the northern American interior and quickly crushing the rebellion through land offensives. For such a success, controlling the Champlain-Hudson corridor was imperative. "The advantage of controlling the Hudson line would have been great," Mackesy observed. "It would have reduced the handicap of operating on exterior lines, for instead of slow communications by sea which were shut entirely in the winter, there would have been a direct land route between the two bases [New York City and Canada]. The unified command which had ceased [Carleton in the north and Howe in the south] could have been restored, and the two armies acted as one."[3] General George Washington's Fabian tactics against Sir William Howe and Horatio Gates' defeat of Burgoyne severed the nexus between the two British fronts.

New Military and Economic Strategies

After the loss at Saratoga, the Empire needed a new strategy for prosecuting the war, a need that would have existed even if France had not become a belligerent. Britain's leaders undertook to develop one that eventually included three elements: negotiated settlement, naval operations, and military pressure.

Negotiating a settlement with the rebels fell to the members of the Carlisle Commission, which owed its creation to the fear that France and the American Congress would form an alliance. Frederick Howard, Earl of Carlisle, led a team that included the Howes (Admiral Richard, Lord Howe, and General Sir William); William Eden, a member of the Board of Trade and brother of Robert Eden, last royal governor of Maryland, and George Johnstone, a Scot and former governor of West Florida. John Berkenhout and Sir John Temple joined the commissioners in New York in August 1778 as secret agents. The ministry gave those commissioners powers to treat with the Congress and, if necessary, suspend all acts since 1763 that affected North America.

The commissioners reached Philadelphia on June 6, 1778. Because the Continental Congress had resolved, on April 22, that anyone, individually or in concert, who reached terms with the commission was an enemy of the United States, their mission was doomed *ab initio*. Sir Henry Clinton's preparations to evacuate the city made its futility all the more obvious. Lord Carlisle requested a conference on June 9, but the Congress responded on the seventeenth that it would negotiate only British withdrawal and recognition of American independence. On October 3, Lord Carlisle directed a futile direct appeal to Americans that offered a general pardon to all people and to civil and military office-holders who applied within forty days, excepting only those who might be responsible for deaths of British subjects after the date of the appeal. All of the members of the commission—except Temple, who remained behind as an agent—departed America on November 27.[4]

The Royal Navy's primary functions, until 1778, were transporting troops and supplies, raiding rebel seaports, and blockading the coast. But the blockade was a manifest failure and probably exceeded the capacity of any navy. Patrolling the extensive Atlantic coastline certainly exceeded Admiral Lord Howe's resources. His assignment required secure access to sources of fresh water and stores, but the British undertook no sustained aggressive campaign to acquire sufficient bases. They evacuated Boston before taking New York City, and did not capture Newport, Rhode Island, until 1776, nor Philadelphia until 1777, the year of Saratoga.[5]

France's much-dreaded involvement altered fundamentally the war's maritime character: the West Indies became, and remained throughout the remainder of the war, the focus of British naval strategic planning.[6] John Montagu, Earl of Sandwich and First Lord of the Admiralty, had long championed that order of priorities, and a powerful West Indian lobby supported him. But they would have been less influential had they not reflected a tenable perception of imperial interest. There was obvious reason to question whether Britain would ever recover the North American colonies; whereas, regardless of the course of hostilities, the Indies were incapable of independent existence, and so would remain some nation's colonies.

Their sugar-based wealth was vast. The British West Indies sent almost 300 ships into London during a normal year, and their imports in 1776 were worth 4,250,000 pounds, compared with the East India Company's 1,500,000. The islands fit more logically into the mercantilistic scheme for empire than did the products of American farms and fisheries. They supplied commodities that the home islands would otherwise have to buy from foreign rivals. And, unlike some American goods, they did not compete with domestically-produced ones. West Indian planters were better customers for British manufacturers than Americans because profits from sugar enabled them to pay their debts.[7] Possessing the Indies would soon repay the war's expenses and help bring the Americans to terms. Lord George Germain was certainly of this mind. "Having them in our possession, instead of cringing to an American Congress for peace," he wrote in his "Thoughts on the Caribbean Stations," dated December 5, 1777, "we shall prescribe the terms and bid America be only what we please."[8] The Indies seemed to promise all of the following: compensation for losses in America; payment for the war; a favorable trade balance; an economic lever to force the Americans to come to terms; and fruitful operations against France.

The bottom line was that the King was willing to come to terms with America "[f]or the chance of conquering the French West Indies and 'avenging the faithless and insolent France.'" As early as the end of January he had been contemplating a complete withdrawal from the rebel colonies, retaining only Canada, Nova Scotia, and Florida.[9] He insisted that Britain mobilize her resources against France, and that plans for providing Clinton with more men to resume land operations in the north were dead. A force of 2,000 or 3,000 men could be retained in America to attack rebel ports, with others committed to maintaining garrisons in New York, Rhode Island, Nova Scotia, and Florida. The new strategy, however, demanded that Clinton abandon Philadelphia. All other troops would become part of the force used in the West Indies campaign.[10]

With George III and his First Lord of the Admiralty relegating the American theater of operations to a poor second in their priorities, the crucial third party in planning a strategy for the post-Saratoga war was Jeffrey, Lord Amherst, who became the King's chief military adviser, replacing recently deceased General Edward Harvey. On March 19, 1778, he was effectively appointed to command of the army with a cabinet seat—although the title of commander-in-chief was withheld out of consideration for the Duke of Gloucester, the titular incumbent. Amherst had a merited reputation for honesty and competence, but his post as commander of the home forces in England and Wales, his unease among politicians, his taciturnity, and the extraordinary demands of an aggressive West Indian commitment diminished his effectiveness as a strategic planner.

Defeat at Saratoga validated the opinions of two important critics of the strategy of 1776-77. William Knox, undersecretary of the American

Department, had believed since the war's outset that attacking the rebels where they were strongest was a mistake, and that trying to recover the northern colonies was not worth the effort. Instead of following Sir William Howe's plan of using Pennsylvania as a base for operations against Virginia, the army should concentrate its efforts where the rebels were weakest: Georgia and the Carolinas. With the Royal Navy dominating the coast, Clinton's army to the north, and the Indians on the frontier, Virginia would be ready to return to the imperial fold. With the South secured, the northern colonies would be isolated.[11]

Charles Jenkinson, later Lord Liverpool, went further and was more influential. He had been a joint secretary of the treasury, was master of the Royal Mint, and became secretary at war in 1778. Like economists Adam Smith and Josiah Tucker, dean of Gloucester, Jenkinson believed that the Americans were so dependent upon British goods that losing the colonies would not necessarily mean losing the American market, and that Britain would profit economically by dispensing with political control of its North American colonies. Dean Tucker argued that a political and military alliance with an independent America "would be more productive of good than an attempt to suppress the 'smothered rebellion.'"[12] Soon after learning of Burgoyne's surrender, Jenkinson urged that, if Britain was going to limit American operations, the wisest course would be to abandon New England and establish the imperial line on the Hudson. He believed, not unreasonably, that New Englanders provided the rebellion's intellectual, ideological, political, and military leadership. However, he erred in assigning Yankee militiamen so much military importance, and that their provincialism would prevent their engaging in operations in the Middle and Southern States if Britain fortified and blocked the Hudson frontier. And he failed, as did most of his contemporaries, to appreciate American capacities for creating a regular military establishment not dependent upon the whims of local militiamen. Yet, his was a remarkable strategic argument.[13]

More unusual was his economic thesis. Piers Mackesy summarized it this way:

> England had no need to control New England's trade. Of all the produce of the rebel colonies only the tobacco of the south was worth monopolising by restrictive trade laws; and of England's exports to America only linen and some silks would suffer if every Act of Trade were repealed. New England would always buy British woollen goods,

hardware and India goods because we sold them cheapest; indeed, if the woollen import figures of Canada and Nova Scotia meant anything, the New Englanders were buying by stealth at that very moment. Most of their other British imports were for re-export to the Spanish Main, and were finding their way there through other channels. New England's own exported products mostly went to foreign markets. . . . New England, in a word, could be cast out of the Empire without damage to Britain's wealth and security. . . .[14]

Exaggerating the impact of Knox's and Jenkinson's arguments would be unwise. But, even among those in government who did follow them closely, the defeat on the upper Hudson revealed the fallacies upon which the strategy of the past two years had relied. The realities behind the arguments appealed to ministers looking for a new way to deal with the rebellion and the internationalization of the war that France's involvement must make inevitable.

The change in priorities was made manifest in the orders Sir Henry Clinton received on March 18, 1778, notifying him that he would receive no reinforcements, and that 8,000 of his men would leave him for duty in Florida and the West Indies. It only remained for him to abandon Philadelphia and take what was left of his field army to New York City. France was now the principal enemy, and Britain would concentrate its greatest efforts in the American South and the West Indies.[15]

The French Connection

The time has come to turn to how victory at Saratoga changed the war for American independence into an international conflict by persuading France to move from covertly supporting rebellion within its traditional foe's empire into openly allying itself with a Continental Congress that had declared itself, and the people it presumed to represent, independent.

France emerged from the Seven Years' War and the Peace of Paris of 1763 reconciled to renouncing colonial ambitions in North America, but she did not accept a status as a cipher in international politics. Before the ink was proverbially dry on the peace treaty, her foreign minister, Etienne-Francois, Duke of Choiseul, was devoting attention and energy to rebuilding French economic, military, and naval resources to take revenge on perfidious Albion and to reverse the balance of power imposed by the treaty.[16]

With a remarkable appreciation of the effect of France's cession of Canada upon the potential for encouraging an independent sentiment among newly-secure Americans, Choiseul planned to fish in what he hoped would become troubled waters, and sent agents to Britain and her restless colonies to report on matters military and political. His successor, Comte de Vergennes, applied his subtle, methodical intellect to bringing the duke's objective to fruition through careful management of relations with Spain and Austria, and to a determination to engage England only with "a sure chance of success."[17] His early reaction to American colonials' discontents was one of cautious interest, which became more responsive to the potential for profiting from those discontents during mid-1775 as Caron de Beaumarchais, functioning as an agent in London, observed through reports and in person that Britain's problems could be exploited to French advantage. During September, Vergennes sent Archard de Bonvouloir, who knew something of America and was fluent in English, to the colonies as a confidential observer, with oral instructions to assure American leaders that France did not covet Canada and would not be hostile to an independent nation on the North American Continent.[18]

Even before Bonvouloir reported back to him, Vergennes approached his King about assisting the insurgents by secretly supplying them with munitions and money. While still preparing to present his ideas in a manner that would overcome the King's scruples, he received, on February 27, 1776, his agent's report assuring him that the colonists were, indeed, preparing to declare themselves independent and would fight to make that declaration a reality, and that Bonvouloir, without committing his master, had given the Americans reason to hope that French ports would be open to their trade and for even more concrete assistance.

Soon after Bonvouloir's report reached the foreign minister, Beaumarchais, who was in contact with Arthur Lee, correspondent of the Continental Congress' Secret Committee of Correspondence, sent Vergennes his "Peace or War" memoir, which the minister passed on to the King. Lee had represented to Beaumarchais "[t]hat if the American insurrectionists should become too discouraged at the futility of their efforts to obtain from the French Ministry aid in the shape of powder and munitions, they might join forces with England and fall on the French sugar islands." The young author and amateur agent suggested to the King that the way to secure those precious islands was to "give help to the Americans, so as to make their forces equal to those of England," and that France provide secret aid to the rebels.[19] The argument helped overcome the monarch's scruples against supporting rebellion.

With cautious persistence Vergennes maneuvered to commit Louis XVI and the nation to his program of revenge against England and aid to her rebellious subjects. To shorten a long and complex story, he succeeded, against controller of finance Baron Turgot's strenuous opposition, in persuading the King: to adopt a policy of convincing Great Britain that France and her ally, Spain, desired peace; to reorganize the army and navy; and to support the Americans' revolution with money and munitions. On May 2, 1776, Louis directed that 1,000,000 livres be made available to the rebels through a fictitious company, Roderique Hortalez et Cie.[20] Charles III of Spain soon matched Louis' contribution for distribution through the same dummy trader. France thus responded to the coldly logical principles of balance-of-power politics by offering aid to Britain's rebellious colonists before any agent of the Continental Congress even arrived in Paris. It did so while preparing to engage her ancient foe [England] in war when the opportune moment arrived.

American Diplomacy

The agents the colonies had employed previously to represent their interests in London were, excepting Benjamin Franklin and Arthur Lee, inadequate to the task of providing diplomatic services for the Continental Congress. America's "foreign office" had its real origin in the secret committee "for the sole purpose of corresponding with our friends in Great Britain, Ireland and other parts of the world," created by the Congress on November 29, 1775.[21] Less than a fortnight later, on December 12, the Committee of Secret Correspondence initiated American diplomatic correspondence when it directed Arthur Lee, in London, to report on European governments' attitudes toward the rebellious Americans.[22]

Youngest of the five famous revolutionary Lee brothers (the others being Philip Ludwell, Richard Henry, Francis Lightfoot, and William), Arthur was well-educated, patriotic, unstable, and an important participant in the new republic's rallying of international support. Sometime during 1775 Lee met Beaumarchais at John Wilkes' house and began the fruitful dialogue that produced Hortalez et Cie's creation and the launching of secret foreign support. Under Silas Deane's management, critical aid flowed to the rebel cause.

July 1776 brought significant change to Franco-American diplomacy. The Continental Congress declared the insurrectionist provinces independent, and it appointed John Adams, John Dickinson, Robert Morris, Benjamin Harrison, and Benjamin Franklin to a committee for drafting a plan for treaties. On July

18, they reported a set of model articles, which the delegates adopted on September 17, and a week later drafted instructions to accompany the "Plan of 1776."[23]

On December 4, 1776, Benjamin Franklin—one of the authors of the "Plan of 1776"—arrived in France. He was the most famous American, and he soon overshadowed Silas Deane and the choleric Arthur Lee. Franklin appealed to the European romantic's idea of what an unspoiled American should be, and aristocratic France throbbed with sympathy for the brave men who were contending for rights flowing from natural law. With Vergennes' connivance the Marquis de Lafayette illegally sailed to join General Washington's army. Prussian Freiherr Friedrich Wilhelm von Steuben left France to offer his professional expertise to the amateurish Americans. Many officers applied to the American commissioners with offers to volunteer—with appropriate rank and pay—and at least twenty-eight entered the Continental Army during 1776-1777.[24] One, the Comte de Broglie, brother of the Marshall de Broglie, aspired to replace Washington and become a dictator, establishing a kind of stadtholderate in the newly-independent land.[25] Bavarian Johan Kalb, who is embalmed in American hagiography as "Baron de Kalb," initially came to America as Broglie's agent and remained to become a major general and die of wounds received at Camden, South Carolina, in 1780.

Franklin, Deane, and Lee devoted themselves during 1777 to increasing the flow of covert assistance, while simultaneously working zealously to persuade their secret ally to accord official recognition to American independence and to enter into a formal alliance against the common foe. On their own initiative they made solemn promises not to make a separate peace with Britain if, as a result of a treaty of commerce and amity, Britain went to war with France and Spain.[26] The Congress soon provided official sanction for a triple alliance, pledging to fight on until Britain was expelled from North America and the West Indies and Portugal was subjugated—making peace only upon the concurrence of all three parties.[27]

From mid-1776 through 1777, France inched toward war, influenced by the varying fortunes of American arms. When the rebels seemed to achieve some success and increase the likelihood of making good their declaration of independence, the French edged a little closer to the brink; Washington's defeats on the lower Hudson and retreat from Manhattan and across New Jersey caused them to draw back. His spectacular recovery at Trenton and Princeton gave some cause for momentary optimism, but his Fabian tactics, Congress' abandoning Philadelphia, and rumors of peace overtures that would reconcile England and her colonists made France and her ally, Spain, hesitate to intrude themselves into a war whose outcome was so problematic. So Vergennes and his Spanish counterparts, first Jeronimo Grimaldi and then Jose Floridablanca, confined their involvement to watchful waiting and keeping the American rebellion alive through covert support.

The Impact of Saratoga

But then everything changed. When news of Burgoyne's surrender reached Paris on December 3, fevered consideration of national interest replaced watchful waiting. Questions about Americans' ability to fight a campaign to a successful conclusion seemed resolved. Adequately armed and provisioned, they might rend the fabric of Britain's empire—and overt Franco-Spanish engagement could help assure that happy end. But France must act quickly: fear of an Anglo-American reconciliation, never far from Vergennes' thoughts, made immediate recognition of the United States and open military and logistical support imperative. On December 17, 1777, and without waiting to consult Floridablanca, the French foreign minister promised the commissioners recognition through a treaty of alliance and commerce that would guarantee independence, and would in turn engage the United States to not accept alluring terms from Britain—terms that would leave France fighting her ancient enemy alone.[28]

The minister's fear that Britain, shocked by the disaster at Saratoga, would try to persuade the American commissioners to accept favorable terms short of independence was realistic. Spies had reported to Whitehall that, before Saratoga, Franklin and Deane would have been receptive to such an overture and were averse to a French alliance; and agent Paul Wentworth met with Franklin and Deane on January 6 to sound them out. They rebuffed him, and Wentworth returned to London to report his failure to Undersecretary William Eden, whose competent secret service agents—including Edward Bancroft, who was to become the commission's secretary—kept Lord North's ministry well-informed about the details of Franco-American negotiations.[29]

For two weeks Vergennes waited for Floridablanca to respond to his proposal that Spain join France in an alliance with the Americans, but the Spaniard opposed recognizing their independence. Fearful that further delay would be fatal to his objectives, the French minister advised the commissioners on January 8 that Louis XVI was disposed to enter into an alliance.[30]

After a month's delay the French and American plenipotentiaries signed two treaties on February 6. One, the treaty of "conditional and defensive alliance," became operative if France and Great Britain went to war. It affirmed, in Article II, that "The essential and direct End of the present defensive alliance is to maintain effectually the liberty, Sovereignty, and independence absolute and unlimited of the said united States, as well in Matters of Gouvernement [sic] as of commerce." The other eleven articles detailed the allies' obligations and rights and made important mutual pledges to "aid each other with their good Offices, their Counsels and their forces," that France renounced future possession of the Bermuda Islands "as well as of any part of the Continent of North America . . ."; that "Neither of the two Parties will conclude either Truce or Peace with Great Britain, without the formal consent of the other first obtained; and that they mutually engage not to lay down their arms, until the Independence of the united states shall have been formally or tacitly assured by the Treaty or Treaties that shall terminate the War," as well as a famous perpetual guarantee of territory.[31] The other treaty, one of amity and commerce, mutually conferred most favored nation trading privileges on the parties.[32]

On March 20, Louis XVI ceremoniously received the Continental Congress' commissioners in his court at Versailles. The treaties and the King's reception transformed the war from a civil war into an international conflict that eventually involved Spain and brought into existence the League of Armed Neutrality—a true revolution in international affairs.

American independence became a reality.

Appendix A

A Junction at Albany, New York, between Burgoyne and Howe? An Examination of the Evidence

Chronology of Events

July 1776: Carleton receives the Order of the Bath;

November 30: Date of Howe's first two letters to Germain;

December 1-13: Howe forces Washington to retreat across New Jersey;

December 9: Burgoyne arrives in England;

December 9-10: Germain receives Carleton's dispatch announcing the end of campaigning and his retreat to Canada for winter;

December 10: Burgoyne delivers Carleton's "Requisitions" and own "Observations" at meeting with Germain and Cabinet;

December 11: Burgoyne meets with the King;

December 20: Date of Howe's third letter to Germain;

December 23: Thomas Paine publishes pamphlet *The Crisis*;

December 26: American victory at Trenton;

December 30: Howe's first two letters reach Germain;

January 3, 1777: American victory at Princeton;

January 10: Cabinet begins discussion of Howe's first two letters;

January 14: Date of Germain's letter of reply to Howe;

January 17 - 20: Howe sends letters to Germain, reporting British defeats at Trenton/Princeton and retreat across NJ, and predicting a major offensive will be needed to end the war;

February 23: Howe's letters of January 17 & 20 reach London;

February 28: Burgoyne submits to Cabinet his memorandum, "Thoughts on Conducting the War from the Side of Canada"; Clinton arrives in England;

March 26: Burgoyne receives instructions from the King; Germain sends instructions to Carleton to remain in Quebec, and to send Burgoyne to join Howe; but no direct order to Howe regarding operations with Burgoyne is sent;

May 18: Germain issues order permitting Howe to first invest Philadelphia, but to return to New York in time to support and rendezvous with Burgoyne;

August 16: Germain's 18 May order reaches Howe, en route to Philadelphia;

Sept. 18-Oct. 17: The Battles of Saratoga;

November: Parliamentary hearings in House of Commons attempt to affix blame for the defeat.

Details of the Scholarly Debate Concerning Burgoyne's Behavior vis-a-vis Carleton

After the defeat at Saratoga, the House of Commons held hearings in November of 1777, including one on the conduct of General Burgoyne. In his "Prefatory Speech" Burgoyne accused Lord Germain of impressing "the public with, an opinion, that I was endeavouring to supplant Sir Guy Carleton in the command of the northern army—an action abhorrent to the honour of an officer and the liberality of a gentleman; and which, thank God, I can prove the irrefragable upon your table . . . ."[1] He then cited Germain's August 22, 1776, dispatch to Carleton ordering him to return to Quebec as governor and to detach Burgoyne . . .

> or such other officer as you shall think most proper, with that part of your forces which can be spared from the immediate defence of your province, to carry on such operations as shall be most conducive to the success of the army acting on the side of New York, and to direct the officer so detached to communicate with you, and to put himself as soon as possible under the command of General Howe.[2]

Burgoyne claimed that he had been informed that Carleton was required to return to Canada, "not only upon the political reasoning which appears in that dispatch, but also, under the commission [of] governor he then held under the great seal, pass the frontier of his province." He argued that the dispatch, although it was not delivered until the spring of 1777, established that the government's decision antedated his own return to England by four months.[3] He also claimed that he could produce at "your bar a tribe of gentlemen, who had imbibed impressions not very favorable proceedings of Sir Guy Carleton in the campaign of 1776," and that he could "shew that I seized numberless, indeed I seized every possible occasion to vindicate the judgment, the assiduity, the activity of that highly respected officer, careless how ill I paid my court, earnest to meet every attack against his fame."[4] Burgoyne was exaggerating his deference to Carleton. He may have actually convinced himself that he had always acted without self-interest toward his former commander. That does not mean, of course, that he in fact did nothing to advance his own interests, even at the expense of his senior's "fame;" merely that he was capable of editing his memory toward a charitable view of his own motives—in which he would not be unique.

Of the crucial December 10, 1776, conversation between Burgoyne and the Cabinet, no record exists except for a single page of Germain's "Precis of Operations & Plans"; and that is noted in the margin as "conversation with General Burgoyne after his arrival in England," concerning Carleton's rejection of the plan for an expedition down the Mohawk Valley.[5] That "Precis" had an important history. Germain dictated it to William Knox more than a year after the interview, at a time when he was defending himself against mounting attacks upon his conduct of the American war. Lord Thurlow, the attorney general, read it while preparing the ministry's case against Burgoyne for the House of Commons inquiry into the campaign's failure.[6] It is weak support for the allegation that Burgoyne seized the opportunity afforded by his meeting with the secretary to intrigue against Carleton.

Details of the Scholarly Background on the Missing Order from Germain to Howe

The authoritative treatment regarding Germain and the missing order to Howe is by Hoffman Nickerson. In 1928, Houghton Mifflin published Nickerson's *The Turning Point of the Revolution, Or Burgoyne in America*, certainly the most influential book on the Saratoga Campaign. Captain Nickerson was a respected military historian, co-author with Colonels Oliver Lyman Spaulding and John Womack Wright of *Warfare: A Study of Military Methods from the Earliest Times*, the first scholarly work on the subject this writer read while at university. A sweeping style—one to which this writer cannot pretend—marked his narrative of events, and with which every study of Saratoga must be compared. The captain enlivened that narrative by populating it with heroes and villains.

And, like Sir John Fortesque, he chose his heroes from among generals: Washington, Schuyler, and Arnold—but not Gates; and the knaves and villains from among venal, interfering members of the Continental Congress and self-indulgent officials such as Lord George Germain. Because Germain did not keep his promise to send the critically necessary letter to Sir William, Nickerson held the secretary responsible for the failure of the plans of which he was principal author.

Nickerson had an explanation for what happened: After Germain's letter to Carleton of March 26 was drafted, Under Secretary William Knox pointed out to Germain that "no corresponding letter had been sent to Howe to tell him of Burgoyne's move. Where at Germaine [sic] authorized him to write to Howe himself and enclose a copy [of the letter to Carleton]." Nickerson continued:

> Germaine's weakness was not laziness—he was anything but lazy; it was an almost religious care not only for official routine, but also for that which ministered to the comfort of his own majestic self, and in general for the ritual of social life. Seeing that Knox's copy of the orders to Carleton was not enough, he had a positive order to Howe drawn up directing that easy-going commander to move up the Hudson. It happened, however, that when he called at his office to sign the order, it had not been fair copied. Now Germaine, together with other peculiarities, had 'a particular aversion to be put out of his way on any occasion,' and just at that moment he was on his way to visit in the country in Kent. Even though he believed the rebels already as good as beaten, a better man would have sat down and waited until the copy was finished. Not so Germaine, who went off leaving his dispatch unsigned. This time his subordinates were as bad as himself. They allowed the all-important paper to be pigeon-holed or mislaid. Probably thinking that because he had meant to sign, therefore he had done so, Germaine was fool enough to forget the whole matter.[7]

Because Nickerson disdained footnotes, identifying his sources can be difficult. He did not cite the Historical Manuscripts Commission's publications, but a check of their volume 6, the William Knox Papers, reveals this entry:

> When all was prepared [Burgoyne's appointment and related documents] and I had then to compare and make up, Lord Sackville [Germain] came down to the office on his way to Stoniland, when I observed to him there

was no letter to Howe to acquaint him with the plan or what was expected of him in consequence of it. His lordship stared and D'Oyley [deputy secretary] stared but said he would in moment write a few lines. 'So,' says Lord Sackville, 'My poor horses must stand in the street all the time, and I shan't be to my time anywhere.' D'Oyley then said he had better go, and he would write for himself to Howe and inclose copies of Burgoyne's Instructions which would tell him all that he would want to know, and with that his Lordship was satisfied as it enabled him to keep his time, for he would never bear delay or disappointment.[8]

Lord Edward Fitzmaurice, in his *Life of William, Earl of Shelburne, Afterwards Marquess of Lansdowne* enlarged upon that entry:

The inconsistent orders given to Generals Howe and Burgoyne could not be accounted for except in a way which it must be difficult for any person who is not conversant with the negligence of office to comprehend. It might appear incredible, if his [Germain's] own secretary and the most respected persons in office had not assured me of the fact, and what corroborates it is that it can be accounted for in no other way. . . . having among other peculiarities a particular aversion to be put out of his way on any occasion, had arranged to call at his office on his way to the country in order to sign despatches; but as those addressed to Howe had not been 'fair copied' and he was not disposed to be balked of his projected visit to Kent, they were not signed and were forgotten on his return home.[9]

Neither of those sources appears in Nickerson's bibliography, but Edward Barrington de Fonblanque's *Political and Military Episodes in the Latter Half of the Eighteenth Century Derived From the Life and Correspondence of the Right Hon. John Burgoyne, General, Statesman, Dramatist* does, and it includes this passage: "A subsequent despatch containing full and explicit instructions to Sir William Howe as to his co-operation with Burgoyne was written, but by one of those shameful acts of neglect, of which history unfortunately affords but too many examples, this document was suffered to be pigeon-holed in London, where it was found, after the convention of Saratoga, carefully docketed, and only wanting the signature of the minister."[10]

The similarities between Nickerson's accounts and the ones just cited indicate that he had consulted them, but included only Fonblanque in his bibliography. Nickerson derived his version from the Knox Papers,

Fitzmaurice's biography of Shelburne, and Fonblanque's biography of Burgoyne, and gave it the respectability that made it part of the historiography of the American Revolution.

Scholarly Treatments Concerning Howe's Perception of his Orders

Two scholars devoted their impressive knowledge to pass objective judgment on Howe's perception of his orders and the consequences thereof: Troyer Steele Anderson and Ira D. Gruber. No one is likely to make their judgments obsolete. Anderson wrote in 1936:

> . . . Howe knew what the expedition was intended to accomplish. He was entirely justified in supposing that Burgoyne's safety was not expected to depend upon assistance from New York. But in his failure to take steps to join hands with Burgoyne after the latter had reached Albany he either overestimated the capacity of Burgoyne's force, or, what is more likely, deliberately accepted a postponement of the completion of the Hudson chain in order to ensure success in Pennsylvania. Although it would be entirely mistaken to assume that Howe sacrificed Burgoyne either through indifference or stupidity, there was, nevertheless, in his correspondence . . . . a lack of enthusiasm for it that leaves the impression that the failure of the government to send Howe reinforcements as numerous as he wished put him in a mood prejudicial to a sympathetic handling of the problem presented by Burgoyne's advance. . . .[11]

Writing thirty-six years later, Gruber rendered this judgment:

> The campaign of 1777 was disastrous for the British—primarily because Sir William Howe had been obsessed with recovering Pennsylvania and incapable of taking prompt or consistent action. Although Germain had not done all he might to ensure that Howe and Burgoyne worked together, it is doubtful Sir William would have abandoned his expedition to Philadelphia under any circumstance. As it was, Howe ignored Clinton's pleas for a thrust up the Hudson as well as Germain's instructions to Carleton. But his obsession with Pennsylvania was not matched with decisive action. He did nothing until June, spent two weeks trying to bring Washington to action in New Jersey and another three in

embarking from New York, chose to go to Philadelphia by the Chesapeake, and did not reach Pennsylvania until September. . . .[12]

These well-informed, nuanced interpretations cannot be improved upon.

Details of the Scholarly Debate Concerning Burgoyne's Understanding of Howe's Intentions

The question remains: Did General Burgoyne expect General Sir William Howe, or a significant part of his army, to advance northward and form a junction with him and St. Leger at Albany? Most students of the campaign answer in the negative, and that only after he experienced setbacks did he insist that meeting a cooperating column at Albany had been a definite expectation. The reasons below convincingly argue against this prevailing opinion.

First, John Burgoyne had a better command of language than either Germain or Howe, and when not resorting to oratorical persiflage, he wrote lucidly and with a careful selection of words. His 'Thoughts' contained careful projections of tactical options for accomplishing the purpose that informed Carleton's 1776 campaign: a junction with Sir William Howe. When he wrote "junction," I suspect that it was a carefully chosen definition of what he intended to accomplish, which was something Carleton had failed to do. Burgoyne intended to meet Sir William or his surrogate at Albany and tender his and St. Leger's services to their new commander to employ in whatever mission he required, including but not limited to retaining possession of the Champlain-Hudson line and the Mohawk Valley. Securing those important river systems would help assure Howe's success, because unless Burgoyne and St. Leger had annihilated both the American Northern and Eastern Departments, the British could expect the rebels to do everything in their power to harass Howe's rear; and most of those rebels would include New England Yankees, the most virulent of the breed. On the other hand, securing the rivers would mean Sir William would not be operating in a strategic vacuum, and could pursue his Southern strategy.

Second, George III's principal military adviser, probably Jeffrey, Lord Amherst, advised the King that the commander of the army from Canada must "force down to Albany and join att [sic] that place," an objective the King identified forthrightly: "As Sir William Howe does not think of acting from Rhode Island into Massachusetts, the force from Canada must join him at

Albany."[13] The King rarely expressed himself in metaphors. He meant that he was approving a plan that intended a junction of the three commands at Albany.

Third, two Germain letters—one, dated March 25 to George, Lord Townshend, Master-General of Ordnance, and another dated April 19 to General Howe—concerned units that had mistakenly shipped to Canada. The first involved forty-six artillerymen intended for Rhode Island. Germain told Townshend that they were to go "by way of Lake Champlain, until they join the army under General Howe, when they will receive his Orders for joining their respective companies."[14] The second concerned 342 Hesse-Hanau chasseurs Howe had requested. They had, instead, gone to Canada, where they became part of "the Detachment ordered down the Mohawk River to Albany and [to] join your Army."[15]

Fourth, Burgoyne told Simon Fraser in a letter dated May 6 that the military operations in which they were engaged were "all directed to make a junction with Howe."[16] Fraser, St. Leger, Polwell, and Hamilton were lieutenant colonels who received "local" brigadier commissions that would expire at the end of the current campaign, when they would revert to their permanent rank. Correspondence among Howe, Burgoyne, Secretary at War William Wildman, and Germain reveals Sir William insisting that those temporary brigadiers revert to regimental commanders, i.e., lieutenant colonels, whenever his, Burgoyne's, and St. Leger's forces merged. All four assumed that the troops from Canada would, at that point, become part of Howe's command.[17]

Fifth, Barry St. Leger wrote a letter to Burgoyne on August 11, while he was besieging Fort Stanwix at the Mohawk Oneida Carrying Place, urging that pressure from Burgoyne (which was physically impossible) would weaken the American garrison and "greatly expedite my junction with either of the Grand Armies." This clearly reflects his shared expectation of a rendezvous at the juncture of the Hudson and Mohawk rivers.[18]

Finally, all of the surviving sources indicate that the officers and men in Burgoyne's army expected to meet a cooperating force at Albany. For example, Lieutenant William Digby of the 53rd Regiment of Foot recorded in his journal entry for May 6, 1777, that the campaign in which he served was "necessary for junction with the Southern army, under command of General Howe."[19] Alexander, Lord Balcarres, testified during the parliamentary inquiry into the defeat at Saratoga that the army expected active cooperation from south of Albany. Major Forbes, whose men made the initial contact with the Americans on Freeman's Farm on September 19, testified to the same effect.[20] The Germans shared that expectation, as Freifrau von Riedesel made clear in her account of discussions conducted during the defeated army's retreat northward.[21] Her husband, Freiherr Friedrich von Riedesel, commander of Burgoyne's German contingent, wrote from Albany to the Herzog von Braunschweig on October 21 that "*Der General Bourgoyne kam von England mit der espressen Ordre zuruck sich die Communication mit der Armee so von New York herauf zu franchiren, es koste auch was es wollé*" [freely translated: "General Burgoyne returned from England with the express orders to establish communication with the army coming up from New York, whatever the cost."][22]

A piece of evidence that seemed to support the contrary argument that General Burgoyne never really intended meeting any of Sir William's army at Albany appears as a part of his later justification for having taken along the large field artillery train that slowed his advance. After observing that it was the same size Sir Guy Carleton intended to employ had he commanded; was consistent with his artillery chief General William Philips' recommendations; and that it met the needs imposed by the type of fighting he expected, Burgoyne added, "but principally the intention of fortifying a camp at Albany, in case I should reach that place, should meet a sufficiency there (as I was led to expect) and should find it expedient to pass the winter there, without communication with new York."[23] That passage appeared to give the lie to Burgoyne's contention that he expected to meet a British force when he reached Albany—until one reads in Gerald Howson's excellent *Burgoyne of Saratoga* this persuasive analysis:

> At first sight, this sounds as if he had inadvertently let the cat out of the bag and that he had all along expected to reach and hold Albany alone. Yet, in the context [in which it had] been said, this surely means that, a junction with Howe's army having been effected and Howe having turned south to attack Philadelphia, a countermove might sever the communication once again during the winter, a contingency that ought to be prepared for. Alternatively, Howe might never be able to get through to Albany at all, being blocked at the Highlands, and Burgoyne would need heavy artillery if he was to keep the city.[24]

Military men were not unique in believing that Burgoyne's 'Thoughts' defined his campaign's mission as a junction with Howe's army at Albany. Some politicians, including the opposition leader, Edmund Burke, also asserted that it did. Very few Britons equaled Burke in knowledge of colonial affairs, and his articles in the *Annual Register*, or *A View of the History, Politics and Literature for the*

Year (year just ended) were mined assiduously by American plagiarists. He told the Commons:

> Ignorance had stamped every step taken during the course of the expedition, but it was the ignorance of the Minister for the American department [Germain], not to be imputed to General Burgoyne of whose good conduct, bravery and skill I do not entertain the shadow of a doubt.

> [If] the intended measure was a conjunction between Howe and Burgoyne, it was to be produced in the strangest way ever heard of the armies were to meet—yes: Howe was traveling southward, and Burgoyne in the same direction.

Charles James Fox, another nemesis of the ministry, was less gentle:

> An army of 10,000 men destroyed through the ignorance, the Obstinate, wilful [sic] ignorance and incapacity of the noble Lord. . . . A gallant general sent like a victim to be slaughtered, where his own skill and personal bravery would have earned him laurels, if he had not been under the direction of a blunderer, which circumstances alone are the cause of his disgrace, was too shocking a sight for humanity to bear unmoved. The General and the House [of Commons] have been imposed upon and deceived: Burgoyne's orders were to make his way to Albany, there to wait upon the orders of Sir William Howe and to cooperate with him; but General Howe knew nothing of the matter, for he was gone to a different country, and left the unhappy Burgoyne and his troops to make the best terms for themselves.[25]

Burke and Fox were speaking in the environment of parliamentary debate, one not free of hyperbole, nor always an unimpeachable source of historic proof. But their recriminations reflected an understanding of the implications of the strategy that had been followed that was shared by other members of Commons.

The sources cited are persuasive that the evidence is strong, but not overwhelming, that Burgoyne consistently predicated his campaign and its objective upon cooperation with a force from New York City with which he would form a junction at Albany.

Believing that does not, however, answer another important question: Had Burgoyne learned before he sailed from Portsmouth in *Apollo* anything that should have told him that other parties to the planning saw his expedition and its objective differently? Before his ship left the harbor during Easter Monday, he did learn that the man-of-war *Albion* was ready to depart for New York; and he sent a message to General Howe describing "the subject of my expedition, and the nature of my orders. . . . From thence I wrote a second letter to Sir William Howe, wherein I repeated that I was entrusted with the command of the army destined to march from Canada, and that my orders were to force a junction with his excellency."[26]

Was he aware when he wrote that letter of the contents of Howe's two letters to Germain of December 20, 1776, and January 20, 1777, documenting Howe's second and third plans and the secretary's response to the first? (There is no reply to the second.) Troyer Anderson believed that he was.[27] Other students, including Piers Mackesy, Don Higginbotham, Rupert Furneaux, and Gerald Saxon Brown agree, assuming Germain and Burgoyne were in regular contact when the minister prepared his letter approving Howe's decision to invade Pennsylvania. Furneaux, without citing evidence, wrote: "Burgoyne, who was in and out of Germain's office in Cleveland Row at the vital time, *must* have learned of Howe's proposed change of plan [emphasis added], although he may have believed Howe would be ordered to support him."[28] Surviving contemporary sources reveal, however, nothing that would indicate frequent personal contacts between the secretary and the general that would lead to the conclusion that they were other than, in Gerald Howson's words, "occasional and rather formal."[29]

A useful piece of circumstantial evidence is what one can learn about contacts between Burgoyne and Sir Henry Clinton during the month immediately preceding the former's departure for Canada. In an interview with Germain shortly after his arrival in London, Clinton expressed an unqualified endorsement of the necessity of supporting Burgoyne's junction with Howe at Albany.[30] Shortly after Clinton returned to New York, the generals dined on at least one occasion. Believing that that they did not discuss Burgoyne's plan and Howe's and Clinton's roles would be ridiculous. William B. Willcox, in his outstanding study of Clinton entitled *Portrait of a General*, cited the relevant memorandum in the general's papers and his entry for March 2, 1777. "No record of their evening has survived," wrote Willcox, "but imagination can picture them talking in the candlelight about the hopes and prospects of the summer, perhaps drinking a toast to their next meeting, on the banks of the

Hudson. Clinton subsequently did everything in his power to bring about that meeting, which by September was Burgoyne's last hope."[31]

If Germain had even hinted to either general that the government did not anticipate a junction, their conversation would have taken an entirely different turn, and Clinton would not have attempted to argue Howe out of his determination to go southward.

Thus, the weight of the evidence suggests that Burgoyne, when he sailed for Canada, had no reason to believe that the objectives defined in his "Thoughts" were no longer controlling. That does not mean that Howe's and Clinton's original mission was to rescue Burgoyne. But it does mean that Burgoyne expected Howe or his surrogate to cooperate in securing the Hudson valley. In short, they and Burgoyne shared that mission.

However, while historian at Saratoga National Historical Park, this author submitted on January 8, 1960, a research report that was generally consonant with conclusions reached by Don Higginbotham, Piers Mackesy, Troyer Anderson, Gerald S. Brown, and Rupert Furneaux that it was only when Burgoyne defended himself and tried to explain why he was defeated that he invented the story of inflexible orders to effect a junction as an excuse for his failure. Because that 1960 report predated the other authors' publications, they bear no responsibility for the interpretation embalmed in *Decision on the Hudson: The Battles of Saratoga*, a publication sold at Saratoga National Historical Park.

This serves as a reminder that a judicious quantity of salt should be applied to what any researcher, reader, or writer—no matter how eminent or confident at the time—commits to the page.

Appendix B

British Order of Battle

BRITISH	
UNIT	**STRENGTH**
General staff	10 – 20
9th Regiment of Foot	542
20th Regiment of Foot	528
21st Regiment of Foot	538
24th Regiment of Foot	528
47th Regiment of Foot	524
53rd Regiment of Foot	537
62nd Regiment of Foot	541
Flank companies of the 29th, 31st, and 34th Regiments	329
Total British Infantry	4,077 – 4,087
Royal Artillery	251
Artillery Recruits	154
Total British Strength	4,482 – 4,492

GERMAN	
UNIT	**STRENGTH**
General Staff	22
Dragoon Regiment	323
Grenadiers	533
Chasseurs (Jagers)	552
Regiment von Rhetz	604
Regiment von Riedesel	646
Regiment von Specht	589
Regiment Prinz Friedrich (Erbprinz)	625
Regiment Hesse-Hanau	700
Total German Infantry	4,594
Total Germans, including Artillery	4,694

Source: *State of the Expedition*, Appendix No. XI, "Army from Canada under Lieutenant-General Burgoyne. Total Rank and File, 1st of July, 1777."

ORGANIZATION OF BURGOYNE'S ARMY			
DIVISION	**DESIGNATION**	**ELEMENTS**	**COMMANDER**
First	Advanced Corps		Brigadier Simon Fraser
		24th Regiment	Major Robert Graves
		Grenadier Battalion	Major John Dyke Acland (20th Regiment)
		Lt. Infantry Battalion	Major Alexander Lindsey, earl of Balcarres (53rd Regiment)
		Ranger Company (marksmen)	Captain Alexander Fraser (34th Regiment)

ORGANIZATION OF BURGOYNE'S ARMY (continued)			
DIVISION	**DESIGNATION**	**ELEMENTS**	**COMMANDER**
RIGHT			
	First Brigade		Brigadier James Hamilton
		20th Regiment	Lt. Col. John Lind
		21st Regiment	Major George Forster
		62nd Regiment	Lt. Col. John Anstruther
	Second Brigade		Brigadier Henry Powell
		9th Regiment	Lt. Col. John Hill
		47th Regiment	Lt. Col. Nicholas Sutherland
		53rd Regiment	Major William Hughes
LEFT			
	First Brigade		General Johann Specht
		von Rhetz (Braunschweiger Regiment)	Major Carl von Ehrenkrook
		von Specht (Braunschweiger Regiment)	Lt. Col. Ernst Spaethe
		von Riedesel (Braunschweiger Regiment)	General von Gall
	Second Brigade		
		Prinz Friedrich (Braunschweiger Regiment)	Lt. Col. Christian Praetorius

ORGANIZATION OF BURGOYNE'S ARMY (continued)			
DIVISION	**DESIGNATION**	**ELEMENTS**	**COMMANDER**
		Erbprinz (Hesse-Hanau Regiment)	General von Gall
Reserve			Lt. Col. Heinrich von Breymann
		Grenadier Battalion	Breymann
		Light Infantry Battalion	
		Braunschweiger Jagers Company	
		Braunschweiger Dragoon Regiment von Ludwig	Lt. Col. Friedrich Baum
Artillery			Major Griffith Williams
		Royal Irish Artillery detachment	
		33rd Regiment detachment	
		Hesse-Hanau Artillery company	Captain Georg Pausch

Source: Lunt., Appendix I, "Order of Battle - The Expedition from Canada-1777"; *Hadden's Journal and Orderly Books: A Journal Kept In Canada and Upon Burgoyne's Campaign in 1776 and 1777, By Lieut. James M. Hadden, Roy Art; Also Orders kept by him and issued by Sir Guy Carleton, Lieut. General John Burgoyne and Major General William Phillips in 1776, 1777 and 1778, With Explanatory Notes by Horatio Rogers* (Albany, 1884), 44-47.

History of Units in Burgoyne's Army

The oldest regiment, the 21st, or Royal North British Fusiliers, "Marlborough's Own," had its origins in Scotland, where it was raised in 1678 during the reign of Charles II. It fought with distinction at Blenheim, Ramilles, Ordemonde, Malplaquet, Dettingen, Louisbourg, Minden, and the relief of Quebec.

The 24th, Simon Fraser's regiment, was raised by Sir Edward Dering, had its first muster on 28 March 1689, participated in the Battle of the Boyne and the fall of Limerick, Blenheim, Ramilles, Ordenonde, Malplaquet, and Warburg.

The newer regiments, the 20th, 9th, 62nd, 49th, and 53rd, formed during the 1750s, later distinguished themselves in Britain's 19th and 20th century wars, including serving with special valor during the First and Second World Wars.

The grenadier and light infantry companies included drafts from the 29th, 31st, and 34th Regiments, all with honorable combat service to their credit.

Appendix C

American Order of Battle

Freeman's Farm, September 19, 1777

AMERICAN	
UNIT	**STRENGTH**
Patersons' Brigade	1,280
10th Massachusetts Regiment	340
11th Massachusetts Regiment	345
12th Massachusetts Regiment	345
14th Massachusetts Regiment	250
Learned's Brigade	1,305
2nd Massachusetts Regiment	491
8th Massachusetts Regiment	366
9th Massachusetts Regiment	448
Glover's Brigade	1,609
1st Massachusetts Regiment	453
4th Massachusetts Regiment	453
13th Massachusetts Regiment	474
15th Massachusetts Regiment	229

AMERICAN (continued)	
UNIT	**STRENGTH**
Nixon's Brigade	1,537
3rd Massachusetts Regiment	384
5th Massachusetts Regiment	428
6th Massachusetts Regiment	372
7th Massachusetts Regiment	353
Poor's Brigade	2, 109 *
1st New Hampshire Regiment	350*
3rd New Hampshire Regiment	384
2nd New York Regiment	280*
Cook's Connecticut Militia	*
Latimore's Connecticut Militia	(Total Connecticut Militia 1,095*)
Morgan's Regiment of Riflemen (brigaded with Dearborn's Light Infantry 300)	578
Artillery	
Stevens' Independent Battalion of Artillery	302
Cavalry	
Connecticut Light Horse	200
Engineers	
Estimates caused by either a paucity or poor quality of data	

AMERICAN (continued)	
UNIT	**STRENGTH**
Baldwin's Detachment of Engineers and Artificers	71
Total American strength (according to return dated October 16 in Gates Papers, NYHS)	8,991

Appendix D

Organization of the American Army at Saratoga

Freeman's Farm, September 19, 1777

Left Wing, (4,000 men in thirteen regiments) commanded by Maj. Gen. Benedict Arnold

Learned's Brigade
Brig. Gen. Ebenezer Learned

2nd Massachusetts Regiment
Col. John Bailey

8th Massachusetts Regiment
Col. Michael Jackson

9th Massachusetts Regiment
Col. James Wesson

Livingston's New York Regiment
(formerly 1st Canadian)
Col. James Livingston

Poor's Brigade
Brig. Gen. Enoch Poor

1st New Hampshire Regiment
Col. Joseph Cilley

2nd New Hampshire Regiment
Col. Winborn Adams

3rd New Hampshire Regiment
Col. Alexander Scammell

2nd New York Regiment
Col. Philip Van Cortlandt

4th New York Regiment
Col. Henry Beekman Livingston

Cook's Connecticut Militia
Col. Thaddeus Cook

Latimore's Connecticut Militia
Col. Jonathan Latimore

Right Wing (5,000 men in fifteen regiments) under the personal command of Maj. Gen. Horatio Gates

Glover's Brigade
Brig. Gen. John Glover

1st Massachusetts Regiment
Col. Joseph Vose

4th Massachusetts Regiment
Col. William Shepard

13th Massachusetts Regiment
Col. Edward Wigglesworth

15th Massachusetts Regiment
Col. Timothy Bigelow

2nd Albany County Regiment,
New York Militia
Col. Abraham Wemple

Organization of the American Army at Saratoga

Freeman's Farm, September 19, 1777 (continued)

17th Albany County Regiment
New York Militia
Col. William B. Whiting

Graham's Regiment of Dutchess & Ulster
County New York Millitia
Col. Morris Graham

Nixon's Brigade
Brig. Gen. John Nixon

3rd Massachusetts Regiment
Col. John Greaton

5th Massachusetts Regiment
Col. Rufus Putnam

6th Massachusetts Regiment
Col. Thomas Nixon

7th Massachusetts Regiment
Col. Ichabod Alden

Paterson's Brigade
Brig. Gen. John Paterson

10th Massachusetts Regiment
Col. Thomas Marshall

11th Massachusetts Regiment
Col. Benjamin Tupper

12th Massachusetts Regiment
Col. Samuel Brewer

14th Massachusetts Regiment
Col. Gamaliel Bradford

Morgan's Corps
Col. Daniel Morgan

Morgan's Regiment of Riflemen
Col. Daniel Morgan

Dearborn's Light Infantry
Major Henry Dearborn

Cavalry
Connecticut Light Horse
Major Elijah Hyde

Artillery
Stevens' Independent Battalion of Artillery
Maj. Ebenezer Stevens

Engineers
Col. Thaddeus Kosciuszko

Baldwin's Detachment of
Engineers & Artificers
Col. Jeduthan Baldwin

Appendix E

American Order of Battle, October 7, 1777

Note: Several factors operate to frustrate an effort to determine the strength of the American units committed during the October 7 fighting. In the first place, more militia were engaged than was the case on September 19. Some regiments were dispatched to Bemis Heights as organic county organizations. Others were formed from drafts from the various townships within the county. Militia were normally organized by classes, and when summoned for service, the men were called up by class. Determining who and in what numbers the men appeared is usually impossible to determine with any comfortable degree of certainty.

Secondly, the records of Richard Varick, the American muster master, are not dependable in determining unit strengths. That is not surprising. He functioned under the pressure of multiple duties complicated by his active participation in the headquarters politics that produced the rupture between Generals Gates and Arnold and his role as a daily source on information and gossip for General Schuyler. The September 19 losses reported by contemporaries and later writers are not consistent with participants' accounts of the battle's intensity.

What follows results from a consciously skeptical effort to use available data for Continental regiments and some judicious guesses based upon available population data and colonial laws requiring the enrollment of all men between sixteen and sixty. The problem is somewhat eased by the fact that most of the men engaged during September 19 were Continentals, and that data records the strengths of the regiments not engaged are sometimes recoverable.

With that lengthy introduction, the following Order of Battle is provided:

Left Wing, formerly Arnold's Division, now personally commanded by General Gates

Learned's Brigade
Brig. Gen. Ebenezer Learned
Strength: Continental: 1,088; Militia, ca. 500
Total = 1,588

2nd Massachusetts Regiment
Col. John Bailey

8th Massachusetts Regiment
Col. Michael Jackson

9th Massachusetts Regiment
Col. James Wesson

Livingston's New York Regiment
Col. James Livingston

Evans' Regiment of New Hampshire Militia,
Col. Stephen Evans

Drake's Regiment of New Hampshire Militia

Poor's Brigade
Brig. Gen. Enoch Poor
Strength: Continental: 1096; Militia: 870
Total = 1,966

1st New Hampshire Regiment
Col. Joseph Cilley

2nd New Hampshire Regiment
Col. George Reid

3rd New Hampshire Regiment
Col. Alexander Scammell

2nd New York Regiment
Col. Philip Van Cortlandt

4th New York Regiment
Col. Henry Beekman Livingston

Cook's Connecticut Militia
Col. Thaddeus Cook
Latimore's Connecticut Militia
Col. Jonathan Latimore

Ten Broeck's Brigade of
Albany County Militia,
Brig. Gen. Abraham Ten Broeck
Strength: 1,845 (militia)

Parts of the following
Albany County Regiments:

Col. Jacob Lansing's 1st Regiment
Col. Francis Nichol's 3rd Regiment
Col. Robert Killian Van Rensselaer's
4th Regiment
Col. Gerrit G. Ven Den Bergh's
5th Regiment
Col. Stephen John Schuyler's 6th Regiment
Col. Abraham Van Alstine's 7th Regiment
Col. Peter Van Ness' 9th Regiment
Col. Henry Livingston's 10th Regiment
Col. Anthony Van Bergen's 11th Regiment
Col. Jacobus Van Schonbeven's
12th Regiment
Col. John MacCrae's 13th Regiment
Col. John Knickerbacker's Regiment
Col. Lewis Van Woert's Regiment

Note: No General Order brigading the Albany County Militia exists. Because of its participation in the fighting of October 7, I assume it served as part of the Left Wing.

Right Wing, Major General
Benjamin Lincoln

Glover's Brigade
Brig. Gen. John Glover
Strength: Continentals: 1,169; Militia: 575
Total = 1,744

1st Massachusetts Regiment
Col. Joseph Vose

4th Massachusetts Regiment
Col. William Shepard

13th Massachusetts Regiment
Col. Edward Wigglesworth

15th Massachusetts Regiment
Col. Timothy Bigelow

2nd Albany County Regiment New York
Militia, Col. Abraham Wemple

17th Albany County Regiment
New York Militia, Col. William Whiting

Graham's Regiment of Dutchess & Ulster
County New York Militia,
Col. Morris Graham

Nixon's Brigade
Brig. Gen. John Nixon
Strength: Continentals: 1,126, Militia: 277
Total = 1,403

3rd Massachusetts Regiment
Col. John Greaton

5th Massachusetts Regiment
Col. Rufus Putnam

6th Massachusetts Regiment
Col. Thomas Nixon

7th Massachusetts Regiment
Col. Ichabod Alden

2nd New Hampshire County Regiment
of Massachusetts Militia

Paterson's Brigade
Brig. Gen. John Paterson
Strength: Continentals: 976; Militia: 277
Total = 1,253

10th Massachusetts Regiment
Col Thomas Marshall

11th Massachusetts Regiment
Col. Benjamin Tupper

12th Massachusetts Regiment
Col Samuel Brewer

14th Massachusetts Regiment
Col. Gamaliel Bradford

South Berkshire Regiment
Massachusetts Militia, Col. John Ashley

3rd York County Regiment Massachusetts
Militia, Lt. Col. Joseph Storer

Warner's Brigade,
Brig. Gen. Jonathan Warner
Strength: 1,768 (militia)

Central Berkshire Regiment Massachusetts
Militia, Col. John Brown

5th Middlesex Regiment Massachusetts
Militia, Col. Samuel Bullard

3rd Suffolk County Regiment Massachusetts
Militia, Col. Benjamin Gill

1st New Hampshire Regiment Massachusetts
Militia, Col. Benjamin Woodbridge

4th Essex County Regiment Massachusetts
Militia, Col. Samuel Johnson

Morgan's Corp of Riflemen
and Light Infantry
Col. Daniel Morgan
(Estimated strength: 730)

Appendix F

A Debate Concerning the Non-Fortification of Mount Defiance (Fort Ticonderoga Operation)

Hoffman Nickerson, citing no sources, provided an explanation that other writers who shared his antipathy for Horatio Gates have found appealing and have endorsed. Allegedly, not fortifying Mount Defiance was a product of Gates' folly in not heeding young John Trumbull's counsel:

> During the previous summer [1776] there had been on the ground an able young officer, not yet twenty-one, whose keen eye and just sense of proportion were one day to make him a notable painter. His name was John Trumbull . . . and he was serving as adjutant-general. Having helped select the Mount Independence position . . . he had become convinced that Mount Defiance was within gun-shot both of Mount Independence and Ticonderoga proper, and one day he said so at the commanding officer's table. Gates and his officers laughed at him, but young Trumbull had stuck to his point and finally gained Gates' permission to experiment by gunfire. Even from the far northern end of Mount Independence, the balls from a double-shotted twelve pounder crashed against the rocky face of Mount Defiance more than halfway to its summit. From the old French fort a six-pounder had thrown a shot almost to the summit itself.

Yet, claiming that the height was too rugged to be scaled by a battery, Gates refused to order its occupation.

Some students of the campaign, albeit a minority, have not believed Nickerson's account. Citing Kosciuszko's May 18, 1777, letter to Gates in John Trumbull's *Autobiography, Reminiscences, and, Letters, 1777 to 1841*, and an undated letter from Gates to General Arthur St. Clair, Paul David Nelson wrote:

A year earlier, Gates had seen the possible danger that Mount Defiance might present and tried, without success, to persuade his superior, Schuyler, to occupy the strategic summit. Col. John Trumbull had also shown that a cannon shot could really reach the fort from the hill. While Gates had commanded there from March to May 1777, he had ordered Col. Thaddeus Kosciusko [sic] . . . to reconnoiter the ground and determine whether guns could be dragged to the top . . . Kosciusko had reported the distinct possibility of placing cannon upon the summit, but before Gates could do anything about the problem he was replaced by Schuyler. After General Schuyler assumed command in early June, the plan was set aside as impractical, and considering the lack of manpower, it is difficult to see how he could have arrived at any other decision. Even after being relieved of command, however, Gates continued to point out the vulnerability of Mount Defiance.

Nickerson's explanation is suspect on several counts, besides his unrelenting bias against Gates. Neither Trumbull nor his father Jonathan criticized Gates for not fortifying the mountain. Nor did either ever hint that the young man had been the butt of ridicule at the commander's table. Both remained on friendly terms with the general, as correspondence in his papers demonstrates. Nickerson was not above inventing episodes, as his dramatic and inaccurate story of General Philip Schuyler's sending Benedict Arnold to relieve Fort Stanwix testifies. Contemporary evidence makes Nelson's account more credible.

But other considerations are important. The two accounts agree that Trumbull demonstrated that Fort Ticonderoga's works were so vulnerable to artillery fire from Mount Defiance as to make the height's occupation essential. But was that really the case? The distance from its summit to Mount Independence is one mile, and to the palisaded star fort and to the original stone fort a mile and a quarter, or 1,760 yards and 2,100 yards respectively—considerably beyond the effective range of field pieces firing solid shot in the Revolutionary War era. Therefore, it is very doubtful that Trumbull or anyone else demonstrated that artillery on Mount Defiance would make the American fortifications untenable.

Sources: Hoffman Nickerson, *The Turning Point of the Revolution: Or Burgoyne in America* (Boston and New York, 1928), 131; David Paul Nelson, *General Horatio Gates. A Biography* (Baton Rouge, 1976), 91.

Appendix G

Battle of Bennington Casualties

Burgoyne's Orderly Book records the loss of six cannon and 1,220 men. German accounts list eighteen officers captured and five killed. Enlisted men killed or captured totaled approximately 600. Of Baum's dragoons, only seven escaped to rejoin the army. However, an unsigned return in the Gates Papers entitled "Account of the Enemy's Loss, in the late Action of the 16th August 1777, in the Walloomsac," contains the most credible data:

Account of Enemy Loss (from the Gates Papers)	
Found dead in the field including Tories	222
Officers killed (not known) (Prisoners) Lt. Col. Baum	1
Major	1
Captains	7
Lieutenants	14
Ensign	4
Cornets	2
Judge Advocate	1
Canadian Officers	2
Surgeons	6
Aidedecamp [sic]	1
Chaplain	1
Baron [?]	1
Of Different Sorts, Wounded Come to hand	100
Not wounded, Rank prisoners British	37

Account of Enemy Loss (continued)	
Hessians	398
Canadians	30
Tories	55
Total	883

If accurate (as its general agreement with rosters suggests), Burgoyne lost at least 730 enlisted regulars and thirty regular officers, six surgeons, and two Canadian officers. The total of 883 men, killed, wounded, and captured represented almost one-seventh of Burgoyne's entire strength.

American Casualties. Out of some 2,200 Americans engaged, the return reports between twenty and thirty killed, and "wounded not known." General Stark reported to the Council of New Hampshire that American losses totaled fourteen killed and forty-two wounded—numbers difficult to reconcile with his description of the fight against Baum that he reported to Gates as lasting "2 Hours, the hotest [sic] I ever saw in my life, it represented one continuous clap of thunder." Stark also praised his men's heroism for fighting "through the midst of fire & smoake [sic], mounted Two Breastworks, that was well fortified & supported with Cannon." He added a confusing note when he reported "about 40 wounded & thirty killed." The ratio of wounded to killed, which during the Revolution was three to one, is too skewed to be credited. Figures found in Washington's writings were seventy to eighty casualties. If those killed numbered about thirty, as Gates' papers and Stark's letter to Gates agreed, the number of wounded was between ninety and 126—still a remarkably low figure for the number of men engaged in so hard-fought a battle.

Stark described his material fruits in his report to Gates as "4 pieces of Brass Cannon, some hundreds stands of arms, Bradd Barrell [sic] Drums, several Hessian swords." He and his militiamen did not intend that the booty automatically become part of the Northern Department's arsenal, and his report to Gates contained this remarkable request: "As I promis'd in my orders, that all the plunder, taken in the enemy's Camp, [I] would be Glad [if] your Honour would send me word what would be the value of the Cannon, & the other artillery Stores above described might be." The men who answered the New Hampshire General Court's call to defend the Grants were determined that they and the fruits of their service would not lose identity in the anonymity of Continental service.

Appendix H

An American Partnership Torn Asunder: Benedict Arnold, Horatio Gates, and the Battle of Freeman's Farm, September 19, 1777

General Discussion

Almost four decades after the Battle of Freeman's Farm, James Wilkinson published an interpretation that, despite the author's character flaws, is a useful contribution to understanding what happened on September, 19, 1777. His observations are excerpted below in a lengthy quotation that provides a reference for commentary. "The battle was perfectly accidental," began Horatio Gates' aide-de-camp,

> neither of the generals meditated an attack at that time, and but for Lieutenant-colonel Colburn's report, it would not have taken place; Burgoyne's movement being merely to take ground on the heights in front of the great ravine, to give his several corps their proper places in line, to embrace our front and cover his transport, stores, provisions and baggage in rear of his left; and on our side the defences of our camp being not half completed and reinforcements daily arriving, it was not General Gates' policy to court action. The misconception of the adverse chiefs put them on the defensive, and confined them to the ground they occupied at the beginning of the action, and prevented a single manoeuvre, during one of the longest, warmest, and most obstinate battles fought in America.

Wilkinson continued:

> General Gates believed that his antagonist intended to attack him, and circumstances appeared to justify a like conclusion on the part of Burgoyne; and as the thickness of the investing wood concealed the

position and movements of either army . . . sound caution obliged the respective commanders to guard every assailable point; and thus the flower of the British army, the grenadiers and light infantry, one thousand five hundred strong, were posted on an eminence to cover its right, and stood by their arms, inactive spectators of the conflict until near sunset; while General Gates was obliged to keep his right wing on post, to prevent the enemy from forcing the flank, by the plain bordering the river. Had either of the generals been apprised of the dispositions of his antagonist, a serious blow might have been struck on our left or the enemy's right, but although nothing is more common, it is as illiberal as it is unjust, to determine the merit of military operations by events exclusively. It was not without experience that the Romans erected temples to Fortune. . . .[1]

Wilkinson's observations have the virtue of being more judicious and objective than the judgments rendered by some students whose partisanship flavors their observations. That it contains factual errors will become apparent, and his interpretation was not infallible. But it represented the judgment of an informed and intelligent witness.

Wilkinson's characterization of the battle's being "perfectly accidental" is an oversimplification. When Fraser's Corps, the artillery, and the [British] right wing of his army crossed the Hudson during Saturday September 13, Burgoyne knew that his adversary was at Stillwater and anticipated a fight; his troops camped that night "in columns in order of Battle."[2] Three days later, while his army lay at Dovegat [Coveville], Burgoyne led a large reconnaissance (Digby claimed it numbered 2,000 men), accompanied by six field pieces. He knew the Americans occupied Bemis Heights and blocked the road to Albany.[3] He knew with equal certainty that he would have to reopen that route by ruse or force, and the deployment of his troops reflected that certainty.

To summarize the British position: Burgoyne was too far from Canada to be reinforced and resupplied; autumn and the end of the campaigning season were rapidly approaching; he could not winter on the upper Hudson; he was less than fifty miles from his objective, where he could winter; Gates and his swelling army in their fortified camp blocked the way. Burgoyne intended to dislodge them.

The British commander, his staff, subordinate commanders, and officer corps had spent their adult lives in military service. While there was, as yet, no Royal Military College nor Kriegsakademie, experience and study had made them professionals. That professionalism was apparent in the manner General

Burgoyne deployed his outnumbered force to attack an enemy entrenched in works of whose extent and strength he had imperfect knowledge. Consciously or otherwise, he employed Pierre de Bourcet's "plan with branches," sending three separated columns to converge against the Americans, an intelligent tactic given his objective and his limited information about Gates' position and deployment. De Bourcet, a French strategic theorist, recommended that a commander divide his attacking force into two or more columns that could reunite quickly to concentrate his full force when required, but in a manner threatening multiple or alternative targets, forcing the defender to divide his strength and compromise his capacity to concentrate his defensive resources. The three-column deployment also provided flexibility, allowing it to respond to one blocked approach by exploiting another, more promising, one.[4]

Terrain, the American position, and the size of his army severely limited the British commander's options. A massed attack in column along the river flats at Jotham Bemis' tavern would have been suicidal. The hilly, wooded topography north of Bemis Heights afforded no ground suitable for massing and advancing either in line or column against the American left wing. De Bourcet offered a theoretical solution.

Burgoyne intended to take, and Gates meant to retain, Bemis Heights. Wilkinson was correct in that neither general anticipated the manner in which the battle developed. Gates expected Morgan to observe, not engage, the British. The term "accidental" was, however, less applicable to Burgoyne. His objective was to force or entice Gates out of his fortifications and to divide his numerically stronger defensive force. In that Burgoyne was partially successful.

Once the fighting developed, neither army displayed impressive tactical skill. Better coordination between Fraser's and Hamilton's columns early in the fight before Learned's Brigade deployed could have overlapped and turned Morgan's and Enoch Poor's left. But Burgoyne and Fraser credited the Americans with more sophistication than they possessed. The American use of an aggressive turning action against the British right made the latter so obsessed with occupying high ground overlooking the battlefield that they failed to employ aggressively their elite corps against the vulnerable American left. When Fraser finally committed his men later in the day, he did so in a limited, reactive manner.

For their part, the Americans made no concerted attempt—even when they had the numerical advantage—to turn the enemy's right flank. There is no credible evidence that Generals Gates, Arnold, Poor, or Learned imposed any kind of tactical direction beyond ordering regiments onto the battle line. The result was reliance upon frontal assault sustained by committing additional men. Stolid, stubborn Freiherr von Riedesel came marginally closer to exhibiting initiative when he attacked the American line's right flank shortly before sunset. But that was more the result of falling in line with Hamilton's left than of foresight on his part.

The courage of the company officers and enlisted men compensated for their commanders' limited effectiveness, repeatedly fighting their way through the smoke, confusion, and terror to attack, withdraw, and counterattack. The Americans faced up to their enemy's deadliest weapon, the bayonet charge, so bravely as to render it indecisive. The Europeans, except briefly during the battle's first phase, tenaciously maintained their order and fire discipline in unfamiliar terrain against a strong enemy and Morgan's expert marksmen. They overcame the odds to outfight the Americans and eventually drive them from the field.

The Role of Benedict Arnold

A comprehensive discussion of the battle of Freeman's Farm requires a careful examination of Benedict Arnold's role. The part played by his division's brigades is obvious. But there are two closely connected questions concerning his personal role. The first concerns whether he personally led his men into battle. The second is whether Horatio Gates prevented him from delivering the "knockout blow" that would have brought about John Burgoyne's defeat and ended the campaign. Both are important questions to which an impressive quantity of ink has been devoted. Yet a review of the evidence with as much objectivity as can be summoned justifies contributing to the volume of print.

"It is worthy to remark," wrote James Wilkinson, whose testimony again provides a starting point for our examination,

> that not a single general officer was on the field of battle on the 19th Sept, until the evening when General Learned was ordered out, about the same time Generals Gates and Arnold were in front of the center of the camp, listening to the peal of arms. When Colonel [Morgan] Lewis, deputy quarter-master general returned from the field, and being questioned by the General, he reported the indecisive progress of the action, at which General Arnold exclaimed, "by G-d I will put an end to it," and clapping spurs to his horse, galloped off at full speed. Colonel Lewis immediately

observed to General Gates, "you had better order him back, the action is going well, he may by some rash act do mischief." I was instantly dispatched, overtook and remanded Arnold to camp.[5]

One of the influential Livingston clan was Robert R. Livingston, an important Revolutionary-era statesman and diplomat closely associated with General Philip Schuyler by kinship and political interest. Two of his relatives played important roles in the Saratoga campaign: a cousin, Henry Brockholst Livingston, was an Arnold aide; and Robert's brother, Henry Beekman Livingston, commanded the 4th New York Continental Regiment. The Livingstons maintained a strong sense of family and did not hesitate to support their kinsmen's interests. In that spirit, Robert R. wrote to General Washington on behalf of his brother on January 14, 1778. His letter reads, in part:

> I take the liberty to inclose to your excellency an extract of a letter to him [Henry Beekman] under general Arnold's direction by a gentleman of his family [staff], he being unable to hold a pen himself. After a warm recommendation of his conduct, both in camp and in the field, and giving him and his regiment full share of the honor of the battle of the 19th of September (in which General Arnold, not being present, writes only from the reports of those who were . . . .)[6]

Henry Brockholst Livingston and his friend, Richard Varick, were Arnold's active partisans during his quarrel with General Gates, and they gave him exclusive credit for every American success on September 19. The former wrote to General Schuyler that Arnold "is the Life and Soul of the Troops—Believe me, Sir, to him and to him alone is due the Honor of our late victory. Whatever share his Superiors may claim they are entitled to none." Echoing him, Varick declared, "This I am certain of, that Arnold has all the Credit of the Action of the 19th, for he was ordering out troops to it, while the other [Gates] was in Dr. Potts tent back biting his Neighbors . . ."[7] Yet while they credited Arnold with making the critical decisions and issuing the orders putting them into effect, they did not represent him as personally leading his division into battle.

To assess their judgments' validity, the testimony of other contemporaries is useful. Colonel Philip Van Cortlandt, another scion of an important New York family with close connections to General Schuyler, was commander of the 2nd New York Regiment, which left its position on the camp's left wing about

4:00 p.m., with orders to extend the line facing the British grenadiers. Van Cortlandt recorded that he received orders from Arnold on his way to the firing line, but he was not specific about whether he received them from the general personally, through an aide, or more probably through General Poor, his brigade commander.[8]

Jared Sparks' papers in Harvard's Houghton Library contain contradictory testimony. When the historian toured the battlefield in 1830, he visited John Neilson, New York militia sergeant and owner of the house in which Generals Learned and Poor made their quarters and the cabin that housed Arnold. His guide was a talkative old veteran named Ezra Buel. Both men served at Bemis Heights. "Arnold was inactive, and took no part," both told Sparks. "In fact, there was no general officer in action. At one time Buel says he saw Genl. Poor, with two or three other officers, quite in the rear of the American Army, and taking no part in the action. The fighting was under the eyes of Morgan, Scamill [sic] and Ciley."[9]

However, the same collection also contains an account written the day after the battle prepared by General Poor. It presents the strongest evidence of Arnold's personal participation in the fighting:

> Arnold rushed into the thickest of the fight with his usual recklessness, and at times acted like a madman. I did not see him once, but S [probably Colonel Scammell] told [me] this morning that he did not seem inclined to lead alone, but as a prominent object among the enemy should present itself, he would seize the rifle-gun and take deliberate aim.[10]

Thus, while he placed his division commander on the battlefield, Poor did not credit him with exercising responsible command. Considering his remarkable testimony is appropriate for three reasons. First, Poor apparently saw nothing of Arnold within the camp, which argues for Arnold's being on the field. Second, Poor reported what he had been told by someone else—probably Scammell, commander of the 3rd New Hampshire Regiment—which was on line with Morgan's riflemen by 1:30 p.m. Third, Poor was not an Arnold partisan. He had been president of the court-martial that acquitted Moses Hazen and ordered Arnold's arrest in December 1776—the same arrest that Gates declined to execute. Poor's evidence was circumstantial and portrays Arnold's conduct in an unfavorable light—but it is important.

Hezekiah Smith was chaplain to Colonel Thomas Nixon's 6th Massachusetts Regiment, a unit of Brigadier General John Nixon's command (the brigade posted on the extreme right blocking the road to Albany and not an active participant in the fighting). In his 1885 editing of Smith's papers, Reuben A. Gould quoted the chaplain as saying that Arnold personally commanded his division. Later writers identified Smith's papers as a source testifying that Arnold exercised that command on the Freeman farm.

Of the American participants cited, three (Wilkinson, John Neilson, and Ezra Buel) unequivocally denied that Arnold personally led his men into combat. Henry Brockholst Livingston and Richard Varick credited him with directing the battle. Neither, however, placed him anywhere but in camp, and Varick's letter credited Arnold with "ordering out troops." General Poor reported that he had been told Arnold participated in the fighting, more as a private soldier than as a division commander. Chaplain Smith said that Arnold commanded his division, but that he was more than two miles from the battle line (and so may not have meant the general exercised personal command on the field). Robert R. Livingston wrote explicitly to Washington that Arnold was not present on the field.[12]

James Wilkinson's unsavory character invites skepticism. The details recounted in his *Memoirs*, however, stand up well when compared with facts established by more respectable sources. He published his book in 1816, while Richard Varick, Henry Brockholst, Henry Livingston, Morgan Lewis, and Robert Troup—men in positions to know whether he lied—were alive. Five colonels who commanded units that fought during September 19 were also alive in 1816: Rufus Putnam, 5th Massachusetts; Edward Wigglesworth, 13th Massachusetts; William Shepard, 4th Massachusetts; Philip Van Cortlandt, 2nd New York; and James Livingston, Canadian Regiment. Henry Dearborn, who commanded the light infantry and was later secretary of war, was also alive and publicly prominent. Yet, a diligent search of contemporary published literature (some of it characterized by controversy and vituperation) and surviving correspondence and personal papers has failed to produce a refutation of Wilkinson's account of the battle.

The confusion and smoke of combat precluded the recognition of individual American officers by British and German combatants. Max von Eelking, editor of the English edition of von Riedesel's correspondence and journals, however, asserted that Arnold personally led the American soldiers. An examination of von Riedesel manuscripts in the New York Public Library's Bancroft Collection and the Niedersaechische Staatsarchiv, Wolfenbuttel, does not support Eelking's statement. The baron's letter to the Duke of Brunswick mentions only one officer by name: Horatio Gates.[13] In none of his papers deposited in Wolfenbuttel did von Riedesel credit Arnold with personal participation, noting only that he had learned that the American troops were from Arnold's Division. Von Eelking took so many liberties when he edited the German's papers that using his work requires caution.

Secondary sources disagree on Arnold's role at Freeman's Farm. One of the earliest to comment was Charles Neilson, who in 1844 contradicted his own father's firsthand testimony by writing that Arnold, on a gray horse, returned from the battlefield and asked Gates for reinforcements. The latter responded, "You shall have them, sir," and immediately ordered out Learned's Brigade, whereupon Arnold rushed back "at full gallop and the men after him in double quick time."[13] Charles Neilson's book embalmed many errors, confusing the events of September 19 and October 7, and inventing dialogue for which there is no corroborating evidence. Believing that he accurately portrayed Arnold as leaving the firing line to ride back to camp for reinforcements rather than sending a courier requires a suspension of critical faculties and reflects a gross ignorance of command practice.

A more serious writer was the Italian scholar Charles Botta, who, without citing a single source, wrote that "Arnold exhibited upon this occasion all the impetuosity of his courage; he encouraged his men with voice and example."[14] Arnold's kinsman, Isaac N. Arnold, penned an extravagant, undocumented story of the general's career that included such details as the color of his horse and verbatim dialogue unreported by any contemporary.[15]

Historian-writer Hoffman Nickerson, as usual, wrote the most influential version of Arnold's personal role. After describing von Riedesel's attack on the American right on Freeman's farm, he followed Wilkinson's account—with one important difference:

> At this moment the Americans were without the dashing leadership of Arnold, who had ridden back to ask for reinforcements. In answer to his request Gates ordered out a whole brigade, that of Learned. Gates and Arnold were for the moment listening together to the sound of firing, Arnold sitting on a gray horse, when Colonel Morgan Lewis, Gates' Quarter-master general, . . . who rode in and reported the action still undecided. Whereat the vehement Arnold exclaimed, "By God ! I'll soon put an end to it!" And spurred off at a gallop. Hardly had he done so, however, when Lewis said to Gates that the latter had better order him back, since the action was going well and Arnold by some rash act might do mischief. Gates therefore despatched Wilkinson, who overtook

Arnold and transmitted Gates' order to return to camp, which Arnold obeyed.[16]

Nickerson ignored contemporary testimonies, of which he was certainly aware, and invoked unreliable Charles Neilson and inventive Isaac Arnold to represent Arnold as having led an unidentified part of his command into battle, then returned to camp to request reinforcements. The captain knew enough military history to know that no responsible general officer would leave his men on the firing line to function as his own courier, returning to solicit support. Nickerson's detestation of Gates led him to enhance Arnold's role.

Christopher Ward's readable *The War of the Revolution* contains a riveting description of Arnold dramatically leading his entire division into battle and securing a victory that fell short of being complete only because Gates thwarted his delivering the knock-out blow.[17] Two of Arnold's recent biographers have categorically placed him at the head of the battle line. Willard Sterne Randall, combining Wilkinson's and Isaac Arnold's versions with other unnamed sources, tells an equally stirring story.[18] Other students have been equally divided.

Benedict Arnold left us a brief written account regarding his role in the fighting. "On the 19th just when advice was received that the enemy was approaching," penned the angry general to his commander just three days later on September 22, "I took the liberty to give as my Opinion that we ought to march out and attack them, you desired me to send Colonel Morgan and the light infantry and support them. I obeyed your Orders, and before the Action was over I found it necessary to send out the whole of my Division to support the attack no other troops were Engaged that day," he continued, "except Colonel Marshals Regt of General Paterson's Brigade."[19]

Arnold wrote nothing suggesting that he had to argue his tactical case with Gates, that he acted on his own initiative, nor that he led his division into battle. Gates desired him to "send" Morgan and the light infantry, and "before the Action was over, I found it necessary to send out the whole of my Division." His statement is consistent with the fact that he committed his troops piecemeal, one brigade at a time, which argues against his personally "leading" them. We know that his subordinate brigade commanders remained in camp. Believing Arnold left his commanders there while he led their men in successive commitments onto the field of battle, returning to camp to bring up reinforcements, strains credulity. If he had, in fact, initiated the American action, had led his men into combat, and been denied requested support,

Benedict Arnold would have reminded Gates of those facts in a letter penned in the midst of the bitter quarrel that erupted between the two generals.

Livingston and Varick did not place Arnold at the head of his troops on Freeman's farm. "[T]his I further know," wrote Varick in a September 22 letter to General Schuyler, "that he [Gates] Asked where the Troops were going, when Scammils Batt marched & upon being Answered, he declared no more should go, he would not suffer the Camp to be exposed." Varick concluded: "Had Gates complyed [sic] with Arnolds Repeated Desires, he would have gained a Genl. & Compleat Victory over the Enemy."[20]

Upon that unsupported allegation, later writers constructed an indictment of Gates' competence. William L. Stone, an early and energetic student of the campaign to whom we owe much, never missed an opportunity to disparage the man who displaced Philip Schuyler. "Arnold was not only the hero of the field, but he had won the admiration of the whole army," Stone wrote, kicking off what would become an influential paragraph:

> There was not a man, officer or private who had participated in the battle, or who witnessed the conflict who did not believe that if Gates had sent reinforcements, as Arnold again and again begged him to do, he would have utterly routed the whole British army. So general was this belief, and so damaging to Gates, that as an excuse to save himself from reproaches coming from every side he gave out as the reason that the store of powder and ball in the camp was exhausted, and the supplies of ammunition from Albany had not arrived. No one could dispute this, yet none believed it.[21]

Mr. Stone may have known of contemporary sources supporting that sweeping interpretation. If he did, he did not identify and cite them.

Sir John Fortesque declared in his magisterial history of the British Army that "Had Gates sent to Arnold the reinforcements for which he asked, Arnold would certainly have broken the British center."[22] Much-traveled Benson Lossing carried that interpretation a step further when he wrote, "Had he [Arnold] been seconded by his commander, and strengthened by reinforcements . . . he would doubtless have secured a complete victory. But for Arnold on that eventful day, Burgoyne would doubtless have marched into Albany at the autumnal equinox a victor. . . ."[23]

Hoffman Nickerson penned the classic indictment of Gates when he accused him of keeping Arnold from rejoining his division and failing to take advantage of von Riedesel's move to Freeman's farm by attacking the column the German commander left behind in the valley and destroying Burgoyne's stores, thus ending the campaign.[24]

Christopher Ward, a better stylist than Nickerson, wrote what is arguably the most coherent condemnation of Gates. Accepting Nickerson's and Lossing's accounts and ignoring all primary sources, he accused the general of refusing to reinforce the men on the battle line, depriving them of Arnold's leadership, and failing to attack Burgoyne's left column after von Riedesel moved to Brigadier General James Hamilton's support.[25]

In summation, those accounts assert that Gates refused Arnold's requests for reinforcements, apparently from among the men posted on his right wing. While no contemporary evidence supports that thesis, it has gained wide acceptance. Even if supporting evidence should surface, Gates could have pled sound strategic reasons for not withdrawing men from the wing that was the key to why he had positioned his army on Bemis Heights: interdiction of Burgoyne's only viable route to Albany. Gates knew from reconnaissance that Burgoyne had posted a column on the road and he was ignorant of von Riedesel's movement from the road to support Hamilton's left.

A Detailed Analysis

Assessing those interpretations, which have been shared by other students, requires reviewing in some detail the sequence of American commitments between 3:00 and 6:30 in the afternoon and evening of September 19. Because the sources are less than precise about timing events, the times that several units departed camp and deployed in the field are approximations arrived at by examining the evidence as carefully as possible and applying the information to determining, as logically as possible, the time required to move regiments in formation under the conditions in existence on the field.

The first American regiment to join the fighting during the second half of the afternoon was the 2nd New York, which left Enoch Poor's Brigade's sector of the camp between 3:00 and 3:30, covered the 1 and 3/10-mile approach march, and deployed on Henry Dearborn's left by 4:30. They were followed, about thirty minutes later, by the 4th New York, which by 5:00 p.m. had deployed between the 1st New Hampshire and Cook's Connecticut Militia. Thirty minutes thereafter, Latimore's Connecticut Militia fell in between Cook and Dearborn to counter Fraser's threat to flank the Americans fighting Hamilton's men on Freeman's farm.[26]

By 5:00 p.m., Fraser was posing a more serious threat to overlap and turn the American main line by advancing the British 24th Regiment, Alexander Fraser's rangers, and the British and German grenadiers about 650 yards, forming a right angle by deploying northward for seventy yards.[27] That was the most dangerous threat the Americans had yet faced, and Arnold and Gates responded by committing the 10th Massachusetts Regiment from Paterson's Brigade and the first brigade-sized reinforcement, Learned's Brigade.[28]

Nickerson, Ward, and Randall cited Learned's deployment to illustrate Gates' culpability in keeping Arnold from exercising personal command on the line at a critical juncture. Nickerson set the tone:

> By recalling Arnold Gates deprived the American troops engaged of command other than that of leaders of unit . . . Had Learned's brigade of over eight hundred effective rank and file been directed by Arnold, or indeed had any other superior officer familiar with the ground and the precise position of the units engaged, been on hand to command them, their intervention might still have brought victory . . . . Lacking such direction they went astray, and instead of joining the action against Burgoyne's centre column, they blundered against outposts of Fraser, leaving their comrades in the centre unaided.[29]

Ward seconded Nickerson with the statement that Learned, "Instead of striking the British center . . . led his men in a futile attack on Fraser's wing and was beaten off. All other aid, Gates refused."[30] Randall repeated the allegation that Learned "blundered" into position against Fraser because Arnold was not permitted to exercise his proper command function.[31] To summarize: if Gates had permitted Arnold to direct the fight from the vantage point of the battlefield, he would have deployed Learned's Brigade against von Riedesel's reinforcement, defeated the baron's attempt to save Hamilton, and decisively won the day.

The interpretation's validity depends upon four assumptions: (1) That Arnold had returned to headquarters from the field for reinforcements and been retained in camp by Gates; (2) That Fraser was inactive, posing no threat to the Americans engaged on Freeman's farm; (3) That Learned's mission was to attack von Riedesel; and (4) That Learned's incompetence made him "blunder" into a "futile" engagement with what Nickerson called Fraser's "outposts."

Contemporary evidence—especially Arnold's own description of how he exercised command—contradicts the first assumption. The fourth assumption is patently ridiculous because Learned, like the other brigade commanders, was in camp and was not on the field. The following observations address the two remaining assumptions. British and German sources testify that Fraser was active during the battle's second phase and that his column deployed westward on line, opposing Latimore, Dearborn, and Van Cortlandt, and before 5:00 p.m. threatened to turn their left. It was in response to that threat—not one posed by von Riedesel—that Arnold and Gates committed Learned's Brigade and the 10th Massachusetts Regiment. Von Riedesel did not receive Burgoyne's order to reinforce the center column until about the same time Learned's Brigade and Colonel Marshall's regiment left Bemis Heights. Thus, his column was not even on the way to Freeman's farm when they marched into battle. Learned's men did not get lost in the woods and blunder into the wrong position; rather, they went where Arnold sent them: to refuse Fraser's threat to flank the American line.

The responsible criticism that critics should level at Gates was for not reinforcing the main line of resistance. He certainly had the units available to do so. General John Glover's 2,100-man brigade occupied the position on Bemis Heights to the right of Arnold's Division. Committing it immediately after Learned's Brigade departed for the front—that is, about 5:30 p.m.—could have strengthened the line at a crucial time. Glover's men could have extended the American left, helping neutralize Fraser's threat from that direction. They could have served a more decisive purpose if they had deployed to the right, reinforcing that flank to meet and probably repulse von Riedesel's attack. Neither Arnold nor Gates knew, of course, that the German had come to Hamilton's assistance until between 5:30 p.m. and 6:00 p.m., but less reluctance on Gates' part to commit more men would have provided a potentially decisive tactical superiority. It is important, however, to remember that there is no credible contemporary evidence that he failed to make effective decisions in spite of Arnold's pleas to do otherwise.

Reinforcing the right would certainly have forced Burgoyne's center to withdraw from Freeman's farm to reinforce the column on the road to Albany. But Fraser's elite corps would have remained a dangerous and unpredictable factor. Fraser and Burgoyne formed a resourceful combination. A headlong charge and pursuit—and Americans had a predilection for headlong action— would have exposed them to attack on their left flank by relatively fresh troops, well-positioned for such an attack. Approaching darkness made even the best-coordinated action hazardous—and that kind of coordination did not mark American performance that day. Assuming that eliminating the British center would have ended the campaign on September 19 is assuming too much.

Including Glover's Brigade, Gates retained in their positions a total of some 4,412 men. His critics condemned him for not employing at least some of them to destroy the remains of the left column after von Riedesel moved to Hamilton's support and seizing the artillery train, bateaux, and supply wagons left on the Albany Road. The charge seems plausible until one considers the time factor. No one in the American camp knew what the left column's situation was until after von Riedesel attacked the American right flank on Freeman's farm—that is, until after 6:00 p.m. Colonel Andrew Colburn, who commanded the reconnaissance on the east side of the river, had rejoined his regiment, the 3rd New Hampshire, and sources do not document intelligence received from parties operating on the western side.[32] Assuming that Gates knew by 6:00 p.m. the size of the enemy force left on the Albany Road, was an attack that late in the day feasible? John Nixon's 1,200-man brigade was the unit closest to the road. Forming it for an effective two-mile-long approach march and attacking in column could not have been accomplished before dark.

As Don Higginbotham observed, Gates accurately took the measure of Burgoyne when he occupied and fortified Bemis Heights.[33] He chose a prudent, economical strategy for frustrating his enemy's designs, one that he was capable of modifying at Arnold's suggestion. As they had in 1776, the two generals complemented each other and achieved a strategic victory that cost their enemy at least 600 irreplaceable men. American losses numbered just 319—substantially fewer than a more aggressive tactic would have produced. Most important, they stopped the advance to Albany and imposed a delay when every delay made American victory more nearly certain. Sadly, within three days ambition, vanity, and petty partisanship destroyed that remarkable American partnership.

Appendix I

Composition of Burgoyne's "Reconnaissance in Force" and Testimony Regarding its Objectives, October 7, 1777

Loyalist Lieutenant Joshua Pell, Junior, detailed the composition:

Captain [Alexander] Fraser's Company: one captain, two subalterns, 50 rank and file;

Canadian Volunteers and Provincials: two captains, four subalterns, 100 rank and file;

British grenadiers: one major, five captains, ten subalterns, 250 rank and file;

24th British Regiment: one lieutenant colonel, four captains, nine subalterns, 200 rank and file;

Total Advance Corps: one lieutenant colonel, two majors, seventeen captains, thirty-five subalterns, 950 rank and file.

Lieutenant Colonel Breymann's Corps: one captain, one subaltern, 100 rank and file.

Detachments from the British regiments of the Line (9th, 20th, 21st, and 62nd): three captains, five subalterns, 300 rank and file;

Detachments from German Regiments, Riedesel, Rhetz, Specht, and Hesse-Hanau: one lieutenant colonel, three captains, seven subalterns, 300 rank and file.

Royal artillery: number of officers not recorded, 100 rank and file.

Total: two lieutenant colonels, two majors, twenty-four captains, forty-eight subalterns, 1,700 rank and file.

(Note: The total rank and file given by Pell exceeds the numbers given by Burgoyne and Riedesel.)[1]

Testimony During the Parliamentary Inquiry Concerning Burgoyne's Objectives, October 7, 1777

During the hearings several of the expedition's officers responded to questioning by the general and commission members. The questions and the witnesses' responses limn a picture of conditions between the engagements and the motives that informed the action that initiated the battle of October 7. The testimony of Captain John Money, deputy quartermaster general, was especially informative. The duties of the 18th-century quartermaster were more diverse and extensive than those of his modern successor. In addition to procuring and distributing stores other than food and clothing, he was the staff officer charged with planning the movement of troops; the layout, organization, and construction of camps; and the supply and maintenance of teams, vehicles, and boats. Captain Money was thus an especially well-informed witness. The transcript of the thirty-seventh and thirty-eighth questions put to him reads:

> 37. Q. What was the nature of their [the American] position to the right with regard to entrenchments?
>
> A. They were posted on a hill that came very near the river. On the top of the hill was a strong breast-work, at the foot an abbatis.
>
> 38. Q. Did it appear to you that that wing was attackable?
>
> A. I do think that we could not have attacked the right wing of the rebel entrenchments without risking the loss of the whole army, and with little probability of success.[2]

More directly germane to establishing Burgoyne's objective was the exchange attending questions forty-five to and including forty-eight:

> 45. Q. Had you an opportunity, after you was [sic] a prisoner, to see the left of the enemy's entrenchments?
>
> A. I had.
>
> 46. Q. Was the ground within cannon shot of the left open and commanding it?
>
> A. All the ground I saw was cleared and entrenched.

47. Q. Was there not ground within cannon shot that would have commanded that entrenchment on the left?

A. There was.

48. Q. Had we gained possession of that ground, and been able to erect batteries of our heaviest guns, would not the whole line of the enemy have been enfiladed?

A. The ground alluded to was entrenched, and commanded the whole of the rebel camp and lines. If the army had got possession of that ground, I do not believe the rebels would have staid one hour in their camp.[3]

Money further testified that American officers told him that General Arnold had expressed the opinion that "If General Burgoyne should ever come near enough [to] their lines [as] to be able to make use of his artillery, that he would certainly possess himself of their camp; that their troops in that case would never stand anywhere. . . ."[4]

John Money's credibility does not depend solely upon his being deputy quartermaster general. He was not the callow scion of an aristocratic family who had purchased a sinecure. His career began in 1760, when he was twenty years old. The next year he participated in the battle of Frelinghausen. Nine years later he received a captain's commission in the 9th Regiment of Foot. In that capacity and as deputy quartermaster general, he served in Sir Guy Carleton's 1776 campaign. After Saratoga, he was exchanged and became a member of Lord Cornwallis' staff. Following service as a major, lieutenant colonel-commandant, major general, and lieutenant general, he became a general in the army on June 14, 1814, by which time he had written extensively on military subjects. Money knew what he was talking about and had the experience to back it up.[5]

Additional testimony contributes to understanding British intentions. One of the deponents was blunt Alexander Lindsey, earl of Balcarres and Crawford, commander of the British light infantry and Fraser's successor to command of the Advanced Corps. His Lordship was not a cooperative witness, refusing to conform his statements to fit anyone's purposes—Burgoyne's or his critics—and he answered every question with terse (and rather refreshing) candor.

Someone, probably Burgoyne, asked: "Does your Lordship think it would have been advisable, in point of prudence, or just to brave troops, who have suffered severe loss, to attack an enemy the morning after that loss [20 September], posted within entrenchments, which it was impossible to reconnoitre?"

Balcarres replied: "That attempt was made on the 7th of October, and did not succeed."[6]

That was not the answer Burgoyne wanted. He had argued after his defeat that an attack without accurate knowledge of Gates' strength and position would have been a blunder. He framed his question to demonstrate that the deployment of October 7, since it failed, was not an attack, but a reconnaissance in force. Lord Balcarres knew otherwise and set the record straight when he bluntly called the movement what it was: an attack against a position that had not been reconnoitered, and was neither a reconnaissance nor a foraging expedition.

General Burgoyne was on the defensive and his parliamentary experience taught him that he faced censure and disgrace. He found being consistent under that circumstance difficult. When he questioned Captain Thomas Blomefield of the Royal Artillery, he reverted to an earlier contention, declaring that he intended "to gain the left of the enemy's entrenchment," and employed revealing language when he asked: "Do you remember the position of the King's troops from the time of the attack of the 7th October?" The captain replied in the affirmative.[7]

Lieutenant Colonel Robert Kingston, Burgoyne's adjutant general and military secretary, had served with his commander since August 1759, except for a period on half-pay during 1774 to 1776, and knew him more intimately over a longer period than any other staff member. He also enjoyed the personal friendship of Phillips, Fraser, and the engineer, William Twiss. If anyone was privy to Burgoyne's intentions, it was Robert Kingston, whose testimony reflects more accurately than any other the perception of Burgoyne's headquarters.

After the colonel had talked at some length about matters leading to the second engagement, Burgoyne posed the critical questions:

> Q. From your conversations with the chief engineer [Twiss], and other circumstances, have you reason to know, that every possible means were used after the action of the 19th to obtain a knowledge of the ground on the enemy's left?
>
> A. I had frequent conversations with the chief engineer on that subject. I believe his attention was given to that point almost every day, and knowledge of that ground I understood to be very difficult to be obtained.
>
> Q. Was not the right of the enemy deemed impractical?

A. I had no opportunity myself of seeing the right of the enemy; but I understand from others, that the position to be too strong to be attacked with any prospect of success.

Q. Did you conceive that the chief purpose of that movement [October 7] was to attain a knowledge of the left of the enemy's position, and if expedient to attack there?

A. I understood it was.[8]

Appendix J

Glossary of Military Terms

Adjutant: Staff officer responsible for official correspondence and records and of all orders except combat orders.

Aide-de-Camp: Personal assistant to a field or staff officer.

Artificer: Soldier mechanics who served with the artillery and engineers performing maintenance and repair of equipment and assisted in building defenses. The Continental Army had two regiments of artillery artificers. One, commanded by Jeduthan Baldwin, was present at Saratoga; the other was commanded by Benjamin Flower, which served with the Grand Army.

Battalion: During the Revolution, regiments consisted of one battalion and the terms were used synonymously. Commanded in the British Army by a lieutenant colonel, in the Continental Army by a colonel or a lieutenant colonel commandant. The standard British battalion had ten companies, while the American battalions varied in size, although they generally conformed to the British standard.

Battalion Companies: In the British Army, the eight companies that remained when the grenadiers and light infantry were detached to serve along with other grenadiers and light infantry in grenadier or light infantry battalions.

Coehorn Mortar: A small, brass, high-angle-of-fire artillery piece, sometimes mounted on wooden blocks.

Column: When soldiers stand shoulder-to-shoulder facing the front they form a *rank* or *line*; when they stand one behind the other, they constitute a *file*. Two or more files make a *column*.

Continentals: The "Regulars" of the American Army as distinguished from state militia. Most of the units actively engaged at Saratoga were Continentals, but the presence of a large number of militia gave General Horatio Gates a valuable deploying flexibility, especially in keeping a strong presence blocking the road to Albany.

Corps: A specialized tactical unit, such as Morgan's Corps of Riflemen.

Division: Two or more battalions/regiments.

Dragoon: Mounted troops who dismounted to fight.

Envelopment: An attack directed against the enemy's flank or flanks—a "turning movement."

Flank Companies: A regiment's light infantry and grenadier companies.

Frontal attack: An assault in which the committed force was distributed to strike the enemy along his entire front.

Fusil and fusiliers: A light flintlock musket developed during the 17th century for artillery guards, leading to the development of a special type of light infantry. Like the grenadiers, they continued to exist as elite units after their original mission had disappeared. Until a few years before the Revolution, infantry officers carried spontoons (a European-style lance), most of which were replaced by fusils.

Grenadiers: Special troops formed into one of the flank companies, named for soldiers who were originally powerful men who threw grenades or "hand bombs."

Howitzer: A short artillery piece with a high angle of fire.

Jagers or Chasseurs: Both terms mean hunters in German and French, respectively. Sharpshooters armed with rifles.

Light Infantry: Special, lightly equipped troops. Because riflemen were especially vulnerable to musket and bayonet attack due to the time required to load, Gates ordered Major Henry Dearborn to organize a 300-man musket-armed light infantry battalion to provide cover for the riflemen.

Matross: A soldier who assisted artillery gunners in loading, sponging, and moving guns.

Militia: State troops whose primary mission was to defend their home state. Part-time soldiers organized into classes that rotated when called into service by either the Continental or state authorities, they were sometimes poorly trained and incompetently led. When motivated and well led, however, they were effective even against regulars, as the fighting at Hubbardton and Bennington demonstrated.

Musicians: Military organizations had musicians who always included drummers. They, by standard beats, signaled commands as well as setting the pace of march, as did fifers and players of the hautboy, a type of oboe.

Musket: The standard shoulder weapon of the 18th century, a smoothbore piece that threw a large lead ball with limited accuracy, but was admirably fitted for the linear tactics of the period. Well-trained men could deliver a volley upon command at a rate of one shot every fifteen or twenty seconds. Effective range was about eighty yards. The caliber of most muskets was .75 inch. It could kill up to 300 yards. Because infantry formed compact masses, accuracy was of secondary importance.

Rank and File: A unit's enlisted men armed and present in a battle line, including corporals and privates but not sergeants and drummers. If one knows the number of rank and file of a British regiment, its total strength can be determined by adding 17.5 percent. Because American overhead was higher, 25 percent needed to be added to arrive at the corresponding number. Conversely, from a known total strength, one can get the number of rank and file by subtracting 14.8 percent from the British and 21.8 from the American.

Redan: A two-sided fieldwork pointed toward the enemy and open in the rear.

Redoubt: A completely enclosed fieldwork surrounding the main entrenchments, covering the main avenues of approach. Two redoubts, the Light Infantry (Balcarres) and Breymann, figured prominently in the fighting of October 7, 1777.

Rifle and Riflemen: The rifle barrel had lands and grooves and was capable of delivering aimed fire, as opposed to the smoothbore musket. It was used in Europe for hunting, but unknown in America until introduced by German and Swiss immigrants to Pennsylvania. It was not considered an effective military arm because of the time needed to reload and because it could not be fitted with a bayonet. Unlike the musket, which could be loaded with a cartridge, the rifle had to be loaded by pouring the proper amount of powder into the muzzle, followed by wadding and a ball seated in a cloth patch. Riflemen were superior to musketeers on certain missions, but no match for them in most battles. For that reason, General Gates ordered Morgan to brigade his rifleman with Dearborn's light infantry.

Appendix K

A Modern Photographic Tour
of Saratoga National Historical Park

This appendix offers readers a photo gallery of many significant and interesting portions of the battlefield at Saratoga. We included this gallery for several reasons.

First, these photos help readers better understand the terrain of the battlefield and so more fully appreciate the ebb and flow of the battle as described in the main text. This is accomplished by numbering each photograph and keying each image to the map that appears on the following page (403). Simply find the number of the photograph on the map to determine where on the field the image was captured. The map also depicts the direction of the camera when the photograph was taken.

Second, this photo gallery can be used as a quick and useful guide when you walk or drive the magnificent Saratoga battlefield.

Lastly, for a wide variety of reasons many people who study and enjoy Revolutionary War history never visit the hallowed ground upon which these important combats took place. Hopefully, these modern photographs will serve as a helpful (though admittedly poor) substitute for a tour in the flesh. And if they prompt a visit, all the better.

In Appreciation: These photos and captions would not have been possible but for the dedicated and timely assistance of Eric H. Schnitzer, Park Ranger/Historian, Saratoga National Historical Park. Eric enthusiastically endorsed the idea of a photo gallery, and enlisted the equally enthusiastic assistance of Jim McKnight, a former photographer for the AP who performs volunteer work at the park. Jim's magnificent photos and Eric's captions are a perfect match, and we believe tremendously enhance the value of Mr. Luzader's outstanding study. Thank you both.

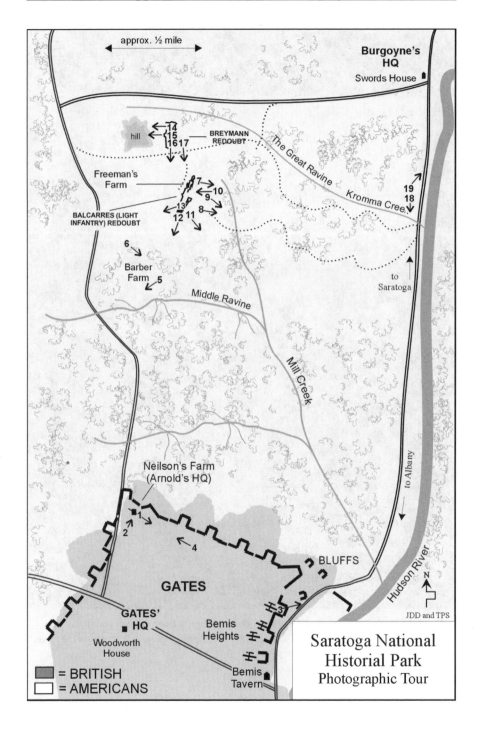

approx. ½ mile

Burgoyne's HQ
Swords House

hill
14
15
16 17
BREYMANN REDOUBT

The Great Ravine
Kromma Creek

Freeman's Farm
7
10
9
13
12 11 8

BALCARRES (LIGHT INFANTRY) REDOUBT

19
18

6

Barber Farm
5

Middle Ravine

to Saratoga

Mill Creek

Neilson's Farm (Arnold's HQ)

1
2
4

BLUFFS

GATES

Hudson River

to Albany

N

JDD and TPS

GATES' HQ
Woodworth House

Bemis Heights

Bemis Tavern

3

Saratoga National Historial Park
Photographic Tour

= BRITISH
= AMERICANS

Photo 1. This view, looking east toward Bemis Heights from the Neilson house porch, overlooks the main Army of the United States encampment ground. The park's tour road is visible in the background.

National Park Service, Saratoga National Historical Park

Photo 2. The John and Lydia Neilson house was built ca. 1776 and served as the headquarters for Major General Benedict Arnold and Brigadier General Enoch Poor. The original house, restored by the National Park Service, exists to this day.

Photo 3. This view, facing northeast and taken from an American army artillery corps battery position on Bemis Heights, overlooks the Hudson River valley. The line of trees on the far side of the field below the bluffs today lines the Hudson River. The commanding view of the valley, afforded by the bluffs, was essential to Army of the United States defensive strategy. *National Park Service, Saratoga National Historical*

Photo 4. Bemis Heights was not the highest point of ground defended by the Americans. This view, looking west from near Brigadier General John Paterson's brigade encampment, gives a good view of the "summit"—the highest point within the defensive network, topped by the Neilson House—upon which Brigadier General Enoch Poor's brigade encamped. *National Park Service. Saratoga National Historical Park*

Photo 5. The Simeon Barber Wheatfield, shown here looking west, is where the major fighting of the second battle began on October 7, 1777. The Royal Artillery light 6-pounder in the foreground is located near where the British grenadier battalion was deployed. Captain Georg Päusch's two British light 6-pounders are located in the field in the background. The distant hill was surmounted by Colonel Daniel Morgan's 'Corps, from which it attacked the British light infantry battalion on the adjacent Joshua Barber farm.

Photo 6. The George Coulter farm is where periphery fighting occurred during the Battle of Freeman's Farm on September 19, 1777. Brigadier-General Simon Fraser commanded the rearguard of the British forces retreating from the Barber farms in this field during the battle on October 7. It was near this area, on the southern side of this field, that Fraser was mortally wounded.

Photo 7. This view, looking east, was taken from the hill upon which the John and Effelina Freeman house stood. It was upon that extensive plateau that the Freemans cultivated their land, and where much of the Battle of Freeman's Farm took place. After that battle, Brigadier-General Simon Fraser's Advanced Corps encamped on the northern side of this field. *National Park Service, Saratoga National Historical*

Photo 8. This wooded branch of the Middle Ravine bounded the southern end of the Freeman Farm. It was on the southern (right) side of this ravine that Colonel Daniel Morgan's riflemen posted themselves on the American line's right flank, and from that position were able to shoot at the flank and rear of the 62nd Regiment of Foot, located on the open field to the west. Attempts made by the 20th Regiment of Foot to dislodge the riflemen were in vain due to their inability to successfully traverse this massive ravine and the abatis thrown up by Morgan's men. The riflemen suffered sixteen casualties in the battle; the 20th Regiment, 116.

Photo 9. This view, looking east, is from the plateau of Freeman's cultivated field from which the 20th Regiment of Foot attacked the riflemen in the woods to the south. It was from the far end of this field that Major General von Riedesel brought reinforcements to the fight, ending the battle of Freeman's Farm in Burgoyne's favor. *National Park Service, Saratoga National Historical Park*

Photo 10. This view, looking west, is from the plateau of Freeman's cultivated field. The sparsely tree-topped hill is where the Freeman house was located (near the trees in the center of the photograph), while the barn was located to the south (at the left edge of the photo). The massive British Light Infantry (or Balcarres) Redoubt was constructed on this height. *National Park Service, Saratoga National Historical Park*

Photo 11. During the battle of Freeman's Farm, both armies fought in the open fields and woods, although American regiments were keener on using the tree line for cover when it was advantageous. This view, over the barrel of a reproduction British light 6-pounder, looks in the direction of where Colonel Thaddeus Cook's Regiment of Connecticut Militia fought the left flank grand-division of the 62nd Regiment of Foot. *National Park Service, Saratoga National Historical Park*

Photo 12. Freeman's Farm, looking south, where the heaviest fighting took place. Both armies fought a mix of open field and wooded actions, although the British artillery was unable to support the infantry sent into the woods. The units primarily engaged here were all three New Hampshire Continental regiments, the 21st Royal North British Fusiliers, the 62nd Regiment of Foot, and Captain Thomas Jones' Royal Artillery detachment. *National Park Service, Saratoga National Historical Park*

Photo 13. This height is near the southwestern edge of Freeman's Farm. Heavy fighting took place here during both battles of Saratoga (September 19 and October 7). After the first battle at Freeman's Farm, British forces constructed a fortification on this hill. Although unsuccessful in his attempt to capture the nearby British Light Infantry (Balcarres) Redoubt during the second battle, Brigadier General Enoch Poor's brigade captured this small satellite fort. Today, this area is called the "Bloody Knoll." *National Park Service, Saratoga National*

Photo 14. Breymann's "Redoubt" was in fact composed of three separate elements: a main curtain manned by the Braunschweig Grenadier Battalion, Light Infantry Battalion von Bärner, and two British light 6-pounders manned by Hessen-Hanau artillerymen; a secondary curtain manned by Captain Alexander McKay's American Volunteers; and a small fort manned by Braunschweig jägers. The force-to- space ratio was dispersed when troops were siphoned off for the October 7 reconnaissance force, leaving the "Redoubt" vulnerable when Americans attacked later that evening. *National Park Service, Saratoga National Historical Park*

Photo 15. Another view from inside Breymann's "Redoubt." See the photo and description on the previous page for more information. *National Park Service, Saratoga National*

Photo 16. It was through this area that Major General Benedict Arnold joined other Continental troops assaulting the open rear of the Breymann Redoubt. Before he did so, two companies of Québec and Montréal French Canadian militia, garrisoning two cabins located in this field, were overpowered by American forces. The four corners of the cabins are today marked with white and red posts, one set of which can be seen here. *National Park Service, Saratoga National Historical Park*

Photo 17. The 1887 "Boot Monument" commemorates the service of "the most brilliant soldier of the Continental Army who was desperately wounded on this spot," at the open rear of the Breymann Redoubt. The view looks southeast, the direction from which Benedict Arnold approached and made his attack. *National Park Service, Saratoga National Historical Park*

Photo 18. This view looks south from atop the Great Redoubt hill overlooking the Great Ravine through which runs Kromma Creek and an entrance road into the park. Despite its name, the Great Redoubt was not a large fortification. It was so named because it overlooked the Great Ravine. *National Park Service, Saratoga National Historical Park*

Photo 19. This majestic view is from the Great Redoubt looking northeast up the Hudson River Valley. Burgoyne's river fortifications, including the Great Redoubt, protected the park of artillery, general hospital, bateaux, Royal Navy detachment, native warriors and refugee families, most of the army's loyalists, artificers, local civilian refugees, and the army's six accompanying officer families. It was down this valley that Burgoyne's army descended, and up this same valley that his army withdrew following the battles of Saratoga.

National Park Service, Saratoga National Historical Park

Notes

1. National Archives, Papers of the Continental Congress, 17 January 1776.

2. Don Higginbotham, *The War of American Independence, Military Attitudes, Policies, and Practice* (New York, 1971), 115.

3. Sir John Fortesque, *A History of the British Army.* Thirteen volumes (London, 1899-1930), III, 165, 243.

4. Douglas Southall Freeman, *George Washington: A Biography.* Seven volumes (New York, 1947-57), IV, 97.

5. Gates Papers, New York Historical Society, Schuyler to Gates, 25 June 1776.

6. Piers Mackesy, *The War for America* (Cambridge, Massachusetts, 1964), 95.

7. Gates Papers, Dr. Jonathan Potts to Gates, 8 August 1776; Gates to Washington, 28 August 1776.

8. *Ibid.,* Gates to Arnold, 13 and 17 August 1776.

9. *Ibid.,* Schuyler to Gates, 18 July 1776, Gates to Schuyler, *American Archives,* 22 July 1776; George Clinton Papers, New York State Library, Albany, Gates to Varick, 16 August 1776.

10. Peter Force, editor, *American Archives: A Documentary History of the Origin and Progress of the American Colonies.* Nine volumes (Washington, 1837-1853), Series 5, volume I, 1123, II, 1039.

11. Gates Papers, Gates to Arnold, 14 August 1776.

12. *Ibid.,* Arnold to Gates, 12 October 1776.

13. Force, *op. cit.,* Series 5, II, 1039.

14. *Ibid.,* II, 224.

15. Willard M. Wallace, *Traitorous Hero: The Life and Fortunes of Benedict Arnold* (New York, 1954), 118.

16. National Archives, "General Return of the Forces of the United States of America Serving in the Northern Department under the Hon. General Gates, Sept 19, 1776.

17. Force, *op. cit.,* Series 5, III, 701

Chapter 1

1. See the Chronology in the Appendix to illustrate how the vagaries of timing affected the events of 1777.

2. British Public Record Office [PRO], *Colonial Office Papers* [CO] 5/93, 609-15, Howe to Germain, 30 November 1776.

3. Ira D. Gruber, *The Howe Brothers and the American Revolution* (Chapel Hill, 1972), 156-57, 179-80, 194, 199-200.

4. Germain Papers, William L.Clements Library, Ann Arbor, Michigan, Germain to North.

5. PRO, CO 5/94, 1-12, Germain to Howe, 14 January 1777.

6. Piers Mackesy, *The War For America 1775-1783* (Cambridge, 1964), 110-11.

7. Troyer Steele Anderson, *The Command of the Howe Brothers During the American Revolution* (New York and London, 1936), 216-17.

8. PRO, CO 5/94, 1-12, Germain to Howe, 14 January 1777.

9. William Livingston, *A Memoir of the Life of William Livingston*, Theodore Sedgwick, editor (New York, 1833), 29.

10. John A. Neuenschwander, *The Middle Colonies and the Coming of the American Revolution* (Port Washington and London, 1973), 29-30.

11. PRO, CO 5/94, 41-50, Howe to Germain, 20 December 1776.

12. *Ibid.*

13. *Ibid.*

14. *Ibid.*

15. Mackesy, op. cit., 92, 98, 112, 116-118, 125, 150-51; Freeman, *George Washington*, IV, 290-94, 321-25, 274-76, 303-09, 311-26, 328-31; Fortesque, *A History of the British Army*, III, 201; Thomas Jefferson Wertenbaker, "The Battle of Trenton," *The Princeton Battle Monument* (Princeton, 1922).

16. Higginbotham, *op. cit.*, 170-71.

17. Gruber, *op. cit.*, 156-57.

18. PRO, CO 5/94, 41-50, Howe to Germain, 20 January 1777.

19. Gerald Howson, *Burgoyne of Saratoga: A Biography* (New York, 1974), 128; James Lunt, *John Burgoyne of Saratoga* (New York, 1975), 109.

20. PRO, CO 42/35, 449, "Memorandum of General Carleton relative to the next campaign communicated to Lt. Genl. Burgoyne to be laid before Government."

21. PRO, CO 43/36, 11-27, "Memorandum & Observations relative to Service in Canada submitted to Lord George Germain."

22. *Ibid.*

23. *Ibid.*

24. *Ibid.*

25. John Burgoyne may have, as most scholars reasonably believed, written his "Observations" with himself in mind as commander of the campaigning army. Be that as it may, he was also obeying orders Sir Guy gave when he entrusted his memorandum to him for transmission to the government. His "Observations" were valuable both to cabinet members and future students in helping understand problems inherent in conducting the war "from the Side of Canada."

26. Alan Valentine, *Lord George Germain* (London, 1962), 155.

27. PRO, CO 42/35, Burgoyne to Germain, 9 December 1776.

28. According to an issue of the London *Chronicle*, Lord Germain received that correspondence at his house in Pall Mall during the evening of the ninth. Howson, *op. cit.*, 314.

29. PRO, CO 43/13, 138, Carleton to Germain, 22 October 1776.

30. See Appendix A for extensive details on this debate.

31. John Fortesque, editor, *Correspondence of George III from 1760 to December 1783*. Six volumes (London, 1927-28), III, Number 1936, Germain to the King, 11 December 1776.

32. *Ibid.*, 1938, George III to North, 13 December 1776.

33. William B. Willcox, *Portrait of A General: Sir Henry Clinton in the War of Independence* (New York, 1964), 130-31.

34. *Ibid.*, 129.

35. *Ibid.*, 131.

36. Willcox, *op. cit.*, 177.

37. *Ibid.*, 133.

38. Fortesque, editor, *Correspondence of George III*, III, Number 1964, George III to North, 15 February 1777.

39. Willcox, *op. cit.*, 335-36.

40. *Ibid.*, 137.

41. PRO, CO 42/36, 37, ff; Germain Papers, William L. Clements Library, Ann Arbor, Michigan; State of the Expedition, Appendix III.

42. Mackesy, *op. cit.*, 10, 14.

43. The former was the more probable consultant. The "conqueror of Canada" was familiar with the northern frontier. Although Harvey, in the absence of a commander-in-chief, shared with Secretary at War Lord Barrington important functions of that post, his influence with Germain and the Cabinet was limited.

44. *Correspondence of George III*, III, Number 1996, "Remarks on the Conduct of the War from Canada; British Museum, Additional Manuscripts, 18, 738, 196 "Remarks on the Conduct of the War from Canada."

45. Lunt, *op. cit.*, 124.

46. PRO, CO 5/94, 41-50, Howe to Germain, 20 December 1776.

47. PRO, CO 5/94, 215, Germain to Howe, 3 March 1777.

48. PRO, CO 42/36, 101-13, Germain to Carleton, 26 March 1777; State of the Expedition, Appendix IV; PRO 30/55, Carleton Papers Number 462.

49. See Appendix A for further details.

50. PRO, CO 5/94, 339-44, Germain to Howe, 18 May 1777.

51. State of the Expedition, Appendix III, "Thoughts for Conducting the War from the Side of Canada, IX.

52. William Cobbett, *The Parliamentary History of England from The Earliest Period to the Year 1803*, 36 vols. (London, 1806-30), XIX: 434.

53. PRO, CO 5/94, 299-303, Howe to Germain, 5 April 1777 (confidential).

54. *Ibid.*

55. State of the Expedition, Appendix X, "Copy of a Letter from Sir William Howe, dated New York, July the 17th 1777."

56. Germain Papers, William L. Clements Library, Ann Arbor, Michigan, Howe to Germain 16 July 1777.

57. During the eighteen days that elapsed before favorable winds permitted Sir William to sail, the two mutually uncongenial generals had several conversations. Following a suggestion offered by his friend, Major General William Phillips, Sir Henry kept a detailed record of everything he said and did. He recorded the conversations as he remembered them, apparently very shortly after they took place. Those records are unusually candid in that they do not omit Clinton's mistaken guesses, nor do they include mention of subsequent events that proved him to be right. He simply recorded the event or conversation; and for the reasons just cited, they are authoritative. Not surprisingly, conversations between him and Howe frequently concerned the northern campaign and the impending expedition against Pennsylvania.

58. Henry Clinton Papers, William L. Clements Library, "Memorandum of Conversation with General Howe, 13 July 1777."

59. Henry Clinton, *The American Rebellion: Sir Henry Clinton's Narrative of His Campaigns, 1775-1782, With an Appendix of Original Documents*, William B. Willcox, editor (Hamden, Connecticut, 1971), 62, "Memorandum of 8 and 13 July conversations."

60. Clinton Papers, "Memorandum of Conversation with General Howe, 8 July 1777."

61. *Ibid.*, Clinton to Harvey, 11 July 1777.

62. Clinton, *op. cit.*, 60-61.

63. *Ibid.*, 64.

64. PRO, CO 5/94, 729-34, Howe to Germain, 22 October 1777.

65. See Appendix A for further discussion.

66. See Appendix A for further discussion of what Burgoyne knew and when he knew it about Howe's intentions.

Chapter 2

1. *State of the Expedition,* 3; *Ibid.,* Appendix IV, xii-xviii, "Extract of a Letter from Lord George Germain to General Carleton, dated Whitehall, 26th 1777," Germain Papers, William L. Clements Library, Ann Arbor, Michigan, 26 March 1777; PRO, 42 / 36, Carleton to Burgoyne, 10 June 1777; Howson, *op. cit.,* 151; Lunt, *op. cit.,* 138.

2. *State of the Expedition,* Appendix I, "Army from Canada under Lieutenant-General Burgoyne, Total Rank and File, 1st of July, 1777 [sick included]."

3. Howson, *op. cit.,* 157.

4. Lunt, *op. cit.,* 141.

5. *Ibid.*

6. *Ibid.,* Appendix I, "Order of Battle-The Expedition from Canada-1777"; *Hadden's Journal and Orderly Books: A Journal Kept in Canada and Upon Burgoyne's Campaign in 1776 and 1777, by Lieut. James M. Hadden, Royal Artillery. Also Orders kept by him and issued by Sir Guy Carleton, Lieut. General John Burgoyne and Major General William Phillips in 1776, 1777 and 1778, With Explanatory Notes by Horatio Rogers* (Albany, 1884), hereafter cited as Hadden, *Journal,* 44-47.

7. Lunt, *op. cit.,* 144; Hadden, *Journal,* 67.

8. *Ibid.,* lxi-lxv.

9. *Ibid.,* xlviii; *Army Lists* (London, 1775-1785); Public Record Office [PRO] Army Lists for 1777 and 1778, 30.

10. *State of the Expedition,* lvi, Appendix, "Extract of a Letter To General Harvey, Montreal, May 19, 1777."

11. *Ibid.*

12. PRO, CO 5/94, Howe to Carleton, 5 April 1777.

13. *State of the Expedition,* 9.

14. *Ibid.,* xviii "Copy of a Letter from Lieutenant-General Burgoyne to Lord George Germain, Dated Quebec, May 14, 1777 [Private]."

15. *State of the Expedition,* PRO, CO 42/36, 401, 402, "24 and 25 May 1777."

16. Ibid., liii-liv, "Extract of a Letter from Major-General Phillips to Lieutenant-General Burgoyne, Montreal, June 5, 1777"; "Extract of a Letter from Major-General Phillips to Lieutenant-General Burgoyne, &c, Dated Montreal June 5, 1777."

17. *Ibid.;* Copy of a Letter from Major-General Phillips Relating to a Horse, Dated June 4, 1777."

18. *Ibid.,* Liii-liv, "Extract of a Letter from Lieutenant-General Burgoyne to Major-General Phillips, Dated Montreal, June 6, 1777.

19. *Ibid.,* "Extract of a Letter to Nathaniel Day, Esq. Commissary-General, Dated Montreal, June 4, 1777."

20. *Ibid.*, lv-lvi, "Extract of a Letter to Sir Guy Carleton, Montreal, June 7, 1777."

21. Hadden, *Journal*, 51.

22. *State of the Expedition,* lx, "Extract of a Letter from Lieutenant-General Burgoyne to General Harvey, July 11, 1777."

23. *Ibid.*, 52; *Continental Journal and Weekly Advertiser,* Boston, 19 September 1777.

24. Hadden, *op. cit.*, "Copy of Gen'l Burgoyne Proclamation."

25. *State of the Expedition*, xxi-xxv, Appendix, "Substance of the Speech of Lieutenant-General Burgoyne to the Indians, in Congress at the Camp upon the River Bouquet, June 21, 1777, and their Answer, translated."

26. *Ibid.*

27. *Henry Steele Commager and Richard B. Morris, The Spirit of Seventy-Six: The Story of the American Revolution told by Participants.* Two volumes (Indianapolis and New York), II, 349, "An Answer to General Burgoyne."

28. *Ibid.*

29. Roger Lamb, *Memoirs of His Own Life* (Dublin, 1811), 135.

30. E. B. O'Callaghan, *Orderly Book of Liet. Gen. John Burgoyne from His Entry Into the State of New York Until His Surrender at Saratoga, 16th Oct., 1777. From the Original Manuscripts Deposited at Washington's Head Quarters, Newburgh Head Quarters* (Albany, 1860), hereafter cited as *Burgoyne's Orderly Book,* 11-13, General Order, Camp Crown Point, June 28, 1777.

31. *Ibid.*, 16-17, General Order, Crown Point, 30th June 1777.

Chapter 3

1. Hoffman Nickerson, *The Turning Point of the Revolution Or Burgoyne in America* (Boston, 1929), 131; David Paul Nelson, *General Horatio Gates: A Biography* (Baton Rouge, 1976), 91.

2. Papers of the Continental Congress, National Archive, Washington, D. C., Gates to Hancock, 11 May 1777.

3. Nickerson, *op. cit.*, 138.

4. *Ibid.*, 123.

5. Philip Schuyler Papers, New York Public Library, St. Clair to Schuyler, 13 June 1777.

6. James Wilkinson, *Memoirs of My Own Times.* Three volumes (Philadelphia, 1816), I, 173.

7. Nickerson, *op. cit.*, 138-39.

8. Wilkinson, *op. cit.*, I, 174-76.

9. *State of the Expedition*, Appendix III, "Thoughts for Conducting the War from the Side of Canada," Narrative, 13.

10. James M. Hadden, *A Journal Kept in Canada and Burgoyne's Campaign in 1776 and 1777 by Lieut. James Hadden, Roy Art.* (Albany, 1884), 306-07.

11. *Burgoyne's Orderly Book,* 11-13, General Order, 28 June 1777.

12. *Ibid.,* 16-20, General Order, 30 June 1777.

13. *Ibid.,* 82, entry 1 July 1777.

14. *Ibid.*

15. *Ibid.,* 24-25, General Order, 3 July 1777.

16. *Ibid.*

17. *Ibid.*

18. *Ibid.,* 26-27, General Order, 4 July 1777.

19. James Phinney Baxter, ed., *The British Invasion From the North: The Campaigns of General Carleton and Burgoyne From Canada, 1776-77. With the Journal of Lieut. William Digby of the 53d or Shropshire Regiment of Foot* (Albany, 1887), 204-05, hereafter Digby, *Journal.*

20. Hadden, *Journal,* 54; *State of the Expedition,* Appendix, xxiv-xxvii.

21. *State of the Expedition,* Appendix, VII, "Journal of the late principal Proceedings of the Army," xxiv.

22. Hadden, *Journal,* 84-85.

23. Wilkinson, *op. cit.,* I, 174-76.

24. Jonathan Gregory Rossie, *The Politics of Command in the American Revolution* (Syracuse, 1875), 158-60.

25. Schuyler Papers, Schuyler to Washington, 18 July 1777.

26. John Jay Papers, New York Historical Society, Alexander Hamilton to John Jay, 13 July 1777.

27. Schuyler Papers, Schuyler to Washington, 18 July 1777.

28. Journal of the Continental Congress, 11 July 1777.

29. Gates Papers, Arnold to Gates, 18 July 1777.

30. Mark Boatner, *The Encyclopedia of the American Revolution* (Crown: New York, 1974), 21.

31. *Ibid.,* 956-57.

32. *Ibid.*

33. *State of the Expedition,* Appendix VII, "Journal of the late principal Proceedings of the Army," xxx.

34. *Burgoyne's Orderly Book,* 28-29, General Order 6 July 1777.

35. Christopher Ward, *The War of the Revolution.* Two volumes (New York, 1952), I, 412; John Williams, *The Battle of Hubbardton: The American Rebels Turn the Tide* (Vermont Division of Historic Preservation), 8.

36. New York Historical Society, *Collections (*1880), 31, "Court Martial of General St. Clair, White Plains, New York, August 28, 1778," hereafter cited as St. Clair Court Martial.

37. *Ibid.,* 87.

38. Wilkinson, *op. cit.,* I, 184.

39. *Ibid.,* 186-87.

40. Hadden, *Journal,* 85.

41. Nickerson, *op. cit.,* 149.

42. *Ibid.,* 150.

43. St. Clair Court Martial.

44. Ward, *op. cit.,* I, 413.

45. *Ibid.*

46. Wilkinson, *op. cit.,* 186-87.

47. *Ibid.,* 187-90.

48. Riedesel Urkunden, "Journal des Feldzugs; Senden, Tagebuch von Senden, Niedersächsisches Staatsarchiv, Wolfenbüttel.

49. Tagebuch von Senden.

50. Ward, *op. cit.,* I, 413.

51. *Ibid.*

52. Nickerson, *op. cit.,* 152.

Chapter 4

1. *Burgoyne's Orderly Book,* 33-34; *State of the Expedition,* Appendix, No VII, "Copy of a Letter from Lieutenant General Burgoyne to Lord George Germain, dated Skenesborough July 15, 1777," enclosing "Journal of the late proceedings of the Army," hereafter cited as "Journal of the late Proceedings of the Army."

2. *Ibid.,* Wilkinson, *op. cit.,* I, 215.

3. Roger Lamb, *Memoirs of His Own Life* (Dublin, 18), 142.

4. *State of the Expedition,* "Journal of the late Proceedings of the Army"; Wilkinson, *Memoirs of My Own Times.* 3 vols. (Philadelphia, 1816), I, 189.

5. Wilkinson, *Memoirs of My Own Times,* I, 189.

6. *Burgoyne's Orderly Book,* General Order, 10 July 1777.

7. *State of the Expedition,* Appendix No. III, "Thoughts for Conducting the War from the Side of Canada."

8. *Ibid.*

9. Nickerson, *op. cit.,* 163; Digby, *Journal,* 273.

10. Ibid.

11. Thomas Jones, *History of New York During the Revolutionary War.* 2 vols. (New York, 1879), I, 137-38.

12. Nickerson, *op. cit.,* 167; Doris Begor Morton, *Philip Skene of Skenesborough* (Granville, N. Y., 1959), 47.

13. *State of the Expedition,* 17-18.

14. *Ibid.,* 18

15. *Ibid.*

16. Baronin von Riedesel, *Berufs=Reise nach America Briefe der Generalin von Riedesel auf dieser Reise und wahrend ihres sechsjahrigen Aufenthalts in America Zeit dortigen Krieges in der Jahren 1776 bis 1785 nach Deutchland Geshrieben* (Berlin, 1800), 135.

17. Robert McCluer Calhoon, *The Loyalists in Revolutionary America* (New York, 1969), 105-119.

18. *Burgoyne's Orderly Book*, 38, General Order, 12 July 1777.

19. See Note 1 above.

20. Hadden, *Journal,* 100-01.

21. Map, "The province of New York and New Jersey, with part of Pennsilvania [sic] and province of Quebec. Drawn by Major Holland, Surveyor General of the Northern District in America. Corrected from the Original by Govr [sic] Pownall, MP, 1776."

22. *State of the Expedition*, 18.

23. Nickerson, *op. cit.*, 167.

24. *Ibid.*, 161; "Journal of the late Proceedings of the Army."

25. *Ibid.*

26. Hadden, *Journal,* 93.

27. *State of the Expedition,* lxi.

28. *State of the Expedition,* Appendix, No VII, xxxv.

29. Lamb, *op. cit.*, 153.

30. Hadden, *Journal,* 93-94.

31. *Ibid.*, 95-6.

32. *Burgoyne's Orderly Book,* General Order, 13 July 1777.

33. Hadden, *Journal,* 95.

34. *State of the Expedition,* 88

35. *Ibid.,* 13.

36. Hadden, *Journal,* 154-55.

37. Nickerson, 496.

38. *Burgoyne's Orderly Book,* 52-55, General Orders, 25 and 27 July 1777.

39. *Ibid.,* 57; Nickerson, *op. cit.,* 179.

40. Nickerson, *op. cit.,* 179.

41. J. Benson Lossing, *Pictorial Field Book of the Revolution.* 2 vols. (New York, 1759), II.

42. National Archives, Washington, D.C, "Compiled Service Records of Soldiers who served in the American Army During the Revolutionary War, Samuel Standish."

43. Jared Sparks Papers, Harvard University Library, "Standish Interview."

44. Nickerson, *op. cit.,* 184-86.

45. Ward, *op. cit.,* I, 496-98; George O. Trevelyan, *The American Revolution.* Six volumes (London, 1909-1914), III, 148-50.

46. Snell, *Strength and Organization of Gates' Army* (Saratoga National Historical Park).

47. Gates Papers, Gates to Burgoyne, 2 September 1777.

48. *Ibid.,* Gates to Trumbull, 4 September 1777.

49. C. T. Atkinson, editor, *Journal of the Society for Army Historical Research* (Winter, 1948), "Some Evidence for Burgoyne's Campaign," 142.

50. *State of the Expedition,* 66, Harrington testimony.

51. John F. Luzader, *Decision on the Hudson: The Battles of Saratoga* (Fort Washington, 2002), 32-34.

Chapter 5

1. Riedesel Urkunden Militargeshichtler, "Journal des Feldzugs," hereafter "Journal des Feldzugs."

2. *Ibid.*

3. *Ibid.*

4. Niedersachisches Staatsarchiv, Der Dienstervieht fur. Oberst Lieutenant Baum uber dem Connecticut Fluss Feldzug, hereafter cited as Riedesel, Bennington Report; *State of the Expedition,,* lxiii -lxvii.

5. *Ibid.*

6. *Ibid.,* 100, Kingston testimony.

7. "Journal des Feldzugs."

8. Howson, *op. cit.*

9. Riedesel Urkunden Report to Herzog von Braunschweig on the Bennington Fight.

10. *Ibid.*

11. Germain Papers, Burgoyne to Germain, 20 August 1777.

12. Riedesel, "Bennington Report."

13. Baronin von Riedesel, *Berufs=Reise,* 134.

14. Riedesel, "Bennington Report."

15. Boatner, *op. cit.,* 1052.

16. Allen Nevins, *The American States During and After the American Revolution* (New York, 1927), 578-83.

17. James Truslow Adams, *The History of New England in Three Volumes, Volume II, New England in the Republic, 1776-1850* (Boston, 1922), 93-107, 181-82.

18. John F. Luzader, *The Saratoga Campaign to 18 September 1777* (National Park Service, 1958).

19. Nickerson, *op. cit.,* 227-28.

20. Ward, *op. cit.,* 424.

21. *Ibid.,* 229.

22. Ward, *op. cit.,* 424.

23. Riedesel, "Bennington Report."

24. *State of the Expedition*, lxx-lxxi, Baum to Burgoyne, 14 August 1777.

25. Riedesel, "Bennington Report."

26. Gates Papers, "Statement of the troops under General Stark."

27. The paucity of eyewitness accounts makes a detailed recording of Baum's defeat tentative. The one offered here is based upon Riedesel's report to his sovereign; Roger Lamb's *Journal;* Burgoyne's *State of the Expedition*, and especially his 20 August letter to Lord Germain.

28. Germain Papers, William L. Clements Library, Ann Arbor, Michigan, Burgoyne to German, dated August 20, 1777.

29. Riedesel, "Bennington Report."

30. *Ibid.*

31. *Ibid.*

32. Digby, *Journal*, 304.

33. Riedesel, *Berufs Reise*, 177-78.

34. Gates Papers, Stark to Gates, 22 August 1777.

35. *Ibid.*; Nickerson, *op. cit.*, 260.

36. *Ibid.* "Account of the Enemy's Loss in the late Action of the 16th August in the Walloomsac."

37. Nickerson, *op. cit.*, 260.

38. Journals of the Continental Congress, 4 October 1777 (not to be confused with Worthington C. Ford's series of the same name. See note 6 under Chapter 6.)

Chapter 6

1. William Livingston, *A Review of the Military Operations in North America* (London, 1757), 42-3.

2. J. N. B. Hewett, *Handbook of American Indians, North of Mexico.*

3. O'Callaghan, *Documents,* I, 765.

4. Papers of the Continental Congress, Schuyler to Hancock, 11 June 1776.

5. *Ibid.*, Schuyler Papers, Schuyler to Washington, 11 June 1777.

6. Worthington C. Ford, et. al., *Journals of the Continental Congress,* 33 vols. (Washington, 1904-36), V, 442. Hereafter cited as *JCC.*

7. Schuyler Papers, Washington to Schuyler, 16 and 26 June 1776; "Letters and Orders," Albany, 26 June 1776; Schuyler to Washington, 17 July 1776.

8. O'Callaghan, *Documents,* VIII, 451.

9. Schuyler Papers, Schuyler to Dayton, 16 July 1776.

10. *Ibid.*, Dayton to Schuyler, 25 July 1776.

11. *Ibid.*, Schuyler to Washington, 1 August 1776.

12. *Ibid.*, Dayton to Schuyler, 1 August 1776.

13. John F. Luzader, *Construction and Military History of Fort Stanwix* (Fort Washington,) 60-61.

14. Schuyler Papers, Schuyler to Elmore, 9 October, 17 October, and 12 November 1776; Ebenezer Elmore, *Journal,* New Jersey Historical Society.

15. Luzader, *op. cit., 63.*

16. *JCC* VI., 1048.

17. Schuyler Papers, Schuyler to de Lamarquise, 13 and 18 March 1777.

18. Gates Papers, "Memorandum, Lamarquise to Gates," no date.

19. Schuyler Papers, Gansevoort to Schuyler, 15 June 1777.

20. Marinus Willett, "Narrative," New York Public Library.

21. Schuyler Papers, Schuyler to Gansevoort, 10 July 1777.

22. Public Archives of Canada, Ottawa, "Transcripts of Colonial Papers," St. Leger to Carleton, 27 August 1777.

23. *State of the Expedition*, Appendix no. III, "Thoughts for Conducting the War from the Side of Canada."

24. Luzader, *op. cit.,* 95.

25. Nickerson, *op. cit.,* 195, 444.

26. Germain Papers, Germain to Carleton, 26 March 1777; "Colonel Claus' Account of the Battle of Oriskany and the Defeat of St. Leger's Expedition in an Original Letter to William Knox, British Undersecretary of State for the Northern Department, dated Montreal, October 11, 1777," New York State Library, Albany, hereafter cited as Claus' Account.

27. *Ibid.*

28. Schuyler Papers, Schuyler to Herkimer, 29 July 1777.

29. *Ibid.,* Schuyler to Gansevoort, 30 June 1777.

30. *Ibid.,* Gansevoort to Schuyler, 4 July 1777.

31. *Ibid.,* Schuyler to Herkimer, 8 July 1777.

32. *Ibid.,* Schuyler to Tryon County Committee of Safety, 10 July 1777.

33. *Ibid.,* Herkimer to Schuyler, 15 July 1777.

34. *Ibid.,* Schuyler to John Barklay, et. al., 15 July 1777.

35. William Colbreath, "Journal of the most material occurrences preceding the Siege of Fort Schuyler (formerly Fort Stanwix) with an account of the siege, etc." negative photostat, New York Public Library, hereafter cited as Colbreath, "Journal."

36. Gansevoort Papers, New York Public Library, von Schaick to Gansevoort, 22 July 1777.

37. *Ibid.,* to van Schaick, 28 July 1777.

38. Colbreath, "Journal."

39. *Ibid.*

40. Marinus Willett, "Orderly Book," New York Public Library.

41. Gansevoort Papers, "Captured British Papers."

42. Colbreath, "Journal."

43. Germain Papers, St. Leger to Germain, 27 August 1777.

44. Colbreath, "Journal."

45. Nickerson, *op. cit.,* 200.

46. Colbreath, "Journal."

47. *Ibid.*

48. *Ibid.*

49. *Ibid.*; *Remembrancer,* 448-49, Copy of a Letter, Marinus Willett to Jonathan Trumbull, 11 August 1777.

50. *Ibid.*

51. *Ibid.*

52. *Ibid.*

53. Public Archives of Canada, "Transcripts of Colonial Papers," St. Leger to Burgoyne, 11 August 1777.

54. Colbreath, "Journal."

55. *Ibid.*

56. Willett, "Narrative"; *Remembrancer,* 450; Claus' Account.

57. Willett, "Narrative"; *Remembrancer,* 459; Claus' Account.

58. Colbreath, "Journal."

59. *State of the Expedition,* Appendix XIII, lxxx, Extract of a Letter, St. Leger to Burgoyne, 27 August 1777.

60. "A Sketch of the Siege of Fort Stanwix," Jared Sparks Collection, Cornell University.

61. Colbreath, "Journal."

62. Claus' Account.

63. *Remembrancer,* 451.

64. Schuyler Papers, Schuyler to Herkimer, 7 August 1777, to Tryon Committee of Safety, 12 August 1777.

65. *Ibid.,* Schuyler to Washington, 12 August 1777.

66. *Ibid.,* Schuyler to Arnold, 13 August 1777.

67. Gates Papers, "Report of Council of War at German Flatts [sic], Aug. 21, 1777."

68. The size of Gansevoort's garrison is difficult to determine. Two hundred men arrived with Willett, 200 more with Badlam, and 100 with Mellen. The number accompanying Gansevoort is unknown, but it was at least 200, making a total of 700 or so a reasonable conclusion.

69. *Remembrancer,* 396-97.

70. Nickerson, *op. cit.,* 273-74.

71. Claus' Account.

72. *Ibid.*

73. Gates Papers, "A return of ammunition and artillery stores taken at the camp before Fort Schuyler, August 21st 1777."

74. *Ibid.*, Arnold to Gates, 23 and 24 August 1777.

Chapter 7

1. Journals of the Continental Congress, 7 June 1775. For Schuyler's biographical data, see Don R. Gerlach, *Philip Schuyler and the Revolution in New York* (Lincoln, Nebraska, 1964) and Martin Bush, *Revolutionary Enigma: A Reappraisal of General Philip Schuyler of New York* (Port Washington, 1969).

2. Nelson, *op. cit.*, 6-9.

3. Journals of the Continental Congress, 17 June 1775.

4. Higginbotham, *op. cit.*, 209-16; Bernhard Knollenberg, *Washington and the Revolution: A Reappraisal: Gates, Conway, and the Continental Congress* (New York, 1940), 50 ff.

5. Worthington C. Ford, "Washington at the Crisis of the Revolution," *Century Magazine,* Vol. 81 (1911), 661-62.

6. Worthington C. Ford, editor, *Writings of George Washington.* Fourteen volumes (New York, 1889-93), 9, 464-65, 468. Until John Fitzpatrick's 1931-41 edition, Ford's was considered the standard compilation.

7. Lyman C. Butterfield, et al., editors, *Diary and Autobiography of John Adams.* Four volumes (Cambridge, 1961), 386-87

8. Alexander Hamilton, *Letters from Alexander Hamilton concerning the Public Conduct and Character of John Adams, Esq.*

9. Jonathan Gregory Rossie, *The Politics of Command in the American Revolution* (Syracuse, 1975), 135-153.

10. Charles Snell, "Gates' Army" (Saratoga National Historical Park, 1958).

11. Journals of the Continental Congress, 18 June 1776.

12. Gates Papers, Knox to Gates [n.d.]

13. Bush, *op. Cit.*, 134

14. Journals of the Continental Congress, 17 February 1776.

15. Papers of the Continental Congress, Hancock to Schuyler, 20 February 1776.

16. *Ibid.*, Hancock to Charles Lee, 19 February 1776.

17. *Ibid.*, Schuyler to Hancock, 1 March 1776.

18. Washington Papers, Library of Congress, Charles Lee to Washington, 5 February 1776.

19. Rossie, *op. cit.*, 86.

20. Journals of the Continental Congress, 27 February 1776.

21. *Ibid.*, 1 March 1776.

22. Washington Papers, Washington to Lee, 14 March 1776.

23. Rossie, *op. cit.*, 95.

24. Edmund C. Burnett, *Letters of Members of the Continental Congress.* Eight volumes (Washington, 1921-36), I, 408.

25. Rossie, *op. cit.*, 99-100.

26. Papers of the Continental Congress, Samuel Chase and Charles Carroll to Congress, 27 May 1776.

27. *Ibid.*

28. Butterfield, *op. cit.*, 391.

29. Higginbotham, *op. cit.*, 170.

30. *Ibid.*

31. Douglas Southall Freeman, *George Washington: A Biography.* Seven volumes (New York, 1949-57), III, 528; Nelson, *op. cit.*, 42-43.

32. Journals of the Continental Congress, 16 May 1776.

33. James Wharton, *Revolutionary Diplomatic Correspondence of the United States.* Six volumes (Washington, 1889), II, 71-74.

34. *Ibid.*, II, 74, 78.

35. Freeman, *op. cit.*, IV, 99.

36. *Ibid.*

37. Papers of the Continental Congress, Washington to Hancock, 19 May 1776.

38. *Ibid.*, Hancock to Washington; Jared Sparks, editor, *Correspondence of the American Revolution.* Seven volumes (Boston, 1853), I, 205.

39. Hancock to Gates.

40. Gates Papers, Hancock to Washington, 20 May 1776.

41. Nelson, *op. cit.*, 53.

42. Rossie, *op. cit.*, 105.

43. Burnett, *op. cit.*, 487.

44. Gates Papers, Adams to Gates, 13 June 1776.

45. *Ibid.*, Washington to Gates, 24 June 1776.

46. Berhard Knollenberg, "Correspondence of John Adams and Horatio Gates, *Proceedings of the Massachusetts Historical Society, October 1940-May 1944*, LXVII (Boston, 1945), 145-46.

47. Rossie, *op. cit.*, 105.

48. *Ibid.*, 124.

49. *Ibid.*

50. Washington Papers, Schuyler to Washington, 1 July 1776, enclosing "Memorandum of Conversation between Generals Schuyler and Gates, 20 June 1776."

51. Journals of the Continental Congress, 8 July 1776.

52. Burnett, *op. cit.*, II, 11, Samuel Adams to Richard Henry Lee, 15 July 1776.

53. Rossie, *op. cit.*, 111.

54. Knollenberg, "Correspondence of John Adams and Horatio Gates," Gates to Adams, 17 July 1776.

55. Papers of the Continental Congress, Gates to Hancock, 16 July 1776.

56. Washington Papers, Schuyler to Washington, 17 July 1776.

57. Washington Papers, "Council of War at Crown Point, July 7, 1776," enclosed in the field officers' protest.

58. *Ibid.*, Schuyler to Stark, et. al., 9 July 1776.

59. Quoted in Rossie, *op. cit.*, 113.

60. *Ibid.*, 112; Washington Papers, Washington to Schuyler, 17 July 1776.

61. *Ibid.*, Washington to Gates, 19 July 1776.

62. Gates Papers, Gates to Washington, 29 July 1776.

63. *Ibid.*, Washington to Gates, 4 August 1776.

64. Washington Papers, Schuyler to Washington, 6 August 1776, Washington to Schuyler, 10 August 1776.

65. *Ibid.*, Washington to Hancock, 17 July 1776.

66. Gates Papers, Gates to Thomas Hartley, 21 July 1776.

67. *Ibid.*, Gates to Congress, 16 July 1776, to Washington, 16 July 1776; Force, *op. cit.*, I, 1126, "General Orders, Ticonderoga, 15 July and 13 August 1776."

68. Gates Papers, Gates to Washington, 28 August 1776.

69. *Ibid.*, Gates to Schuyler, 24 October 1776.

70. *Ibid.*, Arnold to Gates, 16 August 1776.

71. *Ibid.*, Arnold to Gates, 21 August 1776.

72. Force, *op. cit.*, I, 268, Gates to Hancock, 2 September 1776.

73. Papers of the Continental Congress, "Resignation of General Schuyler, 14 September 1776."

74. Rossie *op. cit.*, 127.

75. Journals of the Continental Congress, 14 September 1776.

76. Washington Papers, Washington to Schuyler 30 September 1776.

75. Rossie, *op. cit.*, 128.

78. Burnett, *op. cit.*, II, 105, William Williams to Joseph Trumbull, 28 September 1776.

79. *Ibid.*, 107, Philip Livingston to President, New York Commission, 28 September 1776.

80. Journals of the Continental Congress, 2 October 1776.

81. Schuyler Papers, Hancock to Schuyler, 27 September 1776.

82. *Ibid.*, Schuyler to Washington, 6 October 1776.

83. Papers of the Continental Congress, 26 September 1776.

84. Schuyler Papers, Schuyler to Hancock, 16 October 1776.

85. *Ibid.,* 25 October 1776.

86. *Ibid.,* Robert R. Livingston to Schuyler, 27 October 1776.

87. Rossie, *op. cit.,* 132-33.

88. Journals of the Continental Congress, 23 November 1776.

89. National Archives, Record Groups, "General Return of the Army, 7 December 1776."

90. Gates Papers, Washington to Gates, by order of Robert H. Harrison, 26 November 1776.

91. *Ibid.*, Gates to Schuyler, 6, 8, 15 November 1776; Papers of the Continental Congress, Gates to Congress, 27 November 1776.

92. Anthony Wayne Papers, Wayne to Gates, 20 November 1776.

93. Nelson, *op. cit.*, 73.

94. Gates Papers, Charles Lee to Gates, 13 December 1776.

95. Nelson, *op. cit.*, 74.

96. Gates Papers, William Duer to Gates, 9 December 1776.

97. *Ibid.*, Gates to Washington, 12 December 1776.

98. See Note 86.

99. Nelson, *op. cit.*, 77-78.

100. *Ibid.*, 76.

101. Harry Alonzo Cushing, editor, *The Writings of Samuel Adams.* Four volumes (New York, 1904-1908), III, 326-27.

102. Journals of the Continental Congress, 16 September 1776.

103. Burnett, *op. cit.*, I, 262.

104. Rossie, *op. cit.*, 137.

105. Charles Franklin Adams, editor, *Familiar Letters of John Adams and His Wife Abigail Adams, During the Revolution*, 283.

106. Rossie, *op. cit.*, 137-38.

107. *Ibid.*

108. Journals of the Continental Congress.

109. Rossie, *op. cit.*, 140.

110. Papers of the Continental Congress, Trumbull to President of Congress.

111. *Historical Magazine* (New York, 1857), I, 292.

112. Papers of the Continental Congress, Gates to Hancock, 19 March 1777.

113. Burnett, *op. cit.*, II, 308-09, 311-12.

114. Gates Papers, Hancock to Gates, 29 April 1777.

115. Cushing, *op. cit.*, III, 326-33.

116. Gates Papers, Washington to Gates, 5 February 1777.

117. Journals of the Continental Congress, 20 February 1777.

118. Gates Papers, Washington to Gates, 3 March 1777.

119. *Gazette and Weekly Mercury* (New York), 9 December 1776.

120. Papers of the Continental Congress, 4 February 1777.

121. Journals of the Continental Congress, 15 March 1777.

122. *Ibid.*, 25 March 1777.

123. Schuyler Papers, Schuyler to de Lamarquise, 13 March 1777, to Van Schaick, 25 March 1777.

124. Gates Papers, Gates to Washington, 19 April 1777, Washington to Gates, 29 April 1777.

125. *Ibid.*, Gates to Joseph Trumbull, 22 April 1777.

126. *Ibid.*, Gates to Hancock, 14 May 1777.

127. Schuyler Papers, Varick to Schuyler, 18 April 1777.

128. Gates Papers, Gates to Hancock, 29 April and 11 May 1777.

129. Papers of the Continental Congress, "New York Delegates to the President of the New Convention," 21 April 1777.

130. Journals of the Continental Congress, 17 April 1777.

131. Schuyler Papers, Schuyler to Varick, 26 April 1777.

132. Washington Papers, Schuyler to Washington, 29 April 1777.

133. Gates Papers, Gates to Congress, 11 May 1777; Papers of the Continental Congress, Gates to Congress, 11 May 1777.

134. Papers of the Continental Congress, Schuyler to Congress, 13 May 1777.

135. Burnett, *op. cit.*, II, 357-58.

136. Journals of the Continental Congress, 15 May 1777.

137. *Ibid.*, 22 May 1777.

138. "Trumbull Papers," Massachusetts Historical Society Collection, Seventh Series, I, 51-52.

139. Rossie, *op. cit.*, 150.

140. Journals of the Continental Congress, 18 June 1777; Burnett, *op. cit.*, II, 384, Duer to Schuyler, 19 June 1777.

141. Burnett, *op. cit.*, II, 384-86, James Duane to Schuyler, 19 June 1777.

142. Journals of the Continental Congress, 8 July 1777.

143. Freeman, *op. cit.*, IV, 465.

144. Quoted in Rossie, *op. cit.*, 165.

145. Washington Papers, Schuyler to Washington, 18 July 1777.

146. Papers of the Continental Congress, Hancock to Arnold, 2 July 1777.

147. Journals of the Continental Congress, 26 July 1777.

148. Rossie, *op. cit.*, 163.

149. *Ibid.*, 162.

150. Burnett, *op. cit.*, II, 429-30.

151. Journals of the Continental Congress, 29 July 1777.

152. Whipple Papers, Library of Congress, Lowell to Whipple, 2 August 1777.

153. Rossie, *op. cit.*, 164.

154. Papers of the Continental Congress, Washington to Congress, 3 August 1777.

155. Journals of the Continental Congress, 4 August 1777.

Chapter 8

1. Nelson, *op. cit.*, 106.

2. Charles W. Snell, *A Report on the Organization and Numbers of Gates' Army, September 19 and October 17, 1777, including an Appendix with Regimental Data and Notes* (Saratoga National Historical Park, 1951).

3. Gates Papers, Gates to Washington, 22 August 1777.

4. Snell, *op. cit.*

5. George Clinton Papers, New York State Library, Albany, Gov. George Clinton to Colonel Morris Graham, 1 August 1777 (copy).

6. *Ibid.*

7. *Ibid.*, Clinton to Ten Broeck, 1 August 1777.

8. Gates Papers, General Order, 20 August 1777.

9. Snell, *op. cit.*

10. Gates Papers, "Report of Council of War of German Flatts, August 21, 1777; Gates to Arnold, 22 August 1777."

11. *Ibid.*, Gates to Morgan, 24 August; Gates to Lincoln, 31 August 1777.

12. John C. Fitzpatrick, *The Writings of George Washington.* Thirty-nine volumes (Washington, 1931 1944), IX, 71.

13. Gates Papers, Gates to Lincoln, 31 August 1777.

14. *Ibid.*, Gates to Morgan, 29 August 1777.

15. *Ibid.*, Gates to Lincoln, 31 August; Gates to Hancock, 3 September 1777.

16. *Ibid.*, Stevens to Gates, "A Return of Ordnance Stores wanted in the Northern Department, 19 August 1777."

17. *Ibid.*, Cheever to Gates, 24 August 1777.

18. *Ibid.*, Mason to Gates, 25 August 1777.

19. *Ibid.*, Hughes to Gates, 24 August 1777.

20. *Ibid.*, Mason to Gates, 21 August 1777.

21. *Ibid.*, Heath to Gates, 30 August 1777.

22. *Ibid.*, Mason to Gates, 2 September 1777.

23. *Ibid.*, Stevens to Gates, 3 September 1777.

24. *Ibid.*, Mason to Gates, 5 September; Gates to Schuyler, 10 September 1777.

25. *Ibid.*, Schuyler to Gates, 11 September 1777.

26. *Ibid.*, Varick to Gates, 10 September 1777.

27. *Ibid.*, Lewis to Gates, 1 September 1777.

28. Journals of the Continental Congress, June 1775.

29. E. Wayne Carp, *To Starve the Army at Pleasure: Continental Army Administration and American Political Culture 1775-1783* (Chapel Hill, 1984), see generally, Chapter 3.

30. Gates Papers, "Return of Provisions in Store at Albany, the 31st August 1777."

31. *Ibid.*, Hughes to Gates, 7 September 1777.

32. *Ibid.*, Heath to Gates, 12 September 1777.

33, *Ibid.*, Lincoln to Gates, 12 September 1777.

34. *Ibid.*, Schuyler to Gates, 14 September 1777.

35. *Ibid.*, Lewis to Gates, 14 September 1777.

36. *Ibid.*, Palmer to Gates, 17 September 1777.

37. *Ibid.*, Gates to Arnold, 19 August; Arnold to Gates, 21 August 1777.

38. *Ibid.*, Arnold to Gates, 23 August 1777.

39. Schuyler Papers, Arnold to Schuyler, 21 August 1777.

40. Gates Papers, Gansevoort to Gates, 22 August 1777.

41. *Ibid.*, Arnold to Gates, 21 August 1777.

42. *Ibid.*, Mason to Gates, "Private Intelligence," undated.

43. *Ibid.*, Fellows to Gates, 22 August 1777.

Chapter 9

1. Gates Papers, Library of Congress, Gates to Hancock, 20 August 1777; Lloyd A. Brown and Howard H. Peckham, editors, *Revolutionary War Journals of Henry Dearborn, 1775-1783* (Chicago, 1939), hereafter cited as Dearborn, *Journals*, 102.

2. Snell, *op. cit.*

3. *Ibid.*

4. *Ibid.*

5. Gates Papers, New York Historical Society, Lincoln to Stark, 6 September 1777.

6. *Ibid.*, Stark to Lincoln, 7 September 1777.

7. *Ibid.*

8. *Ibid.*, Lincoln to Stark, 8 September 1777; Lincoln to Gates, 8 September 1777.

9. *Ibid.*, Gates to Lincoln, 10 September 1777.

10. *Ibid.*, Gates to Stark, 10 September 1777.

11. *Ibid.*, Stark to Gates, 9 September 1777.

12. Schuyler Papers, New York Public Library, Henry B. Livingston to Schuyler 11 September 1777.

13. Snell, *op. cit.*

14. Luzader, *Decision on the Hudson*, 40-41; Nickerson, *op. cit.*, 284, 291, 301; Nelson, *op. cit.*, 113.

15. Schuyler Papers, Varick to Schuyler, 12 September 1777.

16. Luzader, *Saratoga Campaign to 18 September 1777.*

17. George W. Womack, "Some Notes on the Continental Army," (First Installment), *William and Mary College Quarterly*, Second Series, XI, No. 2 (April 1931), 91; George Smith, *An Universal Military Dictionary* (London, 1779); J. G. Tielke, *Unterricht fur die Offiziers die sich Feld-Ingeniers bilden.* Two volumes (Berlin), II, 63-64; Edwin

Hewgill, *The Field Engineer or Instructions Upon Every Branch of Field Fortifications,* 2 vols. (London, 1789), I, 187-90, II, 218-19, 246-49.

18. Gates Papers, Gates to Hancock, 15 September 1777.

19. Snell, *op. cit.*; Schuyler Papers, Varick to Schuyler, 12 September 1777.

20. *Ibid.*

21. *Ibid.*, Varick to Schuyler, 8:00 a. m., 11:30 p. m., 16 September 1777.

22. *Ibid.*, Varick to Schuyler, 18 September 1777.

23. For an assessment of Livingston, see Richard B. Morris, *The Peacemakers: The Great Powers and American Independence* (New York and London, 1970), 237.

24. Schuyler Papers, Livingston to Schuyler, 13 September 1777.

25. *Ibid.*

26. *Ibid.*

27. *Ibid.*, 16 September, 3:00 and 8:00 a. m., 11:30 p. m.

28. *Ibid.*, 17 September 1777.

29. *Ibid.*, Varick to Schuyler, 17 September 1777.

30. *Ibid.*, Livingston to Schuyler, 13 September 1777.

31. *Ibid.*, Varick to Schuyler, 15 September 1777.

32. *Ibid.*

33. *Ibid.*, Livingston to Schuyler, 16 September 1777.

34. *Ibid.*, 16 September, 8:00 a. m.

35. *Ibid.*, 17 September 1777.

36. *Ibid.*, Varick to Schuyler, 18 September 1777.

37. *Burgoyne Orderly Book*, 113-14, General Order, 18 September 1777.

38. Gates Papers, Lincoln to Gates, 26 August 1777.

39. *Ibid.*, Lincoln to Gates, 4 September 1777.

40. *Ibid.*, 14 September 1777.

41. *Ibid.*, 18 September 1777.

42. *Ibid.*, Brown to Lincoln; Schuyler Papers, Varick to Schuyler, 21 September (two letters), Varick to Schuyler, 22 September.

Chapter 10

1. Schuyler Papers, "John Freeman Indenture."

2. Public Archives of Canada, Ottawa, Loyalist Claim 448. "Evidence on the Claim of Thomas Freeman, Late of Saratoga, New York."

3. *State of the Expedition,* Appendix II, Map, "The Encampment of the Army under Lt. General Burgoyne at Swords House and the Freeman Farm on Hudson's River near Stillwater, 1777."

4. Schuyler Papers, James McBride Indenture, Albany County Clerk's Office, Albany, Y. Y., "Farms and Surveys A & B."

5. Loyalist Claim 448; Bryan L. Cathcart, editor *Three History Theses* (Ontario Department of Public Records and Archives, 1961), E. Rae Stuart, M. A., "Jessup Rangers: A Factor in Loyalist Settlement."

6. *Ibid.*

7. Minutes of the Commissioners for Detecting and Defeating Conspiracies in the State of New York, Albany County Session, 1778-1781, three volumes (Albany, 1909-10), 263, 296, 303, 408, 596, 600, 602, 609, 615-624; British Public Record Office, London, A. O. 3/276; Beatrice Reubens, *A Fractious People: Politics and Society in Colonial New York* (New York, 1971), 179-211; William Nelson, *The American Tory* (Oxford, 1961), 90-95.

8. Harold L. Peterson, *Arms and Armor in Colonial America, 1626-1783* (Harrisburg, 1956), 160.

9. Quoted in Ernest M. Lloyd, *A Review of the History of Infantry* (New York, 1909), 155; See also Christopher Duffy, *The Wars of Frederick the Great* (Newton Abbot, 1974), 82-85; Brent Nosworthy, *The Anatomy of Victory: Battle Tactics 1688-1963* (New York, 1990), 183ff.

10. *Burgoyne's Orderly Book,* 116, General Order, 21st September 1777.

11. Boatner, *op. cit.*, 403-4.

12. *Journals of the Continental Congress,* II, 89.

13. Aaron Wright, "Journal," Boston Transcript (April 1862); Freeman, *op. cit.*, III, 525-26.

14. Followers of the romantic tradition, especially among American writers, tended to interpret "leading" their men in combat literally.

15. General Burgoyne found himself so involved physically that he compromised his ability to influence events.

16. Wilkinson, *op. cit.*, I, 245-46.

17. Hans Delbrück, *The Dawn of Modern Warfare: Volume IV of the History of the Art of War* (Lincoln, Nebraska and London, 1885), 465.

18. Niedersacchisches, Wolfenbüttel, Germany, Briefschaften und Akten des Generallieutenants Friederich Adolf von Riedesel Freiherr zu Eisenbach, Riedesel to the Duke of Braunschweig, hereafter cited as Riedesel, Briefe 21ten October.

19. *Ibid.*; *State of the Expedition,* Appendix xiv, lxxxv, "Extract of a letter from Lieutenant General Burgoyne to Lord George Germain, dated at Albany 20th October 1777; *Ibid.*, Lord Harrington testimony; 81-83, Major Forbes testimony; Digby, *Journal,* 271-72.

20. Gates Papers, Gates to Lincoln, 19 September 1777.

21. *Ibid.*, Arnold to Gates, 1 October 1777.

22. Nickerson, *op. cit.*, 307-08. Most students of the campaign agree with the cogency of Arnold's recommendation.

23. Ordering tents struck and vehicles prepared to move when the order of battle was issued was normal preparation before imminent combat.

24. Gates Papers, Library of Congress, Arnold to Gates, 22 September 1777.

25. *State of the Expedition,* 81-82; Digby, *Journal,* 272, 19 September 1777; Gates Papers, NYHS, Gates to Hancock, 22 September 1777; Wilkinson, *op. cit.,* I, 245-46.

26. Digby, *Journal,* 272.

27. Wilkinson, *op. cit.,* I, 237-38.

28. *Ibid.*

29. Hadden, *Journal,* 164-65.; *State of the Expedition,* 104, Kingston testimony.

30. Wilkinson, *op. cit.,* I 137; Dearborn, *Journals,* September 19, 1777.

31. *Ibid.*; Wilkinson, *op. cit.,* I, 237-38.

32. *Ibid.*

33. William Cumberledge Wilkinson's Map 19 September, "First and Second Positions of the Army Engaged on the 19th of September."

34. Lamb, *op. cit.,* 199.

35. *Magazine of American History,* II (1878), 108.

36. Hadden, *Journal,* 164.

37. *Ibid.,* 165.

38. Nickerson, *op. cit.,* 311

39. Gates Papers, Arnold to Gates, 22 September 1777.

40. Snell, op. cit.

41. Hadden, *Journal,* 165-66.

42. Wilkinson, Map, 19 September, "Third and Fourth Positions . . . ."

43. *State of the Expedition,* Appendix, lxxxvi, lxxxvii; *Ibid.,* 162-6.

44. *Ibid.,* 41-2, 57, 69-73, 81-83, 103-05.

45. *Ibid.,* 163.

46. Lamb, *op. cit.,* 105.

47. *State of the Expedition,* 163-64.

48. *Ibid.*

49. Charles W. Snell, *A Report on the Strength of the British Army* (Saratoga National Historical Park).

50. Hadden, *Journal,* 166.

51. Riedesel, Militargechichtler Nachlass.

52. Riedesel, "Briefschatten und Akten."

53. *Ibid.*: Tagebuch von Senden, 19 September 1777.

54. Riedesel, Briefschaften und Akten.

Chapter 11

1. Digby, 274 *Journal,* entry for 20 September 1777; Pausch, "Tagebuch Pausch."

2. *Ibid.*

3. Digby, *Journal*, 274.

4. *Ibid.*, 275.

5. Wilkinson, *op. cit.*, I, 251-52.

6. Charles W. Snell, *A Report on the Left Wing of the British Fortified Camp at Freeman's Farm, September 20 to October 8, 1777* (Saratoga National Historical Park, 1950).

7. Schuyler Papers, Varick to Schuyler, 22 September 1777.

8. William Heath Papers, Massachusetts Historical Society, Boston, Glover to Heath, 21 September 1777.

9. Wilkinson, *op. cit.*, I, 235-56.

10. *Burgoyne's Orderly Book*, 2, General Order, Sandy Bluff, 20 June 1777; Hadden, *Journal*, 71-72.

11. Hessische Staatssarchiv, Marburg, Pausch to Baurmeister, 26 November 1777.

12. Hessische Staatsarchiv, Cassel, Tagebuch Pausch, entries 20 September and 8 October 1777.

13. Riedesel, Journals des Feldzugs.

14. *Ibid.*

15. Hessische Staatsarchiv, Marburg, Pausch to Baurmesiter, 26 November 1777.

16. Wilkinson, *op. cit.*, I, 271-72.

17. Jared Sparks, "Journal," Widener Library, Harvard.

18. *State of the Expedition,* Appendix, No. XIV, lxxxi, ff.

19. Clinton Papers, Clinton to Burgoyne, 11 September 1777.

20. Willard Wallace, *Traitorous Hero: The Life and Fortunes of Benedict Arnold* (New York, 1954), 104-05; Gates Papers, Gates to Hancock, 2 September 1777.

21. Schuyler Papers, Arnold to Schuyler, 21 August 1777; Gates Papers, Arnold to Gates, 21 August 1777.

22. Ward, *op. cit.*, II, 522; Willard Sterne Randall, *The Life and Fortunes of Benedict Arnold: Patriot and Traitor* (New York, 1990); Clare Brandt, *The Man in the Mirror: A Life of Benedict Arnold* (New York, 1994), 129, 136; Richard M. Ketchum, *Saratoga: Turning Point of America's Revolutionary War* (Henry Holt: New York, 1997), 385.

23. Rossie, *op. cit.*, 170; Nelson, *op. cit.*, 123-25; Nickerson, *op. cit.*, 330-31.

24. Ketchum, *op. cit.*, 288.

25. Schuyler Papers, Varick to Schuyler, 12 September 1777.

26. Gates Papers, Gates to Arnold, 9 September 1777.

27. Gates Papers, General Order, 10 September 1777.

28. Gates Papers, Gates to Hancock, 20 September 1777.

29. Schuyler Papers, Varick to Schuyler, 21 September 1777.

30. Gates Papers, General Order, 22 September 1777.

31. Schuyler Papers, Livingston to Schuyler, 23 September 1777.

32. Wilkinson, *op. cit.*, I, 254.

33. Schuyler Papers, Livingston to Schuyler, 23 September 1777.

34. Gates Papers, Arnold to Gates, 22 September 1777.

35. *Ibid.,* Gates to Arnold, 23 September 1777.

36. *Ibid.,* Gates to Hancock, 23 September 1777.

37. *Ibid.,* Arnold to Gates, 23 September 1777.

38. Schuyler Papers, Varick to Schuyler, 17 September 1777.

39. *Ibid.,* Varick to Schuyler, 19 September 1777.

40. *Ibid.,* Varick to Schuyler, 22 September 1777.

41. *Ibid.,* Livingston to Schuyler, 23 September 1777.

42. *Ibid.*

43. *Ibid.,* Varick to Schuyler, 24 September 1777.

44. *Orderly Book of Major Stevens,* 25 September 1777.

45. Schuyler Papers, Livingston to Schuyler, 24 September 1777.

46. *Ibid.,* 25 September 1777.

47. *Ibid.,* Varick to Schuyler, 26 September 1777.

48. *Ibid.,* Livingston to Schuyler, 26 September 1777.

49. *Ibid.,* Varick to Schuyler, 26 September 1777.

50. Benjamin Lincoln papers, Massachusetts Historical Society, Houghton Library, Harvard, New-York Historical Society, and New York Public Library; John Glover Papers, Massachusetts Historical Society, Essex Institute, and Columbia University Library; John Nixon Papers, Historical Society of Pennsylvania; Daniel Morgan Papers, Theodorus B. Myers Collection, New York Public Library; Lieutenant Thomas Blake's "Account" in Frederick Kidder, *First New Hampshire Regiment in the War of the Revolution* (Albany, 1868); R. A. Guild, *Chaplain Smith and the Baptists* (Philadelphia, 1886); Joseph Cillet Papers, New York Historical Society; Jared Sparks Collection, Widener Library, Harvard; William L. Stone, *Visits to the Saratoga Battle-Grounds;* "Journal of Oliver Boardman of Middleton, 1777. . . ; Connecticut Historical Society, *Collections* (Hartford, 1899); *Elijah Fishers' Journal While in the War for Independence and Continued Two Years after he Came to Maine, 1775-1784* (Augusta, 1880); "A Narrative of Henry Hallowell of Lynn, respecting the Revolution in 1775, 1776, 1778, 1779 to January 1780" in Howard Kendall Sanderson, editor, *Lynn in the Revolution* (Boston, 1909) "Diary of Enos Hitchcock, D. D., a Chaplain in the Revolutionary War," Rhode Island Historical Society, *Publications, VII (1899 and VIII (1900);* J. M. Hughes, "Notes Relative to the Campaign Against Burgoyne," Massachusetts Historical Society, *Proceedings,* III (February 1853) "Diary of Captain Benjamin Warren on the Battlefield of Saratoga, *Journal of American History,* III (1909); "Diary of Ephraim Squire," *The Magazine of American History,* II ((1878); "The Journal of Ebenezer Wild (1776-1781), who served as Corporal, Sergeant, Ensign, and Lieutenant in the American Army of the Revolution," Massachusetts Historical Society, *Proceedings,* second series, VI (1890); National

Archives, Record Group 93, "Compiled Service Records of Soldiers who served in the American Army During the Revolutionary War."

51. Gates Papers, Arnold to Gates, 27 September 1777.

52. *Ibid.,* Arnold to Gates, 1 October 1777.

53. Schuyler Papers, Varick to Schuyler, 22 September 1777.

54. Lloyd W. Smith Collection, Morristown National Historical Park, Schuyler to Varick, 20 September 1777.

Chapter 12

1. *Burgoyne Orderly Book,* 125.

2. Charles E. Shedd, Jr., *Burgoyne's Objective in the Second Battle of Saratoga* (Saratoga National Historical Park, 1952).

3. Riedesel, Briefe 21ten October.

4. *Ibid.*

5. *State of the Expedition,* 24.

6. Sir Henry Clinton Papers, Burgoyne to Clinton, 25 September 1777.

7. Nickerson, *op. cit.,* 358.

8. *State of the Expedition,* lxxxix.

9. *Ibid.*

10. Riedesel, Briefe 21ten October. The original German: *den 7ten Oktober eine Reconnaissance gegen den lincken Fiendlichen Flugel vorzunehmen, und fande man alsdann solchen inattaquable die Retrite zu denken.*

11. Joshua Pell, "Diary of Lieutenant Joshua Pell," *Magazine of American History,* II (1878), hereafter cited as Pell, "Diary," 110-11.

12. William Cumberlidge Wilkinson, "Plan of the Encampment and Position of the Army under his Exell Lt. General Burgoyne at Braemus Heights on Hudson's River near Stillwater on the 20th Septr. With the Position of the Detachments etc. in the Action of the 7th Oct. And position of the Army on the 8th Oct. 1777."

13. *State of the Expedition,* 49, Balcarres testimony; *Ibid.,* 106, Kingston testimony; Hadden, *Journal,* 62-63.

14. Riedesel, Briefe, 21ten October.

15. Digby, *Journal,* 286.

16. *Ibid.,* 291.

17. *Burgoyne's Orderly Book,* 127-28, General Order, 6 October 1777.

18. Pell, "Diary."

19. Riedesel, Briefe, 21ten October.

20. Oliver Boardman, Journal of Oliver Boardman, *Collection,* Connecticut Historical Society, VII (Hartford, 1899), 228-29.

21. Snell, "A Report on the Number and Organization of Gates' Army."

22. Stone, *Visits to the Saratoga Battle Grounds,* 243, Visit of Ebenezer Matoon, writing in 1835; Ralph Cross, "The Journal of Ralph Cross of Newburyport, who commanded the Essex Regiment at the Surrender of Burgoyne in 1777," *The Historical Magazine,* Second Series, Henry B. Dawson, editor (Morrisania, 1870), 10.

23. Wilkinson, *op. cit.,* 267.

24. *Ibid.,* 268-69.

25. *Ibid.,* 273.

26. *Ibid.*

27. Charles W. Snell, "Primary Sources For Drawing No NHP, SAR," 2015 (1 sheet). Part of the Master Plan, Saratoga National Historical Park, "Troop Movements," Battle of October 7, 1777 (Saratoga National Historical Park). An outstanding example of basic (and almost anonymous) research carried out by park historians of the U. S. Department of the Interior, National Park Service.

28. Dearborn, "Journals."

29. Digby, *Journal,* 287-88; John F. Luzader, "Documentary Study of the Death and Burial of General Simon Fraser" (Saratoga National Historical Park, 1958); *State of the Expedition,* Appendix, xiv, xc.

30. Snell, *op. cit.,* 20-25; *State of the Expedition,* Appendix, xiv, Kingston testimony; Hessisches Staatsarchiv, "Betrachten uber den Feldzug des Generals Burgoyne in Canada und Neu York in einem Schreiben an deselben"; Tagebuch von Specht., 7 Ocotober 1777.

31. Wilkinson, *op. cit.,* I, 272; Henry Dearborn, "A Narrative of the Saratoga Campaign," Typed draft, Fort Ticonderoga Library, Fort Ticonderoga, N. Y.; Stone, *Visits to the Saratoga Battle Grounds;* Samuel Woodruff, "Account of the battle of October 7," 223-27; Nickerson, *op. cit.,* 366.

32. Riedesel, Militargechichtler Nachlass.

33. Pausch, Tagebuch Pausch.

34. Riedesel, Betrachten uber den Feldzug.

35. *State of the Expedition,* Appendix xci, xxci.

36. *Ibid.*

37. *Ibid.,* "Narrative," 26.

38. *Ibid.,* Balcarres testimony, 38-53; Pausch, Tagebuch Pausch, 7 October 1777.

39. Wilkinson, *op. cit.,* I, 271.

40. Stone, *Visits to the Saratoga Battle Grounds*, 227, Samuel Woodruff Account.

41. "Autobiography of Colonel Phillip Van Cortlandt," *The Magazine of American History,* II (1978), 287.

42. Dearborn, "Narrative."

43. Ward, *op. cit.,* II, 529.

44. Fortesque, *op. cit.,* III, 338.

45. Nickerson, *op. cit.,* 365-66.

46. Riedesel, "Betrachten des Feldzug."

47. Wilkinson, *op. cit.,* 271.

48. Rowena Buell, editor, *Memoirs of Rufus Putnam* (Boston and New York, 1903), 67.

49. Benjamin Warren, "Diary of Benjamin Warren," *Journal of American History,* III (1904), 215-16.

50. Wilkinson, *op. cit.,* 271-72.

51. *Ibid.,* 273.

52. Dearborn, *Journal,* 108-09.

53. Dearborn, "A Narrative of the Saratoga Campaign," *Fort Ticonderoga Bulletin,* I, No 5. January 1929, 11-12.

54. H. A. S. Dearborn, *The Life of Major General Dearborn.*

55. Riedesel, Briefe 21ten October. Original German text: "Zugleicher Zeit attaquirte deselbe des Retranchment von Ober"; Lieut Breymann. Welches sich heilt, da der dieser todt Geschlossen wurdem und der Fiend ihm Rucken kam, so importirte der Fiend das Retranchment und bekam Zelte und Equipage. Der Theil der Leute aber is gerited worde. Der Oberst Lieut V Spetch der mit 40 Mann dem Oberstlieut Breymann seconderiren wollte, wurde in die Nacht fur Affair auf.

56. Riedesel, "Betrachten uber den Feldzug."

57. *State of the Expedition,* Appendix xiv, "Extract of a Letter from Lieut General Burgoyne to Lord George Germain, dated Albany 20th October 1777."

58. Digby, *op. cit.,* 291-92.

59. Gates Papers, Gates to Hancock, 12 October 1777.

Chapter 13

1. Digby, *Journal,* 291-92.

2. *Ibid.*; Riedesel, *Berufs = Reise,* 172; *State of the Expedition,* 73, Harrington testimony.

3. Digby, *Journal,* 297-98; Lamb, *op. cit.,* 165.

4. Riedesel, Briefe, 21ten October.

5. Riedesel, *Berufs = Reise,* 172-73.

6. *State of the Expedition,* 169-70.

7. Gates Papers, Gates to Bayley, 14 October 1777.

8. Wilkinson, *op. cit.,* I, 280.

9. Snell, "Organization of Burgoyne's Army . . . ."

10. Riedesel, *Berufs = Reise,* 174.

11. Ketcham, *op. cit.,* 409; Ward, *op. cit.,* II, 533; Nickerson, *op. cit.,* 376.

12. *State of the Expedition,* 74, Harrington testimony.

13. Digby, *Journal,* 302-03.

14. Snell, "Organization of Gates' Army."

15. *State of the Expedition,* 84, Forbes testimony.

16. Schuler von Senden, Tagebuch von Senden.

17. *Ibid.*

18. *Ibid.*

19. Riedesel, *Berufs = Reise,* 176-77.

20. *Ibid.*

21. Howson, *op. cit.,* 277; *State of the Expedition,* 74, Harrington testimony.

22. Wilkinson, *op. cit.,* I, 284.

23. *State of the Expedition,* 74, Harrington testimony.

24. Wilkinson, *op. cit.,* I, 285.

25. *Ibid.*

26. *Ibid.,* 287.

27. *State of the Expedition,* "PLAN OF THE POSITION which the Army under LT. GENL. BURGOYNE Took on the 10th of September [October] and in which it remained till the CONVENTION was signed."

28. Digby, *Journal,* 304.

29. Senden, Tagebuch von Sender.

30. Wilkinson, *op. cit.,* I, 285.

31. Nickerson, *op. cit.,* 380.

32. Wilkinson, *op. cit.,* I, 285-89.

33. *Ibid.,* 289.

34. *Ibid.*

35. Digby, *Journal,* 305.

36. Riedesel, *Berufs = Reise,* 150.

37. Thomas Anburey, *Travels Through the Interior Parts of America, 1776-1781,* two volumes (Boston, 1923), I. Because of strong evidence of plagiarism, use carefully.

38. *State of the Expedition,* APPENDIX No. XV, xcviii-ci, "Minutes of the Council of War held on the Heights of Saratoga, Oct. 12."

39. *Ibid.*

39. *Ibid.*

40. *Ibid.*

41. *Ibid.*

42. *Ibid.,* c and ci.

43. Riedesel, Briefe, 21ten October.

44. *State of the Expedition,* APPENDIX, "Extracts from the Minutes of the last Council of War, excepting the Names of the Officers and the Notes they gave."

45. Riedesel, Briefe, 21ten October.

46. *Ibid.*

47. *Ibid.,*

48. Gates Papers, Burgoyne to Gates, 13 October 1777.

49. *Ibid.,* Gates to Burgoyne, 13 October 1777.

Chapter 14

1. Wilkinson, *op. cit.*, I, 299 ff.
2. Gates Papers, Gates to Burgoyne, 12 October 1777.
3. *Ibid.*, Box 8, Negotiation Documents.
4. Wilkinson, *op. cit.*, I, 311.
5. Gates Papers, Box 8, Negotiation Documents.
6. Wilkinson, *op. cit.*, I, 313.
7. *State of the Expedition*, App. No. XV, "Minutes of a Council of War. Holden on the Heights of Saratoga, Oct. 12," "Minutes of a Council of War consisting of all the general Officers and Captains commanding Corps, on the Heights of Saratoga, October 13, No. 2," "Major Kingston delivered Message to Major-general Gates, October 14."
8. *Ibid.*, No. 3. "Major General Gates' Proposals together with Lieutenant-General Burgoyne's Answers."
9. *Ibid.*
10. *Burgoyne's Orderly Book*, 153.
11. Clinton Papers, Clinton to Burgoyne, 6 October 1777.
12. Gates Papers, Putnam to Gates, 11 and 12 October 1777.
13. Gates Papers, Box 8, Negotiation Documents.
14. *Ibid.,* Putnam to Gates, 11 October 1777.
15. Wilcox, *op. cit.*, 188-89; Clinton *op. cit.*, 80-81.
16. Howson, *op. cit.*, 232-33.
17. Ketchum, *op. cit.*, 422.
18. Gates Papers, Box 8, Negotiation Documents; Howson, *op. cit.*, 232.
19. Wilkinson, *op. cit.*, I, 286.
20. Riedesel, "Briefschaften und Akten."
21. Gates Papers, Box 8, Negotiation Documents.
22. *Ibid.*
23. Wilkinson, *op. cit.*, I, 286.
24. Howson, *op. cit.*, 233.
25. Wilkinson, *op. cit.*, 287.
26. Gates Papers, Box 8, Negotiation Documents.
27. PRO, CO 42/37. 608, PRO, CO 5/94, 718-19; *State of the Expedition*, App. II.
28. Digby, *Journal*, 318-19.
29. James Thacher, *A Military Journal During the Revolutionary War* (Boston, 1828), 128; Ward, *op. cit.*, II, 538.
30. Ketchum, *op. cit.*, 429; Ward, *op. cit.*, 538; Nickerson, *op. cit.*, 399.
31. *State of the Expedition*, App. No XIV, "Extract of Letter from Lt.- Gen. Burgoyne to Lord George Germain, Albany 20th October; *Ibid.*, Second No. XIV.

32. *Ibid.*

33. Nelson, *op. cit.*, 144.

34. Papers of the Continental Congress, Gates to Hancock, 18 October 1777.

35. Wilkinson, *op. cit.*, I, 323-24.

36. Journals of the Continental Congress, 31 October 1777; Gates Papers, Hancock to Gates, 4 November 1777.

37. Nelson, *op. cit.*, 145.

38. *Ibid.*, 147-49.

Epilogue

1. Mackesy, *op. cit.*, 141.

2. *State of the Expedition*, 12-15.

3. Mackesy, *op. cit.*, 143.

4. Carl Van Doren, *Secret History of the American Revolution: An Account of the Conspiracies of Benedict Arnold and Numerous Others drawn from Secret service Papers of the British Headquarters in North America now for the first time examined and made public* (New York, 1941), 116.

5. Higginbotham, *op. cit.*, 242.

6. Wilcox, *op. cit.*, 211. See also that author's "Why Did the British lose the American Revolution?" *Michigan Alumnus Review*, LXII (1956), 121.

7. Mackesy, *op. cit.*, 157, 182-84.

8. Germain Papers, William L. Clements Library.

9. Mackesy, *op. cit.*, 184.

10. *Ibid.*, 185.

11. William Knox Papers., William L. Clements Library, Volume 9, numbers 21-22. See also Mackesy, *op. cit.*, 158.

12. V. H. H. Green, *The Hanoverians 1714-1815* (London, 1949), 358.

13. British Museum, Additional Manuscripts, Liverpool MSS, 187-91.

14. Mackesy, *op. cit.*, 158-59.

15. W. B. Wilcox, "British Strategy in America, 1778," *Journal of American History* (1948), 109 ff.

16. Samuel Flagg Bemis, *The Diplomacy of the American Revolution* (Bloomington, Indiana, 1957), 16.

17. *Ibid.*

18. *Ibid.*

19. *Ibid.*

20. B. F. Stevens, *Facsimiles of Manuscripts in European Archives Relating to America, 1773-1783*, number 1310.

21. Journals of the Continental Congress, 19 November 1777.

22. Burnett, *op. cit.*, I, 165.

23. Journals of the Continental Congress, 17 and 24 September 1777.

24. Heitman, *op. cit.*, identified French officers receiving Continental commissions.

25. Francis Wharton, *op. cit.*, I, 392.

26. *Ibid.*, 260.

27. *Ibid.*, 304; Journals of the Continental Congress, 30 December 1777.

28. Bemis, *op. cit.*, 60.

29. *Ibid.*, 58, 59, 66; Wharton, *op. cit.*, I, 639-51; Fortesque, *The Correspondence of King George the Third*, II, 518, V, 200.

30. Bemis, *op. cit.*, 60.

31. David Hunter Miller, *Treaties and Other International Acts of the United States of America*, eight volumes (Washington, 1921-48), II, 35-40.

32. Vernon Setser, "Did America Originate the Most-Favored Nation Clause?" *Journal of Modern History*, V (1933), 319-23.

Appendix A

1. *State of the Expedition*, 2-3.

2. *Ibid.*, iii, "Extract of a Letter from Lord George Germain to Sir Guy Carleton, dated Whitehall, 22d August 1776."

3. *Ibid.*, 3.

4. *Ibid.*

5. PRO, CO 5/253, "Precis of Operations & Plans."

6. Gerald Howson, *Burgoyne of Saratoga: A Biography* (New York, 1979), 315.

7. Hoffman Nickerson, *Turning Point of the Revolution.*

8. British Historical Commission, *Publications*, VI, William Knox Papers.

9. Lord Edward Fitzmaurice, *Life of William, Earl of Shelbourn, Afterwards Marquess of Lansdowne*, three volumes (London, 1875-76), II. 69.

10. de Fonblanque (London, 1876), 232-33.

11. Troyer Steele Anderson, *The Command of the Howe Brothers During the American Revolution* (New York and London, 1936), 272-73.

12. Gruber, *The Howe Brothers*, 266.

13. Fortesque, *Correspondence of George III from 1760 to Dec. 1783.*

14. PRO, CO 5/163, 183, Germain to Townsend, 25 March 1777.

15. PRO, CO 5/94, 169, Germain to Howe, 19 April 1777.

16. *Journal of the Society for Historical Research*, xxvi (London, 1946), Burgoyne to Fraser, 6 May 1777.

17. PRO, CO 42/36 and 37, CO 5/167.

18. PRO, CO 42/37, 335, St. Leger to Burgoyne, 11 August 1777.

19. Digby, *Journal*, 188.

20. *State of the Expedition*, 51-52, Balcarres testimony; 86-87, Forbes testimony; 117, Kingston testimony.

21. Baronin von Riedesel, *Berufs=Reise,* 180.

22. Riedesel, Briefe, 21ten October.

23. *State of the Expedition*, 15-16.

24. Howson, *op. cit.*, 149.

25. *The Political Magazine and Parliamentary, Naval, Military, and Literary Journal for the Year MCCLXXVII* (London, 1788).

26. *State of the Expedition*, 9.

27. Anderson, *op. cit.*, 227.

28. Rupert Furneaux, *The Battle of Saratoga* (New York, 1977), 87.

29. Howson, *op. cit.*, 148.

30. Clinton, *The American Rebellion*, 60-61.

31. Wilcox, *op. cit.*, 125.

Appendix H

1. Wilkinson, *op. cit.*, I, 239-40.

2. Hadden, *op. cit.*, 144; Digby, *Journal*, 267.

3. *Burgoyne's Orderly Book*, 101-05, General Order, 13 September 1777; Digby, *Journal*, 269.

4. Basil Liddell Hart, *Strategy* (New York, 1991), 95; Martin Van Creveld, *Command in War* (Cambridge and London, 1995), 35-38.

5. Wilkinson, *op. cit.*, I, 243-46.

6. Washington Papers, Robert R. Livingston to Washington, 14 January 1778.

7. Schuyler Papers, Livingston to Schuyler, 23 September 1777.

8. Phillip Van Cortlandt, "Autobiography....," *The Magazine of American History*, II.

9. Jared Sparks Papers, Houghton Library, Harvard.

10. *Ibid.*

11. R. Gould, *op. cit.*, 369.

12. Riedesel, Briefe, 21ten October.

13. Charles Neilson, *An Original, Compiled and Corrected Account of Burgoyne's Campaign, and the Memorable Battles of Bemis Heights, September 19-October 7, 1777* (Albany, 1844), 148.

14. Charles Botta, *History of the War of Independence of the United States of America*, two volumes, translated from Italian by George Alexander Otis (New Haven, 1841), II, 11.

15. Isaac N. Arnold, *The Life of Benedict Arnold: His Patriotism and Treason* (Chicago, 1880), 170-72.

16. Nickerson, *op. cit.*, 215.

17. Ward, *op. cit.*, II, 506-12.

18. Willard Sterne Randall, *The Life of Benedict Arnold: Patriot and Traitor* (New York, 1990), 357-59.

19. Gates Papers, Arnold to Gates, 22 September 1777.

20. Schuyler Papers, Varick to Schuyler, 23 September 1777.

21. William L. Stone, *Visits to the Saratoga Battle-Grounds . . .* , 153.

22. Fortesque, *A History of the British Army*, III, 234-36.

23. Benson J. Lossing, *Life and Times of Philip Schuyler*, Two volumes (New York, 1873), II, 348.

24. Nickerson, *op. cit.*, 315-16.

25. Ward, *op. cit.*, II, 511.

26. Wilkinson, *op. cit.*, I, 239; Henry Livingston Papers, Massachusetts Historical Society, Matthew Clarkson (Arnold aide) to Susan Livingston, 21 September 1777; Henry Dearborn, "Narrative of the Saratoga Campaign, prepared for James Wilkinson in 1815"; Enoch Poor, *Massachusetts Spy or Oracle of Liberty*, Thursday, 9 October 1777, "Extract of Letter from a General Officer, Camp at Stillwater, September 25, 1777; John Glover, *A Memoir of General John Glover of Marblehead* (Salem, 1862), 28; William Heath Papers, Massachusetts Historical Society, Glover to Heath, 21 September 1777; Ebenezer Wild (Sergeant, 1st Massachusetts Regiment of Glover's Brigade), Massachusetts Historical Society, "Journal. . . .; Philip Van Cortlandt (Colonel, 2nd New York Regiment, Poor's Brigade), "Autobiography," *Magazine of American History,* II, 286-87; Schuyler Papers, Varick to Schuyler, 19 and 22 September 1777; Heath Papers, Massachusetts Historical Society, Wilkinson to Heath, 22 September 1777.

27. *State of the Expedition,* xviii-ix, 121-22, 29-30, Balcarres testimony; 42, Money testimony; 51-52, Harrington testimony; 61-62, Forbes testimony; 78-79, Kingston testimony; Hadden, *op. cit.*, 164-66.

28. Gates Papers, Arnold to Gates, 22 September, 1777.

29. Nickerson, *op. cit.*, 315-16.

30. Ward, *op. cit.*, II, 511.

31. Randall, *op. cit.*, 358.

32. See note 27.

33. Higginbotham, *op. cit.*, 194.

Appendix I

1. Pell, "Diary."

2. *State of the Expedition*, 58, Money testimony.

3. *Ibid.*, 59, Money testimony.

4. *Ibid.*, 60, Money testimony.

5. *Ibid.*, 91, Blomefield testimony.

6. *State of the Expedition*, 49, Balcarres testimony.

7. *Ibid.*, 91, Blomefield testimony.

8. *Ibid.*, 106, Kingston testimony.

Bibliography

Manuscripts

Albany County, New York, County Clerk's Office

    Land Records

British Museum, London

    Additional Manuscripts, Add. MSS 344413-15, Aukland Papers

William L. Clements Library, University of Michigan, Ann Arbor

    Sir Henry Clinton Papers
    Lord George Germain Papers

Colonial Williamsburg, Williamsburg, Virginia

    British Headquarters Papers (photographic copy)

Columbia University Library, New York

    John Glover Papers

Connecticut Historical Society, Hartford, Connecticut

    "Journal of Oliver Boardman of Middleton, 1778."
    Jonathan Trumbull, Senior, Papers
    Jonathan Trumbull, Junior, Papers
    Joseph Trumbull Papers

Connecticut State Library

    Trumbull Papers

Cornell University Library, Ithaca, New York

    Jared Sparks Collection

Essex Institute, Salem, Massachusetts

    John Glover Papers

Harvard University, Houghton Library of Harvard College

    Jared Sparks Papers and "Journal"

Hessisches Staatsarchiv, Marburg/Lahn, Germany

    Tagebuch von Pausch

Historical Society of Pennsylvania, Philadelphia

    John Nixon Papers
    Jonathan Potts Papers

Henry E. Huntington Library, San Marino, California

    James Abercrombie Papers

Library of Congress Manuscript Division

    George Washington Papers

Massachusetts Historical Society, Boston

    John Glover Papers
    William Heath Papers
    Benjamin Lincoln Papers
    William Livingston Papers
    Joseph Palmer Papers

Morristown National Historical Park

    L. W. Smith Collection.

National Archives, Washington, D. C.

Journals of the Continental Congress
Papers of the Continental Congress
RG Numbered Records, Miscellaneous Records of the War Department
    Collection of Revolutionary War Records, 1775-1795
Pension Office Records
Service Records of Soldiers who served in the Revolutionary War

New Jersey Historical Society, Newark

Ebenezer Elmer, "Journal"

New York Historical Society

Joseph Cilley Papers
Benjamin Lincoln Papers
Richard Varick Papers

New York Public Library, New York

George Clinton Papers
William Colbreath, "Journal"
Peter Gansevoort Papers
Horatio Gates Papers
Benjamin Lincoln Papers
Robert R. Livingston Papers (Bancroft Collection)
Daniel Morgan Papers (Theodorus B. Myers Collection)
Philip Schuyler Papers
Marinus Willett "Narrative"
Marinus Willett, "Orderly Books"

New York State Library, Albany

George Clinton Papers
Horatio Gates Papers
"Colonel [Daniel] Claus Account of the Battle of Oriskany and the Defeat
    of St. Leger's Expedition"

Niedersachsisches Staatsarchiv, Wolfenbuttel, Germany

    Friedrich Adolph von Riedesel, "Journal des Feldzugs"
    Riedesel Urkunden
    Tagebuch von Senden
    Tagebuch von Soecht

Saratoga National Historical Park, Stillwater, New York

    Nielson Family Papers

Ohio State Library, Columbus

    Arthur St. Clair Papers

Public Records Office, London

    CO 5/93-106, Secretary of State, America, Military Dispatched
    CO 5/94
    CO 5/95
    CO 5/167, Secretary of State to Secretary at War
    CO 5/174, Commander-in Chief to Secretary of State (Germain)
    CO 5/253, Precis, Military Operations against Colonies
    TO 11/387, Treasury Solicitor's Papers
    WO 1/616, Burgoyne Court of Inquiry
    WO 34/110 ff. Amherst Papers
    PRO Library, Army Lists, 1777/78

Printed Original Sources

Albany County, New York, *Minutes of the Commissioners for Detecting and Defeating Conspiracies in the State of New York, Albany County Sessions, 1778-79*, three volumes Albany, 1909-10.

Anburey, Thomas. *Travels Through the Interior Parts of America, 1776-1781*, two volumes. Boston, 1923.

Baldwin, Jeduthan, Thomas William Baldwin, editor. *The Revolutionary Journal of Col. Jeduthan Baldwin.* Bangor, 1906.

Baxter, James Phinney, editor. *The British Invasion From the North: The Campaigns of Generals Carleton and Burgoyne From Canada, 1776-77, with the Journal of Lieut. William Digby of the 53d or Shropshire Regiment of Foot.* Albany, 1887.

Boardman, Oliver. *Journal of Private Oliver Boardman,* Collections, Connecticut Historical Society, VIII (1899).

British Historical Commission, William Knox Papers, Publications, VI.

Burnett, Edmund C., editor. *Letters of Members of the Continental Congress.* Six volumes. Washington, 1923.

Butterfield, Lyman. *Diary and Biography of John Adams.* Four Volumes. Cambridge, 1841.

Cone, Mary. *Life of Rufus Putnam, with Extracts from his Journal.* Cleveland, 1886.

Dearborn, Henry. *Revolutionary War Journals of Henry Dearborn, 1775-83,* edited by Lloyd A. Brown and Howard H. Peckham. Chicago, 1939.

Fisher, Elijah. *Elijah Fisher's Journal, While in the War for Independence and Continued two Years After He Came to Maine, 1775-84.* Bangor, 1880.

Fitzpatrick, John C. *The Writings of George Washington from The Original Manuscript Sources.* Thirty-nine volumes. Washington, 1931-44.

Flick, Alexander, editor. *William Johnson Papers.* Ten volumes. Albany, 1921-51.

Force, Peter, editor. *American Archives: A Documentary History of The Origin and Progress of the North American Colonies.* Nine volumes. Washington, 1827-51.

Ford, Worthington C., et. al., editors. *Journals of the Continental Congress.* Eighty-three volumes. Washington, 1904-36.

Sir John Fortesque, editor. *Correspondence of George II, 1760-83.* London, 1927-28.

Glover, John, William P. Upham, editor. *A Memoir of General John Glover of Marblehead.* Salem, Massachusetts, 1863.

Graham, Joseph M., "A Recollection of the American Revolution," Virginia Historical Register. Richmond, n.d.

Hadden, James. *Journal and Orderly Book.* Albany, 1884.

Hastings and Holden, J. A. *Public Papers of George Clinton, First Governor of New York, edited by the State Historian.* Ten volumes, 1899-1914. New York, 1900.

Hitchcock, Enos. "Diary of Enos Hitchcock, D.D., a Chaplain in the Revolutionary War," *Rhode Island Society Publications,* VII (1899) and VIII (1900).

Lamb, Roger. *An Original and Authentic Journal of Occurrences During the Late American War from Its Commencement to the Year 1783.* Dublin, 1809.

New York Historical Society, "Proceedings of a General Court Martial at White Plains in the State of New York, by Order of His Excellency General Washington, Commander In Chief of the Army of the U. S. of America, For the Trial of Major General St. Clair August 25 1778. Major General Lincoln, President (Philadelphia, 1778, Collections of The New York Historical Society for the year 1880. New York, 1881.

O'Callaghan, E. B., editor. *Orderly Book of Lieut. Gen. John Burgoyne From his Entry Into the State of New York Until his Surrender at Saratoga, 16th October 1777. From The Original Manuscript Deposited at Washington's Head Quarters, Newburgh, NY.* Albany, 1860.

O'Callaghan, Edmund B. and Fernow, Berthold, editors. *Documents Relating to the Colonial History of the State of New York.* Ten volumes. Albany, 1854.

Pell, Joshua. "Diary of Lieutenant Joshua Pell," *Magazine of American History,* II, 1878.

Sanderson, Howard Kendall, editor. "A Narrative of Henry Howell Of Lynn respecting the Revolution in 1775, 1776, 1777, 1778, 1779 to January 17, 1780," *Lynn in the Revolution.* Boston, 1909.

Stevens, Benjamin Franklin, editor. *Facsimiles of Manuscripts in European Archives Relating to the American Revolution, 1773-83.* Twenty-five volumes. London, 1889-98.

Thacher, James. *A Military Journal During the Revolutionary War.* Boston, 1823.

Trumbull, John. *Autobiography and Letters, 1756 to 1841.* New York, 1841.

Van Cortlandt, Philip. "Autobiography of Philip Van Cortlandt," *Magazine of American History,* II. 1878.

Warren, Benjamin. "Diary of Captain Benjamin Warren on the Battlefield at Saratoga," *Journal of American History,* III, 1909.

Wild, Ebenezer. "The Journal of Ebenezer Wild (1776-81), who served as Corporal, Sergeant, Ensign, and Lieutenant in the American Army of the Revolution," *Massachusetts Historical Society Proceedings,* 2nd Series, VI. Boston, 1890.

Journal of the Society for Historical Research. XXVI. London, 1846.

Secondary Sources

Almon, John, editor. *The Parliamentary Register: or, History of The Debate and proceedings of the House of Lords and Commons.* Seventeen volumes. 1775-80.

Anderson, Fred. *Crucible of War: The Seven Years' War and The Fate of Empire in North America, 1754-1766.* New York, 2001.

Anderson, Troyer S. *The Command of the Howe Brothers during the American Revolution.* London, 1936.

Andrews, Charles M. *The Colonial Background of the American Revolution.* New Haven, 1931.

Arnold, Isaac N. *Life of Benedict Arnold, His Patriotism and Treason.* Chicago, 1880.

Atkinson, C. T., "British Forces in North America, 1774-81," *Journal, Society for Army Historical Research,* 16. London, 1937.

Bemis, Samuel Flagg. *The Diplomacy of the American Revolution.* Bloomington, 1961.

Billington, Ray Allen. *Westward Expansion, A History of the American Frontiers.* New York, 1967.

Bland, Humphrey. *A Treatise of Military Discipline*. London, 1743.

———. *Abstract of Military Discipline*. Boston, 1757.

Bloodgood, DeWitt S. *The Sexagenary; Or, Reminiscences of the American Revolution*. Albany, 1866.

Boatner, Mark Mayo, III. *Encyclopedia of the American Revolution*. New York, 1966.

Botta, Charles. *History of the War of the Independence of the United States*. Two volumes. New Haven, 1837.

Brandt, Clare. *The Man in the Mirror*. New York, 1994.

Burgoyne, John. *State of the Expedition from Canada*. London, 1780.

Burnett, Edmund C. *The Continental Congress*. New York, 1941.

Bush, Martin H. *Revolutionary Enigma: A Reappraisal of General Philip Schuyler of New York*. Port Washington, New York, 1969.

Callahan, North. *Daniel Morgan, Ranger of the Revolution*. New York, 1961.

Carp, E. Wayne. *To Starve the Army at Pleasure: Continental Army Administration and American Political Culture, 1775-83*. Chapel Hill and London, 1884.

Clark, Jane. "The Command of the Canadian Army in 1777," *Canadian Historical Review*, X. 1928.

Cobbett, William. *Parliamentary History of England from the Earliest Period to the Year 1803*. Thirty-Six volumes. London, 1806-30.

Commager, Henry Steele and Morris, R. B. *The Spirit of Seventy-six: The Story of the American Revolution as told by Participants*. Two volumes. New York, 1967.

Creasy, Edward S. *The Fifteen Decisive Battles of the World*. London and New York, 1851.

Curry, Cecil B. *Road to Revolution, Benjamin Franklin in England, 1765-75*. Garden City, 1968.

Curtis, Edward. C. *Organization of the British Army in the American Revolution*. New Haven and London, 1926.

de Fonblanque, Edward Barrington. *Political and Military Episodes in the latter Half of the 18th Century, derived from the Life and Correspondence of the Right Hon. John Burgoyne General, Statesman Dramatist*. London, 1876.

Dickerson, Oliver M. *American Colonial Government, 1896-1765*. New York, 1962.

Fitzmaurice, Lord Edmond. *Life of William, Earl of Shelburne, Afterwards Marquess of Lansdowne*. Eight volumes. MacMillian, 1876.

Fleming, Thomas J. *1776: Year of Illusions*. New York, 1975.

Flick, Alexander. *The American Revolution in New York*. Albany, 1926.

Fisher, Elijah. *Elijah Fisher's Journal While in the War of Independence and Continued Two Years after he Came to Maine*. Augusta, 1880.

Ford, Worthington C. "Washington at the Crisis of the Revolutionary War," *Century Magazine*, LXXXI. March, 1911.

Fortesque, Sir John. *History of the British Army*. Thirteen volumes. London, 1899-1902.

Furneaux, Rupert. *The Battle of Saratoga*. New York, 1971.

Gerlach, Donald R. *Philip Schuyler and the American Revolution in New York, 1733-77*. Lincoln, Nebraska, 1964.

Graham, James. *Life of General Daniel Morgan*. New York, 1856.

Gruber, Ira. *The Howe Brothers and the American Revolution*. Chapel Hill, 1972.

Guild, R. A. *Chaplain Smith and the Baptists*. Philadelphia, 1885.

Guthorn, Jeter. *American Maps and Map Makers of the Revolution*. Monmouth, 1966.

Hamilton, Alexander. *The Public Conduct and Character of John Adams, esq*. New York, 1800.

Hart, Basil Liddell. *Strategy*. New York, 1991.

Hatch, Louis Clinton. *The Administration of the American Revolutionary Army*. London and Bombay, 1904.

Heitman, Francis B. *Historical Register of Officers of the Continental Army During the War of the Revolution, April 1775 to December 1783*. Washington, 1914.

Higginbotham, Don. *The War of American Independence, Military Attitudes, Policies, and Practice, 1763-87*. New York, 1971.

———. *Daniel Morgan: Revolutionary Rifleman*. Chapel Hill, 1961.

Holden, James Austen. "Influence of Death of Jane McCrae on Burgoyne, *Proceedings of the New York State Historical Association*, XII. 1913.

Howson, Gerald. *Burgoyne of Saratoga: A Biography*. New York, 1979.

Hughes, J. M. "Notes Relative to the Campaign Against Burgoyne. *Massachusetts Historical Society, Proceedings,* III. 1853.

Jones, Thomas. *History of New York During the Revolutionary War*. Two volumes. New York, 1879.

Keegan, John, *The Face of Battle*. New York, 1976.

Ketchum, Richard M. *Saratoga: Turning Point American Revolutionary War*. New York, 1997.

Kidder, Frederic. *First New Hampshire Regiment in the War of the Revolution*. Albany, 1868.

Knollenberg, Bernhard. *Washington and the Revolution, A Reappraisal: Gates, Conway, and the Continental Congress*. New York, 1941.

Lesser, Charles H. *The Sinews of Independence: Monthly Strength Reports of the Colonial Army*. Chicago, 1976.

Livingston, William. *A Review of the Military Operations in North America*. London, 1757.

Lossing, Benson J. *Pictorial Field Book of the Revolution*. Two volumes. New York, 1858.

Lunt, John. *John Burgoyne of Saratoga*. New York and London, 1995.

Luzader, John F. *Decision on the Hudson: The Battles of Saratoga.* Fort Washington, 2002.

———. *Fort Stanwix: Construction and Military History.* Fort Washington, 2001.

———. *Documentary Research Report On the Saratoga Campaign to September 19, 1777.* Saratoga National Historical Park. 1960.

Lynn, John A. *Feeding Mars: Logistics in Western Warfare from the Middle Ages to the Present.* Boulder, Colorado, 1993.

Mackesy, Piers. *The War For America.* Cambridge, 1964.

Miller, David Hunter. *Treaties and Other International Acts of the United States of America.* Eight volumes. Washington, 1921-48.

Miller, John C. *The Federalist Era.* New York, 1960.

Morris, Richard B. *The Peacemakers: The Great Powers and American Independence.* New York, Evanston, and London, 1970.

Morton, Louis, "The Origins of American Military Policy." *Military Affairs,* XXII. 1958.

Nelson, Paul David. *General Horatio Gates: A Biography.* Baton Rouge, 1976.

Neilson, Charles. *Burgoyne's Campaign and the Memorable Battles of Bemis Heights.* Albany, 1844.

Nickerson, Hoffman. *The Turning Point of the Revolution or Burgoyne in America.* Boston and New York, 1928.

Norton, Mary Beth. *The British-Americans: The Loyalists in England.* Boston and Toronto, 1972.

Nuenschwander, John A. *The Middle Colonies and the Coming of the American Revolution.* Port Washington and London, 1973.

Pancake, John S. *1777: The Year of the Hangman.* University of Alabama, 1977.

Parkman, Francis. *Montcalm and Wolfe.* Two volumes. Boston, 1831.

Patterson, Samuel White. *Horatio Gates: Defender of American Liberties.* New York, 1941.

Peabody, James Bishop. *John Adams: A Biography in his Own Words.* New York, 1973.

Peterson, Harold L. *Arms and Armor in Colonial America, 1526-1783.* Harrisburg, 1956.

Pickering, Timothy. *An Easy Plan of Discipline for a Militia.* Sale, 1750.

Quaife, Milo, Weig, Melvin J., and Appleman, Roy E. *The History of The United States Flag.* Philadelphia, 1966.

Randall, Willard Sterne. *Benedict Arnold: Patriot and Traitor.* New York, 1990.

Riedesel, Baronin von Riedesel, *Die Berufs=Riedesel nach America Briefe der Generalin von Riedesel auf dieser Reise und wahrend ihres sechsjahrigen Aufenthalts in America zur Zeit dortigen Krieges in Den Jahren 1776 bis 1785 nach Deutchland geschrieben.* Hande und Spener, 1800.

Robson, Eric. *The American Revolution in its Political and Military Aspects, 1763-83.* Norton, New York, 1966.

Rossie, Jonathan Gregory. *The Politics of Command in the American Revolution.* Syracuse, 1975.

Schutz, John A. *William Shirley, King's Governor of Massachusetts.* Chapel Hill, 1961.

Scott, John Albert. *Fort Stanwix (Fort Schuyler) and Oriskany.* Rome, New York, 1927.

Shy, John. *A People Numerous and Armed: Reflections on the Military Struggle for American Independence.* Ann Arbor, 1990.

Simes, Thomas. *The Military Guide for Young Officers.* London, 1776.

——. *A New Military, Historical, and Explanatory Dictionary.* Philadelphia, 1776.

Simms, Jeptha. *History of Schohari County.* Albany, 1845.

——. *The Frontiersmen of New York.* Albany, 1883.

Sosin, Jack. *Whitehall and the Wilderness.* Lincoln, Nebraska, 1962.

Spaulding, Oliver Lyman, Nickerson, Hoffman, and Wright, John Womack. *Warfare: A Study of Military Methods from Earliest Times.* Washington, 1937.

Stevenson, Roger. *Military Instructions for Officers Detached in the Field.* Philadelphia, 1775.

Stone, William L. *Life of Joseph Brant-Thayendoga, Including War of the Revolution.* Two volumes. New York, 1838.

——. editor. *Visits to the Saratoga Battlegrounds, 1780-1880.* Albany, 1895.

——. *The Campaign of Lieut. Gen. John Burgoyne and the Expedition of Lieut. Col. Barry St. Leger.* Albany, 1877.

Tielke, J. G. *The Field Engineer of Instructions Upon Every Branch Of Fortification: Demonstrated by Examples which occurred in the Seven Years' War between the Prussians, the Austrians, and the Russians With Plans and Explanatory Notes. Translated from the Fourth Edition of the German original by Edwin Hewgill, Ensign and Adjutant in the Coldstream Regiment of Foot Guards.* Two Volumes. London, 1789.

Trevelyan, George Otto, Richard B. Morris, editor. *The American Revolution.* New York, 1964.

Upton, Leslie F. S. *Revolutionary Versus Loyalist: The First American Civil War, 1774-84.* Waltham, Massachusetts, Toronto, and London, 1868.

Valentine, Alan. *Lord George Germain.* London, 1962.

Van Creveld, Martin. *Command in War.* Cambridge, Massachusetts, and London, 1985.

Van Doren, Carl. *Secret History of the American Revolution.* New York, 1941.

Wainwright, Nicholas B. *George Croghan, Wilderness Diplomat.* Chapel Hill, 1959.

Wallace, Willard M. *Traitorous Hero: The Life and Fortunes of Benedict Arnold.* New York, 1954.

Ward, Christopher. *The War of the Revolution.* New York, 1952.

Weigley, Russell F. *The American Way of War: A History of United States Military Strategy and Policy.* New York, 1973.

Werner, Edgar. *Civil List and Constitutional History of the State of New York.* Albany, 1884.

Wharton, Francis. *Revolutionary Diplomatic Correspondence of the United States.* Six volumes. Washington, 1882.

Williams, John. *The Battle of Hubbardton: The American Rebels Stem the Tide.* Vermont Division of Historic Preservation, 1988.

Willcox, William B. *Portrait of A General: Sir Henry Clinton in the War of Independence.* New York, 1964.

———. "Why Did the British Lose the American Revolution?" *Michigan Alumnus Review,* LXII. 1956.

———. "British Strategy in America, 1778." *Journal of Modern History.* 1948.

Wilkinson, James. *Memoirs of My Own Times.* Three volumes. Philadelphia, 1816.

Willett, William, editor. *A Narrative of the Military Actions of Colonel Marinus Willett.* New York, 1831.

Wolfe, James. *Instructions to a Young Officer.* London, 1768.

Womack, George. "Some Notes on the Continental Army" (First Installment). *William and Mary College Quarterly,* Second Series. Volume XI, Number 2. April 1931.

Young, William, editor. *Maneuvers for a Battalion of Infantry Upon Fixed Principles, by a German Officer.* London, 1766.

———. *The Manual Exercise.* New York, 1780.

———. *Maneuvers, or, Practical Observations on the Art of War.* Volume I. 1770.

Periodicals

The Political Magazine and Parliamentary, Naval, Military, and Literary Journal of the Year. MLXXVII. London, 1778.

The Independent Chronicle and Universal Advertiser. Boston, August 28, 1777.

The Remembrance; or Impartial Repository of Public Events For the Year 1777. London, 1778.

Pennsylvania Evening Post. Philadelphia, Vol. III, Number 398, 453.

New York Journal and General Advertiser. New York, September 8, 1777.

New York Patent and the American Advertiser. New York, September 11, 1777.

Gazette. Boston, September 15, 1777.

Massachusetts Spy or American Oracle of Liberty. Boston, 1777.

Index

337-338, 340; Marquis de
Lafayette, 347; retreat across New
Jersey, 351; Sir John Fortesque,
354
Wayne, Col. Anthony, 48, 143, 169
Wempel, Col. Abraham, 202, 371, 375
Wentworth, Paul, 348
Wesson, Col. James, 126, 136, 268,
371, 374
Westchester campaign, 1
Whipple, Brigadier William, 99, 183,
327
White Plains, battle of, 15
Whiting, Col. William B., 202, 372, 375
Wigglesworth, Col. Edward, 371, 375,
386
Wilbur's Springs, 275
Wilcox, Professor, 15
Wildman, William, 358
Wilhelm von Steuben, Friedrich, 347
Wilkinson, Col. James, xxviii, 50, 53,
55, 214, 228, 234-236, 248-249,
254, 259, 261, 269, 273, 283-284,
287, 290, 292, 307, 309-310, 319-
322, 326-332, 335, 337-338, 380-
383, 386-388
Wilkinson, Lt. William C., 221, 254-
255, 279
Willett, Col. Marinus, 119-120, 122,
127, 132-133, 136, 138, 187
Williams, Maj. Griffith, 34, 366
Williams, William, 165, 174, 202-203
Willoe, Capt. Samuel, 245
Woedtke, Frederick William von, 158
Wolfe, Gen. James, 225
Wood Creek, 47
Woodbridge, Col. Benjamin, 375
Woodruff, Samuel, 287
Woodworth, Capt. Ephraim, 205-206,
218
Woolbridge, Col. Benjamin R., 218
Wooster, Brig Gen. David, 143, 146,
148, 151, 155, 167
Wynkoop, Col. Cornelius, 117

Wynkoop, Capt. Jacobus, 161-162
Yorktown, battle of, xxii
Zion Hill, 61-62, 64-66

About the Author

John F. Luzader served as an Army Ranger during World War II and is a graduate of West Virginia University and the University of Texas. Working with the National Park Service, he conducted extensive archival and ground research for the preservation and interpretation of Saratoga National Historical Park, and served as the NPS's central history office staff historian for the colonial and revolutionary periods. Mr. Luzader lives with his wife Jean in West Virginia.